The Rhetoric of Immediacy

A Cultural Critique of Chan/Zen Buddhism

BERNARD FAURE

PRINCETON UNIVERSITY PRESS

PRINCETON, NEW JERSEY

Copyright © 1991 by Princeton University Press
Published by Princeton University Press, 41 William Street,
Princeton, New Jersey 08540
In the United Kingdom: Princeton University Press,
Chichester, West Sussex

Library of Congress Cataloging-in-Publication Data

Faure, Bernard.
The rhetoric of immediacy : a cultural critique of
Chan/Zen Buddhism / Bernard Faure.
p.   cm.
Includes bibliographical references and index.
ISBN 0-691-07374-0 (CL)
ISBN 0-691-02963-6 (PBK)
1. Zen Buddhism. I. Title.
BQ9265.4.F38   1991
294.3'927—dc20   91-11746

Publication of this book has been aided by grants from the
Suntory Foundation and the Japan Foundation

This book has been composed in Linotron Bembo

Princeton University Press books are printed on
acid-free paper and meet the guidelines for permanence
and durability of the Committee on Production
Guidelines for Book Longevity of the
Council on Library Resources

First Princeton Paperback printing, with corrections, 1994

Printed in the United States of America

10 9 8 7 6 5 4 3 2

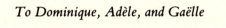

To Dominique, Adèle, and Gaëlle

Contents

Acknowledgments

Offered on the threshold of a book, acknowledgments are in many respects similar to the "dedication of merits" (Sanskrit *pariṇāma*, Japanese *ekō*) performed at the beginning of Chan/Zen rituals. This book may therefore appropriately be dedicated to all the "great and small deities" of the intellectual Olympus and of the academic temples. Among the first category, I would like to single out as cardinal and tutelary deities Michel Foucault, Michel de Certeau, Jacques Derrida, and Yanagida Seizan. As will be apparent to the reader, my thinking has been strongly influenced by their writings. My debt to them, however, goes much beyond literary influence, for their help and/or their example has significantly changed my entire approach to scholarship.

The basic research for this book was conducted during the academic year 1985–1986, a year well spent as a Faculty Fellow at the Society for the Humanities of Cornell University, under the auspices of Jonathan Culler. Research grants from the Japan Fundation and from the American Council of Learned Societies allowed me to spend the academic year 1987–1988 in Japan. While there, I received the help of a number of scholars and individuals, who generously shared their expertise and opened the doors of their institutions. I am particularly thankful to Anna Seidel and Hubert Durt from the Hōbōgirin Institute, Antonino Forte from the Italian School of East Asian Studies, Ishikawa Rikisan and Yoshizu Yoshihide from Komazawa University, and Maeda Naomi from the Institute for Zen Studies, Hanazono College.

Many colleagues and graduate students at Cornell and Stanford also offered useful advice and constructive criticism: Wendi Adamek, Carl Bielefeldt, James Boon, Karen Brazell, Brett de Bary, Kenneth Eastman, David Gardiner, Van Harvey, Victor Koschmann, Dominick LaCapra, Uday Mehta, Steven Sangren, and James Siegel.

Off campus, I have also benefited from the comments of John McRae, Michel Strickmann, Griffith Foulk, Robert Sharf, Anne Klein, and Catherine Bell. The list goes on. Neil McMullin and Wendi Adamek volunteered to read the first drafts of the manuscript and offered many useful suggestions. I have tried, but to no avail, to follow their advice of rewriting my "Frenglish" into standard English. Cathie Brettschneider, of Princeton University Press, has helped me to get closer to that ideal and deserves special thanks. The final revision of the manuscript was made possible by a faculty grant from the Center for East Asian Studies, Stanford University.

Scholarship shares with ritual and neurosis a fascination with details. Although I have tried to behave as a good neurotic, I have no doubt that more advanced readers will find me at fault. Of course, all those whom I have compromised by my acknowledgments should be held partially responsible for whatever errors remain.

Palo Alto
June 26, 1990

Abbreviations

BEFEO   *Bulletin de l'Ecole Française d'Extrême-Orient*. Paris: Ecole Française d'Extrême-Orient.

DNBZ   *Dai Nihon bukkyō zensho* 大日本佛教全書. Ed. Takakusu Junjirō et al. 150 vols. Tokyo: Dai Nihon bukkyō zensho kankōkai, 1931. Reprint. Ed. Suzuki gakujutsu zaidan. 100 vols. Tokyo: Kōdansha, 1970−1973.

DZ   *Daozang* [*Zhengtong daozang* 正統道藏, 1445]. Including the *Wanli xu daozang* 萬曆續道藏 [1607]. 1120 vols. Shanghai: Commercial Press, 1923−1926. Reprint. 60 vols. Taibei: Yiwen yinshuguan, 1962.

DZZ   *Dōgen zenji zenshū* 道元禪師全集. Ed. Ōkubo Dōshū 大久保道舟. 2 vols. Tokyo: Chikuma shobō, 1969−1970.

HJAS   *Harvard Journal of Asiatic Studies*.

IBK   *Indogaku bukkyōgaku kenkyū* 印度学仏教学研究 [Journal of Indian and Buddhist Studies].

JAOS   *Journal of the American Oriental Society*.

JDZS   *Jōsai daishi zenshū* 常濟大師全集. Ed. Kōhō Chisan 孤峰智璨. Yokohama: Daihonzan Sōjiji, 1976.

KDBGKK   *Komazawa daigaku bukkyō gakubu kenkyū kiyō* 駒沢大学仏教学部研究紀要. Tokyo: Komazawa University.

KDBGR   *Komazawa daigaku bukkyō gakubu ronshū* 駒沢大学仏教学部論集. Tokyo: Komazawa University.

QTW   *Qinding Quan Tang wen* 欽定全唐文 [1814]. Ed. Dong Gao 董誥 (1740−1818) et al. 20 vols. Taibei: Huaiwen shuju, 1961.

SKSLXB   *Shike shiliao xinbian* 石刻史料新編. 30 vols. Taibei: Xinwen feng, 1982.

SZ   *Sōtōshū zensho* 曹洞宗全書. Ed. Sōtōshū Zensho Kankōkai. [1229−1235]. Reedition. 18 vols. Tokyo: Sōtōshū Shūmuchō, 1970−1973.

T.   *Taishō shinshū daizōkyō* 大正新修大藏經. Ed. Takakusu Junjirō 高楠順次郎 and Watanabe Kaigyoku 渡邊海旭. 100 vols. Tokyo: Taishō Issaikyō Kankōkai, 1924−1932.

ZBKK   *Zen bunka kenkyūsho kiyō* 禪文化研究所紀要. Kyoto: Hanazono College.

ZZ   *Dai Nihon zokuzōkyō* 大日本續藏經. Ed. Nakano Tatsue 中野達慧. 150 vols. Kyoto: Zōkyō shoin, 1905−1912. Reprint. Taibei: Xinwenfeng, 1968−1970.

The Rhetoric of Immediacy

Prologue

The bottom of our mind is paved with crossroads.
—Paul Valéry, *Monsieur Teste*

If you are walking westward . . . , you forfeit the northern and eastward and southern directions. If you admit a unison, you forfeit all the possibilities of chaos.
—D. H. Lawrence

Unlike Raymond Roussel's *New Impressions of Africa* (Roussel 1963), this book, which could as well be titled *New Impressions of East Asia*, opens a series of parentheses that it proves ultimately unable—but also unwilling—to close. All this makes it rather difficult to know where the tradition (here the Chan/Zen tradition) ends and where scholarship begins—let alone where scholarship ends and I begin. Any historian is to some extent aware that the choice of his or her object of study is not one of pure chance, for there are uncanny affinities between a historian and the period or persons the historian studies: a strange osmosis takes place, which the historian, for the sake of objectivity, usually tries to conceal. But, more fundamentally, one also sees *discursive* affinities between the tradition and its scholarly study; there is a dialogue, an exchange of ideas (the text answers questions, or itself questions the interpreter), a pervasive influence of categories, a retroaction from the object to the subject.

Michael Fischer defines transference as "personal empathetic 'dual tracking'—seeking in others clarifications for processes in the self." He adds that "one needs authentic anchorages that can allow a kind of dual or multiple tracking (between self and other) . . . that can be subjected to mutual criticism or mutual revelation from both traditions. At the same time, one needs a check against assimilating the other to the self, seeing only what is similar or different" (Fischer 1986: 201). Transference takes place in a variety of ways in the present text. It seems to be at work behind most of the text's themes. *Transfert* also means translation, not of one language into another (transfert/transference) but of relics—and there will be much to follow about that topic in Chapter 7. In a sense, a text like this one may be seen as a reliquary—or perhaps as a common grave.

The elaboration of a Chan orthodoxy becomes a metaphor for the writing of a book: just like the tradition, the author ideally fulfills a function of mastery, control, and rarefaction of discourse. This goal, however, can never be fully achieved, and the author, just like the tradition, turns out to be "a mere succession of centers": to attribute to the author only one center would be "to constrain him to a monological, theological position" (Kristeva 1969: 107). Thus in order to deconstruct the tradition, that is, to reveal it in its essential multiplicity, one has to fight against the teleological tendencies of controlled narrative and to give up at least some authorial privileges. In particular, one must abandon the reassuring certitude that one has reached some central thesis, some definitive truth, that will constitute the skeleton of the book and survive it. The multiplication of references (transferences) and quotations (translations of relics) contributes to a destabilization (albeit sometimes a reinforcement) of the central meaning, of the unity of style that most secretly determines that meaning.

Of course, much of this agenda remains wishful thinking, and I continue looking in the traditions under scrutiny for structural constants, one of which might be the dialectic between mediacy and immediacy, or in Chan terms "gradual" and "sudden"—an oscillation that seems to take place not only in these traditions but in my own discourse as well. Whether I like it or not, I find in my own writing some of the rhetorical and theoretical tendencies that I see at work (yet consistently denied) in many Chan/Zen writings. Perhaps, as Umberto Eco remarks, there are times "when a wise man [has] to nurture in himself contradictory thoughts." At any rate, there are analogous relations among certain trends in or levels of Chan/Zen, popular religion, and scholarship. The notion of mediation plays a central role: not only does it describe what is at stake in these discourses, it is also what makes these different trends or levels visible and allows them to communicate.

The gradual/sudden paradigm, which functions as the matrix of the Chan/Zen tradition, can be seen as a dialectical tension between mediate and immediate understanding. It has a certain degree of analogy to the scholar's distinction between respect for tradition (hermeneutics of retrieval) and the critique of all truths as metaphorical and ideological (hence the *tabula rasa*): in other words, the distinction between the ("gradual") acceptance of the mediations provided by a tradition or its ("sudden") rejection. At the methodological level, one might also characterize as "sudden" or "immediate" the unwillingness to enter any structure, that is, to use the mediation of the available methodologies to understand Chan; conversely one might represent as "gradual" the tendency to identify with one particular structure or methodology. To propose an alternative (or "expedient means"?), one could call "performative" (a new variety of the "sudden" move?) the willingness to enter all structures and the ability to move on when necessary.[1]

---

[1] In Chan terms, the first ("sudden") position bears some analogy to the notion of *linian*

The latter attitude, what we may call a methodological "ductility," might take its cue from the *Vajracchedikā-sūtra*'s statement that "one should produce thought without abiding anywhere."[2] There is thus a transference between the Chan notion of the "unlocalized" mind and the "multilocalization" of scholarship—the latter offering, in place of ubiquity or *u-topia*, rather a constellation of possibilities (within which the oscillation between sudden and gradual is but one example). But, as we will see, this very *utopia* is itself localized, a typical product of intellectualism; and we must be aware of this "localization" of both monks and scholars. Many Chan masters were intellectuals, as we are. In this sense they, like us, were at least to some extent *dissociated*—despite their not being Cartesians.[3] Chan practice (at least for certain monks) was, like scholarship (at least for some scholars), a serious game, jesting in earnest. Conversely, one can discern an ascetic imperative or a "monastic" tendency in philological and historical approaches to literate cultures (Boon 1982: 203). These analogies between "subject" and "object" in fact reinforce the necessity of a topological approach. Their very affinities help us to appreciate that properties of fields differ and that scholarship or Chan teachings are always, to some extent, the products of a specific place.

This transferential relationship between the scholar and the Chan tradition that he or she studies may help us then to answer the fundamental question raised by Edward Said and others: namely, how to understand other cultures and religions. It may be that "the dialogue which is established when two cultures meet is not different in quality from that which is implied within any vital tradition or 'form of life,' which is constantly 'transcending itself.' " (Giddens 1976: 58). On the one hand, the gap between two cultures might be less insuperable than the critics of Orientalism have led us to believe. On the other hand, the gaps within a "vital" tradition might be wider than they seem, to the point of leading to what François Lyotard calls a *différend*, that is, "a conflict between [at least] two parties, that cannot be equitably resolved for lack of a rule or judgement applicable to both arguments" (Lyotard 1988: xi). To take a specific example of the culturalist view, Henri Corbin wanted to deny agnostics the

---

("transcending thought"); the third ("performative") position parallels that of *wunian* ("nonthinking," actually flowing with thoughts as they arise); and the second ("gradual") position corresponds to *nian* ("thinking"). Although the Northern Chan notion of *linian* was polemically characterized as "gradualist" by its Southern opponents, it was actually, like *wunian*, a variant of "subitism"—true gradualism being represented by the second position. On these notions, see Zeuschner 1983.

[2] This passage could also be taken as justifying the first, "sudden," position (*linian*).

[3] This statement is *apropos* of Marcel Mauss, who said: "One is confronted with a concept of the world . . . that formulates itself otherwise than we formulate it—or more exactly, than those among us who are *dissociated*, Cartesians, formulate it, since any fortune teller, and even the young polytechnicians and the seamstresses who listen to her, live in a world apart from that of the philosophers" (Mauss 1968–1969: 2:158).

capacity ever to understand gnosticism (Corbin 1967). One can find counterexamples, however, supporting the possibility that the opposition between gnosticism and agnosticism is never as clear-cut as Corbin claimed. In Chan, at least, one can distinguish between a gnostic or sacerdotal pole and an agnostic or rationalist pole.

In anthropological parlance, one may say that any individual belongs to several clans or tribes. Transference is precisely what allows us to understand Chan monks who, like Westerners, appear to be both gnostic and rationalist. Insofar as an analogous rationalization or demythologization process has taken place in Western and Chinese cultures, or that modern thinking is, as Lévi-Strauss claims, an avatar of primitive rationality, we have a perspective on the agnostic dimension of other cultures. On the other hand, insofar as we keep dreaming and are dominated by symbols even in our waking lives, we may have a perspective on Asian forms of gnosticism. Thus the tension in Chan is in some ways analogous to the confrontation in each of us of magical thought and rational thought. Not only does this mean that we perhaps tend to read our problems into Chan philosophy, but it also helps us identify and become sensitive to a similar confrontation in Chan.

Writing of (and about) Chan is necessarily a dual activity, an intertwining of two tendencies: it represents or reproduces more or less truthfully certain ideas or movements of thought, thus aiming at transparency; but it is also an act that produces new thoughts and creates an opaque reality. Whatever its author may say, a book is not merely an image of the world, "a mirror carried along a path," as Stendhal said of the novel; it is another world. (See Deleuze and Guattari 1983: 5.) Hence the necessity of complementary approaches: hermeneutical/structural and performative/semiological; the incessant to-and-fro movement between the seriousness of meaning and the "pleasure of the text," between commentary and rhetoric, between *kōan* and "capping phrase" (*jakugo*).

To turn the observation back again toward the observer, one sees that many academic writings are not only motivated by the claimed sacrosanct search for objective truth but also driven to comply with the constraints of academic discourse, with its unspoken rules, incentives, and rewards. This book is no exception, and it indulges in ritualistic and proleptic devices such as references and footnotes. As is already obvious, it is also a struggle—perhaps a lost battle—with (through) the English language, as well as an acceptance of and a reaction against various aspects of American, French, and Japanese scholarship. My interest in the margins of the Chan tradition stems no doubt from the fact that I feel myself marginal to that tradition and to the academic traditions as well and, at the same time, largely indebted to all of them. Much of this book's content could probably be seen in terms of Harold Bloom's notion of the "anxiety of influence" (Bloom 1973), although I do not feel particularly anxious.

Hence the attempt, or rather the need, to weave together several types of discourse, to have them elucidate each other within the same text.

FROM MARGINS TO MEDIATION

In the course of writing this book, I have worked from one root metaphor to another. The first metaphor I used was that of *margins*, since I had in mind the constitution of Chan as a tradition, and of the Chan tradition as an object or field of study. The problems, the theories found in what is recognized as orthodox Chan writings, impose themselves, to use Pierre Bourdieu's terms, "as a sort of autonomous world" on those who want to enter that field and "who must not only know them, as items of culture, but recognize them, as objects of (prereflexive) belief, failing which they disqualify themselves" (as Chan adepts; Bourdieu 1984: 496). The exclusions that constitute the field of Chan/Zen studies appear to me to be a replication of those that organized Chan/Zen as a single orthodoxy. Heterodox tendencies were repressed and/or relegated to the periphery. And yet the strongest claims for orthodoxy came from marginal figures.

With the development of the "sudden" orthodoxy toward the eighth century, the main tendency that was thereby marginalized was the notion of *mediation* and the various intermediary schemas that derive from it. The elements suppressed or repressed at the core, however, either reappeared at the periphery as the "others" on the margins of Chan (i.e., "popular religion," scholasticism, ritualism, gradualism), or they reinvested and subverted the tradition from inside. If one of the contexts of Chan is indeed popular religion, then we are reminded of Derrida's remark that "context is always at work *within* the place, and not only *around* it" (Derrida 1988: 198). Thus the dialectic between pluralistic or "inclusive" Chan and sectarian or "exclusive" Chan is perhaps replicated by that between pluralistic methodology and "pure" scholarship. Needless to say, my course from margins to mediation was also transferential, moving from traditional Chan scholarship toward methodological eclecticism—prefigured by earlier research on repressed and syncretistic Chan/Zen trends such as the Northern school or the Darumashū. My study of the relations between Chan and popular religion, however, is carried out from the standpoint of the "great tradition" so as to question or unsettle Chan discourse from within. It stresses the internalized relation between the two "poles" that some may call "popular" and "elitist" Chan, although the relation is not limited to these two poles.

METHODOLOGICAL POLYTHEISM

Just as Chan orthodoxy repressed syncretism, scholarly orthodoxy, based on the law of the genre, tends to reject the mixing of genres. One may object to methodological pluralism for a plurality of reasons. One may, for example, argue that although the various approaches used here all aim at redefining, or rather reinventing, a single evasive reality called Chan, each of them, in its specificity, constitutes a new object different from the others, so it may be after all an illusory eclecticism based on indifference that can submit the same object to so many interrogations (Certeau 1980: 73). The superimposition of the objects produced by each perspective creates an ideal, and perhaps fraudulent, object whose outlines are unstable. Yet this may help us heuristically to shift from "linear vision" to "vision in masses." According to Heinrich Wölfflin, "linear vision . . . means that the sense and beauty of things is first sought in the outline," whereas seeing in masses "takes place where the attention withdraws from the edges, where the outline has become more or less indifferent to the eye as the path of vision." Wölfflin thus contrasts "lines of a singular sharpness whose function is to divide" with "blurred borders, which favors the linking of shapes between them."[4] What Wölfflin says of shapes seems to apply equally well to traditions, and if linear vision has shaped the elaboration of the Chan school by a monastic elite, one may surmise that "vision in masses" has commanded the daily practice of the "masses," and that vision should direct the perception of scholars intent on deconstructing the tradition. "Linking shapes between them," as Wölfflin advocates, however, presupposes that there are more or less entities to be linked, and one has to take into account sectarian discourse ("linear vision") as well as syncretistic discourse ("vision in masses") to understand a tradition like Chan in its dialectical tension.

Again, it may be objected that syncretism "is a factitious amalgamation of dissimilar ideas or theses that look compatible only insofar as they are not clearly conceived" (Angenot 1984: 159). I have, I hope, avoided the kind of "accumulation without reworking" criticized by Angenot and reached something closer to what Weber called a *pantheism* or a "polytheism of values"—a notion that implies "not peaceful coexistence but a Homeric battlefield, in which 'different gods struggle with one another, now and for all times to come' " (Jameson 1988: 2:11). At any rate, Angenot's objection implies a rather prejudiced conception of syncretism, one that, unfortunately, is also prevalent in fields such as the History of Religions, Sinology, and Japanology. Texts, methodologies, and traditions are no more exempt from contradictions than are scholars or even philosophers. Actually, they often survive and develop precisely because of them—and contradictions themselves may come to form a system.

Methodological pluralism means here an attempt to mediate be-

---

[4] Heinrich Wölfflin, *Principes fondamentaux de l'histoire de l'art* (Paris: Gallimard, 1966), 25–27.

tween—or rather hold together—conflicting approaches such as the hermeneutical and the rhetorical, the structural(ist) and the historical, the "theological" and the ideological/cultural. My research remains structural inasmuch as I attempt to bring out mental structures, whether these structures turn out to be "long-term prisons" or patterns of a certain freedom, and to show how various levels of Chan practice and doctrine are structured by a few paradigms such as mediacy/immediacy, sudden/gradual, center/margins, orthodoxy/heterodoxy, hermeneutics/rhetoric, description/ prescription, communication/performance. I do not put too much weight on the frequent inversion of signs, on the exchange of positions that takes place—in a blissful amnesia—between various theories or protagonists of doctrinal controversies: the reversals usually take place unnoticed, masked by the false consciousness of a perfect continuity on each side, while the antagonistic structure itself remains basically unchanged. I incline to believe that intellectual history may be the history of variations on a few paradigms or metaphors. On the other hand, I would not want to emphasize these structures at the expense of the dialogical or transferential relationship and the historical or "topological" contingencies. If, as Fernand Braudel pointed out in his debate against structuralism, the historian is the one who would like to rescue from the debate "the uncertainty of the mass movement, its various possibilities for alteration, its freedoms" (Braudel 1980: 76), I would still consider myself a historian of Chan/Zen. Inasmuch as the rhetoricity of Chan discourse is at work in my own writing, the latter has also what J. L. Austin called a "perlocutionary" character, and it is fraught with supplementary (theoretical, moral, ideological) meanings (Austin 1962: 101–132). This multiplicity of purposes is reflected at the microlevel by a perhaps disconcerting oscillation between contradictory statements, and at the macrolevel by the division of the books into two parts, or rather two levels, the first one (Chapters 1 through 4) dealing with the general epistemological and ideological constraints resulting from the Chan/Zen dialectic of mediacy and immediacy, and the second (Chapters 5 through 13) examining various examples of this oscillation or agonistic tension. Chapter 1 is an attempt to delineate the fault that runs through the Chan tradition and that reinscribes itself in its epistemological or ideological discourse. Chapter 2 takes the sudden/gradual controversy as a paradigmatic expression of that fault and tries to reconstitute the various layers of meaning sedimented in that paradigm. Chapter 3 takes up the same epistemological/ideological issue from a slightly different angle—through the concept of the Two Truths—and dwells on the notion of mediation, which is seen as central in the evolution of Chan/Zen. Chapter 4 examines the relations between Chan and popular or local religions characterized by their emphasis on mediation and hierarchy. Despite the claims of sudden or immediate/unmediated Chan, Chan masters were perceived as both masters in a spiritual hierarchy and mediators. Chapters 5 and 6 examine the changes in the Chan conception of the mediator, from the thaumaturge through the trickster to the Bodhisattva. Another form of mediation was provided by the Buddhist cult of relics and icons. Chapters 7 and 8 attempt to show that, despite its much-vaunted iconoclasm, Chan/Zen had a relentless interest in the worship of relics and icons. Chapter 9 pursues this reassessment of the Chan tradition by examining the various aspects of the ritualization of death that turned Zen into a form of "funerary Buddhism." Another important form of mediation, dreams, is examined in Chapter 10. On the other hand, the Chan claim for immediacy paved the way for antinomianism. Chapter 11 attempts, therefore, to show the extent to which Chan antinomianism was put into practice by focusing on the limits of transgression and Chan/Zen conceptions of gender and sexuality. Chapters 12 and 13 take up again the question of ritual mediation by focusing on Chan "polytheism" and liturgy. In the last analysis, however, mediation will appear as merely another rhetorical device. By providing the lineaments of a narrative, it comes to serve—just like the related notion of immediacy that it subverts—a variety of performative functions distinct from its avowed purpose. When both immediacy and mediation are extenuated, however, the narrative fails and the book has to come to an end. One final disclaimer: the semblance of linearity of the above outline is merely for the sake of the reader's convenience and should not be seen as an attempt to save the harmonious continuity of the Chan/Zen patriarchal lineage or the cohesion of its orthodox teaching.

One　　*The Differential Tradition*

The vision of the world is a division of the world.
—Pierre Bourdieu, *Le sens pratique*

It would hardly be an exaggeration to say that everything in Chan revolves around the patriarchal lineage. The stress on lineage, to be sure, is
not specific to Chan, but the paradox here is that of a tradition which, at
its most esoteric level, denies the existence of any *tradita*.[1] Of course, the
patriarchal robe was supposedly transmitted, and so was the Dharma; but
this transmission claims to be in reality a nontransmission, lacking as it
does any specific referent. It is (or should be) a "transmission of mind
through mind" (*yixin chuanxin*): the patriarchal robe is presented as a
mere symbolic token and the mind transmitted as a no-mind. Time and
again, Chan masters have denounced the attempt to follow the paradigm
established by the Buddha. It is, to use a Chan metaphor, as meaningless
as the action of the man who, having dropped his sword in the river,
looked for it at the place where he had put a notch in the gunwale. As the
Zen monk-poet Gidō Shūshin (1325–1388) put it: "How laughable, to
suppose Gautama did something special!/ Quick, let's notch the gunwale
so we can find the sword!"[2] But should we take this denial of Dharma
transmission at face value? Like many other Chan masters, Linji Yixuan,
in his (respectfully recorded) *Sayings*, declares that he has no Dharma to
give to men (Sasaki 1975: 25), only to insist a few pages later that "My
Dharma is that of the correct transmission, a transmission that has continued in a single line through the masters Mayu, Danxia, Daoyi, Lushan
and Shigong, and has spread abroad over all the world" (ibid.: 30). The
notion of a perennial and quasi-sacerdotal tradition was emphasized by
Zen masters such as Dōgen (1200–1253). Yet the most conservative
Chan/Zen masters were well aware that their tradition was an open one,
as Dōgen's master Rujing compassionately said to his rather rigid disciple: "The footprints of the Tathāgata . . . can actually be seen today in
the land of Udyāna in Western India. The room in which the layman

---

[1] See the following passage from the ninth-century Korean master Muyŏm's *Treatise on
the Tongueless Realm*: "[The Chan transmission] has nontransmission for its transmission;
hence it is not transmitted and yet *is* transmitted" (Buswell 1983: 13).

[2] See Burton Watson 1988: 108. Another traditional antitradition metaphor is the story of
the man who, having once caught a hare who had knocked itself out on a tree stump, waited
patiently in the hope that another hare would run into the stump. Against ritualization and
routinization, these stories point out the accidental and nonreiterative character of beginnings.

Vimalakīrti dwelled still exists. The foundation stones of the Jetavana monastery remain as well. But when one goes to sacred remains such as these and measures them, he finds them sometimes longer, sometimes shorter, sometimes extended, and sometimes contracted. Their dimensions cannot be fixed. This is a manifestation of the rush and vitality of the Buddha Dharma itself." (See Waddell 1977–1978: 80–81.)

Recent historical studies have shown that Chan tradition was not simply transmitted from India by the monk Bodhidharma; rather, the patriarchal tradition emerged through a rather complicated process. As is well known, the orthodox view is that the first patriarch Bodhidharma transmitted his new teaching to his disciple Huike (487–593), and that this teaching eventually reached the fifth patriarch Hongren (601–674), through Sengcan (n.d.) and Daoxin (580–651). With Hongren, the rising Chan school divided into two branches, the Northern school founded by Shenxiu (606–706) and the Southern school, the legitimate one, by Huineng (d. 713). Huineng's two main disciples, Nanyue Huairang (677–744) and Qingyuan Xingsi (671–738), became the ancestors of the "five houses" of Chan that developed during the Tang, and of which only two survived after the Song, to become in Japan the Rinzai and Sōtō sects.

Six patriarchs in search of a tradition

This traditional account of early Chan has been questioned by Chinese and Japanese scholars such as Hu Shih and Yin Shun, Ui Hakuju, Sekiguchi Shindai, and Yanagida Seizan.[3] They have shown that the groundwork for the "invention" of a patriarchal tradition was done within the so-called East Mountain school (*dongshan famen*) founded by Daoxin and Hongren and continued by Shenxiu (although later rebaptized Northern school by its rivals). The rising popularity of this school led its adepts to search for more distant origins, and the result was a connection with another group known as the Laṅkāvatāra school, which had developed around a charismatic figure named Fachong (d. ca. 665). Fachong himself had traced his school back to Huike and Bodhidharma, thus linking forever the fates of the two lineages. (See McRae 1986; Faure 1988.) One further step was taken when Shenhui (684–758) claimed that the sixth patriarch was his own master Huineng (d. 713) and not the Northern Chan master Shenxiu. Besides arguing that the Northern school was a collateral branch issued from Hongren, the fifth patriarch, Shenhui tried to convince his audience that his rivals were advocating a gradual teaching, in contrast with the sudden teaching of Bodhidharma and his legitimate heirs. Helped by extraordinary political circumstances (i.e., the An

[3] See Hu Shi 1970, 1975; Yin Shun 1971; Ui 1966a,b,c; Sekiguchi 1969; Yanagida 1967.

Lushan rebellion of 755), he was able to establish Huineng and himself as legitimate heirs to Hongren and the East Mountain school, rebaptized as the Southern school by opposition to Shenxiu's Northern school. It is now clear that Shenhui's allegations tell more about him than about the people he disparaged. His virtuous indignation against a supposedly corrupt Northern Chan appears to have been motivated largely by his own ambition to become the seventh patriarch. The sectarian character of Shenhui has been emphasized by Ui Hakuju, who did not admit Hu Shih's praise of the Southern school's champion. By simply rejecting Shenhui's (and Hu Shih's) claims, however, one still grants their main point, namely, the opposition of two monolithic schools. Things may have been much more complex. To begin with, none of these groups apparently referred to itself as the Northern school. In fact, there is some evidence that Shenxiu and his disciples considered themselves representatives of the Southern school, Southern referring here to Southern India, from where Bodhidharma had supposedly brought Chan. Furthermore, the diagram of filiations or the layout of the various trends on the politico-religious chessboard does not coincide with real philosophical affinities or antagonisms. For example, Zongmi, who claimed to be the fifth patriarch of Shenhui's Heze school, was in many respects much closer to the Northern school than to his proclaimed master Shenhui. Therefore, the demarcation line drawn by historians between the two schools may be purely fictitious or at least unstable. The tree of Shenhui may have hidden the forests of Chan. At any rate, it was another trend of the Southern school, the Hongzhou school founded by Mazu Daoyi (709–788), that eventually became the mainstream of "classical" Chan in the mid-Tang and of Japanese Zen after the Kamakura period.

Unfortunately, this revised "historical" account might itself be nothing more than a useful fiction. At any rate, it fails to question its premises— the notion of a Chan tradition—although it had helped significantly to call into question the claims of that tradition. This retrospective illusion arises from the grip on scholars of metaphors such as the "arborescent model" of tradition.[4] This model assumes the existence of an original tradition that branches off into various schools. A variant of this model— actually an inversion—is the "river model." It seems at first glance more appropriate, since, by taking into account the multiple streams that eventually merge into the mainstream, it leaves room for a multiple origin of the tradition. Yet it still implies a convergence, a teleological thrust toward unity. It may be useful here to remember Foucault's words: "What is found at the historical beginning of things is not the inviolable identity of their origin; it is the dissension of other things. It is disparity" (Fou-

[4] On the "arborescent model," see Deleuze and Guattari 1983: 10ff.

cault 1977: 142). Clearly, Chan was no exception to this rule, and its "primitive" (if not originary) teachings were not simply syncretistic, borrowing as they did freely from a variety of other currents (Mādhyamika, Yogācāra, Tiantai, Huayan, Pure Land, Daoism). They achieved in fact an uneasy "polytheism of values." In this sense, the orthodox claim in a "pure" Chan is an amnesia, an active forgetting of origins, a repression or scapegoating of doctrinal features and historical figures. The (inclusive) hierarchy or (exclusive) unity it achieved was a violent one. Here a doubt may arise: did these affluents ever merge? What if we had, instead of a unique and unified tradition, a plural one? Could we go one step further and imagine that we are confronted with a number of distinct religious currents that would have developed in relative autonomy under a convenient blanket name? If this were the case, it would be another retrospective illusion, due to the eventual success of the orthodox unitary model that through hindsight would have distinguished a plural "early Chan" from the later tradition. Another metaphor sometimes found in Chan texts speaks of a transmission from the uncle to the nephew, that is, from the main line to the collateral line. But, to use that metaphor for our purpose, it would seem that the nephew's parents were actually single children. This metaphorical kinship, which permitted the circulation of men (instead of women, as the anthropologist would deem it proper) between the various "houses" of the Chan tradition, often resulted from retrospective adoptions, in other words, forged lineages.

One could argue that there never was an "early Chan school" in the sixth century, since the Chan tradition was then only a dim (and future) ideological construct. Accordingly, to speak of "early Chan" is an anachronism, although I will still use this expression as shorthand. What a closer scrutiny reveals are different groups vying with each other for official recognition. There were, for example, several "Southern schools" (some of which later became known collectively as the "Northern school"), and the doctrinal differences between them were at times great. In these conditions, can one still speak of them as if they were simply variants of the same teaching? And yet there was undeniably some common ground among all these trends, and the fact that this permitted the (however laborious and conflictual) definition of an orthodoxy justifies us in speaking at the level of representations of a single Chan tradition—at least from a certain point in time, say, the ninth century. At any rate, the Chan patriarchal lineage was eventually successful enough for emerging Buddhist schools to want to affiliate themselves with it. A common feature shared by most of these schools was their desire to distance themselves from the old Buddhist order and to become part of the new Chan establishment. Such was, for example, the case of Mazu's Hongzhou school and of the so-called Oxhead (*Niutou*) school.[5]

If, however, "early Chan" did not exist as a school or tradition, can we at least say that it did exist as a certain type of discourse or literary genre? Early Chan texts are unmistakable in their form and content. "Classical" Chan texts belong to an entirely different genre, although some stylistic features can be traced back to the earlier period: for example, the recorded sayings appended at the end of the biographical chapters of several patriarchs (Guṇabhadra, Bodhidharma, Hongren, and Shenxiu) in the *Lengqie shiziji* (T. 85, 2837), or the fictional dialogues that make up several Northern Chan texts such as the *Zhenzong lun* (T. 85, 2835), can be seen as the forerunners of the "Recorded Sayings" (*yulu*) genre. The more didactic "early Chan" genre continued to develop, although it was somewhat eclipsed by the dominant *yulu* genre during the late Tang. It eventually resurfaced in Song China, as well as in Korea and Japan, under the label of "the convergence of doctrinal Buddhism and Chan" (Ch. *jiaochan yizhi*, J. *kyōzen itchi*).

The emergence of Chan as a "tradition" was prepared by the emergence of Chan as a "style" and, more precisely, as a literary genre. As noted above, "early" and "classical" Chan differ radically in their style and cannot be reduced to a single genre. It would again appear that the Chan lineage, whether doctrinal or patriarchal, is an optical illusion carefully maintained by the later "tradition." Two approaches can be used here to describe the coexistence, first independently and later within a relatively unified system, of these two genres, or of the related doctrinal positions, the so-called sudden and gradual teachings.[6]

One, the socio-historical approach, stresses the conflict between various groups that eventually divided according to theoretically irreconcilable positions and came to justify their divergences in terms of sudden versus gradual. Eventually, these two positions were accommodated at the level of religious practice and tended to form a relatively stable system, and orthodox Chan emerged as a result of this compromise. The other, structural, approach posits the logical priority of the sudden/gradual paradigm and sees in the historical development of Chan only a grad-

---

[5] As Paul Demiéville (1970a: 1314) puts it: "This [Chan] sect . . . had become so institutionalized that it came to define itself in genealogical terms. A monk of the Chan sect was someone who had received ordination from a master belonging to one of the patriarchal lineages of that sect. . . . Although genealogically aggregated to that lineage, that monk could ignore entirely the teachings of Linji. He could study and teach the doctrines of any other ancient school."

[6] Needless to say, the advocates of the *jiaochan yizhi* theory would have denied that their position could be equated with gradualism, since no one wanted to be labeled gradualist in the rhetorical outbid that brought the victory of the "sudden" position.

ual and incomplete enactment, an actualization of some of the potentialities contained in this paradigm. Perhaps there is no need to choose between these two models, since it is precisely an alternation between them that may help us reduce the uncertainties that would remain if we were to use only one model. In Paul Veyne's words, "two models are better than one" (Veyne 1988: 34).

I have examined the structural model elsewhere (see Faure 1986a). I want to focus here on a socio-historical approach that stresses the ideological presuppositions at work in the notion of tradition. The ideological work of the tradition has been to hide the diversity and contingency of its origins behind an apparent consensus of orthodoxy, repeated *ad nauseam* in all the texts. Would-be historians should therefore avoid replicating this view in their own writings and try, on the contrary, to reveal and deepen the inner divide—to the point of showing that it is reflecting (or reflected in) an "outer" difference. Not surprisingly, outside criticisms of Chan are also found within the Chan tradition itself. Whether they arose first within Chan or were simply internalized by Chan in order to meet outside criticisms matters little at this point. More significant is the fact that the fault line between Chan and other schools also passes within Chan itself and the borderline is, as it were, "invaginated," rendering the very notion of tradition problematic. (See Derrida 1979.)

THE SECOND ORDER

Differentiation is not only to be sought in relatively obvious changes, it can also be hidden by an apparent continuity. Similar teachings and behavior or institutions can acquire a radically different meaning when their intellectual or social context is modified in sometimes hardly visible ways. (See Certeau 1975: 166.) The apparent unity of any religious system such as Buddhism is relatively easy to maintain precisely because "the same concepts, the same practices tend to take *opposite meanings* when they serve to express radically opposed social experiences" (Bourdieu 1971a: 316). Chan orthodoxy turns out to be a creation of marginals, a palimpsest or an interpretive arena. Its ambiguity and vitality result from its being, if not entirely blank, at least largely open to reinterpretation. In order to retrieve some of these sedimented meanings of orthodox discourse, it may be necessary to multiply dialectical reversals and to problematize what seemed a nonproblematic interpretation.

Let us begin with the sociological level. A first type of inner differentiation results from what Max Weber called "routinization of charisma." As in other religious trends, a constant dialectic between routinization and nonconformism seems at work in Chan.[7] On the one hand, Chan can be seen as a reaction against what was perceived as a Buddhist *trahison des clercs* (in both senses of clerics and intellectuals). On the other hand, Chan turned into a "tamed heresy." Etymologically, "heresy" means "choice," that is, the refusal to accept the tradition as it is, the questioning of its dogmas. But this questioning itself soon becomes a new dogma, no longer having for the epigones the meaning it had for the founders. The heresy may first turn into a successful heterodoxy, and then finally becomes an orthodoxy. Roles are inverted: the true calling into question might then come from apparently conservative persons or groups. We are confronted with what we may call a semiotics of orthodoxy: certain terms ("sudden," "Southern") are waved as rallying symbols, others ("gradual," "Northern") have as their main aim to devalue adverse theses. This situation was analyzed, within the Chan/Zen tradition itself, by some lucid individuals such as Zongmi (780–841), Qisong (1007–1072), or Juefan Huihong (1071–1128), who show the weaknesses of the prevailing orthodoxy and the complexity of the rival teachings.[8]

The Chan patriarchal lineage reflects the elaboration of a symbolic universe "that unites men with their predecessors and their successors in a totality full of meaning" (Berger and Luckmann 1967: 103). It constitutes a process of legitimation of the tradition and of social hierarchization and eventually effects a defusing or denial of the troubling "provinces of meaning" that derived from individual glimpses of ultimate reality. By the same token, "the empirical community is transposed onto a cosmic plane and made majestically independent of the vicissitudes of individual existence" (ibid.). For example, in an interesting document found at Dunhuang, the patriarchal transmission is shown as taking place in a purely metaphysical realm, the Vajradhātu or Diamond World. (See Tanaka 1983: 587–588; Xu Guolin 1937: 2:139–141.) On the other hand, the characteristic this-worldly attitude of "classical" Chan can also be interpreted in terms of institutionalization, a phenomenon that occurs "whenever there is a typification of habitualized actions by types of actors."[9]

---

[7] According to Weber, "routinization" (*veralltäglichung*) is "the process whereby either the prophet himself or his disciples secure the permanence of his preaching and the congregation's distribution of grace, hence insuring the economic existence of the enterprise and those who man it, and thereby monopolizing as well the privileges reserved for those charged with religious functions" (Weber 1964: 61). Although what Weber calls a "prophet" seems at first glance alien to Chan, by this he means a spiritual master like the Buddha.

[8] On Zongmi, see Gregory 1983; on Qisong, see Chi-chiang Huang 1986; on Huihong, see Gimello 1989a.

[9] Berger and Luckmann 1967: 54. Weber also pointed out that "When religious virtuosos have combined into an active asceticist sect, two aims are completely attained: the disenchantment of the world and the blockage of the path to salvation by a flight from the world. The path to salvation is turned away from a contemplative 'flight from the world' and towards an ascetic 'work in this world' " (Weber 1958a: 290).

This description could certainly apply to the Chan ideal as reflected in the monastic rule attributed to Baizhang Huaihai, who is also well known for his motto: "One day without work is one day without food." Institutionalization is explained in Chan terms by resorting to a variant of the Two Truths model: the success of Chan during the seventh–eighth centuries among laymen was probably both cause and effect of a growing proselytism, which explains the unfortunate necessity of leaving the rarefied atmosphere of ultimate truth ("first-order meaning," *diyi yi*) for the pedestrian realm of conventional truth ("second-order meaning," *dier yi*). This fall into the second order of meaning thus constitutes the founding loss from which the "historical tradition" will grow. It is presented as a duplication, a parody of the original experience, but also as the genealogical flaw of the monastic order: after the Buddha, the primitive community was lost, giving way to second, routinized, "minor" orders. It was restored temporarily with the appearance of the Chan patriarchs—only to be threatened time and again by their epigones. Even the apophatic discourses of Chan on the "second order" turn into semiotic systems and discursive tactics. This predicament is perhaps what caused Yunmen Wen'yan (864–949) to declare, while joining the funeral procession of one monk: "How many dead bodies follow in the wake of a single living person!"[10] The Master undoubtedly, however, considered himself perfectly alive, and by joining the procession he in effect contradicts and reinforces his statement, blurring the distinction between what precedes and what comes after, the master and his epigones, the founder and the tradition. The development of the "encounter dialogues" and the institutionalization of Chan as a tradition self-consciously distinct from traditional Buddhism were in a way attempts to evade the double bind created by success, the paradoxes of an antiinstitutional institution and an antitextual textual tradition. But these attempts, bound to remain purely theoretical, could only fail.

This double bind does not mean, of course, that "pure" or "authentic" Chan masters such as Sengcan, the mysterious "third patriarch," never existed, but they themselves became pawns on a given ideological chessboard, protagonists in a controversy they did not create—or could not help creating. Furthermore, they were in most cases soon set aside, destined to become mere signs of a convenient ideal, a screen behind which life could go on. As Foucault points out, "The successes of history belong to those who are capable of seizing [the] rules, to replace those who had used them, to disguise themselves so as to pervert them, invert their meaning, and redirect them against those who had initially imposed them; controlling this complex mechanism, they will make it function so

[10] Quoted in John Wu, *The Golden Age of Zen* (New York: Paragon Books, 1975), 145.

as to overcome the rulers through their own rules" (Foucault 1977: 151). Other scholars such as Michel de Certeau have stressed the high cost of a genealogy and the loss of the differences that result from the production of a "tradition" (Certeau 1982: 155).

In this manner, the complex reality of Chan was gradually replaced by a simplistic image of its mythic past. This may account for what we will later define as its "essential" duplicity. In this sense, the pious reconstruction of the "golden age" of Zen by post-Meiji Japanese scholars such as D. T. Suzuki was only a replication of a process initiated much earlier. From the outset, or at any rate very quickly, the Chan tradition seems to have been a denial of loss. Its emergence is marked by the nostalgia for a "return to origins" and the awareness that the "pure" practice of the early Chan practitioners, the uncompromising (but rather Hinayanistic) ascesis of the *dhūta-guṇa*, had become impracticable in the new social context in which the Chan school flourished. It is significant that Northern Chan reached its apogee while its "founder," the "national teacher" Shenxiu, was practically kept hostage at the court, asking in vain for authorization to return and to spend his last years in his mountain hermitage.

We seem confronted, at least at the level of representation, with two general types of Chan. This duality results from the attempt to save the, as it were, "theological" aspect of Chan, or the *sui generis* nature of *insight*, at the expense of the "anthropological" aspect or the variety of elaborations (usually seen as degeneration or as corruption of a primordial "ontic seizure"; Jonathan Z. Smith 1982: 42). The inner divide between *spirituels* and clerics is not specific to Chan; it is a recurrent feature of all "spiritual" movements. Once the early controversies are settled, the new majority becomes established and the more conservative or ascetic minority is marginalized or condemned to disappear. While deriving its legitimacy from the renouncers who take their own experience as the only guide and criterion of truth, the tradition actually silences them in order to impose its authority and substitute its own ritualistic access to truth. For example, the so-called *Laṅkāvatāra* tradition chose to remember the "second patriarch" Huike instead of Daoyu, another of Bodhidharma's disciples, who "practiced the Way in his mind and never spoke of it." Sengcan seems at first glance an exception, but precisely because of his anonymity he provided a convenient missing link between the two early Chan lineages. The "silent minority" was perhaps closer to the ideal of Chan, but its silence almost led it to fall into oblivion.[11] Sometimes its representa-

---

[11] In some cases, however, Chan masters were retrospectively elevated to the rank of patriarchs precisely because of their obscurity, which allowed reconstruction of their biographies in the most convenient way. Such is the case with Sengcan and perhaps with Huineng himself. (See Faure 1989: 131–132.) But this apotheosis does not mean that their ideas were gaining recognition.

tives in their efforts to elude prestige and fame, and not to forsake the moon for the finger pointing at it, would turn into "lunatics," and this ideal of a "wild Chan" was endorsed by the now-orthodox tradition as additional legitimacy—at least up to a certain point, past which it was denounced as "naturalist heresy." Yet their (remote) existence proved structurally necessary. Some of them, like Sengcan, were selected to serve as alibis, and their alleged teachings provided a paradoxical foundation for the tradition. Others were less (or more?) fortunate. Of course, we may have here a literary *topos*: they were nevertheless still perceived as masters and, although they apparently did not care to proselytize, they admitted disciples. Yet they consistently refused to become schoolteachers or to represent anything. It seems that in front of any eloquent "master," we can find a "silent" or laconic figure: I mentioned the case of Daoyu, Huike's co-disciple. Another important figure of early Chan that was eclipsed by Bodhidharma and Huike was a "master" named Yuan, about whom nothing is known except a few devastating sayings. In the Northern school, we find someone like Mingzan (fl. 8th c.); and, of course, in "classical" Chan there is Linji's cryptic interlocutor, Puhua. (See Sasaki 1975: 41–49.) We might thus establish a summary typology of three types of Chan adepts: advocates of "sudden" Chan, advocates of gradualism, and "silent" practitioners (true to the "sudden" teaching?), who emulated Vimalakīrti's silence.[12] In the so-called *Treatise of Bodhidharma (Damo lun)*, a master asks his disciple: "What Dharma could I teach you?" (See Faure 1986d: 128.) Clearly, the question is largely rhetorical. Linji, too, and many other Chan masters, teaches constantly that there is no teaching, nothing to obtain, and merely points to the empty place of the absolute, just as the Chan ritual is authenticated by the empty seat of the Arhat Piṇḍola. This move is reminiscent of the strategies of condescension analyzed by Bourdieu. In such strategies, the master is sufficiently assured of his position in the hierarchy to be able to deny the hierarchy, thus cumulating the profits tied to the hierarchy and its symbolic denial (Bourdieu 1984: 497). For all their radical, iconoclastic rhetoric, the teachings of paradigmatic Chan masters such as Mazu, Huangbo, and Linji became the "classics" of a conservative tradition. They served as alibis for the perpetuation, under a "sudden" disguise, of the most "gradual" components of early Chan. Such is also the case of various trends of Korean Sŏn (such as Chinul and the Chogye school) and Japanese Zen

[12] Of course, the question remains as to how to evaluate this silence. For silences are also texts, and as such they are open to a variety of interpretations. Is this silence—as the refusal of the Buddha to the fourteen metaphysical questions (see Lamotte 1944–1980: 1:154), or the "thundering silence" of Vimalakīrti to Mañjuśrī's question about nonduality—the ultimate attitude, a refusal to play the cultural or philosophical game? How do we distinguish it from the silence of Hīnayanist "world renouncers," unconcerned with the salvation of others?

(such as the Darumashū, Yōsai, and Dōgen). The gesture of exclusion that permitted the emergence of Chan orthodoxy had to be repeated again and again within the later tradition, constantly threatened by centrifugal forces. In the process, there was a shift from the open ambiguity of the early teachings to the rather sterile dichotomies of "orthodox" Chan. This dialectic may be expressed by the opposition between ideal types such as "inclusive" and "exclusive" Chan.

An alienating tradition?

Even if one is willing to take seriously the truth claims of the Chan school, it seems difficult to deny that, as with any other religious institution, it came to fulfill specific social and ideological functions. As Berger and Luckmann remark, "To say that a segment of human activity has been institutionalized is already to say that this segment of human activity has been subsumed under social control" (1967: 55). The close relationship between Chan and the state, from the eighth century onward, is well documented. Although Chan fell temporarily from grace, along with the rest of Buddhism, at the time of the Huichang repression (845), it emerged from this political turmoil less severely affected than the other Buddhist schools. But the cost was in a sense higher, for once Chan became the Buddhist orthodoxy, it had to surrender its independence and become part of the imperial administration. In Japan, too, Zen tried to present itself as an ideological instrument that could serve the interests of the country. Although scholars usually look toward the Kamakura figure Yōsai (1141–1215) as an example of this development because of the suggestive title of his main work, "On the Protection of the State through the Promotion of Zen" (*Kōzen gokoku ron*), the work of the Tokugawa Zen master Suzuki Shōsan (1579–1655) is much more significant in this respect.[13]

It is, therefore, important to examine the social aspects of the tradition. Through ordination, a Chan monk could be granted upward mobility in a hierarchical society. This state of affairs may have determined many vocations. Hence the constant (and insufficient) warnings of Chan and Zen masters against "worldly benefits." There was, however, another more subtle infatuation, the consciousness of belonging to the "selected few," of being able to look down upon the common run of unaware worldlings. The technical (and later aesthetic) specialization served to im-

---

[13] On the ideological aspects of Suzuki Shōsan's thought, see Ooms 1985: 122–143. On the Buddhist justification of war, see Demiéville 1956. See also the special issue on *Kōzen gokoku*, *Zengaku kenkyū* 32 (1939). In this context one could also mention the contribution to nationalist propaganda of "Zen thinkers" such as Nishitani Keiji. See the (in)famous *Chūōkōron* "Round Table" in Kosaka Masaaki, Nishitani Keiji, Koyama Iwao, and Suzuki Shigetaka, *Sekaishiteki tachiba to Nihon* (Tokyo: Chūōkōronsha, 1943), 201.

pose an elitist character, what Bourdieu calls "cultural pedigree" (*quartiers de noblesse culturelle*; Bourdieu 1984: 63). This consciousness prevailed even when Chan masters were advocating "commoner Chan."

The free spirit of Chan thus became a kind of *noblesse oblige*, culturally and socially determined. As Bourdieu has shown, the search for symbolic gain may be hidden behind the most seemingly disinterested attitudes. In this connection, one should also recall Weber's remark that even ascetics and mystics are interest groups. Much of the motivation for a monastic career may be found in a search for distinction, although this does not necessarily preclude a genuine spiritual calling. But religious practice itself was deeply affected by sociological changes in the community: actually, the ritual identification of the Chan adept to the patriarchal lineage, first through ordination, later through the "seal of approval," and the certificate of authentication given by the master, came to replace the traditional Buddhist notion of the "path" (*mārga*). (See McRae 1988a.) One may also wonder whether the controversy over the value of *upāya* or "skillful means" to reach awakening does not overlap with a social division whose stake would be somewhat similar to that which, according to Bourdieu, divides the "scholars" (*doctes*), who value apprenticeship, and the "gentlemen" (*mondains*), who value innate talents (Bourdieu 1984: 68).

The definition of masters and disciples, and of what is supposed to be transmitted through them, is primarily social. Despite the constant reference to ultimate truth, it does not acquire its validity from some extra-social criterion but is closely related to status. In some ways, Chan masters are akin to those "masters of truth" of ancient Greece analyzed by Marcel Detienne.[14] In other words, they are not masters because they have realized the truth and can now teach it (although, of course, this may be the case); rather, they can teach the truth because, having been socially defined as Chan masters, what they teach has the performative power of being the truth. Like the author function analyzed by Foucault, the "master function" is a "position" determined by the discourse; it is a function (and not a pure origin) of discourse. In this sense, its performative power requires a broad social consensus. The impassivity of the Zen master calls to mind that of Marcel Proust's character, Monsieur de Norpois, who, "knowing that he will keep in hand the command of the conversation, lets his interlocutor stir, strive, struggle as he likes" (Proust, quoted in Bourdieu 1982: 59).

The increasing importance of title and rank in Chan, at first glance paradoxical in an antinomian teaching, can be interpreted as reflecting a

---

[14] See Detienne 1979a; see also Faure, "Zen and Modernity," *Zen Buddhism Today* 4 (1986): 87.

shift in the locus of power—namely, that symbolic domination, initially located in the individual master, is now located in the institution. Monastic rationalization, together with a certain Weberian "disenchanting of the world," brought about a "reenchanting" of human relationships, that is, a concealment of their naked ideological nature. The master–disciple relationship offers an example of these "enchanted relationships" analyzed by Bourdieu (1980b: 217). Indeed, the ritualization of daily life in Zen monasteries provides many cases of what he calls a "euphemization of symbolic violence," that is, of a "gentle, invisible form of violence, which is never recognized as such, and is not so much undergone as chosen" (Bourdieu 1977b: 192; 1980b: 219). The ritualized staff beatings (*kyōsaku*) during meditation retreats (*sesshin*) and the traditional "thirty strokes" given by the master to his questioners in the *yulu* literature are only the most obvious cases. Chan discipline, particularly in its Japanese, post-Hakuin version, could serve as an illustration of the growth of power of the type analyzed by Foucault in *Discipline and Punish* (1979). According to this model, the individualistic search for freedom lends itself to rationalization and seems to lead paradoxically to increasing hierarchy and domination, which reinforce the social structures imposed from outside the monastery. This, arguably, is too dark a picture and need not be endorsed entirely. But it should help us keep in mind the "radical ambiguity of all traditions" and to take into account, when we have to judge the truth claims of the Chan tradition, the possibility of "systematically distorted communication" (Tracy 1981: 137).

Tradition as kinship

Let us briefly return to the Chan metaphor of the transmission from the uncle to the nephew.[15] Should we, as Thomas Merton suggested, "admit from the outset that uncles have nothing to do with Zen" (Merton 1970: 1)? The importance of Chan discussions concerning lineage may on the contrary allow us to see the Chan school as a kind of symbolical "kin group." It is worth recalling here Bourdieu's distinction between "official" and "practical" kinship and his observation that the two genealogical schemas do not coincide (Bourdieu 1977b: 35; 1980b: 284). Just as the official genealogy remains an abstract schema that legitimates practical genealogical strategies, the notion of "sect" reflects the "official" standpoint, which is the less active position in the concrete reality of practices and exchanges. In many cases, the spiritual affinities of Chan/Zen masters conflict with their official lineage: for instance, the teachings of

[15] See also the verse attributed to Prajñātara (in *Zutang ji*, quoted in Yanagida 1978: 33): "Although China is vast, it has no distinct paths; the main thing is to follow the footsteps of the nephews and grandsons."

Southern Chan masters such as Zongmi, Yanshou, or Chinul were actually closer to Northern Chan; Zen masters such as Yōsai and Muhon Kakushin were immersed in esoteric Buddhism; and Sōtō masters such as Gikai and Keizan remained adepts of the Darumashū criticized by Dōgen. As with the networks of kinship in social life, official and practical sectarian affiliations were strategically used. Genealogies were even manipulated or entirely forged, as we can infer from the biographies of such eminent monks as Shenhui, Zongmi, Wuzhu, or Hakuin. For example, the relationship of Dainichi Nōnin, the founder of the Darumashū, with the Chinese master Fozhao Deguang could be seen as a "distant wedding" (*mariage lointain*), as an alliance of two lineages, with all the strategic considerations this implies. Metaphorically, Japanese masters such as Yōsai and Dōgen also went off to "marry" outside their village, thereby becoming incorporated into a new clan (sect). One could reinterpret in the same anthropological (and slightly parodic) vein a number of traditional Chan "events." Thus Huike cutting his arm to convince Bodhidharma of his sincerity might appear as an example of potlatch (see Mauss 1950: 200) or as a case of submission of the vassal to his lord. This emphasis on sectarian faithfulness should in any case be related to the sacrificial tendencies prevalent at the time in Chinese society and to the cases of self-mutilation described in Buddhist chronicles (which, incidentally, prefigured the rites of passage of the *yakuza* in modern Japan).

One can also discern two contradictory trends in the evolution of the early Chan community; the institutionalization of alms-begging and the attempts to live in autarchy. Begging inscribed Chan in circuits of gift and countergift, such as Marcel Mauss analyzed, and thus located it within the social structure. The tendency to autarchy, on the other hand, aimed at disengaging Chan from social mediations and from the gift circuits, and so it would seem to correspond better to the "sudden" position. But it also entails organized manual work and the administration and development of monastery land, in other words an investment in this-worldly values: thus, in a sense, it contradicts the initial movement by bringing Chan "down to earth."

I WANT now to question the sociological interpretation given above. Of course, routinization is an obvious consequence of institutionalization. The radical, unlocalized rhetoric of Chan, however, has always been the product of a specific place. In other words, routinization is not to be construed as an unfortunate development, an unwanted supplement, but rather as an "essential" component of the most early tradition. All records of early "wandering" Chan masters (such as Huike) are already an idealization. The centrality of "erring" as an early Chan ideal has often been pointed out, but its importance was perhaps always only as an *ideal*. On the other hand, the famous "Pure Rules" of Baizhang Huihai, considered by most Japanese scholars as the birth certificate of the Chan school, could be interpreted as the other face of domestication, the return to structure under the guise of an institutionalization of liminality, to use Victor Turner's terminology (Turner 1974). But was liminality itself ever more than a virtual origin? It is tempting, of course, to interpret the Chan tradition as a reflex of protection, a symbol of sobriety. The rules of Baizhang could then be taken as the sign of a withdrawal under the "sacred canopy" of ritual, another way to tame death and chaos. (See Berger 1969.) If we accept, however, the Chan masters' claim that they speak only out of compassion, one may consider that Chan proselytism resulted from a contamination of the early Chan apophatic stances by Mahāyāna values such as the Bodhisattva ideal. These values marking a return of Chan to society, a reintegration of the renouncer into the world that had been left behind, are symbolized by the tenth Oxherding picture showing Budai "Entering the market place." It is this unstable and unsatisfactory compromise between apophatic eremitism and popular predication that perhaps most enhances the value of Chan as a philosophical and religious trend.

The fact that, sociologically or institutionally, a "routinization of charisma" takes place does not entail a *deviation* at the theoretical level. The banalization of the teaching is time and again counterbalanced by reformative attempts, the resurgence of a process of purification. Yet the question remains: Is there an originary, nonderived, Chan principle at the dawn of the tradition, or is one confronted merely with "traces" in the Derridean sense? According to Derrida, "the trace is not only the disappearance of origin, it means . . . that the origin did not even disappear, that it was never constituted except reciprocally by a nonorigin, the trace, which thus becomes the origin of the origin" (Derrida 1974: 61). Thus differentiation is at play *from the outset*, in a twofold process of routinization and purification. Indeed, it may not be a case of a "pure" teaching becoming "corrupted" because of social factors. The very notion of the original "purity" of Chan seems to have arisen simultaneously with or even posterior to the notion of its "degradation." Thus there is a danger in regarding the institutionalization of Chan as a deviation from a "pure" Chan experience. One would thereby simply replicate a certain type of traditional discourse and end up reintroducing an "essence" of Zen.[16]

---

[16] In another context, this is, for example, the way in which defenders of the Enlightenment such as Jürgen Habermas or Tzvetan Todorov refer to subsequent developments such as nationalism and colonialism as mere "deviations" from humanist individualism, monsters engendered by the sleep of reason, without really addressing, as Foucault and Derrida did, the possibility of the radical ambiguity of the humanist tradition, and without including these "accidents" or "supplements" within the definition of its "essence." (See Habermas 1981, 1986; Todorov, "The Deflection of Enlightenment" [Stanford: Stanford Humanities

Chan/Zen has often been presented as a kind of mysticism. Victor Turner, for instance, relying on D. T. Suzuki, saw in it a good example of a religious teaching founded on what he called *communitas*: "Seeking oneness is not from this perspective to withdraw from multiplicity; it is to eliminate divisiveness, to realize nonduality" (Turner 1974: 203). The opposition between *communitas* and "structure" seems at first glance analogous to that presupposed by Linji's notion of the "true man without a rank," that is, the individual who, among other things, does not get caught up in social and ideological structures. One should be wary, however, of taking an intellectualist view of structure and ritual and seeing institutionalization as mere routinization, thus idealizing *communitas* and mystics as Turner, writing in the sixties, did. It is tempting to dismiss ritual and hierarchy because we can no longer understand their religious purpose. Many interpreters have tended to overreact to the secular approach and have returned to an idealized conception of religious phenomena. At any rate, this oscillation between two poles such as *communitas* and structure, faith and reason, iconoclasm and ritualism, was apparently as much a part of Chan as it is a part of our cultural heritage, and this situation permits a transferential relationship between us and Chan adepts that may, after all, facilitate the kind of "fusion of horizons" advocated by philosophical hermeneutics.

Making a difference

Despite (or because of) its attempts at defining an orthodoxy and stressing nonduality, Chan discourse keeps creating dichotomies such as sudden and gradual, Northern and Southern schools, "special transmission outside the Scriptures" (Ch. *jiaowai biechuan*, J. *kyōge betsuden*) and "harmony between Scriptures and Chan" (*jiaochan yizhi, kyōzen itchi*), "Kōan Chan" (*kanhua chan, kanna zen*) and "silent illumination Chan" (*mozhao chan, mokushō zen*). Leaving aside for now the question of measuring the exact role of methodological "double vision" in these various processes of differentiation, I am here concerned with overriding the unifying ideology of the tradition (but also with accounting for it and making it account for itself).

It was first suggested that the Chan institution emerged at the cost of Chan itself. This distinction between Chan as atemporal experience and

Center, 1989].) A similar attempt was made by Thomas Merton, who, following D. T. Suzuki, emphasized the universalism of Zen and tried to separate the wheat of Zen from the chaff of Buddhism: "I wonder whether one could make Zen enter in some way the framework of structuralist anthropology. . . . Insofar as Zen is part of a social and political whole, insofar as it seems to be connected to other elements of a cultural system, 'yes.' But in that case, what fits in the system is *Buddhism* rather than *Zen*" (Merton 1970: 1). Shall we conclude that to the extent that Zen is "Buddhism" it has *deviated* from its ideal essence?

Chan as cumulative tradition helps us, for example, to understand the debate between partisans of the historical and the phenomenological approaches to Chan as it was replayed in the fifties by Hu Shih and D. T. Suzuki. (See Hu Shih 1953; D. T. Suzuki 1953.) It is now time to relativize this earlier distinction. The "originality" of Chan may be that there is no "originary" teaching, since the Buddha allegedly "never spoke a word during his forty-nine years of predication." But was there even an "originary" or "pure" experience? What we seem to find are "traces" in the Derridean sense of signs pointing to an origin that was never more than virtual. Paradoxically, the very insight that there is nothing to obtain comes to play the role of an original insight, and thus constantly risks becoming hypostasized, even and particularly when signified by the (meaning-full) silence of the Buddha or of Vimalakīrti. Like a dream, the insight cannot be retrieved; it can only be imagined. In this sense, the "original" insight, just like the dream, may exist only as a "trace," something that was never "present" to a fully awakened consciousness, since there is no self that can actually live the experience. Zhongfeng Mingben compares Chan to the original chaos described by Zhuangzi:

> One man came along and put a stroke on the head of Chan. Another put a stroke on the feet of Chan; a third put a stroke in the heart of Chan. Finally yet another man came over and put three dots on top of the three strokes. When we look at it, the Chan thus decorated bears no resemblance to its original face. Later on more people came along and added more dots and strokes to those already there. Occasionally, they would put some of the dots and strokes in the wrong places, and they would start to criticize each other and give names to these, calling them Tathāgatagarbha Chan, Patriarch Chan, literary Chan, heretical Chan, Śrāvaka Chan, worldling Chan, . . . Chan of shouts and sticks. . . . (Chün-fang Yü 1982: 433)

Here Mingben criticizes Zongmi's attempt to classify Chan in a *panjiao* system, that is, a doctrinal hierarchy, instead of pointing out that Chan stands outside any hierarchy. But his comparison of Chan with the realization of primordial chaos (*hundun*) is already off the mark, since Chan's primordial body is here differentiated into eyes, feet, and so on, while this differentiation was the very cause of the death of chaos in Zhuangzi's parable. (See Girardot 1983.) Mingben himself is part of the process he criticizes, and his discourse is recuperated (or even produced) by the larger syntax in which it is inscribed.

The process of differentiation is thus always already at work in every traditional style of Chan, as can be seen from the following description of the three main "houses" of Chan by the Caodong monk Yelu Chuzai (1189–1243): "In the school of Yunmen, the enlightened ones attain it out of (a paradoxical combination of) reticence and incisiveness, and the deluded ones lose it out of discrimination and impulsiveness. In the school of Linji, the illuminated ones attain it out of headlong daring, and the obfuscated ones lose it out of recklessness. In the Caodong school, the wise ones attain it out of fine insight, and the stupid ones lose it out of (involvement in) minute details" (Jan 1982: 383).

The logical necessity of the dialectic of transcendence found in Chan is well expressed in another context by Merleau-Ponty: "A time came when the inner conviction to grasp the principles in their inner evidence ceased to be stimulus to knowledge and became the threat of a new scholasticism" (Merleau-Ponty 1960: 224). Thus Chan practice is sometimes conceived as an attempt to recover the "lesson of this creative act which had instituted a long period of fecund thought, but which had exhausted its virtue" in the pseudo-Chan of the epigones.

The obvious danger here is that of a "foundational" conception of Chan, one that was actually legitimized by the notion of "fundamental awakening" (Ch. *benjue*, J. *hongaku*) and all the "fundamentalist" rhetoric found in the Tāthāgatagarbha trend of Chan. In this sense the Chan tradition is a fictional remembering of origins, that is, an active forgetting of the fact that there never was any pure origin. What may serve as origin is at best an emerging awareness of the differential, deferential nature of awakening. In contrast to the belief in the retrieval of some metaphysical truth through laborious practice, we find the view of those rugged individualists like Linji, who claim that there are no arcana because, as Veyne points out, "if one believes that arcane domains accessible only to others exist, research and invention are paralyzed. One does not dare to take a step all alone" (Veyne 1988: 93). This "immanentist" or "naturalist" Chan, taking its cues from Mādhyamika, has cut off the moorings of traditional Buddhism—"hitching-posts for asses"—and advocates notions such as the "great function." These two types of Chan, of course, are simply tendencies or ideal types and should not be construed as well-demarcated social groups.

The "immanentist" or "naturalist" tendency may itself derive from two opposite premises. It could result from an immanentist conception of the Buddha nature and fundamental awakening, like that of Mazu's school (as interpreted by Zongmi): a case in point is the Senika or "naturalist heresy" (J. *jinen gedō*) so vehemently criticized by Dōgen. It could also derive from the departure from ontology achieved by Mādhyamika Chan: the drift initiated by the rejection of the notion of originary truth led to a moral relativism that was perceived as freedom, an escape from metaphysical bondage.

Despite its "domestication" and the repression of its "heterological" elements, Chan remained plural, if only because of the essential divergence produced at the phenomenological level by the differential nature of awakening and its reinscription in a "metaphysics of presence" that it unceasingly subverts. To understand the dialectical structure of Chan, the dialectic between differentiation and totalization, it might be heuristically useful to start from Bergson's "law of dichotomy": "We call *law of dichotomy* that which seems to provoke the realization, through their mere dissociation, of trends which were at first only different views taken over a single trend. And we will then propose to call *law of double frenzy* the requirement, immanent to each of the two trends once they are realized through separation, that each be followed to its end—as if there was an end!" (Bergson 1935: 316). Apparently, a dichotomization similar to that which characterizes our binary thought processes—the structural division that shows us all phenomena under two different and mutually exclusive aspects—was already at work in Chan, and it has tended to mask the complex reality of this religious phenomenon with "blind windows" such as Northern and Southern Chan. Ideally, we should aim at retrieving some of the as-yet-unpolarized profusion of prereflexive reality; we need therefore to start from the discursive elaborations of the tradition. These elaborations, however, are themselves productive of a second-order reality—and second-order here no longer implies degeneration, as in the sociological critique. Thus the elliptic ideological structure of Chan is not merely the product of our "methodological double vision" but finds its roots in epistemological and psychological processes that seem largely cross-cultural.[17] The paradigmatic opposition appears to be that between un-mediated or nonmediating (sudden) and mediated/mediating (gradual) Chan.

I am concerned here with heuristically widening the gap, "doing the splits" as it were, in order to make the initial difference (that infinitesimal difference that is already, as a famous Chan poem tells us, the *grand écart* that separates Heaven and Earth) reinscribe itself into all kinds of dichotomies. If the movement of the tradition is fundamentally irenic insofar as it tries, by denying it, to close the gap it has opened, then we may as well attempt, agonistically, to widen it—and the degree of iconoclastic pleasure to be taken in this endeavor might actually further our understanding of Chan iconoclasm. This may help us realize that Chan is hybrid, not only for circumstantial reasons, but because it is *also* fundamentally a type of *hybris* that resists any attempt at mastery (and, consequently, unceasingly subverts the *Chan de maîtrise* represented by Chan "masters"). The dialectic is therefore not one of surpassing (which still implies mastery, hierarchy, power) but rather one of subversion—the result of an "inter-

[17] For a discussion of "methodological double vision," see Bell 1987: 97–118; and infra, "Dichotomies in Question(s)," in the Epilogue: 310–14.

stitial thinking," of an active disjunction of monolithic "structures." On the margins of the Chan school, marginalized by it while emanating from it, is the alternative of Chan as "école buissonnière," which we must attempt to bring to the foreground.

This heuristic polarization could find its expression in a number of (not necessarily overlapping) clusters such as inclusive/exclusive, irenic/agonistic, hierarchical/anarchist, sacerdotal/philosophical, foundational/historicist, hermeneutical/performative.[18] For instance, the distinction between hieratic and communal, derived from François-André Isambert's discussion of Catholicism, seems to a certain extent applicable to Chan. Isambert distinguishes between a "hieratic order," legitimated by the use of "sacrality," and a "communal order," characterized by faith and fraternity (Isambert 1982: 271). The combination of these two orders is stable, but their conflictual nature would be lost were one to present them as belonging to a single essence. The communal order requires the perfect transparence of all intermediaries, and any tendency of the latter to acquire a specific opacity is criticized, under the name of "religion," as an obstacle to "faith."[19] In Christianity as in Buddhism, we find a dialectic between hieratization and its opposite, the denial of the sacralization of any system that may interfere in the name of mediation between humanity and ultimate truth (officials, institutions, rites). This polarization is often related to that between the cosmological and the ethical spheres, that is, the assertion of the priority of the world and of the law of things (the Dharma), and that of the priority of human beings and of their creative activity (Gauchet 1985: xiii). But this relation is not necessary. At any rate, we have a constant oscillation between two criteria of truth, and it is this oscillation between the poles of a "twofold truth" that gives the impression—and sometimes is the effect—of a fundamental duplicity.

Interpreters of the tradition are not secure against the dangers of such polarization, either. They may be drawn into the ranks of those who, in the wake of Hegel, attempt to find everywhere the "comfortable binary confrontation." It is a similar disjunction that produces dichotomies such as sacred and profane, doctrine and ritual, and leads us to forget that in real life, as Edmund Leach points out, holidays are always mixed with holy days, and feasts with fasts. Individual cases are always more complex: Dōgen, for example, seems to start from a rather foundational no-

[18] Concerning the foundational/historicist paradigm, see Vincent Descombes, "Les mots de la tribu," *La traversée de l'Atlantique, Critique* 456 (1985): 431. The division within Chan seems to offer some analogies to the *différend* that opposed Jean-François Lyotard and Richard Rorty, and more generally the advocates of postmodernism and the defenders of the Enlightenment. See ibid.: 559–584.

[19] Incidentally, this is precisely the type of dichotomy that Merton, himself an advocate of "faith," made when distinguishing, within Zen, the mystical element (Zen proper) from the "religion" (what he calls "Buddhism"). See Merton 1970: 1ff.

tion of the original Dharma, but his conceptions of the patriarchal tradition and of his privileged historical role, together with his speculations concerning the "actualization" of ultimate truth, lead him eventually to advocate a "historicist" type of Zen. Furthermore, as Bourdieu points out, "beyond the antitheses of 'thinking in pairs', permanence can be ensured by change and the structure perpetuated by movement" (Bourdieu 1984: 164). Thus moral rule and its transgression are not simply opposed but intertwined. If polarized structure is actually an intertwining, then this structure requires an approach different from that which tries, in Lévi-Straussian fashion, to solve the opposition of two terms by a mediation.

The importance of the *dual/duel* in Chan simultaneously points toward and reduces the irreducible plurality, or the multipolarity, of Chan. The two antagonist teachings defined as "sudden" and "gradual" turn out to be accomplices that conceal the complexity of the Chan phenomenon— phenomenological trees that hide the "forests of Chan"—because "in a given cultural context, the coexistence of two antithetical discourses might well be what assures the balance of the system" (Charles 1985: 65).

Instead of the "monotheism" of the One practice (*yixing*) in the orthodox tradition (on which see Faure 1986c), I will attempt to make the "polytheism" of values and practices reappear and to show that neither the "purist" vision of unitarian Zen, nor even the dualism of the "blind windows" found in theories such as the "convergence of Chan and the teachings," faithfully reflects the experience of Chan adepts. The differentiation produces a dissemination, a setting in motion of various paradigmatic pairs that can no longer be assigned to precise and unchanging sectarian positions. Once again, it is important to consider these various examples of "differential Chan" merely as ideal types and to avoid reifying the divisions into groups. Chan is, and always was, an "imagined community." The notions of *distinction* on the social level and of *différance* on the philosophical level may help us to account for this constant production of gaps (*écarts*). As in the Saussurian conception of *langue*, there are no "substantial" entities, only differential *écarts*. And perhaps it is with the sudden/gradual polarity that Chan finally succeeded in "doing the splits" (*le grand écart*). We will in the following chapters explore the epistemological factors that may help explain Chan "duplicity" (in both senses of the term). But it will be helpful to keep in mind the socio-historical background of the tension or polarization between duality and nonduality, between the theoretical assertion of the orthodox nonduality and the constant creation or reinscription of doctrinal dualities, that distinguish orthodoxy and heterodoxies, "sudden Chan" and its "others."

Two   *Sudden/Gradual: A Loose Paradigm*

The rise of Chan orthodoxy is by and large due to the success of the "sudden" teaching. What were the conditions of such a success? Paul Demiéville once suggested that "sudden" and "gradual" were universal categories that preexisted Buddhism in China (Demiéville 1949: 179). For Demiéville, "the antinomy is not only of a psychological or methodological order, it applies to two conceptions of truth itself and actually spreads to all planes of thought." Demiéville went on to argue that it is possible to detect in this paradigm a "kind of transposition in Buddhist terms of the polarity that always divided the Chinese mind and that finds its historical expression in the antagonism between reasonable, scrupulously careful, industrious Confucianism and intuitive, mystical, totalitarian Taoism" (ibid.: 181). Can we, therefore, following Mauss's suggestion that we ought to draw up a list of fundamental categories of human thought, Western and non-Western, enlist the sudden/gradual paradigm as one of them? As Luis Gómez points out, Demiéville omitted to take into account the different cultural contexts in his comparison between subitism and the Christian concept of grace (Gómez 1987: 131). At first glance, the polemical context in which subitism developed seems to argue against the universality of this notion. This polemical factor should not, however, prevent us from considering the sudden/gradual polarity as the projection onto the soteriological plane of a priori logical structures. I shall examine Demiéville's claim and see how useful these categories, whatever their universality, may be for understanding Chinese religion in general. I shall therefore shift my focus from the doctrinal and polemical content of these notions to their socio-cultural function on the one hand and to their epistemological and logical value on the other. Not limiting myself to a strictly Buddhist terminology, I will attempt to express the paradigm in Western terms. Bracketing the traditional interpretations or grafting them onto other discourses may enable us to bring to light neglected aspects of the controversy and perhaps to understand what from the outset systematized it.

The philosophical framework of the controversy was provided by the Two Truths theory: sudden and gradual refer to whether awakening is regarded from the point of view of ultimate truth or of conventional truth.[1] Its soteriological purport was to solve the following dilemma: "Is ultimate reality so distant from and yet so continuous with the mundane that one can have only a mediated and step by step access to it? Or is it so proximate, and yet so autonomous and so utterly unlike our illusions or expectations of it, that one can reach it only all-at-once and only without any mediation whatsoever?" (Gimello 1982: 484).

THE SEMANTIC FIELD

The semantic and philosophical content of the "sudden/gradual" (*dun-jian*) paradigm has caused much ink to flow, and I do not intend to dwell on those aspects of the question. Demiéville's translation of the term *dun* as "subit" (sudden) was criticized by R. A. Stein, who, relying mainly on Tibetan sources, preferred to render it as "simultaneous" (Stein 1987). For the sake of convenience, I shall for the time being keep the usual "interpretations" of "sudden" (*subit*) in rendering the Chinese framing of the problem. Being the product of a complex historical evolution, this term covers several orders of meaning. As it was used in Chan during the Tang, it seems to cover at least three orders of mutually reinforcing (and sometimes conflicting) meanings, depending on whether it qualifies awakening as (1) fast, (2) absolute, and (3) *im-mediate*.

The term first denotes *rapidity*: in this case, it points toward an experience that may be achronical but still defines itself in a certain way in relation to temporality. As early as the fourth century, Chinese Buddhists attempted to demonstrate that it was possible to reach deliverance in this very life, relying for that purpose on Mahāyāna scriptures such as the *Laṅkāvatāra-sūtra*.[2] This first meaning of "sudden" as "imminent" is common to both the Northern and Southern schools and predates their antag-

[1] The Two Truths theory offers a metaphor for Buddhist practice, but it also provides the *metaphorical* (i.e., two-tiered) structure of subitism; gradualism, on the other hand, is characterized by a *metonymic* structure, whereby truth is coextensive with objective reality and unfolds, as it were, horizontally, temporally. This, incidentally, is radically different from the immanent version of subitism, which collapses the two levels of truth, as in Zhiyi's following comment: "Even though we make fine distinctions between shallow and profound, . . . nevertheless the provisional and the ultimate are universally coextensive" (quoted in Donner 1987: 211).

[2] A significant—although somewhat later—example is provided by Huiguang, the author of the preface of an apocryphal text of the Northern school, the *Chanmen jing*. Huiguang relates the despair that overcame him on reading a passage of the *Lotus Sūtra* in which the Buddha Mahābhijñānābhibhu practiced sitting-meditation during ten "small" kalpas without realizing the Buddha Dharma. One can imagine the joy—and the relief—of Huiguang when he eventually discovered the *Chanmen jing*, which advocated very opportunely the doctrine of sudden awakening! (See Yanagida 1961.) Notice that, later on, Chan adepts overturned the difficulty in another way, by stating that it is precisely in "not realizing the Buddha Dharma" and in "not becoming Buddha" that true Buddhahood is to be found. See *Linji lu*, T. 47, 1985: 502; *Wumen guan*, case 9, T. 48, 2005: 294; *Jingde chuandeng lu*, T. 51, 2076: 229.

onism. It seems to represent the Chinese reaction—particularly clear-cut in the Chan school—against Indian dhyāna and the abhidharmic maps of the path. It is over this issue that Indians and Chinese clashed during the so-called Council of Tibet. (See Gómez 1987.) As Buswell points out, however, more than a denial of time itself, *dun* implies a denial of sequence (Buswell 1987: 351).

The term *dun* also refers to "immanent" or "innate" awakening (*ben-jue*), that is, the realization of the transcendent and pure Buddha nature that exists within every being. This new meaning of the term has nothing to do with the first meaning of "rapidity," which expressed only the "conventional truth" (*saṃvṛti-satya*). The faith in the omnipresence of the Buddha nature is no other than Bodhidharma's "Entrance by Principle" (*liru*). According to Demiéville, " 'Sudden' [*subit*], in this sense, . . . implies uniqueness vis-à-vis multiplicity, totality vis-à-vis partiality or particularity; 'subitism' is an absolutism, . . . whereas 'gradualism' implies plurality, accumulation, temporal and spatial determinations, since it corresponds, on the methodological level, to successive and located practices" (Demiéville 1956: 31). Awakening is therefore "sudden" in that it is grounded in the Principle (*li*) and depends on the Absolute—of which it constitutes in a way the "function" (*yong*).

As has been noted, the notion of "innate awakening" attempts to express the paradoxical point of view of absolute Truth, although all points of view are necessarily relative, and all notions are in fact "false notions" (*wangxiang*). As early Chan texts often point out, "only nonseeing is true seeing." Just as the remedy presupposes illness, awakening presupposes delusion. But "innate" (or "sudden") awakening is quite different, for it precedes all false notions such as "awakening" or "practice," just as a healthy person has no use for medicine. As the Chan master Moheyan, the advocate of subitism at the Council of Tibet, put it: "The notions of 'gradual' and 'sudden' . . . are only notions from the mind of beings, false notions, things seen. . . . If one refrains from all notions . . . , 'gradual' and 'sudden' are nowhere to be found" (quoted in Demiéville 1952: 75).

By delving into the conditions of awakening, Chinese Buddhists were paradoxically condemned to fall into a kind of gradualism. Aware of this danger, Chan masters adopted an apophatic stance but did not always avoid the trap. The *via negativa* itself tends to turn into some kind of positivity.[3] Therefore, sudden awakening is a paradoxical "state of grace," an *excessus mentis*, or sometimes simply an act of faith,[4] that allows one to

---

[3] On this question, see "Comment ne pas parler: Dénégations," in Derrida 1987: 535–594.

[4] See the definition given by the *Erru sixing lun*: "Entrance by Principle means that . . . one deeply believes that all sentient beings, profane and sage, possess the same true nature" (Yanagida 1969a: 31).

realize that after all, "false notions" themselves are illusory and that thought does not arise. Being themselves devoid of reality, the adventitious passions covering self-nature cannot defile it. To illustrate the way in which the Buddha nature (or the pure mind) is veiled by passions, Chan masters often use metaphors such as those of the sun hidden by clouds, the mirror covered with dust, or the Maṇi jewel sunk in muddy water—legacies from the Tathāgatagarbha tradition. Gradualism is characterized as a belief in the real existence of these passions and in the performance of practices aimed at their elimination. To this ideal of purification, the sudden stance opposes the simple realization of the intrinsic purity of beings, a purity that makes all practice superfluous. Although Gómez argues that "it would be a mistake to assume that innateness necessarily implies immediacy, to say nothing of suddenness" (Gómez 1987: 95), such a mistake was apparently common in Chan circles.

As is well known, it is on this point that the Northern school was judged to be gradual—on the basis of a verse attributed to Shenxiu, stating the necessity of constantly polishing the "spiritual mirror" in order to restore its original clarity.[5] Aside from the obvious problems with this attribution, it seems that Northern Chan masters were aware of the danger of attachment to notions such as "purity" or "defilement." At the ontological level, both schools almost agreed that a purely "gradual" cultivation can lead only to a "gradual awakening," which is not the ultimate awakening (*samyaksambodhi*). Although they are both gradual in some respects, the verses attributed to Shenxiu and Huineng are both "sudden" inasmuch as the mind is seen as intrinsically pure—and therefore innately enlightened.[6] In other words, if conventional truth can lead to ultimate truth, it is either because it is already absolute, or because, as Jon Elster would put it, true realization is essentially a by-product.[7] Therefore, it seems reasonable to look elsewhere for a more decisive point of divergence between the teachings of the two schools. For this, we now have to consider the third meaning underlying the term *dun* in Chan.

[5] See Demiéville 1987: 13–17. It is interesting that two verses on the same theme are attributed to Huineng in the earlier recensions of the *Platform Sūtra*. While the second one has been selected as a classical example of the "sudden" position, the first one seems as "gradual" as Shenxiu's verse. It is even used by the Huayan master Chengguan (736–839) to summarize the point of view of "gradual cultivation" (T. 36, 1736: 164c; see also Yanagida 1980: 384). Furthermore, there is clearly a hierarchy between the two verses attributed to Shenxiu and Huineng. (See Gómez 1987: 73.)

[6] As John McRae puts it: "The two verses constitute a single unit expressing a rarefied understanding of the 'perfect teaching' of constant Bodhisattva practice" (McRae 1987: 278).

[7] See Elster 1983: 43ff. Likewise, in the dream metaphor of the *Daśabhūmika-sūtra*, the deluded efforts of the dreamer to escape from the river into which he believes he has fallen suddenly cause him to wake up, thus becoming the paradoxical cause of his salvation. (See Demiéville 1954: 432.)

The Chinese *dun* also means *immediate*, that is, etymologically, *unmediated*, "that which works, arises or is reached without intermediary." This notion of "immediacy" seems to be at the core of the controversy between the Northern and Southern schools. Like Huineng in the *Platform Sūtra*, Shenhui denies all skillful means (*upāya*). His criticism of Shenxiu has to do mainly with the fact that the latter—although simply following on that point the example of his predecessor Daoxin—attempted to adapt his teaching to the level of understanding of his audience.[8] It is certain that the Northern school attached a great importance to *upāya*. On this point, it differs, at least theoretically, from its rival. On the other hand, the Southern school was obviously never able to dispense with skillful means. Shenhui's recommendation to read the Mahāyāna scriptures, for instance, is clearly a case of resorting to *upāya*, and it is difficult to accept his self-proclaimed role as an uncompromising representative of "immediate" awakening: his subitism remains in many respects "gradual."[9] This is true as well of other Southern Chan adepts. Even what Zongmi defined as "sudden awakening and sudden cultivation" (*dunwu dunxiu*) remains gradual. (See Buswell 1987: 340.) Linji himself appears to be a "gradualist" when he says: "You must first fathom things yourself, purify yourself, polish yourself; then one day you will awaken" (quoted in Demiéville 1972: 116).

Thus, despite the theoretical one-upmanship that develops concerning skillful means, it does not seem that, in practice, the positions of the two schools were so different. Both were "sudden" (in the first and second senses defined above) and both were to some degree "gradual" (in the third sense). Their divergence was primarily a question of "style"—of rhetoric as well as of practice. Contrary to Shenhui, Northern Chan masters recognized the unavoidable contradiction between their theoretical "subitism" and the concrete necessities of spiritual guidance. While Shenhui's attitude was largely polemical, it may also reflect an effort to escape what could be perceived as a spiritual dead end resulting from proselytism. At any rate, the *de facto* coalescence of various "subitisms" and "gradualisms" does not mean that the distinction between the "sudden" and "gradual" positions collapses, only that it does not overlap with the Southern/Northern schism, or with any such sectarian division. Consequently, the debate on "sudden" and "gradual," by being in the foreground, has contributed greatly to obfuscate the complex evolution of Chan in eighth-century China. This debate acquired another dimension in the Tibetan context, where it underlined the opposition between Chi-

---

[8] On Daoxin's use of skillful means, see Faure 1988: 75–82; Chappell 1983; McRae 1986: 136–144.

[9] See Gómez 1987: 75–86. Gómez, however, argues that Shenhui's gradualism is the opposite of Shenxiu's (ibid.: 89) and so is his subitism (ibid.: 91).

nese and Indian Buddhism.[10] But, as Demiéville has shown, the "sudden/gradual" polarity was so deeply anchored in Chinese culture that the debate soon spread, not only to other Buddhist schools such as Huayan and Tiantai, but also to Daoism, neo-Confucianism, and artistic movements such as poetry and painting. (See Cahill 1987; Lynn 1987.) Shenhui's questionable "genius" was to make full use of this paradigm, the dynamics of which made reconciliation between Chan schools impossible for a time and allowed him to disqualify his rivals.

THE IDEOLOGICAL (DIS)CONTENT

In his "Afterword" to the *Sudden and Gradual* volume, Du Weiming (Tu Wei-ming) writes that "most of Ch'an scholarship is controversial, but the primacy of 'enlightenment' as the ultimate concern of Ch'an training remains unquestioned" (in Gregory 1987: 447). Precisely that primacy is what needs to be questioned. Du Weiming apparently takes at face value the claims of Chan masters about their motivations for practice. Informed by the Confucian tradition, he even considers, despite evidence to the contrary, that the "Sinitic faith in the perfectibility of human nature" underlies sudden Chan (ibid.: 455). Although Chan and Confucianism obviously differ in their theoretical claims, they share a similar elitism, and the social qualifications of their theoretical catholicity have to be examined more carefully.[11] It may be appropriate to analyze the "twofold truth" of subitism and gradualism in terms of the traditional two-tiered model of interpretation of social and cultural constructs. Bourdieu's theory of practice, for instance, represents an attempt to do justice to the two aspects of human experience: the "phenomenological" level of beliefs and representations and the "objective" level at which these beliefs and representations appear as ideological products. (See Bourdieu 1977b: 3.) Since the phenomenological level corresponds in this case to the doctrinal conceptions reviewed above, we now turn to a consideration of the social and ideological uses of these theories. The "middle way," here, is not a neutral (and neutralized) position; it is achieved by a "simultaneous grasp of the two truths," a refusal to reduce one level to the other or to reconcile them in a convenient hierarchy (as Bourdieu, in spite of himself, eventually does).[12] The middle way is itself dual tracked.[13]

[10] On the persistence of a "sudden" opposition, long after the famous (and problematic) Council, see Ōbata 1976.

[11] It also seems difficult to argue, as Du Weiming does (in Gregory 1987: 448), that sudden Chan "has deep roots in Chinese cosmological thinking," when, as we will see later, it is defined essentially by its acosmological thrust.

[12] For a discussion of Bourdieu in the context of Tokugawa religion and ideology, see Ooms 1987. Proceeding along different lines, Paul Ricoeur, although paying lip service to the notion of a balance between the "hermeneutics of faith (or retrieval)" and the "herme-

The socio-political stakes of the sudden/gradual controversies were obviously high. We are told that, because of his attacks against Northern Chan, Shenhui was sent into exile at the demand of a powerful lay follower of Puji. At the so-called Council of Tibet, the partisans on both sides ended by killing each other in the name of emptiness. It is also apparent that the sudden teaching attracted people who had some reason to hope for a "sudden" change of the political situation. This point is corroborated by the list of Shenhui's supporters, most of them ambitious officials. But Shenhui was not a "revolutionary" figure in the popular sense, and his subitism was from the outset elitist. Although "sudden" and "gradual" may not be reducible to a simple logical opposition, much less a sociological one, subitism and gradualism, as ideological constructs, seem to have sociological connotations. If, like Bourdieu's true culture, sudden or innate awakening cannot be acquired but is that with which everyone is endowed at birth, and which only the elite come to realize, then gradual awakening is like the masses' illusion that they will be able to cultivate themselves, to reach the "distinction" of the elite. As Derrida puts it, "the hierarchized opposition between gift and work, between intuition and concept, between the genial and the schoolish modes . . . is homologous to the opposition between an aristocracy and a democracy. . . . Masters and slaves: the *grand seigneur* reaches in one leap and through feeling what is immediately given to him, whereas the people work, elaborate, conceive" (Derrida 1981b: 452). As noted earlier, the controversy over the value of *upāya* for spiritual realization is reminiscent of the opposition drawn by Bourdieu in the Western context between the *scholars* (partisans of apprenticeship) and the *gentlemen* (advocates of "innate talents"; Bourdieu 1984: 68). In the Chinese literary context, it also calls to mind the contrast between the *zuojia* or "makers," "fabricators," and the *yijia* or "liberated masters" (Cahill 1987: 431).

Critics of Chan have often denounced its claim for a "positionless position." Although well aware of the social context of Chan/Zen notions, Victor Turner, who had read D. T. Suzuki, tended to accept them uncritically: "The familiar distinction made in Zen Buddhism between the concepts *prajñā* . . . and *vijñāna* . . . is rooted in the contrasting social experiences I have described, respectively, as 'communitas' and 'structure' " (Turner 1974: 46). As is well known, Turner tended also to idealize *communitas* and remained unaware of its ideological functions. Without

---

neutics of suspicion," aims at an ideal synthesis, what he calls a "depth interpretation," that would transcend both the naive interpretation and the critical (social-scientific or structural) analysis. See Ricoeur 1981: 131. Fredric Jameson argues more consistently for the necessity of grasping simultaneously what he calls the *ideological* and the *utopian* dimensions of cultural artifacts. See Jameson 1981: 235.

[13] I am indebted to John Strong for this expression.

denying the possibility of an ideal subitism that, like laughter and humor according to Bakhtin (1968: 92ff.), completely subverts the dominant (and scholastic) values, we should be wary of confusing it with its ideological parody, which reflects an elitist conception of practice and remains a socially determined category. Whereas awakening, as a religious ideal, is culturally determined, the realization that any such ideal is self-defeating entails an objectification of, and loss of interest in, the cultural game—an awakening to its ideological nature. (See Bourdieu 1984: 250.) In a sense, Chan may be characterized both as "typically Chinese" and as a refusal to be Chinese. At the same time, the denial of the game may in some cases be a "strategy of condescension"—a strategy that, according to Bourdieu, "is possible in all cases where the objective gap between the persons present is sufficiently recognized by all, for the symbolical negation of hierarchy permits one to accumulate both the profits tied to the intact hierarchy and those provided by the purely symbolical denial of that hierarchy" (Bourdieu 1982: 62). The claim of having "no rank" can become one of the (more or less conscious) strategies to get a rank, or to keep it. This may justify the criticism of Dōgen, if not toward Linji himself, at least toward some of Linji's epigones for whom spiritual claims had perhaps become a shortcut for social ambitions. The denunciation of hierarchy and hierarchies may also reflect the ambiguous social status of Chan masters as cultural intermediaries. This ambiguity could result from or account for the "discrepancy between the (symbolically) subversive dispositions . . . and the manipulative or conservative functions attached to their position" (Bourdieu 1984: 366). In this light, one could even consider "sudden awakening" as a "cultural investment." Subitism and gradualism may be two antagonist yet conniving teachings, accomplices in a "conspiracy of silence." As Bourdieu points out, "One of the generic properties of the fields is that the struggle for the specific stake hides the objective collusion concerning the principles of the game" (Bourdieu 1982: 47). The sudden/gradual controversy would appear as the creation of specific stakes, the imposition of the rules of a spiritual game, the designation of a "sacred" (and empty) place or seat: the "seat of awakening" (*bodhimaṇḍa*). The distinction between the elite and the common people was inscribed in the very structure of Buddhist doctrine—with the Two Truths theory. Unlike Mādhyamika, Chan implies a negation of conventional truth from the standpoint of ultimate truth: it emphasizes the ineffable, nonrepresentational, nonsensational, nonfactual nature of awakening. But awakening itself soon becomes a mere referent, an alibi, and apophatic discourse turns into a rhetorical technique that may at times mask the superficiality of the experience.

The rhetorical emphasis on "sudden" (particularly when understood as "simultaneous" and/or "immediate") and the notion of a "simultaneous grasp" of the two truths also reflected an epistemological shift, facilitated by the use of visual and spatial metaphors. It also served to elaborate the notion of immediacy and created a "conspiracy of silence" around medi- ations and the "supplementarity" of traditional practices. It is a revealing case, because it shows the twofold truth of the Two Truths theory and suggests a homology with our own epistemological position. Thus the central issue is not so much at the doctrinal level, where the dichotomy between subitism and gradualism does not explain as much as scholars have tended to think (for example, the schism between Northern and Southern Chan or the gap between "early" and "classical" Chan), but at another, deeper level, because it may be one of the primary inscriptions of the fault line, the "fracture of meaning" (Pollack 1986) that produced Chan as a "differential tradition." At this level, it does actually reflect the differentiation between "inclusive" and "exclusive" Chan, two variants of subitism (or, from another angle, of gradualism). Like Daoism and Tantrism,[14] inclusive Chan is a two-tiered, dialectical discourse, which advocates a process of "fine-tuning" to the traditional symbols, before eventually passing beyond them in a radical *excessus mentis*.[15] Exclusive Chan, on the other hand, is radically nondialectical in its claim to shortcut the whole process. But its possibility is clearly a rhetorical one, in that it is essentially a matter of "style," a departure from a norm that it implies even while denying it. To borrow the metaphor of nudity from the Ko- rean master Muyŏm (799–888), the inclusive subitist (identified here with the gradualist) argues that one must first put on clothes in order to re- move them later, while the exclusive subitist (Muyŏm himself) argues (with his tongue) that, in the "tongueless realm" of sudden Chan, "one does not wear even one strand of thread": if something must eventually come off anyway, then why put it on in the first place?[16] What Muyŏm failed to see is that primitive nudity lacks the erotic touch and the sense of transgression provided by "civilized" denuding, and that he himself was already excluded from the Eden of subitism for having tasted the fruit from the tree of the knowledge of sudden and gradual. If, as subitists argued, the conditioned (*saṃskṛta*) cannot lead to the unconditioned (*asaṃskṛta*), perhaps, paradoxically, only the removal of the conditioned can. Thus the perception of the uselessness of intellectual efforts to solve

[14] One might add early Buddhism, if we depart from the conventional interpretation to follow Paul Mus's insightful discussion in *Barabuḍur*. Mus shows in particular how early Buddhism, akin in this respect to Brahmanistic ritual, was already characterized by the "magical" notion of a break (and inversion) between two levels. See Mus 1935: 66–70.

[15] Concerning the Daoist practice of "inner contemplation" (*neiguan*) to use images before eventually transcending them, and the "cosmologization" of the Daoist body leading to a leap into chaos (or rather *chaosmos*), see Schipper 1983: 186–192.

[16] See Buswell 1987: 330. The same metaphor is used by Linji, who takes his cues from Zhuangzi.

kōans was seen as the paradoxical condition of the unconditional awakening. With Dahui Zonggao, known for his method of increasing doubt in order to achieve a breakthrough,[17] Chan fell back into a variant of the two-tiered subitism (or gradualism) of early Chan. This type of practice remained the mainstream of the later Chan and Zen traditions, although they kept the superlative, "shortcut" rhetoric of "classical Chan." The artificial creation of the "great doubt" advocated by Dahui, although it may actually provide a powerful soteriological means, lent itself to ideological reappropriation and can be seen as a typical strategy of power (not unlike psychoanalytical discourse, as, unwittingly, the dialogue between Suzuki, a distant heir of Dahui, and psychoanalysis confirms).[18]

PHENOMENOLOGICAL ANALYSIS

> [A]s far back as human history goes these two fundamental attitudes can be distinguished: that of the metaphor and that of unequivocality.
> —Robert Musil, *The Man Without Qualities*

It is important to keep in mind that the meaning of the sudden/gradual paradigm is always contextual, and that the contexts are diverse (Chinese, Indian, Tibetan). Sectarian antagonism was not merely the result of a doctrinal divergence, it also used the doctrinal gap tactically, therefore not always consistently, in order to legitimate its "passion for difference." On the other hand, the doctrinal antagonism itself may be seen as the projection onto a doctrinal plane of a more fundamental epistemological fault.

First of all, to what extent can we speak of a controversy or opposition? Is the sudden/gradual paradigm merely a dichotomy? Not surprisingly, the protagonists of the debate were in fact speaking at cross-purposes. I would like to suggest that what became a dichotomy was first perceived as a polarity or complementarity—resulting itself from the "flattening" of two heterogeneous worldviews. If there is indeed an opposition, it cannot be between the "sudden" and "gradual" insights as such but between two hierarchized wholes, two relative "-isms"—"subit*ism*" and "gradu-

---

[17] On Dahui's doubt, see Buswell 1987: 343. Although Buswell contrasts this emphasis on doubt with Linji's emphasis on faith, one may want to distinguish further between Linji's faith in himself, which leads him to question any outside authority, and Dōgen's advocacy of "blind faith" in others—a distinction that presents some analogy to the self-power/other-power (*jiriki/tariki*) paradigm in Japanese Buddhism.

[18] See, for instance, Richard DeMartino, Erich Fromm, and D. T. Suzuki, *Zen and Psychoanalysis* (New York: Grove Press, 1963).

al*ism*"—each form including varying degrees of sudden and gradual elements. Thus, among various possible cases, Zongmi defines as "sudden awakening followed by gradual practice" and "gradual practice followed by sudden awakening" the two positions that were most commonly labeled "subitism" and "gradualism." The founding paradigm—sudden/ gradual—is always already erased; it appears only as a "trace," never in its "pure," original form (precisely because there is no such form). Speaking of the "sudden" is already gradual; even dismissing both subitism and gradualism in the name of a higher, truer "subitism" is already derivative and therefore gradual. It is never equivalent to the ideal, originary "nonthinking," since any a posteriori denial is still a mediation: it can only point toward an always-receding horizon or absolute origin. This "fundamental" or "sudden" awakening is a vanishing point, an ideal origin— but also an ideological construct.

In a sense, then, sudden and gradual never meet, and the sudden/gradual controversy appears to be impossible, for it has no territory. Only varieties of gradualism (some being called subitism) can be opposed to each other. Their hierarchized opposition can take place only at the level of representation, in a type of metaphysical discourse. This theoretical opposition, however, never corresponds exactly to practice, due to what, borrowing a musical analogy from Max Weber, we could call the "pythagorean comma," that is, the difference in music between harmonics and tonalities, "the irreducible fact that ascending-descending tones and formal-logical harmonics are out of cog" (Boon 1982: 84). We are therefore confronted—and this is already gradual—with a twofold model: the "harmonious" and/or agonistic (gradual) level of representation, and the ineffable (sudden) level of "reality." In Buddhist terms, borrowed from the apocryphal *Śūraṃgama-sūtra*: "From the perspective of the absolute, awakening occurs all at once. With this awakening all is extinguished at once. . . . [But] in fact and in practice, extinction is not sudden, and one accomplishes [the way] gradually" (T. 19, 945: 155a; quoted in Gómez 1987: 140). Thus the relation between sudden and gradual seems to bear some analogy to that between the *totum simul* of understanding and the *seriatim* character of experience (Ricoeur 1983: 226), or between the signifier and the signified according to Lévi-Strauss, who argues that whereas the signifier is given all at once, the signifieds are discovered progressively (Lévi-Strauss 1987: 60–61).

Ultimate reality itself, however, inasmuch as it is referred to, is already derived, and (re)presentation is primary—the other scene being forever curtained. Like the holistic model described by Louis Dumont (1970), the sudden/gradual as hierarchized totality exists only as a representation. It is therefore important to avoid hypostasizing "sudden" and "gradual" as two separate, simple positions that could be opposed systematically.

These two terms are used as shorthand for a cluster of polarities—among which we can include essence/function (*ti/yong*), one practice/joint practice, absolute truth/conventional truth—that do not always overlap, except at some irregular points. (See Gómez 1987: 89, 132; Faure 1986c.)

Sudden and gradual seem to point toward two originally different experiences that cannot be reduced to some fundamental—logical or sociological—opposition. Indeed, there can be no sudden/gradual debate. What we witness here is not a controversy but rather what Lyotard calls a *différend* (Lyotard 1988: 9). The "sudden" position is properly irrepresentable; it eludes all representation or performance. Consequently, the differend is final yet never ending, for lack of a common space and a common discourse. There may be councils, but there is no possible reconciliation, no common or neutral ground. Despite (or because of) this, sudden and gradual coexist, "in an obscure economy," within individuals or groups. As Jonathan Culler, in another context, puts it, "each perspective checks the error of the other in an irresolvable alternation or aporia" (Culler 1982: 96).

Once the "sudden" and "gradual" perspectives are reified and hierarchized as representations, however, they tend to follow what Bergson called the "law of dichotomy." We are then confronted with two epistemological models, two variants of "gradualism" (one of which claims to be "sudden"): the hierarchical model that allows for compromise, syncretism, *solution*; and the agonistic model that maintains an unmediated tension and leads to what could be metaphorically termed, to borrow a chemical notion from Wendy Doniger O'Flaherty, a state of *suspension* (O'Flaherty 1973: 317). Although the "sudden" is necessarily para-*doxical*, the entire sudden/gradual controversy takes place in the field of a (more or less sophisticated) *doxa*, in the realm of means and mediation. This is not to deny the truth claim of the "sudden" insight but is simply to stress that such insights tend to be reappropriated by the tradition. It is only too easy to fall into gradualism while still believing oneself to be advocating subitism. Such a "gradualist" advocacy of the sudden might in certain respects be more superficial than a straightforward but lucid gradualism. That the opposition is in actual practice often blurred is reflected by the fact that protagonists in the controversy constantly exchange positions and resort surreptitiously to their rival's arguments.[19]

The global relation between the two sedimented visions expressed by the sudden/gradual paradigm cannot be expressed all-at-once in a single

[19] Thus partisans of gradualism often pass themselves off as advocates of subitism, while partisans of *kyōzen itchi* like Zongmi or Musō Soseki extol the *kyōge betsuden* theory. Musō, for example, explains that if Kūkai, in his *Jūjūshinron*, failed to mention Chan, it is because he recognized that the principle of *kyōge betsuden* transcends all the teachings and he did not want to include it in his criticism of the latter! (*Muchū mondō*, ed. Satō Taishun 1974: 196).

proposition; it cannot itself avoid the discursive, dialectical, step-by-step process. The first task is to reveal the inner differentiation produced and simultaneously masked by the sudden/gradual paradigm. I shall consider below the respective strengths and weaknesses of the various approaches subsumed under the two ideal types called "subitism" and "gradualism." We should in the final analysis keep in mind that "beside the explanation through laws . . . , one must practice the understanding of human freedom" (Montesquieu, quoted in Todorov 1984: 102). Although one may be unable to "explain" the "sudden" point of view, one cannot dispense with trying to "understand" it.

Let us then return to the problem of the cultural or "categorical" nature of the sudden/gradual paradigm. If, as Vico believed, "speech itself provides the key for interpreting cultural phenomena," we may use his distinction between "poetic expression" and "discursive prose" to characterize "sudden" and "gradual" texts and pay attention to the "tropical" nature of the sudden/gradual paradigm (i.e., the fact that it expresses linguistic tropes). The "sudden" and "gradual" seem to correspond to the paradigmatic and syntagmatic axes of discourse, respectively. Commenting on Vico's expression, Hayden White declares, "The effect of these two aspects of speech on consciousness sets up a tension, within consciousness itself, that generates a tendency of thought to transcend itself and to create out of the sensed inadequacy of language to its object the conditions for the exercise of its essential freedom" (White 1978: 203). In other words, the unstable balance, within the same discursive field, between "poetical" or "sudden" speech and "gradual" or "pedestrian" discourse would lead to the intuition of a homologous transcendent (i.e., "sudden") dimension of reality. The comparison of "sudden" Chan with poetry (and dancing) and gradual Chan with prose (and pedestrian walking) was a commonplace in Chinese literature.[20]

Point de fuite? Variations on subitism[21]

As noted earlier, it is paradoxical to speak of a "sudden" perspective, since it cannot be defined, even as an "absence of perspective." As a simultaneous vision of everything it cancels all perspective, while as vanishing point it is what makes all perspective possible. The sudden has no place; it is a displacing of metaphysics. Any attempt to convey it through the syntax of language necessarily turns it into a gradualism, a secondhand

[20] If we follow Vico's definition of the four main tropes (metaphor, metonymy, synecdoche, and irony), we may also consider that, more than with metaphor, "sudden" Chan discourse has affinities with the mode of irony. See *The New Science of Giambattista Vico*, trans. Thomas Goddard Bergin and Max Harold Fisch (Ithaca: Cornell University Press, 1984), 129–131.

[21] *Point de fuite* can be translated as "Vanishing point" or "No escape."

or second-order truth (like the Two Truths themselves). And this syntactical character is not, as Wittgenstein shows, merely limited to linguistic utterances, since even the deictic sign par exellence—pointing with the finger, as did the Chan master Juzhi—remains trapped within a syntax. Even Linji's "shouts and blows," to the extent that they remain signifying practices, turn into a semiotic system.

Although no metalanguage appears possible, some compromise is needed to convey that truth. In principle, the notion of "sudden awakening" is given as the (necessarily inadequate) translation of a genuine "experience," or "intuition," elusive or lasting. It supposedly refers to the irruption of the "other"—the *totaliter aliter*—into the same, or of the same into the other; at any rate it is a radical discontinuity in the flow of everyday life, a positive "catastrophe" attested to in apparent good faith by many practitioners. Thus, within or on the margins of an essentially metaphysical discourse, is preserved the possibility of an excess, of a side step, of a "flight outside of time." Such an experience would entail (or result from) a disarticulation or subversion of the syntax in which the subject remained trapped, but also through which the possibility of its preservation exists. In this sense, the sudden is not the opposite of gradualism but that which subverts the very opposition between subitism and gradualism—just as femininity, according to Shoshana Felman, subverts the very opposition between masculinity and femininity (quoted in Culler 1982: 174). This intuition is essentially evanescent, fugitive, elusive, and it may be experienced or conceived as a "grace of the instant," sudden and total, a kind of "radical metabole" comparable to death. Significantly, both awakening and death are subsumed under the term *nirvāṇa*, "with remainder" (awakening) or "without remainder" (death). In both instances, access to/of the "other" is necessarily characterized by a rupture (if not a rapture). Sudden awakening cannot be the result of an empirical progress. Even when it is preceded by gradual practice, it is not as an effect is preceded by its causes, for it is one of those states that, in Elster's words, are "essentially by-products."[22]

Accordingly, to characterize awakening as a state that could be reached is still to be misled by ordinary language, and Mahāyāna texts constantly

---

[22] According to Elster (1983: 57), "states that are by-products" may resist not only the direct but even the indirect attempts to bring them about (for example, through zazen or kōans), because one runs into the so-called *hammock problem*: "Gently rocking myself to sleep in a hammock, I found that just when sleep was coming, my body became so relaxed that I could no longer sustain the rhythmic motion that led me to sleep, and so I woke up and had to start all over again." Chan solves the problem by positing that something, at the critical point, is taking over and continues to perform the rocking. Another problem, related to the question of what Bourdieu calls the "genesis amnesia" of the *habitus*, is the *eraser problem*: "The technology will not be efficacious unless it includes a sub-technology for erasing from memory any traces it may have left" (ibid.).

warn us against this misinterpretation. Another comparison could be that of laughter and humor.[23] Indeed, awakening is often accompanied by laughter (or sometimes tears). There may be a type of sudden awakening that, like humor, totally subverts all dominant categories (and as such is not itself a category), and another that, reflecting an elitist conception of practice, remains a socially determined category.

In some cases, subitism seems motivated by a critical awareness of the potentially negative effects of the gradualist approach, and it imposes itself as a "utopian" strategy. It challenges the "spiritual hierarchies created by abhidharmic maps of the way" (Gómez 1987: 69), which seem to have become ends in themselves. It also implies a criticism of the naive perception of the world, of the kind of "juvenile ontology" that advocates striving for a remote perfection because it fails to see or believe that everything is already perfect(ed). Chan masters such as Linji were aware of the paradoxical effects of their practice; they knew that meditative techniques tended to produce semblances of presence (Certeau 1982: 14). In spite of their nostalgia for presence, they held visions and other spiritual manifestations in distrust. To them, an awakening perceived as such was not a true awakening. According to this view, although there may be awakened ones, there is no awakening. This "sudden" strategy is reminiscent of the antistructural move described by Victor Turner (1974: 297):

> The important thing for those who use metaphorical means is to build up as elaborately as they may a structure of ideas, embodied in symbols, and a structure of social positions, symbolically expressed, which will keep chaos at bay and create a mapped area of security. . . . Then a metaphorical statement is made of what lies at once between the categories of structure . . . and outside the total system. . . . Here words prove useless, exegesis fails, and there is nothing left to do but to express a positive experience by a negative metaphorical act—to destroy the elaborate structure one has made and admit transcendence.

But the antistructural or apophatic stance itself, despite its discursive disclaimers, eventually turns into a positive mediation. Paradoxically, "it is the attempt to find a meaningful formulation of transcendence that leads ineluctably to statements of radical immanence."[24] Sudden intuition is the realization that any mediation is "supplementary" in the Derridean

[23] For Bakhtin (1968: 94), "laughter is essentially not an external but an internal form of truth; it cannot be transformed into seriousness without destroying and distorting the very contents of the truth which it unveils. Laughter liberates not only from external censorship, but first of all from the great interior censor; it liberates from . . . [the] fear of the sacred, of prohibitions, of the past, of power."

[24] See Michael Sells, "Apophasis in Plotinus: A Critical Approach," *Harvard Theological Review* 78, 3–4 (1985): 54. (I am indebted to the late Larry Berman for this reference.)

sense, that is, both a difference and a deferring (Derrida 1974: 157)—
hence the realization that it presupposes a cultural conditioning, which
cannot possibly lead to a freedom from culture and society. Deconstruction itself, whether in its Derridean or Chan version, is always (structurally as it were) on the edge of turning into a diluted metaphysics of presence and a previsible mental artefact or technique. Awakening is thought
or expected to be completely unforeseen, unthinkable, beyond any ex-
pectation. Sudden awakening is perfectly aporetical in the sense that there
is no way (*poros*) leading to it—hence the criticism of a type of Beckettian
Chan called "waiting for awakening" (*daiwu chan*).

The term subitism refers in the Chan context to diametrically opposed
approaches, the metaphysical and the nonmetaphysical, or the ideological
and the critical: the former, stressing the mind's "essence" and the vision
of one's nature (*jianxing*), remained a "metaphysic of presence," while the
latter, realizing that the desire for truth and truth itself are the very source
of delusion, subverted any form of "presence." Linji's admonitions not to
run everywhere in search of the Dharma or of a true master might be seen
as a refusal to play the cultural game called the "spiritual quest." Sudden
awakening is perhaps simply the cutting of the Buddhist Gordian knot, a
legerdemain that solves the old problem of Buddhist theodicy.[25] This
problem is the following: if ignorance (*avidyā*) and delusion are "without
beginning," as the texts have it, all hope seems vain. Are we truly confronted with "an a priori confusion, so desperately anterior to all efforts
to cure it that these very efforts are done under the sign of confusion"
(Jankélévitch 1960: 153), as the most radical critique of gradualism seems
to imply? To this "central and therefore incurable illness," or "innate delusion," subitism conveniently opposes "innate awakening"—taking the
problem by the other end. According to this view, all practices are skillful
means designed to cure specific illnesses: they cannot reach to the root
and bring true health, because the only true health is not to fall ill. True
awakening would be to realize that, although there is a dharma of illness;
it is as empty as the self. The illness may be incurable, but it is adventitious to the true self. Ignorance, delusions, passions only seem to affect
the subject, but they are ontologically distinct from it, just as the clouds,
in the Chan metaphor, may hide the sun but (unlike sunspots) cannot
affect it.

The gradual perspective

As we have seen, at one level sudden and gradual are neither complementary nor opposed but rather both have totalizing claims as "theoretical

---

[25] On subitism as a "shortcut," see Buswell 1987: 350. Its denial of sequence makes sudden
Chan properly "inconsequent" and thoughtless (*wuxin*).

models," ideal types, virtual poles. At another level, however, they are in
a relation of complementarity (or supplementarity), even if they tend mutually to exceed one another. Only with gradualism may one speak of a
perspective, since the all-embracing vision of sudden awakening denies
all perspective. As with "subitism," there is a twofold truth of "gradualism," since that term refers to two different—yet related—realities: (1) It
designates a fundamental intuition, an implicit epistemology and anthropology, a coherent conception of the world and of awakening; in other
words, a "structuring structure" that is not simply a classificatory category but a directing, organizing epistemological schema open to empirical multiplicity. (2) It is also a product, a reified conception, an explicit
"structured structure"—a doctrine, a manifestation of which may therefore serve as a foil in the agonistic relationship with the rival "sudden"
teaching.

It is difficult to speak of gradualism as of a full-blown worldview, because one is unconsciously influenced by the tradition, which sees gradualism as an accommodation to the needs of the people (which it also *is*
in some cases); or, what amounts to the same thing, as a view superseded by subitism. In any case, it implies the basically negative nature of
gradualism conceived of either as a departure from the norm or as a mere
preliminary phase in a return to it. This type of teleological conception is
still at work in the scholarly evaluation of Northern Chan. (See Faure
1986b.) As noted earlier, subitism and gradualism are encountered on the
sectarian stage and only through the intermediary of reductionistic defi-
nitions. Yet gradualism was *not* actually refuted by subitism, and neither
can it be reduced to a deviation or a preliminary phase of the latter.[26] On
the other hand, at the level of representation, subitism and gradualism
have come to endure through their opposition, as "accomplices," set expressions of a difference that keeps reinscribing itself in these rubrics, as
well as in various other epistemological couples.

The flaws of the old teleological schema appear clearly when one realizes that the sudden/gradual dichotomy is constantly blurred in the actual
practice or discourse of Chan monks.[27] These two terms cannot really
serve as classificatory rubrics and provide rather, in this sense, a loose or
false paradigm that hides more than it reveals the true ideological alliances, the actual regroupings on the sectarian stage. This is not, however,

[26] "Gradual" does not, as R. A. Stein (1987: 42) suggests, necessarily define itself by reference to "sudden," no more than did Northern Chan by reference to Southern Chan (at
least initially): if one wants to detect an influence, it is actually the other way around.
[27] In his chronicle of early Chan, the *Lengqie shizi ji*, Jingjue (683–ca. 750) constantly shifts
between sudden and gradual. At the beginning of his career, he takes as his authority the
"sudden" *Prajñāpāramitā* and ends with a praise of the supposedly "gradual" *Laṅkāvatāra*.
(See Faure 1989: 19–24.) In the same way, Zongmi shifts from "sudden" Chan to the "sudden doctrine" (but eminently gradual *qua* doctrine) of Huayan. (See Jan 1972.)

to deny any value to that paradigm—on the contrary. Inasmuch as the representation of reality is an integral part of that reality, the polarization reflected and effected by this paradigm must be taken into account to understand Chan ideology and practice.

At the representational level, the sudden/gradual paradigm (whether polarity or dichotomy) seems to be the very type of metaphysical opposition questioned by Derridean deconstruction. In this deconstructive strategy, the first step is to reverse the hierarchy while maintaining it. Since one cannot leave this epistemological circle, the important step is rather to enter it correctly. The asymmetry between the terms sudden and gradual is striking: Chan theory gives an inverted image of reality (which is the very definition of ideology), to the point where one could speak of a "linguistic taboo" concerning gradualism: it is never discussed, although it remains unchallenged in actual practice. The entire Chan tradition seems to hinge on this scapegoat mechanism.

Beyond the watered-down and apologetic gradualism described by subitists, which is actually a syncretic version of subitism, there exists another, more basic, gradualism, reflecting a full-blown worldview and a certain conception of the sacred. We compared earlier the metabole of sudden awakening to that of death, a death conceived as necessarily sudden. In most traditional societies, however, "death is not the matter of a moment." As a representation, death is not sudden; it is on the contrary the result of a long process. Robert Hertz, for instance, concludes from his analysis of double funerals that the change in state and status provoked by death must be submitted to a long labor of mourning before being absorbed, ratified by the collectivity (Hertz 1960: 27–86). Could this conclusion perhaps apply to awakening?

In the same anthropological vein, one is reminded of the analysis of the sacred by Hubert and Mauss. (See Mauss 1968–1969: 1:217.) According to these authors, sacred space is structured, and ritual may be interpreted as the progression within that sacred space from the outermost enclosure to the innermost sanctuary. This structure is that of the mandala, a visual device that constitutes in the esoteric tradition a means of access to awakening. In this sacred space, any leap, any break of continuity, would result in a loss of balance that might be fatal. This conception of the world as hieratic and strongly structured was openly called into question by "sudden" Chan. It forms nevertheless a fundamental dimension of archaic religious thought, and nothing permits us a priori to reject or play down that epistemological stance. We have seen that, in contrast to this "structured" sacred, sudden awakening appears as an "antistructure" in Turner's sense. "Gradual awakening" would therefore be a "structure," a form of gnosis, the process of discovery of the ontological structures of reality or the anthropological structures of the imaginary. As the Daoist master Tianyinzi put it: "In the *Yijing*, there is the hexagram 'Progressive Advance,' while Laozi speaks of the 'Marvelous Gate.' When man cultivates his inner perfection and achieves his nature, he cannot expect any sudden enlightenment, rather he must progress gradually and practice the techniques in peace. Thus, the progressive gates have been established."[28]

Another traditional model for the gradual approach would be that of anamnesis. As noted earlier, subitism warns against memory in a realization that it is not a mere retrieval agency but, like imagination, a constitutive power. This model is actually hybrid, in that it takes as its authority an originary perfection—one of the characteristics of sudden awakening—but finds its expression in a gradual return to the source, the gradual undoing of oblivion (something like the completion of a puzzle). This conception finds one of its best illustrations in the *Ten Oxherding Pictures*. Such a "foundational" model, which includes sudden and gradual elements, may be contrasted with the "spontaneous" conception of "sudden" awakening, just as the prodigal son's "return to the fold" may be opposed to the "free" (to distinguish it from merely "deluded") wandering of the Buddhist immortal Budai. Perhaps these different courses bear some analogy to those of the scholastic commentary and of the rhetorical tradition, or, closer to home, to hermeneutical and performative scholarship, respectively. In all cases, the point is either to proceed up to the source in order to control the flow, or to flow along with the source in order to use its strength. There is a version of the *Ten Oxherding Pictures* that makes a synthesis of both models, since it adds to the first (gradual) sequence in which the oxherd searches for, finds, and tames the ox— here from the first to the eighth picture instead of the traditional sequence from one to ten—a second (sudden) sequence that retains its gradualism only through its sequential character, since it deals with the naturalness symbolized by the flow of the seasons and the pot-bellied vagabond Budai, "entering the market place with his arms dangling." (See Ueda and Yanagida 1982.)

One could argue that this kind of "natural" gradualism—as an obedience to natural order and the rhythm of nature, as participation in the flux of life and in respect of the multiplicity of reality—is actually very close to the "sudden" view and very far from traditional Buddhist voluntarism (although the latter theoretically derives from the "sudden teaching").[29] It is gradual inasmuch as it is an awareness of the fact that nature does not

---

[28] See Livia Kohn, "The Teaching of T'ien-yin-tzu," *Journal of Chinese Religion* 15 (Fall 1987): 9.

[29] As the Kamakura Zen master Enni Ben'en put it: "When we truly reside on the way of no-mind, [we go] like blossoms that fall and leaves that scatter before the wind, like the melting of frost and snow in the morning sun—what is there that employs the mind in such events as these?" (See Bielefeldt 1989a.)

make any leap, and it results in entrusting oneself to nature. It is an acknowledgment, or even a eulogy and a quasi-sanctification of finitude, at first glance hardly distinguishable from the way in which Layman Pang, in his famous verse, extols daily tasks such as chopping wood and fetching water as the true Buddhist supranormal powers (*abhijñā*). (See Sasaki et al. 1971: 46.)

This latter model lent itself to what the partisans of a rigorous ascesis such as Dōgen denounced as a quietistic misinterpretation of the "sudden" under the name of "naturalist heresy," a trend that apparently thrived in Chan/Zen and in Japanese Tendai under the influence of the *hongaku* theory. In Chinese terms, the emphasis shifted from an ontological model based on the notion of "essence" (*ti*), through a "functional" model (in which the function, *yong*, was still derived from the essence), to a model affirming the supremacy of the function, and in which the essence remained only as a convenient alibi: such is the Chan of the "great activity," as it developed after Mazu Daoyi (709–788). In a sense, Mazu's Chan marked a return to gradualism, since it no longer advocated seeing one's true nature im-mediately, but mediately, through its function. (See Buswell 1987: 341.) After Mazu, however, the "function" seems to stand alone; it is no longer anchored in an ontology. In this way, instead of an essentialist definition of sudden and gradual, we find two contrasting epistemologies, two models of "self-knowledge": one based on introspective (or retrospective) self-knowledge, the other on a permanent self-invention that seems to entail a denial of self-knowledge (since any knowledge would still be an obstacle to the Dao: true knowledge is nonknowledge, true vision nonvision, and so on).

Gradualism also has a critical dimension. In contrast to subitism, which soars in the rarefied space of absolute truth, gradualism implies a mature recognition of human finitude. Indeed, because of its elitism and its apparent lack of skillful means, subitism lends itself to the same criticism addressed to Kantian morality, that "it may have clean hands, but it has no hands." In a letter to his brother Yun'yan, the Chan master Daowu contrasted the teachings of their respective teachers, Baizhang and Shitou, to a hardware store and to a "store selling pure gold," and he urged Yun'yan to leave "Baizhang's hardware store." Elaborating on this comparison, another Chan master, Yangshan, pointed out the value of mediations: "The hardware dealer deals with all kinds of things, from mouse shit to pure gold. The pure gold dealer cannot meet the demand of those who want mouse shit." (See *Zutang ji* 18, *Jingde chuandeng lu* 11.) A rather similar point was made by the Sōtō Zen master Dokuan Dokugo, quoting the *Platform Sūtra*: "When people with weak capacities hear about sudden awakening, it is like small plants receiving a great rain: they are knocked down and cannot grow" (T. 82, 2597: 565a). One may also, from a gradual perspective, point out another analogy between subitism and deconstruction: both require a structure to subvert, and this subversion is perhaps what permits "gradual subitism" to go beyond the structure while remaining within its closure. Shortcut subitism, on the other hand, is like the deconstructive temptation to affirm that everything is rhetorical and performative and that there is no conventional, constative discourse. This theoretical position proves untenable, and the alleged passage beyond the limit actually remains on this side of it. (See de Man 1979: 119–131.)

Although their semantic fields do not entirely overlap, paradigms such as sudden/gradual or essence/function (*tiyong*) may be seen as the Chinese versions of the Two Truths. This polarity played a crucial role in the development of Mahāyāna Buddhism. It is around it that the plot of scriptures such as the *Lotus Sūtra* and *Vimalakīrti-nirdeśa* revolves. It also plays a major role in Chan doctrinal tracts. In the *Treatise on the Two Entrances*, for instance, it allows Bodhidharma to contrast the Entrances "*via* Principle" and "*via* Practice" while maintaining a fragile balance between the two. (See Faure 1986d.) A similar "twofold entrance" is attributed to Bodhidharma's contemporary Sengchou, in a work actually representative of Northern Chan, the *Xinxin lun*. (See Yanagida 1963; McRae 1986.) Notice, however, that although the two entrances have supposedly an equal status and are logically complementary, they are in each case assigned to different types of practitioners.

According to the *Lengqie shizi ji*, the teaching of the Chan patriarch Daoxin also showed a dual structure, corresponding to the two aspects—sudden and gradual—of practice. Daoxin first establishes a whole range of mental exercises, only to negate them later in the name of "spontaneity." The point of these "spiritual exercises" is to go through all mental artifacts, through the "conventional truths" of *upāya*, before eventually discarding them upon reaching ultimate truth. But the process or itinerary is not irrelevant, for it is somehow inscribed in the arrival point, just as the pilgrim's progress is inscribed in the sacred place—being precisely one of the elements of its sacredness. This is what those who are in too great a hurry to arrive, believing they get straight to the goal by pressing on (or, in the more vivid French expression, "brûlant les étapes"), tend to forget. Daoxin and other early Chan masters remained in line with Mādhyamika orthodoxy, which held that one cannot reach ultimate truth if one rejects conventional truth.[1] Radical advocates of shortcut subitism, however, came to assert that ultimate truth required the rejection of conventional truth, which they saw no longer as mediating truth but as outright falsity.

Guṇabhadra, the Indian translator whom the *Lenqie shizi ji* attempted

---

[1] Mādhyamika itself was often criticized as nihilistic, for its "ontological negativism tended to deny things the minimum of existence they need to remain the basis of retribution" (*Hōbōgirin*, Vol. 1: 75).

to promote as the first patriarch of Chan and the master of Bodhidharma, is credited with a more orthodox conception of subitism when he advocates "seeing the two truths equally and simultaneously." Such a simultaneous, "panoramic" or "panoptic" vision is in no way a static synthesis, since no such *synthesis* is possible. As Neal Donner points out, "the third or middle truth . . . is not truly a compromise, a 'middle way' between extremes as we might first think, but instead emphasizes the paradoxical nature of reality: the truth cannot be reduced to a single formulation."[2] Guṇabhadra's visualism tends to mask the dialectical nature of the two truths, the dynamics that carry ultimate truth into a constant overstepping of itself. Shenxiu expresses the dialectical thrust of his teaching through the notion of "repeated mystery" (*chongxuan*)—borrowed from Laozi, probably through Daoist thinkers such as Cheng Xuanying (fl. mid-7th c.), who had redefined it in terms of Mādhyamika dialectics. (See Robinet 1977: 142–148.)

According to the *Treatise of Bodhidharma*, "the common man sees the ultimate in the conventional, while the sage sees the conventional in the ultimate." (See Faure 1986d: 84.) Apart from the marked taste of Chan masters for chiasmatic formulas, one should retain the dialectical value of this reversal: starting from a static opposition between conventional and ultimate truth—an opposition of the conventional level—the text deconstructs this hierarchy by showing that at a higher level—perceived earlier as ultimate—ultimate truth is still conventional. One could stop here and say that, after all, all truth, inasmuch as it is linguistic, is conventional. But the overstepping of ultimate truth is actually achieved in the name of the same "metaphysical" and metalinguistic exigencies that had temporarily been reified in the concept of ultimate truth. The dialectical movement is, however, actually an oscillation that, once launched, does not stop that easily. Thus, falling always back on this side of the limit, it forces one to be open to doubt and to consider that the very exigency of going beyond may after all be only a more subtle expression of conventional truth. We are reminded of Shenhui pointing out, in a rather dualistic fashion, that there are two kinds of self-deception, the coarse and the fine. While the coarse—clinging to forms—is obvious enough, the fine consists in believing that there exists an awakening, and wanting to reach it. (See Liebenthal 1952: 144.) Shenhui nevertheless seems to imply that the realization of the subtle delusion may put an end to it, and that instead

---

[2] Donner 1987: 205. The notion of a "third or middle truth," however, lends itself easily to reification. Gómez seems at first to see it as a synthesis, a "third and middle position stand[ing] outside the plane in which the other two contrast with each other." But he seems to depart from this quasi-Hegelian model when he adds that "it may even be on that same plane if one stands on it without trying to reduce one extreme to the terms of the other" (Gómez 1987: 122).

of making one fall back into conventional truth, it paradoxically provides the true access to ultimate truth.

Let us return to the "simultaneous grasping" of the two truths, for it may help us understand the structure of early Chan texts. We have just mentioned the dual, two-tiered structure of Daoxin's teaching as it is presented by the *Lengqie shizi ji*. Scholars such as D. T. Suzuki, starting from a retrospective conception of Chan in which Daoxin, the "fourth patriarch," is seen only as a representative of orthodox subitism, have tried to explain away what they saw as a contradiction in Daoxin's teaching by attributing it to interpolations (this convenient interpretive method being itself a kind of twofold-truth hermeneutics): they claim that Daoxin's subitism must have been tampered with by later copyists. Other scholars have tried to do the opposite—although with a similar intent—and have claimed that the "sudden" dialogues attributed to allegedly "gradual" masters such as Guṇabhadra and Shenxiu are entirely apocryphal. There is no denying that there was a lot of tampering with early Chan texts. One may in particular distinguish several textual layers in a text such as the *Lengqie shizi ji*, and the question of its "authorship" is a vexed one (Faure 1989: 73–79). Many early Chan texts never achieved closure, and some, like the so-called *Treatise of Bodhidharma*, were mere anthologies.

Perhaps this genetic approach misses the point. Instead of trying at all costs to reconstitute an original text, it seems more fruitful to consider the composite nature of the work under study as a testimony to the character of a later tradition. The text is given to us as a whole, and we may as well accept it as such. Its "author" or compiler must receive the credit for being able to see as well as we do, and probably better, some of its tensions and contradictions. Interpolations—assuming they are not, as is often the case, the product of hypercriticism—have become an integral part of the text, and they function according to a logic of "supplementarity."

This structural approach may prompt us to reconsider some doctrinal aspects of Chan. The *locus classicus* for the Chan expression of the Twofold Truth is the famous poetic contest between Shenxiu and Huineng in the *Platform Sūtra*. As noted earlier, it is actually a good example of how the *two* complementary truths, having become a *twofold* truth, were reinterpreted by the later sectarian tradition as two antagonistic, dichotomous statements—one being ultimately true, the other ultimately false. The poem attributed to Shenxiu, however, although reflecting conventional truth, was not rejected by his master Hongren but was praised as such.[3] In other words, instead of considering this passage as offering a

---

[3] Incidentally, the reasons given by the author of the *Platform Sūtra* for the way in which Hongren, fearing a riot among his disciples, supposedly hid his true reaction may tell us a

"historical" refutation of Shenxiu by Huineng, one may consider the two verses (actually three) as a "dialectical" exposition of the two truths. It is only the polemical radicalization of Chan that led to the rejection of the conventional truth of gradualism as erroneous and of its alleged representative Shenxiu as heterodox.

The Two Truths paradigm plays a mediating role between the onto-logical/epistemological, and epistemological/hermeneutical levels.[4] It provides a convenient hermeneutical device, allowing us to explain all apparent doctrinal contradictions as the result of a shift between the levels of ultimate and conventional truths.[5] It affirms ontological duality only to negate it—through formulas such as *nirvāṇa* is *saṃsāra*, passions are awakening, and so on. The reverse, however, is equally true: by negating duality, it has already acknowledged it and contributed to its preservation. In other words, its effects might be the contrary of what they claim to be. Derrida has pointed out the ideological effects of the attempts to pass immediately beyond oppositions (Derrida 1972b: 56). On the one hand, the theoretical dualism that serves as a starting point might turn into a rather sterile abstraction. As Merleau-Ponty pointed out in another context, "only a thought that looks at being from elsewhere, and as it were head-on, is forced into the bifurcation of the essence and the fact" (Merleau-Ponty 1968: 113). This kind of thought ignores depth and dia-lectics and remains trapped in the opposition it vainly attempts to col-lapse. In particular, the claim that passions are awakening, characteristic of the so-called philosophy of innate awakening (J. *hongaku shisō*), might serve (and actually did serve, if we are to believe critics of antinomian Chan) to legitimate a kind of apology for the phenomenal world that verges on secularism and monism. On the other hand, the theoretical identity of the two levels leads to their reciprocal contamination: it im-plies that phenomena are absolute, but also (a point usually forgotten) that the absolute itself is "phenomenal" (i.e., historically and culturally determined). (See Staten 1984: 17.)

As it was borrowed from Mādhyamika, the concept of the Two Truths holds a strategic place in Chan discourse. At first glance, since "a message with a double meaning entails a split *destinateur* and a split *destinataire*" (Jakobson 1963: 238), it amounts to a kind of "ventriloquism" that accu-

---

lot about the tense atmosphere of, and the considerable power at stake for, the patriarchal succession. See Yampolsky 1967: 134.

[4] Typical in this respect is Zhiyi's ontologization of *śamatha/vipaśyanā*: "That entities are by nature quiescent is called 'calming' (Ch. *zhi*, Sk. *śamatha*); that, though quiescent, they are ever lustrous is called 'contemplation' (Ch. *guan*, Sk. *vipaśyanā*)" (Donner 1987: 218).

[5] The Twofold Truth theory is a useful strategy for certifying that ultimate truth does not change, even if the (conventional) methods change with time (see, for example, modern Sōtō, as described by Reader 1986). This permits one to connect the most diverse trends and to reconcile divergences.

mulates symbolic profit. Those who use this rhetorical strategy seem, by reconciling the absolute and the relative at little cost, to "cash in" on both sides. This strategy, however, may also reflect the "logic of practice" defined by Bourdieu, "the twofold truth of practices that are intrinsically equivocal and ambiguous" (Bourdieu 1977b: 179; 1980: 201). To reduce everything to ideology would be precisely to fall into one of these traps. The twofold truth can also be seen as an attempt to take into account the fact that, in our daily lives, we move constantly back and forth between incompatible systems. To deny the multiplicity of the models that govern us would fly in the face(s) of a multifaceted reality and would constitute an ideological assertion. Yet this system of double truth is also a "system of double falsity": "For what is true *in principle* never being true in fact, and conversely the factual situation never committing the principles, each of the two instances condemns the other, and condemns it with reprieve by leaving to it competency in its own order" (Merleau-Ponty 1968: 124). One would expect such a critique to have a destabilizing effect on the Chan/Zen metaphysical conception of truth: but whereas in Western philosophy a twofold truth becomes rather a half-truth, the situation seems to be the opposite in East Asian Buddhism. It is also possible to see this accommodation to and domestication of the agonistic aspects of reality as a form of wishful thinking. Wendy Doniger O'Flaherty argues that, in contrast to Buddhism, Hinduism has no use for golden means or Middle Paths. Being a "religion of fire and ice," it seeks rather "the exhaustion of the golden extremes" (O'Flaherty 1973: 82). On the surface, the Chinese case seems different, but perhaps it is not. We have seen that the Middle Way is also the "simultaneous vision of the two truths," wherein each extreme keeps its distinct status. It does not always try to collapse them into one undifferentiated reality. Although it hierarchizes them, it does so very much in the same way—according to Louis Dumont (1970)—that Hinduism does. Early Chan simultaneously bridges and maintains the gap between the two levels. As Gómez puts it, "Northern Chan meditation practice creates a gap, at least implicitly, between the world of enlightenment and the world of delusion. . . . [It] recognizes a doctrine of innate enlightenment and uses it to close the gap—a gap that Shenhui also tries to erase" (Gómez 1987: 95).

Double trouble

In the Chinese case, however, the system has proved unstable and has tended constantly to regress toward a kind of monism. In contrast to the Hindu solution to the conflict of opposites—a "solution" that Doniger O'Flaherty metaphorically describes as a "suspension" (O'Flaherty 1973: 317)—Chinese Buddhism tended to a fusion of the opposites. What was

in Indian Mahāyāna a nonduality became in Chinese Mahāyāna an identity, or at least an interpenetration: "It is not that identity is drowned in
otherness, but it is *necessarily* open to it, contaminated by it" (Staten 1984:
18). Chan extremism was attracted toward nihilism or toward imma-
nentism, that is, in either case, toward an abstraction. For, as Merleau-
Ponty argues, negativism is the other face of positivism, and "in this
reversal remains the same in that, whether considering the void of nothingness or the absolute fullness of being, it in every case ignores density,
depth, the plurality of planes, the background worlds" (Merleau-Ponty
1968: 68). Chan was led to reinterpret in a unilateral way the Mādhyamika
notion of Two Truths and to assert the ultimate reality. Chan kōans, for
example, abound in attempts to express the "first-order truth" (*diyi yi*),
the "ultimate meaning" of Bodhidharma's coming from the West. That
Chan reinterpreted the ultimate in terms of the conventional, thus apparently collapsing them, does not change the fact that by doing so it strayed
from the Mādhyamika conception: its synthesis showed a marked one-
sidedness, and the apparent reversal from the previous stress on Principle
(*li*) to the new emphasis on the phenomenal world (*shi*) should not delude
us: the phenomenal world in question is only nominally so, since it is seen
(theoretically) from the point of view of awakening; its physical relativity
turns into metaphysical truth.

In this way, the desire for transcendence turns into a radical immanence, and the soteriological structure elaborated as an expedient tends to
become an end in itself.[6] One observes toward the eighth century a shift
from the notion of twofold truth as a mediation between equi-vocal practices to the dichotomous and exclusive positions expressed in the various
debates over sudden and gradual, "with marks" (*youxiang*) and "without
marks" (*wuxiang*), and reliance or nonreliance on canonical scriptures.
These extreme positions are often characterized by a symbolic denial of
all differences. But such a denial, although apparently subversive of established powers, amounts to acknowledging them: By "staging the unthinkable part of the social [or of reality], that which establishes rules to
which it is not subjected" (Augé 1982b: 285), such a denial participates or
attempts to participate in this power. Such were, for instance, the practical and ideological effects of the advocacy of "formlessness" (*wuxiang*)
that characterizes sectarian ecumenism—the other side of universalism.[7]
Like all its rivals, Chan posed as ultimate truth (*paramartha-satya*) and
claimed to be an "ultimate Vehicle"—above the struggle of sects and

---

[6] On the "transitive" aspect of early Buddhist cosmology, see Mus 1935: 79–83.

[7] The undifferentiated is not only liminal, as Turner shows (Turner 1969: 94–130), but
properly central—the basis of power, of social differentiation. The return to the undifferentiated is therefore a return to the center of power. The renouncer grasps the pivot of Dao.
This is in part the meaning of Laozi's "uncarved block" or Linji's "man without rank."

teachings. For example, Dōgen, "founder" of a Zen sect, argued that there is no "Zen sect." As with Linji's "man without rank," rhetorical devices such as a "sect without qualities" or a "teaching without characteristics" have always constituted a shortcut to the first rank.

Even when a hierarchical "twofold truth" maintains the complementarity of the two levels, it is usually only as a form of "militant syncretism," a way to have the last word. As in the two-tiered hermeneutical models advocated by scholars as different as Ricoeur and Bourdieu, there is no "prolonged hesitation" or aporia between the two levels. Chan reduces one of the two levels to the other (absolute or immanent), thereby repressing the agonistic tension between them. As with the scholar trying to reduce the text to either ideology or metaphysics, one passes from a twofold truth (two-*fold*, and perhaps also two-edged, truth) to *two* contradictory truths—one of which is eventually reduced to the other. In short, one goes from ambivalence to contradiction and further to reduction. A theory or text claiming to pass beyond the oppositions it has set up, however, is bound to fall short of its goal, and the regression to one pole is not simply, as Bourdieu thinks, due to the one-sidedness of reception. If, as Derrida argues, the characteristic move of metaphysics is to set up a binary opposition and then hierarchically subordinate one term of the opposition to the other, the asymmetry between the two levels is itself ideological or metaphysical. (See Derrida 1972b.) On the other hand, "deconstruction does not subordinate one term to the other. . . . It denies the 'impermeability of the as-such' " (Staten 1984: 17). Even the attempt, however, to maintain the viability of both sides of the opposition equally, to be simultaneously on both sides of the divide or to grasp simultaneously the two truths, may reflect a will to mastery that keeps falling back on one side and turning into another rhetorical effect. Perhaps there is no way out of this predicament, and this is the true paradox of the twofold truth.

THE "NATURALIST HERESY"

> Emptiness, having been dimly perceived, utterly destroys the slow-witted.
> —*Madhyamakakārikā*

An extreme but logical conclusion of subitism is the so-called innate awakening (Ch. *benjue*, J. *hongaku*) theory, according to which "passions are awakening." This theory seems to have led to a form of quietism labeled by its detractors the "naturalist" or Senika heresy (from the name of an Indian heretic defeated by the Buddha). This trend, however, had some patents of nobility in the Chan tradition and was usually even considered its mainstream—or at least its most remarkable development. The *locus classicus* for this "naturalist" approach could be Mazu's famous motto: "The ordinary mind is the Way"; or Linji's advocacy of the "true man without affairs." The emphasis on spontaneity and the inner logic of subitism, however, lent themselves to misinterpretation. They seemed to justify a rejection of all practices, beginning with contemplation: the absolute contemplation (*jueguan*) becomes the "cessation of contemplation" (*jueguan*)—a development permitted by the polysemy of the word *jue*. According to the *Lidai fabao ji*, Wuzhu rejected *en bloc* all practices and all works. Describing Wuzhu's Baotang school, Zongmi writes: "[It] carries out none of the marks of Buddhism. Having cut their hair and put on robes, they do not receive the precepts. When it comes to obeisance and confession, reading the texts, making drawings and paintings of the Buddha, and copying sūtras, they revile all these things as false thoughts. In the halls where they dwell they do not set up Buddha artifacts. Therefore I say they 'adhere to neither the teachings nor the practice' " (Broughton 1983: 39).

The theoretical radicalism of the *hongaku* theory opened what seems to be a potentially self-destructive dialectic. The denial of all works outside the monastery, and of all practice inside, rendered monastic life apparently useless. Monks were the first to realize this, and a number of them gave up monkhood. The emperor and his Confucianist entourage were also quick to seize upon this opportunity to weaken the Buddhist institution. For instance, the persecution of Buddhism by Emperor Wu of the Northern Zhou was somewhat hypocritically justified by the Buddhist notion of nonduality: if truth was to be found equally in the profane and the sacred, the sacred space of monasteries was no longer necessary. (See Kamata 1964.) The tradition admits that, by rejecting *upāya* and refusing any merit to Liang Wudi for the construction of temples, Bodhidharma lost an opportunity to spread the Chan Dharma—the mission for which he had allegedly traveled to China.[8] It is also his rejection of works that explains the defeat of the Northern Chan monk Moheyan (Mahāyāna) at the Council of Tibet and the subsequent failure of Chan to become the dominant ideology in Tibet. (See Demiéville 1952.) Demiéville argues that the decline of Chan in China may be the outcome of its "sudden teaching." This teaching, however, may also have been a great part of Chan's success. Paradoxically, the same *hongaku* theory that on the one hand allowed esoteric or *kenmitsu* Buddhism to assimilate local cults and

[8] Ironically, a little-known source, the "biography" of the sixth-century thaumaturge Fu Xi (alias "Fu the Mahāsattva"), presents Bodhidharma as a builder of temples himself. See *Shanhui dashi yulu*, in *zz* 2, 25, 1: 33b, 26d.

thus to become the orthodoxy in Japan, on the other led Chan/Zen to reject all mediations and thus somewhat hindered its dissemination.[9]

Were the excesses of the *hongaku* theory inevitable or unpredictable? Or can we surmise that such theoretical excesses were possible precisely because of an implicit application of the Two Truths schema (i.e., from a tacit understanding of the sharp distinction between theory and practice)? Perhaps they were possible precisely because they took place in a discursive arena that, although theoretically unbounded, was actually checked by multiple mechanisms. The perfect freedom of "sudden awakening" was actually traversed by the multiple constraints of Chinese society. The first advocates of "sudden awakening" recognized the conditions of possibility for unconditioned freedom—an understanding that, if we are to believe their critics, the advocates of the "naturalist heresy" had lost. But one may wonder whether these "heretics" were not a convenient myth—for their partisans as for their opponents. At first glance, Chan had the same rationale for indulging in the mysteries of sexuality as Tibetan Tantrism. It does not seem, however, that its endorsing of the motto "passions are awakening" ever led Chan to orgiastic behavior. Similarly, with the only, although significant, exception of the Shaolin monks, the potential apologetics of killing found in Chan texts such as the *Jueguan lun* [see Tokiwa Gishin 1973] did not transform Chan monks into warriors, as it did for example in Japan with the monks of the esoteric and Pure Land traditions. On the whole, Chan/Zen was perhaps less affected by these outcomes of the *hongaku* theory than any other sect. Some of the intoxicating effect of this theory, however, may have been felt at times, and Chan monasteries were not always the most moral places, as a later chapter will show. Ennin's diary gives some relatively unpleasant descriptions of the behavior of Chan monks in ninth-century China. The fallout of the *benjue/hongaku* theory, and the potential threat of disorder caused by antinomian monks at times of social and political instability, were acutely perceived by other more conservative Chan monks such as Nanyang Huizhong or Zongmi. It also provided ground for criticism by representatives of other schools.[10]

The paradox of Chan antinomianism is pointed out by its Confucian critics and their modern representatives.[11] Commenting on Layman Pang's famous verse, Fung Yu-lan says: "However, if carrying water and chopping wood are all manifestations of the Wondrous Way, why do

[9] See Matsumoto Shirō, "Nyoraizō wa bukkyō ni arazu" (The Tathāgatagarbha theory is not Buddhism), *IBK* 35, 1 (1986).

[10] See, for instance, the criticism of the Vinaya master Yijing in Takakusu 1970: 51 and 93.

[11] An earlier Confucian criticism is that of the Tang statesman Yao Chong (d. 721); see Yoshikawa 1985: 111–198.

those [Chan masters] who cultivate the Way have to leave the world? Why isn't 'one's service to parents and sovereign' taken to be the Wondrous Way?"[12] Aware of the dangers of antinomianism, the partisans of "inclusive Chan" reaffirmed the harmony of Chan and traditional Buddhist values and the intertwining of the two (or three) levels. Even a disciple of Mazu Daoyi such as Weikuan (755–817), in response to a question by the poet Bai Juyi, is prompted to declare: "I regard the highest illumination as taking the form of obedience to monastic rules when translated into personal conduct, that of doctrine when preached, that of *dhyāna* when enacted in a mental sphere. There are these three applications, but in each case it is the same thing that is applied. . . . The Vinaya is Dharma, and Dharma cannot be separated from dhyāna."[13] In Japan, Dōgen was one of the most severe critics of the "naturalist" tendency (J. *jinen gedō*). In *Hō-kyōki*, the diary of his stay in China, he records the following dialogue with his master Rujing: [Dōgen:] "At the present time head priests in all the monasteries let their hair grow out and wear their fingernails long. What grounds do they have for that? Are we to call them priests? They look very much like laymen. Should we call them laymen? Yet their hair is too short for that. In India and China during the periods of the True and Semblance Dharmas disciples of the buddha-patriarchs were never like this." [Rujing:] "They are truly beasts, lifeless corpses weltering in the pure ocean of the Buddha Dharma" (Waddell 1977–1978: 126–127). But Dōgen's criticism was aimed not only at Chinese monks. In Japan, too, there were Zen monks who rejected the disciplinary rules and kept their hair long, like their Chinese model Hanshan and other "mountain monks." They were apparently perceived as belonging to the Darumashū or "school of Bodhidharma" founded by Dainichi Nōnin, a man who had awakened by himself, without the guidance of a master—in other words a *pratyeka-buddha* (J. *engaku*). (See Pollack 1986: 92.) It is to counteract their influence that Yōsai and Dōgen wrote their treatises. Denouncing Nōnin's lack of proper credentials, these two figures, regarded as the founders of Japanese Zen, were motivated in their stress on Vinaya by the rise of the rival Darumashū and its quietistic interpretation of innate awakening (J. *hongaku*). Ironically, Dōgen was himself later criticized by Tendai monks for being no more than a *pratyeka-buddha* (see *Keiran shūyō shū*, T. 76, 2410: 539c). Yōsai's *Kōzen gokokuron*, in particular, sounds like an indictment of the "false view of emptiness"—as the following passage

---

[12] See Fung Yu-lan, *The Spirit of Chinese Philosophy* (London: Kegan Paul, 1947), 174. See also Charles Fu's criticism of the Chan tendency, *in actual practice*, to "leave the dusty world behind," that is, to forsake morality and works, despite the *theoretical* acknowledgment of the importance of the everyday world ("to carry water and chop wood"). Fu 1973: 395.

[13] See Waley 1949: 99. This passage is quoted in Kamakura Japan by traditionalist Buddhists such as Jōkei (1155–1213). See *Gumei hosshin shū*, ed. Takase Shōgon (Tokyo: Iwanami shoten, 1986), 161.

shows: "Some wrongly call themselves Zen masters, who say that there is neither practice nor cultivation, and that passions, being fundamentally nonexistent, are awakening. What is the use then of practices such as reciting the name of the Buddha (*nenbutsu*), worshiping relics, and holding meager feasts? These people have fallen into the false view of emptiness." (See Ichikawa, Iriya, and Yanagida 1972: 41.) But precisely, as we will see later, Darumashū believers *were* worshiping relics, and this raises some questions about the accuracy of Yōsai's description of their doctrine.

SKILLFUL MEANS

> In a Chan monastery, try to borrow a comb: you
> walk the wrong way.
> —Chinese proverb

In terms of soteriology, the main consequence of subitism was the rejection of "skillful means" (*upāya*). In early Chan, and more particularly in the Northern school, *upāya* seems to have played a major role. One of the main Northern Chan texts, the *Gate of the [Five] Unborn Upāya* (*Wusheng fangbianmen*), quotes a passage from the *Vimalakīrti-nirdeśa* that constitutes the *locus classicus* for the use of *upāya*:

> For a Bodhisattva, to taste the savour of the trances (*dhyāna*), the liberations (*vimokṣa*), the concentrations (*samādhi*) and the recollections (*samapatti*) in the absence of skillful means is bondage. On the contrary, to taste the flavours of the trances and the concentrations while having recourse to skillful means is deliverance. Wisdom not acquired through skillful means is bondage. On the contrary, wisdom acquired through skillful means is deliverance. Skillful means not acquired through wisdom are bondage. On the contrary, skillful means acquired through wisdom are deliverance. (See Lamotte 1962: 233; and T. 85, 2834: 1275b.)

Here, *upāya* and *prajñā* represent the two levels of truth, and the dialectic between them is strongly affirmed. *Upāya* are the means to reach the absolute from the relative, or the means through which the absolute manifests itself in the relative, and through which the Bodhisattva, out of compassion (*karuṇā*), reaches out toward deluded sentient beings. They can be seen as either gradual (from the sentient beings' point of view) or sudden (from the Bodhisattva's point of view). Although, as already noted, Shenhui himself clearly resorted to "skillful means" in his preaching, he insisted on rejecting them as merely gradual expedients and stressed *prajñā* instead. The Northern school attempted to counter Shenhui's criticism by stressing the "unborn" (*wusheng*)—that is, the absolute or sudden—nature of its *upāya*. (See Faure 1988: 60–64.) In contrast to Northern Chan, Shenhui's approach was radically nondialectical, and it paved the way to antinomianism.[14] For instance, the rejection of traditional Buddhist ritual by Wuzhu and his disciples was based on his uncompromising affirmation of the "ultimate" point of view. According to Zongmi's description:

> Their intention in reviling all of the teaching lies in extinguishing perception and becoming the completely real. Therefore, where they dwell they do not discuss food and clothing, but trust that men will send offerings. If they are sent, then they have warm clothing and enough to eat. If they are not sent, then they let hunger and cold take their course. They also do not seek to teach [beings] and do not beg food. If someone enters their halls, they do not discuss whether he is highborn or a thief; in no case do they welcome him, nor do they even get up. In singing hymns or praises and making offerings, in reprimanding abuses, in everything, each lets the other take his course. . . . They merely value no-mind as the ultimate. Therefore I call it "extinguishing perception." (Broughton 1983: 40)

This breach of etiquette did not prevent Wuzhu from attracting high personalities such as Minister Du, who was deeply impressed by Wuzhu's show of impassiveness (Broughton 1983: 28). But, in order to be received well, such flagrant disrespect had to be perceived as a rule of a game in which both interlocutors agree to participate. Bodhidharma, trying to play the game with an emperor who did not understand the rules, failed and had to leave.

Such is the paradox of subitism: because it denies levels, it cannot reach down to the level of beginners. By reducing the four *siddhānta*—that is, the mundane, individual, therapeutic, and absolute teachings defined by the Buddha in the *Dazhidulun* (see Lamotte 1944–1980: 1:27)—to two levels of truth, and stressing the ultimate level, the partisans of shortcut subitism tended to forget that the four *siddhānta* are individually *true* (ibid.:

[14] Antinomianism was already present in Northern Chan with masters such as Mingcan and Tengteng, whose teachings were later incorporated in the Southern Chan tradition. Tengteng's *Song on Understanding the Origin* (*Liaoyuan ge*), for instance, reads as follows: "You cultivate the Way—yet the Way cannot be cultivated. You question about the Dharma—yet the Dharma cannot be the object of questions. Men living in delusion understand neither form nor emptiness. In enlightenment, there is fundamentally neither transgression nor observance. The ultimate principle of the eighty-four thousand Dharma-gates does not leave the square inch. . . . There is no need to study much, nor to discriminate through intelligence. Ignore the phases of the moon or the intercalary months. Passions are awakening, the pure lotus grows in mud and manure. Today, at ease and lively (*renyun tengteng*), tomorrow lively and at ease (*tengteng renyun*)." (See *Jingde chuandeng lu*, T. 51, 2076: 461b.)

31). In this way, they came to forsake the "individual" point of view, which required earlier Chan masters such as Daoxin to preach according to the state of mind of individual disciples. The lack of *upāya* in later Chan was criticized both inside and outside the tradition. Within Buddhism, the most virulent critics were found in the Pure Land and Tiantai sects.[15] Within Chan itself, they were often found among the partisans of the convergence of doctrinal Buddhism and Chan (*jiaochan yizhi*).[16] A good, although late, example is that of Mujaku Dōchū, who reproached the Zen masters of his time for admonishing their disciples to give up learning and for failing to use individually appropriate *upāya*, making everyone simply sit instead. Such Zen masters, Mujaku claimed, were either fakes or idiots. (See Yanagida 1977: 2:1339.) At any rate, the necessity of *upāya* was always felt, and a variety of "sudden" *upāya*, such as the kōan, were established. As Dahui already argued, it is not the expedient that renders soteriology sudden or gradual but the attachment thereto (Buswell 1987: 349).

THE MEANS AND THE ENDS

Et dum querunt medium/ Vergunt in contrarium.
[And while they seek the middle,/ They sink into the opposites.]
—"Licet Eger," in *Carmina Burana*

The Chan claim for immediacy leads us now to examine the question of mediation in Chan theory and practice. Perhaps, as Ikkyū poetically put it: "Though it has no bridge,/ The cloud climbs to heaven./ It does not seek the aid/ Of Gautama's sūtras." But Ikkyū's comparison is a two-edged one, for the cloud is still in many ways bound to the earth, and its heaven turns out to be an intermediary realm.

It is precisely the notion of *mediation* in the ordinary sense that will provide us with a mediation in Jameson's sense, that is, "the invention of an analytic terminology or code which can be applied to two or more structurally distinct objects" (Jameson 1981: 225). Using the same language may allow us to think about these distinct realities in a meaningful

[15] For the Pure Land critique, see Chappell 1986. For the neo-Confucian critique, see Sargent 1957; and Wang Yang-ming's *Instructions for Practical Living*, trans. Wing-tsit Chan 1963: 290, 385.
[16] See, for instance, the following passage of Yongming Yanshou's *Zongjing lu*: "Lately, there are sometimes people who mingle with Chan without grasping its principles. . . . Stressing only the abrupt, sudden [aspect of] Chan style and the acute and new character of [Chan] dialogues, they produce a fantastic wisdom and practice a stupid Chan, misunderstanding skillful means and getting astray from the essential principle" (T. 48, 2016: 417).

way. Like the Chan masters themselves, whose claims of immediacy they have for too long taken at face value, scholars have to learn how to "think out the intermediary," that is, "the mid-point and the mediation, the middle term between total absence and the absolute plenitude of presence" (Derrida 1974: 157). For "immediacy is derived" and "all begins through the intermediary" (ibid.).

Mediation can appear in various forms and on various levels: cosmological, psychological, praxeological. In every case it characterizes the approach of what is ordinarily defined, for lack of a better term, as "popular" or "local" religion, and Chan's refusal of mediations entails a condemnation of local religion. As has often been noted, "classical" Chan tends toward an elitism.

From the outset, Buddhism was Janus-faced. Too often, in an approach typical of what Tambiah calls the "Pāli Text Society spirit," scholars have attempted to focus on the first aspect and to interpret Buddhism as a rationalist doctrine, a kind of Kantism *avant la lettre*. Buddhism, however, inherited from and further developed Hindu cosmology. Taking Mount Sumeru as its axis, the Triple World scheme had its ontological and its soteriological sides. The cosmological hierarchy of the heavens where, owing to their karma, human beings could eventually be reborn was reinterpreted psychologically or spiritually as a hierarchy of the states—defined as the four dhyānas—which the practitioner could reach in this very life through contemplation. Whether on the scale of one lifetime or of innumerable kalpas, it was a gradual ascension during which the adept met various obstacles and received help from all kinds of intermediary and mediating figures: devas, Bodhisattvas, or followers of Māra. While every creature had its own place or Dharma-rank, its limited domain of action, only human beings (and their idealized variants: Bodhisattvas, Buddhas) were endowed with the power of moving along the scale of being(s), of going through all the degrees before eventually transcending the cosmic hierarchy. Abhidharma scholasticism developed, with a luxury of refinements, the list of intermediary degrees—of rebirth or extasis. By claiming its intrinsic emptiness, Mahāyāna took away all justification for this prodigious structure—yet it maintained it, if only *pro forma*. (But, as we will see, forms have a life of their own.)

The Chan denial of hierarchy

The Chan denial of symbolic mediations finds its origin in this Mahāyāna disavowal of the ontological edifice elaborated by Buddhist scholasticism. This does not mean, however, that Mahāyāna came formally to disavow the belief system of "primitive" Buddhism.[17] It merely developed—*next* to it (or behind the scene?)—a system based on quite different premises: the notion of *śūnyatā* revealing the illusory, empty character of any spiritual progression; the collapse of *saṃsāra* and *nirvāṇa*; and so forth. Thus, supplementing (and undermining) a teaching that held the most distant possible contraries, as two poles between which the entire range of mediations could take place, there unfolded with Mahāyāna a teaching that laid down as a fundamental principle the *coincidentia oppositorum* or the fusion of contraries. The most complete expression of this teaching is perhaps the *Vimalakīrti-nirdeśa*, one of the Mahāyāna scriptures most often quoted in early Chan.

As is well known, the notion of *karma* or retribution of acts and the realization of the painful character of all existence constituted two of the major tenets of early Buddhism. The theory of innate awakening, as it developed in Chinese and Japanese Buddhism on the basis of the apocryphal *Dasheng qixin lun*, led to a reversal of these two cardinal truths: the "sudden," that is, innate or unmediated realization of emptiness seemed to cancel all karma, while the equation between *saṃsāra* and *nirvāṇa*, profane and sacred, led to a revalorization of the phenomenal world. This was tantamount to emptying the content of both the traditional notion of the "path"—*mārga*, a long and strenuous spiritual progression—and its corollary, the notion of "Vehicles" or teachings appropriate to individual spiritual maturity, the levels reached over many lifetimes by the postulants to awakening.[18] Sometimes, the subversion of hierarchy can be as efficient as its denial, in particular when the acceptance of the traditional schema is based on inner distantiation. (See Gauchet 1985: 179.) Such an inner distantiation was common to Mahāyāna and to "gradual" Chan, which still defined themselves in relation to the "Lesser Vehicle(s)" (Hīnayāna)—if only to stress their own superiority. On the other hand, "sudden" Chan came to affirm itself as *the* One Vehicle, thereby short-circuiting or bypassing the entire spiritual hierarchy of traditional Buddhism and leaving the frame of Indian thought—a thought or way of thinking that "hierarchizes instead of excluding, the complementarity allowing the loosest and at the same time largest integration of alien elements" (Dumont 1970: 244).

This evolution, however, did not take place overnight, or in linear fashion, due in part to the resistance of traditional mental structures. Even as radical a master as Linji cannot entirely deny karmic retribution. He re-

[17] Although they sometimes do just that; see, for example, in the Chan apocryphal *Yuanming lun* (McRae 1986: 168), the way in which the four disks of Buddhist cosmology are explained (away) as the products of four types of false thoughts.

[18] For a Marxist critique of this process, see Ren 1984a: 54ff. For more details on the Chan subversion of *mārga*, see the contributions of Carl Bielefeldt (1989b) and John McRae (1989).

pudiates it on one level, only to accept it on another—thus making sudden awakening a fundamental exception to what remains otherwise the rule. Dōgen, on the other hand, offers an apology for karma that is perhaps a return, beyond the early Buddhist tradition, to the Hindu conception of karma as ritual act. For Linji, the point is to avoid "creating acts" and to realize the essential emptiness of karma, while karmic retribution is for Dōgen an essential part of an individual practice sustaining the cosmos. Linji vilifies those false masters whom he calls "blind shavepates" and "fox spirits," those who, on pretext of exhorting their disciples to practice, push them to "create karma." For Dōgen, however, it is precisely Linji's "naturalism" that makes him a "wild fox spirit."[19] In the Hindu tradition, the "act" (*karman*) is above all the ritual act, understood as a way to maintain or restore the cosmic balance. The rite aims primarily at obtaining a result, a response, a profit. It is defined by its efficacy, its performative value. It is therefore not surprising if Chan, from the outset, stressed the futility of ritual and the "non-obtention," the gratuity, the disinterest that derive from the principle of emptiness—as it is summed up in particular in the *Heart Sūtra*. Thus Linji's "ordinary man with nothing to do" is someone who does not care about ritual and pays only lip service, inasmuch as it may legitimate his predication, to the doctrine of transmigration. Rites are denounced for their empty formalism, and the *Platform Sūtra* already praised the "informal" or "formless" precepts (*wuxiangjie*; Yampolsky 1967: 141). Demythologization goes along in theory with deritualization. In actual practice, as we will see, things were somewhat more complicated. Both form and formlessness have a certain power, and both types of power proved valuable for the Chan tradition.

Chan substituted its own empty space for the multiple and hierarchized places of the "sacred space" of local cults. (See Faure 1987b.) In similar fashion, it affirmed the "unlocalizable" character of no-thought against

---

[19] Dōgen often quotes in this connection the story of Baizhang and the fox, one of the favorite *exempla* of Chan literature. The fox, appearing to Baizhang as an old man, tells him that he was once a Buddhist abbot who fell into this evil destiny for having asserted that an enlightened man does not fall into causation. He is saved when Baizhang tells him that an enlightened man does not ignore causation. The point of the story is that the true Chan master espouses the theory of karmic retribution instead of denying it in the name of a questionable "inneism" or "spontaneism." Unlike Dōgen's, however, Wumen Huikai's comment seems to undercut the traditional interpretation of *karma*: "If you have an eye to see through this, then you will know that the former abbot did enjoy his five hundred happy blessed lives as a fox." (See *Wumen guan*, T. 48, 2005: 293.) Dōgen returns to this question all the time, for it was at the center of the debate that opposed him to the "naturalist" tendency of the Darumashū. It is moreover significant that the main protagonist of the story is Baizhang, the putative founder of the "pure rule" of Chan monasteries, which contributed so much to the institutionalization and the ritualization of the school. The traditional interpretation of *karma* was also strongly emphasized by later Japanese masters such as Bassui. See Braverman 1989: 26, 78, 85.

the structures of thought or consciousness, by essence localized and lo-calizing. Thinking is actually *taking place*—a lot of place. Consequently, to think is to be assigned to a specific place. This point is nicely illustrated by the various anecdotes opposing a Chan master to a thaumaturge en-dowed with telepathic powers. As long as the Chan master thinks of something, he remains trapped in his thoughts or images, assignable, lo-calizable, seizable by the penetrating vision of his opponent. As soon as he takes refuge in nonthinking, nonabiding, that is, in his true unlocaliz-able nature, however, he becomes unpredictable, properly *aporetic*: no path leads to him anymore. He has left behind all ontological or psycho-logical structure and remains (in his nonabiding way) in the undifferen-tiated (absolute?) realm.[20] Ironically, this capacity to pass beyond (or rather to bypass, since passing beyond still implies a gradation) the entire hierarchy of being (and nonbeing) is what ensures him his eminent posi-tion in the social hierarchy.

Inheriting the spirit of Mahāyāna and pushing it one step further, Chan erased not only the cosmological speculations of traditional Buddhism but also the scholastic scaffoldings of Tiantai and Huayan and the other-worldly visions of the Pure Land school. The former soteriological tri-chotomy, in which the poles of delusion and awakening were mediated by an intermediary world, was gradually replaced by a dichotomous in-terpretation of the Mādhyamika notion of the "two truths." Furthermore, the hierarchy preserved in the Two Truths theory between transcendence and immanence tended to give way to a "transcendental immanence" that soon became a mere immanence in some currents of Chan open to Con-fucian influence. Although a correct interpretation of the "two truths" would have stressed that they were epistemological stances and not dis-tinct ontological realms, the common Chinese interpretation on this point was widely off the mark: in many respects, it is reminiscent of the Platonic conception according to which noumenon and phenomena are ontologically distinct, separated by a yawning gap. (See Liebenthal 1955.) One can doubtless discern in Mahāyāna various attempts at theoretically defining a median and mediatory approach: as with the Tiantai notion of the "three inspections" of the One Mind (*yixin sanguan*), which discerns, between vacuity and illusion, a "provisional" truth retaining a certain de-gree of reality and allowing the passage from one extreme to the other. Notions such as this provided the theoretical justification for a militant

[20] A similar idea is expressed by Linji when he reproaches his disciples for their attach-ment to forms: "What a pity that the blind shavepate . . . grasps at the robe I'm wearing and declares it to be blue or yellow, red or white! When I disrobe and enter the state of purity, the student takes one look and is immediately filled with delight and longing. Then, when I cast off everything, the student is stunned and, running about in wild confusion, cries, 'You are naked!' " (Sasaki 1975: 30).

syncretism that allowed Japanese Buddhism to assimilate the intermediary world of local cults. Chan/Zen offers nothing similar, at least in theory. The motto of Chan could have been Jean-Jacques Rousseau's remark: "For me there has never been any intermediary between everything and nothing."[21] But the rejection of symbolical mediation, in its various formulations, remained a kind of "linguistic taboo" (Collins 1982: 183) that created a wide gap between theory and practice. To see beyond this taboo, we must bracket the doctrine and turn toward other documentary sources such as ritual, myth, and iconography.

The intermediary world

The acosmological character of Chan stands in sharp contrast to the cases of Daoism and local religion, in which we find an extremely developed cosmology—purporting to be a description of what Henri Corbin would call a *mundus imaginalis*. (See Corbin 1958: 7; 1983: 16ff.) For Corbin, the *mundus imaginalis* is a realm that, while not being yet the world of pure intellective intuition, is no longer the empirical world of perception. In this intermediary realm, immanence and transcendence fuse and the "uncorporeal becomes corporeal."[22] This is strongly reminiscent of the visionary teachings of Mahāyāna and of the atmosphere of the Dharma assemblies described in scriptures such as the *Lotus Sūtra*—assemblies during which the Buddha, manifesting himself in his Retribution Body (Sk. *saṃbhogakāya*, J. *hōshin*), preaches the Dharma to the Bodhisattva and to his other disciples. As Mus points out, the seemingly acosmological nature of *nirvāṇa* in early Mahāyana presupposed a cosmology: it was actually a reversal of the latter, not a mere denial. The reversal was "taking place" at an intermediary level, the plane (*dhātu*) to which belonged, for instance, the relics of the Buddha (*śarīradhātu*), which were neither purely immanent nor purely transcendent. (See Mus 1935: 60–84.)

Although the *mundus imaginalis* was at first real for Buddhists, as time went by it tended to become imaginary. Perhaps this phenomenon can be attributed to a loss of faith or of vision, a slow sliding during which access to the "imaginal" was gradually prevented, while the Buddha resigned himself to preach only in his Body of Law (Sk. *Dharmakāya*, J. *hosshin*)

---

[21] Jean-Jacques Rousseau, *Les Confessions*, in *Oeuvres complètes*, Vol. 1, *Bibliothèque de la Pléiade* (Paris: Gallimard, 1959), 332; quoted in Derrida 1967: 157. Although translator Spivak (Derrida 1974: 157) is justified in translating "with me it has always been everything or nothing," she loses Derrida's emphasis on mediation (or lack thereof).

[22] This intermediary world, which is that of Islamic mysticism, could have been ours as well if we had paid more attention to Aristotle than to Plato. Yet Plato himself speaks of the "daemonic" as an intermediate realm between human and divine levels, a realm that "unites the cosmos with itself." See *Republic* 614c, *Statesman* 309c, *Timaeus* 90a; quoted in Conze 1974: 24.

for those initiated into Buddhist esotericism or in his Metamorphical Body (Sk. *nirmāṇakāya*, J. *keshin*) for the common believers.[23] As Edward Conze points out: "A belief in the existence of an intermediary world is attested in all Buddhist scriptures a thousand times. No Buddhist community has ever been without it. It is also, incidentally, reflected in the *trikāya* doctrine. . . . The *saṃbhogakāya* reveals itself only to faith, and shows the Buddhas as they are in the intermediary world" (Conze 1974: 24). Because of its elusive character, however, this intermediary world was easily lost sight of. In Conze's inimitable words: "The facts of the intermediary world are . . . of such a nature that they cannot be dragged into the full light of the day and be inspected, tested and scrutinized by all and sundry at their leisure. They no more survive that treatment than the blushes of a virgin who is stripped naked and raped by passers-by on a crowded street every day between ten and eleven in the morning" (Conze 1974: 30). The intrinsic violence of ordinary language explains why "the intermediary world is spoken of in a language which is known as *saṃdhābhāṣya*, an esoteric, secretive, ambiguous, hidden mode of expression which can also be interpreted as 'twilight language' " (ibid.).

Access to and participation in the *mundus imaginalis* takes place through the agency of creative imagination and symbols. For Corbin, imagination is indeed a "truly central, mediating function due to the median, mediating position of the mundus imaginalis."[24] What about the status of imagination in Chinese Buddhism and more precisely in Chan? Here the Aristotelian schema, which places imagination as median and mediating function between sensation and intellect, may serve as a heuristic counterpoint. Does it not, however, do violence to this schema to apply it to the Buddhist and Chinese contexts? It has often been pointed out that Chinese ontology did not know the Western and Platonic divorce between being and thought, the sensible and the intelligible, and that it therefore had no need of the Aristotelian mediation of imagination. The Chinese supposedly do not separate the real into corporeal and uncorporeal, visible and invisible, rational and irrational, human and divine, true and illusory. (See Gernet 1987: 370–71.) Without polarities of this kind, symbols have no role to play, since by essence they refer to an "other

[23] On the Buddhist *mundus imaginalis*, see Conze 1974: 22–31. According to Conze, there are "four main items which fall traditionally within the intermediary world. They are forces I. neutral to the spiritual life, II. hostile to it, III. beneficial to it, and IV. experiences expressive of the spiritual world" (ibid.: 25).

[24] Whereas Corbin (1958: 139–142; 1983: 27) attributes to a secularization of the "imaginal" into the "imaginary" the apparition of the fantastic, the horrible, the monstrous, the miserable, and the absurd, he characterizes traditional Islamic culture by a tendency to hieratic solemnity and stylization. This sharp contrast reflects an intellectualistic vision. Focusing as he does on an elitist mysticism, Corbin ignores Roger Caillois's distinction between pure and impure sacredness, or between two (overlapping?) intermediary realms, known in Tantric Buddhism as the ways of the "right hand" and the "left hand."

scene"—a scene that in China does not exist. Yet there was a hermeneutic and symbolic tradition, represented for instance by the *Yijing*. But, as François Jullien points out, this tradition was weakened by the notion that the phenomenal and the transcendental could not be objectively distinct. Since "the beyond of representation manifests itself precisely through representation" (Jullien 1982b), such representation could not refer to another reality. All of nature becomes a hierophany, although there is nothing, here, behind or beyond phenomena. For the one who perceives Dao, the real appears in its "suchness"; its "true nature" reveals itself. According to Jullien, at this level, the distinction between an abstract meaning and its concrete representation is no longer relevant, since nothing refers to or represents anything: "The conditions of possibility of a symbolical functioning are here definitively abolished" (Jullien 1984).

The Buddhist use of two-tiered symbols to express reality seems to derive from the central tenet that "things are not what they seem to be." The development of Mahāyāna in China and Japan, however, considerably affected this perception of reality. LaFleur defines the theory of "innate awakening" (J. *hongaku*) as "a way of collapsing the distance between ordinary mind and enlightened mind and, thus, abolishing the dualism that is itself the stuff of delusion" (LaFleur 1983: 21). "Even Buddhist symbols themselves had to be subjected to the *hongaku* insistence that no thing is merely a pointer or means for recognition of another thing" (ibid.: 23).

This state, however, is at best an outcome, a rarely—if ever—reached ideal and not a cultural given. We tend to take representation for reality. Although representation is part of reality and can sometimes modify it significantly, the gap between them remains significant. Nowhere, in East Asia or in the West, do ordinary people live permanently and consciously in emptiness. It is only a Zhuangzi or his idealized sage who can "disport himself all day long within Dao."[25] According to LaFleur, the Buddhist critique of symbols "brought into being a very specific aesthetic mode—one customarily associated with Zen. . . . This recognition is powerful because it represents a renewed simplicity rather than a naive simplicity."[26] One therefore arrives at a poetry or a teaching that rejects

[25] See *Zhuangzi*, ch. 1. The ordinary Chinese would probably have felt about Buddhist emptiness the way William James—perhaps unfairly—felt about Neoplatonism: "The stagnant felicity of the absolute's own perfection moves me as little as I move it." Quoted in Harold Bloom, *Kabbalah and Criticism* (New York: Seabury, 1975), 18.

[26] LaFleur quotes the famous statement by Qingyuan (1067–1120), according to which, before realization, mountains were seen as mountains, and waters as waters; then came the realization that mountains are not mountains and waters not waters; ultimately, the mountains are seen once again as mountains, and waters once again as waters. LaFleur writes: "In a sense, the symbolizing process is itself a digression, a move away from the clear recognition of mountains as merely mountains" (LaFleur 1983: 23). The "mountains of after," as the poet or the Chan monk perceives them, however, are no longer the "mountains of be-

any attempt at discovering a "meaning" to the poem or to reality. Far from being naive, however, this mode of being is eminently aesthetic, and one is entitled to ask what strategy looms behind such a mediate immediacy.

The artificial naturalness that passes in most cases for spontaneity is reminiscent of what Pierre Bourdieu has analyzed under the name of *habitus*. (See Bourdieu 1977b: 72.) At any rate, for the ordinary person still living in delusion, duality does exist, even if it is not as radical a predicament for a Chinese Buddhist as for a Westerner.[27] Therefore, I cannot follow Jacques Gernet when he speaks of "the thesis, heterodox from the viewpoint of Indian Buddhism, of the permanence of mind, which appears at that time [in 6th century China?], and which will *afterwards fall into oblivion*" (italics mine; see Gernet 1987: 371). I feel more inclined to follow Marcel Gauchet, who sees in the radical cut between immanence and transcendence a cross-cultural event and not merely a Western "privilege" (Gauchet 1985: 207). Without finding Gauchet's evidence altogether convincing, it seems clear to me that to claim some Asian epistemological singularity on this point might result simply in an inverted ethnocentrism. Actually, Gernet himself admits that there are indications pointing toward a true dualism: "[The Chinese] oppose the corporeal and the uncorporeal, and note the unextensive character of thought." But in the Chinese case, he argues, "reflexion is not pushed to its extreme consequences." This lack of explicit philosophical *formalization*, however, is not, in itself, sufficient to argue for a radical Chinese singularity in that matter (or mind). Gernet's argument relies on the *Essay on the Extinction of the Mind* (*Shenmie lun*) by Fan Zhen, for whom "mind is a function of the body," or "mind is to the substance [of the body] what the edge is to the knife's blade"; "the hands and the other parts of the body are all parts of the mind" (Gernet 1987: 375). One could as well illustrate a Western non-duality of "bodymind" by quoting William Blake: "For that call'd Body is a portion of Soul discern'd by the five Senses." (See Blake 1966:

---

fore," as the nonawakened mind perceives them. Dōgen stresses this point in *Shōbōgenzō Keisei sanshoku* (T. 82, 2582: 38c–39a). It is precisely through their metaphorical value, as representing the cosmic body of the Buddha, that the mountains can become the cause and content of enlightenment (or enlightened poetry, as in Su Shi's poem quoted by Dōgen).

[27] See the following dialogue between Heidegger and Tezuka: I[nquirer, i.e., Heidegger]: "Your experience, then, moves within the difference between a sensuous and a suprasensuous world. This is the distinction on which rests what has long been called Western metaphysics." J[apanese, i.e., Tezuka]: ". . . Our thinking, if I am allowed to call it that, does know something similar to the metaphysical distinction; but even so, the distinction itself and what it distinguishes cannot be comprehended with Western metaphysical concepts. We say *Iro*, that is, color, and say *Ku*, that is, emptiness, the open, the sky. We say: without *Iro*, no *Ku*" (Heidegger 1971: 14). Admittedly, no Western pair of concepts overlaps with Buddhist notions such as "form" (or "color") and "emptiness"; the fact remains that they are precisely "metaphysical concepts."

149 and 154.) In all likelihood, Buddhists such as Dōgen denied the body–mind duality precisely because they were acutely aware of it and knew that it prevailed among their disciples. Dōgen himself disparaged the body in a way that a Saint Augustine would not have disavowed. He was not an isolated voice, since the entire Buddhist tradition has described the human body as an excremental "skin bag." Linji, for example, uses metaphors such as "bowl bag" and "dung sack" (Sasaki 1975: 29) and recommends to his disciples "not to acknowledge your illusory companion, the body, for it will sooner or later return to impermanence" (ibid.: 15). The ambiguity of the tradition is well reflected by the Tokugawa Zen master Shidō Bunan, who could alternately declare that "the abode of the gods is a person's body" (Pedersen 1975: 111) and that "Buddha is Mind, Hell is the body" (ibid.: 103).

Let us therefore keep in mind that the Chan advocacy of nonduality is not simply a constative statement reflecting a cultural singularity but a prescriptive and largely theoretical answer to a question that, although set in terms appreciably different from those of Western culture, was nevertheless a fundamental given for Mahāyāna Buddhism and for Chinese culture as well. To this question, Chinese local religion and Daoism have given another answer—that of mediation—by recognizing the crucial transformative role of symbols, myths, and cosmology, as well as dreams—those intermediary states between the ordinary waking state and "awakening" in the mystical sense.

Jullien heuristically widens the gap between Chinese and Western cultures when he locates the advent of imagination in the West (Jullien 1986: 33). By so doing, he ignores local religion and the Daoist tradition, for which the *mundus imaginalis* of the *xiang* (images) remained a reality approached through visual meditation. (See Robinet 1979a: 77.) He correctly emphasizes the role of Buddhism, however, in the growing Chinese awareness of the imaginary—as reflected in the emergence of the genre of fiction (the novel; Jullien 1986: 75). This evolution was facilitated by the Buddhist insights into the phantasmagoric character of existence and by the sharp conceptual opposition drawn by Buddhism between illusion and reality. It remains that this evolution reflects a secularization of the "imaginal" into the "imaginary." To be sure, because of the Buddhist revalorization of imagination as an *upāya*, the imaginary was no longer rejected as pure extravagance. As Jullien points out, "the novel *The Journey to the West* is superior, from the standpoint of the revelation of religious intuition, to all the canons of Buddhism and Daoism" (Jullien 1986: 74). But it seems that during a slow process of secularization the imaginary, as it is found in the popular imagery of the *huaben* or *bianwen* and later in *The Journey to the West*, has taken precedence over the "creative"—contemplative or mythical—imagination that gave access to the *mundus imaginalis*. Once *poietic* (in the etymological sense of *poein*, "to do"), imagination has become mimetic; it knows only to "represent" an imaginary world, the credibility of which has considerably diminished. These two types of imagination apparently coexisted—as *upāya*—for a time in Chinese Buddhism. In the Pure Land school and in Tantrism, in particular, visualization of the Buddha and of mandalas played an important part. But the rise of Mādhyamika apophasis and of Chan anoetism struck a fatal blow to the first type of imagination, which survived as a soteriological method only in Daoism, while the "imaginary" persisted and even developed within popular Buddhism and Daoism.

Plato writes that "every demonic being is intermediary between God and mortals. . . . It is only through the intermediary of the demonical that there is a relation between men and gods, either in the waking state or in sleep" (*Banquet* 202D3). In this sense, the Chan practitioner appears as the antithesis of the demonic man: his denial of traditional—Chinese and Buddhist—cosmologies in the name of the "spontaneity" (*ziran*) of the ineffable Dao finds its *locus classicus* in the two verses attributed to Shenxiu and Huineng. While Shenxiu (or rather, the fictitious character that received his name), still immersed in traditional Buddhism, compares mind to a mirror and passions to the dust that tarnish it, Huineng rejects in bulk all these symbols and metaphors to affirm that "from the outset nothing exists." His position seems to entail the futility of any kind of practice or any soteriological mediation: the ideal is pure anoetism or "nonthinking." The Chan accent on personal realization requires the perfect transparency of all intermediaries, or even their disappearance—for intermediaries tend to change from channels into obstacles.

But is it sufficient to negate symbols and other types of mediation to get rid of them? As we will see in later chapters, Chan was not always able simply to dismiss dreams and the imaginary or to ignore intermediary worlds. Despite their denial in principle concerning the other world(s), Chan masters are seen to resort to stories—then widespread—of descent into hell or of ascent into Maitreya's paradise. Above all, it appears that the negation of the symbolic became itself largely symbolic. It turned into an ideology that, while taking the opposite course from traditional mediations, was entangled in the same aporias. Chan masters can be seen as ideologues, not only or always "in the narrow debunking sense of the producers of false consciousness," but in the Jamesonian sense, according to which "Their service to ideology in the vastest sense of daily practices is a virtually demiurgic one, the producing of a whole new world on the level of the symbolic and the imaginary" (Jameson 1985: 373).

Emptiness as Chan texts extoll it is therefore largely symbolic or semiotic. To the objection that this is a reductionist interpretation of "pure"

or "immediate" experience, one could answer by arguing that the allegedly nonsymbolic character of that experience does not entail that it is not
culturally bound. Cultural determination seems to derive from the equiv-
alence between *saṃsāra* and *nirvāṇa*, since any experience of the absolute
should be eminently concrete. Consequently, emptiness tends to become
a rarefied or refined variety of symbolic mediation, and the difference to
become one of modality, not of nature. Moreover, any reference to that
experience, however apophatic it may be, is necessarily estranged from it
and liable to all kinds of symbolic reappropriations.

For instance, it is well known that Zen monasteries strike the visitor by
their simplicity, which seems to reflect the experience of emptiness. At
first glance, they do not offer the iconographical plethora that characterizes the cultic edifices of other Buddhist sects. Iconography is not for all
that absent, as we will see later on. Moreover, the space of the monastery
is all the same strongly hierarchized and pervaded with symbolic values.
Like the Japanese house, the Zen monastery articulates various qualitative
spaces and infuses them with a meaning that structures every moment of
monastic life. As for gardens such as that of the Ryōanji, we know to
what symbolic and semiotic reinterpretations they are submitted.[28]

Paradoxically enough, hierarchy reigns absolute in Zen monasteries,
where the role of mediator is detained by masters who deny the value of
traditional Buddhist mediation, and whose prestige is not entirely free
from symbolic violence. One is far, or so it seems, from Linji's "man
without a rank"—although he was perhaps himself merely a man risen
from the ranks. The Chan/Zen collectivity, like the early Buddhist
samgha, results from what Turner calls an "institutionalization of the transitional qualities 'betwixt and between' defined states of culture." To be
sure, "traces" of the passage quality remain, but because of the monastic
routinization of liminality, "the immediacy of communitas gives way to
the mediacy of culture" (Turner 1969: 107).

This return of the symbolic and the hierarchical was perhaps necessary
to counteract the "naturalist heresy." By rejecting mediation and the hierarchy of the states of being for the *saṃsāra/nirvāṇa* equation, Mahāyāna,
and in its wake Chan, meant to mark the phenomenal world with the seal
of the absolute: in awakening, immanence turns out to be transcendence.
In practice, however, this equation often came at the expense of transcendental values, and it led to legitimating the profane enjoyment of the
world of passions. Although, in a heavily hierarchized society such as
imperial China or Japan, this kind of anarchism had doubtless liberating
effects, it was soon bound to meet its limits.

[28] See Paul-Lévy and Segaud 1983: 70; Casalis 1983: 349–362. Note also the corporeal
symbolism of the Chan monastery, as evidenced, for example, in the *kirigami* or esoteric
documents of the Sōtō tradition. See Ishikawa 1986a: 260.

It may be worth elaborating on the presumed "nondualism" of Chinese thought. I will take my cues from Marcel Gauchet's recent work, titled in homage to Max Weber *Le désenchantement du monde* (*The Disenchanting of the World*). According to Gauchet, the "axial period" (5th c. B.C.E.) was marked by an epistemological fracture that set in motion a dialectic of transcendence and created an ontological duality—a duality replacing the identity of being affirmed by archaic religion. Gauchet contrasts this reversal of structure to the multipartite logic of myth, defining this logic as the "rise of the standpoint of the One, the imputation of the totality of being (*étant*) to a single regulating principle, and, correlatively, as the emergence of a thinking based on constantly renascent oppositions—one/many, sensible/intelligible, matter/form, etc." (Gauchet 1985: 75). Paradoxically, "the advent of the thematic of the One leads toward transcendence and ontological duality, whereas the old economy of multiplicity is the condition of and the key to the representation of a single world" (ibid.: 45). On the one hand, there is the world of myth apparently subject to an anarchic multiplicity but characterized in fact by a rigorous hierarchy of powers, without any solution of continuity between the degrees of being. On the other hand, the ontological division between reality and appearance, the hierarchical affirmation of two planes of reality, then entails a return to the One. Paradoxically, this necessity also finds expression in a dehierarchization inasmuch as the One, instead of being the principle of hierarchy, becomes through this reversal the "other" of hierarchy, the figure of absolute alterity, something that cannot be mediated. The outcome of this process is, according to Gauchet, the radical separation—achieved by Christianity—into two spheres, divine and terrestrial. Other cultures, in particular Chinese culture, attempted to fill the ontological chasm, thereby reaching a more or less successful compromise with the former hierarchical model.

One may reinterpret from this point of view the Chan discourse on nonduality, "returning to the principle," as a makeshift response to the actual situation provoked by the epistemological cut initiated by the doctrine of the Buddha and leading to the theory of the twofold truth. In theory, the two truths are affirmed only to be negated by the Middle Way, which consists in seizing them simultaneously while acknowledging their hierarchy. In practice, however, and more precisely in Chan practice, conventional truth tends to be negated for the sake of ultimate truth. Another response, equally characteristic of Chan, consists in filling the gap by fusing both extremes and by identifying *saṃsāra* with *nirvāṇa*, conventional truth with ultimate truth, the many with the One, which in many cases leads to the affirmation of *saṃsāra*, of the this-worldly, multiplicitous conventional truth. On the contrary, the return to unity as it is extolled implies a previous departure, or even irremediably produces it.

In other words, subitism leads to a dichotomy of the Two Truths type. Inversely, and as paradoxically, the "gradual" bias toward multiplicity seems to prevent any solution of continuity, any "leap," between the world of illusion and that of awakening. Awakening, however, is perceived in both cases as a leap, and the compromise between transcendence and mediation realized by gradualism cannot avoid the reef of ontological dualism. Although it seems to correspond to an attempt to rescue the mediating role of popular religion, it is actually a rearguard battle, and Chan gradualism is already governed by a different logic, which, although not perfectly actualized, provokes nevertheless an irreversible rupture. Despite its theories, and although in its "gradual" version apparently attempting to slip into the mental structures of this "archaic" and pre-Buddhist religion, Chan finally contributed to its repression. By doing so, it participated actively in the "disenchanting of the world" that paved the way to the neo-Confucianist orthodoxy of the Song.

Can we go so far as to say that Chan drives a wedge in the beautiful harmony of being under the pretext of restoring it? Or is the harmony extolled by Chan and its Japanese epigone, Zen, indeed a "return" to primordial nature? In other words, can the effort to make up for ontological duality, since duality there is, finally be successful? To take only one example, can the "disenchanting of the world" be compensated by the symbolic "reenchanting" achieved by Zen aesthetics? It is well known that it is in the so-called art of gardening and its accompaniment, the tea ceremony, that apologists of a "return to nature" have most often drawn illustrations for their advocacy of the harmony of Zen. One may argue, however, that the "exacerbated landscapes" of Japanese "miniature gardens," rather than expressing natural harmony, reflect an attempt at controlling, domesticating nature.[29] The harmony remains indeed always precarious, threatened by the irruption of natural or social forces: one knows the circumstances under which Zen gardens have flourished—or rather have dessicated, since we are concerned here with "dry landscapes" (J. *kare sansui*)—amidst the catastrophes that devastated the Japanese imperial capital.

In all the much-vaunted "Zen arts," one remains in the realm of domesticated, "secondary" nature. The return to fundamental nature, the irruption of primordial forces, the spontaneity deriving from awakening, remain in all likelihood wishful thinking, and the gap between the two ontological orders—reinscribing itself constantly in polarities such as nature/culture, transcendence/ immanence, illusion/awakening—cannot be so easily filled.

[29] I borrow the term "exacerbated landscape" from Hubert Delahaye, "L'espace de la pensée chinoise," in *Espace mental, espace réel* (Paris: Scraffite/Ministère de la Culture, 1984), 6. The utilitarian origin of "miniature gardens" is well documented in R. A. Stein's *The World in Miniature*, which shows in particular that the miniaturization of landscapes had its origin in the Daoist search for longevity (Stein 1990).

Four   *Chan/Zen and Popular Religion(s)*

I have elsewhere examined the Chan conception of space and provided examples of the symbolic violence exerted by Chan on local cults. (See Faure 1987b.) I concluded that this antagonism reflected the conflict, or rather what one could, borrowing Lyotard's term, call the *différend*, between two epistemologies. I also stressed the subversive character of so-called popular religion over against a form of Chan that, under the Tang, had become a quasi-official religion. Now let us qualify this opposition and suggest that neither "popular religion" nor Chan constitutes a monolithic given, and that the fault line did pass not only between them but also through them. The nature of their relationship is therefore complex and dialectical; it is a polarized yet intertwined structure that requires us to move beyond oppositional thinking. My shorthand use of the term "popular religion" is that of an ideal type in the Weberian sense, that is, a *utopia* obtained by emphasizing in one's mind certain elements of reality. But this ideal type is too easily confused with reality. Before proceeding to an examination of its heuristic value, it may be useful to review the semantic field of the term "popular religion."

A Theoretical Parenthesis

One can regroup most recent studies of popular religion into two general types, depending on their positive or negative use of this term.[1] Both are motivated by a variety of reasons—"scientific," religious, political—that may at times contradict each other.[2] Representative of the first type, the

---

[1] A recent survey of the field can be found in Bell 1989a. Among studies of particular relevance see Mikhail Bakhtin, *Rabelais and His World* (1968); Pierre Bourdieu, *Outline of a Theory of Practice* (1977b) and *Distinction* (1984); Peter Brown, *The Cult of the Saints* (1981); Michel de Certeau, *La culture au pluriel* (1980) and *The Practice of Everyday Life* (1984); Nathalie Z. Davis, "Some Tasks and Themes in the Study of Popular Religion," in *The Pursuit of Holiness in Late Medieval and Renaissance Religion*, ed. Charles Trinkhaus and Heiko A. Oberman (Leiden: E. J. Brill, 1974), 307–336; Alphonse Dupront, *Du sacré* (1987); François-René Isambert, *Le sens du sacré* (1982); Dominick LaCapra, *History and Criticism* (1985); Vittorio Lanternari, "La religion populaire" (1982); and Jean-Claude Schmitt, "Religion populaire et culture folklorique" (1976).

[2] Sociologists such as Pierre Bourdieu, Michel de Certeau, and François-René Isambert have called our attention to the fact that this recent interest in "popular religion" is primarily ideological and must be understood in terms of individual strategies in the politico-religious and intellectual fields. It can be argued, as Certeau did, that the objectification of "popular culture" implies (and was historically the product of) a repression of the *people*, in other

apologetic, are authors such as Mikhail Bakhtin, Carlo Ginzburg, or Alphonse Dupront. The second type, the critical and/or disparaging, includes many traditional historians who seem to have inherited their model of religion from Hume.

Hume's "two-tiered model" is precisely what Peter Brown (1981) takes as his target. According to Hume, "it is remarkable that the principles of religion have had a flux and a reflux in the human mind, and that men have had a natural tendency to rise from idolatry to theism, and to sink again from theism to idolatry" (quoted in Peter Brown 1981: 14). In Hume's writings, "theism" and "idolatry" define the two levels of the religion of the elite and the religion of the "vulgar" (official and popular religion in modern terminology), the former being described as "subject to a continuous pressure from habitual ways of thinking current among the 'vulgar' " (ibid.: 17). According to Brown, the basic weakness of the "two-tiered" model is that "it is rarely, if ever, concerned to explain religious change other than among the elite. The religion of the vulgar is assumed to be uniform. . . . It can cause changes by imposing its mode of thought on the elite; but in itself it does not change" (ibid.: 18). In the model criticized by Brown, however, and this differs slightly from Hume's "ebb and flow" metaphor, the circularity has disappeared: popular religion is at times described as "the immobile ground from which Christianity stemmed," at other times as "the lazy ocean of 'popular belief' " on the surface of which the "foam" of religious phenomena such as the cult of saints appears. As an antidote against such metaphorical oversimplifications, Brown suggests one look at the very core of official religion for the source of apparently "popular" phenomena. One would then discover that the famous "ebb" of popular beliefs, their reemergence into official religion, is a largely imaginary phenomenon. Unfortunately, Brown confines himself to criticizing the "trickle-up effect" without discussing the problem of the diffusion of the beliefs of the religious elite—the "trickle-down effect"—into the various popular strata.

Hume's foundational conception is still at work in apologists of popular religion such as Carlo Ginzburg and Alphonse Dupront. Equally worth mentioning is Pierre Bourdieu, who questions the very notion of popular religion, claiming that it exists merely as a reflection, or in the representations, of the dominant culture. We are thus confronted with three conceptions of popular religion: in the first, advocated by Bourdieu, it is perceived as purely residual, a crude copy of the religious beliefs of high culture. The second, found for instance in the works of Mikhail Bakhtin (1968) and Michel de Certeau (1980, 1984), is a somewhat ideal-

---

words, that "popular culture" or "popular religion" have "the beauty of the dead" (Certeau 1986: 119–136).

ized conception of popular religion as popular religiosity, or as a world-view complete in itself. In the third, popular religion, although not purely passive, exists only in relation to high culture, in a bipolar structure. Paradoxically, the emergence of popular religion as a new topic seems to ratify the new relationships of power within academia: it is not merely the discovery of a repressed discourse but the active imposition of a new scholarly discourse claiming to be the orthodoxy.

I shall dwell at some length on Alphonse Dupront's case because it illustrates the ideological nature of the renewed interest in and discourse on "popular religion" among Western scholars. In his recent book titled *Du sacré* (1987), Dupront attempts a phenomenological description of that most elusive reality referred to as "the sacred," which is perceived as the essential characteristic of "popular religion."[3] According to him, the term "popular religion" subsumes three different orders of phenomena: the religions of everyday life, those of the extraordinary, and those of the "cryptical" (i.e., "superstitions"). But whereas the first aspect, "a theoretically total integration of everyday life, is the reality and the life of the Church," the second aspect already presents "noninstitutional margins," while the third aspect, "superstition," is "resolutely outside of the Church" (Dupront 1987: 423). Dupront first attempts to define popular religion negatively, as being "neither a doctrinal body, nor an ecclesiastical body or an ethics" (ibid.: 426); then positively, as a "cosmic religion," which constitutes a "discipline" or "therapy" based on irrational forces and an "assuaging with power" (ibid.: 432). According to Dupront, popular religion is the object of religious anthropology (i.e., the study of *homo religiosus*—a notion apparently considered as a given). Dupront sees festivals and pilgrimages as essential components of popular religion and takes them as universal facts, or the quasi-universal data of religious anthropology. In his view, popular religion is not a historical phenomenon among others: far from being marginal or residual, it is "the basic culture of a religious foundation common to the species" (ibid.: 465). It thus becomes the essence of every religion, the manifestation of a deeper reality that transcends time, cults, and cultures. Dupront's description echoes D. T. Suzuki's definition of Zen as universal and ahistorical. (See D. T. Suzuki 1953.)

Dupront's approach clearly reflects his choices in the politico-religious context of contemporary Roman Catholicism: against the clerics who go on despising popular beliefs, he has chosen to "magnify popular religion for being anthropologically original" (Dupront 1987: 466). His apology, however, cannot hide a fundamental distrust and a certain paternalism.

---

[3] Concerning the notion of the "sacred," see above all Durkheim 1960; Eliade 1959; Dupront 1987; and Jean-Jacques Wunenberger, *Le sacré* (Paris: Presses Universitaires de France, 1981). A good critique of the notion can be found in Isambert 1982: 215–274.

Although conceding that the Church desperately needs to draw from "that immense human reservoir of faith, passion and energy," he holds that the ecclesiastic strategy must be to contain the irrational forces of popular religion—forces that, "in order not to destroy themselves in an anarchic exhaustion or through the sclerosis of practices which have become mechanical . . . , need the order, the discipline, sometimes the safety, if only tacit, of the institution" (ibid.). We are confronted here with an ambiguous idealization, which parades anthropological terminology while in many respects inverting or even merely reproducing the traditional rhetoric as it continues to prevail in the work of many historians. Needless to say, and proleptically speaking, I myself succumb at times to the temptation of idealizing the tradition—for instance when I refer to ambiguous "ideal" Chan figures such as Bodhidharma and Linji.

Paradoxically, a rather atemporal conception of popular religion is also found in a "modern" historian such as Carlo Ginzburg. The image of popular culture proposed by Ginzburg in *The Cheese and the Worms* (1982) is also openly ambiguous. On the one hand, taking as a starting point the "cultural dichotomy" between popular and learned culture, he stresses their circular, reciprocal influence.[4] On the other hand, he congratulates Nathalie Z. Davis for her emphasis "on the active, in fact creative, role of popular classes in matters of religion against scholars who study popular religions from the point of view of the upper classes (or even of the clergy) and see it thus simply as a simplification or perversion, in the direction of magical practices, of the official religion (Ginzburg 1982: 168)." Despite his denials, however, Ginzburg too sometimes yields to the equivocal tendency that consists in hypostasizing the notion of popular religion and stressing the "trickle-up effect," without taking into account the dialectical relationship implicitly connecting every expression of popular religiosity with the religious models stemming from the dominant ideology. (See Lanternari 1982: 121.) The point is stressed by Dominick LaCapra in his comparison of Ginzburg's conception with Bakhtin's:

> Part of the attraction of Bakhtin's conception of an age-old, popular, oral culture is the fact that, despite his periodic invocation of a logocentric metaphysics—he leaves its status relatively "hypothetical" . . . , does not routinize or place excessive "scientific" freight upon it, and uses it rhetorically to motivate often insightful interpretations. Ginzburg, however, demands more of the conception he adapts from Bakhtin. . . . For him, an oral, popular culture, seen

---

[4] See Ginzburg 1982: xvii. Ginzburg goes so far as to criticize Foucault's approach in *Moi, Pierre Rivière* as a "populism with its symbols reversed," resulting from an "absolute extraneousness that places the subordinate class beyond, or, better yet, in a state prior to culture" (ibid.; xix).

either as autonomous or at least as primordial and fundamental, is the *key* to Menocchio's readings and his worldview. (LaCapra 1985: 50)

While tending to idealize popular practices in a Bakhtinian way, Michel de Certeau avoids hypostasizing them as "popular culture." For him, since any discourse tends to reify and to embalm, popular culture has "the beauty of the dead" (Certeau 1986: 119). As an object, it is nowhere to be found: it is more like a nomadic activity, a poaching on the preserves of official culture. Popular or oral culture by its very nature resists all attempts to set it into writing, to turn its customs into an ethnological corpus (corpse). Elusive and "heterological," it haunts the scientific discourse that claims to locate and retrieve it. Far from being irrational, as Dupront and other heirs of Lévy-Bruhl's notion of "primitive mentality" would have it, it appears on the contrary as a form of cunning akin to the Greek *mètis*. (See Detienne and Vernant 1978.) A protean phenomenon, popular culture is the totality of everyday tactics through which subaltern classes reappropriate the discourse imposed upon them. Therefore, it does not constitute a system; or perhaps it does only to the extent that its actors "re-employ a system that, far from being their own, has been constructed and spread by others, and they mark this re-employment by 'super-stitions,' excrescences of this belief in miracles that civil and religious authorities have always correctly suspected of putting in question the 'reason' behind power and knowledge hierarchies" (Certeau 1988: 17–18). As Certeau points out, "a ('popular') use of religion modifies its functioning" (ibid.): dominant discourse is thus *joué* in both literal and figurative senses of the French word: "played," "parodied," and "duped" by those who borrow and revive it, and this parody can be so as to go unnoticed most of the time. As with Bakhtin, we are here in the realm of humor— a realm rebellious against "all the learned or elitist hermeneutics of speech . . . as they have been elaborated over the past two centuries by ethnology, 'the science of religion,' psychiatry, pedagogy and political or historiographical procedures seeking to introduce the 'voice of the people' into the authorized language. . . . These different 'heterologies' (discourses on the other) have the common characteristic of attempting to *write the voice*" (ibid.: 159).

By privileging as he does the myth of a pure orality, however, Certeau tends to fall into the same type of logocentrism for which Derrida reproached Lévi-Strauss in his discussion of *Tristes Tropiques*. (See Derrida 1974: 101ff.) On the other hand, Certeau's critique of all heterologies raises the question of the status of his own discourse.[5] Nevertheless, his approach proves extremely useful for escaping the predicament of the

---

[5] It is perhaps in order to underscore this paradox that the English translation of a collection of his essays has been titled *Heterologies*. See Certeau 1986.

"two levels" and measuring the complexity of popular culture and its subversive tactics. Popular religion in this sense is not so easily localizable and does not overlap with clear social classes or categories. Changing and multifaceted, like the various traditions it subsumes or confronts, it cannot be defined through some immutable referent such as the sacred. Nomadic, forever deprived of territory, it is no less real in its effects.

Pierre Bourdieu, however, reads these characteristics negatively. For him, popular culture (and a fortiori popular religion) is only a myth, a combination of words through which one imposes, willingly or not, the dominant definition of culture. It has no referent but "the scattered fragments of an old erudite culture, . . . selected and reinterpreted in terms of the fundamental principles of the class habitus and integrated into the unitary world view it engenders, and not the counter-culture they call for" (Bourdieu 1984: 395). Despite the relevance of Bourdieu's analyses concerning the role of "distinction" in class relationships and cultural dialectics, his conception of popular culture as residual has the same performative effects as the writings of Hume's epigones, when they present "popular religion" "as in some way a diminution, a misconception or a contamination of 'un-popular' religion" (Peter Brown 1981: 19). Moreover, Bourdieu tends to identify popular culture with lower social strata, while that culture is also the culture of the geographically peripheral fringes of a population, fringes that the constraints of history have sometimes reduced to political—but not necessarily cultural—passivity. Bourdieu himself, in *Outline of a Theory of Practice* (1977), was the first to emphasize the practical logic that governs the values of a dominated culture such as that of Algeria under French rule. He has convincingly shown that the popular worldview persists, if not as *structura structurata*, at least as *structura structurans* or generating schema. His earlier analyses call to mind the works of Certeau (1984) or of Nathan Wachtel (1971) on Native American cultures confronting and subverting Spanish colonization. It is unfortunate that he did not elaborate on this insight after shifting his focus from ethnology to sociology. Moreover, Bourdieu's definition of "distinction" as a will to distance oneself from the *vulgum pecus* actually locates the principle of social differentiation in popular culture—since the latter acts as a foil. If there is "cultural good will" on the part of the lower classes trying to imitate the dominant cultural patterns there is also "cultural bad will" on the part of the elite, and neither pole can be proved to have a privileged role in this dialectical process.

Popular religion and its correlatives

The ambiguity of the notion of "popular religion" derives in large part from the polysemy of the term "popular" itself: in the expression "popular traditions" it connotes continuity and order, whereas in "popular movements" it implies subversion, carnivalization of the established order, and rebellion. Another approach might consist in defining popular religion through its structural relationships with its "others" (i.e., the various terms with which it is paired). If we examine the further implications of the various permutations of the "two-tiered model," three schemas seem to emerge.

In the first case, the uncritical acceptance of this model leads one to conceive of the relationships between levels either in terms of circularity/reciprocity, or in terms of asymmetrical influence, that is, depending on the cases, a mere "trickle down" or "trickle up" from one level to the other. From the opposition between circularity/reciprocity and asymmetry, very different conceptions of popular religion derive: if the "trickle-down" effect is privileged, popular religion will be either a passive acceptance of official religion or a reaction, if not a rebellion, against it. If the "trickle-up" effect is emphasized, official religion may be seen as a kind of domestication of a quasi-permanent and "primitive" religious stock. In all cases, one will tend to consider this dialectic in terms of acculturation—whether through integration or subversion—and extend the notion of acculturation to the coexistence of various temporal strata in the same society.

In the second case, the rejection of the "two-tiered model" may find expression in a denial of all differentiation: official and popular religion are both dismissed in the name of a cultural identity. According to this perspective, not only is the dualistic schema unable to account for reality, but it proves harmful, for it prevents one from asking the right questions. For example, according to Victor Turner, "all traditional antitheses such as . . . 'learned' and 'popular' were rejected alike by the founders of protest religious movements in the name of religious experience or grace" (Turner 1974: 286). Other scholars may prefer to seek the common denominator and consider popular and official religions as idioms from a common language. Dupront, for instance, sees beyond elite and popular cultures, behind the stage where these actors are struggling, a higher reality—religion or religiosity—through which oppressors and victims achieve communion and communication (Dupront 1987: 67). For him as for the Durkheimians, religion, whatever its form, is finally a factor of social integration. As Peter Brown suggests: "Rather than present the rise of the cult of saints in terms of a dialogue between two parties, the few and the many, let us attempt to see it as a part of a greater whole—the lurching forward of an increasing proportion of society . . . toward radically new forms of reverence" (Peter Brown 1981: 22).

In the third case, although a hierarchical structure is maintained, it is considerably diversified.[6] LaCapra, for example, lays emphasis "on the

---

[6] Note in passing that these three approaches more or less correspond, in a Buddhist

complex, often distorted interaction of levels or aspects of culture and the attendant relation between orthodoxy and heterodoxy in social and intellectual life" (LaCapra 1985: 63). For him it is clear that popular, oral culture "was not as homogeneous in its traditions and practices" as Ginzburg, among others, would have us believe. "It harbored inner differences and divisions as well as an internalization of aspects of dominant culture" (ibid.: 55). The latter is not more homogeneous, and one should distinguish between "hegemonic culture(s)" and "dominant culture(s)": "What were the variable relations over time . . . in the interaction among the hegemonic culture(s) of dominant classes, popular culture(s), and high culture(s)?" (ibid.: 58). "If there were . . . reciprocal relations among levels of culture, they took place between segments of popular and high culture. Moreover, dominant and high culture cannot simply be equated" (ibid.: 65). LaCapra concludes that the historian must be alert to the possibility of tensions and contradictions within as well as between levels of culture, including popular culture (ibid.: 64)—a conclusion that we should keep in mind when we examine the relations between Chan/Zen and Chinese/Japanese popular culture(s). The various antitheses such as elite/folk, official/popular, do not overlap exactly and delimit differentiated segments whose dialectical relations are extremely complex: a historical actor can stand at the threshold between popular and learned culture and at the same time between popular and dominant culture.

The internal differentiation of society is examined in detail by Bourdieu in his book *Distinction* (1984). Bourdieu shows that the affinities, resistances, and regroupings that constitute classes are fluid, moving, and contextual. In this tangle of relations, it is fairly difficult to distinguish what is popular and what is not. As Nathan Wachtel points out, one must take into account the ambiguity and the bi- (or multi-) polarity of acculturation: "The same fact . . . may take on opposite meanings depending on the context in which it is inscribed and the project that animates it. . . . The components of acculturation (structural logics, dynamism of the praxis, temporal multiplicity) are indeed constantly at work in the immense historical field that offers an infinite range of heterogeneous cultures."[7] One must retain the structuralist insight that the relation itself is anterior to the terms it defines: one may thus avoid positing popular religion and its interlocutors as unchanging and singular (or monolithic) essences and reifying their relations. Although no epistemological, cul-

context, to the model of the two levels of reality and its alternatives: the fusion of both levels (sudden teaching), and the setting up of a series of mediations between these two ideal poles (gradualism).

[7] See Nathan Wachtel, "L'acculturation," in *Faire de l'histoire: Nouveaux problèmes*, ed. Jacques Le Goff and Pierre Nora, Vol. 1 (Paris: Gallimard, 1974), 142.

tural, or social couple may be considered permanent, the agonistic structure remains essential. It is the principle generating the inner tensions of various fields and the affinities between homologous or isotopic segments in different fields.

THE EAST ASIAN CONTEXT

Are these schemas incompatible, or do they merely correspond to various levels of analysis? What is their value in the East Asian—and primarily Chinese—context?[8] If one adopts the dualistic model (learned culture/popular culture), one is automatically led to raise the problem in terms of internal acculturation, that is, as a problem of "two cultures," of the hierarchization and domination between these cultures. (Le Goff 1980). And the problem can indeed, on a certain level, be raised in these terms. There is no denying that Chan and Zen have been at times part of the culture of an elite, or that, perhaps shifting from elitism to proselytism, they came at other times to adopt various features from the popular cultures they encountered. Certain subversive effects have become visible from the moment Chan—at first essentially aristocratic and metropolitan—became broadly diffused into popular strata or developed in peripheral regions. One should not in the process, however, hypostasize popular religion or culture. The most widespread interpretation tends to privilege the "trickle-up" effect and to see in Chan a synthesis of certain Buddhist currents upon contact with the Chinese "popular" genius. This conclusion seems unwarranted. The situation in China is complicated by the fact that there was not, as in Europe, merely one official religion. The status of Confucianism—whether as official ideology, a teaching of self-cultivation, and/or a religious system—is somewhat ambiguous. Moreover, Daoism and Buddhism also at times played a similar role. At the lower end of the socio-political spectrum, one could perhaps distinguish heuristically between a folk religious culture and several "popular" (or rather "popularized") religions such as popular/folk Buddhism and Daoism. In actual practice, however, all these phenomena are hopelessly intertwined.

On the other hand, the historical or diachronic perspective is indispensable to an understanding of the state of Chinese or Japanese religions at any given time, and it must indeed focus on "great traditions." One cannot, for instance, understand Chinese religion without knowing the classical teachings of Daoism and of cosmological Confucianism (theories of yin-yang and the "Five Phases"). Yet this approach leads easily to an overemphasis on the "great traditions" in which popular religion is seen

[8] For discussions of these methodological issues, see Bell 1989a; Berling 1980; Duara 1988; Freedman 1974; Johnson, Nathan, and Rawski 1985; Lancaster 1984; Overmyer 1980; Sangren 1987; James Watson 1985; Weller 1987; and C. K. Yang 1961.

as only a residue, a heap of superstitions.[9] Such an attitude, inherited from the right-thinking Confucianists and their Western and Christian epigones, is still prevalent in Sinology. Even scholars studying Chinese Buddhism, influenced in spite of themselves by the classical Sinological tradition, tend to pass over "popularized" Buddhism in silence in their attempt to confine themselves to "pure" teachings. But, as R. A. Stein points out in the case of Daoism, "between its practices and those of the prohibited cults, there was not a difference of nature, but only of degree; not of quality, but only of quantity" (Stein 1979: 59). Daniel Overmyer, although relying uncritically on the model of "doctrinal dualism," and finding the difference between great and little traditions obvious, is able to formulate the right question: "Does the scholar choose to affirm or regret the diversity? This is a crucial issue in discussing the history of folk Buddhist sects, for if the monastic tradition is considered superior, the scholar is forced to denigrate the whole development of popular cults in China after the T'ang dynasty and is left without the methodological foundation necessary to understand the role of such folk expression" (Overmyer 1976: 46). And, as we know, this is precisely what happened, in the case of both China and Japan—hence the paucity of studies of Chinese religion after the Tang (and before modern anthropologists), or of Japanese religion after Kamakura. But I would like to reformulate Overmyer's question in the following way: the question is not so much whether there are two levels, or more or less than two, but precisely whether or not we choose to affirm the unity or the diversity, what we are actually doing when we do so, and what the conditions are that determine our choice. In other words, behind any of the models we use, we find again the question of transference, the homology with our psychological or methodological oscillation between monologism, dialogism, and heterology.

The ambiguity of the phenomenon of acculturation stands out clearly, for example, in the development of the cults of Mazu (see James L. Watson 1985; Sangren 1987) and Guan Di (Duara 1988): the same cult can be simultaneously conservative and subversive; it can meet such various— even conflicting—needs as those of the peripheral popular strata and of the centralizing official religion. Like Janus or the eleven-headed Guanyin, the same phenomenon may have two (or more) faces: it can result from a dialectic between two (or more) clearly distinct socio-religious dynamics. In order to counterbalance the historicist perspective, it is

[9] See, for instance, the definition given by R. A. Stein: "Needless to say, the term 'popular religion' here designates everything that does not belong specifically to an institutionalized religion (the State religion, Taoism, Buddhism). Sociologically speaking, this 'popular religion' is not confined to the people but is common to all strata of society, including the imperial court" (Stein 1979: 54).

therefore important to stress the systemic, synchronic aspect of Chinese religion—a religion that, as Maspero pointed out, is not merely a survival or a patched-up syncretism of "superstitions" and Buddhist or Daoist doctrines. In Jean-Claude Schmitt's words: "Nothing is *outlived* in a culture, everything is lived or it is not. A belief or a rite is not the combination of residues and of heterogeneous innovations, but an experience that has meaning only in its present cohesion" (Schmitt 1976: 946).

The bias toward the "great tradition" is not specific to Chinese Buddhism; it goes together with a teleological bias in which the development of the tradition is seen in terms of original purity and irremediable decline. This vision still largely predominates in the history of Indian Buddhism. It is likely, however, that the idealization of "primitive" Buddhism as a "pure" philosophical system reflects the efforts of the partisans of Theravāda to discredit Mahāyāna as a heterodoxy. In Stanley Tambiah's words, "the philosophical abstractions of the canonical *suttas* and the elite scholar monks are often reiterated by the pattern of ideas embedded in myths and popular rites; . . . even the early Buddhism of the Pāli canon and of classical commentary cannot be fully understood unless we see it as an interwoven tapestry of biographical, philosophical, mythological and cosmological strands" (Tambiah 1984: 7). It would be easy to find in the history of East Asian Buddhism equivalents of the "Pāli Text Society spirit"—to begin with, the myth of a "pure" or "classical" Chan.

The "two-tiered model" informs many works on Chinese religion. C. K. Yang, in his *Religion in Chinese Society*, distinguishes two kinds of religion, the "institutional" and the "diffused": "Diffused religion is a religion having its theology, cults and personnel so intimately diffused into one or more secular social institutions that they become part of the concept, ritual and structure of the latter, thus having no significant independent existence. . . . It was in its diffused form that people made their most intimate contact with religion" (C. K. Yang 1961: 294, 296). Although his definition of the "diffused religion," close to the conceptions of Certeau, seems to undermine the two-tiered model, Yang remains trapped in the traditional dichotomy, in which diffused and institutional religions appears as two reified entities. But the most dualistic case is probably that of Wing-tsit's Chan *Religious Trends in Modern China* (1953). Chan argues that "instead of dividing the religious life of the Chinese people into three compartments called Confucianism, Buddhism and Taoism, it is far more accurate to divide it into two levels, the level of the masses and the level of the enlightened." Needless to say, he sees himself as a representative of the latter, thus carrying into Western scholarship the Confucian prejudices against the populace: "The *masses* worship thousands of idols . . . , the enlightened . . . honour only Heaven, ancestors, and sometimes also Confucius, Buddha, Lao-tzu, and a few great historical beings, but not other spirits. The *ignorant* believe in the thirty-three Buddhist heavens, eighty-one Taoist heavens, and eighteen Buddhist hells. . . . The enlightened Chinese flatly reject such belief. . . . [They] are *seldom contaminated* by these diseases. The ignorant people go to deities primarily to seek blessings, the enlightened people worship not to seek favors, but to pay respect" (Chan 1953: 141–143).

It would be easy to show that Confucianism, the religion of the literati and of the State, was never as "rationalist" as Chan would have us believe, and that "the enlightened" were often "contaminated by these diseases" that horrify him. His pejorative rhetoric shows clearly the social origins and the ideological use of his dualistic conception. The crude reductionism of this "enlightened" model, which Chan calls a syncretism or synthesis *"on the highest level,* not on the level of superstition or utilitarianism" (Chan 1953: 185), makes the old schema of the "Three Teachings in One" appear, by contrast, quite sophisticated. Yet his view, however ideological it appears, cannot simply be rejected. It reminds us that the folk/elite dichotomy, although abandoned in a number of recent studies,[10] is an integral part—even if only as a representation—of the Chinese reality.

The "systemic" approach that would provide an alternative to such teleological schemas is not without its inconveniences. It tends to hypostasize a specific historical situation and to overlook the ruptures, the tensions, the centrifugal forces that work upon the system from within or exceed it. As already mentioned, however, the divide is at the very core of the various instances of the so-called popular religion, which is thus both sedative and seditious, simultaneously upholding the social-cosmic order and subverting it. It also passes through Chan, and this fundamental fault is reflected in the constant tension or dialectics between epistemological pairs such as conservative and subversive, inclusive and exclusive, gradual and sudden, or, to use Magliola's terminology, "differential" and "(logo)centric" Chan. (See Magliola 1984.)

Thus the weakness of the "two-tiered model" in the Chinese case results primarily from the fact that both "official" and "popular" religions constitute "structures" (in the Turnerian sense), and these structures are constantly threatened and/or reinforced by subversive marginals: trickster figures such as the Daoist "immortals," "wild" Chan monks, or, in the elite culture, eccentric poets. It should come as no surprise, therefore, that, due to their affinities, these figures tend toward fusion, as in the case of poets *and* immortals such as Dong Fangshuo and Hanshan.[11] In other

[10] See Zürcher 1980; Johnson 1985; Birnbaum 1986; Teiser 1988: 344.
[11] On the other hand, the figure of the "fool" can be perceived as "popular" only because the inversion—as an expression of subitism—is homologous to the carnivalizing aspect of

words, the paradigm hierarchy/anarchy cuts across the two categories of popular and official religions; it does not overlap with them, nor can the dominant term of this paradigm (hierarchy) be identified with either religion. There is an "official" and a "popular" hierarchy, but a popular and an elitist "anarchism" as well. The implicit equations between Chan and antinomianism (denial of hierarchy) on the one hand and between popular religion and hierarchy on the other reflect only the major keys of each tradition and fail to take into account their minor ones. Moreover, what may strike us at first as subversive, both in Chan and in popular religion, may actually turn out to be reinforcing the institutional structure. In this sense, popular religion might provide the necessary freedom and alterity that allow institutional power to assert itself. Like the dialectical relationship between heresies and orthodoxy, Chan and other institutional religions may need the resistance and subversion of popular religion in order to thrive.

As to the question raised by Ginzburg about the circularity or asymmetry between official and popular religion(s), here again two models are better than one, and there is no compelling reason to opt for a strict determinism. There is clearly circularity and reciprocity in some cases between Chan and popular religion(s), while a pronounced asymmetry (privileging the upward or downward movement) may be found in others. Perhaps the very idea of a hierarchy and of vertical movements may be profitably replaced by that of horizontal, multilateral, or multipolar relations. Should we not equally complicate our models, starting from the basic dichotomy (or rather "trichotomy": official, folk, and "popularized" religions), in order to cover the whole range of the spectrum and its various segments and to untangle the hank of affinities and antagonisms subsumed (if not masked) under the relation between Chan and popular religion?

At any rate, in order to hear again the anonymous murmur of popular religious practices, one must first shift the emphasis from the loud and unduly privileged discourse of the "learned" toward popular culture. In the case of Chan, this means that the doctrinal and hermeneutical approach should go hand in hand with an anthropological approach. In order to avoid an inverted methodological scapegoating, however, that would reject the "great texts" of the tradition in the name of the religion "as it is actually practiced," one must also realize that certain apparently "popular" phenomena turn out to be "learned" creations. Admittedly, such an increasingly complex approach risks creating more problems than it is able to solve. Scrutinized in this way, Chan and Zen, or any

popular culture. It remains nevertheless the product of an elitist teaching. On "sudden" inversion, see Stein 1987: 54 and 60.

other tradition, are bound to become, as Nathan Sivin said in the case of Daoism, a "source of perplexity" (Sivin 1978).

The difficulty gets even worse when one moves toward the so-called popular or folk levels. It may, from a holistic standpoint, go without saying that popular religion, in principle totalizing, tends toward a system. Yet one is nevertheless justified, along with the historian, in differentiating the various sedimented temporal strata that compose the system and in speaking in certain cases of archaic survivals, or rather of the archaic origin of certain elements, as opposed to others of a more recent creation and of a more or less learned origin. One is confronting different temporalities, which do not coexist without tension. Another dichotomy, perhaps more fundamental than the learned/popular one, is that of order and transgression. It is found at almost all intermediary levels, which are often only unstable compromises between these two tendencies and which define the pure and impure sacred, the sacred of respect and the sacred of transgression. Whereas archaic religion claimed a perfect adhesion to a preexisting superhuman order, the shift produced by the historical emergence of the State and of salvation religions such as Daoism and Buddhism generated a segmentation of society and a dialectics between the various sectors—a humanization of the sacred that led to the creation of a hierarchized, bureaucratized pantheon, accessible to human requests. As in the case of classical Greece, this mythological proliferation seems to reflect an actual recession of archaic sacrality. To some extent, it paves the way for the Buddhist demythologization. This explains why the Buddhist pantheon merged without difficulty into the Chinese or Japanese native pantheons. This merger was, however, not the case with cosmological theories: the Hindu and Buddhist cosmology made only a few converts (such as the Tang monk-astronomer Yixing) among the Chinese and the Japanese, who had already adopted the yin-yang and Five Phases cosmology.

In the face of such attempts, however, to order chaos and domesticate the ambiguous sacred through *fengshui*, funerary rituals, and ancestor worship arises the world of the sacred of transgression, of black magic or the "left-hand way," of spells and divination, of magical will to power— all the so-called illicit cults, less known but not less real than the Dionysiac realm of the Greeks or the dark worship of Indian Tantrism. Another real tension or dichotomy is the one between local cults and national or "universal" cults, between the "topical" and "choretic" logics of place and space.[12] At first glance, "popular religion" seems to overlap with local, indigenous cults. But what about national cults such as those of Guan Di

---

[12] I borrow these terms from Augustin Berque: "Topical" refers to a place in its singularity, "choretic" qualifies a space in its universality. See Berque 1986: 159–163.

or Mazu? One must realize that the local and the "national" Guan Di sometimes have a veiled antagonism and that Chan will, without contradicting its "official" role, be able to endorse the cult of the latter. (See Sangren 1987.) The very same cult or ritual, for example Mazu's cult or the rituals of "Universal Salvation" (Sk. *ullambana,* Ch. *yulanpen* or *pudu*), brings several levels into play and constitutes in this sense what Marcel Mauss called a "total social fact" *(fait social total).*[13] The ritual itself, usually seen as mediating between different social groups and ontological levels, is also what demarcates or produces them, and it has therefore a logical priority over notions such as "classes" or "religions." But individuals—who are usually standing at the crossroad of several "ways" or oscillating between several "programs of truth"—are perhaps also "total social facts." Moreover, their position in the social field or in the field of cultural production, to use Bourdieu's terminology, may vary considerably. Thus Chan adepts may find themselves on the threshold between learned and popular culture when they interpret in a "spiritual" or "allegorical" sense legends that they do not completely disbelieve. They are equally midway between official and popular religions when they let their prestige as thaumaturges serve the prestige of the State—as did the Northern Chan master Shenxiu. They partake of hegemonic culture when, like Shenxiu's disciple Puji, they compare the Chan patriarchal tradition to the Tang dynastic succession or when, like other Northern Chan masters such as Huian and Yuangui, they confer the Bodhisattva precepts on a local god. They represent elite culture when, like the poet-monks of the Song and Muromachi periods, they indulge in "literary Chan" and consider poetry the highest form of spirituality.

From primitives to Zen, and conversely

As it is used traditionally in the Chinese context, the term "syncretism" covers a plurality of phenomena (synthesis, amalgamation, acculturation) that should be distinguished. Despite or because of its generality, however, it retains a heuristic value superior to that of other available terms, provided one no longer considers syncretic tendencies as a "betrayal of the principles" but on the contrary as the expression of an attempt to respond to the needs engendered by new socio-historical contexts. (See Berling 1980.) The explicative value of this term is usually questioned by those who, like Henri Maspero, privilege the synchronic dimension and argue that the Chinese live their religion as a coherent system and not as an assemblage of heterogeneous teachings: according to this view, Chinese syncretism would be, after all, merely a reductionistic notion im-

---

[13] See Mauss 1967: 78. See also Lévi-Strauss 1987: 25–31.

posed from outside. For Maspero, it is as useless to attempt to decompose Chinese popular religion into its Daoist and Buddhist elements as it would be to decompose French popular religion into "three religions" (Christianity, Judaism, and the cult of the Great Goddess) because the French go to church, celebrate Easter, and receive baptism. Maspero points out that "We see differences in dogma, pantheon, ritual, while [the Chinese] see only differences in specialists within a single religious system" (Maspero 1950: 112–113).

To be sure, historians have tended to accept too uncritically the more or less sectarian declarations of monks and literati as proof of the sometimes difficult coexistence of three great religious traditions: Confucianism, Daoism, and Buddhism. By so doing, they were inevitably led to stress questions of doctrinal orthodoxy and to neglect the popular religion(s), for which these distinctions lost most of their descriptive or explicative value. This imbalance can be corrected by the recognition that the diachronic dimension remains important and that there is a native discourse that may be rightly called "syncretistic," to the extent that it advocates the unity, or rather the harmony, of the three teachings. By the same token, although what Maspero says about popular religion is correct, he is not justified in refusing to take into account the clerical or literati discourse on religion. Moreover, this discourse has contributed greatly to the systematic assimilation by popular religion of doctrinal, mythical, or ritual elements.

It is the ambiguity of the term "syncretism"—applied to two distinct yet related realities, high culture and popular traditions—that explains what one could call the "controversy over Chinese syncretism." If one keeps this term to show there is no solution of continuity between the two conceptions (which do not necessarily overlap with distinct social layers but may coexist within a single individual), it is important to distinguish between two kinds of syncretism: "militant syncretism" and what, for lack of a better term, we will call "popular syncretism." The former describes (or prescribes) the relations between complex ensembles (Buddhism, Daoism), and the latter results from the multiple relationships (fusion, substitution, parallelism) that take place at various levels between particular elements of these ensembles.

The distinction between these two types of syncretism is sometimes difficult. For example, the interaction between Chan and local beliefs may be interpreted as an assimilation of Chan teachings by local culture, or as "militant" syncretism on the part of Chan monks, aiming at the disparagement of local traditions while including them in a purely monastic frame. Thus one witnesses a Buddhist "humanization" of the sacred places of local popular religion. By so doing, Chan can simultaneously conclude an alliance with an official religion intent on defusing local cults by including them in a national cult. As we will see, it is, for example, difficult to interpret definitively, in one direction (sense) or the other, the promotion of thaumaturges marginal to Chan, such as Baozhi or Fu Xi (fl. 6th c.), to the rank of avatars as famous as Guanyin or Mile (Maitreya). Again, although the stories about Huineng's illiteracy or his ethnic origins—he was supposedly from a Liao tribe—are significant, it is not clear whether they point toward a "democratization" of Chan or merely constitute a resurfacing of repressed strata. Huineng's dialogue with the fifth Chan patriarch Hongren, at the time of their first encounter, has been traditionally interpreted as a test given by Hongren and a proof of his social equanimity; but it also reflects the prevailing cultural prejudices according to which "the Southern Barbarians have no Buddha nature." The strong reaction of Hongren's other disciples to Huineng's succession can also be seen as a refusal of an evolution that seemed to lead from "Zen to primitives."[14]

In the following chapters, I shall examine in more detail some examples of the relationships between Chan tradition(s) and Chinese/Japanese popular or local religion(s). The state of the documentation and the complexity of the materials obviously preclude an exhaustive study, and I will limit myself to a few samples. Suffice it to say that for the time being, rather than an opposition—even if dialectical—or a fusion between Chan and local or popular religion, or between Chan and official religion, we can observe an intertwining of—or a transferential relationship among— antagonistic or analogous segments of each of these religious traditions.

[14] The Chan tradition, however, like its Western interpreters, tends to see this evolution as leading "from primitives to Zen." See Mircea Eliade, *From Primitives to Zen: A Thematic Source-book of the History of Religions* (San Francisco: Harper and Row, 1977).

Five   *The Thaumaturge and Its*
            Avatars (I)

What are the exceptional visions that ascetics beg for,
compared to that wonder—to see anything at all?
            —Paul Valéry, *Mon Faust*

If you want the marvelous, then look at the cloudy
skies; above, you do not see that there is any Buddha;
and below you do not see that there are any sentient
beings.

            —*Biyan lu*

Tradition has it that, just before dying, the first "sixth patriarch" and putative "founder" of Northern Chan Shenxiu (606–706) secretly transmitted his Dharma to his disciple Yifu (658–736). After Shenxiu's death, his other disciples were unwilling to accept Yifu's claim to succession, and a fight for succession might have ensued if a charismatic monk named Wanhui had not at that point attested the validity of Yifu's claim.[1] Wanhui himself was not a Chan monk but what we may call a thaumaturge or wonder-worker, particularly famous for his prophetic talents. Yet like his precursor Baozhi who "discovered" Bodhidharma, Wanhui plays a crucial role in the Chan tradition by legitimating masters such as Yifu and Huian. It seems at first glance paradoxical that such a marginal and occult figure would be called upon to support Chan orthodoxy and to legitimate a teaching that was presented as rational and demythologizing. But, in Turner's terms, it is precisely the role of liminal figures to legitimate "structures"—dynastic, sectarian, and doctrinal. We may recall here Ernest Renan's words: "The East sets little value on a sage who is not a thaumaturge." Because he has advanced on the dangerous margins of social order, at the risk of losing himself, the thaumaturge is capable of tapping the reservoir of power at the bottom of human society—and therefore to legitimate social order. (See Lévi-Strauss 1974b.)

THE THAUMATURGE TRADITION IN CHINA

Wanhui is presented as belonging to a tradition that goes back to Baozhi (418–514), and still further back to the Western monk Fotudeng (232–

---

[1] Note, however, that despite Wanhui's support of Yifu's claim, several other disciples of Shenxiu claimed the rank of "seventh patriarch." On that question, see Faure 1988: 131–134.

348!).[2] Many scholars have stressed the interest of the Northern dynasties in the type of "magical" Buddhism symbolized by Fotudeng. (See Yamazaki 1971: 112; Zürcher 1959: 145.) Although the contrast between North and South in this respect has been somewhat exaggerated, it is undeniable that thaumaturges played an important role in dynastic legitimation and in the success of Buddhism. Baozhi contributed to the legitimation of the Liang dynasty in the same way that the Daoist Tao Hongjing (456–536) did. Well known are the two episodes in which Baozhi reveals to a rather dull Liang emperor the true identities of Fu Xi and Bodhidharma as, respectively, manifestations of Maitreya and of Avalokiteśvara.[3] The connivance between the thaumaturge and the Chan masters is well reflected by the commentator on the *Biyan lu*: "This is a case of one acting as the head and the other as the tail." The ambiguity of Baozhi's position in the Chan tradition, however, surfaces in the criticism that follows the above comment: "But when master Zhi spoke in this way, did he after all see Mahāsattva Fu, even in a dream? . . . It was like a cup of fine wine, which was diluted in water by Master Zhi; like a bowl of soup being polluted by Master Zhi with a piece of rat shit" (Cleary and Cleary 1977: 2:426). The author, however, eventually acknowledges the importance of Baozhi for Chan: "Mahāsattva Fu was already dragging in mud and dripping with water; fortunately he had a sympathizer. If not for old Master Zhi, he would probably have been driven out of the country." (See ibid. 2:428.)

Wanhui played a similar role in the legitimation of Chan and of the Tang dynasty. He predicted to Empress Wei that her attempt at usurping the throne would fail. As is often the case, this prediction was made in cryptic terms, and it was only *ex post facto* that its true meaning was revealed. Wanhui appears in the biographies of various other thaumaturges of this crucial period. We are told, for example, that when the Northern Chan master Huian (582–709!) was about to die, Wanhui appeared suddenly and both men, holding each other's hand, had a dialogue in an un-

---

[2] On Fotudeng, who was renowned for his rain-making and other powers, see Arthur F. Wright, "Fo-t'u-teng: A Biography," *Harvard Journal of Asiatic Studies* 11 (1948): 321–371. For a survey of legends related to Buddhist monks as water diviners (*sourciers/sorciers*), see Chen Yuan 1977: 178–190; Soymié 1961.

[3] See *Biyan lu*, cases 1 and 67; *Zutang ji* 18 (ed. Yanagida 1974b: 35); *Jingde chuandeng lu* (T. 51, 2076: 430c). The trio formed by Baozhi, Bodhidharma, and Fu Xi appears in many later sources. In Pen Shaosheng's *Jushi zhuan*, for example, we find the following passage: "When the first patriarch [Bodhidharma] came to China, the circumstances were not ripe. He therefore went to the Shaolin [monastery]. The people thought it was due to an error of Liang Wu[di]. But at the time men such as Baozhi gong and Fu *dashi* had preached the Buddha-mind, taught the dharma of the Greater Vehicle and spread it in the whole country" (quoted in de Bary 1975: 121). On Baozhi and Fu *dashi*, see also Schmidt-Glintzer 1985. For the parallel episode between Liang Wudi and Bodhidharma, see *Zutang ji* 18 (ed. Yanagida 1974b: 35); and D. T. Suzuki 1977: 48.

intelligible language. (See *Jingde chuandeng lu*, T. 51, 2076: 231c.) Baozhi's disclosure of Fu Xi's and Bodhidharma's true identities after their meeting with Liang Wudi is echoed in Wanhui's revelation to the Tang emperor that the Western monk Sengqie, who had just passed away, was actually a manifestation of the Bodhisattva Guanyin. And in the same way, Fengkan—another thaumaturge usually represented with a tiger—would reveal to an official that the "wild monks" Hanshan and Shide were actually manifestations of Mañjuśrī and Samantabhadra.[4]

Démons et merveilles: Early Chan thaumaturges

Watanabe Shōei has argued that the ability of Chan masters to control natural phenomena was the basis of their appeal to the masses (Watanabe Shōei 1975: 161). As even a cursory glance at the biographies of Shenxiu and his disciples shows, thaumaturges played indeed a dominant role in Northern Chan. About half of the wonder-working Buddhist monks recorded by Henri Doré, who relied on the *Shenxian tongjian*, belong to that school. Significant also is the fact that the biography of Shenxiu (to which are appended notes on his disciple Puji and on his co-disciple and posthumous rival Huineng), as well as those of Xuanzang (602–664) and Yixing (673–727), are contained in the *fangzhi* section of the *Jiu Tang shu*, a section reserved for specialists in occult techniques.

Shenxiu's fame seems to have been due among other things to his ability to predict the future. He predicted for instance—although to no avail—a fire that broke out in his monastery. The rapidity with which he was able to gather donations to reconstruct this monastery was also seen as a testimony to his occult powers. Like Wanhui, he predicted the accession of Li Longji (Emperor Xuanzong, r. 712–756) to the throne. According to the *Taiping guangji*, he also foretold his own death several years in advance. Although resulting from an amalgamation of two homonymous figures, the latter story reveals the development of Shenxiu's legend. (See Faure 1983.) His foreknowledge was at fault once, when he failed to anticipate the powerful reaction of the god Guan Di, whose altar he had presumed to destroy. (See Faure 1987b: 351.)

Shenxiu's disciple Puji (651–739) became even more famous in Chinese

---

[4] Makita Tairyō has documented the process of deification that transformed some of these thaumaturges, namely Baozhi, Wanhui, and Sengqie, into avatars of Guanyin. This process, which seems to be a recurring feature of the Tang/Song period, is reflected for instance in an apocryphal text known as the *Sandaishi den* ("Biographies of the Three Great Masters," a title given by Makita to a Stein ms. listed as Giles 6669). The Japanese pilgrims Ennin and Jōjin, among others, noted the popular devotion to Sengqie and Baozhi as avatars of Guanyin and protectors against calamities. (See Makita 1981: 34–38; also Reischauer 1955a: 183.) The three figures came to be worshiped together as a group in a great monastery in Changan. The affinities between them appear in Wanhui's biography, recorded by Zanning in *Song gaoseng zhuan*. Baozhi also became a Daoist deity. See also Makita 1958: 250–253.

folklore, a fame that constituted a posthumous revenge against his rival Shenhui. Under the nickname "Reverend Huayan," he was even raised to the rank of Arhat. It was believed that he was a disciple of Śākyamuni who first appeared in the world at the time of Baozhi and who left with the latter for the Western Paradise. He was also invited by the Queen Mother of the West to take part in the banquet of the Immortals. Apart from his taming of a huge snake (*Shenseng zhuan*, T. 50, 2064: 990; Faure 1987b: 342), the two most well-known stories show him interacting with his former disciple Yixing: in the first, he asserted his superiority over Yixing's divining powers. In the second, he predicted the last visit that Yixing, about to die prematurely, paid him. (See Faure 1987b: 349.)

Yixing was also one of the most famous thaumaturges of the time, although he did not belong strictly to Northern Chan. His *abhijñā* derived also from the practice of esoteric Buddhism, to which many other Chan monks were attracted. He was singled out among Puji's disciples for his extraordinary memory, a talent that he may have developed through mnemonic devices such as *dhāraṇī*. As a thaumaturge, he is remembered particularly for his cryptic prediction of the An Lushan rebellion—"the imperial cart will go ten thousand *li*"—to Emperor Xuanzong.[5]

Early Chan monks such as Huian, Yuangui, and Pozao Duo were famous for subduing local gods and their manifestations as wild animals. The Northern Chan monk Xuanzong, for example, lived as a recluse on a mountain infested with tigers, when he met an old man who told him: "I used to be a man-eating tiger. Owing to your teaching, I have gradually improved and was reborn as a *deva*. I have come to thank you" (*Shenseng zhuan*, T. 50, 2064: 1002). The stories presenting Huineng as a dragon tamer also belong to this tradition. Early Chan seems to have hesitated about which legendary figure to choose as its first patriarch, and the other two likely candidates in addition to Bodhidharma, Guṇabhadra (d. 468) and Sengchou (480–560), were both thaumaturges. Sengchou in particular was famous for having tamed two tigers, thereby provoking the appearance of a well on that very spot.[6] When Jingjue (683–ca. 750), the author of the *Lengqie shizi ji*, emulating Sengchou, visited the site where the latter once lived, the spring, which had in the meantime dried up, suddenly

[5] See Doré 1914–1938: 8:306. The An Lushan rebellion was predicted by several other monks, such as Wanhui and Faxiu (the latter perhaps a hagiographical *splitter* of Shenxiu). See *Shenseng zhuan*, T. 50, 2064: 998b.

[6] According to his biography in the *Shenseng zhuan*, Sengchou, while a novice, had once beaten a *Vajrapāṇi* in order to steal his strength. He also received help from a god in his contemplative practice and was even privileged with a Daoist vision. Having refused to prostrate himself before the emperor, he was condemned to death but was eventually pardoned because of his premonitory talents. At his death, a strange perfume filled the monastery, and hundreds of white birds appeared (T. 50, 2064: 966b).

gushed forth again. (See Yanagida 1967: 597.) This was proof of Jingjue's legitimacy and of his power over the local god.

Another example is Xiangmo Zang ("Demon-subduing Zang"), a disciple of Shenxiu. The *Song gaoseng zhuan* records the meeting between the two men:

> [Shenxiu] asked: "Your name is 'Demon-subduer.' At my place there are no mountain or tree spirits, so will you turn around and become a demon [yourself]?"
>
> [Zang] said: "If there is a Buddha, there are demons."
>
> [Shenxiu] said: "If you are a demon, then you must reside in an unconceivable realm."
>
> [Zang] said: "This Buddha is also nonsubstantial. What is the unconceivable [realm of] being?" (T. 50, 2061: 760a; McRae 1986: 63; see also T. 51, 2076: 232b)

Shenxiu also predicted (or suggested) to Xiangmo Zang that he would take up residence on Taishan, in Shandong. Traditionally believed to be the realm of the dead, this mountain had been the abode of another famous thaumaturge named Senglang.[7] Also worth mentioning is a disciple of Xiangmo Zang, Moheyan ("Mahāyāna"), the Northern Chan monk who represented Chinese subitism at the so-called Council of Tibet. Despite his doctrinal defeat and the subsequent decline of Chan in Tibet, Moheyan found immortality in Tibetan popular culture, where he became one of the eighteen Arhats and is shown accompanied by a tiger.

Thaumaturgic elements in the early Chan tradition reflect its rivalry with and influence by Daoism and Tantrism and the necessity for Chan masters to contribute actively to the legitimation of the ruler through their opportune predictions. Those elements also may have resulted from the constraints of proselytism and of the hagiographical genre. It is perhaps a sign of the slow process of the acculturation of Chan and its subversion by or strategic endorsement of popular beliefs. This process is obviously extremely complex, and to try to outline an evolution necessarily oversimplifies the picture. The present attempt is offered only in a heuristic fashion, in order to reveal the structural logic of those developments rather than their historical occurrence.

The vanishing mediator

In East Asian religious traditions, the mediator par excellence is the thaumaturge, who fulfills the function of what Edmund Leach has labeled the

---

[7] See biographies in *Song gaoseng zhuan* (T. 50, 2061: 760a) and *Gaoseng zhuan* (T. 50, 2059: 354b). On the affinities between Senglang and Xiangmo Zang, see Kamata Shigeo, "Zensha no sōkei: Taizan Sōran to Kōmazō," in *Tamura Yoshirō hakushi kanreki kinen ronshū: Bukkyō no ri no kenkyū* (Tōkyō: Shunjūsha, 1982), 239–248. Concerning Xiangmo Zang, see McRae 1986: 63; Demiéville 1961: 25.

devata. As James Boon points out: "What is inadmissible as fence-sitting in political thought is productive as boundary-straddling in mythic thought. Tricksters, saints, . . . bodhisattva, monks, . . .—such *devata*-types display all sorts of emotive and experiential excesses in order to bridge the necessary gaps of religious cosmology" (Boon 1982: 252). The notion of *devata* types, as opposed to *deva* types, has gained currency in anthropological discourse with Edmund Leach, who defined the two terms as follows:

> One aspect of divinity, which I label *deva*, is that of first cause, the original source of supernatural power. The purpose of all religious activity is to obtain benefit from this ultimate sacred source but, as a rule, direct approach to the deva is felt to be dangerous. In defense against this danger, religions have created a great variety of second-ary gods, goddesses, prophets, and mediums, who are thought to exercise supernatural powers by derivation from the original source and who can, on that account, act as intermediaries between man and God. These secondary deities I label *devata*. (Leach 1972: 305)

Contrasting the roles of the Hindu god Pulleyar and the Buddha in Śri Lanka, Leach further defines two types of *devata*—a distinction that will be helpful for our purpose:

> It is quite appropriate that the Buddha, who mediates between death and the next life, should have a counterpart who mediates be-tween the previous life and birth. . . . And it is appropriate that just as the cult of the Buddha lays stress on the ascetic, the sexless, the repudiation of emotion, the cult of his counterpart should be con-cerned with sex and fertility. One aspect of the relationship between Pulleyar and the Lord Buddha is that Pulleyar is a *devata* of birth, while the Buddha is a *devata* of death. (Leach 1972: 309)

This distinction might be applied in the Chan context to what I call the thaumaturge and the trickster—two contrasting figures who seem to as-sume, respectively, attributes of *devata* of death and of birth. Roles are not fixed, however, and there is a shift from the otherworldly toward the this-worldly, from the *devata* of death toward the *devata* of life, while in some cases *devata* tend to become, like the Buddha himself, *deva* or transcen-dent beings.[8] An example of the first tendency is the way in which the Janus-faced Wanhui, like his twin alter egos/doubles Hanshan and Shide,

[8] An interesting, if somewhat extreme, case of split personality and deification is that of Dōgen, the founder of Sōtō Zen, who in a "new religion" called Nyorai-kyō became the unworthy disciple of a demiurge also called Dōgen. See Kenneth W. Parker, "Okyōsama: Documentation of the Founding of Nyorai-kyō, Japan's First 'New Religion' " (Ph.D. diss., University of Pennsylvania, 1983), 78–80.

became a god of union (*hehe*).[9] Thus Buddhist *devata* figures such as Baozhi, Wanhui, Sengqie, Fu Xi, Bodhidharma, and Budai were progressively perceived as avatars of metaphysical Buddhas and Bodhisattvas.[10] As a mediator, the thaumaturge partakes of two worlds, the two realms of *nirvāṇa* and *saṃsāra*. He is therefore double, Janus-like, and appears simultaneously as a renouncer and cultural hero, as both sustaining and subverting social structure, as marking and transgressing boundaries.

The Buddhist ambivalence toward thaumaturges

The Buddhist thaumaturge is endowed with the six *abhijñā* (Ch. *shentong*) or superknowledges.[11] Commonly recognized as standard by-products of meditation, these *abhijñā* are considered to be essential means of achieving the conversion of others. As the *Visuddhimagga* explains, "the exhibition of miracles is indeed one of the twenty-seven means of ripening the creatures that should be employed by a Bodhisattva." (See Dayal 1975: 115.)

[9] Quoted by Schipper 1966: 91. Schipper notes that Wanhui's cult is still alive in Taiwan, as shown by the following spell for the union of lovers:

> The fifth of the fifth moon of Chen-kuang's first year
> The Holy Bonze Wan-hui from heaven came here;
> He just wanted people to unite somehow.
> Bringing "Union" on earth and a brisk trade for all,
> On Peach Garden's Three platforms his eyes then did fall;
> There, laughing and laughing, and clapping his hands,
> The sound of the bronze drum was stirring the lands;
> The boys and the girls, they loved when they met,
> And go-between's money was not hard to be had.
> With true love forever, no quarrel or strife,
> In all things united, a harmonious life!
> Respectfully I pray the Old Brother Ten-Thousand Turns, the Holy Bonze
> Chang! (Ibid.)

[10] Sengqie and Bodhidharma were believed to be avatars of Guanyin; Fu Xi and Budai, avatars of Maitreya.

[11] These *abhijñā* are (1) wonder-working powers (*ṛdhi* or *siddhi*), which allow a Bodhisattva to pass through obstacles, be ubiquitous, fly through the air, tame wild animals, and perform all kinds of magic transformations; (2) the "heavenly eye" (*divya-cakṣus*), which allows a Bodhisattva to see the death and rebirth of all beings; (3) the "heavenly ear" (*divya-śrotra*), which allows a Bodhisattva to hear all the sounds in the universe; (4) the discernment of the mind of others (*paracitta-jñāna*); (5) the memory of one's own previous existences and those of others (*pūrvanivāsa-anusmṛti-jñāna*); and (6) last but not least the knowledge of the destruction of defilements (*āsravakṣya-jñāna*), i.e., the end of ignorance (*avidyā*), which takes place in the formless realm and marks the attainment of Buddhahood. See Dayal 1975: 107ff. The sources concerning *abhijñā* are extremely numerous. See *Mahāprajñāpāramitā-sūtra* (T. 7, 220: 642c); *Dazhidulun* (T. 25, 1509), trans. in Lamotte 1944–1980: 1:328. See also Vasubandhu's *Abhidharmakośa-śāstra* (T. 29, 1558: 97a) and *Mahāvibhaṣa* (T. 27, 1545: 7). The *Pusa chutai jing*, translated ca. 400 by Zhu Fonian, distinguishes between the imperfect *abhijñā* of the profane or hermits (*ṛṣi*) obtained spontaneously, without study or meditation, and the "holy" *abhijñā* obtained by "excellent men and women" who practice the Way of purity, eliminating the defilements of knowledge. See T. 12, 384; quoted in Demiéville 1927: 296.

Of the six *abhijñā*, only the last one is specifically Buddhist and belongs to the formless realm. All the others are common to both Buddhists and heretics and still belong to the realm of form: they are therefore considered defiled dharma.

The early Buddhist attitude toward *abhijñā* was rather ambivalent. Although the Buddha himself performed miracles, he condemned Piṇḍola for parading his *abhijñā* before laymen and decreed: "You are not, o Bhikkhus, to display before the laity the supreme power of *Iddhi* [Sk. *siddhi*]. Whoever does so, shall be guilty of a *dhukkhata* [Sk. *duṣkṛta*, 'wrongdoing']." (See Horner 1938–1966: 5:142.) John Strong argues that the reasons given by the Buddha for his prohibition against wonder-working are neither clear nor convincing. Asked by King Bimbisāra why he would himself perform what he forbade his disciples to do, the Buddha answered that he had not laid down a precept for himself, and that the precept was intended to apply only to his disciples.[12] According to some sources, the Buddha compared Piṇḍola's act to that of a woman displaying her private parts for money. But Piṇḍola's act was intended not just for display but to convert laymen, and he seems to play here the role of a scapegoat.[13] How are we to distinguish between the Buddha's rule that the performance of magical feats in the presence of laymen will henceforth be a *duṣkṛta* offence, and the tactical move of the heretical master who, while pretending that he has powers, says that he cannot show them? The point is that "the interdiction of the monk's display of supernatural powers in no way denies their ability to perform them, but in fact hints at it" (Strong 1979: 75). According to Strong, we may have here an attempt "to cover up the fact that we have reached the time when ordinary monks simply cannot perform these feats any more" (ibid.).

Therefore, the argument against *abhijñā* needs to be placed in its sectarian context. The problem arises from the fact that *abhijñā* are not specific to Buddhism but are found among the practices of other religious traditions as well. In order to outdo their rivals, the Buddhists resorted to various tactics: either they asserted the superiority or the different nature of their own *abhijñā*, or they downplayed—if they did not entirely reject—them. In any case, the rationalist tendency, which denied *abhijñā*

---

[12] Strong 1979: 74. See also Norman 1912: 3:204.

[13] The same pattern appears in the case of Maudgalyāyana, who, as Soper notes, is usually described as "the foremost of Buddha's disciples in spiritual power acquired through meditation. Late Hīnayāna books present him as a magician, who defeats the two Nāgas Nanda and Upananda by taking first the shape of a Nāga, then that of a tiny being who can fly unseen into their noses and ears. Mahāyāna literature plays him down, partly because magic has become too cheap a commodity. He is one of the group purged and pardoned in the *Lotus*. His spiritual power can carry him only a tiny fraction of the way toward the Mahāyāna truth. In the Sukhāvatī texts, Buddha says that 'all the Bodhisattvas and Arhats in the innumerable Paradises excel my second disciple, Mahā Maugdalyāyana' " (T. 12, 361: 289a; quoted in Soper 1959: 236).

in the name of Buddhist "philosophy," represented merely one trend and was not—as traditional, philosophically minded scholarship would have us believe—the mainstream of early Buddhism. The same point is made by Andrew Rawlinson, who argues that "magic pervades Buddhist cosmology and is not peripheral to it. And such a cosmology naturally gives rise to the Buddha as the ultimate magical being: the *mahānāga*, the one who sits under the tree of enlightenment and transforms the world" (Rawlinson 1986: 145). Thus the supernatural elements in Buddhism cannot be regarded as "fringe benefits adding color and flavour to a great religion," and *abhijñā* may not simply be dismissed as "metaphorical in nature" (Pachow 1986: 99). They belong, and have always belonged, *pace* Pachow and other advocates of "pure Buddhism," to the "fundamentals" of Buddhism.[14]

The development of Mahāyāna increased the ambivalence. On the one hand, its conception of the Bodhisattva as a wonder-working mediator opened the way to its inclusion of fabulous feats. On the other hand, the logic of emptiness undermined these wonders and tended to reduce them all to empty delusions. In contrast to the wrong magic of the heretics, "the magic of the Tathāgata *is the right magic*, since he has fully realized that the entire reality is but magic" (*Bhadramāyākāra*, quoted in Lamotte 1944–1980: 1: 16). Paradoxically, although the Bodhisattva remains a mediator, there is no more intermediary realm. Although he crosses sentient beings to the other shore, sentient beings, as well as the sea of suffering and the other shore, are ultimately all empty—as is the Bodhisattva himself. If the laws of nature are themselves void, there is no supernature, no real miracle that could negate these natural laws.[15] The understanding of emptiness is presented as the supreme *abhijñā*, but it is above all their negation, since it simultaneously includes and cancels them.[16]

The word *abhijñā* was usually translated in Chinese as *shentong*, "spiritual penetration," although a variety of other terms were also used.[17] In

[14] Anthropological studies of Southeast Asian Buddhism (Tambiah 1970, 1976, 1984; Spiro 1970) have incited a few Buddhologists to reconsider the old presuppositions inherited from Burnouf and other nineteenth-century scholars and to attempt to "remythologize" early Buddhism. Despite the danger of falling into the other extreme and the flaws of earlier attempts such as Paul Lévy's *Buddhism: A "Mystery Religion"?* (1968), this approach is useful and likely to yield important insights. Apart from Rawlinson, see Masefield 1986 (reviewed in Harrison 1988) and Tambiah 1984: 45ff.

[15] Thus the use of terms such as "supernatural" powers or "miracles" is somewhat misleading. On "miracle stories," see Koichi Shinohara 1988. On the Bodhisattva as wonderworker, see Gómez 1977.

[16] This immersion in the "source of power" is reminiscent of Mauss's description of *mana* as immersion in Brahman. See Tambiah 1984: 338.

[17] These terms include *shenyi, gantong,* and *ganying.* On *gantong,* see Birnbaum 1986. *Gantong* entails no magical activity; it is a manifestation that occurs spontaneously in response to the purity of the monk. In his concluding section on *gantong,* in chap. 22 of the *Song gaoseng zhuan,* Zanning gives the usual list of thaumaturges (Sengqie, Wanhui, Pozao Duo,

this way, it acquired Daoist connotations, and Buddhist thaumaturges were often depicted as Daoist immortals. The most well-known example is that of Bodhidharma who, although he did not display his powers while alive, revealed his immortal nature by "freeing himself from his corpse" in a typical Daoist manner.[18] The true nature of Bodhidharma as an avatar of the Bodhisattva Guanyin (Avalokiteśvara) was revealed to Emperor Wu of the Liang by another thaumaturge, Baozhi, himself considered an avatar of Guanyin.[19]

The Tokugawa scholar Tominaga Nakamoto (1715–1746) once asserted that, while interest in magic was an Indian characteristic, the Chinese were mainly interested in literature (Tominaga 1982: 22, 97; and 1990: 105). Despite Tominaga's assertion, the main reason for the acceptance of Buddhism by the Chinese apparently had less to do with the appeal of its literature or its philosophical excellence and more to do with the supranormal powers supposedly brought by the practice of Buddhist meditation. Many texts bear witness to the fact that meditation was primarily a means of obtaining *shentong*, and these powers were not always used properly. Moreover, philosophical texts themselves were often used mainly as *dhāraṇī*. The stress on wonder-working increased with the development of Buddhist hagiography. In his *Xu gaoseng zhuan*, Daoxuan mentions many thaumaturges who were simultaneously dhyāna masters, and "extraordinary stories" were one of the main factors in the development of the "biographical" genre in Chinese Buddhism. (See Koichi Shinohara 1988.)

Chan may be seen largely as a reaction against this occultist use of meditation, which it condemned as "demoniac dhyāna." An early Chan chronicle, the *Lengqie shizi ji*, puts in the mouth of the alleged "first pa-

---

Yuangui) and distinguishes *gantong* from the "uncanny" wonders (*guai*) produced through practice by immortals and spontaneously by spirits. " 'Anomalies' [produced by] the *guai* go against the Constant and contravene the Way, but 'genuine anomaly' [i.e., *gantong*] is different" (T. 50, 2061: 855a). It is a fruit of the stage of no–outflows. Birnbaum defines *gan* as the spiritual emanation of a saint, the "stimulus," and *tong* as the "penetration" from spirit realms to earthly realms by the Bodhisattva who are moved to respond by the emanations of the sage. Thus it does not seem that human beings are the agent of the "penetration." *Ganying* is variously translated as "stimulus and response," "spiritual resonance," and "sympathetic response" (Schafer). The *Zongjing lu* defines five kinds of "penetrations": *daotong* ("penetration of Dao"), *shentong* ("spiritual penetration"), *yitong* ("dependent penetration"), *baotong* ("penetration based on karma"), and *yaotong* ("demoniac penetration"; T. 48, 2016: 494ab). For Chinese examples of *gantong*, see Pachow 1986. The *Baozang lun* (T. 45, 1857), on the other hand, stresses the first abhijñā (*datong*) and rejects the four others. On *yaotong*, see Cedzich 1985.

[18] A less well-known story, recorded in the *Uji shūi monogatari*, shows the young Bodhidharma paying a visit to two Indian Immortals engrossed in a cosmic chess game. Note also the Daoist connotations of the Japanese legend of Shōtoku taishi's encounter with Bodhidharma at the foot of Kataoka Hill. See Faure 1988: 145, 160; Nishimura 1985.

[19] See, for instance, in *Uji shūi monogatari* the story titled "Concerning portraits of the Venerable Baozhi." (Mills 1970: 303.)

triarch" Guṇabhadra a warning against those who use these perverse methods, "using demons and spirits to spy on other people's good and bad deeds" while pretending to practice contemplation (T. 85, 2837: 1284a; see also Faure 1990). This reaction had already begun with eminent figures such as the Tiantai master Zhiyi (538–597), who warned against the potential threats of the intermediary realms to the practitioner. In his *Xiao zhiguan*, for example, Zhiyi teaches the practitioner how to distinguish between genuine and false manifestations and warns him that "[He] may come under the evil influence of ghosts and spirits who know of his clinging to their heresies and will increase their power to hold him fast to compel him to realize evil dhyāna and evil knowledge, thereby acquiring the power of speech that impresses worldlings. . . . At his death, he will not meet the Buddha but will fall into the realm of hungry ghosts. If he practises heresies when meditating, he will fall into the realm of hell" (Luk 1964: 143; see also 146). Zhiyi goes on to explain in great detail who these evil spirits are that may upset the meditator (ibid.: 146).

Written a few decades after the *Xu gaoseng zhuan*, early Chan chronicles such as the *Chuan fabao ji* and the *Lengqie shizi ji* attempt to demythologize the notices of Chan masters and can be seen as rewritings of Daoxuan's hagiographical work. For example, while the future "fourth patriarch" Daoxin is presented in the *Xu gaoseng zhuan* as a wonder-worker who can cause water to spring forth and Vajrapāṇi to appear and protect a town, the *Lengqie shizi ji* omits these episodes and stresses Daoxin's doctrinal contribution. In the same work, the Indian translator Guṇabhadra—himself a thaumaturge—contrasts "demoniac" dhyāna with the "contemplation of the Principle."[20] The *Xiuxin yaolun* attributes the following statement to the "fifth patriarch" Hongren: "If you sit [in meditation], you may experience all kinds of good and bad psychological states; enter into any of the blue, yellow, red and white samādhis; witness your own body producing light; observe the physical characteristics of the Tathāgata; or experience various [other] transformations. When you perceive [such things], concentrate the mind and do not become attached to them. They are all non-substantial manifestations of false thinking" (McRae 1986: 127). The *Zongjing lu*, quoting the Tiantai master Zhanran (711–782), declares: "If those who cultivate samādhi suddenly produce *abhijñā*, they must reject them at once. Because these are defiled dharma, that is, illusions" (T. 48, 2016: 497a). A similar point is made by the Japanese monk Enni Ben'en (1202–1280): "To want psychic powers other

[20] The *Lengqie shizi ji*, however, also records the famous story according to which Guṇabhadra had learned Chinese in a dream, through a dramatic divine intervention [T. 85, 2837: 1283c]. A similar episode is found in the biography of Zhixuan, who dreams that a "divine monk" (*shenseng*) cuts off his tongue and replaces it (T. 50, 2061: 743c). In his apparently apocryphal "recorded sayings" in the *Lengqie shizi ji*, Guṇabhadra asks his disciples: "Can you enter into a [water] pitcher or enter into a pillar? Can you enter into a fiery oven?" (See T. 85, 2837: 1284c; McRae 1986: 92; Faure 1989: 111–114.)

than the great wisdom and penetration is the way of Māra and the non-Buddhists. Foxes have psychic powers and transformations, but should we honor them?" (Bielefeldt 1989a).

The Chan discourse on *abhijñā*, if not always the practice, appears relatively consistent. From the time of the early Chan masters to that of such Japanese masters as Mujaku Dōchū, the motto remained "Chan does not revere *abhijñā*." Mujaku devotes a whole chapter of his *Kinben shigai* (unpublished ms.) to this topic. Most of his sources belong to the relatively late genre of the "Records of the Transmission of the Lamp." One such source is the *Jiadai pudeng lu*, from which he extracts Fozhao's words: "In our school, we do not revere *abhijñā*. We revere only the clarity of vision." Mujaku then quotes the story of Yangshan Huiji, as it appears in the *Liandeng huiyao*:

> One day, a strange monk came down from the air, bowed and stood there. The master [Huiji] asked: "Where have you just come from?" "From India," was the reply. "Why do you remain in this world?" "To stroll in the mountains and the rivers." Huiji: "It is not that we do not respect the subtle function of *abhijñā*. [However,] in the Buddha Dharma, it is only after becoming an old monk that one obtains it." The monk said: "I came specially to the Eastern Land to pay homage to Mañjuśrī; and instead, I have met a little Śākyamuni." (*Kinben shigai*, ch. 13)

Another well-known story, quoted by Mujaku from the *Jingde chuandeng lu*, is that of Huangbo Xiyun:

> Once when the master [Huangbo] was travelling to Mount Tiantai, he met a monk on the way. They talked and laughed together like old acquaintances. . . . As they thus travelled along together, when they came to a swollen valley stream, Huangbo planted his staff, took off his hat, and stopped there. The other monk tried to take the master across with him, but the master said, "Please cross over yourself." The other one then gathered his robes and walked upon the waves as though treading on level ground. He looked back and said, "Come across! Come across!" The master upbraided him, saying, "You self-perfected fellow! If I had known you would concoct wonders, I would have broken your legs!" The other monk sighed in admiration and said, "You are a true vessel of the teaching of the Great Vehicle." As his words ended, he disappeared.[21]

Supranormal powers (*shentong*) such as those demonstrated in the foregoing story imply a "penetration" (*tong*), and hence a depth. They are

---

[21] Trans. Cleary and Cleary 1977: 73. See also *Zutang ji*, ed. Yanagida 1974b: 131; Demiéville 1970b: 272 and 1976: 74.

the descending movement of *upāya*, the "skillful means" through which the Bodhisattva reaches out to sentient beings in his attempt to elevate them. In contrast to the magic of the heretics, the "penetration" of the enlightened one is not the conscious exercise of powers but a spontaneous response to beings.[22] We are reminded here of the *Yijing*'s definition of "penetration" (*tong*): "[The sage] is still and unmoving. When he moves, he penetrates [everything]." The *abhijñā* still imply the belief in the existence of different levels of reality and are thus the product of dualistic thinking, as can be seen in Vimalakīrti's criticism of Aniruddha, one of the Buddha's disciples who was famous for his "heavenly eye": "Honorable Aniruddha, this heavenly eye that you possess, is it of constituted mark or of unconstituted mark? If it is constituted, it is the same as the five super-knowledges of outsiders. If it is unconstituted, it is unconditioned, and, as such, incapable of seeing. This being so, how do you see, o Elder?" "At these words," says Aniruddha (who has been reporting the episode), "I kept silent" (Lamotte 1962: 66–67).

Among the six *abhijñā* is the knowledge of others' minds (i.e., the telepathic ability to receive and send mental images).[23] One would expect telepathy to be at the core of Chan, since the Chan transmission is said to take place by "transmitting mind through mind" (Ch. *yixin chuanxin*, J. *ishin denshin*). The reading of other people's minds, however, was constantly played down in early Chan. In a story, whose prototype might be traced back to the *Liezi*,[24] and of which there are several variants, a Chan master is tested by an Indian or Central Asian monk endowed with the power to read minds. At first it appears that the master will be bettered

[22] In a comment appended to Wanhui's biography (*Song gaoseng zhuan*, T. 50, 2061: 824c), we are told that—contrary to the techniques of Daoist immortals, which are only "obtained powers"—Buddhist *abhijñā* are nonintentional. See also the biography of Qin Shi (ibid.: 821c) and the general discussion on *abhijñā* (ibid.: 888b). For a survey of *abhijñā* in *Gaoseng zhuan*, see Murakami Konjitsu, "Kōsōden no shin'i ni tsuite," *Tōhō shūkyō* 17 (1961): 1–17. On the other hand, Buddhists had to take into account the Confucian critique of occultism. Confucians claimed that Laozi's interest in the supernatural merely reflected his lack of understanding of it. According to Huan Xuan, for instance, the Buddhist emphasis on the supernatural, "far from being a proof of excellence, testified to the primitive nature in which the doctrine had originated" (Zürcher 1959: 265).

[23] On this *abhijñā*, see *Abhidharmakośa* vii: 102: "The ascetic who wants to know the mind of others first considers, in his own series, the characteristics of the body and of thought. . . . In the same way, considering the series of another, he realizes the characteristics of the other's body and thought. Thus, he knows the thought of the other and the *abhijñā* arises. When the *abhijñā* is realized, the ascetic no longer considers the body, the *rūpa*; he knows directly the thought." (Quoted in Lamotte 1944–1980: 1:333.)

[24] See *Zhuangzi* vii; *Liezi* 2, xiii. The *Youyang zazu* (ed. Imamura 1980–1981: 4:192) records the paradigmatic encounter between Liezi and the shaman and its Chan variants—featuring Puji and Yijing, Puji and Liu Zhong'yong, Zhishen and Divākara (Rizhao). See Tan Cheng's commentary (ibid.: 194). The influence of the story of Liezi is also visible in Linji's words: "Then, when I cast off everything, the student is stunned and, running about in wild confusion, cries, 'You are naked!' " (Sasaki 1975: 30). Another well-known case, which became a Chan "case" (*kōan*), is the contest between Nan'yang Huizhong (d. 776) and the Indian thaumaturge Daer. See *Jingde chuandeng lu*, T. 51, 2076: 244a.

by the monk, for the latter is always able to tell what he thinks, until finally the master immerses himself in nonthinking, thereby nonplussing his opponent. In one case recorded by the *Lidai fabao ji*, the contest involves several Chan monks and one non-Chinese monk, and it takes place in the presence of the empress Wu. It serves to assert not only the excellence of Chan but also the superiority of Zhishen (609–702), the founder of the Jingzhong school in Szechwan, over his co-disciples Shenxiu and Huian.

Nonthinking may be seen in this context as a refusal to play a type of game—whether that of *abhijñā* or of philosophical debate—in which one was losing and which would decide the future of one's teaching. Such was, for example, Moheyan's strategy at the Council of Tibet. (See Demiéville 1952: 75, 123.) To show that their nonthinking is the very source of all thinking—or even, in the idealist view, of all phenomena— Chan masters after Shenhui clearly distinguished it from "mental cessation" or "detachment from thought" (*linian*). While mind-reading remains dependent on images and forms, Chan stresses no-form. Therefore, returning to the source of power, which is pure potentiality, is considered to be inherently superior to any "manifestation" of power and dispenses with such manifestations.[25]

Whereas the early Buddhist critique of *abhijñā* was aimed primarily at Hinduism, its Chan counterpart was aimed, not only at non-Buddhist traditions such as Daoism and local religion, but at certain trends in Buddhism, such as the Tantric or esoteric school (Ch. *zhenyan, mijiao*), which was then popular in the Tang capitals, even among Chan monks. Eighth-century Tantric masters such as Śubhakarasiṃha, Vajrabodhi, and Amoghavajra considered awakening to be necessarily accompanied by the practice of *abhijñā*. (See Orzech 1989: 97.) Consequently, the denunciation of these powers by Chan masters appears to have been essentially a discursive strategy, a political move at a time when Tantrism and Daoism were in favor at the court and when Chan needed the support of Confucian literati.

One can discern a criticism of Daoist "powers" in Chan hagiography. Sengchou, Bodhidharma's contemporary and hagiographical counterpart, was a thaumaturge famous for taming tigers and causing a spring to appear. He once saw a Daoist scripture materialize out of thin air before

---

[25] Another "power" that relies on images is the ability to remember things past and, more precisely, remembrance of past lives. The advocacy of "nonremembrance" (*wuyi*) in the Baotang school was perhaps a denial of this kind of *abhijñā*. (See *Lidai fabao ji*, ed. Yanagida 1976: 143.) In Tang China there may have been a tendency to play down a kind of clairvoyance that could easily lead to eschatological claims and social unrest. According to Demiéville, "far from being a sign of holiness, the memory of past existences . . . became in Chinese superstition a dangerous faculty against which every man must be secured" (Demiéville 1927: 298). Hence the popular belief that the dead were kindly given the drink of oblivion by the goddess Mengpo.

him, but he chose not to pay attention to it, thereby refusing the opportunity to become an immortal.[26] In similar fashion, Fachang, after discovering a cache of Daoist scriptures on Damei shan, explains to a divine apparition that he is not interested in them—referring to Sengchou's precedent for doing so (*T.* 50, 2061: 776a). Farong, the putative founder of the Niutou ("Oxhead") school of Chan, was also known for his powers. We are told that once while he was meditating in a cave, a huge snake entered, and the monk and the snake stayed together for a hundred days without harming each other. Farong performed all the kinds of feats associated with thaumaturges: he rid Mt. Niutou of its tigers, caused springs to appear, and his preaching and his death were accompanied by all kinds of wonders. The *Jingde chuandeng lu*, however, stresses that Farong—in this respect different from the Daoist recluses living on nearby Mao shan—was able to transcend *shentong*: the text explains that, although at first animals used to bring him food when he practiced meditation, eventually he went beyond this stage of holiness, becoming, as it were, invisible.[27]

The same polemical attitude, but directed this time against Confucianism, informs Liu Mi's *Sanjiao pingxin lun*. The following passage is interesting because it provides a list of *topoi* on Chinese *shentong* and gives a nice sectarian twist to the traditional argument against them:

The Buddha did not find it necessary to discuss the subtle function of the spiritual penetrations (*shentong*). It was only when his disciples arrived in China that they examined this. When Emperor Minghuang [i.e., Xuanzong] asked Yixing about the future of the country, Yixing replied: "The imperial cart has a trip of ten thousand *li* to make, but the gods of the earth and of cereals [i.e., the country] will eventually obtain prosperity [*ji*]." Later, Minghuang had to take refuge in Shu [Sichuan] due to the rebellion of An Lushan. The destinies of the Tang returned to Zhaozong, who first received as a fief the kingdom of *Ji*. Thus everything happened as Yixing had predicted.

[26] To Sengchou is also attributed a small work on dhyāna, the *Chou chanshi yaofang liao youyu* (*Dhyāna Master Chou's Medicinal Prescription for Curing the Outflows*) that parodies an alchemical recipe: "One-third ounce of faithfully receiving [Take swallowing a joyful listening to the Buddha dharma in the midst of thirst]; two-third ounces of pure zeal [Take day-and-night concentration on practice and not falling off]; one-third ounce of Voidness-gate [Take the vision of knowing internal and external]. . . . Grind up the above eight flavors with the axe of kindness, and in the mortar of samādhi finely pulverize them. Take a non-dual silk-strainer. . . ." (See Yanagida 1963: 61–62; Broughton 1988: 161.)

[27] In the *Jingde chuandeng lu*, a famous Northern Chan thaumaturge, Pozao Duo, is shown criticizing the understanding of a monk from Niutou as follows: "It's still the principle of before [Farong] met the fourth patriarch [Daoxin]. Come up with the principle of after their meeting!" (*T.* 51, 2076: 233a). The same work also contains the following dialogue between Nanquan Puyuan (748–835) and a monk: "—'Before Niutou met the fourth patriarch [Daoxin], why were animals making offerings to him?'—'Because he had reached the rank of the Buddha.'—'After he met the fourth patriarch, why did animals no longer come?'—'Even if such is the case, if it were me, I would take one more step' " (ibid.: 227b).

Confucianists hold intelligence and wisdom to be the characteristics of the perfect sage. But can the latter, in the last analysis, bring forth such an anticipatory vision? To this objection, they will certainly answer: "We Confucianists do not esteem this kind of faculty." Have they forgotten that it is said in a *Chronicle*: "Perfect sincerity must entail foreknowledge"? Thus it is clear that they esteem it. But, whatever they may say, they cannot obtain it. (T. 52, 2117: 793a)

Liu Mi then quotes the story of the encounter between Nan'yang Huizhong (d. 775) and the foreign Dharma Master and telepath Daer. The scenario is the same as that of the stories mentioned above, but Liu Mi, dropping the conventional ending, miscasts the story as an apology for *abhijñā*. Quoting a Confucianist source, he attempts to show that, although Confucianists had once been able to achieve such knowledge, they lost this ability:

Now the great Master Bodhidharma, after being buried, returned to the West in his flesh-body. The great master Wanhui, on the other hand, could within a day make a round trip of ten thousand *li*. Qiyu, with only one body, could respond simultaneously to the offerings of a hundred families. Yuance, while alive, could know all the things of the past, present, and future. The Arhat prostrated himself in front of Yangshan [Hui]ji, while the god of the [Central] Peak received the Precepts from [Yuan]gui of Songyue. Tanshi, hit by a sword, was not wounded, while Hanshan disappeared through a stone wall. (T. 52, 2117: 793a)

And Liu Mi concludes:

Whereas life and death, coming and going, all respond to thoughts and intentions, the transformations of *shentong* are unfathomable. Although these [powers] are only the shell of Buddhism, and not something that our school reveres, when one examines other teachings from this point of view, one finds that after all they lack such wonders. It is because they cannot compare with Buddhism in this respect that they try to disparage it. (Ibid.)

THE DOMESTICATION OF THE THAUMATURGE

> Supernatural power and marvelous activity—Drawing water and carrying firewood.
> —Pang Yun, *a.k.a.* "Layman Pang"

Confronting the challenge of the "spiritual penetrations" advocated by other religious trends, Chan monks seem to have attempted initially to meet their rivals on the latter's ground. That is, they first presented themselves as superior thaumaturges. The same logic of subitism, however, that had brought a denial of formal contemplation in the name of absolute, formless contemplation (*jueguan*) and, more generally, a denial of all traditional Buddhist and non-Buddhist teachings or "Vehicles" in the name of the "Ultimate Vehicle," also brought a redefinition of *abhijñā* in a fashion that actually negated them. Consequently, "ordinary" *abhijñā* were criticized in the name of the superior, formless *abhijñā*, that is, the *āsravākṣayajñāna* or knowledge of all defiled dharma (including "ordinary" *abhijñā*).

The story of the conversion of the Song shan god by the Northern Chan monk Yuangui is in this respect extremely significant. When the god threatened to kill him for his lack of respect, Yuangui answered: "I am unborn, how could you kill me? My body is empty and I see myself as the same as you: how could you destroy emptiness or destroy yourself?" And, after conferring the Bodhisattva Precepts on the god, Yuangui explained that true *shentong* is emptiness: "That there is neither Dharma nor master is what is called no-mind (*wuxin*). For those who understand like me, even the Buddha has no powers. He can only, owing to no-mind, penetrate all dharma" (T. 50, 2064: 994b; also Doré 1914–1938: 7:294). Nevertheless, he let the god repay his debt by magically transplanting cedar trees on Song shan. Yuangui warned his disciples not to reveal that episode, for fear of being accused of magic. (See Doré ibid.: 295–296; also Kōichi Shinohara 1988: 147.) In the same way, Pozao Duo's power over the local stove god (again of Song shan) comes not from a specific *abhijñā* but from his realization of emptiness (Faure 1987b: 346). Accordingly, *abhijñā* are simultaneously affirmed and denied, and the real thaumaturge is shown to be the one who refuses to indulge in "ordinary" *abhijñā*.[28]

Linji also opposes Buddhist *abhijñā* to non-Buddhist *abhijñā*: "You say, 'A Buddha has six supernatural powers. This is miraculous!' All the devas, immortals, asuras, and mighty pretas also have supernatural powers—must they be considered buddhas? Followers of the Way, make no mistake! . . . Such supernatural powers . . . are all powers based on karma [*yetong*] or dependent powers [*yitong*]. Such is not the case with the six supernatural powers of a Buddha." But Linji goes one step further, redefining these six *abhijñā* in Chan terms, as one's ability to enter the realms of form, sound, odor, taste, touch, and dharma (or mental objects), without being deluded by them, by realizing their emptiness. Al-

---

[28] This point of view is still echoed in the words of a later Zen master, Shidō Bunan: "If one performs services for the spirits of the dead in a firm state of no thought, even evil spirits are certain to be led to rest. Such exorcism is a sure sign that one has obtained the Buddha way" (Kobori 1970–1971: 4, 1:121).

luding to Layman Pang's famous verse ("Supernatural power and marvelous activity—drawing water and carrying firewood"), he concludes that the Chan adept, although composed of the five defiled skandha, yet has the supernatural power of walking upon the earth.[29] This reinterpretation is typical of early Chan hermeneutics. Eventually, *abhijñā* become for Linji purely metaphorical, serving only to illustrate the freedom of the Chan adept: "Making use of circumstances everywhere you spring up in the east and sink down in the west, spring up in the south and sink down in the north, spring up in the center and sink down in the center, walk on the water as on land and walk on the land as on water."[30]

The argument was later developed by Dōgen, who devoted to the question of *shentong* (J. *jinzū*) an entire fascicle of his *Shōbōgenzō*. Like his predecessors, Dōgen first opposes "genuine," "superior" *abhijñā* of orthodox Buddhism (by which he means Sōtō Zen) to the "inferior" powers described by heretics, Hinayanists, and Abhidharmic scholars. With Dōgen, even the sixth *abhijñā* became a defiled one, belonging to the phenomenal world, limited in time and space. Although he gives a central place to *abhijñā*, these powers beyond comprehension are defined as the "ordinary activities such as drinking tea and eating rice," "cutting wood and carrying water." Elaborating on Pang Yun's verse, he contrasts an inferior, grossly physical Hinayanic *abhijñā* such as "projecting water from one's body" (an allusion to a miracle performed by the Buddha) with the great metaphysical *abhijñā* of "drawing water": "From the upper half of the body flows limitless time; from the lower half the ocean of the Dharmadhātu" (T. 82, 2582: 112a–b).

Dōgen then quotes a dialogue between Guishan Lingyou (771–853) and his disciples Yangshan Huiji and Xiang'yan Zhixian:

> Once when Dagui was lying down, Yangshan paid him a visit. Dagui turned toward the wall. Yangshan told him: "I am your disciple, so please stay where you are." Dagui started to get up anyway. As Yangshan was leaving, Dagui called out his name and Yangshan stopped. Dagui said: "I had a dream. Listen." Yangshan brought a bowl of water and a towel for the master. Dagui washed his face, and then sat down. Xiang'yan then arrived on the scene and Dagui announced: "We are displaying our miraculous powers—Hinayanists

[29] In the epigraph to *China and the Christian Impact* (1985), to illustrate the Confucianist standpoint that informs the Chinese reaction to Christianity, Gernet quotes these words of Linji, or rather Demiéville's gloss: "The true miracle is not to fly in the air or to walk upon water: it is to walk upon the earth." See Sasaki 1975: 22 and 17; Demiéville 1972: 106.

[30] Sasaki 1975: 15–16. A more radical interpretation is that of Linji's contemporary, a monk of Fuzhou named Daoan (793–883), who considered the attribution of *abhijñā* to the Buddha a mere lie. See D. T. Suzuki's *Rinzai no hongaku shisō* (1961), 31, quoted in Demiéville 1972: 108. See also Y. L. Fung, *A History of Chinese Philosophy*, trans. D. Bodde, vol. 2 (Princeton: Princeton University Press, 1953), 403.

have nothing like this." Xiang'yan said: "I was in the next room and overheard." Dagui asked: "Why don't you say something?" Xiang-yan brought a cup of tea. Dagui praised them both, saying: "You two possess miraculous powers superior to that of Śāriputra and Maudgalyāyana."

Resorting to his typical hermeneutical technique of "atomization," Dō-gen glosses all the actions of the encounter, such as "get up," "calling out," "interpreting the dream," "bringing water and a towel." He then quotes a dialogue between Dongshan Wuben and Yun'yan Tansheng, based on Layman Pang's verse: "Yun'yan asked: 'What are your miracu-lous powers and marvelous activities?' Dongshan folded his arms on his chest and stood in front of him. Again Yun'yan asked the same question. Dongshan said: 'Please take care of yourself,' and left." This story, Dōgen comments, demonstrates the miraculous power of understanding through words. He then quotes two traditional Buddhist stories involv-ing the Buddha and a wizard, or Ānanda and Kāśyapa, to demonstrate again that the *abhijñā* of the Buddha are not limited to six and are totally different from those of the heretics (T. 82, 2582: 112b–c), and he con-cludes by quoting verbatim the passage on *abhijñā* in the *Linji lu* quoted above (ibid.: 113a). Thus despite Dōgen's growing criticism of Linji at the time when this text was written (1241), he agrees with Linji's inter-pretation of *abhijñā*. Keizan's position, on the other hand, remained more ambiguous. Although playing down traditional *abhijñā*, he does not deny their reality. Asked by the emperor to explain the "supranormal powers" of the "ordinary man" Bodhidharma, he wrote: "The Buddhist patriarchs always have supranormal powers. As for Bodhidharma, though he was born a prince, he was in reality an incarnation of the Bodhisattva Kannon (Avalokiteśvara). How could he not have had these powers? In Zen, how-ever, one does not stress such powers" (T. 82, 2588: 422). Keizan seems here to pay lip service to Chan orthodoxy, and his autobiographical writ-ings attest to the importance of the occult (dreams, visions, predictions) in his life. Therefore, we should not be too surprised when we see, in the next chapter, that it was within Keizan's lineage that the thaumaturge tradition resurfaced in Japanese Zen.

Six

The Thaumaturge and Its Avatars (II)

THE EMERGENCE OF THE TRICKSTER[1]

One strategy in Chan for domesticating the occult was to transform thaumaturges into tricksters by playing down their occult powers and stressing their this-worldly aspect. Typical of this new ideal of Chan are characters such as Hanshan and Shide, Budai, and Puhua. Thus for several centuries, Chan chose the trickster over the thaumaturge (although there was always much overlap between the two figures), the this-worldly mediator over the other-worldly mediator. And yet in actual practice, the *devata* of life never completely superseded the *devata* of death, as we will see later when examining the Chan cult of relics.

The trickster has a long history in China. We need mention only the legends of Dong Fangshuo and Sun Wukong, who both reached immortality by stealing the peaches of Xiwangmu, the Queen Mother of the West.[2] Another tradition, that of the "strategic folly" of the sage, goes at least as far back as Laozi's description of the man of Dao as a simpleton, or Zhuangzi's derision of Confucianist seriousness in his use of the story of the encounter between Confucius and Jieyu, the madman of Zhu. The song of Jieyu ("Phoenix, o phoenix!/ Your power has weakened . . ."; see *Analects* 18,5) is clear enough: only feigned madness may bring salvation in an insane society. Madness, however, is not merely an expedient; it has

[1] Admittedly, the trickster as it was first analyzed by Paul Radin and other anthropologists presents various features that are absent from the Chan characters under consideration. I believe, however, that the same structural principles are at work here and that, whether we want to call these Chan characters jesters, fools, or otherwise, all these figures can be seen as specific avatars of the more encompassing trickster figure. I have therefore chosen to use the latter term, which allows us to see the relations between monks such as Wanhui and Hanshan and tricksters such as Dong Fangshuo, Sun Wukong, or Jigong. On the trickster, see Paul Radin, *The Trickster: A Study in American Mythology* (New York: Greenwood Press, 1969); Mac Linscott Ricketts, "The North American Trickster," *History of Religions* 5 (1965): 327–350; Robert D. Pelton, *The Trickster in West Africa: A Study of Mythic Irony and Sacred Delight* (Berkeley and Los Angeles: University of California Press, 1980); Lévi-Strauss 1963: 220–223; Wendy Doniger O'Flaherty, "Dionysos and Śiva," *History of Religions* 20 (1980): 81–111; John Saward 1980; Detienne and Vernant 1978; Koepping 1985; David Kinsley, "Through the Looking-Glass: Divine Madness in the Hindu Religious Tradition," *History of Religions* 13 (1974): 270–305; and Kinsley, *The Divine Player* (Delhi: Motilal Banarsidass, 1979).

[2] On Dong Fangshuo, the "divine mediator-buffoon," see K. M. Schipper, *L'empereur Wou des Han dans la légende taoïste* (Paris: Ecole Française d'Extrême-Orient, 1969), 31, 60; Vos 1979: 189–203. On Sun Wukong, see Anthony Yu 1977–1983: 1:7–11.

ontological roots. Thus according to *Laozi* (ch. 20), the sage is a fool because his mind is "muddled and chaotic." In the words of William Willeford, "[Fools] have a magical affinity with chaos that might allow them to serve as scapegoats on behalf of order; yet they elude the sacrifice or the banishment that would affirm order at their expense" (quoted in Girardot 1983: 271). Girardot remarks that "Taoist images of madness are related to the mystical experience of the chaos condition and to the unique effortless freedom of *wuwei*" (ibid.: 269). Elaborating on R. A. Stein's insights (see Stein 1990), he analyzes the symbolic pattern (gourd, calabash, chaos, foolishness) associated with the "banished immortal" figure, and in Chan with figures such as Hanshan or Budai.

The trickster figure had already emerged in Northern Chan, with monks such as Renjian (n.d.) and Mingcan (n.d.). Renjian's nickname, Tengteng ("Volatile"), comes from the last lines of his *Song on Enjoying the Dao* (*Ledao ge*): "Today spontaneous and volatile, tomorrow volatile and spontaneous" (*jinri renyun tengteng, mingri tengteng renyun*). (See *Jingde chuandeng lu*, T. 51, 2076: 461.) He was a monk of the Fuxian monastery in Luoyang who, being invited to the Court by Empress Wu, puzzled her by his irreverent behavior. (See ibid.: 232c.) As to Mingcan, better known as "lazy Can" (Lan Can), he was a disciple of Puji who served as a factotum at the Nanyue monastery. He was famous not only for his laziness but also for his gluttony. He used to wear rags and eat the leftovers of the monk's meals, hence the pun on his name, "Leftover Can." For more than twenty years he slept in the stable with the cattle. The element of dirt in his biography, a hagiographical *topos* that R. A. Stein has illuminated in an interesting way, is something that emphasizes Mingcan's liminality.[3] Every night toward midnight, Mingcan started singing prayers in a loud and melodious voice. One day, an official named Li Mi (722–789) happened to hear his song. Realizing that it did not belong to an ordinary mortal, he went to see Mingcan. After trying to elude the discussion, Mingcan eventually predicted that after ten years Li Mi would become a prime minister. The prediction came true, and Li Mi eventually spoke about Mingcan to Emperor Dezong (r. 780–804), who subsequently sent an emissary to invite this unusual monk to the Palace. When the emissary arrived at the Nanyue monastery, Mingcan was cooking a taro, using cow dung as fuel, and he offered some to his visitor. Then bursting into tears, he exclaimed: "How could I *work* for the Son of Heaven? I don't even think of wiping my tears!" After his true identity

---

[3] See Stein 1970. The topos of the strategic camouflage of the sage is also found in the case of Huineng, who first tried to hide his talents in the kitchen of Hongren's monastery—where he used to forget himself in pounding rice—eventually becoming so light that he had to put stones in his clothes to prevent levitation. Huineng's legend, however, follows the pattern of the thaumaturge, not of the trickster. See Yampolsky 1967: 72.

was disclosed, Mingcan decided to disappear, leaving only a song similar to Tengteng's *Ledao ge* (see *Jingde chuandeng lu*, T. 51, 2076: 461b; Ui 1966a: 516). This song is quoted twice by Linji when he attempts to define the "true man" as one who is "ordinary with nothing to do—defecating, urinating, putting on clothes, eating food, and lying down when tired" (Sasaki 1975: 11). Mingcan, however, remains a wonder-working monk who foretells the future. He once displayed his supranormal strength by moving without effort a giant rock that was blocking the way. We are told that he left the Nanyue monastery riding a tiger in typical immortal fashion. His personage appears therefore doubly ambiguous, participating in and mediating between two mediator figures—the thaumaturge and the trickster, the other-worldly and the this-worldly mediator. The two trends, thaumaturge and trickster, merged in transitional figures such as Budai or the pair formed by Hanshan and Shide. As tricksters, these monks are double: their ambivalent persona contains both comic and uncanny elements, and their smile looks like a grimace. Standing on the threshold between two worlds, they have the potential of reinforcing social structure, or of subverting it. Their wild humor renders them elusive and unpredictable. Carnivalization of this kind is certainly not what the Chan tradition, trying at the time to establish its orthodoxy, needed. On the other hand, the powers and popularity of such personages made them essential, if unpredictable, allies. This may explain why the Chan tradition eventually chose the trickster against the thaumaturge, and why Budai and Hanshan came to supersede, or at least partially eclipse, the rather austere founding fathers Bodhidharma and Huineng.[4] Budai, the "laughing Buddha," even took precedence over Śākyamuni in popular piety. The Japanese representation of Bodhidharma as "Daruma," however, shows that he acquired the symbolic attributes of the Daoist immortal, eventually becoming, in the auspicious form of the one-eyed "Daruma doll," an Asian approximation of Humpty-Dumpty.[5] Was not Bodhidharma perhaps "sitting on a wall" when practicing the elevated "wall contemplation" (*biguan*) that made him famous in Chan circles?

At any rate, the shift of emphasis from thaumaturge to trickster reflects a change from a world-denying to a world-affirming attitude or, to use Leach's expression, a shift from *devata* of death to *devata* of life. This may in turn express the ideological and idealistic shift toward subitism.

[4] On the contrast between the two paradigmatic Chan types symbolized by Budai and Bodhidharma, see Hyers 1973: 25.

[5] One may argue that popular tradition has emasculated Bodhidharma. By giving him this grotesque ("grotto-esque") appearance and turning him into a patriarch, it has rid him of his disturbing strangeness (which nevertheless remains in some representations). Grotesquerie leads paradoxically to the same results as idealization.

Figure 1. Daruma dolls covered with *omikuji* (horoscopes). Darumadera, Kyoto.

Whereas the thaumaturge has to acknowledge evil in order to (gradually) conquer, laughter allows the trickster to (suddenly) dispel evil by merely denying its existence. Although their attributes and functions may overlap to some extent, trickster and thaumaturge do not live in the same world.

Thaumaturges such as Baozhi and Wanhui were reinterpreted as tricksters. R. A. Stein has shown how Sengqie and Wanhui were structurally associated as Chinese avatars of the "Keepers of the Gate" motif (Stein 1981). Wanhui was one of the guests of the Queen Mother of the West (Xiwangmu). By the Song era, he is represented as a buffoon with disheveled hair and a laughing face, of the same type as Hanshan and Shide, with whom, as we saw earlier, he is identified as a "god of union" (*Huohe*, "Harmonious union"). The fecundity element is particularly obvious in the case of the pot-bellied "laughing Buddha," Budai (alias Mile), who is usually depicted surrounded by children.[6]

---

[6] The intercession of another "wild monk" called Hehe ("Double Harmony") gives two daughters to the Princess of the Yue kingdom (*Shenseng zhuan*, T. 50, 2064: 1003b). Concerning the sexual and twin characteristics of trickster figures, see Lévi-Strauss 1974a: 251, and 1985: 201–209.

A bittersweet friendship

A particularly interesting Chan trickster—because of the contrast he forms with Linji—is Puhua.[7] In the *Linji lu*, Puhua plays a secondary role, serving as a foil for Linji. His presence, however, greatly enhances the dramatic value of the work. Moreover, as Yanagida has pointed out, Puhua seems to have seen the "blind spot" of Linji's Chan: whereas Linji became, to some extent, the hostage of power and was forced to preach in front of the governor, Puhua was able to keep his freedom by simulating insanity. The *Linji lu* records several encounters between Linji and Puhua, the first of which is precisely about *abhijñā*:

> One day when the Master [Linji] and Puhua were both attending a dinner at a patron's house, the Master asked: "A hair swallows up the great sea and a mustard seed contains Mount Sumeru. Is this the marvelous activity of supernatural power or original substance as it is?"
> Puhua kicked over the dinner table.
> "How coarse!" exclaimed the Master.
> "What place do you think this is—talking about coarse and fine!" said Puhua.
> The next day the Master and Puhua again attended a dinner. The Master asked, "How does today's feast compare with yesterday's?"
> Puhua kicked over the dinner table as before.
> "Good enough, but" said the Master, "how coarse!"
> "Blind man!" said Puhua. "What's Buddha-dharma got to do with coarse and fine!"
> The Master stuck out his tongue. (T. 47, 1985: 503b; Sasaki 1975: 41)

This dialogue, reminiscent of the encounter between Confucius and the madman of Zhu, implies a strong criticism on the part of Puhua. The criticism becomes even clearer in the following passage:

> One day when the master and the elders Heyang and Mouta were sitting together around the fire-pit in the Monks' Hall, the Master said: "Every day Puhua goes through the streets acting like a lunatic. Who knows whether he's a commoner or a sage?" Before he had finished speaking, Puhua came in [and joined them].
> "Are you a commoner or a sage?" the Master asked.
> "Now, you tell me," answered Puhua. The master shouted. Pointing his finger at them, Puhua said: "Heyang the new bride, Mouta

---

[7] On Puhua, see Yanagida 1969b: 1083–1097. On the *dual/duel* motif, see Faure 1986a: 192–196.

with his granny's Chan, and Linji the young menial, all have only one eye."[8] "You thief!" cried the Master. "Thief, thief!" cried Puhua, and went off. (See Sasaki 1975: 41.)

The story of Puhua's death, as recorded in the *Linji lu*, may have settled any doubt that Linji had about whether Puhua was a saint or charlatan, since it is clearly patterned on the Daoist Immortal's "deliverance from the corpse." Perhaps, however, this story was never told to Linji. The *Zutang ji* (K. *Chodang chip*) contains another biography of Puhua that gives a rather different image of his death and passes over in silence his relation with Linji. (See *Zutang ji* 17.) According to this account, Puhua was not a kind of Daoist immortal who achieved the "deliverance from the corpse" by faking his death, but a man who killed himself by jumping from the top of the city wall. All the later sources, beginning with the *Song gaoseng zhuan* and the *Jingde chuandeng lu*, drop that unhappy end to elaborate on the version in the *Linji lu*. Whatever the case, Puhua was perceived as both a crucial and cumbersome figure by later Chan tradition, a tradition that kept him reluctantly and only in a domesticated form.

Two other episodes are worth mentioning in this respect because they allow us to distinguish the latent rivalry in the relation between Linji and Puhua. In the first, Linji, after offering a meal to Puhua, calls him a donkey. Puhua's immediate response—"Heehaw!"—leaves Linji silent. According to the *Jingde chuandeng lu*, Puhua then commented: "That fellow is one-eyed!" This sounds clearly like a defeat of Linji, and later Chan commentators were well aware of that. Fayan, being asked by a monk about Linji's silence, gives a rather contrived answer: "He merely left the trouble of answering to later adepts." Zhaozhou and Fen'yang too try to save Linji's face by giving their own interpretation of the dialogue. (See *Zhaozhou lu* and *Fen'yang lu*, quoted in Yanagida 1969b.) Finally, Puhua's comment was deleted from the Ming edition of the *Jingde chuandeng lu*. The other episode, which is recorded by the *Zutang ji*, is similar in content. One day, Puhua, having watched Linji resort to his favorite method, which was to beat a monk who came to question him, comments: "He is one-eyed." This seems like a straightforward criticism of the maieutic method of "strokes and shouts," for which Linji and Deshan had become famous. This impression is corroborated by a later commentator, the Tokugawa Zen master Suzuki Shōsan, against Linji and his two acolytes Heyang and Mouta. To a monk who, referring to Puhua's first encounter

---

[8] I follow here Demiéville's translation (1972: 179). Sasaki's translation of this sentence reflects the Zen orthodox interpretation that attempts to save Linji: "Ho-yang is a new bride, Mu-t'a is a Chan granny, and Lin-chi is a Ch'an menial, but he has the eye" (Sasaki 1975: 42). The grammatical structure, however, gives no reason to single out Linji for praise, and neither does the context, as the following discussion will show.

with Linji and his two acolytes Heyang and Mouta, asks him, "Were these three elders truly men who had opened their eyes?", Suzuki replies: "On the contrary, when one sees with Puhua's eyes, the three of them are blind" (*Rōankyō*, ed. Suzuki Daisetsu 1977: 98).

Puhua belonged to a thaumaturge lineage that stemmed from Baozhi, but he was also, through his master Panshan Paoqi, heir to Mazu's lineage. His appearance in the *Linji lu* seems to have been an attempt to connect "eccentric" Chan to Mazu's lineage. Yanagida Seizan (1969b) sees in the figure of Puhua a synthesis of the thaumaturge tradition and of the emphasis on everyday life evidenced in Mazu's teaching. This emphasis, which became the hallmark of mid-Tang Chan, was also a feature of Confucianism. It is the time when Han Yu criticized the emperor for worshiping the Buddha's relic. Contrary to Yanagida, I would interpret Puhua's case as evidence of the repression of the other-worldly element that was present in early Chan rather than as a synthesis. Puhua is not a static synthesis of *abhijñā* and everyday life but an oscillating or pivoting figure through which each trend tries to come to the fore at the expense of the other, and in which the sacred alternately subverts the profane and is repressed by it. Puhua's case may thus be seen as an example of the domestication of *abhijñā* or, inversely, as an obstinate reemergence of *abhijñā* in the discourse of "classical" Chan.

On the margins of Chan

The same might be said in the case of a Chan trickster like Budai, who, however, loses his strangeness in the process. Hanshan and Shide, on the other hand, are doubly marginal *and* liminal figures: marginal to the Chan tradition, but also liminal, on the threshold between the thaumaturge and the trickster. There is still something eerie, other-worldly, about them. And yet, although their friendship was apparently not interpreted as being homosexual, they were readily integrated into popular mythology as *devata* figures, gods of union

Although found in early Chan, the trickster figure seems to have become highly visible by the end of the Tang. This, incidentally, is precisely the time when Chan, according to the tradition, disciplined itself and discarded its unruly aspects. Consequently, the trickster figure is perhaps an inverted image of the actual Chan monk, who has gradually lost his liminal status (or nonstatus). In this sense, despite (or because of) his idealization, Puhua is really one of the last representatives of an endangered species. Like "Lazy Can" and Hanshan, he was actually "poaching" on the Chan preserves. Their "wild Chan" was "ex-centric" in both senses and constituted, parallel to or rather in the interstices of the Chan school, a kind of poaching (an "école buissonnière"). At the time when the "Five

Schools," beginning with that of Mazu, were established and when Chan
became increasingly centralized and narrow, they represented a nomadic
ideal, a kind of "Chan at large," without any fixed lineage. Furthermore,
their apology of pure spontaneity seemed to go against the growing ritualization of Chan. Like other liminal figures, Chan tricksters were
threatening to the orthodoxy, which tried to integrate and exorcise them
as marginals.[9] Emulating their Daoist counterparts, the Eight Immortals,
they refused to be assigned a place in the structure.[10] In his *Song gaoseng
zhuan*, Zanning (919–1001) notices that Puhua was included by Chan
hagiographers in the category called *zansheng*, "miscellaneous saints,"
and he concludes that this proves that Puhua was judged to be rather heterodox (T. 50, 2061: 837b). Strictly speaking, many of these men—
Baozhi, Fu Xi, Wanhui, and Sengqie—did not even belong to the Chan
tradition. In his *General Preface to the Collected Writings on the Source of
Chan* (*Chanyuan juquanji tuxu*), Zongmi, enumerating among various
heterodox Chan adepts those who left "mystical traces" (Zhigong, i.e.,
Baozhi; Fu *dashi*, i.e., Fu Xi; and the poet Wang Fanzhi), says: "Although
all of them are shadows and reflections of the Chan school, . . . one cannot rely on them exclusively to represent the Dharma of Śākyamuni."[11]

Of madness as one of the fine arts

It is also during the Tang, in part due to the influence of Chan and the
renewed influence of Zhuangzi, that originals—or even "madmen"—
flourished in literature and calligraphy as they had not done since the time
of the "Seven Sages of the Bamboo Grove." Calligraphy in particular be-

[9] In this respect, their idealization is parallel to their denunciation. Already in the *Śūraṃ-gama sūtra* (chap. 10), a Chan apocryphal scripture of the Tang, we find a condemnation of the "crazy deliverance of Dhyāna" (*channa kuangjie*), that is, the behavior of the madman characteristic of Chan (and of Tantrism). The *Śūraṃgama* even provides a mantra against these heresies. See Stein 1974: 507.

[10] The liminality of these figures is well reflected in the fact that the new Chan canon relegates them to its annexes: for instance, their *logia* are found in the last three chapters of the *Zongjing lu* (100 juan) or of the *Jingde chuandeng lu* (30 juan). See T. 48, 2016: 937–957; and T. 51, 2076: 429–467.

[11] See *Chanyuan zhuquanji duxu*, in T. 48, 2015: 412c; Broughton 1975: 299–300. In a roundtable discussion on Chan, Shibayama Zenkei pointed out that people like Baozhi and Fu Xi are treated in the *Jingde chuandeng lu* in a special category as "irregulars" whose Chan lineage is not clear. Tsukamoto, responding to Shibayama, remarks: "Your talking about 'irregular' sages brought to mind the Japanese *hijiri* sages who appeared in the aristocratic Buddhism of the Heian period in Japan . . . A lineage of 'sages' similar to this probably existed in China around the time of Bodhidharma." See Tsukamoto Zenryū, Shibayama Zenkei, and Nishitani Keiji, "Dialogue: Chinese Zen," *The Eastern Buddhist* 8, 2 (October 1975): 71. Following this line of thought, one may contrast these two types of Chan monks, as Joseph Kitagawa contrasted *hijiri* and ordinary Japanese monks, through the Weberian opposition of "personal charisma" and "office charisma" or "lineage charisma." See J. M. Kitagawa, "Emperor, Shaman, and Priest," in Kitagawa, *Religion in Japanese History* (New York: Columbia University Press, 1966), 17–22.

came a means of expression particularly well adapted to these marginals. The "mad cursive script" (*dian cao*) was seen as a spontaneous expression of the Buddha nature, a spiritual technique that bore some semblance to the Chan maieutics of the "stick and shout" symbolized by the names of Deshan and Linji. The most well-known calligraphers, who were inspired by Chan, were Zhang Xu (d. ca. 748), nicknamed "Zhang the madman," and Huaisu (725–785). These men had contrasting styles: "Zhang Xu assimilates joy and sadness in his writing, the monk Huaisu eliminates both" (Hsiung 1984: 56; see also 191). Both were perceived, however, as representatives of a similar attitude toward life and society. As Guanxiu put it, "Since the madness of Zhang,/ There has been no more madness worthy of the name./ With master Huaisu, madness has reappeared." Madness, like wonder-working, became a cheap commodity. In his praise of Huaisu's folly, Renhua, not without flattery, contributes to this inflation (or deflation) of madness: "With his unbound freedom,/ Zhang Xu astonished the world./ But his folly cannot compare with master Huaisu's folly, which is the true folly./ It is said, master, that you come from the south of the Yangzi./ I say that you have come from the fantastic country of the Immortals./ You have the genius of folly./ You have the folly of the genius" (ibid.: 213). As one might expect, the Confucianist Han Yu was more critical of this style. In a letter to a Buddhist friend, the monk and calligrapher Gaoxian, he reproached Buddhist impassiveness for leading to the ruin of individuality and of calligraphy and concluded on an ironic note: "But I have heard that Buddhist monks have the gift of magic and various capacities. That you may be capable after all of mastering the technique of calligraphy, it is not in my power to affirm or deny" (ibid.: 119).

The stress on "simplicity" turned into a kind of litany in literate circles. The Chan "artist-eccentric" became a cultural value, his spontaneity or eccentricity turned into a kind of symbolic investment that came to play an ideological role. Despite—or because of—this inherent paradox of a cultivated spontaneity, "wild Chan" (*kuangchan*) survived and eventually influenced Confucianists such as Li Zhi and the members of the radical wing of Wang Yangming's school. The term *kuang* came to refer to an attitude toward society that was perceived as "feigned" (*yang*).[12]

If folly has become a literary pose or a commodity, to what extent is it still really subversive? Or to what extent were the Chan trickster figures domesticated or emasculated? Insofar as nature or naturalness has been co-opted by the ruling classes, true nature can no longer express itself

[12] See Hsiung 1984: 209. Commenting on Wang Bi's admonition of spontaneity, Huang Tsung-hsi warns that "these words are full of savor, and yet they are also extremely difficult to comprehend properly. A slight error could lead one onto the path of madness and eccentricity." (See Huang Tsung-hsi 1987: 580.)

through the paradigm of spontaneity. Despite his eccentricity and his refusal to occupy an official function in the hierarchical structure of Chan, Puhua was posthumously promoted as the founder of a new school that flourished in Japan, the Fuke (Puhua) school.[13] This should alert us to the fact that the jester plays the same function in society as a joker in a game: although it points outside the game, it still belongs to it. In the words of Klaus-Peter Koepping, "Playing around with negativity or with reversion and reversal of symbols in word or action, which is in itself potentially inherent in the rules of language, reveals a hidden truth, that of the close adherence to them, while acknowledging at the same time the existence of rules without which even the game of negativity could not be played. That means even negativity is rule governed" (Koepping 1985: 192). One may even argue that these tricksters played some kind of semiotic, wish-fulfilling function, appearing as heralds of perfect freedom at the very time that that freedom was becoming increasingly restricted and/or theoretical. Whether or not it can be traced back to Baizhang Huaihai (749–814), the elaboration of a Chan monastic rule marked the triumph during the Song of formalization and ritualization of Chan practice. (See Foulk 1989.) Significantly, this elaboration took place precisely at a time when every Chan monk was espousing the superiority of the formless. Perhaps it is in this sense that one may call "classical" this phase of Chan history characterized by "Recorded Sayings" (*yulu*) and "Transmission of the Lamp" (*chuandeng*) literature. The stress on a doctrine of emptiness and formlessness and the parallel development of the ideal of the "crazy Chan monk" might constitute a denial of reality and an inverted image of actual practice. Thus the idealization of personages such as Hanshan and Budai paradoxically reflects a loss of the very experience they symbolize.

Moreover, the stress on everyday life, which facilitated the evolution from "occult" Chan to "wild fox" Chan, is perhaps an index of Chan demythologization. With Layman Pang, Chan has become the religion of "everyday life." The sanctification of ordinary life can also be seen as a banalization of the sacred. It is significant that, at about the same time, Confucianists such as Li Ao and Han Yu launched their attack against "superstitions" such as the cult of relics. Like Confucianism, Chan "enlightenment" contributed to a "decline of magic." Demythologization was achieved theoretically in a number of ways, for example, through the

---

[13] The Fuke school is famous for its use of martial arts and the *shakuhachi* flute. According to tradition, the sect was introduced in Japan by Muhon (Shinchi) Kakushin (1207–1298), a seventeenth-generation heir of Puhua. Kakushin went to China in 1249, studied with Wumen Huikai (the author of the kōan collection *Wumen guan*), and returned to Japan in 1254. According to the *Shakuhachi no tsugibumi*, a document allegedly brought to Japan by one of the laymen accompanying Kakushin, Puhua had served as officer in Xuanzong's army during the An Lushan rebellion. On the value of these claims, see Sanford 1977.

use of abstract concepts (*li/shi*, or the "Five Ranks" of the Caodong tradition) and through Chan "naturalism" or "realism." Many factors—economic, socio-political—may have played their role in this evolution. From the ideological point of view, however, Chan had to affirm *shentong* as a *weapon* in its rivalry with Daoism and indigenous cults when it was trying to gain ground in Chinese society and to expand geographically. Once firmly established, it chose to draw closer to Confucianism and to shift toward the other pole of Chinese ideology.

Just as did the "crazy language" that became the literary genre of Song "Recorded Sayings" and "Histories of the Lamp," the trickster figure served as an alibi within an increasingly institutionalized tradition.[14] It indicates perhaps a nostalgia for a lost primitivism or liminality. Although some trickster figures such as Kakua (n.d.), Kanzan (1277–1360), Ikkyū (1394–1481), or Ryōkan (1758–1831) emerged in Japanese Zen, they did not compare with their Chinese homologues. Despite the development of their legends, they did not become quasi-mythical figures like Hanshan or Budai. Even Ikkyū, for all his popularity, remained human, all too human. Not surprisingly, some of these trickster figures were found on the margins or outside the Chan/Zen tradition. Such is the case of the Tendai priest Zōga (917–1003), well known for his wild behavior.[15] The ambivalent appeal of these personages can be seen, for example, in the fact that Suzuki Shōsan, a Tokugawa Zen master who extolled the Bodhisattva ideal and criticized asceticism and eremitism in the name of dominant social values, did, however, single out for praise Puhua and Zōga (Tyler 1984: 101). Trickster figures, however, always retained a potentially subversive character, and this may explain why they remained the target of criticism and why the domestication process had to be carried one step further, with the progressive displacement of the trickster ideal by the Bodhisattva ideal.[16]

THE BODHISATTVA IDEAL

The Bodhisattva is the figure who, although he could enter into *nirvāṇa*, chooses—out of com-*passion*—to remain in the world of passions. Actu-

---

[14] As James Sanford points out, the merchants of Sakai, where Ikkyū lived, felt pleased that their town had become the home of one of the best jesters in Japan: "Shock is almost a marketable commodity" (Sanford 1981: 46).

[15] See Marian Ury, "Recluses and Eccentric Monks: Tales from the *Hosshinshū* by Kamo no Chōmei," *Monumenta Nipponica* 27, 2 (1972): 161–163; Mills 1970: 362–363.

[16] See, for instance, Bassui's critique: "Then there are the rebels. Calling themselves liberated, they throw away their three types of robes and their begging bowls; they put on courtly hats and criticize the Right Law. They pass through this world deceiving laymen and laywomen. If someone were to rebuke them for this behavior, they would refer to the homeless sages like Budai, Hanshan and Shide, . . . saying that they are like these monks. . . . Though they may be similar to those ancients in appearance, in terms of correct behavior these people are still far from approaching it" (Braverman 1989: 88).

ally, the Buddhist compassion seems a rather detached one, for Bodhisattvas cannot become attached to the idea of existence, and they see the
emptiness of the beings for which they work. The element of compassion
was already present in various personages defined above as thaumaturges
or tricksters. These categories are merely heuristic ideal types, and the
reality of course remains more complex. In the sixth century, Fu Xi, pop-
ularly known as "Fu the Mahāsattva" (Fu *dashi*), attempted self-immolation several times in order to put an end to the evils of his day. The early
Tang witnessed a vogue of self-immolation, and Northern Chan developed on Song shan not too long after the dramatic self-immolation, during the *daye* era (605–616), of a monk named Dazhi. (See Gernet 1959:
552.) Self-mutilation, burning one's head or fingers, seems to have exerted a real fascination in Chan as in the rest of Chinese Buddhism. This
may be why, according to the *Lengqie shizi ji*, the Chan patriarch Daoxin
attempted to reinterpret allegorically the notion of "sacrificing one's
body." At any rate, the most popular Buddhist monks were readily perceived as representatives of the Bodhisattva ideal, and often as actual incarnations of various Bodhisattvas. During the same *daye* era, the Northern Chan monk Huian won fame through his efforts to save from
starvation the men who were working to open the Grand Canal (т. 50,
2061: 823b). According to his stele inscription, "his capacity for humane-
ness was moved by the laity. . . . Consequently, he could not help aiding
the world" (*QTW* 396, 9:5104b). As noted earlier, Huian was also perceived as a thaumaturge. These two images, thaumaturge and Bodhisattva, had become so contradictory by the end of the Tang that they
could not even be accepted as a sign of a split personality. Thus Huian's
"splitters" acquired their autonomy and were treated by the *Song gaoseng
zhuan* as two entirely different biographies, one reflecting the "official"
career of Huian (т. 50, 2061: 823b–c), the other his thaumaturgic activities
(ibid.: 829c). The same thing happened to the biography of his co-disciple
Shenxiu, alias Huixiu. (See *Song gaoseng zhuan*, т. 50, 2061: 755c–756a
and 835b.) Significantly, the "official" Shenxiu had precociously manifested his Bodhisattva spirit: at the age of thirteen during the famine that
afflicted the Honan and Shandong regions as a result of the troubles
marking the end of the Sui, he went to Yin'yang (in Honan) to request
grain from the public granaries (*Chuan fabao ji*, ed. Yanagida 1971: 396).
Whatever the historical accuracy of these early Chan biographies, we
seem to have here a hagiographical *topos* in which social activism is considered an important but preliminary phase of the monk's life, after
which he becomes a recluse and obtains awakening before eventually returning to the world as a "dynastic master." In other words, these three
phases apparently correspond to the traditional tripartite career of the Bodhisattva, in which morality (Sk. *śīla*), manifested by the "perfection of

the gift" (Sk. *dāna-pāramitā*), is followed by the perfections of concentration and wisdom (*dhyāna-* and *prajñā-pāramitā*). In this early Chan context, the *abhijñā* obtained by the Chan practitioner were still perceived as an outcome of the process initiated by his altruism. Isolation and social activism were presented as the two faces or two phases of the same career.

Toward the end of the Tang, however, the Bodhisattva ideal gradually took precedence over the thaumaturge and trickster ideals. The pot-bellied figure of Budai is already a sign of this evolution. As an avatar of Maitreya, he has lost all the dramatic, quasi-traumatic features of his former incarnation, Fu the Mahāsattva. He reflects a more human and somewhat carnivalesque conception of life and society.[17] He would become the paradigmatic figure in Chan practice, the last stage of which is redefined, in the *Ten Oxherding Pictures*, as Budai "returning empty-handed to the market-place" and mixing with the common people.[18] This is a radical departure from the former emphasis on absolute emptiness, a stage that is represented symbolically in the *Oxherding Pictures* as a blank circle, and which is relegated from the ultimate position to the eighth, that is, to the eighth *bhūmi* of the Bodhisattva career.

During the Song, the Tang Layman Pang became a central figure in Chan, together with his Indian model Vimalakīrti. (See Demiéville 1973a.) This Confucianist who had converted to Chan became so popular that he was made the hero of theatrical plays during the Yuan.[19] It is perhaps with a later character, however, a Song monk named Puan Yinsu (1115–1169), that this evolution reached its last stage and that the Chan trickster lost its remaining carnivalizing potential. A contemporary of Dahui Zonggao, Puan was active in Jiangxi.[20] His stele inscription (dated 1179) says that he became popular through his intense social involvement: he used to give medicinal herbs or charms to the sick and contributed to the building of bridges and roads. But as Michihata Ryōshū's work on

[17] On the carnivalesque nature of "pot-bellied" figures, see Bakhtin 1968: 31.

[18] See Ueda and Yanagida 1982: 219 and 235; D. T. Suzuki, *Manual of Zen Buddhism* (New York: Grove Press, 1960), illus. ix and xi.

[19] In one of these plays, written by Liu Junxi toward the end of the Yuan, Pang is presented as a wealthy and generous householder who lends money to the poor. In one instance, he burns the acknowledgment of a debt that has caused the illness of one of his debtors. In another case, passing in front of his stable, he overhears a dialogue between a donkey, a horse, and a cow. As it turns out, all were reborn as animals for having died without repaying their debt to him. Realizing that his wealth was the cause of all this, Pang then decides to throw his possessions into a river and lives afterward as a recluse with his family. This reflection on the evils of money and usury constitutes a strong critique of Yuan society. In a later "Precious Scroll" (*baojuan*), in which the same motives reappear, we learn that Pang had initially acquired his wealth for helping the Five Hundred Arhats. See Sawada 1975: 115–124.

[20] Puan is listed as a wonder-worker in the *Shenxian tongjian*, chap. 18 (see also Doré 1914–1938: 8:313), but his wonders amount to little more than healing the sick with medicinal herbs and incantations.

Buddhist social activities shows, Puan had many predecessors, and it is not clear why he was singled out as an object of worship. Soon after his death, he came to be invoked against all kinds of natural calamities. His cult was first centered on his monastery, the Cihua si, but in 1314, one of his devotees built a temple in Jiangxi—the Huiqing chansi—that became prosperous and contributed greatly to the spread of Puan's fame. Subsequently, in less than two centuries, Puan had become a protector of temples and public edifices and, more important, of sea roads. His popularity increased during the Ming era and reached its zenith during the Qing, an evolution reflected in the increasing length of his title.[21] His posthumous fate reminds us of that of an earlier thaumaturge, Sengqie (d. 710). Actually, there seems to be a structural homology between Wanhui and Sengqie on the one hand and Budai and Puan on the other: whereas Wanhui and Budai became gods of fertility, Sengqie and Puan were both deified as gods protecting navigation roads.

The "socialization" of Chan is reflected in Puan's *Recorded Sayings*. Despite his concession to Chan rhetoric when declaring that all works are fundamentally empty and illusory, Puan seems deeply convinced of the ultimate value of these works. In his *Sermon on Repairing Bridges*, he states that "building bridges is a Buddha act that brings peace to men and causes Heaven to rejoice," and he asserts that those who do so will increase their longevity and deepen their practice of the Way. He thus equates bridge-building with Buddhist practice and attainment of worldly benefits. (See ZZ 1, 2, 25, 3: 281c.)

To suggest how far Puan is from trickster figures such as Hanshan and Budai one need only mention his criticism of those Chan adepts who had interpreted the antinomianism of the "sudden teaching" in a lax sense, namely: "They say that to drink alcohol and to eat meat does not obstruct *bodhi*, and that to commit stealing or adultery does not hinder *prajñā*." He therefore stressed the observance of the Buddhist precepts and of such traditional virtues as filial piety—in this respect very close to another Chan monk of the Song, Qisong (1007–1072). Significantly, although starting from the same premises as the "eccentrics" he criticizes (e.g., the affirmation of concrete reality as ultimate), Puan reached opposite conclusions. Like a Confucianist, he interpreted this reality to mean society and culture, while the "eccentrics" interpreted it to mean nature, as did the Daoists. Therefore, the case of Puan reveals the influence of Confucianist values on Chan and illustrates the full development of the conservative aspects of the "world-affirming" tendency in "classical" Chan, which led to the affirmation of the present society and of one's social

[21] See the preface to *Puan shilu* (1423) by Emperor Chengzu, in ZZ 2, 25, 3: 265a. See also Nagai 1985a: 233–234.

status. This tendency would find its Japanese interpretation in a Zen master like Suzuki Shōsan, who strove to justify in Buddhist (and Zen) terms the social inequalities of his time. (See Tyler 1984: 96–101; Ooms 1985: 122–143).

The opposite antinomian tendency would lead to the hagiographical development of a Southern Song Chan master such as Daoji (d. 1209), alias Jidian or Jigong,[22] the "Vagabond Buddha"—a resurgence of the trickster figure who came to play an important role in Chinese secret societies and marginal social categories. Daoji's "Recorded Sayings" (*zz* 1, 26) became the source of popular novels during the Ming. In contrast to Puan and to official culture, Jigong is a trickster figure who "elevates hedonistic values as a social ideal": he eats meat, drinks intoxicating beverages, gambles, and steals (DeBernardi 1987: 311). His thaumaturgic aspect, on the other hand, is manifest in the way he communicates with his followers, namely, through spirit mediums (ibid.: 320). Not surprisingly, he found his place in oral culture and popular religiosity[23] but was rejected, or at least overlooked, by the Chan tradition. As we have seen, the hedonistic and subversive tendencies reflected by Jigong were perceived as threatening to established Chan. Puan, on the other hand, was welcomed as a paragon of social harmony, and his cult was favored by the people as well as by the emperor. In Japan, his popularity remained for some reason limited to Zen monasteries, where his cult became part of the liturgy. At any rate, the popularity of Puan can be seen as a further step in the domestication of Chan thaumaturgy. The demythologizing elements in Chan and Confucianism paved the way for the kind of rationalist criticism that was to find its full expression in Tokugawa thinkers such as Tominaga Nakamoto.

THE RETURN OF THE THAUMATURGE

With a few major exceptions such as Ikkyū, neither the trickster figure nor the Bodhisattva figure was as successful in Japanese Zen. On the other hand, the thaumaturge reemerged in Japan stronger than ever in China, particularly in the Sōtō tradition. Sōtō hagiographies contain many stories of monks who, thanks to their *abhijñā*, were able to tame

[22] Daoji was the successor of Fohai of the Lingyin monastery. One tradition makes him the co-disciple of Kakua, one of the monks who allegedly brought the teaching of Puhua (J. Fuke) to Japan. See Sawada 1975: 184.

[23] Although there are other similar trickster figures in the Song Chan tradition—for example, Jiuxian Yuxian, "the immortal who loved wine" (fl. 960; see *Jiatai pudeng lu* 24), or Xianhua (alias Zhiyan, d.u.; see *Shenseng zhuan* 9, T. 50, 2064: 1013c)—they never achieved Jigong's popularity. Sawada (1975: 185) suggests that it is because he lived in Hangzhou, a thriving economic and cultural center, that Jigong became the popular symbol of the "wild monks."

snakes and other manifestations of local gods. The themes of these stories are similar to those found in early Chan, namely in Northern Chan. The focus on taming apparently reflects, in both cases, the conflicts these traditions faced when they were gaining new ground and extending geographically across the country. As a result of their contact with local cults, and perhaps due to the influence of esoteric Buddhism, these Zen masters were led again to stress their *abhijñā*. This tendency can already be seen in the Darumashū and in the school of Muhon Kakushin (1207–1298), who disseminated in Japan the teaching attributed to Puhua (J. Fuke). One of Kakushin's disciples, Kyōō Unryō (1267–1341), threw the local god, Hakusan Gongen himself, into the water to teach him how better to protect his monastery against epidemics. The tendency predominates, however, in the lineage of Keizan, with Gasan Jōseki (1275–1365), Gennō Shinshō (1329–1400), and their disciples. A paradigmatic example is that of Ikkei Eishū (d. 1403), a disciple of Tsūgen Jakurei at Yōtakuji. Ikkei once noticed a strange woman who had come to consult Tsūgen and asked her who she was. She answered that she was the dragon of the lake and that she protected the Dharma. Ikkei then said: "I have a question for you. If you answer, you will be saved, otherwise you must leave. Since the Dharma is intrinsically non-Dharma, which Dharma are you protecting?" The woman failed to answer and Ikkei drove her away. Then a violent storm caused the lake to swell, and a huge white snake appeared, which eventually received the precepts from Tsūgen. This story is reminiscent of Yuangui's conferring the precepts on the Song shan god.[24] In Muromachi Japan as in Tang China, gods and spirits yield to the monk's virtue and/or power, introduce them to sacred sites, and help them to build monasteries, receive the precepts from them, and become protectors of the monastery or of the Dharma. (See Bodiford 1989: 400ff.)

Later the rationalist tendencies that developed in Tokugawa Japan, reinforced by Western rationalism, were to "gain right of way" over the occult aspects of Chan/Zen. Tominaga Nakamoto was one of the main critics of *abhijñā*, which he reduced to a type of magic. According to him, "What the heretics called magic and what the Buddha called *abhijñā* are actually the same. His disciples relied on it to transmit his doctrine and resort to it to promote his teaching. Nine-tenths of the Buddhist canon are nothing but *abhijñā*" (*Shutsujō kōgo* 8, ed. Kyōdo 1982: 26, 98; see also Tominaga 1990: 106). And Tominaga concludes: "Although *abhijñā* differ from magic, by and large they are the same thing. . . . Buddhists may seek thereby to spread the Way, while heretics only seek their own profit;

---

[24] There is also a family resemblance to the following story. Malevolent spirits disturb the community of Jitsuan Yusan, but he does not pay them any attention. Later, eight men in official clothes come to pay him homage: they are the Eight Generals, who have been converted by his preaching on the unborn.

as to deceiving people, however, *abhijñā* and magic are the same" (Shut-sujō kōgo, ibid.: 69, 144; see also Tominaga 1990: 176). In the socio-political context of Zen, the abandonment of *abhijñā* might also reflect the fact that once Zen had gained the protection of the local *daimyō*, it became less dependent on the populace and could distance itself from popular beliefs. Having found access to political power, it did not have to advertise its own "powers" any more to convince the people of its legitimacy.[25]

ALL the *devata* types considered above are structured by three poles that we could define as the other-worldly, the this-worldly, and the societal. They are also variants of the conformity/transgression paradigm. The thaumaturge and the trickster are both transgressing the norms of society, but the ascetic thaumaturge still follows the rules of the Buddhist community, while the trickster denies them.[26] The Bodhisattva, on the other hand, emphasizes both the monastic rule and the social norms. The proximity to one of these poles, or the predominance of any one of these components, has permitted a heuristic classification of these ideal figures in the categories of the thaumaturge, the trickster, or the Bodhisattva—at the risk of creating another "fraudulent narrative." The problem remains of how to interpret the place of these figures in the Chan/Zen tradition(s). In particular, the thaumaturge ideal apparently did not arise merely as a concession to popular beliefs, as most scholars would have us believe. It seems that, on the contrary, it was an important paradigm in Chan practice and hagiography, overlapping to some extent with the gradual tendency. But it is clear also that its fate was tied closely to the development of sectarian rivalries (within Chan, but also between Chan and Tantrism, Daoism, or other "heretic" teachings). In this sense, it might serve as an index to Chan/Zen history. In many ways, the trickster (and, to a lesser extent, the Bodhisattva) ideal can be seen as a response to this earlier figure, an attempt to accommodate Chan ideology to the social changes that marked the Tang/Song transition.

[25] A case in point is that of Mujaku Myōyu (1333–1393), who made fun of one of his disciples when the latter came to tell him that he had been initiated for the last eleven years by an incarnation of the Chan master Fuyō Dōkai (Furong Daokai, 1043–1118).

[26] Many Chan/Zen thaumaturges were experts in Vinaya, and as noted earlier, they asserted their power over local gods or spirits precisely by conferring the Buddhist precepts on them.

Seven

Metamorphoses of the Double (I):
        Relics

The signless body exists within the body that has
signs.
                    —Baozhi, *Jingde chuandeng lu*

In twin vases of pallid tourmaline
(Their color colder than the waters of an autumn
        stream)
The calcined relics of Buddha's Body rest—
Rounded pebbles, smooth as the Specular Stone.
                    —Bai Juyi, "The Temple"

Closely related to the importance of the thaumaturge is the existence of a
cult centered on relics and patriarchal images.[1] This may seem at first
glance surprising in a teaching such as Chan, known for its emphasis on
the "formless" and its rejection of devotional practices. In one of the favorite scriptures of Chan, the *Vajracchedikā-sūtra*, the Buddha makes the
point that those who search for him in the realm of forms are deluded.
(See Conze 1957: 88.) Even more surprising, then, is the existence and
veneration of mummies or "flesh-bodies" (*roushen*). As Holmes Welch
remarked: "Indeed the whole concept of the meat-body would seem to
exemplify the antithesis of the doctrine of impermanence and to violate
the spirit in which the bhiksus of Buddhist India were urged to sojourn
in cemeteries, drawing lessons in impermanence from the decomposition
of corpses."[2]

Scholars have tended to regard the Buddhist cult of relics as incongru-
ous and to play it down. Even in Chan, however, there is a trend that has

---

[1] Concerning the cult of relics in Indian Buddhism, see in particular Schopen 1975, 1987,
1988; Pierre Saintyves, "Les reliques du Buddha" in Saintyves 1987: 922–934; *Thūpavaṃsa*
in Jayawickrama 1971. On the cult of relics in the West, see Geary 1978, 1986. See also Peter
Brown, "Relics and Social Status in the Age of Gregory of Tours" in Peter Brown 1982:
222–250. On the cult of the saints, see Peter Brown 1981, 1982; Saintyves 1987; Kaplan
1986.

[2] Welch 1967: 345. The *locus classicus* is probably the following passage of the *Vimalakīrti-
nirdeśa*: "Gentlemen, the human body is transient, unstable, unworthy of confidence and
weak; it is without solidity, is perishable, of short duration, is filled with sorrow and un-
eases, filled with ailments and subject to change. . . . The wise man trusts it not" (Lamotte
1962: 7–13). The contradiction, however, might be a superficial one: in the Hindu context
described by Jonathan Parry, ascetics go to cemeteries in order to, perhaps literally, "feed
on corpses," and they in turn attempt to become "flesh-bodies" (Parry 1982: 86–101).

been largely neglected by orthodox scholarship, intent on arguing the originality and purity of "iconoclastic" Chan. This trend, which we may call "sacramental" or "regalian,"[3] is particularly conspicuous in early and middle Chan. Although it was later repressed in the official discourse—if not in the practice—of "classical" Chan, it eventually reemerged in Japanese Zen, and more particularly in the Sōtō sect. This may be another example of what Carl Bielefeldt has called, in the context of Chan meditative practice, a "family secret" (Bielefeldt 1986: 147). Consequently, what is generally characterized by Japanese scholars as the medieval shift toward "funerary" Chan/Zen may not constitute so much a "revolution" as the resurfacing of a tendency already at work in early Chan.

Not surprisingly, the pattern that emerges here bears a strong resemblance to what we have observed for the thaumaturge tradition. It is indeed the other side of the same coin: the power actualized in living thaumaturges as *abhijñā* was believed to pass after their death into their relics, their charisma being, as it were, objectified and disseminated.[4] What Schopen (1987) says of the Buddha, that he and his relics do not appear to have been thought of as separate things, is true of Buddhist saints as well. At the level of representation, however, there was an oscillation between relics as "subjects," that is, as a living presence, and relics as "objects" or commodities. (See Geary 1978: 531.) The power of relics may be interpreted as a variety of post mortem *abhijñā*, and their importance in Chan might reflect the belief that both *abhijñā* and relics were by-products of meditation and proofs of enlightenment.[5]

The "relics" par excellence are the crystalline fragments (*śarīra, dhātu*) left after the cremation of the body (*śarīra*).[6] In the broadest sense, however, relics indicate all the remnants of an eminent monk. One can thus distinguish between "bodily relics" (hair, nail clippings, ashes, bones, "flesh-body") and "contact relics" (begging bowl, staff, robe, text—or even places or "traces").[7] The early Mahāyāna claim that sacred texts such

[3] In the large sense, *regalia* are material objects that confer upon their possessors the right to the throne. Not only did the possession of the patriarchal robe or relics entitle Chan masters to ascend the "Seat of the Dharma" (a seat in principle superior to the throne), but it also, as we will see, served to legitimate emperors.

[4] As Steven Kaplan remarked in another context, however, death remains the "great divide" between the "holy man" and the "saint," and both figures do not perform the same function in the "economy of the sacred" (Kaplan 1986: 11).

[5] The source of the relic did not have to be dead, and there are cases of the "premortem" efficacy of relics. According to the Vinaya tradition, for instance, the hair of the Buddha, cut by the barber Upāli, allowed Prince Gopālī to be victorious in war. See *Hōbōgirin*, s.v. "Buppatsu," Vol. 2: 170b. See also T. 23, 1435: 415 and *Shejia pu*, T. 50, 2040: 66.

[6] "*She-li* is the technical term for the highest and most developed state of spiritual life, the state where the vital juices are transformed into small brilliant 'jewels', which may be found after the cremation of the body" (K. L. Reichelt, quoted in Prip-Møller 1982: 172). For a recent description of these relics in the Southeast Asian context, see Tambiah 1984: 109.

[7] See Schopen 1987: 203; Renou and Filliozat 1985: 2:605. In this sense, the cave where

as the *Lotus Sūtra* are superior, as objects of worship, to the *śarīra* of the Buddha, need not—as is usually the case—be construed as a departure from relic worship but rather as a shift from a certain type of relic to another.[8] Gregory Schopen may be right when he argues that in India, the cult of the book arose in antagonism to the cult of the Buddha's relics (Schopen 1975: 147–181; Hirakawa 1963). In East Asia, however, both cults are mere variants of the same "sacramental" tendency.[9] The sacred texts, after all, are often described as the "*śarīra* of the Buddha's Dharma Body." The canon is the verbal substitute of the Buddha, just as the relic is his corporeal substitute.[10] Yijing, for instance, distinguishes two kinds of *śarīra*: the corporeal relics of the Buddha and the *gāthā* on the Chain of Causation. (See Takakusu 1970: 150–151.)

A particular case, to which we will return in the next chapter, is that of the self-mummified body, which is seen by Buddhists as a result of saintliness, and more precisely as a proof that the powers of morality, concentration, and wisdom permeated and transmuted the entire body of the deceased.[11] At first glance, *śarīra* and "flesh-body" seem incompatible, since the production of *śarīra* implies cremation and that of the mummy some kind of inhumation. Yet *śarīra* and mummy can be seen as variants of the same phenomenon, a phenomenon familiar to anthropologists under the name of "secondary burial."[12] In China as in many traditional cul-

---

Bodhidharma allegedly practiced wall-contemplation can be considered a relic. A combination of place and object can be seen in the stones where the Buddha's footprints, or his shadow, were found. The most famous is the one near the "stūpa of relics" at Pāṭaliputra. That it is not simply considered, as were later copies, as a "symbol" of the Buddha but as a "hierophany" is clear from the fact that it had magical properties and was coveted by several princes. See *Hōbōgirin*, s.v. *Bussoseki*, Vol. 2: 188. See also Falk 1977. On the shadow of the Buddha as his "double," see Lamotte 1944–1980: 1:553. As we will see, there is also a "shadow-stone" of Bodhidharma, near his cave on Song shan.

[8] The *locus classicus* is the *Lotus Sūtra*'s following passage: "Where the sūtra are, one must erect seven precious stūpa, and not deposit relics in them. Why? Because they contain the whole body of the Buddha." See Schopen 1975; Hirakawa 1963; Mitomo Ryōjun, "An Aspect of Dharma-śarīra," *IBK* 32, 2 (1984): (4)–(9). On the different kinds of relics, see Renou and Filliozat 1985: 2:605. In the *Keiran shūyō shū*, a fourteenth-century Japanese Tendai encyclopedia, we find for instance a distinction between *śarīra* of the "living body" (cultic utensils, staff, bowl) and "*śarīra* of the Body of Law" (sutras; *T.* 76, 2410: 844b). In Korea, the *śarīra* of the Buddha are enshrined at T'ongdo-sa, which is known as the Buddha-Jewel monastery, while the woodblocks of the Korean *Tripiṭaka* are stored at Haein-sa, the Dharma-Jewel monastery (Buswell 1983: 89).

[9] The *Platform Sūtra* or Dōgen's *Shōbōgenzō* were relics in the same way (or almost) as *śarīra*: the entire work had become a *sign* and, as objectified charisma, a source of spiritual power.

[10] On the Dharmakāya as a substitute verbal body, see Mus 1935: 56–83.

[11] See *Koji ruien, Shūkyōbu*, 1: 241, 251. Already in India, relics were believed to be "infused with morality, concentration and wisdom" (Schopen 1987: 204–206). *Śarīra* come in three colors: white (bone *śarīra*), black (hair *śarīra*), and red (flesh *śarīra*). Although Arhats and Bodhisattvas also leave *śarīra*, the hardness of these relics is said not to equal that of the Buddha's *śarīra*. See *Koji ruien*, ibid.: 243.

[12] Or perhaps better "double burial," in the double entendre that, as we will see later,

tures, the goal of double burial was to obtain an incorruptible body, whether in the form of purified bones or of a mummy. Seen in this light, self-mummification appears as a particular case, the goal or sometimes the by-product of provisory burial. Like the ritual setup of the mummy, the cremation of the corpse and the inhumation of *śarīra* correspond to the second burial: far from destroying the body, they are perceived as recreating it, thereby reincorporating the dead at a higher ontological level (Hertz 1960: 20). As Bloch and Parry put it, "The first disposal is associated with the time-bound individual and the polluting aspects of death, and the second with the regenerative aspects which recreate the permanent order on which traditional authority is based" (Bloch and Parry 1982: 11).

What was the place of these funerary practices in Chan/Zen, and how can they be reconciled with the "sudden" ideology? According to Hertz, "the very existence of a cult of relics presupposes the notion that between the collectivity of the living and that of the dead there is no absolute solution of continuity" (Hertz 1960: 44). In China as in the Christian West, "relics were the main channel through which supernatural power was available for the needs of ordinary life. Ordinary men could see and handle them, yet they belonged not to this transitory world but to eternity."[13] Like the vertical slab (*colossos*) of ancient Greek tombs (see Vernant 1965: 2:67), the stūpa or reliquary functions as a kind of *axis mundi*, a place where heaven and earth communicate through the remains of the deceased, who is perceived as a living presence.[14] Stūpa were in this way used to "humanize" a sacred place, and at the same time to "sacralize" human institutions. Relics imply a *mediation* with the other world, a mediation that seems at first glance to contradict the Mahāyāna coincidence between *saṃsāra* and *nirvāṇa*. Here again we are confronted with the limits of ideology, the inverted relation between the doctrine and the values underlying practice. Relics also mediate between two opposite attitudes: the fascination of death and its "taming." They bring death into the world of the living, but they also assure the continuity of life into death, the regeneration of life through death, thereby contributing to blur the distinction, to collapse death and birth, to bridge the gap between both realms. Conversely, by abbreviating the intermediary period between death and the apotheosis of the second burial, cremation seems to symbolize the "sud-

---

relics are also perceived as a "double" of the deceased. On "secondary burial", see van Gennep 1960; Hertz 1960; Huntington and Metcalf 1979: Bloch and Parry 1982.

[13] Richard Southern, *Western Society and the Church in the Middle Ages* (New Haven: Yale University Press, 1953), 31.

[14] As Schopen shows, the stūpa itself was considered a legal person (Schopen 1987: 206). On the symbolism and worship of stūpas, see Adrian Snodgrass, *The Symbolism of the Stūpa* (Ithaca: Southeast Asia Program, Cornell University, 1985); Hirakawa 1963: 57–106; Durt 1987: 1223–1241.

den" teaching:[15] it reduces to a minimum the transition between death and rebirth (for ordinary people), or between death and awakening (for monks).[16] In a way, then, *śarīra* and mummies bring to a dead end—at least symbolically—the process of rebirth. They result in a somewhat paradoxical bifurcation: an upward movement of spiritualization, leading to *nirvāṇa*, the achievement of immutability; and a downward movement of materialization, a return to the realm of change, to the world of cults. Unlike that of Christian relics, their meaning is not primarily eschatological. (See Schopen 1987: 203.) They symbolize (or effect) sudden awakening; the ultimate realization or "transformation" of the saint; a reincorporation into a higher, absolute, ontological plane; but they also achieve mediation for the worshipers by channeling the saint's power and bringing it down to earth. To the extent that this transformative power, ritually activated, allows the practitioner to achieve a spiritual breakthrough, the relics have a soteriological function. As the poet Wang Wei, speaking on behalf of Jingjue's disciples in his epitaph for the deceased Chan master, writes: "We still rely on his *śarīra* in the hope of obtaining awakening" (Yanagida 1967: 519). In this sense, as Mus pointed out, the cult of *śarīra* does not so much contradict the notion of *nirvāṇa* as it complements it (Mus 1935: 82–83). Ideally, the relic (or the stūpa) is merely "a temporary support, from which, through a projection impossible to specify, one hopes to leap toward a supreme transcendence" (ibid.: 79). In common practice, however, the virtue of the relics seems predominantly magical— to bring worldly benefits to the worshiper: the mediation they provide

[15] Ironically, the production of *śarīra* is sometimes said to require a "gradual" awakening. See, for example, Tambiah 1984: 110: "The process of body purification takes a long time; if an *arahant* lives long enough after his attainment, there is an opportunity for the body to eliminate his 'toxic ingredients' by virtue of the mind's regular withdrawal into the most profound depths of concentration and hence the likelihood of his ashes turning into relics after his death"—contrary to the *arahant* whose attainment is "sudden" and who does not live long enough after his attainment.

[16] In both cases, cremation is perceived as rebirth: on the plane of delusion, or ideally, on a higher plane, *nirvāṇa*. Although in Japan the dead are called "Buddhas," the general belief is that they may be reborn in one of the six lower destinies (*rokudō*)—and, it is hoped, as human beings. Van Gennep disagrees with Hertz about the meaning of cremation: he argues that it does not create a new body but simply accelerates the dissociation of psycho-physical components. His argument is supported by early Buddhist attitudes toward the body. As Seidel points out, cremation was for Indian Buddhists the expression of a desire for annihilating the world and the illusory self. (See Seidel 1983a: 585.) A similar idea is found in Chinese monks such as Jiehuan (see *zz* 1, 47, 3: 337), who argues that cremation is good because it allows the easy separation of the "spirit" (*shen*) and of the "vital soul" (*po*). But the two points of view (Hertz vs. van Gennep) are not necessarily incompatible, and both are found in Buddhist practice: cremation was perceived by Indian Buddhists as dissociation/annihilation, and/or as re-creation/reincorporation. In the Chinese context, with the development of relic worship and the resistance of the Confucian ideology to the notion of annihilation, the Hertzian motif of "recreation" seems to have become predominant.

tends to become an end in itself, displacing the ideal of transcendence by an ideology of thaumaturgic immanence.

The Cult of *Śarīra*

From the outset, *śarīra* were highly valued in Indian Buddhism, and the tradition has recorded the "war of the relics" that was barely avoided after the death of the Buddha.[17] These relics, and countless other *śarīra*, were eventually divided among the contestants and enshrined in eight stūpas, around which a cult soon developed. (See Przyluski 1935–1936.) Tradition has it that King Aśoka ordered the erection of 84,000 stūpas to enshrine these relics, one of them being the famous stūpa of Ayuwang shan (Mount of King Aśoka) in China.[18] Relics such as the tooth or the finger of the Buddha became popular in Asian Buddhist countries,[19] and the "Memorial on the Bone of Buddha" written by Han Yu (786–824) to protest against the veneration of one such relic by the Tang emperor Xianzong bears witness to their extraordinary popularity.[20] Chinese Buddhists also came to worship the relics of the "very special dead" (Peter Brown 1981: 69). Despite Han Yu's claim, relic worship was not simply a concession to "vulgar superstitions": as in India (Schopen 1988: 535), it represented an official monastic conception and a powerful instrument of monastic and imperial legitimacy.[21] An important aspect of the cult was

[17] The seven "great relics" of the Buddha were his four canine teeth, the two collar bones, and the frontal bone. See Hastings 1924, s.v. "Relics": 659ff.; *Thūpavaṃsa* in Jayawickrama 1971: 34. The first "sacred theft" was that of the two teeth of the Buddha stolen by two *rākṣasa* from the god Śakra (T. 1, 1: 48b) who himself had spirited one from Droṇa, the brahman who divided the relics among the eight kingly contenders. (See *Thūpavaṃsa*, ibid.: 41.) The *Fayuan zhulin* records that one of these teeth arrived in China at the time of the Qi emperor Wen Xuan. According to another tradition, one tooth was recuperated by the god Weituo (var. Nacha), who gave it to the Vinaya master Daoxuan. This relic played an important role in Chan. It was transmitted to Japan under the reign of Emperor Saga. (See Péri 1916: 53; Soper 1948: 25.) Another tooth had been brought from Khotan by Faxian in 475, but it was stolen in 522 and is not recorded thereafter.

[18] On the history of Ayuwang shan's reliquary, see *Ayuwang zhuan* (T. 50, 2042); Alexander C. Soper, "Japanese Evidence for the History of the Architecture and Iconography of Chinese Buddhism," *Monumenta Serica* 4, 2 (1940): 639–646 and 669–678; Soper 1948: 39. For an interesting description of the relic itself, see Xu Yun's autobiography (1988: 41). Xu Yun describes the relic as it appeared differently to him each time he saw it, because "its size and colour varied according to the visitor's sense organ and its field" (ibid.: 42)—in other words, according to individual karma.

[19] On the tooth of the Buddha, see *Hōbōgirin*, s.v. "Butsuge," Vol. 3: 203b–205a.

[20] See *Lun fogu biao*. See also Homer H. Dubs, "Han Yü and the Buddha's Relic: An Episode in Medieval Chinese Religion," *The Review of Religion* 11 (1946): 5–17.

[21] The tooth of the Buddha, for example, played a very important role in the legitimation of the Liang, Zhen, and Sui dynasties. See Tsukamoto 1975: 3:109–128. See also *Fozu tongji*, T. 49, 2035: 460–461. During the Song, almost every year a relic of the Buddha was offered to the court by Indian monks. See Jan 1966a: 6, 2:144ff.

the practice of self-immolation or self-mutilation (see Gernet 1959): by sacrificing one's own body or part of it in front of the Buddha's relics, one magically produced another, immortal, body.[22]

Another related practice consisted in copying a Buddhist scripture with one's own blood. Inasmuch as a canonical scripture was perceived as the Dharma Body of the Buddha, this practice can perhaps be explained, not simply as a devotional excess, but as a methodical attempt to become— by blood transfusion—a Buddha, and to create an immortal scriptural body for oneself. A well-known example is the case of Hanshan Deqing (1546–1623) who, before eventually succeeding in self-mummification, spent two years (1579–1581) copying the *Avataṃsaka-sūtra* with his own blood,[23] reversing literally the French expression *se faire un sang d'encre*. (See Hsü 1979: 72.) Although Hanshan's motivations were admittedly complex—inspired by the sacrificial ideal of the Bodhisattva, his desire to venerate the memory of his parents and to practice penance—this does not necessarily preclude the logic of transubstantiation outlined above. The fact that Hanshan's copy of the *Avataṃsaka* was perceived as a *śarīra* is evidenced by the imperially sponsored prayer assembly held on Wutai shan, during which the scripture was installed in a stūpa. As we will see, it is also during the time he was copying the sūtra that Hanshan experienced "shamanistic" dreams through which his body was purified and regenerated (Hsü 1979: 73). Another interesting case is that of Hanshan's contemporary Zhixu (1599–1655), who not only copied on seven occasions various Mahāyāna scriptures such as the *Avataṃsaka-sūtra* and the apocryphal *Fanwang jing* with his own blood, but relentlessly practiced other forms of self-mutilation, burning the top of his head up to eight times, and his arm up to twenty-eight times during a period from his twenty-sixth to his fifty-sixth year. (See Zhang Shengyan 1975: 224–233.)

"Saintly" *śarīra* were apparently produced in two different ways: by cremation and by "emanation." Besides the classical method through cremation, there is in China a long tradition of "materialization" of *śarīra* as

---

[22] These rituals seem to have their scriptural paradigm in the *Lotus Sūtra*. Concerning this question, and the vogue of self-immolations in Chinese Buddhism, see Gernet 1959. On the practice of burning one's skull and/or fingers at the time of ordination, see Groot 1893: 217–228. For a denunciation of these practices, besides the Confucian pamphlet of Han Yu, see Yijing, in Takakusu 1970: 195.

[23] The practice of copying sūtras with one's own blood was advocated by the *Avataṃsaka-sūtra* itself. (See T. 10, 279: 845c.) Other *loci classici* include the *Foshuo pusa benxing jing* (T. 3, 155: 119b), the *Dazhidulun* (T. 25, 1509: 178c), and the apocryphal *Fanwang jing* (T. 24, 1484: 1009a). On other occasions, Hanshan seems to have copied various other scriptures (*Lotus Sūtra*, *Vajracchedikā*, *Fanwang jing*) with his blood. (See Zhang Shengyan 1975: 228.)

a result of faith or meditation. *Śarīra* were said to have appeared in the hands, in the mouth, between the eyebrows, in the hair, or in the clothes of fervent believers. They even appeared at the tip of a brush, from the characters of a sūtra, or between the eyebrows of a Buddhist statue.[24] The *locus classicus* seems to be the biography of Kang Senghui (fl. 3rd c.), a Sogdian monk, who, after many days of intense meditation, together with his disciples, managed to avoid the death penalty by producing finally a single grain of *śarīra*, harder than a diamond, in the presence of the emperor. (See T. 52, 2106: 410b; Shih 1968: 23–25.) The *Lengqie shizi ji* records the case of Xuanze, one of Huian's co-disciples, who was immersed in dhyāna when "suddenly each of his eyes emitted a *śarīra* with five-colored light rays"—proof of his awakening. (See Faure 1989: 90.) Another Northern Chan monk, Yuangui, obtained *śarīra* in a dream.[25] By the middle of the Tang, the number of *śarīra* had significantly increased. The *Fozu tongji* records, for instance, that when the construction of the Qianfu si pagoda was completed (744), the monk and thaumaturge Chujin performed the Lotus samādhi (*fahua sanmei*) ceremony and obtained 3,070 grains of *śarīra*. By the Song, even Daoist masters began to produce *śarīra*: Zhang Baiduan's cremation yielded thousands of grains.[26] *Śarīra*, however, were used as a weapon in the Buddhist propaganda against other religions. Despite his attempt to interpret Chan in Confucian terms, the Chan master Qisong, in his *Tanjin wenji*, attributes the superiority of Buddhism over other teachings to *śarīra*.[27] Similarly, the Japanese Zen master Kokan Shiren (1278–1346) remarks in his *Genkō Shakusho*: "*Śarīra* are specific to Buddhism and are not mentioned in Daoist and Confucian books. . . . I have heard that they result from the impregnations of *śīla*, *samādhi* and *prajñā*. . . . It is natural that Confucius and Laozi would have lacked them and that preachers would have few and dhyāna masters many" (DNBZ 62, 470: 110).

[24] See Zhen Hua, "Fota gaolüe," in Zhang Mantao 1978: 282–285.
[25] See *Da Tang Zhongyue dong Xianjusi Yuangui ji dechuang*, in SKSLXB 7: 4849b.
[26] The inflation in the numbers of relics obtained by cremation in the Chan school is reflected in the references provided by Mujaku Dōchū. He lists cases where one obtains 16 grains (biography of Anzhu Hua), 300 grains (Sengcan), more than 1,000 grains (Chishou, Xinghua), five-colored *śarīra*, a cremation yielding five-colored *śarīra* and intact teeth and tongue, *śarīra* having the size of beans (Qingzhuo), *śarīra* falling like rain after a cremation (Wuzu, Huiri Neng), and finally "innumerable *śarīra*" (Yiyuan Yongning; *Chōtei funō*, s.v. "Shari," unpublished ms., Hanazono College).
[27] T. 52, 2115: 518c. Qisong's claim is reminiscent of Liu Mi's argument about *abhijñā* (T. 52, 2117: 793), but whereas Liu Mi and other Buddhists remained ambivalent about *abhijñā* because they were also found in non-Buddhists, *śarīra* were always reserved in principle for Buddhists. The same point is made by the Song emperor Renzong in his *Eulogy of Śarīra*. (Quoted by Zhen Hua in Zhang Mantao 1978: 284.)

Superiority depended not only on the number of śarīra obtained but on their size and quality. According to the *Dahui Pujue chanshi zongmen wuku* (*Arsenal of the School of dhyāna master Dahui Pujue*): "When the eminent monks [*zunshu*] of all directions die, their entire body is washed in fire and one obtains a great number [of śarīra]. But only in the case of Zhenjing's śarīra did one obtain five-colored crystals, large as beans and harder than a diamond."[28] Another interesting case is that of Wuming (d. 795): "The flesh was destroyed by fire, but the crystallized bones remained in an upright position and appeared clean and bright. The members and joints stayed tightly connected and were shining and smooth like jade" (Rhie 1977: 20). A rather extreme example, in this case of the relation between śarīra and a practice based on perfect "nonthinking," is the story of the parrot's śarīra: during the Tang, a Mr. Pei had a parrot who could recite the name of the Buddha (*nianfo*). When the parrot died, its body was cremated and yielded more than ten grains of śarīra. An eminent monk named Huiguan erected a stūpa for the bird, and the *chongshuling* Wei Gao (d. 794 or 803) wrote an "Inscription for the funerary stūpa of the parrot."[29] Wei Gao's interest in these relics is significant when one recalls that he was instrumental in the development of Chan in Szechwan and in the Nanzhao kingdom and wrote an epitaph of Shenhui.[30] The cult of śarīra has remained a constant in Chinese Buddhism. When Xu Yun died, in October 1959, at the auspicious age of 120, "over a hundred large relics of five different colours and countless small ones which were mostly white" were found in the crematory oven, and subsequently

[28] See *Dahui Pujue chanshi zongmen wuku*: 6, ed. *Chanxue dacheng*, vol. 3. The text further tells us, in a way reminiscent of Kang Senghui's story, how these śarīra were tested on an anvil with a hammer and left their imprint on both without being crushed. It also mentions that Zhenjing's disciple was eventually mummified, and that his flesh-body is still visible. Finally, it records a story concerning Fozhao Deguang (1121–1203), the master through whom the Japanese master Dainichi Nōnin and his Darumashū were authenticated. We are told that Fozhao burned statues of Arhats and found śarīra afterward. This story forms an interesting contrast with that of Danxia Tianran (739–824), the paradigmatic iconoclast, who, having been reproached for burning a Buddhist statue, justified his act by saying that, since no śarīra were likely to be found in it, he was simply burning a piece of wood to warm himself. (See *Song gaoseng zhuan*, T. 50, 2061: 773b.)

[29] See *Xichuan yan'e sheli taji*, QTW 453, 10: 5858; see also, in the Dunhuang ms. Stein 3835, the case of a bird who produces śarīra naturally.

[30] See Yanagida 1988b: 24. Shenhui's relics were also important in the success of the Southern school. According to Zongmi (*Yuanjue jing dashu chao*, in ZZ, Taibei ed., 14: 553b), on the night of Shenhui's death, the governor of Zhizhou and imperial commander of the Eastern Shannan, Li Guangzhou, saw Shenhui's seat fly in the sky and heard a voice telling him to go to the Kaiyuan monastery to pay homage to Shenhui. The next year, Shenhui's "whole body" was enshrined in a stūpa (at Longmen or in Kaiyuan monastery). Shenhui's grave, recently discovered at Longmen, contained a bowl but unfortunately no patriarchal robe.

placed in a stūpa. (See Xu Yun 1988: 212.)

Śarīra were also a major feature of Korean Buddhism. According to the *Samguk yusa*, the first *śarīra* were sent to Silla by the Liang emperor in 549. The founder of the Vinaya school, the Silla monk Chajang, brought back to Korea relics of the Buddha, most of which he enshrined at his monastery, the T'ongdo-sa, known thereafter as the Buddha-jewel temple (Ha and Mintz 1972: 225). Tooth relics of the Buddha were also brought from China on several occasions thereafter and played an important role in the legitimation of Korean dynasties (Ha and Mintz, ibid.: 226–234). We are also told that when Chinul (1158–1210), the reformer of Korean Sŏn (Chan), died, his complexion remained as if he were alive during the seven days of the funerals. After his cremation, his disciples found thirty large multicolored relics and innumerable smaller pieces (Buswell 1983: 33). After the fourteenth century, any worthy monk was expected to leave *śarīra*, and many stūpa attesting to the prevalence of this belief—a belief still alive and well—can be found in Korean Buddhist temples.

In Japan, the first *śarīra* are mentioned by the *Nihonshoki* in connection with the reigns of Emperor Bidatsu and Empress Suiko. (See *Koji ruien, Shūkyōbu* 1: 245.) The cult of relics seems to have developed with the legend of Shōtoku taishi. According to this legend, a tiny reliquary containing a *śarīra* of the Buddha appeared in the palms of the infant Shōtoku, when, at the age of two, he joined his hands in prayer and, turning to the east, called the Buddha's name (*Shōtoku taishi denryaku*, in DNBZ 71, 546: 126–140). *Śarīra* played a significant role in Nara and Heian Buddhism, and even more so in the Kamakura period with the development of the ideology of the "Final Dharma" (*mappō*). We are told that Taira Kiyomori and Minamoto Yoritomo secretly worshiped relics of Ayuwang shan (Yanagida 1981a: 179). A document titled *Nyorai hashari denrai* (dated 1367) records how a tooth of the Buddha that had been brought back from India by Xuanzang was brought to Japan by Gishin and transmitted by Annen and Enchin, eventually reaching the Fujiwara clan (*Gunsho ruijō* 716: 19). The Sennyūji, founded by the Vinaya master Shunjō (1166–1227), also claimed to be in possession of the tooth of the Buddha transmitted by the Vinaya master Daoxuan (596–667).[31] *Śarīra* were also con-

---

[31] According to Shunjō's biography, when he returned to Japan in 1209 after a twelve-year stay in China, Shunjō brought three grains of *śarīra* of the Buddha, one grain of the Bodhisattva Samantabhadra, and three grains of a saint named Ruan. See Ishida 1972: 240. On the story of the *śarīra*, see the Nō play *Shari*, attributed to Zeami. The *Wakan zensetsu shidai*, on the other hand, mentions that the *śarīra* in the possession of Engakuji was also the one given by the god Nacha to Daoxuan and brought to Japan by Ennin. (Quoted in *Koji ruien*, s.v. "Sharie," *Shūkyōbu* 2: 119. See also *Butsuga shariki*, ibid.: 117.)

spicuous in the Zen tradition, although scholars have tended not to see them. We know, for instance, that Yōsai transmitted three grains of *śarīra* of the Buddha to the shōgun Minamoto no Sanetomo (r. 1193–1216) and that they became the basis of ceremonies (*sharie*) held at various Kamakura monasteries.[32] It is also revealing that the first text written by Dōgen upon his return to Japan dealt with the *śarīra* of his late master and friend Myōzen (1184–1225), which he brought back from China.[33]

It is apparently in the Darumashū, however, that the cult of relics played the most prominent role. This role is now documented by the recent discovery of a scroll relating the transmission of the relics of the six patriarchs and of the Bodhisattva Samantabhadra (Fugen Kōmyō)[34] in Sanbōji, the headquarters of that school. The transmission was carried on continuously at least until the fifteenth century.[35] The emphasis laid on these relics might reflect an attempt by the Darumashū to gain a legitimacy that had been questioned because Nōnin had not gone to China like other contemporary Zen masters.

The transmission of the Chan patriarchs' *śarīra* had not taken place in Sanbōji alone. We know that Gikai (1219–1309), a Darumashū adherent who became Dōgen's disciple and second successor, transmitted the *śarīra* of the Bodhisattva Samantabhadra and of the sixth patriarch Huineng to his disciple Keizan Jōkin (1268–1325). Keizan eventually placed them in a reliquary called Gorohō (Peak of the Five Elders), together with other regalia of the Sōtō sect, in Yōkōji, a monastery founded on the Noto peninsula. Far from being a way of shedding a Darumashū connection, as

[32] See *Azuma Kagami*, under the date of 1212 (*kenryaku* 2); quoted in Nōtomi 1985: 447–451. In his *Kōzen gokoku ron*, Yōsai records the miracles caused by the relic of Ayuwang shan. See T. 80, 2543: 15c.

[33] See *Shari sōdenki*, in DZZ 2: 395. Dōgen reports that, after Myōzen's cremation, three grains of white-colored *śarīra* were found, and that this was the first time this happened in the case of a Japanese monk in the six centuries since the introduction of Buddhism in Japan.

[34] On the *śarīra* of Samantabhadra, see Shunjō's biography (Ishida 1972: 416). These *śarīra* were obtained by pilgrims who went to Emei shan, the abode of Samantabhadra in Sichuan. Shunjō obtained one grain of *śarīra* from one of these pilgrims, a Sichuan monk who claimed that, after praying for seven days on that mountain, he had found between the palms of his joined hands several grains of five-colored *śarīra*. See also the banner inscription of Yuangui, which records that a youth in a blue robe appeared in a dream to the Northern Chan master Yuangui and gave him *śarīra*. When he awoke, Yuangui actually found seven grains of *śarīra*. The author of the inscription notes that "this realization was brought about by Samantabhadra's divine power." See SKSLXB 7: 4849b.

[35] The total numbers of *śarīra* grains recorded in this document seems to have been eight, two each of Bodhidharma and Huineng and one each of the four other patriarchs. An entry dated 1218, however, records 37 grains (perhaps due to fragmentation) and states that these *śarīra* had been brought from China at the time of Dainichi Nōnin. The next entries show a steady increase in the number of grains and the attempt to keep them at Nōnin's monastery, the Sanbōji. A relatively late entry concerns not the *śarīra* themselves but the transmission of the robe of the Chan master Dahui Zonggao, from whom Nōnin descended. See Faure 1987a: 37–38.

Sōtō scholars have claimed, the fact that Keizan buried all the regalia in his possession should be construed as an act of worship, an attempt at reconciling the two trends he had inherited by sanctifying them. After Keizan's death, both his and Dōgen's ashes were dispersed in seven Sōtō monasteries.[36] In this case, again, the temple records concerning these ashes clearly reflect the attempts by various temples to gain legitimacy.[37]

Relics, however, soon became a cheap commodity. A case in point is that of Shōgen (d. 1311), a disciple of Enni Ben'en. After Shōgen's cremation, his disciples were surprised to find several grains of *śarīra*. One of the disciples argued that *śarīra* were no longer respected—particularly when found only in a small number—and he convinced his fellows not to mention them to anyone. The relics were divided between the disciples and hidden. Subsequently, they began to produce miracles, and the skeptical disciple had to admit that he had underestimated the virtue of his master. (See *Genkō shakusho*, DNBZ 62, 470: 110.) Nevertheless, his skepticism may be symptomatic of a growing tendency to treat *śarīra* no longer as subjects but as mere objects. At any rate, it reflects the tendency to require an increasing volume of production.

THE ICONOCLASTIC REACTION

The cult of relics, however, was not unanimously accepted in Chan—not any more, for that matter, than in early Buddhism.[38] The attempt to localize the sacred could of course be seen as contradicting the "sudden" Chan emphasis on the "unlocalized." It reintroduced a kind of mediation

[36] These monasteries are Eiheiji, Yōkōji, Daijōji, Shōbōji, Sōjiji, Kōshōji (during the Edo period), and Hōkōji (during the Meiji era). See Kawaguchi 1984: 10–12. In the case of Shōbōji, along with Dōgen's and Keizan's *śarīra* were transmitted three grains of alleged *śarīra* of the Buddha (which were eventually broken and thereby proved inauthentic), one sacred stone given by the avatar of Kumano, and the robe of Bodhidharma, transmitted by Rujing to Dōgen and his successors.

[37] A recent example is that of Hōkōji, a Sōtō temple in Aomori prefecture, where the relics (*shinkotsu*) of Dōgen were enshrined in a three-story pagoda (erected in 1949). The temple tradition traces its foundation back to the *shikken* Tokiyori. It contains three *śarīra*: one has been placed within Dōgen's statue in the pagoda; the two others were placed in the *kaisandō* or "Founder's Hall." Hōkōji equally claims to possess relics of the Buddha. See supplement to *Chūgai Nippō*, 5/20/1988. (I am indebted to Ian Reader for this information.)

[38] According to the strict Theravāda orthodoxy, the *ānatman* theory implies a denial of relics: the body (hence the *śarīra*) of a person is not that person's self. This point has been made time and again and is still prevalent among scholars. André Bareau, for instance, considers that the cult of relics was a belated concession to naive faith. For Bareau, the cult emerged around the second half of the fifth century B.C.E., and consequently all the stūpa and *śarīra* related to the Buddha are "apocryphal" (Bareau 1975: 184–187.) Bareau's historicist approach, however, misses another point, superbly made by his predecessor Paul Mus, which is that at the ideological level, relics (or icons) are "a support for mystical transpositions, through which something of the Buddha could be reached, despite, or on the margins of, the 'reserved question' of annihilation" (Mus 1935: 78).

that had to be negated in the name of "immediate" and "unmediated" Chan. Like the Daoist sage, the true Chan master was supposed to walk without leaving any trace. Yet Bodhidharma left one straw sandal in his grave. This was too much, or too little. Even in the Daoist tradition, only inferior immortals practiced the so-called deliverance from the corpse, while superior ones simply vanished. Although the Daoist model of the immortal certainly influenced the early Chan conception of relics, the model of the Buddha, itself patterned after that of the *cakravartin* king, played a major role. As Bareau points out, offerings to the stūpa of the *cakravartin* and of the Buddha suggest that their mode of presence, beyond death, was perceived as essentially different from that of common mortals on the one hand, or of Brahmanic gods on the other. (See Bareau 1975: 183.) There is some evidence that early Chan masters were considered *cakravartin* kings.[39]

For the most uncompromising subitists, however, a "true man without rank" could not be mummified and recuperated as a symbol of legitimacy by a collectivity: a true Chan master should leave no relics, not even a death *gāthā*.[40] Actually, many such *gāthā* express for the record their author's last wish not to have his *śarīra* become an object of devotion. Thus Zongmi instructed his disciples to give his flesh to birds and animals, to burn his bones into ashes, and to throw the ashes away. (See Jan 1972: 21.) In the same way, Zhiduan (d. 969), a Chan master active in Fuzhou, told his disciples: "As to my ashes, scatter them at the four corners of the forest./ Don't select for my grave a donator's land" (Demiéville 1984: 57). Qinghe (fl. toward the end of the 10th c.) wrote: "After my death, take my bones and give them to worms and ants. Don't erect a grave or a stūpa."[41] His disciples first followed his order, but seeing (or imagining?) that worms did not touch the corpse, they eventually incinerated it and enshrined the relics in the Hall of Images (*yingtang*) of the Kaiyuan monastery in Quanzhou.[42] In most cases, these last wishes were not respected

[39] See for instance, the stele of Puji (651–739): " 'Great master of the four seas'—such is the title of our Sagely Literate and Divinely Martial Emperor (Xuanzong) of the *kaiyuan* [period]. 'He who has entered into the wisdom of the Buddha and gloriously rules over the myriad dharmas'—such is the title of the seventh generation of the Chan school, Master Dazhao" (*QTW* 262: 3b; see McRae 1986: 65; Faure 1988: 132).

[40] This criticism reinforced that of rationalists such as Han Yu or Chu Dajun. Writing about the "hair relic" of Huineng, enshrined in a stūpa in the Guangxiao monastery in Canton, Chu Dajun argued that since Huineng was ordained after becoming the sixth patriarch, it is because Buddhas consider their skin and hair as impure that Huineng abandoned his hair. Therefore, people who worship these relics have forgotten their true meaning. See Chu Dajun, *Guangdong xinyu* (Taibei: Taiwan xuesheng shuju, 1968), 3: 1065.

[41] A similar order was given by the fourth Niutou patriarch Fachi (637–702), but the context in this case was radically different: Fachi thought the animals that would eat his body would gain rebirth in Pure Land. Contrary to Zhiduan, he believed the virtue of the saint is something substantial that can be physically propagated.

[42] See Demiéville 1984: 63. Demiéville also gives the verse written by one of the Chinese

by disciples eager to keep their master's *abhijñā* under their own control. The master's own critique strikes us at times as somewhat rhetorical, as in the following dialogue between Huangbo and a monk:

> [The monk:] "Since the body of the Buddha is not composed, it is beyond numbers. How then could it be divided into eight portions [during the 'war of relics']?"
>
> [Huangbo:] "If you hold such a view, you can see only the apparent relics [of the Buddha], not his true relics."
>
> "Do these relics exist inherently, or are they due only to his merits?"
>
> "They neither exist inherently nor are due to his merits."
>
> "If so, why are the Tathāgata relics, if only refined, 'everlasting golden bones'?"
>
> The master then admonished [his interlocutor]: "How can you pretend to study Chan when you hold such views? Have you ever seen bones in the sky? The mind of the Buddhas is like space. What is the use to search for bones in it?"
>
> "But I do see relics now. What kind of dharma are they?"
>
> "It is your false notions that make you see relics."
>
> "But you, master, don't you possess such relics? Could you show them to us?"
>
> "It is difficult to see the true relics of the Buddha. If you could only, from the top of your ten fingers, reduce into dust the Transcendent Mount [Sumeru], then you would see the true relics of the Tathāgata." (*Chuanxin fayao* 1976: 47–48)

In the same vein, the *Jingde chuandeng lu* reports an interesting dialogue revolving around Sengqie's mummy: "The guardian of the stūpa was about to close its gate when someone asked: 'Since this is the great master of the three worlds, how can he be locked in by his disciple?' The guardian did not answer. [Fayan's comment: 'The great master is locked in, the disciple is locked in.']" (*T.* 51, 2076: 434c). Several other dialogues involve the guardian of Huineng's stūpa. The fact that relics became the topic of so many "encounter dialogues," even to be criticized therein, attests to their importance.[43]

Often the critique is expressed through an allegorical interpretation of the cult of stūpa and *śarīra*. In Shenxiu's *Guanxin lun*, for instance, the

---

masters who introduced Chan to Japan, Wuxue Zuyuan (Mugaku Sogen): "Do not scatter cold ashes on the empty hill" (ibid.: 92).

[43] More ironic is the fact that a dialogue intended to criticize the Chan cult of relics—such as Nan'yang Huizhong's dialogue on the "seamless stūpa," as opposed to the ordinary stūpa—became the source of a funerary feature specific to Chan/Zen, the erection of the so-called *muhōtō* graves. On the symbolism of the seamless stūpa, see *Muhōtō kirigami* in Ishikawa 1986b: 208–209; Matsuura 1976: 484–499.

stūpa is interpreted as the human body.[44] This line of interpretation is developed by Japanese masters such as Bassui: "There are none among Buddhas and ordinary people who are not in possession of the sacred bones. The body is called the shrine and Buddha nature is the bones. When you see into your own nature . . . , your body and self-nature are no longer two: the bones and shrine are one. . . . Hence one who clearly sees this doesn't think of the physical bones of the Buddha as the true sacred bones." Bassui refers to the famous self-referential passage in the *Lotus Sūtra* according to which the place where the sūtra is contains the Buddha's whole body (see Schopen 1975) and concludes: "Thus, while one possesses true original nature, the bones of the Buddha, in an undeluded dharma body, not being aware of this, he keeps the ashes of another. Carefully guarding sacred bones is in violation of the essence of Buddhism." (See Braverman 1989: 34–35.)

A slightly different line of approach is taken by the *Zutang ji*, in its biography of the Chan master Dadian Baotong (732–824). The story can be read as a recuperation of the Confucian iconoclast Han Yu, but its criticism is more nuanced. We are told that when the emperor worshiped the finger bone of the Buddha, he and his officials saw a five-colored light. Everyone said: "This is the light of the Buddha." Only Han Yu denied that this was the light of the Buddha. "If this is not the light of the Buddha," the emperor asked, "what is it?" Han Yu was unable to answer and was subsequently exiled to Zhaozhou (in Guangdong). When he arrived there, he searched for some eminent Chan master and was directed to Dadian. When he met the master and told him his story, Dadian confirmed him in his opinion that what the emperor saw was not the light of the Buddha. "Then what was it?" asked Han Yu. "It was the light of transformation of Indra, Brahma, and the Eight assemblies of Heavenly Dragons." "Had someone like you been in the capital at the time," said Han Yu, "I would not have had to come here." Han Yu further asked: "I still wonder if there is a light of the Buddha." "There is," said Dadian. "What is it?" Han Yu ventured to ask. Dadian called his name, and Han Yu assented. "Look!" said Dadian, "Do you see it?" "At this point," said Han Yu, "I no longer understand." "If you did," said Dadian, "this would be the true light of the Buddha." And Dadian went on to explain that this true light, which transcends all senses and categories, even the distinction between sacred and profane, is what allows one never to be deluded. Han Yu is said to have become subsequently enlightened about the truth of Chan (*Zutang ji* 5, ed. Yanagida 1974b: 93). Here again, the phenomenal characteristic of the relic—its five-colored light—is denied in the name of

---

[44] See McRae 1986: 200. In the esoteric tradition, the fivefold stūpa (*gorinnotō*) is later symbolically identified with the body of the Buddha Vairocana. The body of the practitioner immersed in samādhi, on the other hand, becomes metaphorically a "living grave."

the noumenal reality—the superior radiance—of the Dharma Body of the Buddha, understood in Chan terms as the luminous mind. The slightly condescending treatment of Han Yu in the *Zutang ji* must not hide the fact that the authors of this text shared with Confucianism the same elitist approach and the same fundamental distrust of popular religiosity.

Many Chan followers must have shared the doubts expressed by the Minister Li Se in his preface to the funerary inscription for the Indian (yet almost Chan) monk Zhikong (Dhyānabhadra): "The Master's relics were divided into four portions. . . . [It] is not clear whether the Master Chih-k'ung can really be thought of as dwelling here, or elsewhere. But ought not his relics to be considered simply like a grasshopper's discarded shell, and disregarded? Or that his disciples might have a chance of displaying their gratitude was it right that an effort should be made, despite the circumstances? These questions weighed heavily upon me" (Waley 1931–1932: 375). The cult of relics reveals the tensions that existed within the Chan tradition but also the affinities or the alliances that could take place between some of its segments and Confucianism.

Eight

**Metamorphoses of the Double (II):
"Sublime Corpses" and Icons**

Twirled flower, gentle smile.
Vulture Peak is right here
In this mountain, Kāśyapa waits for Maitreya's
    spring
Who drinks his poison down, knows its virtues
    well.
In India, China and Japan, he sits; the same old wild
    fox.

—Ikkyū, *Kyōunshū* 165

No one agrees to be buried alive, and the splendor of
the tomb does not make the sojourn more wholesome.

—Charles Nisard, *Histoire des livres populaires*

The appearance of "flesh-bodies" contributed to blur the distinction between the relics of the Buddha and those of the saints, since mummies
were Buddhas. The relation between relics and mummies is drawn explicitly in the *Song gaoseng zhuan*'s account of the discovery of the remains of
a Northern Chan adherent, Layman Ding, by a Western monk named
Anqing (T. 50, 2061: 830a):

Shi Anqing was originally from the Western land. In *kaiyuan* 15
(727), he wandered toward the east and arrived at Ding. . . . He directly inquired about the whereabouts of Layman Ding. The towns-
people reported to him that the latter had died three years ago and
was buried outside the town. They added: "This man was a lay Bodhisattva. He constantly strove in his *brahmacaryā* practice and became the disciple of the dhyāna master Puji on Song shan." He said:
"Since I have obtained that profound Dharma, I will die while sitting
with joined hands." And he suddenly passed away. The bells of the
temples of Caocheng rang of themselves, without having been
struck. [An]qing went to the grave and opened it. At that moment,
a five-colored cloud of vapor rose above the grave. [Anqing] then
took [Ding's] bones: they all had a golden color and were linked—
forming a chain of about five *chan*. . . . [Anqing] planted trees
around the *stūpa* to enclose it. All the people were very surprised.
Sometime later he died there.

Zanning's comment runs as follows: "The remains of all sentient beings depends on a cause and are the fruit of their practice. While, in an ordinary body, the joints are not communicating, the bones and joints of the Bodhisattva of the ten *bhūmi* are mutually connected. . . . As to the Buddha, his whole body is a *śarīra*. In the present case, the bones had the form of a chain. In other words, he went beyond the stage of the common man but did not yet reach the tenth *bhūmi*; this is the body of Narāyaṇa with eight arms." Although Zanning's esoteric reference to Narāyaṇa eludes me, it seems clear that by saying that the whole body of a Buddha is a *śarīra*, in other words is incorruptible, he is referring to a "flesh-body." Therefore, self-mummification is an index of buddhahood for the practitioner, and perhaps its cause—or at least a source of worldly benefits—for others.

Mummies have attracted the attention of Japanese scholars since the discovery of a group of mummified Buddhist monks in Northern Japan (Yamagata prefecture).[1] Most of these mummies were the remains of Shūgendō practitioners, whose practice was patterned after the legend of Kūkai's "entering samādhi" (*nyūjō*), thereby becoming a "Buddha in this very body" (*sokushinbutsu*). The oldest of these Buddhist mummies in existence today is that of Kōchi Hōin (d. 1363), preserved in Niigata prefecture; the most recent is that of Bukkai Shōnin (d. 1903, also in Niigata).[2] In his ethnographical essays on Northern Japan, *Hokuetsu Seppū*, Suzuki Bokushi (1770–1842) describes and sketches that mummy as he saw it in 1838 (477 years later):

Kōchi's mummy is counted as one of the twenty-four wonders of Echigo. Though it has been mentioned in various works, none of them provides illustrations—which I have seen fit to do here. My drawing records what I saw myself, when I traveled to lower Echigo last year. All that is visible is the face. The hand and feet cannot be seen, and a temple regulation prohibits too close an approach. The mummy's eyes are closed, as if in sleep, with wrinkles at the corners. The head covering and robe the mummy now wears cannot be the

[1] See Hori 1962; Andō 1961; Naitō 1974; Matsumoto Akira 1985; Kosugi Kazuo, "Nikushinzō oyobi yuikaizō no kenkyū," 1937; Mochizuki 1958–1963: 10:s.v. "Nyūjō butsu." For a description of these mummies, see Sakurai and Ogata 1983.
[2] Also in existence are four twelfth-century mummies of the Fujiwara family, a powerful clan in Northeastern Japan. The fact that all these mummies were found in Northern Japan has to do with cultural conditions (the development of Shūgendō in Hokuriku and Tōhoku), but perhaps also with climatic conditions necessary for their preservation. The southernmost *sokushinbutsu* actually preserved seems to be those of Myōshin at Yokokura-dera (near Gifu) and of Dansei in Ōhara (on the northern outskirts of Kyoto). Chinese cases of self-mummification, however, were found principally in Southern China, and I have recently, thanks to Victor Mair, come across the description of a Vietnamese mummy (near Hanoi). See Igor Lisevich, "The Smile of an 'Immortal' Elder," *Sputnik* 11 (1989): 110–113. Other mummies are found in Southeast Asia, but they are lacquered or covered with gold.

original ones. Yet this is certainly a wonder of Echigo, unheard of in other provinces. (Suzuki Bokushi 1986: 281; see also Sakurai and Ogata 1983: 216)

In his commentary, Momoki (Santō Kyōzan, 1765–1831) notes:

There are, in China, mummies similar to that of Kōchi. When the Tang-dynasty monk Yicun died, his corpse was placed in a casket, from which it was lifted each month to have the nails and hair trimmed. The body had not decomposed even after one hundred years. Later, during the rebellions and uprisings at the end of the dynasty, it was cremated. The Song-dynasty Chinese Peng Cheng records in his collection of poems and tales *Moke Huixi* that the monk Wumeng of Ezhou was not buried, and his nails and hair grew just as did those of Yicun—until the corpse was touched by the hand of a woman. This phenomenon is mentioned in *The Five Miscellanies*, where many opinions about mummies are offered, but the whole idea is an insult to Śākyamuni's teachings of the impermanence of all compound things, and cannot be praised. (Suzuki Bokushi 1986: 283)

CHAN "FLESH-BODIES"

The Chinese monk to whom Suzuki referred, Xuefeng Yicun (822–908), was a native of Quanzhou (Fujian) and a well-known figure in the Chan tradition. His case is not exceptional. Beginning with the fourth patriarch Daoxin (d. 651) and the sixth patriarch Huineng (d. 713), many Chan masters turned or were turned into mummies or "flesh-bodies" after their death.[3] Although this phenomenon is in no way restricted to Chan, the number of cases recorded in this school is extremely high. Not surprisingly, thaumaturges such as Baozhi, Wanhui, and Sengqie were all self-mummified, although with varying success. We know that Baozhi's body "retained fragrant odor and a countenance pleasant to look at," but his mummy seems to have disappeared relatively soon. The same thing happened to Wanhui's body: although the *Jingde chuandeng lu* tells us that at the time of his death, "a strange perfume raised, and his whole body remained supple," we know that he was buried in 709 in the Xiangxi monastery, west of the capital.

[3] As mentioned earlier, the "first patriarch" Bodhidharma was credited with several works on the attainment of immortality. See, for instance, Sekiguchi 1969: 488–492. Some of these works found their way into the Daoist canon, although none was recorded in the Chan tradition. At any rate, Bodhidharma, as a true (Daoist) "Immortal," is said to have obtained "deliverance from the corpse" (*shijie*) and therefore did not leave a "flesh-body." On the "deliverance from the corpse," see Robinet 1979b.

The fourth patriarch Daoxin (580–651), who might be considered the actual founder of the Chan school, seems to be the first recorded case. After his death, his body was put in a stūpa on Huangmei shan. The next year, according to the *Chuan fabao ji*, "the stone doors opened of themselves and his countenance was as majestic as when he was alive. His disciples subsequently added lacquered cloth [to the body] and did not dare to close the doors again. They cut stone and engraved a tablet. Du Zhenglun, president of the Department of the Imperial Grand Secretariat, composed the text praising his virtue." (See Yanagida 1971: 380.) This, incidentally, would also make Daoxin the first known case of a lacquered mummy.[4] The *Fozu tongji* notes that Daoxin's master, Sengcan, died "standing erect" and that a stūpa was erected on his relics at the Shangu monastery.[5]

We know that Daoxin's successor, Hongren, was concerned with the construction of his stūpa, and this suggests that he intended to follow his master's example. The *Song gaoseng zhuan* (T. 50, 2061: 755b) simply mentions that Hongren's disciples placed his "whole body" in a stūpa but makes no reference to his mummification. A later work, the *Tanxue zhijin* (*Knowing the Fords on the Way to Knowledge*; 1827), by Xiancheng Ruhai, is more explicit and says that the "true bodies" of Daoxin and Hongren are preserved on the mountains of the fourth and the fifth patriarchs, respectively. On the other hand, Huineng's case is well documented, and the existence of his mummy probably contributed significantly to the success of the Southern school, if not to his posthumous promotion as "sixth patriarch." This mummy, which can still be seen—together with that of the Ming Chan master Hanshan Deqing—in the Nanhua monastery at Caoxi, has often been described, and the Caoxi local gazeteer contains many poems about it. Some of the most interesting descriptions were given by the Jesuit missionaries Ricci and Longobardo, who were contemporaries of Hanshan. Here is how Father Trigault, Ricci's biographer, describes in terms inspired from the *Golden Legend* Huineng's mummy and the Nanhua monastery:

> This institution had its origin with a man named Lusu [*Luzu*, the "Patriarch Lu," i.e., Huineng], some eight hundred years ago. They say that he lived on this very spot and that he acquired a great repu-

[4] The *Xu gaoseng zhuan* gives a slightly different version of the discovery of Daoxin's mummy: "Three years after [his death], his disciple Hongren and others went to the stūpa, opened it, and saw him sitting upright as in the past. Then they moved it to the original place, where it still seems to exist" (T. 50, 2060: 606b).

[5] Qisong also notes that "Li Chang, prefect of Huihenan, obtained the relics of the third patriarch, the great master Can" (*Chuanfa zhengzong ji*, T. 51, 2078: 768b). But the records concerning the "third patriarch"—let alone the tradition recorded by the *Baolin zhuan* (801), according to which these *śarīra* and the stele proving their authenticity were discovered by Shenhui—are patent forgeries.

tation for sanctity because of his unusually austere manner of living. He wore iron chains against his flesh, and he was continually sifting rice and lightly pounding it, the way they do. In a single day he would prepare enough of it for a thousand temple dwellers, or conventuals. His flesh became so torn and mutilated by the iron chains that it was actually putrefied and running with maggots, and if one of them fell he would replace it and say, "Can you find nothing to gnaw? Why are you thinking of deserting me?" His body is enshrined in this magnificent temple, which was built in his honor, and the people, who venerate his memory and whatever belonged to him, come here on pilgrimage from all corners of the realm. . . . The temple ministers also showed them the body of Lusu, enveloped in that peculiar shiny bituminous substance, known only to the Chinese. Many say it is not his body, but the people believe that it is and they hold it in great veneration.[6]

Huineng's actual mummification has not been recorded, and we know only that his body was eventually lacquered.[7] The earliest document, an epitaph written by Wang Wei at the demand of Shenhui, simply tells us, "At an unknown date he told his disciples that he was about to die, and at once a mysterious fragrance permeated the room and a bright rainbow appeared. When he had finished eating, he spread his sitting-cloth and passed away." Again, on an unknown date, the "seat of his spirit" [*shenzuo*] was moved to Caoxi, "and his body was placed, seated, in an unidentified place" (Yampolsky 1967: 67).[8] Much of the material of Hui-

---

[6] Gallagher 1953: 222–223. See also Spence 1984: 211. According to the *Shoushen ji* (quoted by Doré 1914–1938: 7:257), Huineng's body "exhales a very suave smell, the bust is not in the least dessicated [but was it not lacquered?] and seems as if luminous." This omission about the lacquering of Huineng's mummy, and Ricci's comment that "many say that it is not his body," might raise doubts about the authenticity of the mummy, as about the nature of the entire Huineng legend. But the point is that there *was* a mummy, which most people believed to be Huineng's "flesh-body," and the legend concerning it appeared very early. The existence of this mummy, whether or not it is authentic, might as well be seen as a result or as a cause of the success of the Southern school.

[7] A Guangdong archeologist, Xu Hengbing, thinks that Huineng was mummified following what was to become the standard procedure. According to this technique, when his death approaches, the priest, wearing a *kaṣāya*, sits down cross-legged and enters into *samādhi*, stopping all intake of food or drink. After his death, his body is placed on a wooden seat inside two urns tightly shut. The seat is set above quicklime and wood charcoal, and through an orifice in it the juices resulting from the decomposition of the corpse fall on the quicklime, producing a constant hot vapor that dessicates the corpse—ultimately resulting in a cross-legged "flesh-body." In the case of Huineng, the subsequent molding covering of the flesh-body with clay (mixed with) incense and lacquered cloth, and the consolidation of its neck with metal leaves, are said to have been done by his disciple Hongbian. (See *Renmin ribao*, November 1, 1990. I owe this reference to the kindness of Victor Mair.)

[8] Although Yampolsky translates the term as "sacred coffin," *shenzuo* had a technical meaning in Chinese religion and implies the presence of an enduring principle in the corpse or an effigy of the dead.

neng's legend appears in the *Sōkei daishi betsuden* (zz 2B, 19, 5: 483a), a later work that was lost in China but was fortunately brought to Japan by the Tendai monk Ennin. This work, dated 782, was the product of the disciples of Xingtao (var. Lingtao), the keeper of Huineng's stūpa at Caoxi. It was therefore written primarily to establish the legitimacy of the community centered around Huineng's relics, a community apparently different from that in which the *Platform Sūtra* was compiled. This strategy proved successful, since Caoxi became a thriving pilgrimage center. After the Huichang proscription of Buddhism in 845, it came to replace, at least in Chan, the pilgrimage to Wutai shan. (See Suzuki Tetsuo 1985: 54.)

The first well-recorded lacquered mummy is that of Huineng's contemporary Sengqie who, although not a Chan monk himself, was later co-opted by the Chan tradition. The *Fozu tongji* has, for the year 710, the following entry: "When master Sengqie died, a royal decree ordered that his body should be lacquered and a stūpa should also be erected at Jianfu si. Soon after this, a foul smell pervaded the city. An edict ordered the body to be sent to [his former monastery at] Sizhou. At once, a fragrant breeze blew over the imperial capital.[9] The emperor asked Wanhui: 'Who was Sengqie?' Wanhui replied: 'He was an incarnation of Guanyin' " (T. 49, 2035: 372c). Sengqie's case became a paradigm for later generations, and the preservation of his mummy in Sizhou contributed greatly to his deification.[10] In the eleventh century, a Japanese monk and thaumaturge named Jōjin (1011–1091) came to pay homage to Sengqie's mummy and, when he himself died in China, his mummified body was in turn lacquered and covered with gold dust.[11]

In 757, when Emperor Xuanzong was driven to Sichuan by the An Lushan rebellion, he ordered a Chan monk from Silla, master Chuan, to found a monastery in Chengdu for the prosperity of the empire. Later this Korean monk died on Jiuhua shan (present Anwei) at the age of ninety-nine. "His body did not decay and his skeleton kept together as if bound by a golden chain." The mummy worshiped today on Jiuhua shan seems to be that of a different monk, since according to the local tradition it goes back only to the Qing. Another Korean monk, Wuxiang (K. Mu-

[9] Geary (1978: 114) notes that at the time of the *translatio* of St. Mark in 827, his body emitted a fragrance that spread over the entire city. The same thing happened when the relics of St. Nicholas were transferred from Myra to Bari in 1087.

[10] Several self-immolations and miracles took place around Sengqie's stūpa. See for instance *Song gaoseng zhuan*, T. 50, 2061: 822, 992.

[11] In his *San Tendai Godaisan ki* (DNBZ 72, 577), Jōjin records his visit to Puzhaowang monastery on the ninth month of 1072 and describes Sengqie's mummy as he saw it. On another occasion, he also describes the mummy of the thaumaturge Baozhi. (See Soper 1948: 41.) On Jōjin's biography, see *Genkō shakusho* 16 (DNBZ 62, 470: 150b). See also Naitō 1974: 68.

sang), became famous in Sichuan and in the early Chan tradition as one of the founders of the Baotang school,[12] and there seems to be some overlap between his biography and that of master Chuan.

Self-mummification was usually achieved by entering the final samādhi, and it is significant that in the Indian context, *samādhi* designates metonymically both the spiritual state of the ascetic and the grave in which he is buried alive. (See Parry 1982: 97.) Mummification was also sometimes the outcome of a dramatic death. According to the *Fozu tongji*, "Shanxin, a disciple of Mazu Daoyi, one day told his followers: 'Other offerings are incomparable with the offering of one's body.' Thereafter he cut off his foot with a sharp-edged knife and placed it on the table. He died subsequently and was followed in death by two of his lay disciples who had been attending him. Having heard this, the regional commander sent officers with presents and covered their corpses with gold." We are told that "thereafter, prayers offered by the people brought immediate response." These suicides were apparently not perceived as a kind of "bad death" that inspired horror and fear of malignant ghosts. They should of course be seen against the backdrop of self-immolations in Chinese Buddhism. (See Gernet 1959; Jan 1965.) But the point that particularly concerns us here is the fact that these three Chan adepts were mummified just after their suicide.

Another famous mummy is that of Yunmen Wen'yan (864–949), the founder of the Yunmen school. The *Fozu tongji* tells us simply that his body was buried in the abbot room of the monastery. The body of one of Yunmen's disciples, Daan, was recovered with clay after his death (978) in the "Old Datong monastery" (*Datong kusi*) in Guangzhou. According to a stele inscription dated 964 (*Guangdong tongzhi* 204, 6:3472), in 963, a man named Ruan Shaozhuang saw Yunmen in a dream. Yunmen asked that his stūpa be opened. When this was done, he appeared "as if alive." His mummy was subsequently transferred to the king's palace to be worshiped there. The monastery was baptized Dajue si, Monastery of the Great Awakening, and Yunmen received his posthumous title of Chan master Kuangzhen. From this inscription, it is clear that Yunmen had close relations with the court of the Southern Han and that his community was prosperous. The Yunmen school became with the Linji school one of the two dominant trends of Chan during the Song, and this may have had something to do with Yunmen's powers "beyond the

---

[12] Concerning Musang, see *Lidai fabao ji* (т. 51, 2075: 184c–196b); *Song gaoseng zhuan* (т. 50, 2061: 832b); Yamaguchi 1973; Broughton 1983: 21–27; Buswell 1983: 77; Jan 1979: 47–60. For a description of Dizang's mummy on Jiuhua shan, see Powell 1989: 28. There are other mummies on Jiuhua shan, one of them being that of Wuxie, a Buddhist monk of the Ming. See also M. W. de Visser, "The Bodhisattva Ti-tsang (Jizō) in China and Japan," *Ostasiatische Zeitschrift* 2 (1913): 289–292.

grave." Another document, the *Stele Inscription of the Re-arraying of the Master-patriarch Kuangzhen of Yunmen Monastery*, tells us that when Yunmen died, "his disciples received his 'whole body' and erected a stūpa; then they took the body out of his coffin [*gan*] and lacquered it. This was more than eight hundred years ago. During that time, the people, near and distant, officials and common folk alike, prayed to him for rain or for good weather, and he helped them silently and performed many miracles" (*Yunmen shan zhi*, 230). The inscription also records how a group of about forty parishioners cooperated to regild the mummy with lacquer and gold. Another interesting fact in Yunmen's biography (T. 47, 1988: 575b) is that his self-mummification is implicitly compared to Mahākāśyapa's waiting for the coming of the future Buddha Maitreya: "When Maitreya comes, [Yunmen] is likely to reappear, to establish a place of practice on the Three Peaks and to depart again."[13]

Another Chan monk to mention in the context of the Maitreya belief is Budai (d. 916). Little is known of him, but he was considered—and perhaps saw himself—as an incarnation of Maitreya. Toward the beginning of the Song, it was reported that Budai's body had been preserved intact in the monastery where he died. (See *Jingde chuandeng lu*, T. 51, 2076: 434b; Chapin 1933: 51; Ishii 1987: 33.) Perhaps the existence of this mummy explains the retrospective connection with Maitreya and the subsequent popularity of the pot-bellied monk. At any rate, these are the only Chan cases that we can clearly associate with Maitreyan eschatology.

Let us conclude this visit to the catacombs of Chan history (but not of Chan monasteries) with a few more cases. Yuanzhao (811–895) was a monk of the Fengshan monastery in Luoyang who died at eighty-four. After five years, his stūpa was opened and it was found that his hair had grown and he looked "as if alive." His body was worshiped during seven years but was eventually cremated, and his *śarīra* were scattered in almost a thousand grains (T. 50, 2061: 784c, quoted in Demiéville 1984:41). The tradition also has it that when the Caodong (Sōtō) master Hongzhi Zhengjue (1091–1157) died in a sitting posture, *śarīra* emanated from his teeth and hair. His "integral body" was inhumed in the East Valley on Tiantong shan, and it was said that "all those who venerate the stūpa and look for *śarīra* see their wishes fulfilled" (*Fozu tongji*, T. 49, 2035: 427a; Ishii 1987: 320). Although all these cases of self-mummification date from the Tang or Song, the practice seems to have persisted during the Ming. One of the well-documented cases for the "orthodox" Chan tradition is

[13] The "Three Peaks" is an allusion to Mt. Kukkuṭpāda ("Cockfoot"), where Mahākāśyapa was believed to have entered *samādhi* in order to wait for Maitreya. See App 1989: 16. On Kāśyapa and Maitreya, see Lamotte 1944–1980: 1:191–196. On the origin of the legend, see *Fu fazang yinyuan zhuan* (T. 50, 2058: 301a).

that of Hanshan Deqing (1546–1623),[14] whose mummy was enshrined near that of Huineng at the Nanhua monastery, together with that of one of his contemporaries named Dantian ("Cinnabar Field").[15]

The above examples attest to the importance of flesh-bodies in the Chan tradition. These mummies represent a variety of factions (e.g., the Baotang, Hongzhou, Niutou, Yunmen, and Caodong schools) and of conservation techniques. But this trend was cutting across sectarian boundaries. Outside the Chan tradition, the most well-known examples are those of Zhiyi (538–597), Xuanzang (602–664), Kuiji (632–682),[16] and Śubhakarasiṃha (637–735),[17] who played a major role in the formation of the Tiantai, Faxiang, and Zhen'yan schools, respectively. To understand their significance, it is necessary to recall briefly the contexts in which they emerged. For this, it may be useful to distinguish—arbitrarily perhaps—between the "semantic" and the "pragmatic" dimensions. (See Tambiah 1984: 5.) Whereas the semantic context refers to the changes of meaning of the "flesh-body"—and of death in general—in the collective mind, the pragmatic context refers to the various functions it came to play in dynastic or sectarian politics.

THE SEMANTIC EVOLUTION

We should first point out an important difference in the Japanese cases. In Japan, the cult of the so-called *sokushinbutsu* had a distinct eschatological connotation and was explicitly linked to the belief in the future Buddha Maitreya (J. Miroku) and to the legend of Kūkai's "entering samādhi" (*nyūjō*) on Mt. Kōya in 835.[18] With the exceptions of Yunmen and Budai,

[14] Mummies have been produced in China much later, the last example being recorded in Taiwan in 1976. See Welch 1967.

[15] See *Zhongxiu Caoxi tongzhi* 5: 626. Ishii (1987: 33) mentions other examples recorded in the *Jingde chuandeng lu*: Lingshu Rumin of Shaozhou (d. 918), Huangbo Hui, and so on. See also *Beishan lu* (T. 52, 2113: 610–614).

[16] There is also on Tiantai shan an imperial mummy said to be that of the first Qing emperor Shizu (1644–1661). See P. W. Yetts, "The Disposal of the Dead in China," *Journal of the Royal Asiatic Society* (1911): 699ff. On Kuiji, see *Fozu tongji*'s entry for the year 830: "On a request from Yilin, an Attendant of the Imperial Carriage, the stūpa of Master Cien [Kuiji] was excavated for repairs. When the tomb was dug, a fragrance pervaded the place. The original body of the master was still reclining on a brick platform. His forty teeth [*sic*] were still intact and his face looked alive" (T. 49, 2035: 385a).

[17] On Śubhakarasiṃha's "flesh-body," see Chou 1944–1945: 271–272.

[18] According to the *Dazhidulun*, after the *parinirvāṇa* of the Buddha, his disciple Mahā-kāśyapa entered into *nirodhasamāpatti* on Mount Kukkuṭapāda, waiting for the coming of the future Buddha Maitreya in order to hand him down the robe of Śākyamuni. When the time finally comes, Maitreya and his disciples discover a Lilliputian Mahākāśyapa (Hīnakāśya-pa?), and Śākyamuni's robe hardly fits Maitreya's finger. This comic scene rests on the belief that since the world in the age of Maitreya has returned to perfection, the life span and body size of human things are much larger than in the corrupted age in which Śākya-muni appeared. See Lamotte 1944–1980: 1:191–196. On Maitreya, see Sponberg and Hard-

this does not seem to have been the case in the Chinese examples mentioned. This Maitreyan background of Japanese mummies may explain partly the lack of flesh-bodies in Japanese Zen.[19] Although fascinated by Kūkai's example, Ikkyū did not attempt to emulate him: "The living son of Great King Dainichi,/ Able to pass the gate of death at will./ His spirit shares a long night's watch with Kāśyapa./ Autumn winds, spring rains; then moonrise at dawn" (*Kyōun shū* 333; Sanford 1981: 141). The contrast with Chinese Chan is striking, although to my knowledge no one has pointed it out. In order to shed some light on this contrast and its significance, let us retrace briefly the Chinese evolution of the mummy cult.

Mummies have been found in China long before the emergence of Chan. The discovery of the tomb of the Lady of Tai (d. ca. 168 B.C.E.) at Mawangdui in 1972 has provided new evidence of the sophisticated techniques used in ancient China for the preservation of the body, and of their Daoist background.[20] But natural mummification, although equally influenced by Daoist techniques of immortality such as the abstention from cereals, seems to have been largely a Buddhist phenomenon. Paul Demiéville (1965: 169) has noted the paradoxes of such a Buddhist sacralization of the body, and of its absence in Confucianism and Daoism—two doctrines emphasizing the cult of the dead or the preservation of the body. As mentioned earlier, the ideology behind Chan mummies was apparently different from Buddhist or Daoist eschatologies. But perhaps the Maitreyan ideology is a rather superficial ideological addition: even in the

acre 1988. The legend of Kūkai's "entering *samādhi*" appears in textual form at the turn of the eleventh century. See Miyata 1970: 132–139 and Joseph M. Kitagawa, "Master and Savior," in his *On Understanding Japanese Religion* (Princeton: Princeton University Press, 1987), 197. One case of mummification that had apparently nothing to do with Maitreya was that of Yūtei Hōin (1591–1683), a Shingon monk who identified himself with the Buddha Yakushi and became the object of a healing cult at Kanshūji (Fukushima prefecture). Matsumoto Akira (1985: 147ff.) points out a number of other Japanese cases (among which he includes that of Zōga and his disciples) apparently related to the Pure Land doctrine. He also notes a change of attitude toward death: whereas the mummification of Yuihan, a monk of Kōyasan who believed in the Pure Land, was an object of repulsion, that of another monk of Kōyasan, Rinken, a few decades later, was welcomed by the disciples of the latter, who enshrined the mummy in the main hall, without concern with the pollution of death. According to Matsumoto, this change may be related to the reforms introduced into Shingon by Kakuban (1095–1143), a contemporary of Rinken.

[19] Here again are a few exceptions: that of the Sōtō Zen master Anzan Kichidō (d. 1677), who "entered samādhi" in a cave on Mt. Fuji (see his biography in *Nihon Tōjō rentōroku*, 1727); and that of a layman, Shinshū Gyōjun, who entered a Zen monastery after the death of his wife and practiced abstinence from cereals for many years before eventually entering into samādhi on the seventeenth anniversary of her death. His mummified body was discovered by villagers and became the object of a cult. (See Matsumoto Akira 1985: 190ff.) They were, however, practitioners of both Shūgendō and Zen, and they illustrate the syncretism between Zen and the cult of Mt. Fuji.

[20] See Needham 1974–1983: 5, 2:299–304 and illus. 1330–1334; S. C. Kung, "Some Mummies Found in Western China," *Journal of the Western China Border Research Society* 11 (1939): 105–111; Pokora 1985; Kosugi 1937.

case of Kūkai, it seems that the logic at work is as much one of immanence (healing through contact with a mummified mediator) as of eschatology.

The first recorded case of Buddhist self-mummification, that of a
monk of Dunhuang named Chan Daokai, who died in 395 after a seven-
year fast on Luofou shan, shows us that flesh-bodies were still interpreted
through Daoist metaphors such as the "cicada leaving an empty shell."[21]
They were apparently an object of repulsion and awe and were for that
reason abandoned in mountain caves, far from the human world. This
situation changed toward the beginning of the Tang. For instance, when
the *de facto* founder of the Tiantai school, Zhiyi, died in 597, his mummy
was enshrined in a memorial hall. The evolution of the funerary practices
also paved the way for this change. Thus the stūpa, which was until then
essentially a reliquary for the ashes, became the place where the body was
inhumed. Consequently, the attitude toward the corpse changed from
disgust to respect and devotion. After Śubhakarasiṃha's death in 735—
he was lying on his side like the Buddha—the mummification of his body
was interpreted in purely Buddhist terms: its incorruptibility was seen as
a result of its impregnation by morality, concentration, and wisdom.[22] As
noted earlier, this interpretation was usually given in India to the relics of
the Buddha.[23] Like the relics, the mummy (though dead) is perceived to
be in a very real sense *alive*; or, to put it differently, the mummified Chan
master is not simply dead, he *exists* as a dead master.[24]

The death of Sengqie in 710 marks a turning point: from that time
onward, mummies were usually lacquered. In most known cases, the lacquering took place relatively late, after the process of mummification had
followed its natural course. With the lacquering of the body, the attitude
toward the dead changed drastically. The corpse became more of a rep-

---

[21] See Michel Soymié, "Biographie de Chan Tao-k'ai," in *Mélanges publiés par l'Institut des Hautes Etudes Chinoises*, Vol. 1 (Paris: Presses Universitaires de France, 1957).

[22] See *Song gaoseng zhuan*, T. 50, 2061: 716a; Chou 1944–1945: 270.

[23] Therefore, one cannot oppose the Indian case, in which *śarīra* would be merely a "symbol" of the dead Buddha, and the Chinese case, in which relics would be "alive." As Doris
Croissant (n.d.) and Anna Seidel (1988) have argued, however, the *śarīra* cult in China also
has pre-Buddhist origins—for example, in the tradition, apparently nonattested in Chan,
that the Five Organs (*wuzang*) were the repositories of life. Originating in Daoism, this
tradition found its way into Buddhism with the representation of the five viscera in sculptures such as the Śākyamuni of Seiryōji (Shakadō) in Kyoto. Note also—although this
seems to be a different phenomenon—the role played in Buddhist hagiography by the
tongue of the deceased monk, which often remains intact after cremation and sometimes
continues to move (usually to recite the *Lotus Sūtra*). See Gernet 1959: 557.

[24] According to the tradition, when a banquet for a thousand monks was held for the
death anniversary of the Tiantai patriarch Zhiyi, an additional monk showed up. When
Zhiyi's mausoleum was subsequently opened, it was found empty. See *Fozu tongji* (T. 49,
2035: 601; Jan 1966b: 18). Other cases include mummies (or icons) who sweat, like the ash
icon of Wuxiang (K. Musang), or the mummy of Yuanlin at Lingxuan monastery (see *QTW*
510, 11: 6573b).

resentation and somewhat lost its gruesome character as a corpse. Thus it gradually "surfaced," being brought from under the stūpa to its upper part and eventually, in many cases, to a special hall. (See Kosugi 1937; Demiéville 1965.) The portrait of the dead was supplemented by the dead man himself, who thus became his own effigy, an auto-referential sign. The mummy however, did not supersede the portrait; on the contrary, the presence of the dead seems reinforced by its dissemination into various "substitute bodies." This "iconization," which has led Kosugi Kazuo to speak of "flesh-body icons," reached its extreme manifestation in the subsequent development of what he called "ash icons," representations of the dead made by mixing earth and ashes to model realistic statues of the deceased. This new method followed that of the custom of cremation.[25] In this context a significant, if somewhat paradoxical, case is that of the Korean monk (Wuxiang Musang, d. 762). The notice of the *Song gaoseng zhuan* 19, describing the wonders associated with a temple bell, records Wuxiang's postmortem iconization: "*Śarīra* mixed with earth were modeled on his appearance [*xiang*] and made into his true form; on that day, all the faces sweat." It seems therefore that several statues were made with the ashes. It is somewhat ironic that a monk called Wuxiang ("formless")[26] would become the model for a representation (*xiang*).

Another significant case is that of Sengqie's disciple Mucha, who apparently hoped to follow his master's example. Having failed to mummify correctly, he was eventually incinerated. A memorial submitted in 884 to the throne by Liu Rang, governor of Sizhou, however, reported that while Mucha's stūpa was being repaired, 800 grains of relics were found. These *śarīra* were presented to the Throne and an edict ordered that a representation of Mucha be made with them. This icon was called the "True Image" (*Fozu tongji*, T. 49, 2035: 389c). The method adopted in his case allowed his recuperation as an eventually powerful object of worship and his being put next to his lacquered master.[27]

This method was probably adopted to meet the religious needs of the people and the sectarian interests of the monks, and to palliate the scarcity of "natural" mummies. These "ash icons" appear toward the mid-eighth century, when lacquered mummies had already become popular.[28] They mark the last stage of the development of the mummification process in China, itself a result of relic worship and of technical developments such

---

[25] Hertz (1960: 125 n. 96) signals similar examples of "ash icons" among the Quichue.

[26] The notice, in a customary way, calls him simply Xiang—turning the paradox into a pun.

[27] See also the biography of Shucao in *Song gaoseng zhuan*, T. 50, 2061: 857b.

[28] The *Shenseng zhuan* tells us, for instance, that after the death of Xianhua, a clay image was made with his ashes, and those who looked at it obtained *śarīra* (T. 50, 2064: 1013c).

as the dried lacquer in the artistic domain. (See Kosugi 1937: 116–119; also Demiéville 1965; Croissant 1986.) Thus mummies became a special kind of icon: as the mortuary associations receded to the background, mummies proceeded from the stūpa to the memorial halls—or rather the *mausoleums*.

Once it had become an icon, the mummy competed with, and could eventually be replaced by, other icons. Whereas several types of "representation" have vied with each other in the Chinese "image halls" (*ying-tang*), portraits seem to have won out in Japanese monasteries.[29] Just as the mummy, once lacquered, acquired some of the characteristics of the icon, however, the icon or statue acquired some of the characteristics of the mummy. The iconization of the mummy was also a "mummification" of the icon. This "iconization" process may explain why there are practically no mummies in Japanese Zen. As mentioned above, all the mummies of Buddhist monks discovered in Japan belong to the Shūgendō tradition and are a ritualistic reenactment of Kūkai's *sokushin jōbutsu* ("Becoming a Buddha in this very body"), itself based on Maitreyan eschatology and the legend of Mahākāśyapa. As noted earlier, the account of Kūkai's entering into samādhi on Kōyasan is actually a legend that took its final form in the eleventh century. Toward the same time, however, the Tendai monk and "trickster" Zōga (917–1003) did achieve self-mummification at Tōnomine (in Yamato, present Nara prefecture), thereby becoming the first Japanese *sokushinbutsu*.[30] Another interesting, if somewhat dubious, case is that of Yōsai, who is said to have "entered into samādhi" (*nyūjō*)—that is, become a *sokushinbutsu*—at Kenninji. Behind the mausoleum in which his body was supposedly preserved is also an "animate icon" of him, which was installed (*anza*) and had his eyes "pointed" (*tengen*) in 1744—together with a statue of the Shōgun Yoriie—by Ungai Tōjiku (1630–1730), on the occasion of the five-hundredth anniversary of Yōsai's death.[31]

BONES OF CONTENTION

After considering the "semantic" level of the Chan cult of mummies, we now turn to the "pragmatic" level—in other words, the use of mummies

[29] A few "ash icons" are recorded—for instance, those of Daidō Juen of Jijūji (Yamaguchi prefecture) or Zuigan of Ankokuji (Gifu prefecture). Nevertheless, the custom of inserting ashes or relics (among other things) in a cavity made in wooden statues prevailed. See "Chinsō to Zenshū chōkoku," in Kawakami, Yoshikawa, and Furuoka 1979: 171.

[30] Zōga's presence may have been a motivation for the coming to Tōnomine, two centuries later, of the members of the Darumashū that were to become Dōgen's disciples. The *Genkō shakusho* indicates that the method used in Zōga's mummification—placing the body in an earthenware urn and exhuming it after three years—had been introduced from China. See DNBZ 62, 470: 122a.

[31] See Itō Tōshi, "Kenninji annaiki," *Zen bunka* 32 (1964): 55.

and relics as commodities in the sectarian context, what we could call the "politics of mummification." What factors contributed to such an evolution? Was relic worship a concession to popular superstitions, as scholars, following in the wake of Confucianists such as Han Yu, have tended to believe? Although there might be some element of truth in this view, it is far from sufficient to explain the change described above. As in the Western case of relic worship analyzed by Peter Brown (1981), it seems that the Chinese interest in flesh-bodies was primarily a concern of monks and expressed a highly structured awareness of death.

Behind these monastic concerns, we can detect intense sectarian stakes. Relics were from the outset "bones of contention," as the legends related to the deaths of the Buddha and of his disciple and cousin Ānanda amply show. It is not by a mere coincidence that most of the mummies recorded in the Chan tradition happen to be the "founders" of new schools. In all likelihood, the mummies of these "patriarchs" were used as a device by their successors (and owners) to attract the devotion of believers. One may in some cases also wonder to what extent these attempts at self-mummification were free decisions of the individual or reflected the pressure and expectations of the community. In other words, were they not ritual suicides, and at times more or less consenting sacrifices, as in the Daoist calls to immortality analyzed in the case of Mao shan by Strickmann (1979: 136) or in some of the *sokushinbutsu* of the later Shūgendō tradition? The question must remain open. But clearly the self-mummified Chan master, however independent and undisputed he may have been in his lifetime, became after his death a collective property, a disputed commodity.

These fights over a corpse, fights whose history is at least as long as that of Buddhism, can be seen behind stories such as that of the deceased Sengqie, whose posthumous refusal to be enshrined in the capital—far from his community in Sizhou—was manifested in his corpse's stench. Apparently, Sizhou monks were reluctant to deprive themselves of this inexhaustible source of symbolic (and magical) gain, and they eventually succeeded in convincing the emperor of their rights over Sengqie's mummy. The same pattern emerges in the story of Wuliao (787–869), a Chan master from Quanzhou (Fujian). The *Fozu tongji*'s entry for the year 876 records that "twenty years [*sic*] after its completion, [Wuliao's stūpa] . . . fell down owing to a flood in a hill stream. His disciples then saw that the corpse of the master had suffered no physical deterioration. When the Prince of the Min State heard this news, he sent a messenger and took the corpse to his house to worship. Immediately some bad smell came out from that corpse. After the prince had offered some incense and prayed, and it had been reenshrined at the original place at Guiyang, a fragrant smell came out soon after its restoration. So all the people of that city went out and paid homage to the stūpa." The *Fozu tongji* also mentions that Wuliao's disciple Huizhong (817–882) was buried near his stūpa and that "both stūpas are worshiped by the scholars and common people just as Sengqie is" (T. 49, 2035: 389a–b).

Huineng's two bodies

The case of Huineng is particularly significant in this context. The Caoxi community possessed a wealth of relics of the sixth patriarch: "contact relics" such as the robe and the bowl, his "waist-hanging stone" and his staff, but above all the relic *par excellence*, Huineng himself—"in the flesh." The "first patriarch" Bodhidharma had unfortunately, for his successors, achieved "deliverance from the corpse," leaving an empty grave behind him: apparently, the "single sandal" allegedly found in his grave never became an object of worship. Worse, the legend had located his grave not on Song shan—a stronghold of Northern Chan where his nine-year wall-contemplation was said to have taken place—but on a nearby mountain, Xiong'er shan in Henan. The creation *ex nihilo* on Song shan of sacred vestiges such as Bodhidharma's cave or his "shadow stone" were makeshift epiphanies that could not entirely replace *śarīra*, much less an actual flesh-body. Song shan could not compete with Caoxi on that ground, and this may be one of the factors that contributed to the decline of Northern Chan. The canonization of the *Platform Sūtra*, the only "sūtra" not attributed to the traditional Buddha, reflects the confidence of Southern Chan monks that the sixth patriarch, since he had left a "flesh-body," was actually a Buddha in his own right. Thereafter, there developed a tendency to consider Chan patriarchs as "old Buddhas"—or even abbots of Chan/Zen monasteries as living Buddhas.

While the *Platform Sūtra* simply says that Huineng "died on the third day of the eighth month [of 713], and in the eleventh month the 'seat of his spirit' (*shenzuo*) was received and interred on Mount Caoxi," the *Jingde chuandeng lu*, written almost three centuries after the event (1004), makes an allusion to what seems to have been a controversy over Huineng's body:

> At this time at both Shaozhou [where he lived] and Xinzhou [where he died] sacred pagodas were erected and none of the monks or laymen could decide [where the body was to be enshrined]. The prefects of each county burned incense together and offered an invocation: "Wherever the smoke from the incense leads will be the place to which the Master wishes to return." The smoke from the incense burner rose and moved straight in the direction of Caoxi. On the thirteenth day of the eleventh month, the Master's body was en-

shrined in its pagoda. He was seventy-six years old. Wei Qu, the prefect of Caoxi, wrote the text for his monument. (See Yampolsky 1967: 86.)

In 1477, Huineng's body was transferred from this "precious stūpa" (*baota*) to the "Sixth Patriarch's Hall" for better preservation. According to Hanshan's *Caoxi zongxing lu* (quoted in Tokiwa 1972: 79), this was the result of a dream that the Governor of the Commandery had, and in which Huineng appeared and asked for his relocation. Apparently, there were many other *translationes* of Huineng's mummy in the course of its long history: one of them was witnessed by the Jesuit Longobardo, who describes how Huineng's "flesh-body" was brought to Shaozhou in order to put an end to a long drought that was plaguing the city: "So [the inhabitants] gave up hope in the city gods, and for the occasion they brought in a celebrated monster from the country. Its name was *Locu* [Luzu]. They paraded it about, bowing before it and made offerings to it, but like its counterparts it remained deaf to their pleading. It was this occasion that gave rise to the saying, 'Locu is growing old.' " The importance of Huineng's mummy in popular religion is attested by the *Song gaoseng zhuan* (988), according to which, during the Five Dynasties (907–960), the flesh-body of the sixth patriarch was always carried to the city (Shaozhou or Canton) at the time of the *shangyuan* festival (the fifteenth day of the first lunar month) for the prosperity of the people (*T.* 50, 2061: 755c).

Huineng's mummy was apparently threatened several times. There is first the well-known story, spread—if not invented—by Shenhui, that a Northern Chan master paid someone to sever the head of the sixth patriarch, and that this attempt failed. Another attempt was reportedly made in 722 by a Korean. According to the Chinese tradition, it also failed. The *Jingde chuandeng lu* (1004) records what seems to be an *ex post facto* "prophecy" (assuming that the attempts at stealing Huineng's head are "facts"): "His disciples, recalling the Master's prediction that someone would take his head, put an iron band and a lacquered cloth about his neck to protect it. Inside the pagoda was placed the 'robe of faith' handed down by Bodhidharma, the robe and bowl presented by Emperor Zhongzong, the figure of the Master modeled by Fangbian, and various Buddhist implements. The pagoda attendant was placed in charge of these."[32]

According to the Korean tradition, however, the attempt was successful and Huineng's head (Ch. *dingxiang*, K. *chŏngsang*, J. *chinsō*) was taken

[32] See Yampolsky 1967: 86. According to the *Jingde chuandeng lu*, Huineng's reliquary was destroyed by fire during a war at the beginning of the *kaibao* period (968–975), but his body "was protected by the monk in charge of the pagoda and suffered no injury whatsoever" (ibid.: 87).

to Korea, where it is today enshrined in a mausoleum at Ssanggye-sa (on Chiri-san), a monastery tracing its lineage to Mazu Daoyi through the Sŏn master Hyeso (a.k.a. Dynastic Master Chingam, 773–850).[33] We are told that a disciple of Ŭisang named Sampŏp, having read in the *Platform Sūtra* Huineng's prediction that someone would steal his head, concluded that this prediction was about him and decided to steal the head for the glory of Korean Buddhism. He received a large amount of money from a Buddhist nun named Pŏpchŏng, allegedly the wife of the famous general Kim Yusin, embarked for the Tang on a merchant boat, and landed eventually at the Kaiyuan monastery in Hongzhou. There he became a friend with Kim Taebi, and both men hired Zhang Jingman to steal Huineng's head. The head was successfully taken to Yŏngmyo-sa in Korea, the residence of the nun Pŏpchŏng. Then a monk (Huineng) appeared in a dream to Sampŏp and expressed in a poem his desire to be enshrined on Chiri-san. Sampŏp went therefore to Chiri-san with Kim Taebi and built a mausoleum for Huineng and a hermitage for himself, in which he practiced for eighteen years, reciting the *Platform Sūtra*, until his death. Sampŏp's "whole body" was inhumed by his disciples at Un'om-sa. Nukariya Kaiten (1930), of course, denies all credibility to this account, which, according to Chŏn Posam, reflects the intense faith of the Korean Buddhists toward the sixth patriarch and the *Platform Sūtra*.[34] Whatever we make of this Korean claim, it is clear that the attempt to steal Huineng's head was not intended to destroy the mummy. It aimed merely at stealing its power, a power often believed to reside in the head (or in the bones and viscera). To some extent it succeeded: various miracles—such as the emission of light—were said to have taken place at Huineng's Korean mausoleum, so that no one ever dared to open it. (See Yi 1955: 1:32.) The relic of Ssanggye-sa has been compared to that of the head of the Buddha on Wutai shan, and in 1980, a delegation of Taiwanese Buddhists made a pilgrimage there. There are famous Western parallels to this case, such as the heads of John the Baptist, St. Benedict, or St. Martin.[35]

[33] See *Sŏnjong yukcho Hyenŭng taesa chŏnsang tongnae yŏn'gi*; and *Ssanggye-sa yŏksa* (manuscript, Komazawa University Collection); Chŏn 1989; Yi 1955: 1:94, 2:139; Nukariya 1930: 60; and Chung 1987.

[34] Another Korean master, Toŭi (d. 825), came to China in 784. He visited Caoxi and, coming to the "Hall of the Patriarch" (i.e., Huineng's mausoleum), opened its door, prostrated himself three times, and left. See Yanagida 1978: 29.

[35] See Saintyves 1987; Geary 1978. The resemblance between Buddhism and Christianity was already pointed out one century ago by the German anthropologist Adolf Bastian in his discussion concerning the legends around the death of Ānanda: "We must either admit that some of our circumspect forefathers were imposed upon, or that St. John the Baptist had more heads than that of which he was so cruelly deprived, as well as several of their favorite Saints having each kindly afforded them with two or three skeletons of their precious bodies, circumstances that frequently occurred because, says Father John Ferand of Anecy: 'God was pleased so to multiply and reproduce them, for the devotion of the faithful.' " See Bastian (quoting Brody) 1871: 134. The resemblance goes even further in the Chinese context:

Dissemination of charisma and sectarianism

But Huineng left other coveted relics, namely his bowl and robe, and, perhaps as important, a text: the *Platform Sūtra*. Their importance as regalia can be seen from the various attempts, by the emperor or by other Chan schools, to acquire them. As in the medieval West, "translations" of relics paved the way for *furta sacra*—pious or not so pious thefts. (See Geary 1978.) The contest for the other relics of the sixth patriarch, and their role in dynastic legitimation, is reflected in the stories according to which, in 760, the emperor Suzong sent an envoy to Caoxi asking that Huineng's robe and bowl be enshrined in the imperial palace;[36] then, in 765, Huineng appeared in a dream to the emperor Daizong asking for the return of his robe and bowl to his monastery. In response to this dream, the emperor ordered the Grand General of Defense Liu Chongjing to return the robe to Caoxi, saying: "I regard it as a [dynastic] treasure. Let it be installed properly at the head temple, and be strictly guarded by special priests, who have been recipients of the main tenets of the teaching. Great care must be taken so that it is not lost."[37]

Another story, spread by the Baotang school in Sichuan, links dynastic and sectarian legitimacy. It claims that Empress Wu, after requesting Huineng to send the robe to court so that she might worship it, handed it down to another disciple of Hongren named Zhishen (609–702), the putative ancestor of the Baotang school. In compensation, Wu allegedly sent Huineng another robe and a gift of five hundred bolts of silk. According to the *Lidai fabao ji*, the robe was thereafter transmitted from Zhishen to Wuzhu (d. 774), the *de facto* founder of the Baotang school. This claim might have been made to counterbalance not only the claims of Huineng's community in Caoxi but also those of another Chan community

Jesuit missionaries sometimes became mummies. Such are the cases of Father Feliciano da Silva (d. 1617), whose body was found intact and emitting a suave fragrance, and of Father Martino Martini, whose body was found intact in 1679, eighteen years after his death, but returned to dust when worshiped as an "idol." See Pfister 1932–1934: 1:84 and 259; quoted in Gernet 1982: 125. Contrary to Christians, however, Buddhists apparently avoided resorting to miracles to multiply flesh-bodies—even to settle disputes over the possession of a saint's body. On the other hand, as noted earlier, *śarīra* were easily multiplied by "emanation," a process somewhat similar to the hagiographical techniques leading to the production of "composite saints."

[36] The link between various relics or Buddhist regalia and imperial legitimation is well illustrated by the imperial orders to bring to the court the mummy of Baozhi, a sandalwood image of the Buddha, the Five Hundred Arhats of Lushan, and Aśoka's reliquary. See Soper 1948: 25, 41.

[37] See Yampolsky 1967: 87. In Japan, the impressive statues of fifteen generations of Ashikaga shōguns in Musō Soseki's mausoleum at Tōjiin (Kyoto) attest to this linkage of spiritual and military power, beyond death, through the intermediary of "animated" sculptures. Of course, as in the better known cases of Kūkai, Hōnen, and Shinran, the efficient presence of Musō's *śarīra* was also believed to bring personal salvation to the dead disciples and became the motivation for a "burial ad sanctos." See also Schopen 1987.

of Sichuan, that of Wuzhu's alleged master, the Korean monk Wuxiang (Musang). The latter branch could indeed boast of possessing several important relics, since they had made "ash icons" in the perfect resemblance (*xiang*) of Wuxiang by mixing his ashes with clay. Despite those assets, the Baotang school did not succeed in supplanting Caoxi. As the *Jingde chuandeng lu* puts it: "Although in later years people did steal the robe, they did not get far with it, and it was always retrieved. This happened several times."[38] According to Shenhui, "The robe and the Dharma are transmitted by one another and there is no other transmission." (See Gernet 1949: 110.) Accordingly, the robe is not just a symbol: like Huineng's other relics, including the *Platform Sūtra*, it is the *embodiment* of the Chan Dharma. But Shenhui's emphasis on the transmission of the robe as the *only* valid one reveals the concurrence of these various relics and embodiments.[39] Often, however, these various "embodiments" (relics, robe, text, portrait, verse) reinforce each other in an "orgy" of presence and legitimacy.

The pattern observed in Huineng's case repeated itself in that of his distant follower Hanshan Deqing (1546–1623). As soon as Hanshan died, the monks of Nanhua monastery placed his body in a coffin (*gan*) and built a mausoleum. One of his disciples, however, had a stūpa erected at Lu shan and succeeded in 625 to have the body removed there. It took almost twenty years for the monks of Nanhua monastery to convince the authorities to return the body to Caoxi, on which occasion the mummy emerged from its coffin. According to the official responsible for the translation, Liu Qixiang, the coffin doubled in weight when approaching from Caoxi, which led him to suspect that Hanshan wanted to reappear in the form of a "flesh-body" (Hsu 1979: 100). The Hanshan Hall, where the mummy was enshrined, afterward became a flourishing pilgrimage center. Thus Hanshan's mummification allowed him to acquire the status of Chan patriarch that his unorthodox filiation might have otherwise prevented. Without his mummy, the Caoxi school could not have revived as it did, nor would the Nanhua monastery have become a thriving "prayer temple" (*daochang*)—actually one of the most famous cultic centers in Qing China.

[38] See Yampolsky 1967: 87. According to the *Lidai fabao ji*, Huineng said to his disciples: "Because of this robe, I have almost lost my life many times. The robe was stolen three times from the great master [Dao]xin, three times from the great master [Hong]ren, and six times from me" (T. 51, 2075: 182c). Concerning the transmission of the robe and its function as a dynastic talisman, see Seidel 1983a, and "Den'e," in *Hōbōgirin*, Vol. 7 (forthcoming).

[39] In *Shōbōgenzō Den'e*, Dōgen writes: "As to relics, *cakravartin* [kings] possess them, lions possess them, men, *pratyeka*-buddha, etc., possess them. But they have no robe [Sk. *kaṣāya*]; only the Buddhas have one. Imbeciles worship *śarīra* but ignore the *kaṣāya*, and few are those who know that one must preserve the *kaṣāya*" (T. 82, 2582: 56c). See also *Kesa kudoku* ("The Merits of a *kaṣāya*"): "A *Kaṣāya* should be regarded as if it were one's master or the Buddha's *stūpa*" (ibid.: 54a; Yokoi 1976: 102).

Relics were not only a way for a community to attract donations in times of prosperity; they were also a way for the community to defend itself against spiritual or physical aggression in times of adversity. Thus, in 1047, when the rebel Tang He, passing nearby the monastery, attempted to profane the grave of Yunmen, the body of the latter appeared in space. Then Tang He, having suddenly realized his error, was convinced to surrender by the head monk of the monastery. This manifestation of Yunmen's power was the reason he was granted the title "Great Master Juehua" in 1093.[40] Doré (1914–1938: 7:257) records that in 1276, under the rule of Kubilai Khan, soldiers opened Huineng's mummy with a sword. When they saw that the heart and the liver were perfectly preserved, however, they dared no longer profane his remains. Another interesting case is that of Jingshan Faqin (714–792), a patriarch of the Niutou school and a teacher of the emperor. After his death, Faqin was buried under a stūpa. In 901, when a rebellion broke out and Jingshan was occupied, the stūpa was excavated and the rebels found Faqin's body placed inside two earthenware jars. Long hair covered his face. The rebels ran away at the sight of this frightful revenant, and the mummy was reenshrined under instruction of the prince of the Wuyue kingdom. According to the *Song gaoseng zhuan*, "A stūpa was erected over his 'integral body' at the Longxing Jingyuan. . . . In this stūpa one can nowadays see his image, it looks as if alive" (T. 50, 2061: 765a). These stories look strikingly similar to those of *furta sacra* and *translationes* of relics in the Christian West. (See Geary 1978.) Yet there is no literary tradition of "sacred thefts" on the grand scale in Chan/Zen.

Perhaps the most recent case of *furtum sacrum* is that of the alleged mummy of Shitou Xiqian (700–790), in whom the tradition sees a second-generation successor to Huineng and the ancestor of the Caodong lineage.[41] It was brought to Meiji Japan at the time of the Chinese revolution (1911) by a Japanese dentist and Zen/Shūgendō adept named Yamazaki Takeshi. Yamazaki had found the mummy in a monastery in Hunan and rescued it from a fire that devastated the monastery. Despite the monks' protests, he was eventually able to smuggle it to Japan in a Mitsui ship. After Yamazaki's death, the mummy was forgotten in a trunk until rediscovered by Matsumoto Akira in 1960. After examination by a group of experts, it was handed over in 1975 to Sōjiji (in Yokohama), one of the two headquarters of the Sōtō tradition, where it still is today.[42]

[40] See *Yunmen shan zhi*, ed. Chen Xuelu, in *Zhongguo fosi shizhi huikan*, Vol. 6 (Taibei: Mingwen shuju, 1980), 22.

[41] Xiqian's mummy is mentioned neither in the *Song gaoseng zhuan* (T. 50, 2061: 764a) nor in any other source.

[42] See Matsumoto Akira 1985: 202–207. Although the Sōjiji authorities are somewhat reluctant to acknowledge its presence, I was able to see the mummy in 1988. The body was lacquered, and the cloth on which the lacquer was applied remains visible. The preservation was not good: the face has been blackened by fire and shows various wounds. The limbs, at

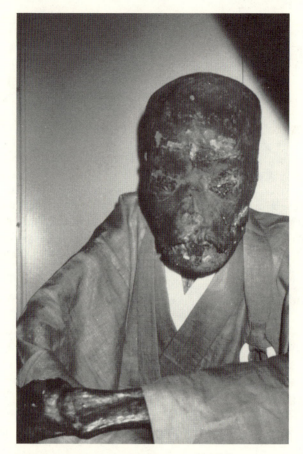

Figure 2. Mummy of Shitou Xiqian. Sōjiji,
Yokohama.

FROM all these examples, we may conclude that the cult of relics and
mummies, if it served well the popularization of Chan and Zen, also implied a "humanization" or "demythologization" that often went against
certain local beliefs in *cosmic* or *divine* mediators such as dragon kings,
stellar deities, or mountain gods. Mediators became idealized men, patriarchs whose power was manifested in the relics. Characterized by a substitution of a human figure for a place (Dupront 1987: 98), that is, the
replacement of mythical bonds by human relationships, this evolution

_____

one time detached from the body, had to be tied up to the trunk. For a comparison with
other Japanese mummies, see Ogata Mamoru, "Waga kuni sokushinbutsu seiritsu ni kan-
suru shomondai," *Niigata daigaku igaku gakushikai kaihō* 15 (1962): 16–30 and illus. 14–15.

established a new "geography of the sacred," a new network of pilgrimage that superseded or simply doubled the old one, giving it new meaning by anchoring it in new places—such as stūpas or "Image Halls." Moreover, as in the Christian context (see Peter Brown 1981: 88–89), relics were mobile; even mummies could travel at times. This mobility was both geographical and social, permitting a "transfer of sacredness," not only from one place to another, but also from the local community founded by the patriarch to the various groups that gained control over his relics. As with the "dividing of incense" in China (see Sangren 1987), the "dividing of *śarīra*" ensured the spreading of new cultic centers.

Beyond narrow sectarian or political concerns, characterized by the attempt to bring the accessibility of the sacred in one place and for *one group* (Peter Brown 1981: 86), these examples may reflect a larger societal change, a change in the relations of Chinese people to death. It is difficult at this stage to document this change, but recent work by Teiser and others seems to confirm that the Tang/Song transition was marked by a significant evolution in funerary practices and representations of the other world. It is possible that, in China as in the West, "an intellectual breakthrough of the first order lies behind what is too often presented as a belated concession to the mindless weight of 'popular belief' " (Peter Brown 1981: 78). At any rate, the Chan/Zen tradition remained haunted by the presence of the dead, a presence that it chose to repress. In this sense, the case of Shitou's mummy at Sōjiji is paradigmatic: worshiped, yet hidden from the public, it reflects the ambivalence of Chan/Zen toward its own "metaphysics of presence." Indeed, the very attempt to animate, breathe life into relics and icons might be seen as a metaphor for the empowerment with meaning of the tradition itself (as Dharma *śarīra*). But perhaps the same nagging doubt remained in some minds that both physical and doctrinal *tradita* might be after all nothing but dry bones and dead ashes.

ICONS AND CHINSŌ

> In the "tasteless Void" he has sketched his countenance,/ Touching the surface of Emptiness he had transmitted his image.
> —Huiyuan, *Foying ming*

The Zen tradition is well known for the stern "realism" of its portraits (J. *chinsō* or *chinzō*).[43] Art historians have often marveled in particular at

---

[43] The term *chinsō* (var. *chinzō*) originally referred to the *uṣṇīṣa* or protuberance on the top

the "true to life" character of Zen portrait sculpture. (See Mōri 1977: 88.) Even to the casual observer, these "representations" of the dead master, with their inlaid eyes glittering in the dark, produce an eerie feeling because, as does a mummy, they look "as if alive." Actually, these sculptures are not portraits in the Western sense; rather, like their aniconic counterpart, the relics, they constitute *substitute bodies*. They are not merely "realistic," they are *real*, pointing to no reality beyond themselves.[44] At first glance, the metaphoric logic of Western representation, in which one thing stands for another, seemed apt to describe the two-tiered structure of Buddhist cosmology. As Huiyuan, speaking of the Buddha, said, "There [in *nirvāṇa*] is his [real] body, here on earth is his shadow."[45] This metaphorical logic, however, was replaced in ritual practice by the logic of metonymy and synecdoche, in which the shadow or trace becomes as real as the body, *is* this very body. Thus icons came to be perceived, no longer as a "metamorphosis body" (*nirmāṇakāya*) "standing (or sitting) for" the true "Dharma-body" (*Dharmakāya*), but as the Dharma-body itself. Chan discourse, however, fluctuated between metaphor and metonymy, transcendence and immanence, endlessly replaying the *fort/da* game of absence and presence.

Nevertheless, Buddhist icons are imbued with the powers of the dead, animated or empowered by them. This empowering, resulting from a ceremonial "opening of the eyes" (Ch. *kaiyan* J. *Kaigen*) of the statue,[46] is often sup-

---

of the head, one of the thirty-two marks of a Buddha. See Hubert Durt, s.v. "Chōsō," *Hōbōgirin*, Vol. 5: 421–430. This *uṣṇīṣa* was said to be invisible. See Durt, "Note sur l'origine de l'*Anavalokitamūrdhatā*," *IBK* 16, 1 (1967): 450–443. There is at least one case, that of the Korean story discussed above concerning Huineng's head, in which the term refers to a corporeal relic. It is not clear how and when it came to designate portraits of Chan/Zen masters. Japanese art historians distinguish five types of Zen *chinsō*: (1) *kyokuroku*—the most common: a portrait of the master sitting cross-legged on a chair, holding a flywhisk (J. *hossu*) or bamboo staff (*shippei*), or with his hands forming the meditation *mudrā*; (2) *han-shinzō*, a bust of the master; (3) *ensōzō*, a portrait enclosed in a circle; (4) *kinhinzō*, a portrait of the master standing; and (5) *dōshaku jinbutsu gafu*, a portrait of the master in a natural setting or with animals. See Kawakami, Yoshikawa, and Furuoka 1979: 166–167. On Zen *chinsō*, see *Dictionnaire historique du Japon*, s.v. "Chinzō ou Chinsō," Vol. 3 (1974), 59–60; Mochizuki 1958–1963: 4: 3632–3633; Iijima Isamu, "Chinsō ni tsuite," *Museum* 80 (1957): 17–20.

[44] A similar "point" is made for Chinese portrait paintings by Spiro 1988: 5–14. According to Spiro, the famous statement by the fourth-century painter Gu Kaizhi on dotting the eyes of a portrait ("What conveys the spirit and conveys the likeness lies precisely in these dots") must be understood in the context of ritual empowerment (ibid.: 1).

[45] See Walter Liebenthal, "Shih Hui-yüan's Buddhism as set forth in his Writings," *JAOS* 70 (1950): 258.

[46] On the "opening of the eyes," see Gombrich 1966: 23–27; Hans Ruelius, "Netrapratiṣ-ṭhāpana—eine singhalesische Zeremonie zur Weihe von Kultbildern," in Heinz Bechert, ed., *Buddhism in Ceylon and Studies on Religious Syncretism in Buddhist Countries* (Göttingen: Van-denhoeck and Ruprecht, 1978), 304–334; Gombrich, "The Buddha's Eye, the Evil Eye and Dr. Ruelius," in Bechert, ibid.: 335–338. The rite was already known in early Buddhism (*Mahāvaṃsa*, *Visuddimagga*) and even in Brahmanism (see Renou and Filliozat 1985: 1:573). It appears in Buddhist esoteric texts translated in Chinese during the Tang (see T. 21, 1227:

plemented by the actual presence of relics inside it.[47] When criticized for burning a Buddha statue, the paradigmatic Chan iconoclast Danxia Tian- ran (739–824) replied that he was merely looking for relics, and that, if there were none, the statue was no more than a piece of wood. (See *Song gaoseng zhuan*, T. 50, 2061: 773b.) Although not entirely to the point, his retort attests to the importance of *śarīra* in Chan iconology and reveals the metonymic logic at work. In China, the statue of the Chan master Hong- bian (d. 862) already contained *śarīra* (Mōri 1977: 8). One of the first Jap- anese *chinsō* (1275), that of Muhon (a.k.a. Shinchi) Kakushin (d. 1298), contained several relics (ibid.: 26, 88). Such is also the case with Dōgen's statue enshrined at Kōshōji in Uji (on the southern outskirts of Kyōto).[48] Sometimes the relics were not postmortem *śarīra* but relics left by the master while alive. A well-known case is that of the *chinsō* of Ikkyū Sōjun (1394–1481), on the head of which real hair—belonging probably to Ikkyū himself—was implanted.[49]

Mummies were only one modality—if the most impressive one—of the lingering presence of the dead patriarchs. Even the so-called *nirvāṇa*

148c), and its performance is recorded in Japan for the *kaigen* ceremony of the Great Buddha of Tōdaiji, performed by the Indian monk Bodhisena in 753. No mention of it, however, is found in earlier Chinese documents. Gombrich also describes the parallel rite of "closing the eyes" of a statue to make it temporarily powerless. According to a later *kirigami* of the Sōtō tradition, the parallelism is such that one cannot "dispatch" the spirit of a statue if one does not know by which method it was empowered at the time of the *kaigen* ceremony. Sugimoto further describes two types of "eyes opening": "abstract" or "according to the principle" (*ri kaigen*) and concrete or "according to the phenomena" (*ji tengen*). The term *kaigen* is actually reserved for the former, while the latter is called, properly speaking, "pointing the eyes" (*tengen*). Whereas the "concrete" opening resembles the ritual described by Gombrich and others, the "abstract" opening is performed through the use of mantra and mudrā. In the "concrete" pointing, the priest projects his own power (*jiriki*), that is, the Buddha in himself, into the icon while pointing the eyes; whereas in the "abstract" opening, he summons another power (*tariki*), that of the cosmic Buddha, into the icon. (See Sugi- moto 1982: 92.) Consequently, when "closing the eyes" of the icon, the priest will dispatch the spirit within the icon back to its original abode, that is, the metaphysical realm in the "abstract" ritual, or his own body in the "concrete" ritual. The latter is the most common in Sōtō Zen, while the former is used primarily in Shingon. Similar rituals are performed for mortuary tablets (*ihai*, *sotoba*). For more details on the esoteric rites of empowerment, see Strickmann 1989.

[47] On the "live icon," the belief in the coming to life of statues, see Delahaye 1983; Frank 1986; Strickmann 1989. As noted earlier, the notion of the statue as a substitute or double is reminiscent of the Greek *colossos*, on which see Vernant's, "La catégorie psychologique du double," in Vernant 1965: 2:65–78. See also Dupont 1989; Kantorowicz 1957; Giesey 1987. For Western examples (*exempla*), see Saintyves 1987: 935–945 ("Les images qui ouvrent et ferment les yeux"). On the Chinese image as a double, see Spiro 1988; and Miranda Shaw, "Chinese Landscape Painting," *Journal of the History of Ideas* 49, 1 (1988): 197–204.

[48] Dōgen's face is very different from the usual portraits, and the Kōshōji monks claim that since the statue was made by one of Dōgen's disciples, it is probably the truest likeness. It is worshiped and offered food daily.

[49] See Mōri Hisashi: "The thought process involved in such a practice corresponds exactly to that involved when inserting the possessions or actual remains of the subject into hollow portrait statues" (Mōri 1977: 44).

Figure 3. Chinsō of Musō Kokushi.

without remainder turned out to leave a remainder after all. Ancestral tablets and icons were functionally equivalent to the "flesh-body" and eventually provided convenient substitutes.[50] Portraits thus became the locus and proof of immortality, if only because, like Christian icons, they were animate (and sometimes literally animated). They functioned according to the metonymic/synecdochical logic of the *pars pro toto*, a logic manifested in the case of statues by the presence or "live" relics within them. As noted earlier, in China and Japan statues and portraits were be-

---

[50] See Kobayashi Taichirō, "Kōso sūhai to shōzō no geijutsu," *Bukkyō geijutsu* 23 (1954): 3–36. The portraits (*chinsō* or *shin*) of Chan/Zen were functionally similar to the Chinese mortuary portraits (*dashou*) and other "seats of the spirit" (*shenzuo*) described by Groot 1982: 1:113–114. On the "pointing" of the funerary tablet, see 214–217.

lieved to be alive, once the rite of "opening the eyes" was performed.[51] Many cases have been recorded of statues that sweat, cried, moved, or walked. (See Delahaye 1983.) A similar rite of "pointing" empowered the ancestral tablets (J. *ihai*) or the stelae of deceased masters, which also occupy a prominent place in Zen temples. According to the epitaph of the Northern Chan master Faru (d. 689), "[As in the case of] the Śākya[muni] image of King Udayana,[52] the activities of generations of masters are engraved on a Buddha tablet." (See Yanagida 1967: 489.) Significantly, Matsuura (1976: 460–500) concludes his study of Zen iconography with a chapter on "human substitutes" (*daijinbutsu*) that includes hierophanic artifacts such as the so-called three tablets (*sanpai*), the *chinsō*, the *shin* (an effigy of the dead abbot used at his funerals), the *ihai*, and the *muhōtō* ("seamless stūpa"). Reminiscent of the Greek *colossoi* analyzed by Vernant,[53] all these can, in a certain sense, be seen as "substitute bodies" or "doubles." As Strickmann (1989) points out, the consecration of an icon is a birth; but simultaneously, by its "suspended animation" in *samādhi*, it is the creation of the living dead—in other words a mummy. In this way, death is controlled and serves to regenerate life. Like mummies, icons provide a channel between immanence and transcendence, between the visible and the invisible, and at the same time they renegotiate the demarcation between the two realms. Not only can they be looked at, but they are themselves endowed with the power of vision—a power so great that, at the time of the "eyes opening" ceremony, the priest has to be shielded from the icons' gaze and looks at their reflection in a mirror. (See Gombrich 1966.) But, most of all, the vision of the icon is transformative. As J. Gonda points out in the Indian context, the spectator is believed to benefit from looking on a mighty being: by participating in its essence, the spectator is purified or raised to a higher level (Gonda 1970: 55; see also Eck 1985). On the other hand, as in the case of *śarīra* (see Xu Yun 1988: 42), the efficacy of the icon depends on the faith and karma of the worshiper and/or on proper ritual reactivation. The latent power of the icon becomes manifest only under certain objective and subjective circumstances. As the Kamakura monk Myōe put it, "When you think of an object carved of wood or drawn in a picture as a living being, then it *is* a living being" (Morrell 1987: 60). A Chinese poem titled "The Gate of Worshiping Relics, Images and Stūpas" suggests that the icon serves as a support for the Buddha as well as a focusing mechanism for

---

[51] The same is true in India. For Hinduism, see Eck 1985: 52; for Theravāda Buddhism, see Gombrich 1966.

[52] On this first—and animated—image of the Buddha, see Soper 1948: 25.

[53] One may add to this list the Chan monk's staff (*khakkhara*). In the Daoist "deliverance from the corpse," the staff becomes explicitly a double of the Immortal that is mistaken for the latter and put in the coffin in his place. See Robinet 1979b.

the believer: "[An image] will express our feelings, concentrate our thoughts, [make them] compassionate and loving;/ *It brings down [the Buddha's] spirit* and portrays his likeness, wiping clean all dust and doubt."[54]

Transmission or diffusion?

As the individual master had been an embodiment of the Dharma during his life, so was his *chinsō* after his death. The *chinsō* thus came to play, as did the *śarīra* and other relics, an important role in the transmission, or rather the diffusion, of the Dharma. It is well known, for instance, that through the mediation of two disciples, Dainichi Nōnin received in 1189 a portrait of Bodhidharma on which the Chan master Fozhao Deguang had written a eulogy together with the robe of Dahui Zonggao. Furthermore, before returning to Japan, Nōnin's disciples also had a portrait made of Deguang on which they asked the master to inscribe a verse. As we saw earlier, Nōnin had also, probably on the same occasion, received the *śarīra* of the six patriarchs and of the Bodhisattva Samantabhadra. The writing of a verse by a Chan master on a portrait (his own or that of an earlier patriarch) may be seen as an alternative form of "pointing" an icon—a proof of transmission "sealing the faith" (*yinxin*). Similarly, Dōgen returned from China in 1227 with a portrait of his master Rujing. Although he later complained about the commodification of *chinsō*, to which he attributed the decline of Linji (J. Rinzai) Chan, he clearly shared with his contemporaries the "ideology of thaumaturgic immanence" that gave rise to the vogue of icons. He was in all likelihood merely reluctant to share its symbolic gains with other schools—in particular with the Darumashū. (See *Shōbōgenzō Shisho*, T. 82, 2582: 69b.) Similar in this sense to the patriarchal robe, these portraits were not simply proof of transmission, as is generally believed, but were its medium and *palladium*.[55]

In a recent paper, Foulk, Horton, and Sharf (1990) have attempted to demonstrate that transmission was not the primary purpose of the *chinsō*—at least not in the usual sense according to which the *chinsō* is seen as the proof of a "transmission from mind to mind" and as a private memento cherished by the disciple. I agree entirely with their analysis that

---

[54] Richard Mather, "Hymns on the Devotee's Entrance into the Pure Life," *JAOS* 106, 1 (1986): 93. (italics mine) In India, the body of an ascetic who has "entered *samādhi*" [in both senses of a grave and one's spiritual state in it] while alive is believed to be still the occasional habitat of his soul, which wanders freely through the three worlds. See Parry 1982: 96. See also Levin 1930.

[55] According to *Le Petit Robert: Dictionnaire alphabétique et analogique de la langue française*, a *palladium* is (1) a statue of Pallas considered by Trojans as a guarantee of salvation for their city; hence (2) shield, guarantee, safeguard.

the possession of a *chinsō* was in itself insufficient to claim spiritual transmission or awakening. It was the device, however, that allowed the ritual transmission of the master's charisma to take place and that provided access to it, thereby linking magically the possessor of the *chinsō* to the mainstream of the tradition perpetuated by his master. The *chinsō* thus lays the ritual ground on which the rarefaction of legitimate authority through succession documents (*shisho*) could take place as a specific case. As Foulk, Horton, and Sharf point out, the *chinsō* must be placed in the funerary context. But so does the patriarchal transmission: by receiving the seal (*inka*) of the master, the disciple becomes his double, symbolically killing him according to the funerary logic expressed by the French expression *le mort saisit le vif.* Likewise, the transmission of the patriarchal robe was never merely—despite Shenhui's claim—the "proof" of the "mind-to-mind" transmission but functioned as a relic, a magical device transforming the disciple into his master (i.e., into the Buddha). This logic of metonymy and dissemination is not negated by the multiplication of *chinsō*, nor to a lesser extent by that of robes and *inka*. Paradoxically, the single transmission was permitted by it and later deconstructed by it. Rather than transmitting the Law to a single successor, the master is disseminating it—and himself by the same token, since the *chinsō*, being his "Body of Law," is both his Law and his body. (See Mus 1935: 698, 728.) With their multiplication and diffusion to monks and laymen alike, however, *chinsō*, like *śarīra*, lost their privilege of conferring legitimacy on a specific lineage and came to serve merely as instruments of ritual affiliation with the Chan "blood lineage," or even as talismans and amulets, forms of "objectified charisma" somewhat similar to the effigies of Thai monks studied by Tambiah (1984).

Functionally interchangeable with the *chinsō*, the *shin* (Ch. *zhen*, "truth" [in painting]) or portrait of the dead master "is the substantial image of the Dharma" (*Sho ekō shingi*, T. 81, 2578: 661). Here again, the general practice consistently contradicted the official teaching—repeated after many others by Mujaku Dōchū (*Zenrin shōkisen*, ed. Yanagida 1979: 1:196a)—that the true *chinsō* is no chinsō, or conversely that the "truth" (in painting; *shin*) is not true, because the true characteristic, form, or aspect (Ch. *xiang*, J. *sō*) is not a characteristic, form, or aspect that can be seen.[56] In many respects similar to the effigy (*shouxiang* or *dashou*) of Chi-

---

[56] On *chinsō*, see also Matsuura 1976: 468; T. 9, 278: 507a; T. 30, 1579: 568c. On *keshin* (*kashin*), the rite of hanging the mortuary portrait (*shin*) during the various phases of a Zen abbot's funerals, see *Keizan shingi* (T. 82, 2589: 779b). That this portrait was perceived as a double is clear from the fact that it was the object of the ceremony, even while the dead body was in the coffin nearby. As in the case of Roman emperors (Dupont 1989) or French kings (Giesey 1987), the body of the Chan/Zen master seems divided into *ossa* and *imago*, into a mortal body and an immortal metonymic body. Studying royal funerals in sixteenth- to seventeenth-century France, Giesey describes the processes that led to the dissociation of

nese funerals, the *shin* functions as a substitute body. (See Groot 1982: 1:113.) Like the Western kings studied by Kantorowicz (1957) and Giesey (1960, 1987), the Chan master had apparently two bodies: one physical, perishable body and one social, imperishable body. It is for the second body that the ritual is performed: as in the funerals of the king, "the focus of the ceremony shifts away from the encoffined body and centers upon the lifelike representation of the deceased" (Huntington and Metcalf 1979: 168). Thus the portrait serves as support for the social body of the deceased master, until the latter is properly reincorporated—through cremation or mummification—into his purified body, the *śarīra* or the flesh-body, thereby becoming a "collective" ancestor and a source of regeneration. The portrait anticipates this state of affairs and continues to operate in parallel with the relics afterward.[57] The "realistic fallacy" about *chinsō* and *shin* comes from the linguistic drift from "truth" (*shin*) to "true likeness" but, more generally, from an aniconic conception of "objectified charisma" (the *śarīra* or stūpa) to an iconic one (the *chinsō*). As Chinese painters such as Gu Kaizhi knew well, true likeness lies not in physical resemblance but in "animation" or ritual empowerment. In a sense, the "realism" of portraiture marks a decline of ritual symbolism. Hence perhaps Mujaku's claim that all true portraits are nonportraits. Therefore, the "realistic" portraiture of the Ōbaku sect in Japan can be seen as the end of the iconization process of the double that leads from *śarīra* and symbolic relics through flesh-bodies to *chinsō*.

Figures of the double

Similar in many respects to the *chinsō* of the Chan/Zen master, the icons of the gods worshiped in Zen monasteries differ nevertheless in their ritual function; they protect the monastery, or some part of it: the meditation hall, the Dharma hall, the kitchen, the bathroom, and the toilets. The presence of these gods in their icons is achieved by ritual empowerment through invocation. Thus these icons are perceived as having "spiritual power" (*ling*), and they belong to the category of the "double." This heuristic category provides a common link (*ling*) among relics, mummies, dream apparitions, Arhats, gods, and icons; it helps explain why the "response" of the spirit of deceased masters or of gods to the requests addressed to their relics or icons usually takes place in dreams or apparitions: all these "doubles" are functionally and/or psychologically related.

---

the "two bodies" (i.e., the corpse in the coffin and the effigy of the dead king) to the extent that, after the death of Henry IV in 1610, priests and magistrates vied with each other to march at the sides of the effigy (the living king), leaving the coffin (the dead king) to professional handlers. (See ibid.: 38–47.)

[57] This is different from the Roman case, where the wax effigy of the emperor was burned after his reincorporation as a god. See Dupont 1989.

The icons are, in the strict sense, the visible bodies of the gods, their "traces"—although "trace" here implies an invisible presence, not an absence.[58] Just as, according to William Blake, the body is the visible part of the mind, the icon or relic is the visible part of the Buddha's or Chan master's Mind or "Body of Law." As Menzan, in a text concerning a bronze image of an Arhat, put it: "I have heard that when the Tathāgata Śākya[muni] was in this world, king Prasenajit had the first image of the Tathāgata made, and that it was in every respect identical to the living Buddha and had the same virtues. Now, we have here an image of an Arhat. How could it differ at all from the true Arhat? Both have the same virtues." (Quoted in Michihata 1983: 227.) Inheriting the Platonic conception of *mimesis*, art historians tend to devalue these images as "artistic representations," thus missing the point (i.e., the pupil in their eyes).[59] The ritual presence, latent or manifest, of the gods in their icons is another figure of mediation that sustains the notion of "worldly benefits" (*genze riyaku*).

DESPITE the radical difference of soteriological context, the Chinese "question of icons," like its Christian counterpart, appears to have been a controversy over the position of the sacred in society. Chan's much-vaunted "iconoclasm" was aimed essentially at "superstitions" that seemed to result in a "hemorrhage" of the sacred—and, by the same token, in a banalization of charisma and a devaluation of sectarian legitimacy. Accordingly, a rationalist or aesthetic interpretation of Chan iconology would be misleading. Chan/Zen monks were in fact trying to limit the proliferation of sacred symbols and to reserve for themselves the privilege of the possession of selected symbols or icons such as *śarīra* and mummies. Their iconoclasm was therefore a relative one, although the

---

[58] The legend concerning the first representation of the Buddha, a wooden statue made on the order of king Prasenajit (or king Udayana) while the Buddha had gone to visit his mother in heaven, seems to indicate that it was conceived as merely a replica (*pratima*) of the missing original. But this interpretation is belied by the end of the legend, which tells how the statue got up to welcome the Buddha when he returned. See *Gaoseng Faxian zhuan*, T. 51, 2085: 860b.

[59] This rite of consecration by "opening the eyes" can be related to a detail in the story of Piṇḍola's apparition and appearance. As Strong points out in his description of Piṇḍola's encounter with king Aśoka, "with his white brows covering his pupils, Piṇḍola sits before Aśoka in much the same way as an unfinished 'blind' Buddha image. It is, therefore, a moment of great importance in the text when, we are told, with king Aśoka bowing down before him, 'the elder lifted up his brows with both hands and gazed straight at the king.' The point is clear; in the cultic situation established by Aśoka and confirmed by his offerings and devotion, the live Piṇḍola is consecrated, i.e., sacralized in much the same way as an image of the Buddha. And just like the Buddha image, at the precise moment of its consecration, Piṇḍola re-presents or 'makes present,' cultically speaking, the Buddha who is absent in Nirvāṇa" (Strong 1979: 85). And Strong concludes: "Such a dis-covery of the presence of the ultimate object of devotion in the immediate focus of devotion, whether that be an image, a stūpa, an icon or, as in this case, a man—a monk, comes as no surprise to the historian of religions; it is, to a great extent, characteristic of all cultic situations" (ibid.).

most radical among them, carried away by the rhetoric of immediacy, attempted to deny any symbolic mediation. By so doing, however, they tended to forget that the aniconism of early Chan—another expression of its subitism—functioned as a ritual inversion and marked the ultimate phase of a process that could not dispense with its preliminary iconic— and gradualist—phase without losing its meaning.[60] Even then, they still relied on the notion of a lineage of Chan patriarchs having realized one-by-one the formless truth—a notion that made sense only in the context of a funerary ideology centered on ancestor worship, an ideology for which every patriarchal generation is only the embodiment of a perennial Dharma, the *lex incarnata*. Each patriarch is thus himself already an icon, a particular form of the formless, a metamorphosis of the primordial dou-ble—the Buddha: sitting cross-legged on his chair, every Chan master is a double of the Tathāgata and of his alter ego, the *cakravartin* king, and he is in turn duplicated in his cross-legged disciples; whereas the Buddha, as manifested in his icons, may be seen as a mental projection of the concrete monks and as a ritual projection of their Buddha nature. In this way, the logic of dissemination has come to supplement—and to displace—the early Chan metaphysics of presence. Between these mirror images power circulates endlessly, from mind to mind and from body to body, and this circulation is paradoxically enhanced by the ritualization of death.

---

[60] Likewise, as we will see shortly, the postmortem awakening of Chan monks cannot be achieved without the ritual dramatization of the preliminal and liminal phases of the funerary ritual.

Nine   ***The Ritualization of Death***

> Where the red fire burns through the body, there
> sprouts a lotus, blossoming within the flames.
> —Zen funerary sermon

> "Buddha" is what we call what remains alive/ After
> the body has thoroughly died.
> —Shidō Bunan, *Sokushin ki*

Although death is experienced as a sudden event, it is also perceived at
the level of collective representations as a gradual process. The question
of relics has led us—in theory—beyond the threshold of death, to what
we could call the "postliminary" phase of the death process or, after Arnold van Gennep (1960: 146–165), the "reincorporation" phase of the funerary rite of passage. We must now return to the preliminary and limi-
nary phases of the death process, or in van Gennep's terms the
"separation" and "liminal" phases of the funerary ritual, and examine the
evolution of Chan/Zen attitudes toward death itself. Some Japanese
scholars, such as Tamamuro Taijō, have pointed out that, from the fourteenth century onward, Zen became increasingly concerned with death
rituals—to the point of becoming a major trend of so-called funerary
Buddhism.[1] Although useful, the sociological approach of the phenomenon, with its emphasis on the "popularization" of Zen, fails to explain
entirely the predominance of Zen rituals and to account for the shift from
a "philosophy of life" to funerary ritualism in terms of Zen's own dynamic.[2] Therefore, the question remains: How did the advocates of "pure
Zen" come to be regarded as specialists of impurity?

THE CHAN DENIAL OF DEATH AND THE AFTERLIFE

> "—Is there a hell or not?" "—There is, and there is
> not."
> —Dazhu Huihai, *Dunwu yaomen*

Let us first examine briefly the Chan ideology concerning death before
showing its limits. Although the contemplation of the corpse as a symbol

---

[1] See Tamamuro 1963; Ishikawa 1987c, 1987d; Tachibana 1964.

[2] At first glance, this funerary ritualism contradicts Chan/Zen subitism, and it was indeed
criticized by some Chan/Zen masters as nonorthodox. See, for instance, *San'an zatsuroku* in
zz 2B, 21, 2: 182a, quoted in Tachibana 1964: 221.

of impermanence was exalted in early Buddhism as a gruesome *memento mori*,[3] the cyclical nature of *saṃsāra*—with its two alternating phases of birth and death—tended to attenuate somewhat the ineluctability or irreversibility of death itself, reduced to one link in a larger chain of events. Death was furthermore relativized by the notion of the constant arising and cessation of psycho-physical aggregates and the belief that the true break in the stream of consciousness was the result of awakening. Reinforcing the no-self theory of early Buddhism, the Mahāyāna doctrine, as exemplified by the Heart Sūtra, further blunted the scandal of death by denying its ontological reality: in emptiness (*śūnyatā*) there is neither birth nor death, neither coming nor going. Accordingly, temporality and finitude were ultimately negated as karmic delusions. Mahāyāna Buddhists could have made theirs the Roman motto: "Non fuit, fuit, non sum, non curo" (I was not, I was, I am not, I do not care). The Mahāyāna standpoint is illustrated by the response of the Northern Chan master Yuangui to the threat of the Song shan god: "I am unborn, how could you kill me?"—or by the death verse of the Chan master Lingmo (747–815):

> Subtle matter is truly permanent;
> It has fundamentally neither birth nor extinction.
> The *Dharmakāya* is perfectly still;
> How could it come and go?[4]

This denial of the reality of death led to a theoretical rejection of funerary rituals: at first glance, Chan seems to advocate an experiential transcendence (awakening) and to deny the ancestral or mythical transcendence produced by mortuary rites.[5] Chan's idealistic (Mind-Only) stance—paradoxically reinforcing its this-worldly tendency—also led to a denial of the intermediary worlds of Buddhist eschatology. One *locus classicus* of this denial is the following passage of the *Treatise of Bodhidharma* (*Damo lun*): "Some, by discrimination in their own mind, create tigers, wolves, lions, poisonous dragons, evil spirits, the generals of the five destinies, King Yama, the ox-head guards and the sound-of-cold hell. . . . Merely realize that whatever mind discriminates is [only] forms. . . . If you realize that these forms are not real, then you will obtain lib-

---

[3] See, for instance, the "ten perceptions of putrescence," in *The Path of Freedom by the Arahant Upatissa*, trans. from the Chinese by N.R.M. Ehara, Soma and Kheminda (Kandi, Sri Lanka: Buddhist Publications Society, 1977), 132–138. This tradition continued in China, Korea, and Japan. See Sanford 1988.

[4] See *Zutang ji*, ed. Yanagida 1974b, ch. 4:84; and the variant in *T.* 51, 2076: 254b. See also Demiéville 1984: 32.

[5] I borrow these notions from Chidester 1990: 134.

eration."[6] In a similar fashion, the Pure Land was reinterpreted as Mind-Only (and thereby emptied of its eschatological content) by early Chan, and this interpretation influenced Pure Land masters such as Fazhao (fl. 8th c.).[7] Although this teaching must have had a profoundly liberating effect at a time when the Buddhist belief in hell was becoming more prevalent, it clearly failed to address the problem of theodicy. Conversely, one may argue that the intensification of the descriptions of hell and paradise reflects a radicalization of traditional Buddhism in the face of a certain "recession of faith" or growing agnosticism—of which Chan may be one expression.[8] Bernard Groethuysen has shown that this was precisely the case in the Western context of the post-Reformation; he quotes Bossuet's criticism of the Quietists: "The world is full of their hymns in which hell and damnation are despised" (1968: 79). The same criticism could apply to Chan "quietism," and it was indeed voiced by Pure Land masters such as Huiri (680–748). (See Chappell 1986: 169.)

Many counterexamples reveal the ambiguity and the complexity of Chan in this domain as well. Chan's idealistic stance is expressed in the famous story in which Huineng tells two monks who were arguing about a flag that was blowing in the wind that it is neither the flag nor the wind that moves but their own minds.[9] Yet not all Chan monks were as detached as Huineng concerning the Pure Land. Fachi (637–702), the fourth patriarch of the Niutou school, was also known as a Pure Land believer. As noted earlier, he ordered that his corpse be abandoned to wild animals and insects so that, by assimilating its virtue, they may produce the thought of awakening (T. 50, 2061: 756c; T. 51, 2071: 120a). The Niutou school is one of the most radically antinomian trends in early Chan, and Fachi's case shows the paradoxical coexistence, within the same school—and perhaps the same individual—of fundamentally contradictory attitudes toward death and the other world. Another significant example is that of Huangbo Xiyun (fl. 9th c.), who, despite his typically Chan denial

[6] See Faure 1986d: 110. See also ibid.: 133. Ironically, a later *baojuan* attributes to a demiurgic Bodhidharma the creation of the Ten Kings of Hell. See David Johnson, "A Paochüan on the Theme of Mu-lien Rescuing his Mother: The *Yu-ming Pao-chüan* and its Performance Context," 1990: 33 (unpublished paper).

[7] See, for example, Shenxiu's *Guanxin lun* (T. 85, 2833: 1273a), *Lengqie shizi ji* (T. 85, 2837), *Platform Sūtra* (T. 48, 2008: 342b; Yampolsky 1967: 156), and *Dunwu yaomen* (ed. Hirano 1970: 197). On Fazhao, see in particular Tsukamoto 1976: 459ff. On the relations between Chan and Pure Land, see Chappell 1986; Faure 1988: 76–83.

[8] On the evolution of Chinese Buddhist conceptions of the other world, see Teiser 1989. See also Michihata Ryōshū, "Tonkō bunken ni mieru shigo no sekai," in Makita and Fukui 1984: 501–536.

[9] For an ironic critique of Chan idealism, see Fayan Wen'yi's response to a monk arguing that everything, including the stone in front of them, was an objectification of his mind: "Your head must feel very heavy, if you are carrying a stone like this in your mind." Quoted in Nyogen Senzaki and Paul Repps, eds., *Zen Flesh, Zen Bones* (New York: Penguin Books, 1957), 71.

of other realms, was perceived as a kind of psychopomp able to bring the Prime Minister Pei Xiu back to life.[10]

The ambiguity of Chan/Zen conceptions of the afterlife appears most clearly in a document recently discovered in the Kanazawa Bunko collection and relating to the founder of the Darumashū, Dainichi Nōnin. In this text, the *Jōtō Shōgakuron*,[11] Nōnin borrows from the popular Chinese genre of "descent into hell" stories (see Demiéville 1976): on his way to the infernal tribunal, a certain Wang comes across the Bodhisattva Dizang (Jizō) who tells him that he can avoid the sufferings of hell simply by reciting the following verse: "If you wish to know all the Buddhas of the Three periods, you must contemplate the nature of the Dharmadhātu and know that all things are the creation of the mind." Wang is then taken to King Yama, who, after hearing his verse, releases him. Nōnin's comment is strongly reminiscent of the passage in the *Treatise of Bodhidharma* quoted above: "Clearly, hell is a product of mind. If you understand this, then hell is empty." "When you see marks, in all places you see demons." (See Faure 1986d: 89, 106.) But the point to note here is that the value of Dizang's verse derives from its use as a mantra rather than from its doctrinal content, potentially leading to the realization of emptiness. Or should one perhaps say that the doctrine is precisely what empowers the mantra—as in the *Heart Sūtra* or in the Verse on Causality?[12] At any rate, the realization that hell is empty could not as such prevent Wang from confronting Yama. Nōnin seems to imply that delusion has become too real to vanish through a simple intellectual realization, or even a spiritual insight—it has to be fought on its own terms. This story illustrates the process through which Chan/Zen teachings were modified to take popular beliefs into account—and possibly were subverted by these beliefs. The belief in karmic causality and dedication of merits, however, a fundamental feature of the popular religious landscape, was also crucial in "framing" the Chan teaching on spontaneity and emptiness. In Kamakura Japan, Zen funerary rituals reveal a type of devotional teaching closer to the "Other Power" (J. *tariki*) of the Pure Land sects than to the much-vaunted "self-power" (J. *jiriki*) of Zen apologetics.

---

[10] Here is the *Zutang ji*'s account of the story: "One day, the Prime Minister Pei [Xiu] felt indisposed and suddenly died. The master [Huangbo] happened to be there; he did not leave him, and remained sitting at his bed-head. After a long time, the Minister recovered consciousness and told what had happened to him in the other world: 'When I entered the dark world, I had feet but I did not walk; I had eyes but I did not see. After having walked for about forty-five *li*, I became tired; suddenly I saw a pond and wanted to enter it. There was an old *heshang* who did not permit it and shouted. This is why, master, I see you again.' The master said: 'If you had not met that old monk, Prime Minister, you would have gone to the dragon's abode.'" Huangbo, if the old man is indeed his double, appears here as a shamanic intercessor. (Quoted in Demiéville 1970b: 278; see also 1976: 73–74.)

[11] See Shinagawa Kenritsu Kanazawa Bunko 1974: 204.

[12] On the mantric use of the *Heart Sūtra*, see Lopez 1990.

The ambiguity of the tradition is sometimes reflected in a single individual. In his *Jishō ki*, for instance, the Zen master Shidō Bunan (1603–1676) takes a Confucian stand against the occult: "Someone asked why 'Confucius did not speak about strange phenomena, feats of strength, disorders or spirits.' I said, 'These things do not exist for the sage.' " (See Pedersen 1975: 126.) In another work, *Sokushin ki*, Bunan writes: "What is outside of the self is Buddha. It is just like empty space. Therefore, when you die, 'returned to Emptiness' is written on your mortuary tablet" (Kobori 1970–1971: 4, 1:116). Yet the realm of emptiness is quite populated, if we are to believe another of Bunan's statements:

> Someone said: "The spirits of the dead are here in this world and I am sure that they cause the destruction of both individuals and families." I said: "There are four kinds of spirits. The first are 'ghosts of the country.' These are the rulers of the country from long ago, who still have the desire to communicate with their successors. The second kind are called 'ghosts of the yard.' . . . The third kind are called 'ghosts of the house.' . . . As far as these are concerned, if you leave the place where they are, there is no danger. 'Ghosts of the family' you can't escape no matter where you go, but if you call a virtuous Master and hold a memorial service for them, everything will be all right." (Pedersen 1975: 114)

The funeral paradox

The ambiguity is revealed even more vividly by Chan/Zen funerary rituals. Did Chan monks believe in their funerary rites, and if so, to what extent? One might argue that belief follows ritual—"Kneel down and you will believe"—or even that ritual already carries with it a certain type of implicit representation that, even when it seems to the observer to contradict explicit beliefs, may never come into open conflict with those beliefs for the participant. The ambivalence of the Chan tradition toward death, and the double discourse that ensued, is usually explained away as a utilitarian device for the conversion of the people, a "skillful means" (*upāya*) that did not necessarily reflect the profound conviction of the literate monks—or even, in the worst case, as a form of clerical hypocrisy. While these interpretations may have some validity, they are insufficient. Indeed, the contradiction between agnostic and funerary Chan was clearly felt—and carefully played down—by various spokesmen of the tradition.[13] Although the Two Truths paradigm could also be used to

---

[13] For instance, funerary rituals and the patriarchal cult implied a form of ancestor worship that seemed in blatant contradiction to the Buddhist teaching on impermanence. In particular, the custom of the imperial conferment of *posthumous names* for deceased masters,

assert the coexistence of several—equally vital—conceptions of truth as a basic fact of religious life, in most cases it conveniently served to allow the tradition to evade the difficulty created by the *agonistic* coexistence of contradictory beliefs and/or rituals.

THE RITUAL DOMESTICATION OF DEATH

The dominant impression left by Chan/Zen documents is that of an increasing ritualization and collectivization of death. As a form of mediation, ritual simultaneously hides and reveals death: it marks its apotheosis, but it also diffuses or defers its suddenness by turning the corpse or its substitutes into signifiers. In the Chan/Zen case, these signifiers point toward a form of ancestral, corporate transcendence rather than to the much-vaunted experiential, individual transcendence of awakening. We also witness what we could call an undramatization of death (as a traumatic event) through its "dramatization" (as ritual performance). This ritualization affects all the "stages" (in both senses) of the death process. Let us turn to the preliminary stage—itself a three-act sequence consisting of the prediction of death, the final words, and the ritual "entrance into samādhi" (J. *nyūjō*).

Preliminaries

PREDICTION OF THE TIME OF DEATH

From very early times, the death of a Chan master was staged as an epoch-making event—the ritual reenactment of the Buddha's *parinirvāṇa*. The first task of a truly enlightened master—as such fully endowed with *abhijñā*—was to foretell, not only his forthcoming death, but the precise

---

from the Tang onward, implied their aggregation to the lineage of Chan (and imperial) ancestors. Early Buddhist ascetics, however, did not perform any funerary ritual, in accordance with the Buddhist notion of death as a return to nothingness and with the Indian notion that the ascetic, at the time of his initiation, had already "died to the world." Likewise, some conservative Chan masters asked that their ashes be dispersed and no grave be erected. As Schopen (1987) has argued, however, the Buddhist ideology of impermanence was from the outset contradicted by another ideology, that of the relics. Hence, as noted above, there are two conceptions of cremation: as destruction (or even punishment) and as creation of an immortal body (*śarīra*). The fact that the inhumation of Buddhist monks persisted despite the development of cremation during the Tang bears testimony to this hesitation about cremation. Inhumation was clearly connected to ancestor worship, which perhaps explains the traditional (Confucian) funerals of Chan "patriarchs" such as Shenxiu. Cremation aimed at the same goal through the production of relics, but the former Buddhist or non-Buddhist associations (destruction of individuality and of bodily integrity) lingered and led eventually to its proscription by the Confucianists in China. A recent example of this Chinese repulsion was the protest against Zhu Enlai's cremation. See Wakeman 1988: 260.

time of his "transformation."[14] We are told that Hongren, the fifth patriarch, watched carefully over the completion of his funerary stūpa and
decided to delay his death so that it would not fall on the anniversary of
the Buddha's *parinirvāṇa*. A later Chan master, Lin'yang Zhiduan, advanced the date of his death for the same reason (see *Chanlin sengbao zhuan*
10). Hongren's successor, Huineng, allegedly predicted his death one
month in advance, left a long departing poem, and made a prediction
concerning the future of his school (Yampolsky 1967: 174). Another interesting case, mentioned earlier, is that of Puhua, whose predictions
seemed to fail several times. Puhua was able by this stratagem both to
predict his death and to avoid the ritualization that usually accompanies
the death of a master: when he actually passed away, all the usual bystand-
ers, having grown skeptical, were gone.[15] At any rate, death predictions
were popular: among the twenty wonders of Song China, the Japanese
pilgrim Yōsai counts the fact that "many monks know the time of their
death" (Ichikawa et al. 1972: 88).

An interesting aspect of this increasing ritualization of the prediction of
one's death is a four-verse *gāthā* with strong Daoist overtones known as
"Great Master [Bodhi]dharma's [Method for] knowing the time of one's
death" (*Daruma daishi chishigo*):

As soon as you realize that there is no dripping in the Jade Pond,
You proceed to catch the divine light at the bottom of waves.
[To find out about] impermanence, you must listen to the drums of
   the skull;
If you can count their beats, you will know the number of days that
   remain before you die. (Suginoto 1982: 324)

First transmitted and glossed in Tendai esotericism, this verse later became part of the Sōtō esoteric transmission.[16] One tradition has it that
Saichō (767–822) received it while in China from his master Daosui, and
another says that it was transmitted to him through his Japanese master
Gyōhyō (722–797)—the same master who had initiated him into Northern Chan.[17] In the Sōtō school, the verse was handed down in the way
esoteric teachings were commonly transmitted, namely through initia-

[14] For predictions of death outside the Chan tradition, see Naruse Yoshinori, "Shi no
yogen ni tsuite," *IBK* 31, 2 (1983): 122–123.
[15] See Ikkyū's poem: "Who could walk beside Deshan and Linji? That old man from
Zhen[zhou] really startled the crowds. Some die in meditation, some on their feet, but he
beat them all. Like a distant bird call, his bell rang faintly" (*Kyōun shū* 126; Sanford 1981:
147).
[16] Another Sōtō document gives a variant of this verse attributed to the Buddha himself
and titled *Bussetsu saidai ichi kudoku enman chishigo kyō*. This "sūtra" also contains a *dhāraṇī*
that saves all sentient beings. See Ishikawa 1986b: 199.
[17] On the Northern Chan influence on Saichō, see Faure 1988: 149–154.

tion documents known as *kirigami* ("paper strips").[18] There is no doubt that it was already known in the early Kamakura period, since Yōsai mentions it if only to reject it as apocryphal. In his *Kōzen gokokuron*, Yōsai stages the following dialogue with a disciple:

> Someone asked again: "In our country of Japan, there is the '*verse of the prediction of the time of death*' by the great master [Bodhi] dharma. What about its authenticity?" I answered: "As to the method you are mentioning, its words have been compiled by demons with dull faculties. As to the way of death and rebirth, in our school coming and going, life and death, are held to be fundamentally equal and, from the outset, there is no principle of birth and extinction. Those who believe that they can know the time of their death are deeply mistaken in regard to the way of our patriarchs, and this is a true nuisance." (T. 80, 2543: 10a)

The virulence of Yōsai's criticism suggests that this verse was widespread at the time—and perhaps within the Darumashū itself, a school that was strongly influenced by Tendai esotericism and is the main target of the *Kōzen gokokuron*. This would explain the transmission of the verse in the later Sōtō tradition, which can be seen in many respects as a resurgence of the Darumashū. The verse is also recorded in the Tendai encyclopedia, *Keiran shūyō shū*,[19] and its transmission in Japan is traced back to two priests, otherwise unknown: a certain Fanshang and a Yōjin *shōnin* of Chinzei (Kyūshū). According to Dong Jun's *Zuoqiao*, "Since that time there has been a secret tradition according to which the 'Jade Pond' means the mouth, and the 'bottom of the waves' the eye. To 'listen to the drums of the skull' means that, on the eve of the New Year, one covers one's ears with both hands and knocks on one's head a number of times corresponding to the number of days and months in the coming year. When one reaches the point where there is no sound, this day, is the time of one's death. There is also a method of cultivation, but I cannot describe it here." (Quoted in Ichikawa et al. 1972: 396.) The Sōtō gloss of the verse is more detailed and provides the ritual setting. The method presents two steps: first, the practitioner finds out whether or not he will die in the coming year by checking with his finger the presence (life) or absence (death) of bubbles in his saliva. An alternative way is to press his eyeballs:

[18] Concerning these documents, see Sugimoto 1982; Ishikawa, "Chūsei Sōtōshū kirigami no bunrui shiron," 1983, 1984a, 1985a, 1986a and b, 1987a and b; Kuroda 1989.
[19] See T. 76, 2410: 779c, 781c. The *Keiran shūyō shū* mentions other oral traditions concerning the symptoms of an approaching death: for example, the fact that things are perceived in a yellow light is a forerunner of the Yellow Springs, that is, the Chinese underworld (T. 76, 2410: 779c).

if this produces light, it means life; if not, death. In the second case, the practitioner can find the exact month, day and hour of his forthcoming death by knocking as described above on his head. The Sōtō gloss concludes with an ambiguous statement: "The above verse was certainly not composed by the great master Bodhidharma; it is a later interpolation. If you want to attract the faith of the people, you attribute a text to the master patriarch. Although it was not composed by him, if you cultivate according to this method, you will obtain spiritual efficacy (*ling'yan*)" (*sz* 18, Shūi, 546). In his attempt to separate Zen esoteric teachings from "superstitions," Menzan too points out the unorthodox nature of the *chishigo kirigami* and traces them back to the Shingon tradition (*sz* 15, Shitsuchū, 197). At any rate, the popularity of this method and its attribution to Bodhidharma suggest the vitality, on the margins of Chan/Zen orthodoxy, of an esoteric trend concerned with Daoist techniques of divination.[20]

DEATH VERSES

The second task of the dying Chan master was to leave a "death verse" or *gāthā* (J. *yuige*), after having clarified his teaching for his disciples for the last time and designated his successor. (See Yanagida 1973; Demiéville 1984.) The death verse is symmetrical to the awakening verse: together they mark the beginning and end of the master's preaching. Both were recorded relatively early. One of the earliest known examples is the cryptic "departing words"—not yet a verse in the strict sense—of the Northern Chan master Shenxiu (d. 706): "Folded, bent, straightened" (*T.* 85, 2837: 1290b). The most well-known "awakening verses" are those of the Indian and Chinese Chan patriarchs, verses linked by the metaphor of the blossoming flower. These clearly apocryphal poems allowed the neo-Confucian critic of Chan, Zhu Xi (1130–1200), to note the irony that Indian patriarchs could be so well versed in Chinese prosody. (See Sargent 1957: 147.)

A death verse testifying to his degree of enlightenment was expected from anyone who wanted to be considered a master. These poems, whether or not they ever originated as spontaneous expressions of an enlightened mind, became increasingly codified. It was expected that they state the age of the dying monk and illustrate his detachment toward death. Some masters tried to react against this increasing ritualization and what they must have perceived as an intrusion of worldly concerns into their last moments. But very few could, like Puhua, avoid this drudgery, or simply say, as Zhouxun (d. 1134) did, "I have made no verse" (*T.* 50, 2062: 921a).

---

[20] Apparently a number of Daoist methods of longevity were also attributed to Bodhidharma. See, for instance, *Damo chanshi zhishi liuxing neizhen miaoyong jue,* in *Yunji qiqian* 59 (*dz* 689). See also Sekiguchi 1969: 488–492.

This statement, which Demiéville (1984: 68) interprets as "typical" of Chan antiritualism, was actually atypical: it risked being seen by the disappointed disciples as a mere admission of failure on the part of the master and could have dealt a potentially fatal blow to his school.

Thus, ironically, Chan masters who disapproved of such ritualization had to express their reluctance by way of the very medium they criticized. Yuanwu Keqin (1063–1135), for example, declared:

> Having already reached the effortless state,
> Why should I have to leave a verse?
> I only have now to yield to circumstances
> Farewell! Farewell![21]

But precisely to leave a verse was to "yield to circumstances." Keqin's contemporary Dahui Zonggao (1089–1163) expressed similar feelings:

> Birth is thus
> Death is thus
> Verse or no verse
> What's the fuss?[22]

Yet, despite their strong reservations about doing so, both Yuanwu and Dahui eventually wrote "departing verses"—for, as Dahui said, "without a verse, I could not die." Their individualistic contempt of conventions had to give way to the power of tradition—perhaps because it was itself part of the tradition. In the case of Japanese masters, the difficulty was compounded by the requirement that they write their poems according to the rules of Chinese prosody.[23] The results were not always of the greatest originality. The verse attributed to Dōgen, for instance, is a variant of that attributed to his master Rujing (1163–1228):

Rujing:

> For sixty years, my sins have filled heaven.
> Suddenly, I fall all alive into the Yellow Springs.

[21] See Mochizuki 1958–1963: 2:1142a; Demiéville 1984: 69.

[22] See *Dahui Pujue chanshi yulu*, in T. 47, 1998a: 863a; Yanagida 1973: 229; Christopher Cleary 1977: xx.

[23] See the examples given by Mujū Ichien's *Shasekishū* (end of chap. 10, "Felicitous Final Moments among Followers of Kenninji [i.e., Yōsai's]"), including verses by Yōsai, Lanqi Daolong (Rankei Dōryū), and Enni Ben'en. See *Shasekishū*, ed. Watanabe Tsunaya 1966: 450–459; Morrell 1985: 262–265. In one case, that of an illiterate disciple of Wuzhun Shifan named Venerable Hosshinbō, his attendants remarked that the verse lacked one line: "At this he shouted inarticulately and expired" (Morrell 1985: 264). For Chinese cases of "Auspicious Signs at the Time of Death," see *Fozu tongji* 54 (T. 49, 2035: 473b–c). Another revealing case is that of the master who, when his disciples asked for his verse, wrote "I do not want to die." When the disciples, shocked, asked for another better verse, he wrote "Truly, I do not want to die!" and passed away. (Quoted in Chidester 1990: 134.)

Ah!
I, who never cared about birth and death.
> (See Demiéville 1984: 87–88.)

Dōgen:

> For fifty-four years
> I illuminated the First Heaven.
> Suddenly I have smashed into pieces the whole universe.
> Ah! My whole body has no place to hold to!
> I fall all alive into the Yellow Springs.
> > (See Yanagida 1973: 187–189.)

Admittedly, intertextuality is not mere plagiarism, and Chinese poets have traditionally made use of quotations to express freely their own feelings.[24] Yet even though Dōgen's poem seems to reflect an understanding radically different from Rujing's, its formulaic nature diminishes considerably its originality, if not its poetic value. There are cases in which one may indeed suspect straightforward plagiarism, as in the death verse of the Shōgun Tokiyori, a verse strikingly similar to that of the Chinese Chan master Xiaoweng Miaokan (1177–1248), who died fifteen years earlier on Ayuwang shan. Tokiyori's case may not be isolated, for apparently the custom of leaving death poems often became an empty—but not less efficient—ritual by the thirteenth century. In the *Nomori kagami* (1295), for instance, it is severely criticized for having become a mere show. (Quoted in Yanagida 1973: 9.) Yet it had important ideological and political consequences. A departing verse was not simply intended to testify to the master's enlightenment; it was *producing* it and contained, in the litteral sense, its "essence." As such, it was also a *relic* "embodying" ultimate truth, and it sometimes competed with other Chan regalia used in the transmission of the Dharma such as the robe or the *chinsō*.

DEATH POSTURE

Another important element in the Chan *ars moriendi* is the final posture. Ritualization extended to the ultimate moments of a Chan/Zen master's life. His death became a public event, and he was required to die in a seated posture in order to show, not only that he was intent on practicing until the end and that he was facing death in the quiet composure of *samādhi*, but also that he had become ritually identified with the paradig-

---

[24] This is one of the modes of creative variation in poetic composition that the Chinese, by analogy with Daoist alchemy, called "appropriating the embryo" method (*duotai fa*) or "changing the bones" method (*huangu fa*). See Lynn 1987: 387.

matic Buddha (the historical Buddha having died lying on his bed).[25] So powerful was this model of "sitting *samādhi*" that it came to supersede all the others.[26] One may, however, discern voices of dissent regarding the dominant model. The *Lengqie shizi ji*, for example, reports that the Chan patriarch Sengcan, before passing away, told his disciples: "Everyone holds it to be valuable to die in a sitting posture. As for me, life and death, coming and going, depend on my will. I will therefore die standing." And he died holding the branch of a tree.[27] Also worth mentioning is the case of Miaopu (1071–1142), who drowned himself while playing the flute on a sinking craft, leaving the following verse:

> To die while sitting or standing
> Cannot compare with death by immersion.[28]
> First, one saves wood for the fire;
> Second, one saves oneself the trouble of digging a hole.
> (*Da Ming gaoseng zhuan*, T. 50, 2062: 926b)

Usually seen as an extreme illustration of perfect freedom in death, the ritual suicide of some Chan masters is reminiscent of Chinese Buddhist self-immolations and later Japanese self-mummifications (*sokushin-butsu*).[29] Not only were these individual suicides collective in the Durk-

---

[25] The most extreme case is that of the National Teacher Daitō (Shūhō Myōchō, 1282–1337), who, according to his hagiographer, had been unable during his entire life to sit properly in *zazen* due to an infirm leg. Approaching his last moment, he deliberately broke his leg in order to achieve the proper *zazen* posture. See also the similar case of Yunmen Wen'yan, in App 1989.

[26] A few cases of "lying *parinirvāṇa*" were still recorded (Śubhakarasiṃha during the Tang, Myōe in Kamakura Japan), but they have become exceptions and are outside the Chan tradition. Perhaps the predominance of "seated *parinirvāṇa*" has something to do with mental associations between the dead master and the (usually seated) Buddhas of the statuary: like the deceased, the wooden Buddha is supposedly in a state of suspended animation or *samādhi*. See Strickmann 1989.

[27] T. 85, 2837: 1286b. See also the precedents of Saṅgharaksa and Saṅghanandi in Demiéville 1954: 364 and 382.

[28] Although there seems to be no direct relationship, this story is reminiscent of the Japanese custom of drowning oneself in a sinking boat in order to reach the Pure Land of Kannon, the island of Fudaraku (Sk. *Potalaka*) believed to lie off the coast of the Nachi/Kumano area. The collective and sacrificial, as it were, Girardian (see Girard 1977) components of the latter case are illustrated by the story of the man who resolved to drown himself and then, having come to his senses when he contacted the cold water, swam frantically back to the shore. Despite his protestations, he was put afloat again by his followers and eventually drowned. On the belief in Fudaraku, see Nei 1986: 209–214.

[29] One could cite a number of examples of "freedom in [from] life and death." See, in particular, the case of the monk who "inaugurates the stūpa" of his master and becomes a "flesh-body" (T. 50, 2061: 584). On self-immolation, see Gernet 1959; Jan 1965. In Japan, the *Genkō shakusho* records one case of immolation by fire in its section on "The practice of endurance" (*ningyō*) and gives the *loci classici* for self-sacrifice (*Lotus Sūtra* and apocryphal scriptures such as *Fanwang jing* and *Śūraṃgama-sūtra*). See DNBZ 62, 470: 133–134. The *Koji ruien* attempts a distinction between heretical and legitimate forms of self-immolation and self-mutilation. See *Shūkyōbu* 2: 717.

heimian sense, they were staged as *public events*. (See Michihata 1980: 99–100.) These masters (or their disciples and hagiographers) were still trying to set a model for posterity, and their resistance to a specific form of death still contributed to the general ritualization process.[30] As Bloch and Parry put it: "What had at first appeared as supremely individual turns out to be the product of socially-constructed emotions and beliefs" (Bloch and Parry 1982: 3).

All these examples suggest that even in a school whose teaching was usually considered to be the most individualistic, the death of the master—that paradigmatic individual—and more precisely his cremation or "conspicuous consumption" (in the literal sense as well) became (or perhaps simply remained) an essentially collective phenomenon reflecting the concerns and expectations of the whole community. It becomes clear that, even more so in the case of a master than in that of an ordinary person, the deceased is also "a social being grafted upon the physical individual" (Hertz 1960: 77). Perhaps the most striking feature of this collectivization of death in Chan and Zen was the auction of the deceased master's personal belongings in order to pay the fast-growing cost of the funerals—a custom that can be illustrated by the funerals of Keizan's master Gikai (d. 1309). (See Bodiford 1989: 440.) We should therefore depart from the methodological individualism that leads us to believe that death and salvation concern only the individual. They also concern the collectivity, for which salvation means primarily continuity despite individual deaths.

The liminal stage: Chan funerary ritual

Let us examine now how ritualization affected the liminal/liminary stage, that is, the funerals of the forty-nine-day period during which the deceased was believed to travel through the Buddhist limbo before being eventually reborn.[31] We will take our cues from Robert Hertz's observation that, in many cultures, the corpse may be considered an index for the soul or spiritual component (Hertz 1960: 83). One obvious problem is how to reconcile funerary ritual with the *anātman* or no-self theory that allegedly forms the core of the Buddhist teaching. Like most other Buddhists, Chan monks recognized the persistence after death of something

[30] Although Ikkyū died in his sleep in 1481, he was still able to leave the following death verse: "Who in Japan teaches the True Law?/ Good and bad are made one by false wisdom./ Crazy Cloud knows the smell of his own shit./ Long letters of love, short poems of passion." (See *Ikkyū zue shūi* 743–747, quoted in Sanford 1981: 288.)

[31] It is not by pure coincidence that the Awakening of the Buddha is said to have lasted forty-nine days. As we will see below, the liminal phase of the death course is described symbolically as both a gestation (leading to rebirth) and a spiritual awakening (culminating in *nirvāṇa*).

called "intermediary being" (*anantarabhāva*, J. *chūū*, *chūin*), an entity that was easily mistaken for an enduring self.[32] At first glance, Dōgen's verse, referring as it does to his falling "fully alive" into the Yellow Springs, seems to suggest the persistence beyond death of some kind of clear consciousness. So does the common reference, in the context of Zen funerary rituals, to the "true man without rank" (J. *mui no shinnin*). As one Zen funerary sermon puts it, "The moon sets, but does not leave the sky." (Quoted in Bodiford 1989: 461.) Yet Dōgen himself spent a good part of his life criticizing the "substantialist" or "Senika" heresy, that is, the belief in the indestructibility of the spirit. It seems that the *anātman* theory was, to use Steven Collins's expression, a "linguistic taboo" whose primary function was to assert religious and sectarian difference (Collins 1982: 183). In most cases, it remained a kind of wishful thinking that did not really threaten the common belief in an afterlife.

Apart from the *Chan'yuan qinggui* compiled in 1103 by Changlong Zongze (n.d.), our main sources for the Chan/Zen funerary rituals are the *Jixiu Baizhang qinggui*, compiled under the Yuan (and its Tokugawa commentary by Mujaku Dōchū), the *Keizan shingi*,[33] and the *Sho ekō shingi* (1566).[34] The specificity of Chan funerary rituals cannot be traced back earlier than the *Chan'yuan qinggui*. Prior to that time, Chan masters such as Shenxiu and his disciple Puji were buried according to rites that were essentially Confucian, and we have no documentation for ordinary monks.[35] By the twelfth century, Chan rituals had come to include

[32] On this notion, see André Bareau, s.v. "Chūū," in *Hōbōgirin*, Vol. 5: 558–563; Collins 1982: 225–261.

[33] As Griffith Foulk points out, the *Keizan shingi*, despite its title, is not strictly speaking a *shingi* ("Pure Rule") but a collection of essays on ritual topics. See Foulk 1989.

[34] Another important source of documentation are the so-called *kirigami*. According to Ishikawa's classification, we find six kinds of "funerary *kirigami*" dealing with (1) rites immediately following death: for example, postmortem ordination; (2) the funerals proper: for example, transfer of the body through the Four Gates of the cremation ground, lighting of the funerary pyre (*ako*), sermon for the spirit of the deceased (*indō*); (3) the grave; (4) the spirits of the dead; (5) death during pregnancy; and (6) the ordination of spirits and animals.

[35] Although the early Buddhist tradition has it that the Buddha told his disciples to leave his funerals to the care of laymen, it also claims that the cremation rite was performed by his main disciple, Mahākāśyapa. See Bareau 1971: 175–265. On this question, see also Schopen 1990. The funerals for Indian monks seem to have been relatively simple. According to the Chinese pilgrim Yijing: "Three years' mourning or seven days' fasting [as in China] are not the only way in which a benevolent person is revered after death. . . . According to the Buddha's teaching, when a priest is dead, after one has recognized him to be really dead, on the same day his corpse is sent on a bier to a cremation place and is there burned. While the corpse is burning, all his friends assemble and sit on one side. . . . The 'Sūtra on Impermanence' [*Anityatā-sūtra*] [T. 17, 801] is recited by a skilled one, as short as a page or a leaf, so that it may not become tiresome. . . . Then they all meditate on the impermanency. On returning to their residence they bathe together in their clothes, in the pond outside the monastery. . . . They cleanse the floor with powdered cow dung. All other things remain as usual. There is no custom as to putting on a mourning-dress. . . . It is not right for a priest to lay aside the noble teaching of Śākya the Father and follow the common usage

a number of elements borrowed from Pure Land and esoteric Buddhist teachings. The *Chan'yuan qinggui* distinguishes clearly between the funerals of eminent monks (*sonshuku*) and those of ordinary monks (*bōsō*), who died before realizing awakening. These rituals became in Japan the model for the funerals of laymen and laywomen that will be described below. (See Ishikawa 1987d: 139.)

The funerals of Chan/Zen priests ideally involved nine rites (although, according to circumstances, this number was often reduced to seven or less): placing the body in a coffin (J. *nyūgan*); transfering the coffin from the abbot's room to the *Hattō* or Lecture Hall (*igan*); closing the coffin (*sagan*); hanging a portrait of the deceased above the altar (*kashin*); having a wake in the form of an individual consultation with the deceased master (*tairei shōsan*); removing the coffin to the cremation ground (*kigan*); offering a libation of tea (*tencha*); offering a libation of hot water (*tentō*); and lighting the funerary pyre (*ako, hinko*).[36] While a specific officiating priest is selected for each phase, all ceremonies present the same basic ritual components: tea offering (*tencha*), lecture of *dhāraṇī*[37] (*nenju*) and sūtras (*fugin*), dedication of merits (*ekō*), burning of incense.

Unlike the enlightened masters (*sonshuku*), whose religious goal had already been fulfilled during their lifetime, the ordinary dead—monks/ nuns or laymen/laywomen—were the objects of specific rites designed to help them achieve the deliverance they failed to realize while alive. The most important phases of the ritual were thus the postmortem ordination (in the case of a lay person), the sermon at the side of the corpse (*indō*), the circumambulation of the coffin around the cremation ground (*unyō sansō*), and the lighting of the funerary pyre (*ako, hinko*). In Japan, all these rites came to take place at the cremation ground, where a temporary edifice was built, which was divided into two spaces connected by a fenced corridor: the coffin room (*gandō*) and the cremation ground proper (*hiya*), with four symbolic doors and a hexagonal crematory oven in the middle. (See Figure 4.) This spatial division nicely reflects the tripartite structure of the rites of passage described by van Gennep (1960): rites performed in the coffin room ("separation"), ritual transfer to the cremation ground ("liminal phase"), and cremation ("incorporation").

handed down by the Duke of Chou, crying and weeping many a month, or wearing the mourning dress for three years." (See Takakusu 1970: 81–82.) Yijing's criticism of Chinese customs must be read against the backdrop of the sumptuary funerals of Buddhist monks such as Shenxiu.

[36] For more details, see Tamamuro 1963: 122; Fujii (1977): 3–4. For a sequence based on *Chan'yuan qinggui*, see Bodiford 1989: 425–463. On *tencha*, see *Hōbōgirin*, s.v. "Chatō," Vol. 3: 281–283.

[37] These *dhāraṇī* are usually the *Senju sengen daihishin daranikyo* (Ch. *Qianshou qian'yan dafeixin jing*, T. 20, 1060: 106–111) and the *Ryōgonju* (Sk. *Śūraṃgama-dhāraṇī*, T. 19, 945: 139–141).

These ritual innovations were eventually adopted by the other sects of Japanese Buddhism.[38]

The structure of the *indō* rite is rather paradoxical. Taking place at the beginning and at the end of the funerary process, it consists of preaching to the deceased about the emptiness of his attachments, which he has because of his illusion of selfhood (Fujii 1977: 21). But in order to assert the nonexistence of the self, the rite has to posit the existence of a dead spirit who listens to the sermon. Judith Berling interprets these funeral sermons as an example of "acculturative syncretism": "They would begin and/or end with a Buddhist statement of the ultimate emptiness of all souls, but the middle portion treated the souls as though they existed to assist mourners in their profound grief" (Berling 1980: 27). This may be a case of subversion of Mahāyāna dogmas by ritual practices, or merely an example of the clerical attempt to give philosophical meaning to ritual—or both. At any rate, this dialectical process reflects the tension between the two levels of understanding.[39] Particularly important, in this context, is the rite of hanging the portrait of the dead master (*shin*). The Chan/Zen ideology of presence, however, finds its limits in the sectarian manipulations of the ritual. In Sōtō Zen, for instance, the *indō*, while taking the form of "consultations" (*sanzen*) and "dialogues" (*mondō*) with the animate portrait of the master, became a pretext to assert the teachings of the sect and came to fulfill the same sectarian purpose as the earlier kōan ritual.

Other examples of sectarian statements may be found in the symbolism of the funerary site. Inscribed on the four banners erected at the sides of the site (*shihonbata*) and on the ceiling that covers it (*tengai*) were four-sentence verses such as:

Due to delusion, the three worlds are completed;
Due to awakening, the ten directions are empty.
From the outset, there is neither east nor west;
Where could there be a north and a south?[40]

---

[38] As noted earlier, another funerary symbol that arose in Chan is that of the "seamless stūpa" (*muhōtō*, also called "egg stūpa," *rantō*), which first appears in a Chan "encounter dialogue" between Nan'yang Huizhong (d. 775) and Emperor Daizong. (See *Jingde chuandeng lu* 5, т. 51, 2076: 245a.) On the legends surrounding these stūpas, see Suzuki Bokushi 1986: 259.

[39] This contradiction is not simply an oversight but reflects the fact that the dialectical affirmation of emptiness is essentially parasitic and cannot stand alone. This bears some analogy to the way in which the theoretical assertions in this book and others, usually found in the opening and concluding chapters (or in footnotes like this one), are constantly negated by the text itself, where the old categories constantly reemerge. But they in turn deconstruct these categories in the process, and deconstruction remains dependent on discursive constructions, just as the Middle Way rests on the two extremes.

[40] See, for example *Sho ekō shingi*, т. 81, 2578: 662. This typically Chan poem is reminiscent of Huineng's line, "Fundamentally, there is not a single thing," and the last two lines

The following verse on impermanence reflects a more traditional Buddhism:

All the *saṃskāra* are impermanent;
They are dharmas that arise and are destroyed.
When the [process of] arising and extinction is itself extinguished,
The quiescence-and-extinction becomes bliss.[41]

The development of the symbolism of the cremation site was a Japanese innovation (Seidel 1983a: 582). As mentioned earlier, while in the case of monks the procession goes from the Dharma Hall to the cremation ground, in the case of laymen the latter is divided into two parts, one for the coffin (*gandō*) and the other, the cremation ground proper (*hiya*), for the crematory. (See the figure in *Sho ekō shingi*, T. 81, 2578: 661.) The *hiya* has four gates, symbolizing the four stages of the practice of the Buddha: (1) production of the thought (of awakening), *hosshinmon* (east); (2) practice, *shūgyōmon* (south); (3) awakening, *bodaimon* (west); and (4) *nirvāṇa*, *nehanmon* (north). Buddhist symbolism seems to have merged with Japanese beliefs. According to Gorai Shigeru, Buddhism merely recontextualized the *shimon* structure, which is a survival of the *mogari*, a funerary structure destined to keep the soul of the dead.[42] In the Zen ritual, however, the coffin is carried three times clockwise around the room (*unyō sansō*), passing through all the doors and thus symbolically through all the stages from delusion to *nirvāṇa*. (See Fujii 1977: 21.) The threefold circumambulation corresponds to the three *pradakṣiṇā* around the Buddha or his stūpa.[43] It implies (and simultaneously creates) the presence of a

---

may have been used as a criticism of the Northern/Southern controversy. On the symbolism of the banners, see Fujii 1977: 91–92.

[41] These four verses are glossed in the following way: the first verse comes from the *Āgama-sūtra*; it is the precious vehicle to climb to Heaven. The second verse comes from the *Mahāprajñāpāramitā-sūtra*; it is the bridge of wisdom to be reborn in the Pure Land; the third verse comes from the *Avataṃsaka-sūtra*; it is the causes and conditions attained by the ultimate Buddha; the fourth verse comes from the *Mahāparinirvāṇa-sūtra*; it is the formless ground of "This very mind is the Buddha" (T. 81, 2578: 663b). Four verses with a similar content are also written on the four banners on the coffin: "All conditioned dharmas/ Are like a dream, an illusion, a bubble, or a shadow;/ They are like the dew or like lightning;/ You should examine them like this." See *Sho ekō shingi*, ibid.: 663a; see also *Chan'yuan qinggui, zz* 1, 2, 16, 5: 457c.

[42] See Gorai Shigeru, "Sō to kuyō," *Tōhōkai* 112 (1973): 34–42; on *mogari*, see also Macé 1986: 323–352.

[43] Yijing gives a different interpretation of the *pradakṣiṇā* (*unyō*): "Once I heard an explanation of a learned man in China, that the 'walking round towards the right' means to have one's right hand inside the circle (he makes) . . . , and that, in fact, therefore, when one walks round towards one's left-hand side, the 'walking round towards the right' has been accomplished" (Takakusu 1970: 141–142). Yijing rejects that opinion, arguing that *pradakṣiṇā* means walking counterclockwise. According to Indian commentators, however, this type of circumambulation is called *prasavya*, not *pradakṣiṇā* (ibid.: 141 n.2). This interpretation is the one found in the Sōtō *kirigami*. Another Chinese Vinaya master, Daoxuan, gives contradictory explanations, which may have in part to do with the fact that he is describing

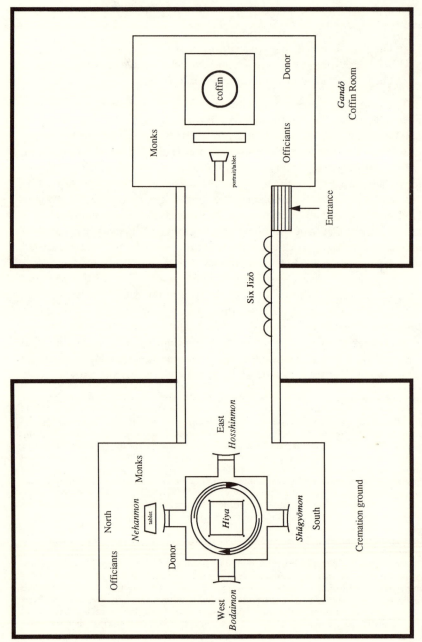

Figure 4. Schema of the cremation ground.

Buddha (the deceased) at the center of the cremation ground: the first circumambulation signifying the veneration of the Buddha, the second the annihilation of all illusions, the third the acquiring of sublimation. (See Falk 1977: 291.) Traditionally, the circumambulation of the four cardinal directions also means the conquest of the fifth, the center (or zenith). The symbolism of the "four gates" is also traced back to the four "encounters" that set up Śākyamuni on his spiritual quest: the young prince, on four different occasions, exited the royal city in a different direction, through the East, South, West, and North gates, meeting on each occasion, respectively, a sick man, an old man, a corpse, and an ascetic. Another tradition has it that, after the *parinirvāṇa* of the Buddha, his coffin was carried seven times around the city of Kuśinagara. According to the *Kirigami of the Four Gates*: "By opening the four gates one transcends the three times [past, present, future]. Hell and all the other receptacle worlds have the same circular form. This is what is called coming out of a circle into a circle. The three *pradakṣiṇā* express the three dots of the mind: *dharmakāya*, *prajñā*, and *vimokṣa*.[44] After the three turns toward the right, one can make three turns toward the left.[45] This symbol was

in some cases the (clockwise) circumambulation of the Buddha, in others the (counterclockwise) circumambulation of the ordination platform. See Mochizuki 1958–1963: 1:611a.

[44] According to various commentaries, the "three dots" of the mind refer to the three dots of the ideograph *xin* (J. *kokoro*), an ideograph chosen for its resemblance, in cursive script, to the Sanskrit (*siddham*) letter "i" (ॐ or ꣾ), the vowel that, in the esoteric Buddhist tradition, was considered the "root sound" and symbolized the origin of everything. (See Sugimoto 1982: 89, 235.) See *Mahāparinirvāṇa-sūtra* (T. 12, 374: 376c): "What is it that is called the secret store? It is like the three dots of the letter *i*. If they are lined up horizontally, they do not constitute an *i*. If lined up vertically, they also do not constitute an *i*. It is like the three eyes of Maheśvara. . . . I [i.e., the Buddha] am also like this. The Dharma of liberation is not *nirvāṇa*. The Body of the Tathāgata is not *nirvāṇa*. *Mahāprajñā* is not *nirvāṇa*. The three dharmas are each different and none of them [alone] is *nirvāṇa*. . . . Thus the three dharmas [together] for the sake of sentient beings are called entering into *nirvāṇa*." (See Broughton 1975: 143.) These three dots are symbolized in the Sōtō tradition by three connected circles expressing the three interrelated aspects of ultimate thruth: "The upper circle represents the true essence of formlessness, i.e., the virtue of the *Dharmakāya*. The circle with the character *myō* ["subtle"] in it expresses the subtle character of formlessness, i.e., the virtue of *prajñā*. The circle with the character *shin* ["mind"] in it expresses the mysterious function of formlessness, i.e., *vimokṣa*. These three circles are the three dots of the 'round i.' " Because of the mystic virtue of this Sanskrit vowel, by writing, pronouncing, or hearing it, one reaches into the origin of things, formlessness, that is, *nirvāṇa* or Buddhahood. This is why, we are told, the officiating priest knocks three times on the coffin, before drawing a clockwise circle for more certainty. Similarly, before "opening the eyes" of a Buddhist icon, or "pointing" a grave or a mortuary tablet (*ihai*), the priest visualizes three times the character *shin*, or the three dots of the "i" (eye?). In both cases, he ritually creates a Buddha, an immortal double of himself or of the dead. These esoteric rituals were rejected by Menzan in his attempt to demythologize the Sōtō tradition. See *Tōjō shitsunai danshi kenpi shiki* in *sz* 15, *Shitsuchū*: 197–218. See also Kushida 1977: 79–80.

[45] According to another document: "In the past one turned three times toward the right, then three times toward the left, to signify the unity of life and death and the freedom of coming and going. Nowadays, one makes only the three turns toward the right." (Quoted in Sugimoto 1982: 132; Ishikawa 1987b: 165–167.) In other words, just as the clockwise

used to signify the identity of *saṃsāra* and *nirvāṇa*, of going with the current [*jun*] or against it [*gyaku*]." (See Sugimoto 1982: 132; Ishikawa 1987b: 166.) Another *kirigami* supposedly transmitted by Meihō Sotetsu (1277–1350) describes the procession from the room of the coffin to the cremation ground.

> From the room with shutters [*shitomi*], one must go around the hall toward the left. . . . The left means going against the current, death. The svastika turning toward the left symbolizes the four marks: birth, old age, illness, and death. Those who transcend all marks are called Buddhas. The subtle mark is round and clear and transcends all names and marks. Having turned around the hall, one proceeds directly to the cremation ground, and one turns around it three or seven times. In Buddhism, to follow the current means to go from the first to the tenth *bhūmi*, to obtain all the fruits of subtle awakening and to enter the *nirvāṇa* without remainder. Such is the meaning of the cremation of the saints. Buddhism considers that to die is to follow the current [*jun*], while Confucianism considers that it is to go against the current [*gyaku*].[46]

This ritual overkill should not make us forget that in other contexts the circumambulation of the coffin aims at preventing the deceased from finding his or her way back. Although the ambivalence characteristic of funerary rituals dealing with the liminal phase does not appear in Chan/Zen funerals, we should not conclude that it is entirely absent. The very redundance of positive symbolism is perhaps indeed an indication to the contrary.

The *ako* ("lowering the torch") rite, performed as are the rites marking the end of the liminal phase at the "*nirvāṇa* gate" (*nehanmon*), is based on the legend of the Buddha's funeral.[47] According to tradition, Śākyamuni's disciples tried in vain during one week to light his funerary pyre. When Mahākāśyapa, however, who had been absent at the time of the Buddha's death, returned to lead the ceremony, he was greeted, so we are told, by auspicious signs (the Buddha's feet emerging from the many-layered shroud and disappearing again), and the pyre lighted by itself.

---

turns signify the upward movement from *saṃsāra* to *nirvāṇa*, the counterclockwise turns signify the downward movement from *nirvāṇa* to *saṃsāra*. The Bodhisattva goes in both directions, returning to the world after enlightenment.

[46] Quoted in Ishikawa 1986b: 205. Another passage in the same document states: "The procedure for circumambulating the cremation ground is different for saints and ordinary people. The saints turn three times toward the right, or seven times. This is because they see death as natural [*jun*], coming to life as unnatural [*gyaku*]. . . . Common people turn toward the left because they see death as unnatural, coming to life as natural" (ibid.).

[47] According to Mujaku Dōchū, the term *ako* is used when there is just one funerary sermon, *hinko* when there are several. See Yanagida 1979: 1:574b.

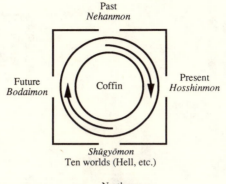

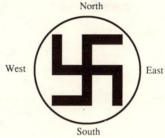

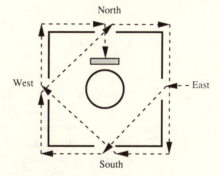

Figure 5. The Four Gates and funerary circumambulation.

(See Fujii 1977: 3.) The point here is that the cremation rite (i.e., the rein-corporation) must be performed by the successor, or rather, that the rite *makes* or confirms the successor.[48] Another paradigmatic story tells of the Chan master Huangbo and his mother, whom he had abandoned in order to practice Chan. Once, on a begging tour, he happened to pass through

---

[48] See also *Senshi nyūmetsu kirigami* in Ishikawa 1986b: 206.

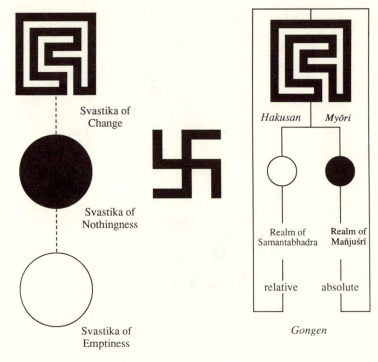

a. The three aspects of reality   b. Symbolism of the Hakusan god

Figure 6. Symbolism of the *Svastika* in Sōtō Zen.

his village, but because of the darkness, his mother first failed to recognize that he had returned. Soon her maternal instinct moved her to go out in search of him, but she drowned in a river. Knowing this, Huangbo came to the spot and drew a circle with a torch before throwing it into the water with a shout.[49] Then the body of his mother floated to the surface, and she was eventually reborn in paradise. This story is usually

[49] As we saw above, the symbolism of the circle is omnipresent in Chan, and particularly in Sōtō Zen. The symbolism of *ako* in general, and of the torch in particular, is found in many Sōtō *kirigami*. Several of these documents stress the relation between the cremation rite and the pair formed by Śākyamuni and Mahākāśyapa. A "Kirigami of the Torch," for example, interprets the story of the transmission to Mahākāśyapa in funerary terms. The story, often quoted in Sōtō literature, is that the Buddha once held up a flower in front of the assembly. Everyone was puzzled, except Mahākaśyapa, who smiled. The Buddha therefore transmitted the "Treasure of the Eye of the True Law" (*Shōbōgenzō*) to him. According to the esoteric interpretation of this story, the Buddha is the officiating priest, while the smiling disciple is the dead. The flower, symbol of the mind, is itself symbolized by a circle. To hold up the flower means to integrate the dead into the lineage of the *Shōbōgenzō*, as in the case of the postmortem ordination, which is sometimes interpreted as exiting the circle of sentient beings to reenter the circle of Buddha's disciples. See Ishikawa 1987b: 172.

given as the origin of the Chan practice of throwing the torch onto the funerary pyre with a shout.[50] Yet the elaborate descriptions of the ritual hardly mention the cremation proper—and neither do the sermons.[51] The actual transformation of the master's body—unlike that of the common corpses in Indian Buddhism—seems to be a taboo for Zen discourse and meditation. The negative symbolism of the cremation process (as dissolution) has been replaced by an irenist ideology of reincorporation and transformation into a Buddha. Today the *ako* is even more "symbolic," in the sense that the officiating monk no longer uses a real torch but a mere stick with a red end.

After the thirteenth century, the ritual sequence described above was progressively extended to laymen and laywomen, who were tonsured and ordained postmortem (*mutsugo sasō*) before passing through all the stages from *indō* to *ako*. When possible, the ordination took place just before death, becoming a kind of Extreme Unction. Thus, for example, the Regent Hōjō Tokimune (1251–1284) was tonsured on his deathbed by Mugaku Sogen (Ch. Wuxue Zuyuan, 1226–1286). (See Collcutt 1981: 70–73.) These posthumous ordinations became the pretext for sermons (Ch. *pushuo*, J. *fusetsu*), which came to form the bulk of Chan/Zen "Recorded Sayings" (Ch. *yulu*, J. *goroku*). (See Levering 1987b; Bodiford 1989: 449.) An important element of the ordination was the transmission of a lineage chart (Ch. *xuemo*, J. *kechimyaku*), which came to serve as a magical talisman, providing salvation for the dead by allowing them to join the "blood line" of the Buddha (Bodiford 1989: 418). In other words, the lineage chart was no longer—if it ever was, even in the case of living monks—the symbol of awakening, but was its magical cause. The incorporation of the dead into the lineage of the ancestors is well attested graphically by Sōtō *kirigami* (see Ishikawa 1986b: 188), in a fashion strikingly similar to premortem ordination.

The ceremony of "depositing" (or "pacifying," *ankotsu*) the bones is a rite of reincorporation of the dead, marking the end of the liminal phase. Yet it reproduces in itself the liminal phase: during ten or fifteen days, offerings of tea and hot water were made to the relics before putting them into a reliquary in the presence of the entire community. (See Seidel 1983a: 582.) The last important stage in the funerals—a superfluous precaution, it would seem, after a cremation—was the "closing of the grave"

[50] See Fujii 1977. According to a *kirigami* of the Pure Land sect found in the Kanazawa Bunko collection, the *Hyakutsū kirigami*, this episode was also the origin of the *indō* rite. Before throwing his torch in the river, Huangbo said: "The source of the great river [*saṃsāra*] has dried up, and it can no longer hide the Five Sins. When one child leaves his family, nine generations ascend to heaven. If these are false words, all the Buddhas have told lies." See Ishikawa 1987a: 192.
[51] For an elaborate description of the Chinese cremation ground, see Prip-Møller 1982: 163–175.

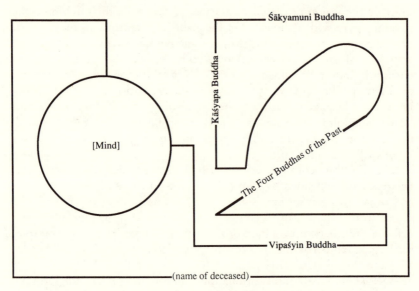

Figure 7. Symbolism of postmortem ordination.

by burying talismans at the four sides, probably as much to prevent the spirit of the deceased from returning as to prevent malevolent spirits ("foxes and wolves") from intruding into the grave. The "closing" formulas, written in Chinese, were *jiji rulü ling* ("Promptly, promptly [obey], in accordance with the statutes and ordinances," the formula used to implement an official edict)[52] and *shizi hong* (Sk. *siṃhanāda*, J. *shishiku*, "the Lion's Roar"), that is, the teaching of the Buddha, the "lion of the Śākya," the mere utterance of which is said to frighten the heretics. (See Ishikawa 1986b: 189.) Whereas the second of these is unmistakably Buddhist, the first one—the most frequently used—has a long history in Chinese popular religion. (See Seidel 1987: 39–42.) Both are often found in the *kirigami* of the Sōtō tradition. These talismans became particularly important in the cases of inauspicious deaths—such as death during pregnancy and accident, or in the case of services performed for outcasts (*hinin*). In some *kirigami*, for instance, the above formulas are supplemented by specific injunctions aimed at cutting all relationships with the deceased and his/her living relatives.[53] They seem to reflect the expansion

[52] According to Seidel (1987: 39–42), these ordinances presupposed the existence of a code of law governing the relations with the other-world or with the spirit hierarchy, and their purpose was "to exorcise malefic influences on behalf of the living and to gain release from culpability on behalf of the dead." See also Ikeda On, "Chūgoku rekidai bōken ryakkō," *Tōyō bunka kenkyūsho kiyō* 86 (1981): 193–278.

[53] For a similar example in the Taiwanese context, see Ahern 1973: 172.

of Sōtō in the lower strata of society during the fifteenth and sixteenth centuries. (See Ishikawa 1987a: 189–192.)

From Defilement to Purity

It seems that the ritual sequence examined above—from defilement to purity—repeats itself historically or ideologically with the shift observed in Sōtō during the Tokugawa period from "mixed" to "pure" Zen. Tamamuro and others have argued that it is as a result of its social and territorial expansion in medieval Japan that contemplative Chan became "funerary Zen." Like their predecessors, many of the Zen monasteries of the medieval period—such as Tenryūji and Tōjiin in Kyōto—were *bodaiji*, temples for the performance of services for the peace (i.e., awakening, *bodai*) of deceased patrons or for placating the spirits of past enemies. The evolution of Chan/Zen funerary rituals in China and Japan can be summarized as a shift from lay funerals for Chan monks (as in the case of Shenxiu),[54] to specifically Chan funerals for Chan monks (during the Song), and finally—at least in the Japanese context—to Zen funerals for laymen (from Kamakura onward).[55] The major change appears to have taken place during the fourteenth–fifteenth centuries, with the spread of the Sōtō sect in the provinces and its subsequent development of rituals for laymen and laywomen of all social ranks (including outcasts, *hinin* or *eta*). These rituals were both a cause and a result of the "popularization" of the Sōtō teaching. Consequently, Zen monks, and Sōtō monks in particular, became specialists of impurity and had to confront the question of the pollution of death. Buddhist monks, however, always had a deep concern with purity, and they may have accepted reluctantly the role of undertakers: after its introduction into Japan in the sixth century, more than a century was necessary before Buddhism came to take over a role until then assumed by the priests of what would later become Shintō.[56]

[54] In Indian Buddhism, funerals seem to have been limited to the recitation of the *Anityatā-sūtra* (*T*. 17, 801), and the care of Buddha's relics was left to laymen. In China, the funerary rituals described in a Buddhist encyclopedia such as the *Shishi yaolan* (1019) are still predominantly Confucian (see *T*. 54, 2127: 307–310). On this question, see Ishikawa 1987a.

[55] During the Song, funerals for laymen were often performed by professionals called "good friends" (*shan'you*, Sk. *kalyāṇamitra*) or "incinerating laymen" (*huo juzhi*), whose status was halfway between that of monks and laymen. In Japan, this function was taken over by the monks. During the Tokugawa, however, Sōtō Zen monks retroceded part of their dubious privilege as undertakers to another category of "specialists in impurity," the *chōri*—a kind of outcast group (*hinin*). For a description of their function, see *Chōri yuisho sho*, quoted in Satō Shunkō 1986–1987: 149. See also *Dictionnaire historique du Japon*, s.v. "*Chōri*" (Tokyo: Kinokuniya, 1975), 3: 100.

[56] As is well known, it is the cremation of Empress Jitō in 703—only three years after the inaugural cremation of the Buddhist monk Dōshō—that marks the Buddhist takeover of imperial funerals, characterized until then by the performance of the *mogari* ritual. On this question, see Macé 1986: 368–383.

The customary characterization of Shintō as a tradition concerned from the outset with ritual purity is a myth—or at least a relatively late ideological product. (See Macé 1986: 380.)

One way Zen monks tried to deal with the problem of the impurity caused by their contact with death might be seen in the development of the Hakusan cult in the Sōtō tradition. The function of this cult in Sōtō seems to have been primarily one of purification after funerals. (See Satō Shunkō 1986–1987.) The so-called *Chinju kirigami*, a document that was often transmitted within the Sōtō sect during the medieval period, explains how one may purify oneself upon returning from funerals by reciting two poems while facing in the direction of the shrine dedicated to the Hakusan god. There is in popular culture another Hakusan (Shirayama), which seems to present some functional similarities to the Hakusan of the *kirigami*. In the popular context, Hakusan refers to the structure—made of bamboo and of white cloth—into which the corpse was introduced during the *mogari* ritual (Miyata 1979: 126–134). This is strongly reminiscent of a Shūgendō rite performed during the Hanamatsuri festival, in which young men and women clothed in white are secluded in a square building called Hakusan. According to Gorai, to enter this Hakusan means to enter the Pure Land, and the practitioners are thereby returned to this world purified. (See Gorai 1983.) In these two cases, Hakusan appears as a cultural artifact in a ritual of rebirth. Therefore, despite differences in ritual, these variants of Hakusan might be seen as a means of inverting values, a way to change death into life, or pollution into purity.

Apparently, this inversion/purification rite was also the primary function of the Hakusan cult in the Sōtō ritual (Satō Shunkō 1986–1987). Later Sōtō tradition gave a radically different interpretation of Hakusan. In some variants of the *Chinju kirigami*, Hakusan is interpreted in terms of the Sōtō dialectics of the Five Ranks, and the funerary aspects of the myth are played down. As the Sōtō tradition developed in close contact with Hakusan Shūgendō, the Hakusan god came to be worshiped as a protector of the Sōtō community. Significant is the story in which he helps Dōgen, on the eve of the latter's departure from China, to copy the *Biyan lu* ("Emerald Cliff Record") overnight. (See Faure 1987a: 51; Durt 1983: 607.) This story, which depicts a protector god that is completely different from the deity of local cults, seems to reflect the change that took place in Sōtō during the Tokugawa period, when Eiheiji became once again the head temple of the sect and when the image of the "patriarch" Dōgen was revised. Contrary to the aforementioned *Chinju kirigami*, later *kirigami* relative to Hakusan omit the reference to funerary ritual and purification. The most drastic change, however, came with Menzan Zuihō (1683–1769). Always intent on demythologizing the Sōtō tradition and criticizing the "superstitions" that had crept into the esoteric transmission of the *kirigami*, Menzan subsequently rejected the *Chinju kirigami*, as most other *kirigami*, as "unworthy of belief." For him, the Hakusan god was no longer the tutelary deity described by the *kirigami* but a more abstract protector of the Dharma.[57] As a result, the connections between Hakusan and funerary rituals were eventually severed. Menzan's attitude reflects the evolution of the Sōtō sect, at a time when, owing to the *danka* system established by the Tokugawa, it was solidly entrenched in the provinces and no longer needed to pose as "funerary Buddhism" (Satō Shunkō 1986–1987). Once well in favor with the local authorities, it could leave the pollution of death to others. For that, it needed to rid the name of Hakusan of its mortuary associations. It is against such a backdrop that Menzan's advocacy of a return to the "pure Zen" of Dōgen's *Shōbōgenzō* must be placed. In this sense, one may perhaps say that the "philosophy" of the *Shōbōgenzō* hides many skeletons (to begin with, Dōgen's) in its cupboard.

LIKE any ritual, Chan/Zen funerary rituals are multilayered, polysemic, and multifunctional. Their main function for the collectivity might well be, as Hertz claimed, to reaffirm order and continuity in the face of the scandal of death—or perhaps to use the latter as an opportunity to create an ideal (and illusory) order.[58] The expression of social order by differentiation of status was manifested in the medieval period by the multiplication of *kaimyō* (mortuary titles) specific to all layers of society, down to the outcasts (*hinin*). In this sense, "the society of the dead structures the society of the living" (Huntington and Metcalf 1979: 65)—and inversely. Furthermore, the hierarchical structure of the monastery was expressed in the careful choreography of the ritual, a performance divided into various "acts" during which each of the main participants came in turn to the forefront. Funerals were not only a way for the Chan/Zen collectivity to redefine itself ritually after the disruption caused by the death of one of its members; in the case of an abbot, they also served the more narrow ambitions of his would-be successors.

At another ideological level, funerary rituals can also be seen as an attempt to accelerate the process of death. They are a compromise with the irreversibility of change, a reality conveniently denied at the theoretical

[57] See Menzan's, *Tōjō shitsunai danshi kenpi shiki* (1749), in *sz* 15, *Shitsuchū*: 197–218; Satō Shunkō 1986–1987: 157.
[58] What Bloch and Parry say of "society" seems to apply, *mutatis mutandis*, to the Chan/Zen "sect": "This social order is a *product* of rituals of the kind we consider rather than their cause. In other words, it is not so much a question of Hertz's reified 'society' responding to the 'sacrilege' of death, as of the mortuary rituals themselves being an occasion for *creating* that 'society' as an apparently external force" (Bloch and Parry 1982: 6).

level.[59] They offer a mediation between perfect order (the world of awakening) and pure—or rather impure—chaos: the world of *saṃsāra*; they incorporate the dead into a cyclical pattern, thereby subsuming the discrepancy of death in a process that allows the continuation of individual life. As mentioned earlier, if the fate of the corpse serves as an index for that of the spirit, the acceleration of the process that leads to immutable ashes or relics (and sometimes mummies) symbolizes the reintegration of the spirit in the eternal world of truth. The reality of death as a slow and unpleasant process of transition from one stage to another is to a certain extent denied, but by the same token, it is, however little, reintroduced. As Bloch and Parry point out, "the ideology has to be put to work in the very world which it denies, and it must therefore be compromised. This compromise is manifested symbolically and this explains certains aspects of the funerary rituals, . . . which take the form of the reintroduction, in certain ritual contexts, of what had enthusiastically been denied in others" (Bloch and Parry 1982: 39).

Incidentally, while borrowing many elements from popular culture, Chan/Zen rituals did not incorporate the sexuality/fertility symbolism that often constitutes a characteristic of the popular attitude toward death—or only in an implicit way, through the traditional ascetic belief that the regeneration of life through sexuality is a cause of death. Bloch and Parry have, however, convincingly argued that the denial of sexuality did not imply that of fertility—on the contrary.[60] In contrast with Indian ascetics who, being already ritually dead to the world, do not need funerals, the importance of the funerary ritual in Chan/Zen implies that the rise of Chan masters to patriarchal status had made them denizens (or perhaps captives) of this world, for whom (despite disclaimers) ancestral transcendence came to take precedence over experiential transcendence. Being mystically identified with the lineage, that is, with the entire *collectivity* of his forebears, or with a death-transcending double or effigy, the individual Chan master tended to lose his individuality and could therefore become a source of regeneration. (See Bloch and Parry 1982: 35.) For instance, the fact that the flesh-body of Huineng was carried in the countryside in times of drought bears testimony to its association with rain and fertility. Furthermore, the relation between death and procreation is clearly described in some *kirigami*. As Parry points out, "it is only to be expected that the beliefs and practices associated with cremation are pervaded by the symbolism of embryology" (Parry 1982: 80). The theme of

[59] In *Shōbōgenzō Genjō kōan*, for instance, Dōgen develops the notion, advocated first by Sengzhao (384–414?), of the immutability of things. (See T. 82, 2582: 24a.)

[60] See Bloch and Parry 1982: 19. On the relationship between asceticism and sexuality, see Wendy Doniger O'Flaherty, *Śiva: The Erotic Ascetic* (Oxford: Oxford University Press, 1980).

death as parturition, mentioned by Parry in the Indian context (ibid.: 85), is also present in Japanese Buddhism.[61]

To a certain extent, then, funerary rituals, with their notion of an intermediary period, reintroduced in Chan the notion of ontological change (*devenir*). Death constitutes an intrusion of reality into the Chan utopia—and funerals are an attempt to deny this reality or to create anew that utopia. While the forty-nine-day intermediary period can be seen as a ritual extension of the moment of death and a concession to change, it is also, when compared with the traditional three-year mourning period, a drastic reduction of the liminal phase. In the Japanese context, after cremation replaced *mogari*, death became more punctual and disjoined: the rites of *mogari* took place around the corpse; those of the forty-nine days take place in monasteries.[62] Unlike the *mogari* ritual, the Buddhist ritual operated a disjunction between the state of the deceased's body and the destiny of the soul, thereby rendering the metaphorical relationship between the corpse and the soul more abstract. By accelerating the process of transformation, cremation suppresses or at least diminishes duration. At the same time, decay is increasingly denied and feared, losing whatever purpose it may have had in the *mogari* ritual. François Macé has shown that from the eighth century onward—after having been first exalted, then tamed—death came to be feared and despised. Accordingly, the corpse, having lost its function of reference to the destiny of the soul, was rejected into the realm of defilement and evil (Macé 1986: 397).

Zen, however, contributed to a partial rehabilitation of death by inverting its meaning—from a purely negative event to a positive occasion for awakening. The Zen master's appeal to popular imagination was due

---

[61] On Japanese Buddhist embryology, see James Sanford, "Spiritual Embryology in Shingon Buddhism," 1989 (unpublished paper). In the Sōtō tradition in particular, the parallelism between death and birth, constantly affirmed in the Buddhist notion of *saṃsāra* ("life-and-death"), is reinforced by *kirigami* dealing with conception. According to these documents, the fetus develops by periods of seven days, during which the Thirteen Buddhas, by turns, make the parts of its body. If it dies *in utero*, the Buddha of the corresponding period is the intercessor to whom one should pray. See Ishikawa 1986b: 201–203. This periodization replicates that of the liminal phase of the funerary ritual, during which the dead, as "intermediary being," proceeds toward rebirth through the Ten Hells, with the assistance of the Thirteen Buddhas. A *kirigami* attributed to Keizan expresses in Tantric terminology the characteristically Chinese belief that the flesh (the decaying element) is female, while the bones are male: "The seed of humans is constituted by the union of the two fluids of the father and the mother. The seed of the father is white and gives the bones; it is the blood of the Five Hundred Worthies of the *Vajradhātu*. The seed of the mother is red and gives the flesh-body; it is the blood of the Seven Hundred Worthies of the *Garbhadhātu*." See Ishikawa, ibid. Thus the cremation, producing quintessential bones, is indeed an incorporation into "patriarchal," that is, male, lineage. The case of the "flesh-bodies" is more ambiguous. On flesh and bones and their relation to gender in Chinese religion, see James L. Watson, in Bloch and Parry 1982: 155–186.

[62] See Macé 1986: 377. On cremation, see Seidel 1983a: 573–577; Ebrey 1989a; Groot 1982: 3:1391ff.; Prip-Møller 1982: 163–175.

to his apparent power over death. This privilege was an expression (1) of the combined effects of the Chan/Zen "character planning"—an everyday practice conceived as a preparation for death (was not *satori* itself perceived as a form of death, in which true life would be found?); (2) of the extension to funerary ritual of the dialogical structure and paradoxical language of Chan dialogues, which suggested transcendence of death; and (3) of the theory of "innate awakening" (*hongaku*), which denied the ultimate reality of death. Ironically, this denial and apparent mastery of death, source of the ritual composure that rendered Zen funerals so impressive to a lay audience, nourished the Chan/Zen fascination with the paraphernalia of death (e.g., relics). The emergence of a Chan discourse on death, while reflecting a strategic adaptation to popular needs, also reflects Chan's inner dynamics. What has perhaps changed is that the implicit consensus that limited the theoretical extremism of subitism, the fluid "double truth" of the logic of practice, now needs to be made explicit in "black and white."

Zen could not remain entirely exempt from the defilement associated with death. This is why, after purifying itself by its funerary rituals, the Sōtō sect attempted, more radically, to purify itself from them by returning to the "pure Zen" of Dōgen. By the same token, it weakened its privileged relationship with popular culture—a relationship that it has tried more recently to resurrect by intense proselytizing. More generally, by accepting the common prejudice against the defilement of death and retreating into an elitist utopia of "dry landscapes"—where decay cannot prevail—Japanese Zen lost the funerary ground to other Buddhist sects (Pure Land and Nichiren) and to the so-called New Religions.

Ten   *Dreams Within a Dream*

Il faut vouloir et savoir rêver.

—Baudelaire

You have not awakened to wakefulness, but to a previous dream. This dream is enclosed within another,
and so on to infinity.

—Borges, *Labyrinths*

Relics and icons reintroduced presence and mediation in a world emptied
by the Buddhist philosophy of emptiness and selflessness. Another aspect
of the Buddhist "metaphysics of presence," and a crucial mode of mediation, is provided by the intermediary world of dreams. Despite the
Chan/Zen rhetoric of immediacy, dreams seem to have played a significant role in the life of Chan/Zen communities. Like poets, according to
Cocteau, many Chan masters "took their orders from the night." It is this
role of dreams in Chan and Zen that I now attempt to evaluate.

METHODOLOGICAL CAVEAT

To understand the place of dreams in Chan is not an easy task, for this
understanding is mediated by various cultural and methodological presuppositions inherited from the Enlightenment. The most obvious are
the ethnocentric universalism that devalues dreams in the name of reason
and the prevalent agnosticism that usually informs the scientific attitude.
The dominant approach is the psychoanalytical one, based on Freud's *Interpretation of Dreams* or Jung's discussion of archetypes.[1] Despite their
usefulness, and because of their universalism, both theories are clearly
ethnocentric. The socio-historical approach, on the other hand, pays
more attention to the specificity of each cultural context and stresses the
contextual meaning of dreams.[2] Roger Bastide, for instance, contrasts the
continuity between dream and reality in traditional societies with their
inverted relation in Western societies. While in our culture dreams are

---

[1] See Brill 1966: 179–549; C. G. Jung, *Dream Analysis: Notes on the Seminar Given in 1928–
1930*, ed. William McGuire (Princeton: Princeton University Press, 1984). See also: Foucault and Binswanger 1984–1985.

[2] See G. E. von Grünebaum, "The Cultural Function of the Dream as Illustrated by Classical Islam," in Grünebaum and Caillois 1966; Bastide 1972; Le Goff, "Dreams in the Culture and Collective Psychology of the Medieval West," in Le Goff 1980: 201–204; and Le
Goff 1988.

perceived negatively as an instrument of evasion from a socially defined reality, in other cultures they serve as an instrument of social and/or cosmic integration in a larger reality. Therefore, we are not prepared to understand how dreams can be simultaneously incorporated in reality or be a reflection of the transcendental and produce history (Bastide 1972: 39).

Our cultural presuppositions lead us to oppose dream and reality and to associate dreams with irrationality and subjectivity. Even the hermeneutic revalorization of dreams since Freud holds them to be cryptic revelations of disturbed mental states, failed attempts at individuation. "To us," writes G. E. von Grünebaum, "the symptomatic, revelatory, 'prophetic' significance of the dream points inward to the dreamer (and to his society), not outward into areas of reality inaccessible by rational or 'natural' means. . . . The great change that has made the dream an instrument for introspection and (collective) self-cognition, rather than an instrument for cognition of 'outside reality,' has in some ways detracted, in other ways added, to its significance within our own culture" (Grünebaum and Caillois 1966: 21).

The psychoanalytical theory fails to take into account the fact that the meaning and function of dreams are culture-specific and that they have drastically changed with the general transformation of Western culture itself. The borderline between the real and the unreal is a shifting one, and dreams do not always fall on the same side of that line. Furthermore, starting from the assumption of illness, psychoanalysis tends to focus on the pathological and/or therapeutic aspects of dreams and to leave aside dreams that do not fit in this schema. The content of the dream, however, seems to depend largely on the degree of social integration. For instance, while dreams of temptation are common during the initial stages of religious practice, bearing witness to the difficulty of breaking with the former social milieu, they tend to give way in later stages to dreams of a more spiritual nature (Bastide 1972: 15–17). Yet even Arhats were believed to have wet dreams.

The Western cultural history of dreams helps us to understand how, when dreams become synonymous with delusion, a society can be "frustrated of its dreams." Jacques Le Goff, in particular, has well shown how, with the disappearance of the pagan intermediary realm of the "daemonic," dreams progressively lost their ambivalence—an ambivalence symbolized by the Homeric image of the "two gates" (of horn for true dreams, of ivory for false dreams)[3]—and became, with Christianity, the object of an increasing distrust and finally of an unequivocal condemna-

---

[3] See the famous dream of Penelope in *Odysseus*, Song xix, verse 560ff. Quoted in Le Goff 1988: 196.

tion. Thus, during the Middle Ages, "daemonic" dreams became demoniac, they "swung over to the side of the devil" (Le Goff 1988: 203).

These attempts, however, to reassess with historical objectivity the
evolution of dreams in Western society reflect a fundamentally agnostic
approach, and Henri Corbin is not entirely unjustified to think that, "in
one respect or another, the causal reduction of visionary dreams to a psychological, sociological, historical explanation derives from agnosticism"
(Corbin 1967: 382). On the one hand, an agnostic seems bound to mis-
understand gnosticism and the true value of dreams in a "gnostic" culture, that is, a culture that takes dreams seriously as revelations and
stresses their performative nature or transformative power. To understand what Corbin means, we must recall his notions of a *mundus imaginalis* and of "creative imagination." (See Corbin 1967: 402; 1983: 7–40). In
this view, dreams give a privileged access to the intermediary world and
have a higher ontological status than the world of ordinary reality. Such
a conception—that of Shiite Islam as described by Corbin—was apparently not alien to Buddhism or to East Asian cultures. On the other hand,
a gnostic like Corbin is likely to overlook the dream's ambivalent effects.

Taking dreams seriously, however, does not mean that one can play
down their ideological functions. The fact that dreams provided an access
to a higher reality did not prevent them from being manipulated by the
dreamers themselves—and by others—for all kinds of more down-to-
earth purposes. Dreams are ambiguous because they are both a collective
and an individual phenomenon, which may serve the interests of tradition
but also threaten them. Insofar as they tend to assert the imaginary world
of popular culture or to reflect "an aspiration to *personal religion*,"[4] they
seem to subvert social and religious orthodoxy. Yet they are often at the
source of orthodoxy. The soteriological value of dreams remains problematic: because of their fundamental ambivalence, dreams can always
constitute a stumbling block on the path—justifying Freud's famous
statement that "the dream is the guardian of sleep," not its disturber. (See
Brill 1966: 287.) For the community, too, the dream turns out to be a
two-edged sword: it may provide an opportunity for change or an argument against it, increase collective control over individuals but also undermine it.[5] To the question "what speaks in the dream?"—the collective

[4] As Le Goff points out, the development of dream has been closely linked with the vogue
of the trip to the other world and the importance of *individual judgment* after death" (Le Goff
1988: 227).

[5] For example, Myōe's process of individuation through dreaming, as Kawai (1990) interprets it, is only the other side of the collectivization of Myōe's dreams. In this sense, one
may speak of a "*communauté de rêve*": Myōe's dreams were anxiously waited and interpreted
by his disciples, for they influenced all the important decisions. Dreams were thus the governing principle of the medieval *samgha*, and as such they were the property of the collectivity, not of the individual.

or the individual, the social (Freud) or the cosmic (Jung)?—there is no easy, or rather no single, definitive answer.

ASIAN DREAMS

Dreams undeniably play a major role in Asian cultures.[6] The Indian approaches to dreams, as they found their ultimate philosophical expression in the *Yogavāsiṣṭha*, have been well documented by Wendy Doniger O'Flaherty. Chinese and Japanese lores are also rich in dreams of all kinds. In early Buddhism, dreams were prominent in the hagiography of the Buddha. The most well known is of course Śākyamuni's mother's dream of a white elephant piercing her side when she became pregnant. The main events in Śākyamuni's life, his awakening and death, were announced to his disciples by premonitory dreams. Before awakening, he himself had several such dreams, and so did his father and his wife. At the time of the Buddha's *parinirvāṇa*, an ascetic named Subhadra had ominous dreams that he first misinterpreted as announcing his own death. Doniger O'Flaherty mentions a variant of the "lotus growing out of the mud" parable, a story in which Gautama dreams that he walks on a great mountain of shit but is not dirtied by it (O'Flaherty 1984: 153). She notes that, within Buddhism, the Sarvāstivādins and the Theravādins, as well as Tibetan Buddhists, paid close attention to dreams.[7] In Tibetan Buddhism, dreams permit one to reach the *bardo* or intermediary world.[8] "Seizing one's dreams" is thus recognized as a valuable soteriological means, as long as the practitioner is aware that "dreams, like gold, may be either wholesome or harmful."[9] In Indian Buddhism we also find an attempt at classifying dreams according to their origin. According to the *Samantapāsādikā* (T. 24, 1662: 760; trans. Bapat and Hirakawa 1970: 356–358), a commentary on Vinaya often quoted in Chinese sources (see

[6] For India, see the masterly book by Doniger O'Flaherty 1984. The literature on China is extensive. See Roberto K. Ong 1985, 1988; Carolyn T. Brown 1988; Strickmann 1988; Laufer 1931: 208–216; Waley 1970; D. F. Miao, "The Dream in Chinese Literature," *The China Journal* 20, 2 (February 1934): 70–75; Eberhard 1971; David R. Knechtges, "Dream Adventure Stories in Europe and T'ang China," *Tamkang Review* 4, 2 (1973): 101–119; Romeyn Taylor, "Ming T'ai-tsu Story of a Dream," *Monumenta Serica* 32 (1976): 1–20; Donald Harper, "Wang Yen-shou's Nightmare Poem," *HJAS* 47, 1 (1987): 239–283; Dell R. Hales, "Dreams and the Daemonic in Traditional Chinese Short Stories, in W. H. Nienhauser, *Critical Essays on Chinese Literature* (Honolulu: University of Hawaii Press, 1976), 71–87; Schafer 1965; Anthony C. Yu, "The Quest of Brother Amor: Buddhist Intimations in *The Story of the Stone*," *HJAS* 49, 1 (June 1989): 55–92; Michel Soymié, "Les songes et leur interprétation en Chine," in *Les songes et leur interprétation* (Paris: Seuil, 1959), 295–301; Jean-Pierre Drège, 1981 a and b; Yoshikawa 1985. On Japan, see Saigō 1972.

[7] See also Alex Wayman, "The significance of dreams in India and Tibet," *History of Religions* 7 (1967): 1–12; and Kapstein 1989.

[8] See Nakazawa Shin'ichi, *Iconosophia* (Tokyō: Asphalt Books, 1986); Kapstein 1989.

[9] See *Māyādhvakrama*, by Niguma, quoted in Kapstein 1989: 33. On the ambivalence of dreams, see also O'Flaherty 1984: 161.

Youyang zazu 2: 124), dreams are of four kinds: (1) dreams induced by the disorder of the four great elements (*mahābhūta*) that constitute the body; (2) dreams caused by things seen during the day; (3) images induced by divine beings; and (4) dreams that are prognostics, resulting from good and evil karma. The first two kinds are unreal, the last two real.[10] Therefore, as in the West, dreams were ambiguous, since they could arise from good or evil causes.

In China and Japan, despite the tradition of Confucius's dreams of the Duke of Zhou (*Lun'yu* vii, 5), Confucian orthodoxy passed an unfavorable judgment on dreams. In another vein, Daoist philosophers such as Zhuangzi and Liezi asserted that "the true man does not dream."[11] Liezi mentions six types of dreams: the true dream, the premonitory dream, the dream with thought, the dream while awake, the good dream, and the dream of anguish—all the result of an inbalance of yin and yang, and to believe in them is to ignore the relationships of changing realities (*Liezi* iii, 4; see also *Youyang zazu* 2: 124). Yet these rationalist interpretations did not prevent the people from believing that dreams were channels of communication with the invisible world. The practice of incubatory dreams, for instance, was apparently widespread in the temples of the Chenghuang god. (See Laufer 1931: 211.) Although the Chinese were aware that dreams can never be simply "recalled" but are in fact mediated by—and structured as—language, this did not prevent them from interpreting dreams. An interesting illustration is found in the following story from a *Key of dreams* found in Dunhuang: a man consulted a diviner three times, telling him that he had dreamt of a straw dog. Each time, the diviner's prediction, based on the dream, was realized. The man then confessed that he had actually invented the dreams to test the diviner, and he asked the diviner how his predictions came true. The diviner replied that when the mind is activated, it manifests itself through words—thus there is no difference with a true dream. (See Drège 1981a: 247.)

Did Buddhism negatively influence the Chinese attitudes toward dreams? Analyzing the story of a Buddhist (and Chinese?) monk in the *Yogavāsiṣṭha*, Doniger O'Flaherty asks: "What would the story of the monk's dream be like if it were told by a Buddhist and therefore lacked the substructure of Godhead? The closest the Buddhist could come was the *Laṅkāvatāra-sūtra* and certain zen *kōans*, but there are no *narratives* on the grand scale of the *Yogavāsiṣṭha*. Without God (or, at least, gods), there can be no story, no myth" (O'Flaherty 1984: 245). In order to find dream narratives "on the grand scale" in China, one must perhaps turn toward

[10] See also the five kinds of dreams described in the *Dazhidulun* (Lamotte 1944–1980: 1:373).

[11] See *Zhuangzi* iii,2; *Liezi* iii,5. For other references, see *Taiping yulan*, 4:1962–1979.

Mao shan Daoism, a teaching entirely based on oneirical revelations.[12] In Mahāyāna Buddhism, however, the stress on emptiness obviously deprived the oneirical background worlds (*arrière-mondes*) of any ontological basis—in the same way, actually, as it did for the phenomenal world as a whole. References to dreams are many, but dreams in this context are only a negative metaphor for the emptiness of existence.[13] Chan inherited that attitude, but as we shall see, this theoretical position was far from reflecting the reality of practice.

The dream metaphor

Although dreams are ordinarily denounced as pure illusion in Mahāyāna Buddhism, this was not always the case: as long as the existence of an intermediary world was recognized, dreams had an ontological status and a soteriological value. In the *prajñāpāramitā* sūtras or in the *Lotus Sūtra*, the Buddha preaches the Law in a dream. (See T. 8, 224: 459b; T. 8, 227: 569c; T. 8, 228: 651a; T. 9, 262: 39b, 110a.) Even in the *Dazhidulun*, the so-called vision of the Buddha in a dream is asserted as a means of awakening (T. 25, 1509: 597c). As Stephan Beyer puts it, "The metaphysics of the *prajñāpāramitā* is in fact the metaphysics of the vision and the dream: a universe of glittering and quicksilver change is precisely one that can only be described as empty. The vision and the dream become the tools to dismantle the hard categories we impose upon reality, to reveal the eternal flowing possibility in which the Buddha lives" (Beyer 1977: 340). Only gradually did the "visions in a dream" described in scriptures such as the *Panshou sanmei jing* (T. 13, 418: 875c, 897c) lose their positive connotations and become hallmarks of delusion. A transitional stage (or intermediary position) is reflected in a dialogue between Huiyuan (334–416) and Kumārajīva (ca. 344–413) in the *Dasheng dayi zhang* (T. 45, 1856: 134b). Huiyuan argues that the metaphorical use of the dream in the *Panshou sanmei jing* is misleading: since the dream is a deluded mental state, the Buddha seen in a dream can be only an illusion and such illusions cannot lead to awakening. Kumārajīva replies that, although one may still not be detached from worldly desire, if one practices according to the scriptures, the Buddhas that may appear in one's dream or *samādhi* are utterly real (T. 45, 1856: 134c).[14]

To be sure, it is only through the experience of dreams that the comparison of reality with a dream becomes possible, and in this sense dreams

---

[12] See Strickmann 1977, 1988; Yoshikawa 1985: 59–110.

[13] In major Mahāyāna texts such as the *Dazhidulun* or the *Vimalakīrti-nirdeśa*, one finds a list of fourteen comparisons that illustrate the emptiness of everything: mirage, bubble, trunk of a banana tree, dream. See Hattori Masaaki, "Yume no hiyu ni tsuite," IBK 3, 1 (1954): 252–254; and *Buppō yume monogatari*, in Miyasaka (1964): 216–225.

[14] See also Motobe 1979: 373–376.

are indeed acknowledged. To find interest in the dreams and to want to explain them—as I do here—one must assume that the phenomenal world has some reality. Conversely, it is because dreams have invaded reality—resulting in an identification of the two planes instead of their polarization—that one may lose all desire to "explain the dream within the dream." By becoming, as it were, "ontological," the dream has deprived the real world of its reality, it has "derealized" the ontological realm. The comparison of reality with a dream, however, or rather the contamination of reality by a dream, undermines in return the ontological or soteriological value of dreams.

Yet an illusory dream may have real effects. These effects can be good, as when one "realizes prajñā in a dream." The *Zuting shiyuan* (reedition 1154), for example, quotes the following dialogue between Śāriputra and Subhūti: [Śāriputra:] "If one practices the six *pāramitā* in a dream, does it contribute to supreme awakening?" [Subhūti:] "If there is profit when one practices the six *pāramitā* during the day, there must be profit during the dream too." (See *Chanxue dacheng* 4: 2327b.) But the effects can be negative, too, as in the Yogācāra discussions of the nocturnal emissions provoked by the (purely illusory?) *incubi* and *succubi* of Buddhism. These obsessions of monks infatuated with purity call to mind the temptations of Saint Antony. As is well known, one of the bones of contention of the third Buddhist council was the question of whether Arhats had wet dreams, and whether these dreams had moral consequences.

The lack of an elaborate discourse on dreams in Mahāyāna does not indicate an absence but rather the pervasive influence of dreams on the theoretical level. We might recall here Merleau-Ponty's remark that philosophical idealism turns easily into its opposite, realism—both being expressions of a similar negation of mediations (Merleau-Ponty 1968: 68). The once potentially truthful dream was gradually relegated to the realm of delusion. But we shall shortly witness the persistence, or even the resilience, of the old ontological or cosmological schemes in the dreams of Chan/Zen.

DREAMING IN CHAN/ZEN

Buddhists felt compelled to deny as demoniac all revelatory dreams involving celestial maidens—the most cherished dreams of Daoist aspirants to immortality.[15] To call them demoniac, however, was still to recognize

[15] See K. M. Schipper, *L'Empereur Wou des Han dans la légende taoïste: Le Han Wou-ti nei-tchouan* (Paris: Ecole Française d'Extrême-Orient, 1965). As Doniger O'Flaherty points out, in the Indian context, these "succubic" dreams "may be regarded as a threat [to yogins . . . headed for *mokṣa*] or as a reward [to folk heroes committed to *saṃsāra*]. The dream may therefore represent an initiatory test—conveying [to the ascetic] powers that should be re-

their reality, whereas, according to the ultimate teaching of Mahāyāna or "sudden" Chan, one need not take into account such illusions. The radical Mahāyāna position is well expressed by a Chan text attributed to Sengchou's alter ego, Bodhidharma. According to the *Damolun*:

"Is awakening to realize *nirvāṇa* "with remainder" [Ch. *youyu niepan*, Sk. *sa-upādiśeṣa-nirvāṇa*] and to obtain the fruit of Arhatship?"

"This is only a realization in a dream."

"Is awakening, then, to practice the six Perfections, to reach the fullness of the ten *bhūmi* and the ten thousand practices, to realize that all dharmas are without birth or extinction, without consciousness or knowledge, without thought or understanding?"

"It is still only a dream—because anything that implies thought, discrimination, speculations and projections of one's own mind is only a dream. When you awaken, there is no more dream; but when you dream, there is no awakening. These are only false notions of the mind, of the intellect and of consciousness, wisdom in a dream. When you awaken according to the Dharma, there is absolutely no self-consciousness, nor after all anything [worth calling] awakening. The correct awakening of the Buddhas of the three periods is [the product of] the conceptual discrimination of sentient beings. This is why I call it a dream." (See Faure 1986d: 82.)

Commenting on Zhuangzi's dream of being a butterfly, Mujū Ichien (1226–1312) stresses that yesterday's reality and today's dream are not different. In light of the principle of emptiness, all the mental states of *saṃsāra*, all the positions in the Triple World, are a dream. (See Morrell 1985: 96.) If everything is illusory, degrees in illusion are illusory too, and the whole Buddhist cosmological scaffolding crumbles. The same point is stressed by Shidō Bunan (1603–1676), in a versified reply titled "To a person who asked about dreams":

Dreaming while asleep, dreaming while awake,
Oh, this world of dreams.
When you make no distinctions,
Your dream is broken.

(Kobori 1970–1971: 3, 2:104)

Yet the Mahāyāna notion of "Seeing the Buddha in a dream" (J. *muchū kenbutsu*)[16] and its Chan/Zen version of "Explaining the dream in a

---

jected or [to the prince] magic powers that are highly prized" (O'Flaherty 1984: 161). Indian Vinaya considered these dreams morally evil: as the *Samantapāsādikā*, in its inimitable way, puts it, "If the semen is released from its original source, . . . and when it comes out even to the extent of what a fly can be satisfied with, then the person becomes guilty of a Saṅghādisesa offence." See Bapat 1970: 356. On the Chinese context, see also Schafer 1965.

[16] For references to this technical term in *Mahāprajñāpāramitā* literature, see Motobe 1979.

dream" (J. *muchū setsumu*) were ambivalent and could serve as well to affirm dreams as to deny them. The very notion of a "dialogue in a dream" (J. *muchū mondō*), giving its title to the collection of Musō Soseki's "Recorded Sayings," may be read in two different ways: does such discourse cause one to sink into an always deeper dream or does it, on the contrary, help to dissolve it? Dreams are a form of thinking, and we have here a variant of the alternative between thinking and nonthinking, that is, between two conceptions of thought—as ambivalent or as purely negative.[17] This alternative overlaps with the sudden and gradual standpoints. While subitism remained the prevalent orthodoxy, the gradual standpoint, as we will see below, also found its partisans.

While the collapse of the distinction between dream and reality tended to undermine the ontological status of both, it also, paradoxically, contributed to revalorize dreams. As the Japanese poet Saigyō put it:

> Since the "real world" seems
> To be less than really real,
> Why need I suppose
> the world of dreams is nothing
> Other than the world of dreams?

(LaFleur 1983: 6)

In a similar way, Ryōkan's master wrote:

> Dreaming, we talk about dreams.
> Thus we seldom know
> Which is, and is not, dreaming.
> Let us, then, dream as we must.

(Yuasa 1981: 171)

It is precisely through a revelatory dream that Saigyō understood that the Way of poetry was all right for him to practice: "Not seeing this in a dream,/ I'd have been deaf to truth" (LaFleur 1983: 2.) As LaFleur remarks, "Buddhists made it their business to point out that it is not a matter of a black-or-white difference between waking consciousness and dream consciousness but rather of both of them being *on a continuum* of consciousnesses. To them our ordinary juxtaposition of only two types of consciousness divided sharply into the categories of reality and dream was inadequate, itself an illusion" (ibid.: 5). Partisans of sudden Chan, however, were theoretically reluctant to accept the continuity of consciousness that seemed to derive from speculations on nonduality—and therefore the provisional value of "expedient means." For them, just as

---

[17] In a document contained in the *Zhongxiu Caoxi tongzhi* (1: 387), the "Record of the Restoration of the Guanyin Hall" by Fang Guolong, a Chan-like distinction is made between true dreams based on nonthinking and false dreams based on thinking.

thinking could never lead to nonthinking, dreaming could not lead to dreamlessness—much less to awakening.[18]

The lack in Chan texts of any thorough discussion of dreams and their effects may have to do with the fact that oneirology was perceived as the trademark of "popular religion" and Daoism. It does not mean that Chan masters had no interest in dreams, or that there was no evolution in their conceptual understanding of the phenomenon. Dreams constitute a *topos* of Chan literature. One of the most well-known passages is that of Yang-shan Huiji's dream:

> The master [Yangshan], after falling asleep, dreamt that he entered the palace of Maitreya. All the seats were occupied, except the second one. He sat down there. A worthy monk [*bhadanta*] then struck a hammer and said: "It is the turn of the 'second seat' to speak." Yangshan got up and said: "In the Law of Mahāyāna, one rejects the four sentences and one severs the hundred negations. Listen well, listen well!" The monks left. Yangshan awoke and told his dream to Guishan [Ling'you], who said: "You have reached the rank of the saint." (*Yangshan yulu*, T. 47, 1990: 583a)

This rather ambiguous passage has been abundantly commented on. Characteristically, the tendency has been to play down the oneirical component of the story and to consider it a mere literary framing of a specific Chan teaching. In the *Congrong lu*, for example, a commentator asks: "Tell me, who occupied the first seat?" (See case 90; T. 48, 2004: 285b). Even as a literary device, however, the story implies that Chan masters, as other Buddhists, could visit Maitreya's Tuṣita Heaven in their dreams—and this must have struck a number of readers.

But in theory, dreams remained a negative metaphor, and the "absolutization" of the dream through the Mahāyāna dialectics of nonduality was not its absolution. In the fascicle *Muchū setsumu* ("Explaining the dream in a dream," 1242) of his *Shōbōgenzō* (T. 82, 2582: 161–163), Dōgen for instance says that the dream has paradoxically more reality than reality. He develops this logic of "supplementarity" in the same way that, in other chapters, he reinterpreted expressions such as "only a painted dragon can bring rain," or "only a painted rice cake can satiate hunger": "Since the wonderful Dharma of all the Buddhas is only transmitted from Buddha to Buddha, all the dharmas of dream and awakening are ultimate reality. In awakening as in the dream are found the initial thought of

---

[18] An intermediary position is expressed by the Song syncretist Li Daochun, who believes in the possibility of a gradual achievement of nothought: "To do away with the mind of arising and extinction, one must start from the cumulative practice of no-thought. When that has been sufficiently mastered, one can achieve the state of dreamlessness" (Berling 1980: 41).

bodhi, the practice, *bodhi* and *nirvāṇa*. Both the dream and the awakening are ultimately real, there is no great or small, no superior or inferior" (ibid.: 162c).

These are, however, theoretical positions—and rhetorical propositions. Such statements should not be misconstrued as a real article of faith concerning the revelatory nature of dreams. Actually, Dōgen's discussion of dreams in *Muchū setsumu* might be an example of what Harold Bloom (1973) has called the "anxiety of influence," and it needs to be seen against the background of earlier Chan teachings such as that of Dahui Zonggao (1089–1163). Dahui represented the traditional Mahāyāna understanding that the dream is the result of false notions, and that the whole world is but a dream: inverting the Hegelian equation of the rational and the real, he concluded that "all the dream is real, all the real is a dream." For Dahui, "when one says that the perfect man has no dreams, this lack does not belong to being and non-being, it means only that dream and no-dream are one" (Araki 1969: 176). But in the end, the great dream that is the origin of both dreams and reality must be rejected: "All the Buddhas have explained a dream. The six patriarchs too have explained a dream. . . . In the dream one reaches awakening. This is why what the Buddhas and the six patriarchs explained is not a dream. . . . Why? Because dream and awakening are one, word and silence are one, explanation and non explanation are one. Thus it is said: the two come from the one, but one must not even keep the one" (T. 47, 1998(a): 897a). Dahui expands on this point in a letter to his lay follower Zeng Tian'yu:

> I understand that you dreamed of burning incense and entering my room at night, and everything went so smoothly. Don't interpret this as a dream: you must realize that you really entered my room. Haven't you read how Śāriputra asked Subhūti: "To expound the six Perfections [*pāramitā*] in a dream or awake, is it the same or different?" Subhūti said: "The meaning of this is profound, I cannot explain it. But since the Mahāsattva Maitreya happens to be in this assembly, why don't you go and ask him?" Ah! Didn't he speak too much! Xuetou said: "At that time, if he hadn't let him go, but had followed up giving him a thrust—'Who says Maitreya?' 'Who is Maitreya?'—then we would have seen the ice melted and the tiles scattered." Ah! Xuetou too speaks too much. If someone asked: "When the Retired Military Governor Zeng dreamed he entered your room, tell me, was this the same or different from [entering] when awake?" I'd immediately say: "Who is entering the room? Who is witnessing it? Who is dreaming? Who is telling the dream? Who is it that doesn't interpret it as a dream? Who is it that really

entered the room?" Ah! I spoke too much too! (Araki 1969: 28; Christopher Cleary 1977: 117)

Like Yangshan, Dahui eludes the questions raised about the nature of the dream by referring them, in typical Chan fashion, to the subjectivity of the person who raises them. This position seems informed by Yogācāra idealism, which maintains that everything is a dream, and only the dreamer is real.

Quite different is the position advocated by a later figure such as Chewu Jixing (1741–1810), a Chan master strongly influenced by the Pure Land tradition. For Chewu, the ambiguity of dreams is ontologically grounded and soteriologically crucial.[19] One can discern in his teaching a return to a hierarchy of dreams and to a cosmological conception of awakening: some dreams lead into reality, others lead into delusion:

> There was a Chan master who asked: "All dharma are like a dream. The *Sahā* world is itself a dream. So is the Pure Land. Since all are equally only one dream, what profit can there be in cultivating this?"
>
> I answered: "This is not so. Before the seventh *bhūmi*, one cultivates the Way in a dream. Ignorance is a great dream. Even the awakening [of the tenth *bhūmi*] is still sleep. There is only one individual, the Budddha, for whom one may begin to speak of 'great awakening.' When, in the dream, eyes are not yet opened, suffering and pleasure are [as if] the same. Because of this dream, one experiences the extreme sufferings of the *Sahā* [world]. How, when dreaming, could one experience the subtle pleasures of paradise? Even more so with the dream of the *Sahā* world.
>
> "If one enters the dream following the dream, one dreams and dreams again. One is carried away by the whirlpools and one sinks into illusion. [But] in the dream of paradise, one enters awakening from the dream. Realizing this, one realizes further, and progressively one reaches the great awakening. The dream is the same [in both cases], but its reason is altogether different."[20]

Dreams and hagiography

If the Chan theory of dreams remains relatively unformulated, the discourse on dreams proliferates in hagiography—a genre cutting across the boundaries of Chan and traditional Buddhism. We are told, for instance,

---

[19] This stress on dreams was apparently a feature of the Pure Land tradition. See Roberto K. Ong 1985: 93ff.

[20] See *Chewu chanshi yulu*, in zz 109: 760; also quoted in Kamata 1986: 83.

that the Indian translator Guṇabhadra, after dreaming that his head was cut off and replaced by that of a Chinese, awoke speaking fluent Chinese. (See *Gaoseng zhuan*, T. 50, 2059: 366a; Shih 1968: 151.) These hagiographical dreams were in most cases premonitory dreams. As we have seen earlier, Chan masters often had a premonitory knowledge of their death. Many of these dreams had a political significance and played a role in the legitimation of Chan. In some cases, they involved laymen—as when Huineng appeared to the emperor in a dream and asked him to return the patriarchal robe to Caoxi. Another layman dreamt of Yunmen Wen'yan requesting that his stūpa be opened by an official: on this occasion it was found that the master had become a "flesh-body." Mummies have in this way inspired Chinese officials with numerous dreams. (See Demiéville 1965; Roberto K. Ong 1985.) In most cases, dreams of this type serve to legitimate a particular individual or school—as when Lingtan, a descendant of Empress Wu Zetian, saw in a dream a monk who told him to consult Shenhui; or when, in Kamakura Japan, a member of the Taira family dreamt that an Arhat had arrived from China—a dream announcing the coming of Wuxue Zuyuan (J. Mugaku Sogen, 1226–1286).

DREAMING PRACTICE

Despite the theoretical denial, the soteriological significance of dreams was often recognized in the daily practice of Chan/Zen masters. Dōgen's attitude toward dreams seems ambivalent. According to *Shōbōgenzō Shisho*, when Dōgen visited Yuanzi (alias Yuancai) at the Wannian monastery on Tiantai shan, the latter told him of a dream he had, in which he was advised by the Chan master Damei Fachang to transmit his Dharma to the first worthy foreign monk he encountered. Apparently unimpressed by the man and his dream, Dōgen politely declined the offer. Yet Dōgen himself, some time later, while staying on Damei shan on his way back from Tiantai shan, had a dream vision of Fachang, and he came to believe that he had received Fachang's Dharma in this dream (T. 82, 2582: 71a). Keizan, on the other hand, was a monk who "lived his dreams," or perhaps better "dreamt his life."[21] Although upholding the Mahāyāna tenet of emptiness (*śūnyatā*), Keizan lived in a world impregnated with very real dreams. He shared this worldview with many Buddhists of the Kamakura period, for whom dreams were the privileged means of com-

---

[21] In this respect, Keizan differed from Dōgen, at least the Dōgen of the Sōtō tradition, not the fictional character in Inoue Hisashi's play, *Dōgen no bōken*, whose recurrent dreams— in which he is both the Kamakura Zen master and a murderer in a modern psychiatric institution—lead to hopeless schizophrenia.

munication with the invisible world.[22] He was very close in this respect to masters such as Myōe, a contemporary of Dōgen and patriarch of the Kegon school, for whom "dreams are truly to be awed." Both men have left detailed records of their dreams. These records, the so-called *Yume no ki*, constituted a specific literary genre of the time, particularly popular in the Tendai tradition.[23]

Myōe's Record of Dreams

Like Yōsai and Shunjō, Myōe stood on the margins of the Chan and Shingon traditions. One of his disciples, Shōjō, wrote a compendium of Chan, the *Zenshū kōmoku* (ed. in Kamata and Tanaka 1971), that was strongly influenced by the syncretistic teachings of Zongmi. Myōe kept a record of his dreams over a period of thirty-five years. Whether during his sleep or during his meditation, he experienced all kinds of dreams or visions. Many of them were ordinary dreams, while some clearly had a sexual content. In one of the most interesting, he dreams that he has found a Chinese female doll, who bursts into tears because she is homesick, and turns in the palms of his hands into a living woman. Someone then accuses her of consorting with snakes, but Myōe does not believe it, although he admits that she may also have a snake's body. He interprets his dream as referring to Zenmyō (Shanmiao), a dragon goddess protecting Buddhism (Tanabe 1983: 381–383). The story of the platonic love between the Korean Hwaŏm (Huayan) master Ŭisang (625–702) and a Chinese girl named Shanmiao had obviously made a strong impression on Myōe. When Ŭisang had to leave China to return home, Shanmiao threw herself into the sea, turned into a dragon, and protected Ŭisang's boat all the way to Korea, where she eventually turned into stone.

Apparently, Myōe had many dreams involving women: "In a dream one night, five or six ladies came. We were on close terms and they respected me. I have been having many, many dreams like this" (Tanabe 1983: 386). In a few instances, he has explicit sexual relationships with a woman.[24] One dream at least, reminiscent of *chigo* stories of love between

---

[22] On this question, see Saigō 1972. Keizan, however, was sometimes ambivalent about visions. In his *Zazen yōjinki* (T. 82, 2586: 413a), for instance, he states that visions of the Buddha and other similar phenomena induced by meditation are a form of illness.

[23] See, for instance, the mention of such *yume no ki* in the diary of the Japanese pilgrim Jōjin in Waley 1970: 369. Myōe's *yume no ki* has been translated into English by George Tanabe (1983: 337–426) and into French by Frédéric Girard (Paris: Ecole Française d'Extrême-Orient, 1990). For a Jungian analysis of Myōe's dreams, see Kawai Hayao, *Myōe: Yume o ikiru* (Kyoto: Shohakusha, 1987); see Kawai 1990 for an English translation by Marc Unno. See also Okuda 1978; Kubota Jun and Yamaguchi Akiho, eds., *Myōe shōnin shū* (Tokyo: Iwanami shoten, 1981), 47–102.

[24] See, for example the "Dream of the Princess," in which, after performing a ritual at the residence of the lord of Hōshōji (Kujō Kanezane), Myōe seems to forget his priestly func-

a monk and a beautiful youth, has a homosexual undertone. (See ibid.: 357.) Myōe has been labeled the "purest monk in Japan," and it is clear that, despite (or because of) his oneirical fantasies, purity was his primary concern. One of his main purposes in recording his dreams seems to have been to find auspicious signs concerning the progress of his purification. In some cases, sexual dreams were given a religious interpretation—as in the dream of the Chinese doll/woman, interpreted as an apparition of Shanmiao, or in another dream in which a noble lady who wants to get close to him is retrospectively perceived as a manifestation of the Buddha Vairocana. (See ibid.: 397.) The most striking example is a dream in which Myōe meets a "fat noblewoman" whose appearance "was truly in conformity [with the teachings], and whose every aspect revealed the Dharma." Myōe writes: "I stayed overnight with her and engaged in sexual intercourse. Everyone said that the ceremonial act would certainly become a cause of enlightenment. We embraced each other. There was deep compassion." Myōe concludes his account by noting that "the emotional atmosphere of this ceremonial act was in accord with a commentary on the *Avataṃsaka-sūtra* authored by the Chinese Huayan patriarch Fazang." (See Kawai 1990: 90.)

Myōe also records a number of dreams or visions with a more specific religious content. In some of them he has visions of Arhats (Piṇḍola, Mahākāśyapa), Bodhisattvas, or various deities. He also describes several vivid "dreams of ascent" like the following: "During my meditation in the sixth month, I ascended to the Tuṣita Heaven. I polished a golden tub before the altar of the Bodhisattva Maitreya and placed some aloes in the tub. There was a Bodhisattva there who bathed me."[25] In another seance of meditation, after asking for a good sign that he was making spiritual progress, Myōe has the following vision:

> My body and mind became quiescent in the midst of *samādhi* as had happened earlier in the sixth month. There was a pole made of lapis lazuli hanging from the sky, and I think it was hollow like a tube. I grabbed the end, and someone pulled me up. I maintained my hold and seemed to have reached the Tuṣita Heaven.
>
> My face suddenly became like a bright mirror. My entire body gradually became like one. I felt perfectly whole, like a bead-jewel of quartz.
>
> I rolled to another place. I was waiting for a voice, and someone said: "All the Buddhas have entered into you. You have now attained

tions: "Then I engaged in a highly improper act of intimacy with someone whom I thought to be the lord's princess. I carried her in my arms and together we got into a carriage." (See Tanabe 1983: 362.)

[25] See Kawai 1990: 179; Tanabe 1983: 386. This dream was so important that Myōe returned to it in another work, the *Kegon Bukkō zammaikan Meikanden*. See Kawai 1990: 169.

purity." Following this my body was enlarged. I was adorned by a
decoration made of the Seven Jewels hanging about two yards above.
I emerged from my meditation. (See Kawai 1990: 182–183; Tanabe
1983: 390.)

The dream is accompanied by revelations concerning the fifty-two
stages of the Bodhisattva's career, and Myōe concludes his description
with these words: "I must think about this. It is difficult to record this
with brush and paper."[26] In another dream of the same type, he climbs on
the top of a cosmic pagoda and contemplates the entire universe: "The
sun, moon, stars and houses were far below me, and I felt that I had gone
beyond the *Akaniṣṭha* Heaven. Then I descended back down to the earth."
(See Kawai 1990: 86.)

Dream and reality tended to merge in Myōe's life. His reliance on
dreams led his disciples to believe that he had visionary powers. One of
them, Kōben, records that Myōe, in his forties, often fell asleep during
the day and was thus able to read other people's minds. Other stories
relate how, on various occasions, he woke up to tell his attendants to rush
outside the monastery to save an insect or a wounded sparrow. All this
points to the practice of "directed dreaming," a type of practice that
would probably have been rejected as "demoniac dhyāna" by an advocate
of "pure" Chan/Zen. From the "sudden" point of view, Myōe had fallen
in the "Black Mountain's Cave of Demons." Although he cultivated his
visionary powers, however, Myōe did not become infatuated with them.
When one of his disciples referred to him as a reincarnation of a Bodhisattva, he scolded him, arguing that whatever powers he may have were
nothing special and were the natural by-products of his assiduous practice: "It is just the fact that you drink water if you are thirsty, and you go
near the fire if that is what you want." (See Kawai 1990: 115–116.)

A realistic dreamer

Although Keizan never wrote a "record of dreams" as such, one finds a
number of extremely interesting dreams in his *Tōkoku ki*—a chronicle
describing the circumstances of the foundation of Yōkōji at Tōkoku in
Noto peninsula: "In one dream I saw the halls of a temple. And in front
of the door was a great tree where one hangs sandals. Then I knew that
the wandering monk had to return the money of his straw sandals and
that this was an excellent place. I received this place, desiring to make it
my resting place until the end of my life" (*JDZS* 392).

[26] This dream is also recorded in the *Meikanden*: the main difference is that the lapis lazuli
pole is held by the three Bodhisattvas Samantabhadra, Mañjuśrī, and Avalokiteśvara, who
pull Myōe up to Tuṣita Heaven. (See Kawai 1990: 169.)

Keizan had this dream in the spring of 1312, while spending the night in the house of the lay couple who had donated the land to build Yōkōji. In 1213, when he began to build a straw hut on the hillside, he had the following dream:

> That night, I had a dream in which the eighth Arhat, the venerable Bhajalabhadra, came to reveal to me that he had entered this mountain and examined it. He concluded that, although this was not a well-known place, it was actually an excellent site, which was even better than that of Eiheiji: "The site where Eiheiji is built is a valley, a place where obstructing divinities dwell. This is why, since ancient times, there have always been troubles. Such is not the case with this mountain. You will be able to spread your teaching here at your will."[27]

The dream here justifies *ex post facto* Gikai's and Keizan's departure from Eiheiji and makes clear that Keizan's community in Noto was, despite appearances, as orthodox as that of Dōgen's successors at Eiheiji. Although this does not mean that he was not sincere or that his dreams were not genuine, one of their functions is obviously to legitimate him and his teaching.[28] Keizan may be a dreamer, but he is a realistic one, and his dreams generally serve him well. Particularly significant is the fashion in which Keizan received the transmission of the Dharma:

> In the past, I obtained the fruit of Arhatship during the time of the Buddha Vipaśyin, and died in the Himalayas, north of Mt. Sumeru. I became the deity of the Kubara tree, a four-legged animal with a dog's head, an owl's body, the belly and tail of a snake.[29] Although I was a tree-spirit, I had obtained the fruit, and lived thereafter on the Himalayas, together with the fourth Arhat Subinda, in the continent of Uttarakuru. Owing to these affinities with the northern land, I have now been reborn here as a parishioner [*ujiko*] of Hakusan. . . . Having obtained the fruit, during five hundred lives, I appeared in

[27] *JDZS* 392–393. Although the superiority of Yōkōji is attributed here to geomantic factors, there were times when Keizan's dreams convinced him to neglect basic geomantic rules. For instance, when one of his disciples remarked that it was inauspicious to build a mausoleum—the *Gorohō*—above the Buddha Hall, he replied that everything he had done at Yōkōji had been based on dreams. See *Tōkoku ki*, in *JDZS* 409.

[28] We already noted the prediction of the Arhat. Similarly, it is after Kannon appeared to him in a dream and instructed him that Keizan transformed Sōjiji into a Zen monastery. See *Sōjiji chūkō engi*, in Ōkubo Dōshū, ed., *Sōtōshū komonjo*, Vol. 1 (Tokyo: Chikuma shobō, 1972), 33–34. Also significant in this respect is a dream in which Keizan received the approbation of Gien, the former abbot of Eiheiji, whom he had left to follow Gikai at the time of the so-called controversy of the third generation. See *Tōkoku ki*, in *JDZS* 401.

[29] Keizan's description is reminiscent of the Greek *chimera*: "Her forepart lionish, her tail a snake's, a she-goat in between." See Ginevra Bompiani, "The Chimera Herself," in Feher 1989: 3, 1:375.

the world in order to spread the Dharma and to help sentient beings. (*JDZS* 395–396)

Keizan goes on to describe his oneirical initiation:

> Bodhidharma entered my dream as I was bathing in the pure water that gushed out from the stone, under my seat. I was naked, so he gave me his robe and produced in me the thought of awakening.
>
> Maitreya entered my dream as I had been reborn three times on a blue lotus and took me with him in the sky. The *deva*, playing *gigaku* music, came to welcome him. Maitreya led me to the inner sanctuary of the Tuṣita heaven and helped me reach the stage of nonreturn.
>
> Śākyamuni entered my dream as I was manifesting my body at the time of the preaching of the *Ratnakūṭa-sūtra* and taught me the three deliverances—from time, mind, and phenomena." (Ibid.: 396)

Here again, as in Yangshan's dream, the negation of the phenomenal world is based on its ultimate assumption in a dream: paradoxically, Keizan owes his freedom from time, mind, and phenomena to an experience that involves these three aspects of reality. But the point is that, by receiving the transmission, Keizan is ritually identified, first with an Arhat, then with three ideal figures of Mahāyāna Buddhism and Chan—namely, the Indian patriarch who first transmitted Zen to China, the Buddha of the past, and the Buddha of the future. In the spiritual progression described or enacted by his dream, Keizan moves from the relatively low status of an Arhat, to that of a patriarch, and finally of a Buddha.

Dreams of ascent and voices of dissent

Although they take place in a Buddhist framework and serve some sectarian or individual purpose, the dreams experienced by Myōe and Keizan have clear "shamanistic" overtones.[30] The "ascent symbolism" is found in many other Chan dreams, usually in connection with the palace of Maitreya. Particularly significant in this context is the case of the Chinese Chan master Hanshan Deqing (1546–1623). In his autobiography, Hanshan records three important dreams. The first one, experienced at a time when he was engaged in copying the *Avataṃsaka-sūtra* with his blood, revealed to him the magnificence of the *Dharmadhātu*. In the sec-

---

[30] Myōe once had a dream in which he was eaten by two wolves. When they finished eating him, however, he found to his surprise that he was still alive, and he awoke, soaked with sweat. On another occasion, when he was ill and refused to take care of himself, an Indian monk appeared in a dream and gave him a potion to drink, after which Myōe recovered (Kawai 1990: 70 and 89). Another significant case is that of Keikai, the author of the *Nihon Ryōiki*, who records a dream in which someone skewers his corpse with the branch of a tree and turns it over a fire so that his soul is thoroughly roasted (*Nihon Ryōiki*, in Nakamura 1973: 282).

ond dream, Hanshan, like Keizan, ascended to Maitreya's paradise. He noticed a huge pavilion in which all kinds of human activities took place, "including the ugly and trivial affairs of the human world." As soon as he wondered how these trivial scenes could take place in such a supposedly pure world, the pavilion moved away from him and returned only when he realized that purity and impurity were generated by his own mind. He was then taught by Maitreya the difference between discriminating consciousness (*vijñāna*) and undiscriminating wisdom (*prajñā*). But the most interesting dream is the last one, in which Hanshan was invited by Mañjuśrī to a bathing party on the northern terrace of Wutai shan: "I was led to a bathing room where I removed my garments and was ready to bathe. Someone was already in the bath and, as it turned out, the person was a girl. I abhorred the sight and had no desire to bathe. The girl in the bath deliberately changed her appearance and became a man. I joined him" (Luk 1971: 90). Hanshan was eventually washed by the man, and the water poured over Hanshan's head cleansed his five viscera, leaving his body as transparent as a crystal cage. Then an Indian monk brought tea in half a skull, filled with blood and brains. After his initial repulsion, Hanshan was convinced to eat the brain. He eventually drank the blood, which tasted like ambrosia and penetrated every pore of his body. After rubbing his back, the Indian monk suddenly clapped his hands and Hanshan woke up, drenched in perspiration, but feeling extremely clean and relaxed (ibid.; Hsu 1979: 73).

Besides the homosexual overtones and the shamanistic elements of this fascinating dream, the similarity to Keizan's dream is striking. According to Hsu Sung-pen, the three dreams may be seen as expressions of the Huayan philosophy as Hanshan understood it while in the process of copying the *Avataṃsaka-sūtra*. Although this may be true in the first case, it seems somewhat reductionistic to see, as Hsu does, the second dream as an illustration of Yogācāra philosophy, and the third as a description of Tantric ideas and practices. Because of his desire to interpret these dreams according to a hermeneutic model, Hsu tends to look at them as a mere justification for Hanshan to involve himself in worldly affairs. The "shamanistic" dreams of Myōe, Keizan, and Hanshan, however, are not mere doctrinal illustrations or convenient alibis; they are essentially transformative.[31] Two other interesting "ascent dreams" or visions are those of

[31] To be sure, the doctrinal element is sometimes important. We have seen how Myōe was taught in a dream the meaning of the fifty-two stages of the Bodhisattva career. In the Chan tradition, one may mention the dream of the Chan master Zhifeng of Wuyun shan (Hangzhou). Zhifeng once dreamed that he ascended Mount Sumeru and saw three Buddhas sitting next to each other. He prostrated himself at the feet of Śākyamuni, then of Maitreya. But he did not know the third Buddha, nor how to pay homage to him. Then Śākyamuni told him: "He is the Buddha Siṃhacandra, the assistant of Maitreya." Zhifeng

the contemporary Chinese master Xuyun. In the first one, while meditating at the Ayuwang monastery in 1897, where he was worshiping the relic of the Buddha, Xuyun is taken on a dragon's back to an elevated place that seems to be Tuṣita, "where the mountains, streams, trees, and flowers were most beautiful to behold, with palaces of an exquisite grandeur." Seeing his mother in a room, he told her to ride the dragon to the Western paradise. After this incubatory dream, he continues his devotions to the relic, and eventually burns one of his fingers as an offering. (See Xu Yun 1988: 41.) The second dream takes place one year before Xuyun's death in 1952, while he is in a coma after being beaten by Communists. He dreams that he has entered the inner room of Maitreya's palace and listens to the future Buddha expound the Dharma. Maitreya eventually tells him that he should return temporarily to the human world, which he does reluctantly (ibid. 140). Although these dreams clearly have a symbolical or doctrinal content, their "meaning" or significance may be hidden rather than revealed by symbols.[32] Admittedly, we cannot help interpreting and adding meaning to facts, which are themselves already interpretations. By trying to fit these dreams in the Procrustean bed of doctrinal or psycho-biographical interpretation, however, we necessarily miss their performative nature. Some of the most important changes in the history of East Asian Buddhism were the result of dreams: in China, this foreign teaching was legitimated by a dream of Emperor Ming of the Han dynasty; in Japan, the monastic rule about the celibacy of monks was reformed after the revelation Shinran received from the Bodhisattva Kannon at Rokkakudō.[33] In this sense, as Georges Duby once remarked, "the trace of a dream is as real as the trace of a footstep."

Perhaps we need to distinguish between two models: the hermeneutical model that leads to the "Keys of Dreams" and oneirology—or psychoanalytic "dream interpretation"—and the performative model that recognizes the transformative nature and the performative effects of events

---

then paid homage. After awakening, he examined the Buddhist canon and his dream proved true (*Jingde chuandeng lu*, T. 51, 2076: 422b).

[32] Keizan also recorded dreams with doctrinal content. It seems that, like Myōe, he expected from the dream, not only an omen, but also a kind of gnosis. During one sermon, he alludes to the fact that he has, during a dream, been able to "meet men inside the mirror," and that, "entering into the illusion-like *samādhi*, he has performed Buddha's work within a dream." In another dream, he reads a passage from the *Ratnakūṭa-sūtra* and finds out, after waking up, that the two variants (oneirical and "real") of the passage are complementary (*Tōkokuki*, in *JDZS* 399).

[33] In this dream, Kannon told Shinran that if, because of his karma, he would transgress the precept forbidding sexual relations with women, she would manifest herself as a woman and become his lover—serving him until the end of his life, when she would lead him to the paradise of Amida. (See Stein 1986: 56; Dobbins 1990: 184.)

such as Keizan's or Hanshan's reception of the Dharma in a dream.[34] Like a ritual, a dream is performative not only because it may be transformative but also because it modifies social structures. Chan masters appear as "elite dreamers," and it becomes clear that, despite theoretical denials, there is a hierarchy of sleepers and of dreams. (See Le Goff 1988: 218–220.)

Dreams seem to have developed in Zen—in particular in the Sōtō tradition—together with a "return of/to the sacred," a resurgence of local cults. As we saw earlier, this resurgence itself accompanied the geographical expansion of the Sōtō school in the fourteenth–sixteenth centuries.[35] We may recall here Doniger O'Flaherty's statement that dream narratives "on the grand scale" need the existence of gods. But this return of dreams, this displacement of the limits between real and unreal, profane and sacred, in favor of the latter, was only temporary. With the increasing rationalism of a society witnessing the rapid growth of the merchant class and in which, with the importation of Western rationalism, the disenchantment of the world was under way, dreams were bound to fall back into the realm of delusion. This rationalist tendency, already present in Chan, found one of its most vivid expressions in the work of the Tokugawa thinker Tominaga Nakamoto. Tominaga provides an interesting analysis of induced dreams as a manifestation of *abhijñā*, which in a typical fashion he rejects as delusion and magic:

> According to Zhao [Yushi]'s *Bintui lu*: "When [Su] Dongpo was prefect of Yangzhou, he dreamt that he went into the mountains when a tiger attacked him. At that moment, a Daoist priest [*daoshi*] shouted at the tiger and drove him away. The next morning, a Daoist priest came to ask, 'Weren't you frightened by your excursion last night?' Su Dongpo exclaimed: 'You rascal! I should break your back with my staff. Do you think I don't know your nocturnal techniques?' Surprised, the Daoist priest withdrew." Come to think of it, this too is magic. In all cases, past and present, when people have been deceived by dreams, it is with these techniques. Such was, for

---

[34] For a similar performative/shamanistic dream in the Confucian context, see the case of Wang Gen in Huang Tsung-hsi 1987: 174. Premonitory dreams constitute an intermediary type, since they involve interpretation but have marked performative effects. Such are, in Keizan's case, besides the prediction of the Arhat Vajraputra, the dream in which he sees a majestic monastery cover the entire valley of Tōkoku; or the dream staging an *enoki* with luxurious vegetation and swollen waters. Incidentally, Keizan gives a Freudian interpretation of this dream when he sees it as an oneirical transposition of the word *unsui*, "clouds and water," used metaphorically for Chan monks. He concludes: "How strange! waking and sleep unite, dream and awakening are in harmony" (*Tōkoku ki, jdzs* 398).

[35] Keizan received twice in a dream oracles from a kami—the god Hachiman (Yawata) in the first case. Both are poems and were apparently given—or at least recorded—in *manyō-gana* (a Japanese syllabary using Chinese characters). Keizan notes that the use of these "nonconventional characters" is in itself auspicious (*Tōkoku ki*, in *jdzs* 405, 409).

example, the case when Katyayana taught the Greek King,[36] when the Han emperor Ming dreamt of a golden man, when the Tang [emperor] Xuanzong saw in a dream the letters "Chujin" in the sky,[37] when Suzong dreamt of a monk chanting [the name of] the Tathāgata Baosheng,[38] when Daizong dreamt that he visited a mountain temple, when the Song [emperor] Weizong dreamt of a divine cloud,[39] or when Shenzong dreamt of a wonder-working monk riding a horse through space. All these [dreams] were nothing but magic. (Tominaga 1982: 28, 100; see also Tominaga 1990: 109)

Although Tominaga borrows these references from the *Fozu tongji*, his interpretive strategy is interesting: rather than rejecting these stories as apocryphal, he still seems to believe in telephatic dreams but rejects them as manipulations of the minds of credulous emperors by cynical monks. Ironically, his position is reminiscent of that of early Chan masters such as Nan'yang Huizhong, who played down psychic powers. At any rate, his examples illustrate the ways in which the dream works as a mechanism through which cultural borrowings or subjective experiences can become elements of general culture. Many cases of self-immolation or self-mutilation were the consequences of "supernatural" dreams. (See, for instance, *Genkō shakusho*, in DNBZ 62, 470: 133–134.) Dreams are also seen to mediate between the realms of death (*thanatos*) and sexuality (*eros*), and this may to some extent justify the digression that follows on the Chan/Zen "history of sexuality."

[36] The Chinese term *Xila* is a transcription of *Hellas*. See T. 53, 2122: 534a.
[37] See *Song gaoseng zhuan*, T. 50, 2061: 864c. On the importance of Xuanzong's dreams for the rise of Daoism, see Duyvendak 1947: 102–108. On imperial dreams, see also R. Taylor, "Ming T'ai-tsu's Story of a Dream," *Monumenta Serica* 32 (1976): 1–20.
[38] See *Fozu tongji*, T. 49, 2035:375c.
[39] Ibid.: 420c.

Eleven   *Digression: The Limits of*
Transgression

> Moreover, the kinship that I find between myself
> and Zen monks has nothing to encourage me (they
> don't dance, don't drink, don't . . .). . . . The most
> attractive Zen monks were chaste.
> —Georges Bataille, *Oeuvres complètes*

In such extremely hierarchized societies as China and Japan, the Chan
claim for immediacy was bound to have some perverse effects, and the
limits of transgression were soon reached. As noted earlier, with its affirmation of passions, the "naturalist" tendency in Buddhism seemed to
pave the way for moral laxity. As with all antinomian teachings, it lent
itself easily to a justification of worldly desires.[1] For example, the theory
of "innate awakening" (J. *hongaku shisō*) was one of the main theoretical
justifications for the changes that took place in medieval Japanese monasteries and that allowed, among other things, the emergence of the so-
called warrior-monks (*sōhei*). Therefore, not surprisingly, this "naturalist" tendency was perceived as a threat by the more conservative monks,
both within and outside the Chan/Zen tradition.[2] Yet there was no way
to deny that antinomianism was central to Chan and in perfect harmony
with the "sudden teaching."

This tendency is criticized, for example, in the apocryphal *Śūraṃgama
sūtra* (*Shouleng'yan jing*, T. 19, 945), a text widely read in Chan during the
Song.[3] Although this text contains many Tantric elements, such as a *dhāraṇī* that is supposed to bring sudden awakening, it stresses the danger of
desire and mentions, for example, the cases of a nun and a monk who,

[1] For a review of the Confucian criticism of Chan "naturalism," see Fu 1973: 375–396.

[2] With the significant exception of the Shaolin monastery in China, however, Chan/Zen
monasteries have never been known for their warrior-monks. (See Demiéville 1957: 362.)
Perhaps this was due to the success of "literary Chan" in the so-called Five Mountains. But
the main reason is probably that in Japan, Zen monasteries, in contrast to Shingon, Tendai,
Nichiren, or Jōdo monasteries, did not need to protect themselves because they enjoyed the
support and protection of the feudal lords. Thus because it was protected by the local *daimyō*, Eiheiji could prosper in the immediate proximity of two major Shingon and Tendai
monasteries well known for their *sōhei*. On the other hand, the *samurai* were not primarily
attracted by the martial values of Zen, as D. T. Suzuki and others have stressed. On the
contrary, as *parvenus*, they were trying to acquire cultural patents of nobility, and Zen,
precisely because of its intellectual tendencies, provided them the cultural legitimacy they
needed.

[3] According to tradition, it was first transmitted by the Northern Chan master Shenxiu.
(See Demiéville 1952: 44.) In Japan, too, it became popular with masters such as Enni
Ben'en (1202–1280).

acting out of the belief that all phenomena are empty, fell into hell—the nun after having sexual relations, the monk for committing murder.[4] Chapter 9 of this sūtra, in particular, refutes heretical teachings that stress that desire is *bodhi*, the human body is the Dharmakāya, the organs of senses are Pure Lands, and the sexual organs are the "true abodes" of *bodhi* and *nirvāṇa*.[5]

Conflicting interpretations regarding desire were found in early Chan. The denial of desire is expressed in the story of the bath given by the empress Wu Zetian to Shenxiu: when the Chan monk, attended by young female servants, remained master of himself, Wu commented: "Only after he enters the water does one see the great man."[6] This comment can perhaps be interpreted metaphorically, the hot water signifying the passions that leave the sage unmoved. To be sure, Shenxiu was almost one

[4] See Stein 1974: 504. This story is symmetrically opposed to that of the two monks Baojing and Baoqin, in the *Vimalakīrti-nirdeśa* (T. 14, 474: 523a). To hide the fact that Baoqin had had sexual relations with a village girl, Baojing killed the girl. When both monks confessed to Upāli, they were told that their sins could not be forgiven. They went then to consult Vimalakīrti, who told them that he could accept their repentance if they would show him their sins. Realizing that their sins were ultimately empty, the monks reached awakening. The same scenario is found in early Chan texts such as the *Treatise of Bodhidharma*, but the actual description of the sins is omitted. (See Faure 1986d: 130–132.) See also Yongjia's *Zhengdao ge*: "There were two *bhikṣus*: one broke the precept on celibacy; the other, the precept against killing./ But Upāli's firefly wisdom only tightened the knot of wrongdoing./ The mahāsattva Vimalakīrti instantly removed their doubts,/ Like the hot sun which melts both frost and snow." (Quoted in Buswell 1983: 330.)

[5] The latter interpretation was prevalent in esoteric works such as the *Adhyardhaśatikā-prajñāpāramitā-sūtra* (*Liqu jing*, translated by Amoghavajra; T. 8, 243), which affirms love between the sexes and argues that "desire is itself pure," since everything, including "the exquisite rapture" of sex, belongs to the pure realm of the Bodhisattva. R. A. Stein points out that Yixing, in his commentary on the *Mahāvairocana-sūtra* (T. 39, 1796: 579), glosses *bhagavat* by *bhaga*, which means "woman" and "refers to the origin" (Stein 1975: 483). Stein mentions the equation between desire and *bodhi*, Dharmakāya and the human body, the organs of senses and Pure Lands, sexual organs and "true abodes" (*zhenzhu*) of *bodhi* and *nirvāṇa*. This is precisely the type of interpretation condemned as "heretical teachings" by the Chinese *Śūraṃgama*.

[6] See *Zuting shiyuan*, chap. 1: 12; *Zutang ji*, ed. Yanagida 1974b: 348a. The story is also quoted in the *Genkō shakusho*, together with that of a monk (actually an avatar of the Bodhisattva Avalokiteśvara) who had sexual relations with an empress in order to convert her to the true Dharma. See *Genkō shakusho* 9: 113a. A similar story is told by the Indian monk Zhikong (Dhyānabhadra) in his autobiography, trans. Waley 1931–1932: 363: "In that land, the ruler is an infidel, and knowing my vows debarred me from violence and lechery, he ordered a dancing-girl to bathe with me in the same pool. I showed complete indifference, being no more affected than if I had been a corpse. The king sighed, saying: 'This is certainly an unusual man.'" Another, more recent, case of sexual temptation—rehearsing Māra's temptation of the Buddha—is given in Xuyun's biography (Xu Yun 1988: 10): "At night, I felt someone touching my body. I woke up and saw a girl beside me taking her clothes off and offering her naked body to me. I dared not speak and promptly got up, sitting crosslegged, reciting a mantra. She dared not move after that." A final quote from the Tokugawa Zen master Shidō Bunan: "Once when my master was bathing, a woman washed him back and front, all parts of his body. I feel this to be a rare event among our own people" (*Sokushin ki*, trans. Kobori 1970–1971: 4, 1:122).

hundred years old when this event allegedly took place, but the empress, well known for her sexual appetites, was hardly younger. The point might also be that the Bodhisattva, immune to desire, must immerse himself in the world of passions.

On the other hand, the affirmation of desire in Chan is clearly (and somewhat polemically) established by another story featuring the Empress Wu and three disciples of the fifth patriarch Hongren—Shenxiu, Huian, and Zhishen. When the empress asks them if they still have passions, Shenxiu and Huian reply negatively. Zhishen, however, wins Wu Zetian over by answering that to be alive is to have passions. The conflicting interpretations of the motto "The passions are awakening" (J. *bonnō soku bodai*)—and their practical consequences, observance or transgression of the Buddhist precepts—were the source of a recurring problem in Mahāyāna. The theory of the Two Truths seemed to relativize Buddhist morality. The superiority of transgression as a proof (and test) of enlightenment found its *locus classicus* in the *Dazhidulun*'s story of the two Bodhisattvas Prasannendriya and Agramati. Despite his strict observance of the precepts, Agramati eventually fell into hell, while Prasannendriya, who advocated the identity of passions and awakening, became a Buddha. (See Lamotte 1944–1980: 1:399; also T. 15, 650: 758–761.) As R. A. Stein points out, the concept of "revulsion" (*paravṛtti*) seems to underlie the notion that, instead of denying the passions, desire, and sexuality, one can transmute them. This "revulsion" is what allows the Bodhisattva to perform sexual acts without being defiled. In the Indian *Śūraṃgama-sūtra* translated by Kumārajīva, a Bodhisattva makes love to the daughters of Māra to save them (Stein 1974: 504–506).

This paradigm is reinscribed in many later hagiographies, for instance, those of the Korean masters Wŏnhyo (617–686) and Ŭisang (625–702): while Ŭisang's strict observance of the precepts prevented him from succumbing to temptation and returning the love of the young Chinese girl Shanmiao, Wŏnhyo broke the precepts and even visited brothels.[7] Another rationale for transgression, inspired by Daoism, is found in a Chan text such as the *Jueguan lun*: "Question: Can there be any condition under which libertinage is possible?" "Answer: The heaven arches over the earth. The element of Yang unites itself with that of Yin. A privy accepts leakage from above. Spring water pours into gutters. If the mind works in the same manner, in no place where it functions will it meet any obstruction. If passion arouses discrimination, even your own wife will defile your mind" (Tokiwa Gishin 1973: 14). Paradoxically, passions (from

---

[7] This tradition seems to have been well preserved in Korea. For a recent case of "unlimited action," see Jung-kwang 1979.

the Latin *pati*, "to suffer") are acceptable insofar as they are no longer passions—there being no "subject" to suffer from them.

TALES OF MONASTIC DERELICTION

> Those who hide [their sins] are called monks, those
> who desist from [committing them] Buddhas.
> —Retired Emperor Shirakawa

There is no denying that moral laxity prevailed at times in East Asian Buddhism. This situation gave rise to anti-Buddhist persecutions like that of Huichang (845) but also to a widespread anticlericalism, which found expression in satires such as *Monks and Nuns in a Sea of Sins*—which opens on the following song, titled "The Happiness of Monks":

> Don't tell me that monks are joyous;
> Strong and violent, that's what they are!
> Wearing the robes,
> And with their heads shaven and shiny,
> They act as if they were important.
> But they are bald, on top as below;
> And the two stones, below and above, are equally shiny.
> Bald and naked, naked and bald—
> Indeed, all monks are two-headed.
> . . . Heads protruding, they search for cracks,
> And summon charming girls,
> Revealing the true shape of "Buddha's tooth."[8]

The subversion of the Chan tradition may also be seen in popular stories (*huaben*) such as the one titled "Chan master Wujie has illicit relationships with Red Lotus" (*Wujie chanshi si Honglian*), whose protagonists are the young girl Red Lotus and two Chan monks, the one-eyed Wujie (Five Precepts) and Mingwu (Clear Realization), who happened to be former incarnations of the famous Song poet Su Shi (alias Su Dongpo) and of his friend, the Chan master Foyin Liaoyuan (1032–1098). (See *T.* 49, 2036: 673b.) Wujie was the superior of the Jingci Xiaoguang monastery in Hangzhou, and Mingwu was his disciple. Once, a female baby was abandoned at the gate of the monastery, and Wujie entrusted her to one of his monks. The child, baptized Red Lotus, turned eventually into a beautiful young girl. Wujie, who had forgotten her existence, happened to see her one day and fell suddenly in love. He told the monk to bring her to his

---

[8] See *Sengni niehai*, quoted (in Latin!) in van Gulik 1974; Howard S. Levy 1975: pt. 2:11.

quarters, and he subsequently took her virginity. The eloquent versified account of the defloration concludes as follows: "What a shame that the sweet dew of *bodhi*/ Has been entirely poured into the corolla of Red Lotus!"

But, the story goes on, while sitting in dhyāna, Mingwu saw with his "eye of wisdom" that Wujie, by defiling Red Lotus, had transgressed the precept against fornication and, in one instant, ruined years of pure behavior. The next day, he invited Wujie to a poetic meeting and took as a topic the lotus flowers in full bloom. His own poem ended with the following verses: "In summer, to admire lotuses is truly delicious,/ But can the red lotus be more fragrant than the white?" Realizing that he was discovered, Wujie took leave and wrote a farewell poem, then died while sitting in dhyāna. Knowing that Wujie, because of his karma, would be reborn as an enemy of Buddhism, Mingwu decided to follow him into death. He was reborn as the poet-monk Foyin, while Wujie was reborn as the poet Su Shi, "whose only shortcomings were not believing in Buddhism and abhorring monks."[9] Fortunately, upon meeting Foyin, Su Shi was converted and soon enlightened, eventually becoming a Daoist immortal known by the name of Daluo Tianxian.[10] As to Red Lotus, we are told that she was saved, too.

The story of Su Shi's awakening is one of Dōgen's favorite examples, and it gives its title to the chapter *Keisei sanshoku* of the *Shōbōgenzō*.[11] Dōgen probably ignored the above version of Su Shi's antecedents, since he did not understand colloquial Chinese. The story was apparently well known by the time he visited China, more than one century after Su Shi's death. The legend of Wujie's reincarnation as Su Shi is quoted for example in the *Lengzhai yehua* by the Chan master Huihong (1071–1128).[12] At

---

[9] Su Shi is given as the author of a famous anticlerical pun (*bu du bu tu, zhuan du zhuan tu, zhuan tu zhuan du*), nicely rendered into French as: "Qui n'est pas pernicieux n'est pas religieux, et qui n'est pas chauve n'est point fauve. De même, qui quitte la religion quitte la corruption, et en abandonnant la tonsure on quitte l'ordure." See Lanselle 1987: 37, 61. Su Shi and Foyin also became the pretexts of further carnivalization in a literary genre popular after the Song and consisting of comic dialogues analogous to Japanese *manzai*. See Sawada 1975: 180.

[10] See *Qingpingshan tang huaben* (Shanghai: Gudian wenxue chubansha, 1957), summarized in André Lévy 1978: 1:57–60. See also Dars 1987: 425; Iriya 1958: 197–203. The story is recited as a "precious scroll" (*baojuan*) by two nuns in the *Jingpingmei* 53; see the translation by André Lévy 1985: 2:613.

[11] The title of this fascicle, "The Sound of the Valley Stream, the Forms of the Mountains," refers to that of the poem written by Su Shi after his awakening. For more details, see Faure 1987c: 121–142.

[12] The *huaben* is quoted in other Song works and in later collections of stories such as the *Xiugu chunrong* and the *Yanju biji*. A variant appears in the *Jinpingmei, juan* 73. (See André Lévy 1978: 1:59.) See also the *huaben* titled "Master Foyin four times composes for Qinniang" (*Foyin shi si diao Qinniang*), in which Foyin, a poet who became a monk because of a whim of the emperor Shenzong, resists the advances of Qinniang, a singer whom Su Shi has hired to seduce his friend and thus force him to unfrock. Impressed by Foyin's example,

any rate, the two contrasting images of Su Shi are typical of the selective memory of the "great" and "little" traditions and of the Janus character of their heroes. There are many other stories about the depravity of Buddhist or Chan monks.[13] Although one must of course suspect the bias of these anticlerical sources, clues are found in Buddhist sources as well. In his diary, the Japanese pilgrim Ennin (794–864) describes the laxity of Chan monks he happened to meet. Moreover, the criticism of "meat eaters and fornicators" is also found among Chan monks themselves. For example, there is Puan, whose criticism is quoted verbatim in the—perhaps not so different—context of Tokugawa Japan by the Ōbaku master Chōon Dōkai (1630–1682): "And today there is an empty-minded Zen school, people who, without having the proper awakening, explain that to drink wine or eat meat, and to commit adultery is no obstacle for the enlightened nature."[14] Such an attitude was apparently widespread in Japan long before the Tokugawa. Ikkyū Sōjun has a poem titled "For Students of Pretense," which reads:

> Sex in the temple, the Zen of demons.
> Calling followers in for a "mysterious satori."
> That modern leper, Yōso.
> Amidst universal sin, I alone follow nature.
>
> (*Kyōun shū* 351; Sanford 1981: 135)

Ikkyū sharply contrasts his own "naturalism" with the moral laxity prevailing in Zen monasteries, a laxity that he associates with his co-disciple Yōso. We must, however, keep in mind the polemical context of such criticisms. At any rate, both types of "naturalism" were conflated by later tradition—and the *Kyōun shū* was for that reason forbidden.

The dereliction of the Buddhist clergy during the Tokugawa has often been described, in official documents as well as in the works of novelists. According to Kumazawa Banzan's *Usa Mondō*: "In recent years, from the time of the ordinance banning Christianity on, a faithless Buddhism has flourished. Since throughout the land everyone has his parish temple (*dannadera*), unlike in the past, monks can freely indulge in worldly affairs without concern for either discipline or scholarship. . . . The freedom with which they eat meat and engage in romantic affairs surpasses that of secular men" (Watt 1984: 190).

Su Shi is converted to Chan. In a variant recorded in the *Jinlian ji*, however, it is Qinniang who turns away Foyin. See ibid.: 2:621–622.

[13] Another example is found in Lanselle 1987: 33–65.

[14] See Dieter Schwaller, "Der Text *Mukai Nanshin* des Japanischen Zen-Mönchs Chōon Dōkai," 1987 (unpublished paper). As noted earlier, a representative of this trend of Chan during the Song was the "trickster" Daoji (Jigong). Particularly significant in this context is the story of Jigong's "encounter-dialogue" with courtesan Hongjian and its resemblance to the story of Wujie and Red Lotus quoted above.

This anticlerical vision is reflected in the urban(e) novels of Saikaku Ihara. In *A Bonze's Wife in a Worldly Temple*, the heroine, a young courtesan, recalls: "In the course of time I urged this one religion [i.e., sexual indulgence] on temples of all the eight sects, and I may say that I never found a single priest who was not ready to slash his rosary [break his religious vows]" (Saikaku 1956: 149). Although Zen did not belong to the "eight sects" of traditional Buddhism, it is unlikely that it was very different in this respect.

Sexual relations were only one aspect of transgression, which included also the breaking of the precepts on intoxicants and vegetarianism. The eating of meat and fish was apparently condemned by Japanese authorities as a sign of the corruption of the Buddhist clergy.[15] We know, for example, that several monks were implicated in 1409 in a scandal related to the eating of fish and meat and were sent into exile (Tsuji 1944–1955: 5:66–67). The drinking of sake, under the name of "water of *prajñā*," was also widespread. It was strictly forbidden in 1419 at Shōkokuji. The following year, the prohibition was extended to all Zen monasteries. The same year, a Korean envoy reported in his *Rōshōdō Nihon gyōroku* about a temple where monks and nuns slept in the same hall. And, as we will see, cases of homosexuality ("sodomy") were apparently relatively common.[16] Even so, the degeneration of Buddhist monasteries during the Tokugawa might have been somewhat exaggerated. A good part of Tsuji's evidence is provided by anti-Buddhist tracts and by the accounts of Christian missionaries. (See ibid.: 10:404.) Even though it may have some basis in fact, his account of a degenerated Tokugawa Buddhism, which became the received opinion among Japanese historians, is too close to the official interpretation of the puritan Meiji ideologues—intent on offering Buddhism as a scapegoat—not to raise a few questions.

CHAN/ZEN ATTITUDES TOWARD SEXUALITY

Although sexuality—or more precisely its castigation—played a predominant role in Indian Vinaya, it was elided in Chinese Vinaya and Chan/Zen "Pure Rules." With the development of Bodhisattva Precepts and the interiorization of morality, the emphasis is laid on a "formless repentance"

[15] See Tsuji 1944–1955: 5:67–70, 10:446–493; Wakatsuki Shōgo, "Edo jidai no sōryō no daraku ni tsuite: Sono shorei," KDBGKK 2 (1971): 5–19.

[16] One may even wonder whether the custom of priests marrying women was not to a certain extent a compromise in order to reduce pederasty and other types of semi-clandestine loves such as those described by Ihara Saikaku. As is well known, the first well-recorded case of a monk taking a wife is that of Shinran (1173–1262). Marriage, however, was legally forbidden for monks until Meiji, although monks often entertained female servants or concubines. Significantly, even after monks were permitted to marry, celibacy continued to be required for nuns.

that aims at realizing the emptiness of sins and delusion rather than on the actual, "phenomenal" or "formal" transgressions. Already present in early Chan, for example in early Chan texts such as the *Treatise on the Five Unborn Upāya (Wusheng fangbian men)* or the *Platform Sūtra*, this tendency lent itself to laxity—as is suggested by the criticism of the Tokugawa Zen master Dokuan Dokugo against monks who neglect Vinaya and Buddhist doctrine on the authority of Huineng and the *Platform Sūtra* (T. 82, 2597: 565a).

Actually, Indian penitentials already showed a propensity to elide the detail of the transgressions. For example, in the Vinaya discussion of two ambiguous cases of illicit talk with a woman, the head monk asks the community: "Venerables, I finished reading the two ambiguous cases. I now ask you this question: Venerables, are you pure regarding that matter? . . . Once, twice, thrice. . . . The venerables are pure regarding the ambiguous cases—so do I interpret their silence" (Rhys Davids and Oldenberg 1881: 229.) Although the *uposadha* ceremony was more a ritual recitation of the *prātimokṣa* rules, a reaffirmation of community, than an actual public confession, such an interpretation of silence paved the way for the development of a subtle casuistry. And yet, Indian Vinaya is fairly outspoken about sexual matters—since at least five of the thirteen recognized cases of penitence fall under that rubric.[17] Sexual intercourse is strictly prohibited, "even with an animal." But more than "bestiality," onanism seems a major concern, and the texts forbid "the emission of semen by design, except by a person sleeping" (Prebish 1975: 54). We are told that the Buddha once scolded a monk in the following terms: "Imbecile, you raise your hand publicly to receive alms, . . . and then, with the same hand, you commit horrors!" To avoid this, the Buddha declared: "If a monk, by touching his genital parts, makes semen flow, he must confess his error before the community and submit to canonical penitence" (Wieger 1951: 350–351). There are even clauses about the rejection of eunuchs (considered as passive homosexuals) and hermaphrodites (ibid.: 467, 471). Homosexuality, however, is strangely overlooked and, at any rate, seems more acceptable than heterosexuality.

On the other hand, the only Chinese monastic regulations to address explicitly the question of sexuality seem to be those of the Ming Chan master Zhuhong. In his *Ten Things for the Cultivation of the Self*, Zhuhong describes the "seventh thing" as follows: "Do not go near women: If one enters into friendship with young nuns, adopts a woman from the outside world as a godmother, goes frequently to relatives' homes to visit relatives or dependents, or even if one lives with his mother who is not yet

---

[17] The five cases are (1) onanism, (2) fondling, (3) saucy talk, (4) "platonic" love, and (5) playing the role of a go-between. See also Rhys Davids and Oldenberg 1881: Part 1; Prebish 1975: 52.

seventy, oblivious of ridicule and suspicion; all these are regarded as being near women." (See Yü Chün-fang 1981: 205.) Zhuhong is also famous for his double-entry moral bookkeeping. In his *Record of Self-Knowledge* (*Zizhi lu*), he puts a price on every good and bad deed.[18] On the whole, however, perhaps because of Confucian influence, Chinese and Japanese monastic rules remain extremely abstract and euphemized when compared with Indian Vinaya.

IMAGES OF WOMEN

> If Buddhists scorn the feminine body, I think it has originally to do with a degradation of morals. . . . In the countries of the redheads, men behave as son-in-laws adopted as heirs; they hold women as their masters. It must have been the same in India.
> —Tominaga, *Shutsujō kōgo*

The transgression of the rules against "fornication" presupposes the presence of women within the monastic community or on its margins. Not surprisingly, it is Ānanda—the handsome Ānanda, so sensitive to feminine charms—who is held responsible for convincing the Buddha to admit the first woman, Śākyamuni's own aunt and foster mother, into his monastic community. The basic misogyny of Buddhism—or at least of its Elders (Sk. *Sthavira*)—is revealed by this episode, which shows (retrospectively) the reluctance of the Buddha to accept women in his community and his prediction of the decline of Buddhism because of the presence of women.[19] After the death of the Buddha, Mahākāśyapa reproaches Ānanda, not only for his intervention on behalf of women, but also for his lack of respect for the Buddha: "You have shown to women the mark of cryptorchidy of the Buddha after he entered into *parinirvāṇa*. Is this not shameful?" (See Lamotte 1944–1980: 1:96.)

Ānanda's role as a scapegoat is well illustrated by the opening chapter

[18] This is how Zhuhong evaluates the following "Miscellaneous bad deeds":

167. To have sexual intercourse with extremely close kin counts as fifty demerits.

168. To have sexual intercourse with a prostitute counts as two demerits.

170. To have sexual intercourse with a nun or a chaste widow counts as fifty demerits.

171. If upon seeing a beautiful woman of a good family, one desires to make love to her, count two demerits. (This is for lay people. In the case of a monk, no matter whether the woman is related to oneself or not, of good family, or of lowly origin, to commit such an offence will be counted uniformly as fifty demerits, and to have the desire to make love to her will be counted uniformly as two demerits. (Yü Chün-fang 1981: 252)

[19] For a detailed and nuanced study of the early Buddhist attitudes toward women, see Sponberg 1989. Sponberg distinguishes in this respect four major strands, what he calls soteriological inclusiveness, institutional androcentrism, ascetic misogyny, and soteriological androgyny (ibid.: 8).

of the apocryphal *Śūraṃgama-sūtra*. In this episode, which provides the
pretext for Buddha's sermon, Ānanda is shown about to succumb to
temptation and is saved *in extremis* by the intervention of Mañjuśrī, acting
on the order of the omniscient Buddha. Later tradition has accepted as
such the negative judgment passed on Ānanda in the *Śūraṃgama*, although this episode might have been one of the main reasons for the popularity of the scripture, and readers may have enjoyed the story itself
more than its morality. There is at least one monk, Ikkyū (1394–1481),
who reacted against this morality. In a poem titled "Portrait of an Arhat
at a brothel," he writes:

> That Arhat, detached from passions, is still far from Buddhahood.
> One trip to a brothel would bring him great wisdom.
> Quite a laugh; Mañjuśrī reciting the *Śūraṃgama*,
> Having long ago forgotten the pleasures of his youth.[20]

In another, autobiographical, poem titled "The Heresy of Lust," he returns to the same theme:

> Whose song carrying over the brothel revelry?
> A song of youth that swirls my head.
> Then a dawning never seen by Ānanda.
> A means to enlightenment, this fading Autumn Moon.
> (*Kyōun shū* 336; Sanford 1981: 157)

"Great traditions"—whether Buddhist or not—tend to define themselves against women (and the body, namely, the feminine body), which
is often perceived as the representative of local religion. Chan is an interesting case, since its subversive and "sudden" components would at first
glance seem to offer some analogy to what has sometimes been perceived
as characteristic of a feminine religious experience. (See Bynum in
Bynum, Harrell, and Richman 1986.) Yet the Chan/Zen attitude in this
domain has remained in fact rather conservative. In early Buddhism,
women were considered intrinsically lustful and defiled; they were the
daughters of Māra, the Tempter. As the Buddha, in the *Aṅguttara Nikāya*
(III: 67), put it: "Monks, a woman, even when going along, will stop to
ensnare the heart of a man; whether standing, sitting, or lying down,
laughing, talking, or singing, weeping, stricken, or dying, a woman will
stop to ensnare the heart of a man. . . . Verily, one may say of woman-
hood: it is wholly a snare of Māra." Although it could not affect Shenxiu,
the mere sight of women bathing made the famous hermit Unicorn lose
all his painfully acquired powers.[21] Another paradigmatic example is that

---

[20] See *Kyōun shū* 255, trans. Sanford 1981; Arntzen 1986: 255.
[21] See *Konjaku monogatari shū*, trans. Bernard Frank, *Histoires qui sont maintenant du passé*
(Paris: Gallimard, 1968), 73. The same thing happens to a nun (ibid.: 117).

of Upagupta's disciple. The third Indian patriarch Upagupta had warned one of his most devout disciples against women. The disciple, convinced that he had already attained enlightenment, felt offended. Later on, as he was crossing a river, he was compelled to rescue a woman who was carried away by the current. Aroused by her contact, he forgot his monastic vows: "Forcing her to the ground, he lay between her legs, intent on violating her—and at that moment he looked at her and found that instead of a woman he had hold of the holy sage who was his master. Aghast, he tried to pull away, but Upagupta held him fast between his legs, and cried out, 'Why do you torment an aged priest in that manner? Are you the saintly man who has gained enlightenment and is untainted by sexual desire?' The disciple was overwhelmed with shame and struggled to get free from Upagupta's legs, but they held him in a vice-like grip and would not let go. As the master went on upbraiding him, a crowd of passers-by gathered to watch, and the disciple was overcome with shame and mortification."[22]

Upagupta's "skillful means" were particularly effective, and the disciple understood the lesson. This episode is interesting to compare with that of Ānanda's temptation in the apocryphal *Śūraṃgama-sūtra*. Upagupta shows more humor than the Buddha: the latter was probably too serious to use such a dirty trick. Although Upagupta had some characteristics of the trickster, he remained a strict ascetic, unlikely to become in popular imagination a god of union like tricksters such as Wanhui—who, "believing neither in Buddha nor in Dao, . . . just wanted people to unite somehow." Upagupta's story, which appears in Zhiyi's *Mohe zhiguan*, is quoted by Dōgen in the chapter *Shizen biku* ("A Monk at the Fourth Dhyāna") of his *Shōbōgenzō*, but it has lost its subversive humor: "Actually the woman was Upagupta in disguise. When the monk discovered this, he was filled with great shame and prostrated himself before his master" (Yokoi 1976: 157). Dōgen merely wants to provide examples of monks who wrongly believe themselves to have attained Arhathood; he is not interested in the issue of sexuality, or in dwelling on the transgression of the precepts.

The Chinese also commonly perceived women as a potential threat to men's physical and spiritual powers. Robert van Gulik shows how conceptions derived from Daoism led to a belief in a kind of sexual vampirism (van Gulik 1974). Daoism, however, stressed the necessary complementarity of the sexes and gave an important role to women in its rituals. Although the Mahāyāna logic of nonduality similarly led to the theoretical equality of men and women, it apparently did not raise women's status. The Two Truths theory provided an argument to explain away

[22] See *Uji shūi monogatari*, trans. Mills 1970: 396.

sexual differences at the absolute level while retaining them at the conventional level. As Ikkyū put it: "As for the skin, what a difference between a man and a woman!/ But as for the bones, both are simply human beings." But contrary to the "absolutist" interpretation of many Chan/Zen masters, Ikkyū knew that, according to Mādhyamika orthodoxy, the conventional truth was *necessary*, and he was able to enjoy skin-deep differences. Most Zen masters seem to have shared Shidō Bunan's attitude: "I abstain from contact with women because the mind of a beast still remains with me." (See Kobori 1970–1971: 4, 1:122.) Very few Chan/Zen monks indeed were able to claim, as did the Korean "mad monk" Jun-kwang, to have transcended "bestiality" and to put into practice their theoretical ecumenism.[23] The *locus classicus* for Buddhist sexual equality may be found in the Devadatta chapter of the *Lotus sūtra*, in which the eight-year-old daughter of the *Nāga* king Sagara attains enlightenment through Mañjuśrī's guidance; or in the *Vimalakīrti-nirdeśa*, where the archetypal Arhat, Śāriputra, is ridiculed by the Nāga girl in a way that anticipates the humor of Wu Cheng'en's *Journey to the West* (see Anthony Yu 1977–1983) or Ikkyū's poems quoted above. But significantly, the heroines of these stories are Nāga girls, that is, fictive and nonhuman females. The misogyny of Buddhism was too deeply entrenched to be shaken by mere theoretical contradictions or fictional subversion. Despite—or because of—the theoretical equality it posits between the sexes, Chan was an essentially masculine discourse, defined by its patriarchal tradition: for all the talk about robes, there are no women, no matriarchs there.

The rhetoric of equality

To be sure, in Chan rhetoric, distinctions such as that between men and women were denied "not only any ultimate importance in themselves, but also any relevance to enlightenment" (Levering 1982: 19). But precisely such a statement is essentially rhetorical: just like the equality between passions and awakening, it is denied in practice or in discourse as soon as it seems to threaten the established order. In Chan as in other traditions, the equalization of the sexes in principle coexisted with the monopolization of authority by men. (See Weber 1964: 104.) Miriam Levering quotes Dahui and Dōgen, who, although representing opposite trends of Chan, seem to agree in their ecumenical approach. Speaking

[23] See the following dialogue between Lewis Lancaster and Jung-kwang: "I finally asked him, 'Did you do all those things mentioned? Did you have sex with animals?' 'Yes,' he answered, 'all sentient beings have the Buddha nature. Why make distinctions?'" (Jung-kwang 1979: 10). In another dialogue, the Korean monk explains: "I never hurt anyone by my actions. I am a 'Buddhist mop.' A mop is something that gets dirty itself but makes everything it touches clean" (ibid.: 10).

about his successful lay student, Lady Tang, Dahui declares: "Can you say that she is a woman, and women have no share [in enlightenment]? You must believe that this matter has nothing to do with [whether one is] male or female, old or young. Ours is an egalitarian Dharma-gate that has only one flavor" (*Dahui pushuo, zz* 1, 31, 5:455a). And he concludes: "For mastering the truth, it does not matter whether one is male or female, noble or base. One moment of insight and one is shoulder to shoulder with the Buddha" (ibid.: 433b, in Levering 1982: 20).

After mentioning other declarations of Chan/Zen masters such as Yuanwu, Bassui, and Jakushitsu, Levering concludes: "The teaching of the school appears to have been clear and consistent over the centuries" (Levering 1982: 22). But is this really the case? Levering goes on to discuss the story of Moshan Liaoran (*Jingde chuandeng lu* 11, Levering ibid.: 27), who happens to be (surprisingly?) "the only nun who is given a record in the *Jingde chuandeng lu*."[24] Levering asks why Chan and Zen "included these stories in preaching and teaching at a time when their societies were putting more emphasis on Confucian education as a path of self-cultivation, while at the same time failing to educate women, or to allow women to become leaders or teachers." Precisely, Chan egalitarianism served perhaps a strategic purpose in the larger context of Buddhism's rivalry—and complementarity—with Confucianism. Buddhism attracted women who wanted to run away from their gender-determined roles. A paradigmatic case is the legend of Miaoshan, which contributed to turn a (predominantly male) Bodhisattva, Avalokiteśvara, into a female deity, Guanyin. Unlike Daoism and popular religion, or even Tantrism, Chan did not give a positive value to femininity. Yet early Chan attracted a large number of aristocratic women, beginning with Wu Zetian. Empress Wu was the only Chinese woman who succeeded in symbolically becoming a man—by taking the title of emperor and passing herself off as an incarnation of Maitreya. (See Forte 1976.) A close scrutiny of Chan epigraphy reveals a number of eminent nuns who reached awakening, but they are usually recorded simply as Chan masters and the stele omits mentioning their gender. An interesting case is that of the two Tiantai nuns (and blood sisters) who challenged the Northern Chan master Puji even before Shenhui did. But their challenge has been (almost) erased from the official record.[25] At any rate, the Chan rhetoric of equality was the consequence not only of its theoretical premises but also of its need for aristocratic

---

[24] Other paradigmatic women in Chan texts include Linzhao, the daughter of Layman Pang, or Zongzhi, Bodhidharma's disciple, who is said to have obtained the "skin" (?) of her master. Dōgen elaborates on these cases in *Raihai tokuzui*. See Levering 1982; Bodiford 1989.

[25] It was preserved by chance in the fragments of an epigraphic collection by the Korean master Ŭich'ŏn. The elder of the two sisters is presented as a thaumaturge and an avatar of Samantabhadra. See Saitō 1973: 839–840.

support. The sudden increase of references to women in Dahui's sermons reflects the fact that a number of them were addressed to influential nuns or laywomen. Levering notes that Dahui counted five nuns and one lay-woman among his fifty-four Dharma-heirs. Yet Levering shows very well that Dahui's rhetoric of equality cannot stand up against the rhetoric of masculine heroism commonly associated with the spiritual quest. Awakening gave a woman the opportunity to become a "great man" (*da-zhangfu*).[26] Despite the large number of women having reached awakening under Dahui, none of them appears in the official lineage of Dahui's school. The impulse for an egalitarian Chan seems to have come largely from lay circles—as suggested by the popularity of stories in which Lin-zhao, the daughter of Layman Pang, outwits even her father.

In his early proselytic years, Dōgen too advocated the equality of the sexes. Consider, for example, the following passage in the *Shōbōgenzō*: "What demerit is there in femaleness? What merit is there in maleness? There are bad men and good women. If you wish to hear the Dharma and put an end to pain and turmoil, forget about such things as male and female. As long as delusions have not yet been eliminated, neither men nor women have eliminated them; when they are eliminated and true reality is experienced, there is no distinction of male and female" (Terada and Mizuno 1975: 1:326, Levering 1982: 31). Perhaps this does not sound like vintage Dōgen, like the man who advocated the "true man (and woman?) with a rank." Perhaps also this talk about equality reflects precisely a male viewpoint. At any rate, once proselytism gave way to the concern for a narrow monastic community, the equality between man and woman—just like that between monk and layman—soon disappeared from Dōgen's discourse. Dōgen apparently had only a few female disciples, and perhaps it is for them that he spoke the sermon recorded in *Raihai tokuzui*, or wrote the *Shōbōgenzō* in "feminine" script (*kana*).[27] But, like his model Śākyamuni, he remained aware of the dangers of a feminine presence in the saṃgha and would probably have sided with Mahā-kāśyapa and other conservative Arhats against Ānanda. Keizan seems to have been more willing to put into practice this theoretical equality. We know, for instance, that he built a nunnery, Enzūin, on the land of Yō-kōji. This nunnery was entrusted to the woman who had given him the land, and who had in the meantime become his disciple under the reli-

[26] See Miriam Levering, "Lin-chi (Rinzai) Ch'an and Gender: The Rhetoric of Equality and the Rhetoric of Heroism," 1988 (unpublished paper).

[27] On the relation of *kana* to the Zen tradition, see Tetsugen (1854–1904), who gives as examples the waka exchanged by Prince Shōtoku and a mendicant (alias Bodhidharma) at Kataoka, the poem sent by the wife of Emperor Saga (r. 810–823), Empress Danrin, to Yanguan Qian (d. 842), and the subsequent coming to Japan of Yanguan's disciple Yikong (Gikū), the second Chan master (the first one being Daoxuan/Dōsen, a Northern Chan monk and Vinaya specialist) to teach in Japan (*Tetsugen zenji kana hōgo*, 41).

gious name of Sonin. Of his relationship with her, Keizan says that they were "as close as the iron and the magnet" (*Tōkoku ki*, in *JDZS* 395). Yet despite Keizan's interest in the spiritual guidance of female disciples, nuns were still on the margins of the male monastic community. Despite her importance in Keizan's life, and his attestation of her awakening, Sonin was not counted among Keizan's Dharma-heirs.

Remarkable women

There are, however, a few types of women playing significant roles, if not in the Chan/Zen institution, then at least in Chan discourse. One is the old woman—a woman who has lost her femininity, and who is often shown teaching lessons to monks. Perhaps her closeness to death has made her a liminal figure, who, like the Chan master, can as such serve as a mediator.[28] A well-known example, often quoted by Dōgen, is that of the old woman who refused to give a rice cake to Deshan Xuanjian because he could not solve her kōan. A similar episode happened to the young Huangbo Xiyun, who was outwitted by an old laywoman. When he asked her to take him as a disciple, she replied that, having a body afflicted with the five obstructions, she was not a receptacle for the Dharma. She then directed him to Baizhang, under whom Huangbo eventually reached awakening. The old woman herself had apparently studied Chan with Nan'yang Huizhong. (See Demiéville 1970b: 272.) Despite its revalorization of the woman's role, this story implies that even an enlightened laywoman could not presume to take monks as disciples.

A figure closely related to that of the old woman is the mother who serves as a spiritual guide to her son. Keizan, for instance, tells us how he overcame his karmic obstacles thanks to the prayers of his mother to Kannon, and how he inherited from her his faith in this Bodhisattva. It is in memory of his mother that he founded Enzūin, a pavilion dedicated to Kannon and to the salvation of all women (*Tōkoku ki*, in *JDZS* 406). The situation, however, was not always so harmonious. The abandoned mother haunts Chan literature (or Buddhist literature in general). The paradigm here is the story of Buddha's going to the Tuṣita Heaven to preach to his dead mother, or of Maudgalyāyana (Ch. Mulian) rescuing his mother from hell. But the salvation of the mother often remains wishful thinking, and she has to be sacrificed for the awakening of her son. We have seen earlier how Huangbo's mother drowned when trying to run after her son. Another case often mentioned in Chan literature is that of Huineng, who abandoned his old mother in order to study with Hongren. As one can imagine, such stories sounded horrifying to Confucian-

---

[28] A striking case is that of Sōtōba Komachi, in Kan'ami's Nō play. See Arthur Waley, *The Nō Plays of Japan* (Rutland, Vt.: Charles E. Tuttle, 1976), 114–124.

minded Chinese, who must have read them as illustrations of Linji's famous words: "If you meet your parents, kill your parents." Advocates of Chan such as Zongmi or Qisong worked hard to prove that Buddhist filial piety not only did exist but was even superior to Confucian filial piety because it included the larger family of humankind.[29] They overlooked in their ecumenism, however, the primary function of filial piety—namely, to preserve and differentiate familial lineages.

At another pole is found the virgin—a role that seems sometimes to have sexual or incestuous overtones. Such is, for example, the case of Miaoshan, an incarnation of the Bodhisattva Guanyin, who came to play a predominant role in Chan/Zen. (See Dudbridge 1978.) Like Mazu (the goddess, not the Chan monk), Miaoshan was a virgin who refused to marry and died a premature death. The same theme is expressed in a popular *huaben* titled "How Lotus became a Buddha in a flowery Palanquin" (*Huadeng jiao Liannü Fo ji*). The interest of the story is increased by the way in which Chan monks are defeated in their "encounter dialogue" with a seven-year-old girl, just as the Arhat Śāriputra had been defeated by the daughter of the dragon king in the *Vimalakīrti-nirdeśa*. One day, Lotus stops a procession led by the Chan master Huiguang, the superior of the Nengren monastery, and asks him the following question: "The daughter of the dragon king became a Buddha when she was eight by offering a precious pearl. Why couldn't I, without a pearl, become a Buddha at seven?" People think that she has become mad. A few days later, she interrupts a sermon of Huiguang with the same question. Huiguang answers by drawing a circle with his finger. She is taken back home by her father. Years later, when she turns sixteen, she returns to the Nengren monastery for the Lantern Festival and asks the monks: "Which is the brightest of the lamps in this temple?" "That in front of the Buddha." "This is the lamp of the Buddha; where is that of the mind?" She then slaps in the face the nonplussed monks, who go and complain to Huiguang. She has then another verbal sparring with him and makes him blush with her last repartee: "Get a chap who will pay the debt!" When she turns eighteen, her parents decide to marry her to the son of a neighbor. On the day of the wedding, after leaving a departing poem alluding to her "Buddha body," she dies in meditation posture in her palanquin. The two families argue over her relics, when Huiguang, claiming her as his disciple (despite his defeat), comes to take her remains back to the monastery. Significantly, Lotus is presented as the reincarnation of a pious old woman, a specialist on the *Lotus Sūtra*.[30] The agonistic nature of

[29] On this question, see Kenneth Ch'en, "Filial Piety in Chinese Buddhism," *HJAS* 28 (1968): 81–97.

[30] See André Lévy 1978: 1:69–72; Iriya 1958: 71–80. Notice the resemblance between the stories of Lotus and of Mr. Ma's "wife," namely, the fact that both die before their wedding is consummated.

her relationships with society (through her encounters with the monks and her passive resistance to her parents) and the final recuperation of her body by the Chan master seem to offer a paradigm of how the voice of women was eventually silenced by institutionalized Chan, although Buddhism offered to some of them a relative freedom from the duties of their gender.

At the third pole, where the male fantasies play themselves out most clearly, one finds the woman as a whore. The most significant case is again that of Guanyin/Kannon. As Stein has shown, the erotic allusions are obvious in various legends concerning Guanyin, which were apparently widespread in Chan circles. (See Sawada 1975: 147–152.) Such is, for example, the story of Guanyin as the wife of Mister Ma (Malang fu), celebrated by Ikkyū in one of his poems (*Kyōun shū* 62, in Yanagida 1987: 40). A man named Ma had a wife who fornicated with every man she met, thereby ridding them forever of desire. (See *Fozu tongji*, T. 49, 2035: 380c.) This story is usually associated with another image of Guanyin, "Guanyin with the fish-basket," which appears in the work of the Chan master Zhouyai (fl. 11th c.).[31] The theme is also developed in a collection of stories discussing sexual problems in Buddhism, "How Kāśyapa climbed down from the mountain to marry a nun," recorded in the *Xinbian Zuiweng tanlu* (ca. 1226) by Jin Yingzhi.[32] Despite the importance of the sexual theme in Chan literature on Guanyin between the twelfth and fourteenth centuries, this theme cuts across sectarian boundaries. We need simply to recall that Shinran's decision to marry was based on a dream in which Kannon appeared to him and said that she would manifest himself/herself as his wife in order to save him. We also noted earlier the return of repressed sexuality in the dreams of monks such as Myōe. Equally worth mentioning is the existence in Sennyūji—a monastery founded in Kyoto on the Chan model by the Vinaya master Shunjō—of a superb statue of Guanyin/Kannon as Yang Guifei, the courtesan who helped to bring to an end the reign of the Tang emperor Xuanzong (r. 712–756).

Ikkyū and women

Despite (or because of) these "returns of the repressed" and the "philosophical femininity" of its subitism, Chan/Zen remained essentially a male chauvinist discourse, well characterized by what Bataille calls a "virilité bousculante." The subversive tendencies in Chan overlap to some

---

[31] Concerning these two figures, see Sawada 1975: 143–162; Stein 1986: 54–61. Stein also unravels the intricate sexual connotations of Guanyin's thousand hands and eyes by tracing the legend back to its Hindu prototype (ibid.: 34–54).

[32] See *Xinbian Zuiweng tanlu* (Shanghai: Gudian wenxue chubanshe, 1958), 33, quoted in Stein 1986: 54.

extent with the rise of women in Chan/Zen communities—or on the margins of them. Nevertheless, misogyny is fundamental among Chan ascetics, always worried about incontinence and the subsequent spiritual impotence, and the "fathers" were always concerned with the cohesion of their male community. Transgression, however, is intertwined with morality, and figures such as Ikkyū are the exceptions that confirm the (Chan) rule. In a poem in praise of Dharma master Kuiji of Cien monastery, Ikkyū writes: "Kuiji excelled in *samādhi*, but also in wine and meat, in scriptures and in beautiful women. To equal a *zasu* with such pupils, in the [Zen] school, there is only Sōjun" (*Kyōun shū* 161, in Yanagida 1987: 92). Ikkyū has a number of poems celebrating sexual desire, love, women, and the female body. In one poem titled "Sipping a beautiful woman's sexual fluids," he writes: "Linji's followers don't know Zen./ The true transmission was to the Blind Donkey./[33] Love play, three lifetimes of sixty long kalpas./ One autumn night is a thousand centuries" (*Kyōun shū* 537; Sanford 1981: 160). Another poem, titled "Taking my hand to be Shin's hand," tells of his late love for the blind singer Shin and seems to allude to masturbation: "How is my hand like Shin's hand?/ Self-confidence is the vassal, Freedom the master./ When I am ill, she cures the jade stalk,/ And brings joy back to my followers" (*Kyōun shū* 543; Sanford 1981: 164; see also Covell 1980: 227). Masturbation is even more explicit in an earlier poem, titled "The Calf": "My naked passions, six inches long./ At night we meet on an empty bed./ A hand that's never known a woman's touch,/ And a nuzzling calf, swollen from nights too long" (*Ikkyū zue shūi*, quoted in Sanford 1981: 287). Finally, a metaphoric poem titled "A Woman's body has the fragrance of a narcissus": "One should gaze long at King Chu's hill, then ascend it./ Midnight on the jade bed amid regretful dreams./ A flower opening beneath the thrust of the plum branch,/ Rocking gently, gently between her water-nymph thighs" (*Kyōun shū* 542; Sanford 1981: 167).

SODOM AND GOMORH

> The teacher of the seven Buddhas is a boy five feet tall/ Whose hair hangs down to his shoulders like clouds.
>
> —Zen master Godaichi Shūgaku, inscription on a scroll dated 1455

[33] This is an allusion to the episode of the transmission of the True Dharma Eye by Linji to his disciple Sansheng. See Sasaki 1975: 62. Ikkyū returns to the theme of "sexual fluids" in another poem concerning Shin: "I'm infatuated with the beautiful Shin from the celestial garden:/ Lying on the pillow with her flower stamen,/ My mouth fills with the pure perfume of the waters of her stream./ Twilight comes, then moonlight's shadows, as we sing our new song" (*Kyōun shū* 541; Covell 1980: 225).

Despite their different reactions to Buddhist teachings, Jesuit missionaries in China and Japan agreed in their condemnation of the moral depravity of Buddhist monks, and more precisely in their denunciation of "sodomy"—this "sin of intellectuals and clerics" (Ariès and Béjin 1982: 95). Homosexuality seems to have been widespread among both Chinese and Japanese societies, or in any case less repressed than in Europe, where it had been strongly condemned by the Church since Thomas Aquinas and was punishable at the stake.[34] "Sodomy" is one of these categories, often paired with circumcision in the Western imagination, that define primarily the "Other." As Jonathan Spence (1984: 222) points out, such practices were ordinarily associated with the paradigmatic Other, Islam,[35] although Luther had given a broader extension to the term "Sodomites,"[36] by which he meant "Turks, Jews, papists and cardinals" (ibid.). Francis Xavier felt horrified by the "abominations of the flesh" he discovered in Japan, and to see that "great and abominable sins are held in such slight regard." But this situation was even more prevalent in the Buddhist clergy:

> There are fewer sins among the laity, and I see that they are more subject to reason than those whom they regard as priests, whom they call *bonzos*, who are inclined to sins abhorrent to nature, and which they confess and do not deny; and this is so public and manifest to all, both men and women, young and old, that they do not regard it as strange or an abomination, since it is so very common. . . . We frequently tell the *bonzos* that they should not commit such a sin, and how much they offend God; and everything we tell them amuses them since they laugh about it and have no shame when they are reproached about so vile a sin. These *bonzos* have many boys in their monasteries, sons of *hidalgos*, whom they teach how to read and write, and they commit their corruptions with them; and this sin is so common that, even though it seems an evil to them all, they are not upset by it. (Schurhammer 1982: 84)

Xavier's successor, Torres, discussed this point in his controversy with Zen monks: "They said that this might be so with respect to women, but it would not be so in respect to boys, since there is no consequent shame to their relatives, and still less to the boy, when one commits sodomy

[34] In Manila, Chinese homosexuals were burned alive by the Spaniards at the end of the sixteenth century. See Spence 1984: 227.

[35] As such, the "Mohammedans" were both "sodomites" and "circumcised," while the Buddhist bonzes, perhaps because of their resemblance to Christian missionaries, were able to avoid symbolic circumcision.

[36] Originating in the Bible, where it applies to the behavior of the men of Sodom, this term refers as much to the type of intercourse said to be "against nature" (*more canum*) as to homosexual intercourse (*masculorum concubitus*), also said to be "against nature." See Ariès and Béjin 1982: 84.

with him, since he has no virginity to lose, and sodomy is not a sin" (Schurhammer 1982: 287).

Matteo Ricci gave a similar description of the Chinese and strongly condemned the so-called Hanlin way[37]:

> In China there are those who reject normal sex and indulge in depravity, they abandon sex with women and instead they corrupt young males. This kind of filthiness is not even discussed by wise men in the West, for fear of defiling their own mouths. Even the wild animals only make their bonds between female and male, none of them overturn the nature heaven gave them. Men who are like this never blush for shame, how sinful these men have become. The members of my humble society retain all their seed, and do not plant it out in the fields. If you doubt the wisdom of this, how much more should you question throwing it away in a ditch or a gutter. (Spence 1984: 229)

This condemnation was all the more necessary, since Jesuits themselves were soon accused of behaving "against nature." (See Spence 1984: 225.) At any rate, we are fortunate to have the Jesuit account, however biased, on a question about which Buddhist sources remain relatively silent.

The sword and the chrysanthemum

The promiscuity between master and disciple, which so horrified the Jesuits, was already evident in the Tang—if we are to believe Yijing's Vinaya prescriptions. For example, describing the rules concerning the "voiding of the bowels," Yijing mentions in passing that "To save trouble a priest always washes himself; but he who has a page can let the latter wash him." (See Takakusu 1970: 92.) Inasmuch as the term "sodomy" in the Jesuits' mouth, however, was first of all an insult addressed generically to heretics of all kinds, we cannot rely entirely on their testimony to decide whether homosexuality was really an issue in Chan and Zen monasteries.

The evidence concerning Chan/Zen in particular is rather scarce, in part because of the use of "secret words" or euphemisms (such as *kiku*, "chrysanthemum," for the anus) related to male homosexuality. (See Hirazuka 1987: 32–35.) But there is no reason to think that, at least around the seventeenth century, the situation in Zen monasteries was very different from that in other Buddhist institutions. And in China, the popularization of Chan after the Song and the blurring of sectarian borders had

---

[37] Ricci fails, however, to point out that the famous Hanlin Academy was not a Buddhist institution but a Confucian one.

rendered that distinction unnecessary. Paradoxically, certain sexual habits considered "against nature" by the Christians may have been affected by the Chan/Zen "naturalist" teaching. But they must also be placed in their institutional, social, and cultural contexts.

Was homosexuality as prevalent in China and Japan as missionaries claimed? Or was it, as in Europe, merely "the sin of intellectuals and of clerics"? For China, opinions differ widely.[38] Traditionally, it has been associated with the southern province of Fujian, "where homosexuality was supposedly so prevalent that a euphemism for male homosexuality was the 'southern persuasion' (*nanfeng*)" (Ng 1987: 68). According to a supposedly "objective" testimony, that of the medical doctor Matignon, "paederasty is extremely widespread in the Middle Empire. All classes of society give themselves up to it, and all ages, youth as old people, are fond of it."[39] In his masterly study of Chinese sexuality, however, Robert van Gulik thinks that it is difficult to credit the affirmations of many foreign observers, according to whom China would have known, in the eighteenth century and at the beginning of the twentieth century, "an unrestrained display of homosexuality and paederasty" (van Gulik 1974: 78). Van Gulik attributes this wrong impression to the fact that the social etiquette of the time was relatively tolerant of public manifestations of homosexuality.

Opinions also differ as to how homosexuality was perceived by the Chinese. Angela K. Leung concludes that China, during the sixteenth–seventeenth centuries, "tolerated homosexual practices and considered them 'normal.' "[40] Homosexuality was not perceived as a sin or a moral failure. While it was condemned in Christianity for its *malizia*, its violence against nature and God's plans, there was in China no such notion of "counternature."[41] Like other nonprocreative practices, it was judged merely on social grounds. The situation seems to have been somewhat similar to that in Roman antiquity described by Paul Veyne.[42] As Leung points out, the active/passive opposition stressed by Veyne in the Roman case played apparently no significant role in Chinese culture, where the yin/yang complementarity involves relationships of equality (Leung 1984: 660). Nevertheless, as in Rome, the moral judgment that was passed on a particular homosexual relationship had essentially to do with

[38] For a recent synthesis, see Hinsch 1990.

[39] Dr. J. J. Matignon, *Superstition, crime et misère en Chine* (Lyon: Stock, 1902), 255, quoted in Leung 1984: 662.

[40] Leung quotes Matignon's remark that homosexuals have never been persecuted in China—at least not until the twentieth century—and that the only reproach addressed by public opinion to pederasty is to have a baneful influence on eyesight (Leung 1984: 662–663).

[41] On the history of Western homosexuality, see Boswell 1980.

[42] See Paul Veyne, "L'homosexualité à Rome," in Ariès and Béjin 1982: 41–51.

the social positions of the partners involved and with the potential social disorder that may result from "excesses." As a Ming juridical manual makes clear, "A man must abstain, as much as possible, from having relationships with handsome youths and from having female servants, so that everything works all right in the conjugal bed."[43] Van Gulik notes that, according to the *Gaiyu conggao* by Zhaoyi (1727–1814), there was in the Northern Song a class of men who earned their lives as male prostitutes. In the years *Zhenghe* (1111–1117) of the Northern Song, a law punished them with one hundred bamboo strokes and a penalty, but their activity continued. Zhaoyi, however, also points out that this marked the apogee of homosexuality in China.[44] Van Gulik argues that the rise of puritanism under the Qing drastically modified the situation. Vivienne Ng mentions several cases recorded in the *Xingan huilan* (Conspectus of Criminal Cases) "involving the seduction of young boys or young men by their Confucian teachers, and seduction of neophytes by Buddhist monks." Analyzing a case of male rape in 1815, she concludes that "male homosexuality was being punished as well as the crime of rape. The harsher punishment for the unchaste victim suggests that perhaps homosexuality was regarded by the Qing government as a worse evil than female unchaste behavior. Iconoclastic men were more subversive to the state than immoral women."[45] Attempting to explain what she sees as Qing homophobia, Ng suggests an analogy to Europe where "the onset of homophobia in the late Middle Ages coincided with the rise of absolute government" (Ng 1987: 68). In his study of monastic life in modern Chinese Buddhism, Holmes Welch stresses that monasteries are relatively free of sexuality: "Monks were forbidden by their vows to have any form of sexual outlet. If detected, it meant a beating and expulsion for the monk and discredit for the monastery" (Welch 1967: 116). His informants told him in particular that homosexuality was very rare and was considered "low taste" (*xialiu*). Welch notices that the monastic diet contributed to reduce sexual desire, and that a light was kept burning in the meditation hall and other dormitories to discourage "laxity." And he concludes, perhaps too hastily: "Given their diets and beliefs, it seems more likely that the monks of China were able to adjust themselves more easily to continence than their counterparts in Europe" (ibid.: 118–119). It is possible, however, that under such circumstances, homosexual attraction often found an outlet in some kind of Platonic love.

[43] Leung 1984: 665, quoting Huang Zhengyuan's *Record of Ming Juridical Cases* (Taibei: Academia Sinica, 1979), 933.
[44] Van Gulik 1974: 210. See also *Duan xie bian*, in *Xiang'yan congshu* (Collection of Writings on Perfumed Elegance), 9th series, Vol. 2 (Shanghai: Guoxue fulun she, 1909–1911).
[45] See Ng 1987: 69; and M. J. Meijer, "Homosexual Offences in Ch'ing Law," *T'oung Pao* 71 (1985): 109–133.

Therefore, the missionary description of the moral depravity of Chinese Buddhist monasteries seems to have been somewhat exaggerated. To be sure, there were many anticlerical stories circulating among the Chinese people in which corrupt monks were giving themselves over to homosexuality or pederasty. But in most of these stories the monks, once discovered, are severely punished, and this may reflect the fact that, as van Gulik and Ng argued, the Qing rule marked a drastic change in the public perception of male homosexuality.

Similar studies on how homosexuality was treated in Japanese juridical codes are just beginning to appear.[46] There are, however, many fictional accounts of the depravity of Japanese Buddhist monks—a number of which deal explicitly with male homosexuality. (See Saikaku 1990.) According to the *Ōjō yōshū* of the Tendai monk Genshin (942–1017), homosexuals fall straight into hell. According to Buddhist tales known as the *Chigo monogatari*, however, it does not seem that homosexual relationships were regarded as a moral issue in themselves. To be sure, they were condemned as moral transgressions or worldly attachments, but their gravity was apparently lesser than that of heterosexual relationships. In the best-known *chigo monogatari*, titled *Aki no yo no monogatari* (1377), a love affair between a Miidera monk and a youth leads to a war between Enryakuji and Miidera and the subsequent destruction of Miidera. But eventually, after the suicide of the youth, the monk realizes the Buddhist truth of impermanence and reaches awakening. In the conclusion, the whole affair is presented as a rather costly *upāya* of the Bodhisattva Kannon to bring about the monk's salvation (Childs 1980: 129; Guth 1987: 18). In most other *chigo monogatari*, morality is preserved in a similar way. In one of them, however, the *Chigo Kannon engi*, the Bodhisattva Kannon manifests herself as a young novice to reward the devotion of a monk. Here again, the novice dies after three years of an idyllic master–disciple relationship but later emerges from his coffin in the form of the eleven-faced Kannon. As Margaret Childs points out, this text suggests a kind of sanctification of homosexual relationships within the Buddhist community.[47]

Probably the most famous (and the most carefully hidden) source for the history of Buddhist homosexuality is the *Chigo zōshi nanshoku emaki* (1312) attributed to the author of the equally famous "Animals scroll," Toba Sōjō, and preserved in the Sanbōin of Daigoji.[48] One of the stories revolves around a man from Saga, near Kyoto, who, having un-

---

[46] See, in particular, Pflugfelder 1990a and b.

[47] See Margaret H. Childs, "Sexuality and Salvation," paper presented at the annual meeting of the Association for Asian Studies, 1987.

[48] The text has been edited, together with a few censured illustrations, by Takahashi Tetsu 1965: 193–199.

derstood the way of non-action, discards Confucian texts (the Three Histories and the Three Classics), penetrates the arcana of Tendai, and understands that "passions are awakening" (*bonnō soku bodai*), that good and evil are nondual, that *nirvāṇa* and *saṃsāra* are identical, and that all dharmas are empty. Then, following his own mind, he starts chasing young boys (Takahashi Tetsu 1965: 195–196). Here indeed is a vivid description of the consequences of "naturalism."

According to the preface of the *Nanshoku yamamichi no tsuyu* (quoted in Hirazuka 1987: 50), "To stop at cherry blossoms when one thinks of flowers, or at women when one thinks about 'form,' such a one-sidedness is due to one's ignorance of the unique and ultimate path of equality." Thus Buddhist non-duality was invoked to justify bisexuality. The pun about "form" (*shiki*, meaning also "sex") was also frequently implicit in the quotations of the famous passage of the *Heart Sūtra*, "Form is Emptiness, Emptiness is form" (J. *shiki soku ze kū, kū soku ze shiki*), to the point that the term *Kōya shingyō* (The *Heart Sūtra* of Kōya[san]) came to be used as a euphemism for homosexuality. Despite its more frequent association with the monks of the Shingon sect, it seems that the phenomenon was also quite common in Zen monasteries.

A tradition attributes the origin of homosexuality in Japan to Kūkai: "Since the time of Kammu Tennō, when Kōbō Daishi [Kūkai] returned from China, homosexuality has flourished. In the monasteries of Kyōto, the 'Five Mountains' of Kamakura, the four great temples of Washū and Kōshū [Yamato and Edo], and all the temples of the capital, homosexuality [*shūdō*] has become widespread. Later on, not only the Buddhists, but also the nobles, the warriors, and all, without distinction of rank or wealth, have become familiar with it."[49] According to a variant, homosexuality was revealed by Mañjuśrī in India and by Kūkai in Japan. Another tradition traces the origins of homosexuality as far back as mythological times, to the legend of the two friends Otake no mikoto and Amano no mikoto. Homosexuality, however, was apparently perceived as a Buddhist characteristic, if we are to believe a text titled *Yakeiyu shamisen* (1628), according to which "love between women is the mystery of the Way of the kami, love between men is the mystery of the Buddha Dharma" (quoted in Hirazuka 1987: 39). Another common saying has it that Jizō prefers the "love of women" (*nyoshoku*), Yakushi the "love of men" (*nanshoku*).[50] But the most important patron of Japanese Buddhist homosexuals is not Yakushi but the handsome Mañjuśrī (because of a pun

[49] See Hirazuka 1987. See also Georg Schurhammer, "Kōbō daishi," in *Zeitschrift für Missionswissenschaft Münster* 12 (1922): 89, and "Die Yamabushi," ibid.: 206–228.

[50] The terminology reflects the typical male view of the Japanese, since *nanshoku* refers clearly to "love between men," while *nyoshoku* seems to refer to a man's attraction to women rather than lesbianism.

on his Japanese name, Monjushiri, *shiri* meaning "buttocks"). In Saikaku's "The Almanac Maker's Tale," the heroin Osan replies to Mañjuśrī: "You may indeed, Lord Monju, understand love between men, but so far as womanly passion is concerned, you cannot have the slightest knowledge" (Saikaku 1956: 95). Another story, found in Hiraga Gennai's *Konnan shigusa*, tells how King Yama had decided to forbid homosexuality, when one of the Ten Kings, the "King Turning the Wheel" (*tenrinnō*), defends it by arguing that it is less baneful than heterosexuality.

Most authors seem to agree that male homosexuality was relatively well accepted in Japanese society and became a prevalent feature of Japanese monastic life. It was seen as a kind of compensation for the prohibition against the presence of women in monasteries, a prohibition particularly reinforced under the Tokugawa rule. According to Hirazuka, its transgressive nature diminished with time, so that it was eventually perceived as a privilege of the monks. Buddhist homosexuals were known under a variety of names, such as *shūdō*, *kasshiki*, *tera kosho*, and *Monju Bosatsu* (by reference to their patron, the Bodhisattva Mañjuśrī). Names such as *tera kosho* and *kasshiki* referred to functions usually performed by mignons. A number of *senryū* or satiric poems such as the following deal with the topic: "The handsome woman goes to the city, the handsome man to the temple." In "A Bonze's Wife in a Worldly Temple" (Saikaku 1956: 148), Saikaku's heroine remarks: "Now this period was the very 'noonday of Buddhism'—and indeed even at noon the priests disported themselves with their temple pages."

Although most of the materials deal with Shingon, the situation may not have been drastically different in Zen, as the popularity of figures such as *nawa Monju*, Mañjuśrī as a youth, seems to suggest. (See Guth 1987: 13–16.) The term *kasshiki* is specific to Zen and designated in Chan monasteries the young boys charged with announcing meals etiquette in the refectory. In Zen monasteries from the Muromachi period onward, it came to refer to young postulants beginning their training under the supervision of the abbot. (See Collcutt 1981: 245–247.) Like the *tera kosho*, they had long braids and wore make-up (white powder on the face, stylized eyebrows, and lips colored in red) and lavish silken robes. Although Mujaku Dōchū, in his notice about *kasshiki* in *Zenrin shōkisen* (ed. Yanagida 1979: 1:319b), does not elaborate on the specific problems raised by this category of novices, *kasshiki* apparently often became causes of sexual rivalry among elder monks.[51] According to a source quoted by Hirazuka (1987: 16), "The *kasshiki* are novices, young men. Since Heaven and Earth

[51] Another of Mujaku Dōchū's works has a rubric "homosexuality" (*nanshin*), but interestingly enough all the references are to non-Buddhist Chinese texts. See Mujaku, *Saiseki kijishū*, Vol. 3 (unpublished ms., Library of Zen Bunka Kenkyūsho, Hanazono College, Kyoto).

were produced, among the animals and plants there is Yin and Yang. In the way of the flesh, too, there is love of women and love of men. Through the harmony of these two ways the world comes into being."[52]

The strongest case for the dereliction of Zen monasteries has been made by Tsuji Zennosuke. As evidence, besides the letters of Jesuit missionaries, Tsuji quotes a number of official edicts. For example, in 1303, the *shikken* Hōjō Sadatoki (1270–1311) promulgated an edict forbidding the admission of *kasshiki* in all monasteries. Ashikaga Yoshimochi (1368–1428) also decreed that, in the rules of Shōkokuji, novices and *kasshiki* were to be forbidden robes, white powder, and lipstick. From these documents, it seems that the custom of keeping mignons had become widespread, and that there was much competition among monks to get the beautiful adolescents. It was also in part because of the relation between monks, warriors, and the aristocracy. Monasteries like Shōkokuji were places where the shōgun held his parties. According to the *Inryōken nichiroku*, in 1627, "when the practice of the whole monastery was perturbed because of a *kasshiki* of Chōtokuin named Shōkō, an edict ordered the latter to be transferred from Chōtokuin to the distant Kenseidō." A Tenryūji record dated 1458 indicates that the abbot of this monastery was held responsible for a disturbance provoked by *kasshiki*. And the many love letters and poems recorded—if not in the Gozan literature, at least in diaries such as the *Hekizan nichiroku*, written by a monk of Tōfukuji—bear witness to the role played by *kasshiki* in Zen monasteries (Tsuji 1944–1955: 5:70). Outside the monastery, however, Zen monks could find other resources, as the following story told by Saikaku suggests: "[O]ne year, wealthy priests assembled in the capital from all over the country to commemorate the 350th anniversary of the death of Zen master Kanzan, first rector of Myōshinji. After the religious services were over, they went sight-seeing at the pleasure quarters on the dry riverbed. They fell in love with the handsome youths there, the likes of which they had never seen in the countryside, and began buying them up indiscriminately without a thought for their priestly duties." Saikaku blames these wealthy Rinzai Zen priests for inflating the price of boy prostitutes. (See Saikaku 1990: 190.)

Zen masters themselves were adamant in denouncing the degeneration of their school. According to Manzan:

It is said in the *Kudoku enmangyō* that "The monks of the final period [of the Dharma] will indulge in concupiscence, and adultery [*in'yoku*] will flourish; day and night they will rape young boys. Although their outside appearance will be that of monks, inwardly, they will not differ from heretics." There may be a difference between men

[52] See also *Koji ruien, Shūkyōbu* 2: 1217, for a description of the *kasshiki* of Myōshinji.

and women, but what they think, as a karmic cause, is the same thing. When I consider those who dwell in the monasteries of the world, I see those who keep novices and young boys and who will not avoid [the punishment] mentioned by this sūtra. Even if you must keep relations with these monasteries, consider carefully what they teach you. If you have to approach these people, be careful not to catch their stink."[53]

Ikkyū, too, in an allusive poem titled "The strife about the novices and the *kasshiki* of Shōkokuji," laments the events that have brought about the ruin of the monastery.[54] In several other poems, he admonishes monks against lewdness and homosexuality. (See *Kyōun shū* 284, 285, 286, 343, 350.)

Homosexuality was repressed, not as a sexual act in itself, but for its social consequences, and in particular for the disturbances it caused in monastic life. A distant effect of the misogyny of early Buddhism, it was seen as both a cause and a sign of spiritual degeneration. This characterization, perhaps more accentuated in Japanese Buddhism, may have been, if not provoked, at least to some extent justified by alleged misinterpretations of the "innate awakening" (*hongaku*) theory and the corollary notions that "This very mind is the Buddha" (*sokushin zebutsu*) or that "passions are awakening" (*bonnō soku bodai*)—in other words, by the transgressive spirit that was perhaps the most valuable, but also the most dangerous, element of Chan.

BESIDES illustrating the problems resulting from the literal interpretation of "naturalist" or antinomian theories and the negative effects of Zen collusion with the ruling classes, the question of Buddhist (homo)sexuality has revealed some of the gaps in Chan/Zen traditional discourse. Contrary to Daoism or Tantrism, Chan/Zen never considered the sexual act (or the sexual organs) a gate to a higher reality. Unlike in Christianity, sexuality never really became in Chan/Zen the object of an elaborate discourse, despite a relatively similar process of individuation, studied in the Western case by Foucault. Perhaps this is precisely because, in the Chan/Zen case, the individuation process was always denied theoretically and emerged only as a side effect of the discipline. The return of the repressed *Eros* was perhaps part of a larger phenomenon, the return of the gods in Japanese Buddhism.

[53] See Kagamishima 1978: 100.
[54] See *Kyōun shū* 279, ed. Yanagida 1987: 157. See also no. 265, "Shōkokuji's Younger Priests in Turmoil," in Covell 1980.

Twelve   *The Return of the Gods*

The responses of Chan and Zen to the question of sex and gender reflect their degree of integration in the Chinese and Japanese socio-cultural contexts, respectively. Another example of acculturation is the Chan/Zen responses to local religion. The territorial expansion of Chan in China and Korea from the seventh century onward, and later in Japan, created a tension between this new orthodoxy and local cults.[1] This tension resolved itself in a kind of polytheism, which was at odds with the theoretical agnosticism—or even the implicit atheism—of Chan,[2] but it reflected its inherent "polytheism of values." Let us then attempt to evaluate the discrepancy or the articulation between the practices and the representations in the context of the Chan "militant syncretism" and examine the role(s) that the gods of the popular pantheon came to play in the ritual life of Zen monasteries.

It will be useful to introduce a few terminological distinctions. The first distinction is between "tutelary gods," which have a local origin, and "gods of the monastery," which are found in most Buddhist monasteries and have lost their localized character. We are concerned here essentially with the Chinese and Japanese gods, since Hindu gods already integrated in the Buddhist pantheon were no longer perceived as alien figures by most Buddhists.[3] The tutelary god found its most elaborate definition in

[1] On the relations between Chan and Chinese religious traditions, see Faure 1987b. On the development of Chan/Sŏn in Korea, see Buswell 1983 and 1989b.

[2] Yanagida, for example, often speaks of a Chan "atheism." Demiéville, when he praises Linji's "humanism," intends to make a similar point: "As to Linji's originality, it seems to me that it lies especially in a typically Chinese, I would almost go as far as to say Confucian, humanism. He relates everything to man." (See Demiéville 1972: 17–18 and 141–142.) This vision of Chan derives partly from the Western discourse on Buddhist atheism. See, for instance, Catherine Weinberger-Thomas, "Le crépuscule des dieux: Regards sur le polythéisme hindou et l'athéisme bouddhique," *History and Anthropology* 3 (1987): 149–176.

[3] Some of them were in fact completely naturalized: the best known examples are Mahākala and Sarasvatī, who became popular in Japan, and particularly in Zen temples, under the names of Daikoku(ten) and Benzai(ten). Other examples, more limited to Buddhism, include Idaten (Weituo, erroneous transcription of Skanda), Kishimōjin (Hārītī), Kichijōten (Lakṣmī), Gozu Tennō (the tutelary god of the Jetavana grove, hence of its Japanese replica, the Gion sanctuary) and his daughter, the "deity of the year," Nentoku (var. Saitoku). Many were never individualized and were worshiped as a group: the Four Guardian Kings (J. Shitennō), the Two Benevolent Kings (J. Niō), the eighteen *rākṣasa*, and the Twelve Heavenly Generals. Also worth mentioning are the astrological deities: the gods of the two poles, of the seven luminaries or nine luminaries (Sk. *graha*, J. yō), of the twelve palaces, of the twenty mansions, of the sun (Sk. Sūrya, J. Nichiten), and of the moon (Sk. Candra, J. Gatsuten).

Japan in the *chinju* institution. Like most other Buddhist temples, Zen monasteries had on its precincts a sanctuary (*chinjusha*) dedicated to the local kami.[4]

A further distinction is that between tutelary gods (J. *chinju*) and monastery gods (J. *garanjin*) on the one hand and "gods protecting the Dharma" (J. *gohōjin*) on the other. As Mochizuki (1958–1963: 4:1616a) puts it: "The Four Guardian-Kings are gods protecting the Dharma, not tutelary gods [*jinushi no kami*]. We call 'tutelary gods' the gods of heaven and earth [*jingi*] who protect the place that they own." Shōkokuji, for instance, has two sanctuaries, one dedicated to Hachiman *qua* tutelary god, the other to Benzaiten *qua* goddess protecting the Dharma. In some cases, these categories seem to overlap or to become confused: in Tōfukuji, the *garandō* is occupied by statues of Śakra and Indra, who are *gohōjin*.[5]

The notion of tutelary gods led in esoteric Buddhism to that of "temporary manifestations" or avatars (*gongen*) and "bright deities" (*myōjin*). A third distinction is therefore that between the *chinju, garanjin,* or *gohōjin* on the one hand and the *gongen/myōjin* on the other. The tension between the two groups is apparent in Zen, where attempts to redefine the status of a god as *chinju, garanjin, gohōjin,* or *gongen* reflect the fluid balance of forces between what we may call the "rationalist" and the "hieratic" tendencies. While the "rationalist" tendency, intent on playing down the individuality and autochthonous nature of the god, attempted to downgrade and "deterritorialize" the *gongen*, redefining it as a *chinju*, a *garanjin*, or even as a *gohōjin*, the "hieratic" tendency did the opposite and attempted to elevate the *chinju* to the rank of a *gongen* and to increase its territorial jurisdiction.

Like the rest of Buddhism (see Mus 1935; Rawlinson 1986), Chan was from the outset both philosophical and mythological, rationalist and magical. The "psychologization of the Heavens" that took place in early Buddhism resulted in the partial acceptance of the gods into a Buddhist framework, but also in their emasculation (Smart 1981). Despite its growing pantheon, Mahāyāna Buddhism was essentially atheistic in the sense that it did not recognize any ultimate reality in the gods.[6] The *Dazhidulun* argues that the omniscient Buddha is superior to Indian gods such as Śiva and concludes: "The destiny of the world depends on causes and conditions; this is why the sage does not rest on the gods" (Lamotte

---

[4] For example, Shōkokuji and Tenryūji in Kyoto recognized as their tutelary god Hachiman, who had in the meantime become "the great Bodhisattva." See Jacques May, s.v. "Chinju," in *Hōbōgirin*, Vol. 4: 327.

[5] See ibid.: 328.

[6] The Buddhist criticism of the gods has been summarized by Etienne Lamotte 1944–1980: 1:140ff.

1944–1980: 1:141). The Mahāyāna concept of emptiness undermined the symbolic hierarchy of both Hinduism and early Buddhism, and later of Chinese religion. Nevertheless, in Japan at least, the ideological surgery destined to turn gods into eunuchs was not entirely successful, and gods were at times able to regain some of their potency. Zen "purism," although on the surface radically opposed to Shintō "purism," might be seen as an ideological reaction against, and a radical sectarian departure from, the symbolic framework of esoteric Buddhism. Yet, Zen and Shintō both attempt to sever the relationships between Buddhism and the gods in the name of an ideal orthodoxy—forgetting that the pure voice of orthodoxy could have emerged only from the anonymous rumor of a Buddhified pantheon.

MILITANT SYNCRETISM

Being, as it were, the *lex animata*, the Chan master disposed of superior *abhijñā*, which allowed him to convert or defeat the local gods. The paradigmatic example is that of the Northern Chan master Yuangui, mentioned earlier, who conferred the Bodhisattva precepts to no less a deity than the god of Song shan. A similar episode is found in the biography of Yuangui's master, Huian (T. 50, 2061: 823b). While in Yuangui's case the threat comes from the god, in other cases the symbolic or physical violence comes from the monk. Another well-known example is that of Shenxiu's disciple Pozao Duo ("Po the Stove-breaker"), whose nickname is the result of his smashing the altar of the Stove God on Song shan. Instead of being instantly punished, Duo is thanked by the god—who appears in the shape of a young man—for having destroyed his delusion by his discourse on emptiness. Shenxiu had more difficulties when he attempted the same feat with the altar of another powerful god, Guan Di. In an attempt to placate the angry god, he had to offer him the position of "god of the monastery." (See Faure 1987b: 351.) Once solidly entrenched, however, Chan masters no longer felt it necessary to placate or convert the gods and could simply ignore them.[7] Huangbo condemned as "perverse activities" all ascetic practices "worthy of heretics who fear the gods, the demons, and the spirits of water and earth" (see Carré 1985: 86), and his successor Linji could claim that "there is no Mañjuśrī on Wu-tai shan" (Demiéville 1972: 84).

The stories of conversion of the gods were well known in Japan, and

[7] These gods are those of "popular" and "official" religions. The gods and immortals of Daoism were also sometimes indebted to Chan monks, as the following story suggests. A Northern Chan monk, having discovered Lilliputian winged immortals, captures one of them. Realizing that these immortals behave as humans, he finally releases his prisoner. The next day, he receives the visit of an emissary of the "Three Pure Ones," who thanks him. See *Youyang zazu*, ed. Imamura 1980–1981: 4:85.

they served as prototypes when Zen, spreading in the provinces, had to find a *modus vivendi* with Japanese gods.[8] Sōtō monks, in particular, undertook to convert the entire Japanese pantheon. A document titled *Jukai eshiki* (dated 1862) explains how all the numinous beings of Japan—from Amaterasu, Sumiyoshi, and Hakusan Gongen to large snakes, mountain witches, and Tengu—received the Zen precepts and converted to Sōtō.[9]

Once they received the precepts, tutelary gods were to submit to monastic discipline, and infractions were punished—apparently more severely than in the case of monks. Although the attitude of Chan/Zen monks toward tutelary deities was usually one of respect and devotion, the precarious status of the monastery god can be inferred from the following story involving the Tang "trickster" Tiantai Shide and a powerless monastery god (*qielanshen*):

> There was a temple dedicated to the god protecting the monastery. Every day, the monks would put food on the altar, but it was eaten by birds. Shide beat [the statue of the god] with his staff, saying: "You can't even protect your food. How could you protect the monastery?" That night, the god appeared in the dreams of all the monks, saying: "Shide has beaten me!" The next day, the monks realized that they all had the same dream. The entire monastery was in confusion and a letter was sent to the sub-prefecture of Jiazhou. A document from the commandery came that said: "The Sages, the recluses, the avatars of Bodhisattvas should receive honorific distinctions. We thereby confer to Shide the title of Sage." (See *Zenrin shōkisen*, ed. Yanagida 1979: 1:175a; *Jingde chuandeng lu*, T. 50, 2076: 434a.)

This kind of spiritual blackmail had a long tradition in China. Japanese Zen masters carried on the tradition. Even a powerful figure such as the Hakusan god was not above humiliation: we are told that Kyōō Unryō (1267–1341) once threw the statue of this deity into the water for having failed to protect the monks of his monastery from an epidemic. Needless to say, the epidemic stopped right away. (See Hanuki 1962: 46.)

CHAN/ZEN MYTHOLOGICAL IMAGERY

Gods were present in the believers' minds through iconography, and, as we have seen, iconography played a significant role in a supposedly aniconic or iconoclastic school such as Chan. The best documentary source

---

[8] That these stories were modeled after Yuangui's story is revealed by a *kirigami* titled *Shinrei jukai no kirigami*, ed. in Ishikawa 1985b: 30.

[9] See sz, "Zoku zenkai": 380a–382b, and "Sekkai yōmon": 225; see also Ishikawa 1984b, 1985a; Hirose 1983; Hanuki 1962. For the Rinzai sect, see Suzuki Shōkun 1987; Matsumoto Shōten 1969.

on Chan/Zen iconography is probably Mujaku Dōchū's *Zenrin shōkisen* (1741), which devotes a whole section to the "spiritual icons" (*reizō*) found in Zen monasteries.[10] We are confronted here with an impressive cohort of deities.[11] Although the *Zenrin shōkisen*'s list is by no means exhaustive,[12] it defines the three main kinds of spiritual icons: those who protect the Dharma, those who play a role in the life of the monastery, and those who protect the individual after death.[13]

Let us briefly examine one category, that of the "gods of the monastery" (Ch. *qielanshen*, J. *garanjin*). As noted above, their function partially overlaps with that of the local god but still remains distinct. They may originally be local gods who, becoming displaced, acquired a higher status and mediate between localized and unlocalized cults. There can be

[10] For a detailed study on Chan/Zen iconography, see also Matsuura 1976.

[11] Mujaku's list includes (1) the Buddha Śākyamuni; (2) major Bodhisattvas such as Avalokiteśvara (Ch. Guanyin, J. Kannon), Mañjuśrī (Ch. Wenshou, J. Monju) and his manifestation as the "divine monk," *shenseng*, and Samantabhadra (Ch. Puxian, J. Fugen); (3) Arhats such as Mahākāśyapa and Ānanda, Piṇḍola and Kauṇḍinya, or the Sixteen Arhats as a group; (4) Chan masters such as Bodhidharma, Baizhang, Linji, and Puan; (5) famous monks and laymen such as Badhabhadra, Fu the Mahāsattva (Fu *dashi*), and his two sons Pujian and Pucheng; (6) protectors of Buddhism such as the Vajrapāṇi Miji ("Secret traces," Sk. Guhyapāda, one of the two "Benevolent Kings" keeping the monastery gate—the other being Nārāyaṇa), the Sixteen Good Deities (*yakṣasa*), Brahmā, Śakra and the Four Kings, and the Eight Great Heavenly Generals; (7) tutelary gods such as Weituo Tianshen, the God of the monastery (*qielanshen*) and the God of the place (*tudi gong*), the Bodhisattva Daquan Xiuli (J. Daigenshuri), the dragon god Zhaobao Qilang (J. Shōhō Shichirō), the "Great Emperor Zhang" (Zhang Dadi), and the "God of War" Guan Di; (8) gods concerned with human destiny and karmic retribution such as the Ten Kings of Hell, the stellar divinity Huode xingjun (J. Katoku Seikun, an avatar of the Chinese god Shennong, who protects monasteries against fires), Changbu Panguan (the clerk of hell, also considered a guardian deity), Ganying Shizhe (J. Kannō Shisha, the official in charge of destinies, an acolyte of Śakra also considered a protector of Zen monasteries), Kuangye shen (Skt. Aṭavaka, J. Daigensui, one of the sixteen *rākṣasa*), and Hārītī (J. Kishimōjin, an ogress who became a child-giving goddess after being converted by the Buddha); (9) miscellaneous figures such as the Venerable Yuegai, the youth Sudhana, the General Weitian (Iten, whom Mujaku distinguishes from Weituo, Idaten), the official in charge of the meals of the community (J. Kansai Jisha), Naizhong, and Luesheng Dafu.

[12] Other important Buddhas and Bodhisattvas worshiped in Zen monasteries include Amida (Sk. Amitābha), Ashuku (Akṣobhya), Yakushi (Bhaiṣajyaguru), Dainichi (Vairocana), and Hōshō (Prabhūtaratna); Miroku (Maitreya), Daishisei (Mahāsthāmaprāpta), Kōkuzō (Ākāśagarbha), and Jizō (Kṣitigarbha); a number of *vidyārāja* (J. *myōō*, "Kings of Wisdom") such as Fudō (Acala), Aizen (Rāgarāja), or Ususama (Ucchuṣma) were also borrowed from esoteric Buddhism. Important gods not listed by Mujaku are Caojun (the Stove God), Benzaiten, Daikokuten, or Sanbō kōjin.

[13] Despite the theoretical rejection of heaven and hell by Chan/Zen masters (including Keizan), the importance of hell in Chan/Zen monasteries is well documented. An examination of Chan popular predications during the Song shows that it was easier to attract the people's interest with stories related to karmic retribution than to convey the essential teachings of Chan. One may note in particular the importance of the *shuilu* ("Water and Land") Assemblies, rituals of offerings to *preta* that combined the theory of karma and the notion of filial piety. According to Nagai (1985b: 292), the main points stressed in these predications were (1) incitement to practice sitting meditation (2) observance of precepts and vegetarian feasts, (3) ancestor worship, and (4) worldly benefits (J. *genze riyaku*).

more than one *qielan*—Kenchōji of Kamakura, for example, had five, all of Chinese origin: the "Great Emperor" Zhang (Zhang Dadi, J. Chō tatei), Daquan Xiuli (J. Daigenshuri), Changbu Panguan (J. Shōbō Hangan), Ganying Shizhe (J. Kannō shisha), and Zhaobao Qilang (J. Shōhō Shichirō).[14]

Zhang Dadi, sometimes assimilated with Daquan Xiuli, was the tutelar deity of Guizong monastery on Lu shan, and he was also worshiped in many small sanctuaries. It is in one of them that the Chan master Luanqi Daolong (Rankei Dōryū, 1213–1278), about to leave Tiantong shan for Japan (1246), vowed that if he succeeded in founding a monastery there, it would be dedicated to the Great Emperor Zhang.[15] Daolong eventually founded Kenchōji in Kamakura, but the main monastery dedicated to Zhang was Kenninji in Kyoto.

ZhaoBao qilang, the "Seventh Son of Zhaobao (shan)," has also been assimilated with Daquan Xiuli. He is, like the latter, a protector of navigation and the tutelary god of Zhaobao shan, a mountain near Ayuwang shan (Mount of King Aśoka), in Zhejiang (*Zenrin shōkisen*, ed. Yanagida 1979: 1:180). He is also identified with the Daoist master Tao Hongjing (452–536). As we noted elsewhere, he is famous in the Sōtō tradition as the dragon king who protected Dōgen on his return trip from China.[16]

Daquan Xiuli is often represented in Sōtō Zen monasteries together with Bodhidharma. He is dressed in Chinese fashion and holds his right hand above his eyes to scrutinize the horizon. Some legends make him a double of Mahendra, the elder son of King Aśoka; but this attempt to connect him with India seems to derive from his role as tutelary god of Ayuwang shan and guardian of the Buddha's relics.[17] He is said to have helped Dōgen copy the *Biyan lu* in one night on the eve of the Zen master's return to Japan, but he was later superseded in this role by the god of Hakusan. Despite its frequent presence in the *butsuden* of Zen monasteries, however, and in contrast with its counterpart Bodhidharma, Daigenshuri plays a relatively minor ritual role. Hubert Durt argues that the importance of Daigenshuri comes from his role as a symmetrical and contrasting figure vis-à-vis Bodhidharma in the ideological context of the transmission of Chan/Zen in the "three countries." While Bodhidharma is credited with the transmission of Chan from India to China, Daigenshuri symbolizes the transmission from China to Japan. According to

[14] Gods are multifunctional and may fall into various categories: thus, as noted earlier, Changbu Panguan and Gangying Shizhe protect simultaneously the collectivity and the individual. On the "superscription" of symbols, see Duara 1988.

[15] The story tells how Daolong once met in the mountain a strange man who told him that his fate was to go east. He later met him again on the eve of embarking for Japan. See Mujaku's, *Zenrin shōkisen*, ed. Yanagida 1979: 1:181.

[16] See Durt 1983: 608. Shōhō Shichirō is first mentioned in *Keizan shingi* in connection with Daigenshuri (T. 82, 2589: 427c); he also appears in the *Sho ekō shingi* (T. 81, 2578: 642b).

[17] See Menzan, *Tōjō garan shōdō anzōki*, chap. 1 (quoted in Satō Shunkō 1987: 123).

Durt, the important role played by this god derives from the fact that, although the transmission of Chan to Japan could not be, as in the case of Bodhidharma, attributed to a single individual, all the Chinese and Japanese masters involved in the transmission had at a given time studied in the monasteries of Zhejiang and had probably relied on Daigenshuri's protection both as tutelary god and as protector of navigation. He was therefore well qualified to become a symbol of the Chan transmission to Japan (Durt 1983: 609).

Another interesting source for the iconography of Chan during the Song period is provided by the "Twin Pagodas" of Zayton, studied by Ecke and Demiéville. The rich iconography of these pagodas of the Kai-yuan monastery in Quanzhou (Fujian) seems to illustrate the "Gate Keepers" motif studied by R. A. Stein or the Arhat motif studied by M. W. de Visser. It represents, on the five levels of the pagodas, most of the combinations of these themes. The first impression could be that expressed by Visser about the representations of Arhats: "These instances are sufficient to show the absolutely arbitrary way in which the artists treated the emblems and symbols of divine power of the different Arhats. There was no fixed rule, and everybody painted them as he liked" (Visser 1923: 128). Taking his cues from Lévi-Strauss, however, R. A. Stein has shown that such was not the case, and that the combination of motifs in figures such as Guanyin or the Gate Keepers is always significant. The two pagodas seem to constitute incomparable material for a structuralist study of the kind realized by Stein. Such a study, however, is still prevented by the fact that, despite the erudition of Ecke and Demiéville, a number of figures remain unidentified. Another, more fundamental, reason has to do with the fact that we are confronted with a kind of "loose symbolism"—deriving from what Bourdieu (1977b) calls the "logic of practice"—that resists attempts to push the analysis of analogies beyond "family resemblances." At any rate, most of the couples represented belong either to traditional Buddhist mythology or to Chan hagiography. There is no clear hierarchical order, and twin Vajrapāṇi (in the Chinese version, *Ha/Heng*, i.e., "Sniffler"/"Snorter") are interspersed with Bodhisattvas (Mañjuśrī and Samantabhadra, Candraprabha and Sūryaprabha, Avalokiteśvara and Mahāsthāmaprāpta), mythical figures (Nāga and Asura, Sun Wukong and the Dragon King), and Arhats or Arhat-like figures and sometimes Chinese rulers.[18] The only figure borrowed from Chinese mythology

[18] The list includes Mahākāśyapa and Ānanda, Fazang and Piṇḍola, Shide and Hanshan, Xuanzang and Liang Wudi, Bodhidharma and Liang Wudi, The "Venerable of Hualin" and Prince Zhaoming (son of Liang Wudi), Hualin Ying and Yicun, Sengchou and an Arhat, Mulian and Zhiyi, Mulian and Guangmu, Weituo and Pancika?, Budai and Puhua, Puhua and Piṇḍola, Fotudeng and an Arhat, Xiangyan and an Arhat, the tiger tamer and the dragon tamer Arhats, and so forth.

seems to be Sun Wukong, the divine monkey popularized by the *Journey to the West*. (See Anthony Yu 1977–1983). Indeed, the most striking characteristic of this Chan "mythology" is its "human," non-"mythical" aspect. Dragons and tigers are merely a reminder (remainder?) of the natural powers revered in archaic religion, and the imaginary world of Chinese archaic religion(s) seems conspicuously absent. Most of these figures are actually saints, monks, or laymen famous for their charisma: the holy man seems to have superseded the god, even when he has borrowed from the god iconographic or structural elements. The iconography of the pagodas seems to reflect a stage when Chinese local gods have become "monastery gods" and "protectors of the Dharma." This evolution corresponds to the "standardization of the gods" in the larger context of Chinese society. Although not perfect, this formalization is what allows the kind of structural approach exemplified in such a masterly way by Stein.

Stein has shown in particular how the pair formed by Mile (Budai) and Weituo, the two Keepers of the Gate in Chan monasteries, was structurally analogous to—and could be seen historically as a Buddhist reunification of—a Hindu pair formed by the two sons of Śiva, Gaṇeśa and Skanda.[19] Stein has also revealed the affinities between the *qielan* god and the hagiographical pair formed by Sengqie and Wanhui (Stein 1981: 281). As noted earlier, the Western monk Sengqie ("Saṃgha," 629–710) became a god of navigation, while his friend Wanhui (d. 711) was identified with the god of happiness and sexual union (*huohe*). In another study on Guanyin, Stein has analyzed the sexual connotations of this "female" Bodhisattva. (See Stein 1986.) These connotations are most obvious in the Kangiten figure, but also in the Thousand Arms Guanyin and the motifs of Guanyin with the fish basket, let alone the story of Malang fu ("The Wife of Mr. Ma") and the theme of Guanyin as a harlot. As noted above, these stories were apparently widespread in Chan circles, and they probably met certain psychological needs by allowing a sublimation of desires denied by Chan's official asceticism.

[19] In his evil manifestation, Gaṇeśa is known as Vināyaka, and the latter, according to the Tantric tradition, was tamed by an avatar of Avalokiteśvara, who assumed the same form in order to have sexual intercourse with him. Partly because of these strong sexual components, this representation of the *bête à deux dos*, called Nandikeśvara (J. Kangiten or Shōden), was held secret in Tantrism. In Japan, it was worshiped mainly in the so-called Tachikawa heresy. Because of the puritanism of the Meiji restoration, however, Kangiten has become a *persona non grata* in Buddhist studies. One of the finest iconographic examples known today is that of a wooden statue—unfortunately kept hidden in Tōjiin, a branch temple of Tenryūji. It was apparently inherited from Ninnaji, an important Shingon monastery, on which ground Tōjiin was founded by Musō Soseki in the fourteenth century. It is worth noting, however, that Zen monks such as Musō were also well versed in Buddhist esoterism, and one cannot discard the possibility that Kangiten played a role in the rituals of medieval Zen.

While Daoist Immortals were completely *hors-système*, the gods belonged to the social system and could—to a certain extent—be summoned and controlled. Between these two poles, the Arhats (Ch. Luohan, J. Rakan) occupied an intermediary position. For example, in contrast to the Immortals, Piṇḍola can be invited, although he does not necessarily come. It seems that in Chinese Buddhism, and more particularly in Chan, the cult of the Arhats, iconographically influenced by that of the Daoist Immortals, came to supersede that of the gods of popular religion. Perhaps they offered a kind of transcendence and personal relationship that popular gods, however powerful or frightful, did not offer.

THE CULT OF THE ARHATS

At first "protectors of the Dharma," Arhats also became "gods of the monastery."[20] Some of them—Kauṇḍinya, Subhūti, Piṇḍola, or Mahākāśyapa—at times shared with the Bodhisattva Mañjuśrī or various other figures (Daoan, Vajrabodhi, Budai) the function of "divine monk" (*shenseng*), a double or idealized projection of the Zen monk, whose statue is usually placed in the middle of the monks' hall. Their importance in Chan/Zen is vividly illustrated by the statues of the Sixteen Arhats in the Buddha Hall of Manpukuji, the head temple of the Ōbaku sect. The cult seems to have first developed around the figure of Piṇḍola Bhāradvāja, the first Arhat—and the only one to present an individualized character.[21] Piṇḍola was famous for his *abhijñā* and for his gluttony, and his demonstration of the former to satisfy the latter is given as a cause for his staying in this world after the departure of the Buddha and his other disciples. In China, Piṇḍola's cult can be traced back to the Vinaya master Daoxuan (596–667). Despite (?) his gluttony, Piṇḍola represents the ideal monk, and his ritual role is reflected in his function as protector of the kitchen and the bathroom. His popularity outside the monastery reflects in some cases an ambivalent attitude toward the monks, as in the following story quoted by Menzan. Two men who have taken shelter in a Buddhist temple are saved *in extremis* by an oracle spoken by a statue of Piṇḍola from a man-eating tiger who has taken the appearance of an old monk. In Japan, where his figure was associated with those of Jizō and Yakushi as a "god of happiness," Piṇḍola became popular as a healer saint and he is still present

[20] On this question, see Lévi and Chavannes 1916; Visser 1923; Strong 1979; Michihata 1983; Harada Kōdō 1988.

[21] According to the *Sankagakushō shiki*, there are three kinds of Buddhist temples: purely Mahāyāna or Hīnayāna temples, and dual temples practicing a mixture of Hīnayāna and Mahāyāna. Mañjuśrī is worshiped as Prior (*jōza*) in Mahāyāna temples, while Piṇḍola is so worshiped in Hīnayāna temples. In dual temples, however, both are alternately worshiped as Prior, the former on the days of the Mahāyāna *upoṣadha*, the latter on those of the Hīnayāna *upoṣadha*. (See *Koji ruien*, *Shūkyōbu* 2: 106.)

today—as *nadebotoke* ("the Buddha to stroke")—in most "prayer temples."

The cult of the Arhats as a group apparently derived from that of Piṇḍola—through a spatialization that led first to the notion of the Four Great Arhats (Mahākāśyapa, Kuṇḍopadhanīya, Piṇḍola, and Rahula). According to Lévi and Chavannes (1916: 273), the further spatialization of these four symbolic characters explains the later figure of Sixteen Arhats. Already in existence by the fourth century, the cult took off toward the end of the Tang after Guanxiu (Chanyue *dashi*, 832–912) saw in a dream the image of the Sixteen Arhats, which became the basis of all later representations. From the outset closely related to Chan, the cult became very important in Japan during the Kamakura period. Representations of the sixteen or *eighteen* Arhats were placed in the gate-building (*sanmon*) of the main Zen monasteries (Tōfukuji, Nanzenji, Daitokuji, Shōkokuji). The addition of two figures to the traditional list of sixteen has been much studied and seems to reflect a popularization of Chan.[22] This populariza-

Figure 8. The Five Hundred Arhats. Arashiyama, Kyoto.

[22] The two additions were emblematic figures of Chinese popular religion, the dragon tamer and the tiger tamer. Their identity varies: Nandimitra (the man who fixed the Sixteen Arhats tradition) and Piṇḍola (a doublet of the first Arhat, Piṇḍola Bhāradvāja); Dharmatala (i.e., Dharmatrāta, an error for Bodhidharma) and Hva shang (Moheyan *heshang*, the Northern Chan master who represented the Chinese side at the Council of Tibet); Xuanzang and Budai. See in particular Lévi and Chavannes 1916; Demiéville 1978; Siegbert

tion is even truer for the motif of the Five Hundred Arhats, which developed largely outside Chan/Zen monasteries in response to popular piety. The cradle of Southern Chan, the Baolin (i.e., Nanhua) monastery in Caoxi, had a representation of the Eighteen Arhats that was praised by the Song poet Su Shi, while the Jesuit Matteo Ricci described its Five Hundred Arhats in less admiring terms. (See Ricci 1953: 223.)

During his stay in China, the Vinaya master Shunjō (1166–1227), because of his resemblance to the seventeenth Arhat, was given a painting of the Eighteen Arhats by Guanxiu. Another painting—the oldest in Ja-

Figure 9. One of the Sixteen Arhats (Nāgasena).
Manpukuji, Kyoto.

Hummel, "Der Dickbauchbuddha," *Acta Orientalia* 48 (1987): 157–167; Lessing 1954): plates.

pan—attributed to Li Longmin (d. 1106) was brought by Chōnen, the abbot of Seiryōji (in Saga, on the Western outskirts of Kyoto). As Michihata Ryōshū points out, it is somewhat strange that the first two paintings acquired by the Japanese were precisely the most famous. Dōgen also brought back from China an image of the Sixteen Arhats attributed to Li Longmin. In Tōfukuji, Minchō (Chō Densu) painted the Five Hundred Arhats after the models of Guanxiu and Li Longmin, and this representation has also become famous. Despite their cultic importance in Chan/Zen, the Arhats rarely became a topic of discussion in Zen texts, perhaps because the cult of these Hīnayāna figures contradicted so blatantly the ideals of Mahāyāna and Chan's reputed iconoclasm. That a contradiction was felt between Chan theory and practice is amply reflected in the question asked by a monk to the Chan master Suiwei Wuxue (n.d.),[23] a disciple of the famous "iconoclast" Danxia Tianran (739–824): "Danxia was burning wooden Buddhas. Why do you worship the Arhats?" (T. 51, 2076: 313c). In the chapter of the *Shōbōgenzō* titled *Arakan* ("The Arhat," 1242) Dōgen gives a very Mahayanistic reinterpretation of the term and does not even mention the cultic significance of the Arhats. This attitude is replicated by recent scholars such as Harada Kōdō (1988), who attempts to interpret symbolically the Sōtō cult of Arhats from the point of view of practice—as an exhortation to oneself to reach the fruit of Arhatship. Even if this kind of rationalization were correct, it still would not explain why Zen would have forsaken the Bodhisattva ideal to return to the Arhat ideal. The "conspiracy of silence," however, is broken as soon as one looks into the ritual or hagiographic materials.

According to the preface of the *Kōzen gokoku ron*, Yōsai saw the image of an Arhat reflected in his bowl during his first visit to Tiantai shan. Subsequently, he offered tea to the Five Hundred Arhats. His friend Shunjō did the same. (See Ishida 1972: 413.) The Five Hundred Arhats of Tiantai shan were particularly renowned, and they are mentioned by an earlier Japanese pilgrim, a monk of Miidera named Jōjin (well known himself for his *abhijñā*, his "Record of Dreams" and the "flesh-body" he left in China after his death), in his *San Tendai Godai sanki* (1072). According to Jōjin, the Five Hundred Arhats lived near a "rock bridge," which only "pure" monks like him were allowed to cross. (See Morris 1970: 369.) As a later Japanese commentator remarks, "among the Chinese pilgrims, eight or nine out of ten had to stop half-way, while most of the Japanese pilgrims were able to cross."[24] Apparently, the crossing of

[23] As in the case of Wuxue Zuyuan, his name—synonymous with Arhat (*wuxue*, Sk. *aśaikṣa*)—suggests a strong connection with the Arhat cult.

[24] Another well-known case is that of the above-mentioned Shunjō. See his biography in Ishida 1972: 413. For a modern description of the bridge, see Fong 1958. The first mention of a "rock bridge" appears in the *Gaoseng zhuan*'s biography of a monk named Tan'you—a

the bridge had become a ritual authentication for Japanese monks. The passage ends with words of praise for Chōgen, Yōsai's companion, who was able to cross (Michihata 1983: 275). While the text does not mention Yōsai, we know from other sources that the latter, when he himself crossed the bridge, had a vision, not of Arhats, but of two "blue dragons," and a revelation that he had, in a former life, been an Indian monk who lived in the Wannian monastery on Tiantai shan.[25] According to a later source, however, the ceremony performed in the Sōtō school for the Arhats had been transmitted by Yōsai, who had been instructed in the ritual by the Arhats themselves while standing on the rock bridge, together with Chōgen (ibid.: 283). All this took place during the three days that Yōsai spent on Tiantai shan during his first trip to China. On his second trip, some twenty years later, Yōsai returned to Tiantai shan and stayed there for five years. He restored several buildings, including Zhiyi's stūpa and the stūpa of Yōsai's putative former self, the Indian monk Jixiangdan. There are, however, no further accounts of his relationships with the Arhats, even after he returned to Japan. But the fact that they remained a central concern for Yōsai is clear from the priority he gives them in his liturgical calendar.

Dōgen was clearly aware of Yōsai's precedent. According to the Sōtō tradition, he himself saw Arhats on Tiantai shan and later at Eiheiji. In Menzan's commentary to Dōgen's biography, the *Kenzei ki*, it is said that, during a ceremony dedicated to the Arhats in 1249, their images and statues suddenly emitted a light that indicated they had accepted the offerings, as they had done once on Tiantai shan. (See Michihata 1983: 461.) The Sixteen Arhats themselves appeared on the branches of an old pine tree in front of Eiheiji.[26] As Dōgen himself put it: "As other examples of the apparition of auspicious signs, there is only the [story of the] rock

biography, however, that does not refer to the Arhats but simply to "those who have attained the Dao." The Five Hundred Arhats appear in the *Song gaoseng zhuan*'s biography of Puan (770–843; T. 50, 2061: 880b).

[25] In its enumeration of the "wonders of China," the *Kōzen gokokuron* says: "On Tiantai shan, live Arhats appear, and from their footsteps a light emanates. . . . On the Rock Bridge, blue dragons appear, and their apparition is a sign of rain" (Ichikawa, Iriya, and Yanagida 1972: 88). Michihata points out that Yōsai became well known for his performance of rain rituals and suggests that he might have been predisposed toward this apparition by Jōjin's description of the Rock Bridge as blue in color and having the shape of a dragon (Michihata 1983: 283). The biography of the Zhu Tan'you (fl. 4th c.) suggests that the legend predated the cult of the Arhats. After failing to cross the bridge, the Indian monk heard a voice telling him to come back after ten years. When he returned, he eventually met the mountain god (*Gaoseng zhuan*, T. 50, 2059: 396a).

[26] This tree, known as the "Arhat pine tree" (*Rakanshō*), still exists today, and the fan held by one of the Arhats is kept among the treasures of Eiheiji. Another addition to Dōgen's legend was the assertion made by Menzan in his *Teiho Kenzeiki* that the old man that Dōgen met in front of the Arhat Hall on Jing shan and who advised him to visit Rujing on Tiantong shan was actually an Arhat. (See Michihata 1983: 212.)

bridge on Tiantai shan in Taizhou, in the great country of Song. On other mountains, this is yet unheard of. On this mountain [Kichijōsan, the location of Eiheiji], [the Arhats] have already appeared several times. This is truly an auspicious sign. It means that, in their deep compassion, they have repeatedly offered their protection to the men and the Dharma of this mountain" (*DZZ* 399).

The apparition of the Arhats was for Dōgen proof that Eiheiji was the only place in Japan where the Buddha Dharma had been correctly transmitted and could compare only with Tiantai shan in China. Ironically, it is also through the revelation of an Arhat that Keizan Jōkin was able to claim the superiority of his newly founded Yōkōji over its powerful rival, Eiheiji. The role played by the Arhats in Keizan's life and in the rituals of Yōkōji and Sōjiji is well documented by records such as the *Tōkoku ki*. The importance of the eighth Arhat Vajraputra in Keizan's dreams is particularly intriguing.[27] As mentioned earlier, the only well-individualized Arhat was Piṇḍola, and one would expect to find him instead of his rather obscure double in the founding story of Yōkōji. The fact remains that the success of Keizan's branch, and by the same token of the Sōtō school itself, was due to the protection by an Arhat. A ceremony for the Arhats was performed on the fifteenth of each month at Yōkōji. This ceremony is still performed today in the Sōtō sect, and it closely follows the ritual established by Keizan (rather than that transmitted by Yōsai and Dōgen).[28]

Although he advocated a return to Dōgen's "pure Zen" and was instrumental in the demythologization of the Sōtō tradition, Menzan himself devoted an entire work, the *Rakan ōken den* (1754), to the wonders performed by the Arhats in response to human solicitations. Containing over one hundred hagiographical notices, this work is the primary source for the legends concerning the Arhats in China and Japan. The first notice concerning Japan is that of Nichira, a Korean general who became the tutelar deity of Mount Atago and was as such seen as a *gongen* of Shōgun Jizō.[29] Menzan makes a pun on Nichira's name, which he interprets as "Japan's Arhat": *Nichi* (= *Nihon*) (Nichi + hon) + *ra* (*rakan*). (See Michihata 1983: 192.) Another semantic association (Arhat = *aśaikṣa*, Ch. *wuxue*, J. *mugaku*) seems to be the basis of the story according to which an Arhat appeared in a dream to Hōjō Tokiyori to predict the coming of Wuxue Zuyuan (Mugaku Sogen, 1226–1286). Menzan himself had an in-

---

[27] This importance is attested by the fact that the story is repeated three times in *Tōkoku ki*, in entries dated 1318, 1320, and 1323. See also Azuma 1983.

[28] For a description of this ritual, see Visser 1923: 182–196.

[29] See Anne-Marie Bouchy, "Comment fut révélée la nature véritable de la divinité du Mont Atago," *Cahiers d'études et de documents sur les religions du Japon* 1 (1976): 9–48; and Visser 1923: 85–92.

teresting dream encounter with an Arhat. At the end of his work, he records a dream he had before a summer retreat. Fearing that for lack of advertising, few monks would come to this retreat, Menzan had started a religious service for the Eighteen Arhats. On the night of the sixth day, he dreamt that he received a visit from an eminent Zen master, Ōbaku Kōsen, accompanied by more than twenty monks. After offering tea to his dignified visitor, he asked him for a sample of his calligraphy but woke up just when an acolyte was preparing the ink. At the end of his seven-day service, Menzan began rolling up the scrolls representing the Arhats when he noticed that one of them was represented exactly as the man he saw in his dream, holding a brush in his hand while an acolyte was preparing the ink. Menzan then realized that his prayer had been granted. The following days, monks began to arrive from the Rakanji ("Monastery of the Arhats") of Usa in Bizen. Needless to say, the summer retreat was a success, with a turnout of sixty-eight worthy monks (Michihata 1983: 228).

ZEN AND THE KAMI

Despite its theoretical denial of mediation, Zen was more favorable to the "protecting gods" than were the Pure Land sects.[30] This was in part due to its relationships with the State and to the necessity, for Zen masters such as Yōsai, of performing rituals for the welfare of the country. The *Genkō shakusho*, a history of Japanese Buddhism written by the Rinzai Zen master Kokan Shiren (1278–1346), an heir of Enni Ben'en, includes a section on "gods and immortals" (*shinsen*) with notices on five Japanese kami (Amaterasu, Hakusan Myōjin, Tanjō Myōjin, Shinra Myōjin, and Tenman Daijizai Tenjin, i.e., Sugawara Michizane) and "eight immortals," actually Buddhist ascetics (although some of them were clearly influenced by the Daoist quest for immortality).[31] With one exception, all these "immortals," like the kami, are Japanese. As is clear in his discussion of relics and elsewhere, Kokan Shiren was advocating the superiority of Buddhism over Confucianism and Daoism, and his Buddhist replication of the famous "eight immortals" must be interpreted in this light. The Arhats play a relatively minor role in his work, perhaps because he was aware that they had been co-opted by the Sōtō school. Shiren was also deeply immersed in esoteric Buddhism, and his work reflects a strong influence of the *honji suijaku* theory. All the kami mentioned play

---

[30] See Suzuki Shōkun 1987; Ishikawa 1989; and Hosokawa Gyōshin, "Shinran no shingi-kan," *Nihon bukkyō gakkai nenpō* 52 (1987): 231–248.

[31] Tanjō Myōjin is the tutelary god (*jinushi-gami*) of Kōyasan, Shinra Myōjin the protector of Miidera. On the treatment of Japanese gods in *Genkō shakusho*, see Osumi Kazuo, "*Genkō shakusho* to shingi," *Tōkyō joshi daigaku hikaku bunka kenkyūsho kiyō* 48 (1987): 23–33.

a significant role in esoteric Buddhism. They are not simply, as in the earlier tradition of Chan, protectors of Buddhism, but more fundamentally they are themselves manifestations of Buddhas (*gongen*). Although initially a tactical move to overcome native resistance, this ennobling of the kami was to have far-reaching consequences.

Hakusan Myōjin also played an important role in medieval Buddhism and was a key factor in the territorial expansion of the Sōtō school. Shiren explains that this god is actually a manifestation of Izanagi—one of the two primordial gods of Japanese mythology—who should have taken precedence over his daughter Amaterasu. If such is not the case, it is because, as a *gongen*, he manifested himself after Amaterasu. Other traditions consider Hakusan Myōjin an avatar of the Bodhisattva Kannon. As mentioned earlier, Tokugawa Sōtō reformers such as Menzan attempted to reduce the role of this powerful god to that of a "protector of Buddhism" and to interpret him in philosophical terms. (See Satō Shunkō 1986–1987.)

Tenman daijizai tenjin is the honorific name of Sugawara Michizane, a famous Heian official. Following his death in exile, Michizane had become a powerful malevolent spirit (*onryō* or *goryō*) that was appeased only by raising him to the status of a god. His earlier Confucian attributes may explain why he eventually became the God of Literature. This mythological figure is an interesting combination of elements borrowed from Hinduism (Iśvara), Confucianism, and local beliefs in *onryō*. (See Iyanaga 1983 and 1985.) The development of Michizane's legend in medieval Zen plays a strategic role and serves a wide variety of purposes.[32] In particular, the story of the Chan master Wuzhun Shifan (1178–1249) transmitting the robe to Michizane seems to have been actively propagated in Zen circles by the disciples of Enni Ben'en (including Kokan Shiren), Muhon Kakushin, and Keizan Jōkin.[33] At the time of the territorial expansion of Rinzai (Kakushin) and Sōtō (Keizan) Zen, this story advantageously associated Zen with the flourishing Tenjin cult. In the capital, where the "Five Mountains" (*gozan*) had become centers of neo-Confucianism and literature, it served the claims of those Zen masters who advocated the harmony of the "three teachings" (Buddhism, Confucianism, and Daoism, later replaced by Shintō) or the harmony of Chan and poetry. (See Harada Masatoshi 1987.)

[32] See Borgen 1986: 327.

[33] According to the legend, Michizane appeared in 1241 to Enni and asked to become his disciple. Enni suggested that he should be directly initiated by Wuzhun. Michizane flew to China and received instruction and the robe from Wuzhun, then returned to Japan. See Borgen 1986: 327; Harada Masatoshi 1987. Suzuki Bokushi criticizes this legend: see Suzuki Bokushi 1987: 283. The legend is based on a dialogue between Wuzhun and a Chinese "monastery god"—not yet Michizane—found in *Xu chuandeng lu*. It is quoted by Menzan in his *Tōrin goroku* (T. 82, 2598: 600b).

Another example of transmission of the Dharma to a kami involves the goddess Amaterasu and the Zen monks Muhon Kakushin (Hottō *kokushi*, 1207–1298) and Beppō Daiju (1321–1402). When the latter, a monk in the lineage of Enni Ben'en, visited the Ise sanctuary, he had a revelation from Amaterasu, who told him that she had formerly received the robe from Kakushin.[34] According to his biography, Kakushin had once received this robe from Tiantong on Tiantai shan and later offered it to Amaterasu. Another disciple of Enni Ben'en, Kanpō Shidon (1285–1361) had transmitted the precepts and the *kāṣāya* to Kamo Daimyōjin, who in return had offered him a *sogari* robe.[35] According to Mujaku, the god Hachiman appeared to Enni Ben'en when the latter returned from China. It is also Hachiman who invited the Chinese master Wuxue Zuyuan (Mugaku Sogen), a disciple of Wuzhun Shifan, to come to Japan.

The importance of the kami in medieval Japanese Buddhism is attested by another work from a disciple of Enni, the *Shasekishū* of Mujū Ichien. This work also shows the importance of the notion of "worldly benefits" (*genze riyaku*). Another testimony more specifically related to Zen is found in the recently rediscovered texts of the Darumashū. The *Jōtō shōgakuron*, for example, explains that "Whatever is asked for will be obtained" (*Kanazawa bunko shiryō zensho* I: 204), while an anthology of popular Zen sermons by masters such as Yōsai, Myōe, Kakushin, and Musō Soseki, also found at Kanazawa Bunko, provides a discussion of the *honji suijaku* theory and the problems of karmic retribution (ibid.: 229).

One difference between Chan and Zen with regard to the role of the popular pantheon may have to do with the fact that, while Chan masters during the Song were addressing a Confucian and urbanized audience, Zen masters of the Kamakura and Muromachi periods, more particularly those of the Sōtō school, were proselytizing in the provinces. In China, the syncretistic "Three in One" (*sanjiao yizhi*) doctrine, in all its apparent tolerance, had a rationalist, demythologizing thrust, and so did the indigenous "great traditions." The Daoists themselves shared the concerns of the literati in regard to the so-called illicit cults of popular religion. In Japan, where the local traditions were never really threatened by a Confucian or Daoist "Enlightenment," the situation was different. Although they were increasingly manipulated by Buddhist monks, the kami remained unpredictable, as the Buddhist priest Dōkyō (d. 772) found out when his attempt to seize power failed because of a negative oracle from Hachiman.

The kami seem to fall into two main rubrics, depending on whether they are regarded as protecting gods of the place (*chinju*), the monastery

[34] See *Amaterasu taishi sōden kesa ki* (1382), in *Tōfukuji monjo*, quoted in Harada Masatoshi 1987: 383.
[35] See *Kōchi kokushi Kanpō oshō gyōjō*, in *Zoku gunsho ruijū* 9, 2, quoted in ibid.: 383.

(*garanjin*), or the Dharma (*gohōjin*), or as avatars of the Buddhas and Bodhisattvas (*gongen*, *myōjin*). Although they overlap—a *chinju* can be, or
become, a *gongen*—these two rubrics suggest the coexistence in Zen of a
few important, relatively well-defined gods and of a large number of
smaller, functional gods who serve purely ritual purposes and are not well
individualized. As noted earlier, one of the most important gods for the
Sōtō school was Hakusan Myōri Daigongen. (See Matsuura 1976: 440.)
Also worth mentioning are Sumiyoshi Myōjin and Kōjin. Sumiyoshi
Myōjin was a god of navigation and of literature.[36] Kōjin's figure borrows many elements from esoteric Buddhism. He was worshiped as the
guardian (*garanjin*) of Sōjiji (in Noto peninsula) under the name Sanbō
daikōjin. This name alludes to his role as protector of the "Three Jewels"
(Sk. *triratna*, J. *sanbō*). Kōjin is a Tantric divinity usually regarded as a
nefarious god (*arabuha kami*) who is better left alone, but the local legend
records how he appeared from a pond in Sōjiji to Taigen Shūshin, a second-generation disciple of Keizan, and vowed to protect the monastery.
He is typically a ritual god who protects the fire from any impurity. (See
Henmi Baiei 1974: 1103–1107.) Another similar figure is *Huode Xingjun*
(J. Katoku Seikun, or Shōkun), an avatar of the Chinese god Shennong,
whose spatial symbolism—that of the South—refers to its power against
fire. He appears in the *Keizan shingi* as a protector of the Zen monasteries
against fire and other calamities.[37] He usually has a tablet in the Southern
part of the *butsuden*, and sūtras are read on his account on the fourth and
eighteenth of every month. His cult seems to have developed for apo-
tropaic reasons from the belief that, when he appears, he sets fire to
monasteries.[38]

The ritualization of Chan reflects the growing importance of the gods
in monastic life and the process of hieratization.[39] The ritualization of the
gods was accompanied by a "deification" of ritual. In contrast to this hi-

[36] Sumiyoshi's Japaneseness is well reflected in Zeami's Nō play *Hakurakuten*, where the
god supersedes the Chinese poet Bai Juyi: "The God of Sumiyoshi whose strength is such/
That he will not let you subdue us, O Rakuten!" See Arthur Waley, *The Nō Plays of Japan*
(Rutland, Vt.: Charles E. Tuttle, 1981), 207–215.

[37] See *T.* 82, 2589: 437b; Mujaku's *Zenrin shōkisen*, ed. Yanagida 1979: 1:177. See also *Sho
ekō shingi*, *T.* 81, 2578: 620b. In China, this god is mentioned in the *Xuanzhuan qinggui*,
compiled in 1317 by Yuanzhong Mingben.

[38] See Mujaku's *Zenrin shōkisen*, ed. Yanagida 1979: 1:177. Another similar figure, hardly
individualized, is the "god of hot water and fire" (*zhu tanghuo shenming*), who appears in
Sōtō rituals dedicated to Weituo.

[39] This hieratization might also be the product of the "esotericization" of Zen. As Iyanaga
Nobumi (1985: 737) suggests, Sino-Japanese Tantrism—in this respect different from Chan,
which had misinterpreted the Two Truths theory—did not so much attempt to tame local
gods as to identify them with conventional truth, and therefore use them in its equation of
ultimate and conventional truths. See also S. Ruegg, "Rapports entre le bouddhisme chinois
et le 'substrat religieux' indien et tibétain," *Journal Asiatique*, 252, 1 (1964): 77–95, esp. 85
and nn. 10–12.

eratic tendency—and intertwined with it—the rationalist tendency inherent in the monastic worldview tended toward a demythologization of the tradition and a routinization of ritual. To give just one example, the reinterpretation of the Hakusan cult in Sōtō can be seen as a renewed attempt to "emasculate" the kami, since the earlier attempts had failed because of the *honji suijaku* theory (particularly, and not surprisingly, in the case of female deities such as Amaterasu). This reinterpretation is characterized by a shift from what was essentially a purification ritual dealing with the pollution of death to a redefinition of the Hakusan god as a "guardian of the place" or, even more abstractly, a "protector of the Dharma."

As we saw earlier, this syncretism has a long history of ideological and symbolic violence. The dialectical tension is reflected in the function served by the gods, who were either integrated (and emasculated) in Buddhism as "protectors of the Dharma" or given a more important—if still, at least at the beginning, subordinate—role in what came to be known as the (previously mentioned) *honji suijaku* theory. The inner dynamics of the *honji suijaku* contributed to the subversion of the two-tiered model and led to a multitiered model, in which the local or indigenous gods could regain their status of equality with the foreign Buddhas, and sometimes eventually gain the upper hand in the symbolic contest. The symbolic violence of the contest, usually euphemized, sometimes appears explicitly—as in these stories, quoted by Mujaku, where Guan Di cuts the tongue or the head of a novice. (See Mujaku quoting *Kenmonroku* in *Zenrin shōkisen*, ed. Yanagida 1979: 1:190.) In any case, native kami such as Amaterasu, Hachiman, and Kasuga were considered interlocutors to be treated with respect (even more than Guan Di, who was after all only a deified ghost, like Sugawara Michizane). The Japanese pantheon lacked the clear hierarchy of the Chinese pantheon, and Japanese gods could not be dismissed as petty officials. The "functional" nature of the kami is not as readily apparent as that of their Chinese counterparts.[40] Mythology—at least the narrative concerning the gods—was more developed in Japan, while Chinese mythology consists mainly of stories about saints promoted to the rank of heavenly bureaucrats. As does the ritual, the gods constitute an interpretive arena. (See Duara 1988.) The dialectic between sacralization and desacralization, ritualization and antiritualism, overlaps with that between the emancipation and the subjugation of the gods. Ironically, the process of containment and rationalization initiated by the *honji suijaku* theory—in its attempt to categorize the kami, first as *chinju*,

[40] For an attempt at a structural analysis of Japanese mythology taking its cues from Dumézil's study of Indo-European mythology, see Yoshida Atsuhiko, "La mythologie japonaise: Essai d'interprétation structurale," *Revue de l'histoire des religions* 140 (1961): 47–66, and 141 (1962): 25–44, 225–248. For a more Lévi-Straussian approach, see Ouwehand 1964; Macé 1976; and Lévi-Strauss himself, 1985: 73–87.

then as *garanjin* and *gohōjin*—eventually paved the way for a return of the kami as *gongen*. The problem raised by the resistance of Japanese gods is well exemplified by the tradition whereby the Ise shrine was forbidden to monks. Buddhist writers attempted to attenuate the negative effects of this interdiction. Kokan Shiren, for example, reports how Emperor Shōmu asked Gyōki (668–749) to present one grain of *śarīra* to the Ise shrine, and how, on the seventh day, the shrine opened and the voice of Amaterasu declared that, owing to this gift, she had found salvation. We are told that, subsequently, Amaterasu appeared in a dream to the emperor and revealed to him that she was actually an avatar of the Buddha Vairocana. Shiren uses this story and similar legends to prove that Amaterasu is not, as Shintō sectarians would have it, hostile to Buddhism.[41]

The initial stage of the process of rehabilitation is exemplified by Yōsai's attitude toward the kami. Yōsai's *Kōzen gokoku ron* merely mentions that prayers were offered to the local god of Kenninji on the second and sixteenth of each month. Although Yōsai was in many respects more a representative of traditional Buddhism than an innovator, and was well versed in the esoteric rituals of Shingon and Tendai, he does not seem to have viewed the local gods through the grid of the *honji suijaku* theory. Because of his knowledge of rituals, Yōsai was believed to have power over the gods. In one instance, his prayers for rain brought an instantaneous response from the dragon gods. A light emanated from his hands, and the rain fell. On all the drops of rain on the blades of grass, Yōsai's image was reflected. This demonstration of his power was the cause of the emperor conferring upon him the name Jōyō ("On the leaves"). According to the *Genkō shakusho*, however, Yōsai, having on another occasion been accused of causing a typhoon, replied that he had no such power and that typhoons were caused by the god of wind. Admittedly, the story could simply be read as an easy (and somewhat cynical) justification on Yōsai's part. But if one considers his cultural context or the fact that he was highly respected by fervent adepts of the gods such as Myōe, there is a good chance that his statement was sincere. At any rate, the kami came to play a significant role in Zen hagiography and ritual.

On the other hand, despite his nationalism and his increasing criticism of Chinese Buddhism, Dōgen never mentions the Japanese kami. His attitude toward lesser deities, informed by the polemical *Lotus Sūtra*, is clearly negative. One of the few passages where he mentions them is a warning not to be taken in by them: "There are many people who, out of fear, take refuge in the deities of mountains, forests, trees, gardens, non-Buddhist shrines, and so on. Taking refuge in such deities, however, is of

---

[41] See *Genkō shakusho*, in DNBZ 62, 470:162. See also Musō Soseki's *Muchū mondō*, ed. Satō Taishun 1974: 35.

no value whatsoever, for it is impossible to free oneself from pain and suffering in this way." (See Yokoi 1976: 130.) In another text, the *Tokudo ryaku sahō*, in which he enumerates the advantages of monastic ordination, Dōgen claims that merely by taking the precepts, one gains the highest merits and transcends the three spheres and that, by the same token, the gods of Heaven and Earth become protectors of the Dharma. Like Yōsai and his Chinese predecessors, Dōgen seems thus to consider the gods of the indigenous pantheons merely convenient vassals of Buddhism.

The situation is radically different with Keizan, who, as noted earlier, was convinced that he had been a tree spirit in a former life and that he owed to his karmic connections with the Northern continent of Uttarakuru his rebirth as an *ujiko* of the god of Hakusan. According to Keizan's *Tōkoku ki*, the god of the mountain where he built Yōkōji was Inari, and the monastery was entrusted to the protection of Shōhō shichirō and of the kami of Keta jinja (Daichinju ichinomiya). Keizan also revered Bishamon (Vaiśravaṇa, i.e., Kubera) and Karaten (Mahākala, i.e., Daikoku in his Indian form, another aspect of Kubera). According to the *Sōjiji chūkō engi*, the three "avatars" (*gongen*) protecting Sōjiji were the god of Hakusan, Sannō (the tutelary deity of Mt. Hiei), and the Bodhisattva Gyōki.

The invocation of kami for the consecration of Yōkōji is representative of ritual invocations of both Sōtō and Rinzai schools. In this document, the merit of the ritual is dedicated to the great Goddess Amaterasu, the seven generations of heavenly kami, the five generations of earthly kami, the ninety-six generations of human emperors, various stellar deities, the various *daimyōjin* protecting the imperial capital, the great and small gods (*shingi*) of the country, the protector of the Dharma ("great roof-beam," *daitōryō*) Hakusan Myōri Gongen, various minor local gods, Katoku Seikun and the eighteen gods protecting the monastery against calamities, Shōhō Shichirō Daigenshuri (as one single deity), Bishamon (Tamonten), Daikoku (Karaten), Shomen Jisha, Inari, Hachiman, and a host of minor deities. (See *Keizan shingi*, ⲧ. 82, 2589: 437b). Thus it is in the context of the ritual dedication or "deflection" of the merit gained (Sk. *pariṇāmana*, J. *ekō*), and more precisely in the propitiatory devotion, that the gods, Buddhist and non-Buddhist, are invoked, usually together with the Buddhas and Bodhisattvas. The list is open and varies with the circumstances. In Zen, these rituals consist mainly of sūtra recitation (*fugin*), and one of the most often recited texts is the so-called *Śūraṃgama dhāraṇī* found in the apocryphal *Śūraṃgama-sūtra* (ⲧ. 19, 945: 134a)—an invocation to the Buddhas, Bodhisattvas, and gods of all convictions for the attainment of awakening. The usual dedication of merit ends with the formula: "We also make suppliant offerings to the tutelary deity of this temple, and to all the Dharma-protecting gods, with prayers that the true Dharma will flourish, that all nations shall dwell in peace and harmony, that the precincts of this temple shall be tranquil, and that all karmic conditions shall be felicitous." (See Foulk 1988.)

Gods also played an important role in the fundamental ritual of Zen, meditation. As Shunjō, in his *Zazengi*, puts it: "In this method of *zazen*, it is necessary to have a protecting deity. In Tang China, the dragon king of Tianmu shan specially protects dhyāna practitioners. This dragon king is actually a manifestation of Shundei Kannon." (See Ishida 1972: 407.) The ritual role of the gods is well illustrated by a story concerning the Chan master Zhifeng, mentioned earlier for his dream of ascending Mount Sumeru. One day when he was ill and sitting in meditation in the Samantabhadra Pavilion, a god came and kneeled down in front of him, presenting himself as the "god protecting the precepts." Asked by Zhifeng what kind of karmic cause was responsible for his present illness, the god replied that he could see only a minor offense—the fact that Zhifeng usually threw away the water of his bowl instead of drinking it. After Zhifeng amended his ritual misbehavior, his illness disappeared (T. 50, 2076: 363a). Another well-known testimony to ritual correctness is the Arhat Piṇḍola, whose acceptance of the ritual offerings in the monastery's kitchen and bathroom serves to overcome the doubts of the monks as to their spiritual progress. The *Shasekishū* shows, not only the blessings given by the kami to their followers, but also their revenge against those who do not believe in them or do not treat them properly. Mujū Ichien had in mind particularly the adepts of the Pure Land schools who thought that their bond with Amida permitted them to dispense with the worship of other spiritual intercessors.[42] The will of the kami had to be taken into account even by holy monks such as Myōe, who had to cancel his pilgrimage to India after receiving a negative oracle from the Kasuga god. This was the price one paid to become, like Myōe and Jōkei (Gedatsu shōnin), the god's beloved children, his "Tarō and Jirō." (See Morrell 1985: 84.) Even if the *Shasekishū*'s passage can be read as a piece of religious propaganda in favor of traditional Buddhism, its attitude—or Myōe's and Jōkei's attitude—toward the kami cannot be reduced to a purely utilitarian strategy. The gods were present in the daily life of Kamakura Buddhists, and their curses were powerful. Although skeptical minds may always be found, there are times when social conditions make it rather inconvenient to be openly an agnostic.

The Kamakura period was such a time. The growth of a national ide-

---

[42] Mujū merely echoes the criticisms of traditionalist Buddhists such as Myōe and Jōkei. See, for instance, Jōkei's paragraph on "The Error of Turning One's Back on the Holy Gods of Shintō," in "Hossō's Jōkei and the Kōfukuji Petition," Morrell 1987: 79. See also the passage of *Shasekishū* titled "A Pure Land Devotee Punished for Slighting the Gods," in Morrell 1985: 97–103.

ology in response to the Mongol invasions led to the belief that Japan was the "country of the gods" (*shinkoku*). (See Grapard 1982.) The acculturation of Zen during the Kamakura and Muromachi periods with schools such as the Darumashū—whose founder, Dainichi Nōnin, had awakened without a master and received the Chan transmission without going to China—led to a greater importance being given to the kami. Zen monks were eager to show their patriotism when Japan was threatened by the (Buddhist) Mongols, and they joined with other Buddhist schools in the rituals for victory that resulted in the timely destruction of the Mongol armada by "divine winds" (*kamikaze*). They also had to respond to the criticism of the new Shintō sectarianism and other "nativist" movements and to speak the language of the people they attempted to proselytize, that is, primarily, the *bushi*. This may explain the frequent use of the kami in the kōans of the Rinzai school. (See Suzuki Shōkun 1987.) Kami also played a significant role in both Rinzai and Sōtō esoteric transmissions. A number of *kirigami* of the Sōtō school transmit the esoteric interpretation of kami such as Sumiyoshi Myōjin or Hakusan Gongen. Yet these documents reflect the ambivalence of Zen toward the gods. Gods have indeed become a central part in Zen's symbolic system, but they are redefined in abstract, philosophical terms. A case in point is a prediction allegedly made by Sumiyoshi Myōjin to Dōgen after the latter returned from China in which the god "demythologizes" itself.[43]

Gods, ghosts, and ancestors

The rationalizing tendency in Japanese Buddhism—criticized by Motoori Norinaga as the hallmark of *karagokoro* (Chinese spirit)—is well represented by a Togugawa Zen master such as Shidō Bunan: "Someone said: 'This country is the country of gods. To stop practicing the Way of Gods, which we have been blessed with since antiquity, and to practice the Way of Buddha is a great mistake.' I said: 'That is foolish. What are called the gods of this country are also Mind. . . . Besides, the abode of the gods is a person's body. This abiding of the gods is what we call the illumination of the heart. This is Mind' " (Pedersen 1975: 101). In another dialogue about Shintō, Bunan declares: "*Takamagahara* is the self of man. That the kami dwell in you means your mind is clear" (Kobori 1970–1971: 4, 1:117). Yet Zen masters such as Bunan, like their Chan predecessors, devoted a large part of their energy to convert kami. They became the "masters of the gods," thereby acknowledging their existence, and sometimes becoming their mouthpiece. Bunan's last statement could perhaps

---

[43] Another example is an interpretation of the name of Hakusan Myōri Daigongen in terms of the Sōtō metaphysical theory of the Five Ranks. See Sugimoto 1982: 348–350; Ishikawa 1985a: 128–140.

be reversed ("That your mind is clear means that the kami dwell in you") to argue that, in the actual practice of Chan/Zen, there are cases in which the state of mind brought by ritualized meditation bears a strong resemblance to forms of possession, or more precisely of what Gilbert Rouget calls "transe communielle," since the fact of identifying oneself with the founder of a sect "corresponds perfectly to the definition of possession." (See Rouget 1980: 354–374.) Seen in this light, the Chan motto, "This very mind is the Buddha," acquires a new meaning.

Next in importance to the kami as forces of nature were the spirits of the dead (and more precisely the category known as *onryō*). We have already noted that the most famous *onryō*, Sugawara Michizane, received the Chan Dharma from Wuzhun Shifan. Zen masters came to perform the role of exorcists against malevolent spirits. Fumon Mukan (1212–1291), for instance, drove away the ghosts of the imperial villa, which became subsequently a major Zen monastery—Nanzenji. (See *Genkō Shakusho*, 101c.) As exorcists, Zen monks shared affinities with Shūgendō practitioners—with whom they were sometimes confused. A case in point is that of Gennō Shinshō (1329–1400), a disciple of Gasan Jōseki who exorcised the spirit of the "killing stone" (*sesshō seki*). This spirit was that of a nine-tailed fox, who had already incarnated itself several times in various beautiful women of India and China, the last one being Tamamo no mae, a concubine of Emperor Toba. Driven away by the *onmyōdō* master Abe no Yasunari, the fox had taken refuge in a stone on the roadside and killed the passers-by—until Gennō converted it.[44]

Even when Zen masters did actually resort to the cult of kami merely as *upāya*—as most Japanese scholars, influenced by an elitist conception of Chan, tend to believe—the means often came to prevail over the end, and the preachers sometimes lost the inner distance that may have made them "masters of the gods." In most cases, the relations between Zen masters such as Gennō and the kami were not purely utilitarian but reflected their involvement with the spiritual world and symbolic system of Shūgendō. (See Ishikawa 1984b.) We see them as agnostics only because we have forgotten the vital function of rituals and Pascal's remark that ritual performance tends to create belief. Like Quesalid, the skeptical shaman described by Lévi-Strauss, Buddhist monks were sometimes caught at their own games. (See Lévi-Strauss 1963: 167–185.) One may consider that, not unlike the *onryō*, Chan and Zen monks were sometimes "deified" in order to channel their potentially harmful energy. If, as the legend claims, the "scandal" provoked by Bodhidharma (i.e., his rejection of traditional Buddhist practices) resulted in his untimely death, one may come

[44] See Anne-Marie Bouchy, "Le renard, élément de la conception du monde dans la tradition japonaise," in Marie-Lise Beffa and Roberte Hamayon, eds., *Le Renard: tours, détours et retours*, Special Issue of *Etudes mongoles . . . et sibériennes* 15 (1984): 9–70.

to see in a different light his later "deification" as an avatar of Guanyin as a way of placating his angry spirit. It may not be necessary, however, to invoke Girardian scapegoats. (See Girard 1977.) One may recall Robert Hertz's discussion of the necessity for society to protect itself against any threat to order (Hertz 1960: 81–83). Perhaps *satori* represents precisely such a challenge. Although utterly ritualized, meditation and its ultimate result—awakening—tended to transform Chan monks into *energumènes*, that is, etymologically, men possessed and moved by an unpredictable energy. This may explain why, after their death, Chan patriarchs became the object of an ancestor worship that seems designed to reintegrate them into a kind of familial structure. This impression is accentuated by the "realism" of their iconographic representations (*chinsō*), connected, as we saw earlier, with the cult of relics (and in particular with mummies). Also worth mentioning in this context is the existence of the so-called living gods (*ikigami*), men worshiped as living epiphanies. Not only did gods sometimes resist assimilation, but charismatic monks themselves, by becoming "like gods," tended to acquire the disturbing characteristics of otherness. A well-known example is that of a monk of the Saijōji named Dōryō (alias Myōkaku), a disciple of the founder Ryōan Emyō. According to the legend, at the death of his master in 1411, Dōryō made a vow to protect the monastery and subsequently became a Tengu—worshiped under the name of Dōryō Gongen.[45] The Saijōji (Odawara-shi in Shinagawa prefecture) is today one of the most important "prayer temples" (*kitō jiin*) of the Sōtō sect.[46] Dōryō's case bears some resemblance to that of the Tendai monk Ryōgen, who remained alive in popular devotion in his demoniac manifestation (*tsuno daishi*), a fearful appearance/apparition intended to frighten evil spirits.[47]

To UNDERSTAND the process of hieratization that developed parallel (or in reaction) to the routinization of the sacred in Chan/Zen, we will have to examine the function(s) of ritual. Against a Zen theology that tended to deprive the gods of their transcendence and consider them accessories to the ritual, Japanese religion, with the emergence of Shintō nativism,

---

[45] See Kanaoka Shūyū, ed., *Koji meisetsu jiten* (Tokyo: Tōkyōdō shuppan, 1970), 120.

[46] For a history of this temple, see *Koji ruien, Shūkyōbu* 4: 244. Other examples of *kitō jiin* include Akibadera (today Akiba jinja, on Akibayama near Nagoya), dedicated to Sanshakubō Daigongen, a protector against fire; Myōgonji (Tōyōkawa-shi, in Aichi-ken), dedicated to the Dakini (Inari); Kasuisai (Shizuoka-ken) and Kashōzan (Gumma-ken), dedicated like Saijōji to a Tengu; Zenbōji (Yamagata-ken), dedicated to the dragon god; Shūgenji (Shimane-ken), dedicated to the Seven Gods of Fortune and in particular to Daikoku; Osorezan, centered on funerary (and mediumistic) rituals and Jizō worship. See Watanabe Shōhei 1986.

[47] See Murayama 1976: 61–75. Murayama, however, does not address the symbolic significance of Ryōgen's metamorphosis and gives a purely historical explanation of it—as symbolizing the fact that this reformer of Enryakuji was opposed to the "evil monks."

led to a drastic remythologization that affected all sects of Buddhism, including Zen.

Yet despite the hieratization paradoxically permitted in Zen by the *honji suijaku* theory, if we attempt to place Chan/Zen mythology along the spectrum between two poles characterized respectively as mythological and ritual, it is clear that Chan and Zen fall closer to the ritual pole. In other words, they provide examples of what Lévi-Strauss calls an "implicit mythology," that is, a discourse in which the mythological element is subordinated to the ritual and the gods do not possess a strong individuality.

Chan polytheism remained an interpretive arena, populated by figures of the double—reflecting the dialectical tension between sameness and otherness, ritual identification and ritual estrangement, self-control and loss of self. The multivocality or "superscription" of the gods reflects the fluid dialectic—of emancipation and subjugation, sacralization and desacralization, territorialization and deterritorialization—that characterizes Chan/Zen discourse. The same dialectic was at work in the case of the thaumaturge. The fluidity of these figures—gods, Arhats, *onryō*, and even Chan masters—seems to illustrate the Buddhist teaching of no-self. Ironically, after the initial taming of the gods by the thaumaturge, both fell victims to the "disenchantment of the world" and the routinization of charisma resulting from monastic rationalism. Like the "standardization of the gods" in the Chinese pantheon, the development of a Chan mythology was actually the effect of a demythologizing tendency. In Japan, the inclusion of the gods in a symbolic system such as the *honji suijaku* theory marked a further banalization. Yet this theory—combined with the side effects of ritualization—paradoxically paved the way for a resurgence of the gods, precisely at the time when Zen, spreading in the provinces, appealed to thaumaturges again. Thus the stage was set for a second encounter between charismatic Chan masters and rebellious kami. The hagiographical exuberance of the fourteenth–sixteenth centuries bears testimony to this process. After this ultimate confrontation, while the major kami regained their independence—or at least their prestige—under the aegis of Shintō nativism, the other minor deities, duly tamed and hierarchized, continued a precarious existence in the shadow of Zen ritual. The agnostic tendencies of Chan—reinforced during the Tokugawa by Confucian and Western influences, then by the Meiji dissociation of Shintō and Buddhism—contributed to deprive Zen of its popular appeal by "humanizing" it, to detach it from the mainstream of Japanese religion by promoting the elitist ideal of a "pure" Zen.

Thirteen Ritual Antiritualism

> Zen devotion doesn't disgust [as does Spanish or
> Indian devotion]. However Zen monks chant, they
> incense images and masters, and like Christians take
> a vow of chastity and poverty. [Crossed out: "Ugh!"]
> —Georges Bataille, *Oeuvres complètes*

> The meaning of ritual is deep indeed. He who tries
> to enter it with the kind of perception that distin-
> guishes hard and white, same and different, will
> drown here.
> —Xun Zi, *Basic Writings*

The answer to the question whether or not truth can be mediated through
symbols—that is, whether symbols might express truth or lead to it—has
a direct bearing on the importance attributed to ritual. I use the term "ritual" loosely, perhaps abusively, as shorthand for a variety of practices
characterized by repetition and a qualitative difference from everyday
acts. I am not concerned, however, with defining (and objectifying)
Chan/Zen ritual as such, but rather with the "ritualization" of Chan/Zen
life. As Gómez points out, "The Buddhist tradition has an ambiguous
relationship with Buddhist ritual—practicing it with its institutional right
hand, condemning it with its doctrinal left" (Gómez 1987: 119). While
the Chan theoretical claim for immediacy, in particular, paved the way
for antiritualism, it also led to the opposite stance—as was the case in the
Sōtō absolutization of ritual. In the conception transported to the West
by D. T. Suzuki, Zen is a radically antinomian teaching free from any
formalism or ritualism. Suzuki himself, however, had to admit that life
in Japanese Zen monasteries is a far cry from that idealized version for
Western consumption.[1] Yet, although he came to denounce in his late
years the antinomianism he had earlier praised, he still held that rituals
are "mere excrescences" that do not affect the "essence" of Zen. His vision remained to the very end imbued with a nostalgia for naturalness
and a deep bias against ritualism.

[1] See D. T. Suzuki 1965.

ANOTHER RITE CONTROVERSY

Although most scholars have acknowledged the importance of ritual in Chan/Zen, they never shed completely their intellectualist bias against it.[2] According to the dominant interpretation, the scandal of Chan/Zen ritual is redeemed only by its motivation. At best, ritual is seen as a pious lie, an *upāya* performed for the sake of the unenlightened; at worst, as a compromise with the spirit of the times, a way for Chan/Zen proselytism to meet the needs of the people and to adjust to a changing socio-political order. According to this line of argument, although the high-flown teaching of "sudden Chan" may have been attractive to an intellectual elite, it proved too difficult for the common people. Therefore, just as the Buddha himself had to administer the powerful *pharmakon* of emptiness at homeopathic doses, or replace it temporarily with the placebo of the Four Noble Truths, Chan masters had to repackage their metaphysical teaching in the form of symbolical rites. We are thus asked to believe that rituals were introduced only to make the teachings more appealing to the *vulgum pecus*. "Pure Zen" is presented as rejection of ritual, while "syncretistic Zen" is seen as ritualistic (and, by the same token, inauthentic).

As we saw earlier in the case of thaumaturgy, the demythologizing interpretations of modern Chan/Zen scholarship are deeply indebted to the tradition itself. Demythologization plays a predominant role, for example, in the traditional understanding since Menzan of the evolution (often qualified of degeneration) of the Sōtō school after Dōgen. With Gikai, and more notably with Keizan, rituals borrowed from esoteric Buddhism came to the forefront. The ritual syncretism endorsed by Keizan included worship not only of tutelary deities but even of figures such as the Linji (Rinzai) master Puan (1115–1169). By misconstruing the discursive strategies of Chan/Zen as a "first sign of objectivity" and reinscribing these interpretations in another context, that is, scholarly discourse, one actually reproduces the ideology sedimented in them.

It seems that Chan/Zen scholarship has not yet confronted a basic methodological problem now rather well discussed by many anthropologists and a few historians of religions:[3] our prejudice against ritual as empty formalism and our stress on doctrine. As Mary Douglas points out, one must guard against projecting onto other cultures our Western distrust of formalism (1970b) and strive to go beyond the "compensation

---

[2] See, for instance, Jinbo Nyoten, "Zen to gishiki," in *Zen*, Vol. 3 (Tokyo: Yuzankaku, 1941); Hasebe 1972; Shiina 1972; Ōtani 1937; Matsuura 1971; Kamata 1986.

[3] See, for example, Staal (1985) or Jonathan Z. Smith (1982: 42) on "the traditional 'bugaboos' of 'habit,' 'dogma' and 'magic' which have resulted in the vast majority of religious phenomena remaining unintelligible to most Western scholarship."

theory" that "treats the symbolic order as a secondary result of the social order, as purely expressive" (Douglas 1970a: xiv). Systems of representations have their own dynamic, which sometimes reinforces the social structure but also sometimes undermines it.

Although things are beginning to change in the field of East Asian religions, in part due to the impetus of Daoist studies,[4] there has been a conspicuous absence of studies on Chan ritual, particularly when compared with the plethora of discussions on Chan thought.[5] It is time to move away from what we may call the Romantic or Protestant view of Zen and to pay due attention to the "sacramental" tradition that developed side by side with the "spiritual" or "intellectual" understanding of Chan. Erasmus was perhaps right to believe that "to place the whole of religion in external ceremonies is sublime stupidity" (quoted in Jonathan Z. Smith 1987: 101), but precisely it remains to be proved that Chan/Zen ceremonies (or any religious ritual for that matter) are ever purely external. According to Douglas, "sacraments are not only signs, but essentially different from other signs, being instruments. This touches on the belief in *opus operatum*, the efficacious rite, whose very possibility was denied by the Protestant reformers" (Douglas 1970a: 48.) A positive reevaluation of ritual, however, must avoid falling into the opposite extreme of giving an idealized, almost mystical, image of ritual as purely integrative power that brings the individual and society in harmony with the cosmos. We tend to overlook the fact that ritual also participates in hegemonic manipulations, or at least may become the object of ideological reappropriation. It may have liberating or cathartic effects, but it also contributes to bind, contain, divide. As Bourdieu remarked, a rite of passage is also, and perhaps primarily, a rite of demarcation. We have seen, for instance, that the Buddhist rite of closing the grave aimed as much to prevent malevolent spirits from entering the grave as to prevent the dead from returning to this world. In this sense, the function of the ritual, like that of the Great Wall or of modern freeways, is ambiguous: it simultaneously connects and separates, prevents people from entering and from leaving.

The discrepancy between Suzuki's view of an ideally antinomian, "unruly" Zen and the actual practice of Zen monasteries, dominated by a strict rule, is not simply the result of Suzuki's idiosyncratic understanding of Chan. It can indeed be traced back to early Chan, a doctrinal trend that

---

[4] For Daoism, see Ōfuchi Ninji, *Chūgokujin no shūkyō girei* (Okayama: Fukutake shoten, 1972); Schipper 1985; Lagerway 1987; Michael Saso, *Taoism and the Rite of Cosmic Renewal* (Pullman: Washington State University Press, 1972); Strickmann 1981–1985; Bell 1983 and 1988. For Buddhism, see Kamata 1986; Fujii 1977.

[5] See, in particular, Kagamishima et al. 1972; Collcutt 1983; Foulk 1987b and 1989; Sharf 1989.

emerged in the religious context of Vinaya monasteries—if largely in re-action to their ritualism. In this sense, at least, Suzuki is faithful to the tradition: to all appearances, early Chan was "mixed" and fairly ritualis-tic. The legend showing Bodhidharma proudly dismissing Liang Wudi's attempts to accumulate merits by his pious works is counterbalanced by the *Luoyang qielan ji*'s mention of a more conventional Bodhidharma, a Central Asian monk who spent three days in prayers in front of the Yongning stūpa in Luoyang. (See Yang Hsüan-chih 1984: 20–21.) The "sacerdotal" tendency of the *Chuan fabao ji*, a work purporting to trans-mit the "Jewel of the Dharma" and not simply a new philosophy or prac-tice, is also balanced by the more "doctrinal" content of its contemporary, the *Lengqie shizi ji*. The contradiction or counterpoint may at times be found within the same text, and this has led scholars to speculate end-lessly about possible interpolations and the "right" interpretation. That this contradiction was already felt within the Chan school itself is sug-gested by stories such as the following, featuring Huangbo Xiyun and one of his disciples, the future emperor Xuanzong (r. 846–859):

> The master was in Yanguan for a ceremony, together with the em-peror Dazhong, who was then a novice. The master ascended to the altar and prostrated himself in front of the Buddhas. The novice said: "Detached from the quest of the Buddha, detached from the Dharma and detached from the *saṃgha*, here you are, Master, prostrating yourself: what are you seeking?" Huangbo answered: "Detached from the Buddha, from the Dharma and from the *saṃgha*, I am still prostrating, as you can see." The novice asked again: "What can be the use of ritual acts?" Huangbo slapped him. "This is too coarse!" said the novice. "Where do you think you are, to speak of coarse-ness?" said Huangbo, slapping him again. The novice then left. (*Chuanxin fayao*, Taibei ed. 1976; see also Carré 1985: 96)

The Chan critique of ritualism

Chan is usually presented as an attempt to interiorize Buddhist practice and as a criticism of the empty formalism of the Chinese Buddhist estab-lishment. A characteristic example of interiorization is the "formless re-pentance" advocated by Daoxin and his successors. In his *Guanxin lun* (*Treatise on Mind Contemplation*), also known as *Poxiang lun* (*Treatise on Breaking the Forms*), Shenxiu claims that rites such as the casting and erect-ing of images, the burning of incense, the offering of flowers, the burning of memorials lamps, the circumambulation, and the holding of vegetar-ian feasts must be interpreted "spiritually" (*guanxin shi*), that is, through the hermeneutics of the Two Truths (*li/shi*; T. 85, 2833: 1271b; McRae

1986: 200). Is this to be read as a rationalization of spiritual practice, an attempt to save the ritualistic aspects of Buddhism in the face of a growing criticism, or as a first step toward their complete denial? According to Shenxiu:

> My own view is that [Buddhists] nowadays are shallow of understanding and only know the virtue of formalistic effort. They waste a lot of money and inflict injury on the countryside in their incorrect [manner of] constructing images of stūpas. They waste human labor in piling up wood and earth and in painting [their monasteries] blue and green. They expend all their mental and physical energy [in this pursuit], destroying themselves and misleading others. Having no understanding of the shamefulness [of their actions], how could they ever be enlightened? (McRae 1986: 201)

Shenxiu's understanding of ritual seems itself at first glance rather shallow. Even when he does not condemn ritual, he certainly does not do it justice. But reducing Shenxiu's teaching to this statement does not do justice to Shenxiu either. At any rate, behind and despite this theoretical denial of ritual, there was apparently a continuing practice, in particular of repentance rituals.[6] No Buddhist school could have dispensed with these rituals and remained prosperous, at a time when the State was intent on using Buddhism as an instrument of socio-political control. A similar point can be made about the denial of meditation, and of religious practice in general, during the Tang. (See Bielefeldt 1986.) One may also note the importance of ritual for Hongren's disciples, in particular in Sichuan, with Zhishen and his successor Wuxiang. On the other hand, Wuzhu, the founder of the Baotang school, also in Sichuan, was severely criticized by Zongmi for his rejection of all ritual. It may be worth recalling that Zongmi, although he claimed to be heir to Shenhui's Heze school, had actually inherited from Wuxiang's lineage. The predicament into which Wuzhu's uncompromising antinomianism put his heirs is well reflected by the *Lidai fabao ji*'s attempt to connect Wuzhu to Wuxiang. In an interesting passage, Wuzhu's antiritualism is legitimated (and relativized) by the ritualistic Wuxiang as a higher standpoint, yet one that must ultimately be abandoned by the Bodhisattva intent on helping others. (See Yanagida 1976: 170.)

Scholars have been quick to argue that the antiritualist view is well supported by representatives of the tradition such as Shenxiu or Wuzhu. But this point, instead of serving as evidence of Chan practice, is precisely what should have been questioned in the first place. How can we take the

---

[6] In Northern Chan in particular, we can infer the existence of these rituals from documents such as the *Datong heshang qili wen*, attributed to the same Shenxiu. See Shiina 1972: 269–274.

iconoclastic rhetoric at face value, when it became itself part of orthodox discourse and turned into a highly formalized ritual? Significantly, a closer examination shows that most of the interpretations provided by recent scholarship were foreshadowed by the Chan/Zen tradition itself. The sources provide justification for an outright rejection of ritual, a deemphasis of ritual as *upāya* or as a subsidiary, "supplementary" development; or a criticism of ritual as inferior to meditation and as leading to a vulgarization of the true teaching, an empty formalism. The multivocality of the tradition is illustrated by the fact that, depending on the sources (or sometimes in the same text), we seem to find (at least) two contradictory or complementary moves (or moments): an attempt toward an interiorization of ritual and a blatant denial of any ritual in the name of spontaneity. The kind of interiorization exemplified above by Shenxiu's *Guanxin lun*, a work that criticizes the "empty" vocal recitation of Buddha's name, without denying the *nianfo* (J. *nenbutsu*, "commemoration of the Buddha") as such, was characteristic of early Chan, and it was later radicalized by masters such as Linji. This criticism of the "invocation" was often reiterated, most notably by Dōgen in the *Bendōwa* chapter of his *Shōbōgenzō*. Dōgen was perhaps too much of an intellectual to realize that the *nenbutsu*, except for a minority of "authentic" Pure Land monks, was usually perceived by his contemporaries, not as lip service to the Buddha, but as a very efficacious *dhāraṇī*. At any rate, he would probably have dismissed it just the same. In his *Gakudō yōjinshū*, he rejects all methods aimed at obtaining spiritual powers (Sk. *abhijñā*, J. *reiken*) and worldly profits: "One must not practice the Buddha Dharma in order to obtain spiritual power [*reiken*], one must practice it for itself" (т. 82, 2581: 3b). As we have seen, this is one of the grounds on which he condemned those who take refuge in the gods. (See *Shōbōgenzō Kie sanbō*; т. 82, 2582: 291c; Yokoi 1976: 130.)

Dōgen may be a good example of the seeming discrepancy between theory and practice—or between various theories and various practices. Although, in his early teaching, he denied any kind of ritual, he was one of those who eventually did the most for the ritualization of Zen. With their antiritualistic bias, many Sōtō scholars conveniently play down these ritualistic achievements and prefer to quote passages such as the following as expressing the "essence" of Dōgen's Zen: "From the start of your training under a wise master, have no recourse whatsoever to incense offerings and worshipful prostrations, recitation of the Buddhas's names, repentances, or sūtra reading: just sit in meditation and attain the dropping off of mind and body." This selective reading still prevails, despite the central role of ritual in many chapters of the *Shōbōgenzō*[7] and in

---

[7] Ritual prevails namely in the chapters *Raihai tokuzui* (т. 82, 2582: 33c–38b) and *Gyōji*

the *Eihei kōroku*, not to mention Dōgen's ritualistic compendium, the *Eihei shingi*. Judging from *Shōbōgenzō Kankin*, for example, Dōgen was practicing sūtra readings for the birthday of the emperor, and donors were coming to the monastery to order sūtra readings on their behalf. In *Eihei kōroku*, there is also a "major convocation" (*jōdō*) during the rainy season concerned with the prayers for good weather. In the *Chiji shingi*, we find dedications of sūtra readings to the Stove God (*sōkō fugin*) and to the local god (*dochidō fugin*) at the opening and closing of the ninety-day summer retreat (*kessei ango*). The *Eihei shingi* also contains a graphic representation of the talisman (*risshun daikichi*) used for the ritual of the spring equinox—a representation often found in the *kirigami* of the later Sōtō tradition.[8] All these elements seem to undermine the official theory according to which the Sōtō school had to wait until Keizan to see its Zen "diluted" by prayer services (*kitō*).

In the Rinzai tradition, we find a similar ambivalence toward ritual. Although himself well versed in the esoteric rituals of the Shingon school, Musō Soseki criticized the Zen adepts of his time for having fallen into laxity and worldly ambitions and performing only *kitō*, and he advised them to return to the fundamentals (*t*. 80, 2555: 501b). In one of his "dialogues in a dream," he describes how Buddhist esotericism based on *kaji* (i.e., ritual identification with the Buddha Vairocana through mantras and mudras) gradually declined and turned into something like the methods of the yin-yang teachers (*onmyōdō*). After telling how the shōgun Tokimune, instead of offering prayers against the Mongol invasion remained composed and spent his time discussing Dharma matters with Zen monks such as Wuxue Zuyuan (Mugaku Sogen), Musō asks: "Isn't this the reason why the Mongols did not destroy our country?" (Kraft 1981: 82, 85). To him, *kaji* are merely *upāya* to guide foolish people. While Shingon reveals *siddhi* with a material aspect, Zen leaves *upāya* of this type to doctrinal schools and teaches the original nature directly (ibid.: 83). Consequently, Musō sees the use of *kaji* in Zen monasteries as a karmic cause for the downfall of the Zen Dharma (ibid.: 84).

According to Tamamura Takeji, despite Musō's warning, the majority of his disciples—beginning with his successor Shun'oku Myōha—entered the "five mountains" (i.e., the officially sponsored Zen monasteries of Kyoto and Kamakura) and spent most of their time performing ceremonies for the shōgun and the nobility. Although these ceremonies were accompanied by sermons in the form of Zen dialogues (*mondō*), they were

---

(ibid.: 127a–144b), and in the later recension in twelve chapters, which may be Dōgen's spiritual legacy. See Yokoi 1976.

[8] This talisman reflects the influence of the esoteric teaching on the symbolic value of the Sanskrit letters. Not surprisingly, Sōtō scholars have attempted to show that this document is a later interpolation.

highly formalized. They resulted in a decline of private consultations (*sanzen*) and of the collective life in the monks' hall. The life-style of monasteries was drastically modified by the construction of monastic buildings (*tatchū*) centered on the funerary stūpa of the founder of a "branch" and on the relative autonomy of these various branches (Tamamura 1976–1981: 1:931; see also Kawakami, Yoshikawa, and Furuoka 1979: 168–170).

In his *Enkan wanigosui shū*, Bassui Tokushō (1327–1387) rejects as devoid of meaning all *dhāraṇī* and exorcisms: "One realization [*santoku*] of the Way of no-mind is superior to myriad incantations [*kitō*]."⁹ Bassui stressed the superiority of *zazen* over all formulas, claiming that the mind trying to dispel external evils becomes itself an inner evil (Braverman 1989: 36). Tōrei Enji (1721–1792), in his *Goke sansho yōrōmon* (1788), also emphasized that *zazen* is the right entrance and that rituals are merely accessories (T. 81, 2576: 617a). This denial of incantation did not prevent him, however, from drawing a list of the merits acquired for oneself and for others by sūtra readings (ibid.). The opposition between the two approaches to ritual is well reflected in the controversy between Menzan Zuihō and Tenkei Denson concerning the ritual or nonritual nature of the transmission of the Dharma. While Menzan held that this transmission is a ritual (and somewhat magical) delegation of powers effected by the transmission of the succession documents, Tenkei emphasized the importance of awakening. (See Kagamishima 1978: 61–66).

As noted earlier, ritual is usually played down in Zen as a necessary evil, a concession to the common people and to local customs.¹⁰ To be sure, rituals aimed at "worldly benefits" (*genze riyaku*) greatly contributed to the popularity of Chan and Zen: the most thriving centers of the Sōtō sect, for instance, have been "prayer temples" (*kitō jiin*) such as Akibadera, Saijōji, Ryūgein (Kashōzan), or Myōgonji (Enpukusan). This purely functional interpretation, however, does not explain why, in so many cases, Zen monks selected such "unpopular" or "esoteric" objects of worship as Katoku, Ubusama, or Daigenshuri. Buddhist rituals such as the burning of one's head or fingers were often perceived as strange and alien to the local culture. Significant in this respect is the way Zanning argues that incense burning is not a Buddhist innovation but goes back to

---

⁹ See Ichikawa, Iriya, and Yanagida 1972: 212; Braverman 1989: 36.

¹⁰ The importance of prayers (*kitō*) for the popular appeal of Zen and the essential role of faith were stressed by Enrō Ōryū (1720–1813), the twenty-second abbot of Kōshōji (in Uji). In his *kana hōgo* titled *Jūroku dōmyō* (Sixteen Bell Sounds), he tells the story of the man who misread the famous *Vajracchedikā* passage, "Unsupported by anything should a thought [mind] be produced" (J. *ō mushōjū, nishō goshin*) as "Three *shō*, two *shō*, five *shō* of wheat" [*omugi sanshō, nishō, goshō*], and the *dhāraṇī* "*Arinari, tonari, anaro, nabikunabi*" as "*Ana no aita konabe*" ("A small pan with holes"); yet, owing to his faith, he was able to achieve a spiritual experience. When his error was pointed out, however, he read again the passages, correctly but self-consciously, and no longer achieved any insight. Quoted by Sakurai Shūyū, "Zenshū ni okeru kitō," *Daihōrin* 45, 5 (1978): 138.

ancient Chinese rituals of the Zhou dynasty (*Da Song sengshi lüe*, T. 54, 2126: 241b).

Chan/Zen Liturgy

Only from the Song onward is the ritualization of Chan/Zen as an independent school relatively well documented. Japanese scholars, however, have tended to read back into early Chan a situation that was characteristic of Song Chan and Japanese Zen. Thus most scholars are still trying to argue for the existence of Baizhang's "Pure Rule" (*Baizhang qinggui*). The fact remains that the earliest text available is the *Chanyuan qinggui* (1103). This question has been discussed elsewhere (see Bielefeldt 1988 and Foulk 1987a), and I do not intend to dwell on it here. At any rate, from the twelfth century onward, various sources were available, the most important being the *Qixiu Baizhang qinggui* (ca. 1361).[11]

The earliest Japanese description of what was to become Zen ritual is probably that given by Yōsai in his *Kōzen gokokuron*. In this important pamphlet, Yōsai defines the annual ceremonies (*gyōji*) of his school in sixteen paragraphs.[12] Except for the ceremonies related to the *Shingon-in* and to the *Shikan-in*, which remind us that Yōsai always remained (at least in his mind—and body) an orthodox student of esoteric Buddhism, all ceremonies seem related to Zen practice. Significant is the ritual of "entering the room" (*nyūshitsu*), presented by Yōsai as the main charac-

---

[11] Other sources include the *Xuanzhuan qinggui* (by Zhongfeng Mingben), the *Eihei shingi*, and the *Keizan shingi* for the early Sōtō tradition; the *Sho ekō shingi* and the *Shōsōrin shingi* (by Mujaku) for the Rinzai tradition; the *Ōbaku shingi* for the Ōbaku tradition; and Mujaku's encyclopaedia of monastic life, the *Zenrin shōkisen*. The *Shōsōrin shingi* by Mujaku (1653–1744) is the normative work for Rinzai ritual. These *shingi* are divided into five sections: (1) *tsūyō shingi*, basic rules for monks; (2) *nichibun shingi*, rules for everyday sūtra readings (dedicated to local gods, patriarchs, the Fire god [Ch. *huode*], General Wei, Puan, and *chinju*); (3) *getsubun shingi*, rules for the liturgical calendar; (4) *rinji shingi*, rules for irregular events; and (5) *ekō*, dedication of merits, which explains the destination of sūtra readings (T. 81, 2579: 690a–718c).

[12] These are (1) *Shōsetsu dōjō*: prayers for the emperor's longevity. (2) *Nenju*: recitation of the names of the Ten Buddhas for the benefit of all. (3) *Dochi shinji*: ceremonies for the tutelary gods. (4) *Hōon* (repaying blessings): sūtra readings for the current and late emperors. (5) *Nenchū getsuji gyōji* (monthly assemblies): the first month, Assembly for the Arhats (*Rakan-e*); the second month, Assembly for the Relics (*shari-e*); the third, Great Assembly; the fourth, Assembly for Buddha's birth and Summer equinox (*kekka*); the fifth and sixth, *Saishō-e*; the seventh, eighth, and ninth, *Hannya-e*; the tenth, reception of the Defenses; the eleventh, winter solstice; the twelfth, Great Assembly of Buddha's name (*butsumyō daie*). (6) *Angochū gyōji*: ceremonies of the retreat period. (7) *Dokukyō*: daily sūtra readings. (8) *Shingon-in gyōji*: ceremonies of the Shingon Pavilion. (9) *Shikan-in gyōji*: ceremony of the Shikan Pavilion. (10) *Nyūshitsu*: "Entering the Room." (11) *Fusatsu* (poṣadha): bi-weekly sermon on the precepts (*sekkai*). (12) *Junryō*: monthly sermon by the master. (13) *Kaiyoku*: ceremony of "Opening the Bath." (14) *Kishin sai*: banquet organized for the late emperor or for the late master. (15) *Kanke no sasai*: banquet for an official family. (16) *Tenzō*: ritual turning (eight times) of the revolving *Tripiṭaka* (T. 80, 2543: 15a–b).

teristic of his school. The emphasis on this practice seems to have been a Japanese phenomenon. Actually, in the Chan tradition, the essential ritual was rather the *jōdō*, "ascending the [Dharma] Hall" (Ch. *shangtang*, also called "Great consultation," J. *daisan*), during which the master conferred the essentials of his teaching on his disciples. The "ascending the Hall" ritual seems to correspond to Yōsai's *junryō* rather than to the *nyūshitsu*. It is perhaps under the influence of the Tendai oral tradition (*kuden*) that the transmission of the ultimate teachings became a private affair, held "within the room [of the Abbot]" (*shitsunai*).[13] At any rate, Yōsai understood ritual primarily as *gyōji*, "ceremony." With Dōgen, on the other hand, the ritual field greatly increased, and a new word, *gyōji* (written differently), gradually prevailed. In later Sōtō tradition, the latter *gyōji* eventually came to include the meaning of the former and was used to designate "sustained practice" as well as ceremonies proper.

Incantatory Zen

Two of the essential components of the ceremonies were prayers (*kaji, kitō*) and incantations (*dhāraṇī*).[14] Their presence need not be attributed only to the influence of esoteric Buddhism. It is well known that Yōsai was well versed in Tantric *dhāraṇī*, and he himself quotes the *Śūraṃgama-sūtra* for its famous *dhāraṇī* (T. 80, 2543: 3a). But he had many predecessors in this respect: already during the Tang, Shenxiu's disciples were attracted to esoteric masters such as Śubhakarasiṃha and Vajrabodhi, and the epitaph of one of them, Zhida (d. ca. 713), records that he was a master of *dhāraṇī*. (See Faure 1986b.) One cannot overestimate the im-

[13] Note the importance of the *jōdō hōgi* (ceremony of ascending the Hall) and of the *hattō* (Dharma Hall), which came to supersede the *butsuden* (Buddha Hall) in Zen monasteries— supposedly since Baizhang. According to *Wujia zhengzong zan*, for instance, Deshan did away with the *butsuden*. Removed in this way from iconic space, ritual was "demythologized." The *shangtang* (J. *jōdō*), originally intended to express the ultimate truth in a dialogue between master and disciples, soon became ritualized/routinized (perhaps toward the Northern Song, and generalized during the Southern Song). Some *shangtang* were regular, others not. See Foulk 1987b: 75; Sharf 1989: 31–35.

[14] These *dhāraṇī* were usually formulas taken from texts such as the apocryphal *Śūraṃgama*, the *Mahāprajñāpāramitā*, *Kannongyō*, *Vajracchedikā*, and so forth. The *Ryōgonju* or *Śūraṃgama dhāraṇī* was read during the so-called *Śūraṃgama* Assemblies (*ryōgon-e*), assemblies held from April 13 to August 13. After the Ming, this ritual became particularly important in the Pure Land tradition, but it continued to serve as a bridge between various schools (Kamata 1986: 301). Another important *dhāraṇī* is the *daihiju* (Dhāraṇī of Great Compassion), from the *Senju sengen Kannon Dāraṇikyō* (*Nīlakaṇṭhaka*), a short sūtra translated during the Tang, which permits one to gain merits such as good rebirth, longevity, and prosperity of the family and of the country (T. 20, 1060: 107a). Another major ceremony is the *tendoku* of the six hundred *kan* of the *Mahāprajñāpāramitā* or of the *Hannya Rishūbun*, or, when abbreviated, the *Heart Sūtra* or the *Shōsai Myōkichijō darani*. This ceremony was originally supposed to burn all passions by the fire of the wisdom of emptiness but, according to Japanese scholars, it has "degenerated."

portance of mantras and *dhāraṇī* or, more generally, of sūtra readings in Chan/Zen.[15] In *Shōbōgenzō Darani,* Dōgen stresses the value of prostrations and claims that the supreme *dhāraṇī* is the *dhāraṇī* of *samādhi* (although it is not clear whether he means samādhi as *dhāraṇī* or *dhāraṇī* spoken while in *samādhi*). On the other hand, Musō Soseki explained that sūtra readings (*fugin*) were a Japanese innovation. He pointed out that the three daily sūtra readings performed in Zen monasteries were not performed in China, that they began at the time of the Mongol invasion and are not fundamental to Zen. (See Satō Taishun 1974: 54–55.) The same point is made by Bassui. (See Ichikawa, Iriya, and Yanagida 1972: 212; Braverman 1989: 58.)

Incantations were a necessary component of Buddhist rituals for the protection of the State. According to the *Baizhang gui sheng song,* a text appended to the *Chanyuan qinggui,* "those who wear the monastic robe [lit. "robe of the field of merit"] have since ancient times avoided the corvee. If it is not with their prayers, how could they respond to the [blessings] of the State?" Like other Buddhist schools, Chan came to play a role in the protection of the State through its sūtra readings, prayers, and so forth. By the time of the compilation of *Qixiu Baizhang qinggui* (ca. 1341), prayers (*kitō gyōhō*) were already well established and formalized.[16] The use of *dhāraṇī* and other *kaji kitō* was related to the notion of "worldly benefits" (*genze riyaku*). Although the official doctrine was to deny the notion that Chan could bring any benefit in this world, the increasing emphasis on immanence in Chan/Zen teachings certainly had the effect of revalorizing ordinary life and social values. By the late Tang, the rise in influence of laymen brought about the rehabilitation in Chan discourse of the "common man." In Japan, at the time when Dōgen was advocating "pure Zen," other Zen adepts were trying to meet the popular demand for an "easy way" (not necessarily out). This attitude is reflected in works of the Darumashū such as the *Jōtō shōgakuron,* which contains a section on *genze riyaku* titled "Whatever you ask for you will get." (See Shinagawa Kenritsu Kanazawa Bunko 1974: 204.)

RITUAL OMNIPRESENT

Ritual, however, did not end with the performance of ceremonies at the nodal points of the liturgical year, month, or day. Ritualization extended

---

[15] On the relations between Chan and Tantrism, see Tanaka 1981; Hirai Yūkei, "Tonkō shutsudo gigi bunken yori mita mikkyō to zen," in Bukkyō minzoku gakkai, ed., *Bukkyō to girei* (Tokyo: Kokusho kankōkai, 1977), 139–162.

[16] The *Chixiu Baizhang qinggui* was printed in Japan by Kokyō Minsen (d. 1360) and became the basis of monastic life in Zen institutions. Mujaku's *Shōsōrin shingi* (3 kan) lists all the prayers used during services. In *Zenrin shōkisen,* too, are listed all kinds of "meteorological" or "agricultural" prayers—for good weather, rain, and snow; against eclipses and insects (*mushi-okuri*).

to many other aspects of monastic life. In the Sōtō sect in particular, it reached the most remote sectors of private life—or what remained of it. First seen by Dōgen as an expression of awakening, ritual eventually became awakening itself, to be manifested in all aspects of everyday life. But, first of all, it extended to the paramount spiritual practice itself, meditation.

Meditation as ritual

If we see meditation not as a form of knowledge (*jñāna*) but rather as a form of ritual activity (*karman*; Staal 1985: 29), we are better prepared to understand why it had to be denied, along with other forms of *karmic* behavior, by Chan masters such as Linji. Admittedly, there are some trends in Indian Buddhist meditation like *vipasanna* in which knowledge plays an important part. This intellectual tendency is precisely why Chan rejected Indian dhyāna. (See, for instance, Demiéville 1952: 63–77, 130–139.) Sitting meditation (*zazen*) can also be seen as a ritual of identification—a ritual leading to a type of trance induced by specific words or sounds. Scholars have tended to ignore the "musical"—"performative"—aspects of Chan meditation (bells, wooden sticks, songs, psalmodic recitation of kōans).[17] The oral/aural component is well reflected by the formula that usually accompanies the awakening experience in Chan biographies: "Under the words of the master, he reached insight." Despite the stress on "natural" awakening—an experience provoked by the sound of bamboo, the vision of peach flowers, the sound of the mountain stream—these insights, like trances, were culturally or socially determined. There is also an important "oral tradition" in Chan, and this might have to do more with the power of sound than with meaning.[18]

The emphasis on no-thought was an attempt to elude the psychological content of meditation. The alternative was to focus on the bodily posture itself. This may explain the flourishing in Song China and Kamakura Japan of texts titled *Zazengi* and *Zazenshin*. (See Bielefeldt 1988.) It is in Sōtō that the formalization of *zazen* was carried to its extreme. The increasingly formal approach to Zen points to the importance of considering Chan/Zen a *gestuelle* (what the Japanese call a *kata*) rather than a doctrine, a formalization of the bodily postures, the four "dignified

---

[17] On Buddhist initiation music, see Rouget 1980: 145.

[18] The importance of hearing is emphasized in early Chan by Shenxiu. See *Dasheng wu-sheng fangbian men*, T. 85, 2834. It is also a significant feature of the apocryphal *Śūraṃgama*, a text whose propagation has been traditionally traced back to the same Shenxiu. (See T. 50, 2061: 738b; Demiéville 1952: 44.) A similar emphasis on the oral/aural aspects of the teaching is found for the Theravāda tradition in Tambiah 1968 and 1970. See also Harrison 1988: 256–264, apropos Masefield's 1986. The book shows that, even in early Buddhism, "the realization of the goal of the path turns out, in the case of *most* recorded occurrences, also to be the result of hearing the teaching of the Buddha" (Harrison 1988: 260, also 262).

attitudes." And, as Bourdieu pointed out, formalization is rarely exempt from ideological motivations. As an initiation rite, zazen is not only a rite of *passage* placing the practitioner in the liminal phase, it also institutes a difference of nature by institutionalizing liminality. (See Bourdieu 1977b: 128–129.)

Some aspects of Chan meditation are reminiscent of what Gilbert Rouget calls "initiatic trance of depossession"—"depossession" being defined as an "altered state of consciousness, transitory and obeying a cultural model" (Rouget 1980: 95). Such depossession is a preliminary step to possession, that is, "the invasion of the field of consciousness by the *other*."[19] The emphasis on emptiness in Mahāyāna might preclude the understanding of meditation as a form of trance or possession. Despite linguistic traps and trappings, however, and the wide experiential range of both meditation and trance, the experiences may overlap on various points. Sitting Chan (*zazen*) can also be seen as a ritual reenactment of the Buddha's awakening, or even, as in esoteric Buddhism, as a ritual identification with the cosmic Buddha. As noted earlier, sitting meditation—as ritual or mystical identification with the Buddha in *nirvāṇa*—is also a form of "suspended animation" or temporary death. Like the *samādhi* of the mummy or of the icon, it is supposed to regenerate life. In other words, we have an iconization of the practitioner, in some respects similar to the iconization of the "flesh-body." The practitioner has metonymically become, like the *śarīra*, the stūpa or the icon, a "living grave," and has in this way—at least symbolically—transcended time and death.

Kōans also played a significant part in this ritual process. As Tambiah, in his study on the performative aspects of ritual, remarked about them: "Whether literally meaningful or not . . . , the prime value of these repeated sayings is their therapeutic value as 'focusing' mechanisms. . . . The repeated formulae as 'supports of contemplation' or transporters into a trance state do so, not by a direct assault on the actor's senses and inflicting an immense psychic toll on him or her, but by a more indirect conventional illocutionary employment of them as instruments of passage and as triggering mechanisms" (Tambiah 1981: 141). One might reinterpret in this light the notion of *sokushin zebutsu* ("This very mind is the Buddha") as pointing to a trance experience—that may even bear some analogy to the *sokushin jōbutsu* ("Becoming a Buddha in this very body") ritual in Japanese esoterism—and Chan awakening as a ritual affiliation with patriarchal lineage. The importance of the ritual encounter between master and disciple in the so-called dialogues (Ch. *wenda*, J. *mondō*) has

---

[19] In Tibetan meditation, practitioners are warned that they will be frightened by the realization, or rather the intrusion, of their true mind that will appear as the *other*, as a dazzling, awesome light. (See Evans-Wentz 1954: 106–131.) Incidentally, in the Tibetan translation of the *Damolun*, Bodhidharma's "wall contemplation" (*biguan*) is rendered as "abiding in light." This translation suggests that early Chan meditation was perceived—at least by Tibetan Buddhists—as something akin to Tantric meditation. See Broughton 1983: 11, 59.

often been pointed out, but we should also stress that, with the institutionalization of Chan, these lively *tête-à-tête*—and sometimes almost deadly *corps-à-corps*—became essentially a collective affair and, like meditation itself, an elaborate ritual of identification with the past Buddhas and patriarchs. In both cases, this ritual defines a sacred area and operates a transsubstantiation of sorts. (See, for instance, *Bendōwa*, in T. 82, 2582: 16a.) Like its hyperboles—self-mummification or immolation by fire—*samādhi* transforms the practitioner into a lamp, and this may be one of the meanings of the "transmission of the lamp" metaphor. Therefore, the Chan rejection of ritual in favor of kōans or sitting meditation is not to be construed as a denial of ritual as such but merely as a strategic rejection of "mixed" ritual in favor of a "single" ritual. Just as the iconoclasm or aniconism of Chan turned out to be a mirror image of its iconism, Chan antiritualism remains essentially a ritual move.

The above interpretation may be found a bit farfetched, trying as it does to accentuate heuristically the ritual elements of Chan/Zen practice, in order to correct our inveterate tendency to project our modern, antiritualistic state of mind into a medieval practice or theory. Admittedly, there is always in these symbolic matters a risk of hermeneutic overkill—and Zen monks were not the last to succumb to it, as Sōtō *kirigami* show. Most of the time, however, the logic of practice that I have attempted to retrieve is non-explicit and subliminal. After all, much in Chan/Zen was not ritualized, and much in Chan/Zen ritual failed to make (ideological) sense. The fact that practitioners may not be aware of the full implications of their practice must be taken into account, but it does not entitle us to present our models for an accurate description of reality. We have to negotiate a middle way between two kinds of anachronism: accepting the Chan antiritualistic stance because it reinforces our own bias; or rejecting it entirely, and reading too much into the symbolism of ritual. Strategically, I have followed the second line of approach and attempted to reveal a surplus of meaning. This does not mean that there was no room for ideological manipulation and circumstantial improvisation. As in Plutarch's story quoted by J. Z. Smith, many mules have probably got into Chan ritual or doctrine just because they happened to be there at a specific time. (See Jonathan Z. Smith 1982: 53.) In the end, the "irreducible excess of the syntactic over the semantic" remains (Derrida 1981a: 221). Ritual is never hermeneutically transparent; it retains its opacity for the participant as for the observer because of the basic serendipity of ritual innovation.

The ritualization of life

By trying to redefine *all* everyday actions as sacred and providing strict rules even for the most trivial bodily functions, the Sōtō school pushed the ritualization of monastic life one step further. This tendency, already in germ in Mazu's notion that "the ordinary mind is the Dao," found its paradigmatic expression in Layman Pang's verse quoted earlier. The meaning of ritual in Chan life derives from the "innate awakening" (J. *hongaku*) theory, according to which all acts are expressions of the ultimate reality, and therefore belong to the sacred sphere. In this sense, routinized ritualization becomes a betrayal of that fundamental experience.

There are important differences between Sōtō and Rinzai concerning attitudes toward ritual. Whereas in Sōtō, in virtue of the "identity of principle and realization" (*shushō ittō*), *gyōji* fully embody or manifest "innate awakening," there remains in Rinzai a distinction between *gyōji*—ceremonies proper—and other ritualized aspects of practice. As Griffith Foulk (1988) points out, the doctrine of the identity of practice and enlightenment had in Sōtō the effect of sanctifying traditional ceremonial and ritual forms and encouraging their meticulous preservation: "Dignified deportment is the Buddha Dharma, proper ritual procedure is the essential principle" (*igi soku buppō, sahō kore shūshi*). The Sōtō understanding of *gyōji*—as "observances that manifest enlightenment"—was severely criticized by the Rinzai master Tōrei Enji (1723–1794): "Our [Rinzai] school only esteems exertion in proper mindfulness [i.e., kōans]; it does not esteem dignified deportment [*igi*] and the external forms of practice [*gyōsō*]. . . . Deportment and forms are the practice of the Hīnayāna [*shōjō no gyōji*]" (*Shūmon mujintō ron*, T. 81, 2575: 604b).

The Sōtō approach led to a rather different scholarly interpretation of ritual, well exemplified by Hasebe Kōichi (Hasebe 1972). From the premise that the patriarchs are the embodiment of truth, Hasebe concludes that ritual is a kind of hierophany, the expression of an inner realization, and a subjectivization of the Dharma. According to him, the mythic episode in which Śākyamuni held up a flower in front of the Assembly, while expressing the ultimate Chan truth, may also be seen as the origin of Chan ritual. Hasebe attempts to distinguish ritual of the first order (as practice of the Way, *shūdō girei*) and of the second order (as ceremonies for the sake of the common people, *sangyō girei*). Although a degradation, the second type of ritual is still useful for returning to the first. Consequently, both types of ritual stand in a relation of complementarity—as expressions of the Two Truths. First-order ritual is seen as typically Chan, insofar as Chan is said to emphasize "function" over "substance" and to fully express, embody, or perform the truth. Therefore, since ritual is equated with "function," there can be no Chan without ritual. At the same time, it is necessary to warn constantly against the stultification of second-order ritual, and therefore apparently to deny ritual. Hasebe contrasts the importance of ritual in Sōtō texts such as the *Shōbōgenzō* (*Gyōji, Senjō, Gyōbutsu igi*), *Eihei shingi*, *Keizan shingi*, and so forth, with its denial in Chan texts such as the *Linji lu*, the *Chuanxin fayao*, or the *Xuemo lun*. For him, the only difference is whether one chooses to stress the fundamental experience (as in Rinzai Zen) or its expression (as in Sōtō Zen). Hasebe's approach, however, is fraught with problems. Suffice it to say that, contrary to what he implies, Chan critics of ritual had in mind all types of ritual, that is, of repetitive actions, as a departure from the sacrosanct spontaneity and would probably have condemned Dōgen's *shingi* as well.

Ritual is usually strictly delimited in time and space. In monastic life, too, despite the tendency observed in Sōtō Zen to ritualize an always larger sphere of activities, some profane areas necessarily remain. The very existence of sacred space relies on that of a profane space. Transgression, after all, implies a demarcation line, and Zen monks are well known for their jaunts in red-light districts. Selective ritualization (*gyōji*, ceremonies) defines a sacred/profane dichotomy, while totalizing ritualization (*gyōji* as "sustained practice") leads to integral immanence and rejection of transcendence. Were ritual omnipresent, however, it would paradoxically lose much of its efficacy—its very *raison d'être*. Instead of sacralizing monastic life, the utopian ideal intent on regulating entirely the daily activities of the monks would probably produce a deadening repetitiveness. Here again, ideology seems to find its limits, unless what seems to be the failure of ritual—the impossibility of total sacralization—is actually its success, the creation of a discrepancy between the ideal and the real and the making guilty of individuals who fall short of the ideal.

Ritual as Ideology

Let us assume that Zen ritual is not merely the "function" of an "essence," the embodiment of the Chan principle, or the expression of the ultimate meaning. What, then, are its meaning(s) and function(s) or, to use Tambiah's terminology, its semantic and indexical aspects? (See Tambiah 1981: 153.) To be sure, as Catherine Bell points out, ritual is not simply at the critical juncture "wherein some pairs of opposing social, or cultural forces come together" (Bell 1987: 95). If we see meditation itself as a form of ritual, the opposition between ritual and meditation tends to disappear. Insofar as awakening itself is a ritual reenactment of (or identification with) the Buddha's awakening, a ritual affiliation with the Chan patriarchal lineage, and a sacralization of everyday life, ritual cannot be relegated to a secondary or "supplementary" position. Furthermore, if we recognize that ritual is itself a form of thought (*ideology*) or writing (in the Derridean sense of "spacing"), there is no need to oppose ritual and doctrine —either as action and thought or as ethos and worldview—as conative and cognitive aspects. The tension becomes one between two strategic modes in a fundamentally elliptic (in both senses) discourse.

The main ideological function of ritual has to do with the fact that, although it is a "restricted code which shortens the process of communication by condensing units into pre-arranged forms" (Douglas 1970a: 54), this code is not only a system of communication, it is also a system of control (ibid.: 55). If ritual unites, it also differentiates—being perhaps "above all an assertion of difference" (Jonathan Z. Smith 1987: 109). In this light, the proliferation of ordination platforms in early Chan might be as significant as the doctrinal controversy between Northern and Southern Chan staged (from such a platform) by Shenhui at Huatai (732). One of the effects of ritual is to distance the practitioner from the profane world. Even in such deceptively simple actions as eating and drinking, ritualization aims at adorning everyday life and redefining it as "the Way" (*igi soku buppō*), or absolute reality. (See Bourdieu 1977b and 1990b.) Recalling Foucault's analysis of power extending through discipline to all aspects of individual life, one may also come to see ritual as an integral part of the technologies of power. Even *samādhi* does not escape this predicament, since, as Marcel Mauss once noted, mystical states themselves are necessarily rooted in bodily techniques and, as such, are social facts (Mauss 1950: 386). The body becomes the repository of a basic teaching, which will survive all doctrinal changes, since its transmission "from body to body" bypasses the written teaching and prevails even on the Chan transmission "from mind to mind." As Bourdieu points out in his discussion of the "negative rites of ascesis," "all groups entrust to the body, treated as a memory, their more precious trusts, and the way in which, in all societies, initiation rites use the suffering inflicted on the body makes sense when one knows that . . . people adhere all the more strongly to an institution since the initiatory rites it imposed on them were severe and painful" (Bourdieu 1982: 129). This recognition of physicality in and through ritual seems to contradict the Chan emphasis on mind, a form of "mentalism" that—not surprisingly—implied a denial of both body and ritual. The sacralization of the body reflected in the Chan cult of relics and "flesh-bodies" was *paradoxical*, not only because it seemed to depart from Chan *ortho-doxy* but because it laid more emphasis on *praxis* than on *doxa*. On the other hand, ritualization and the subsequent "somatization" are perhaps causes or by-products of Chan/Zen sectarianism, forms of differentiation perceived as necessary correctives for the dominant discourse that tended to collapse all differences into the harmony of the "One Mind."

Chan/Zen ritual may be what Bourdieu calls an *habitus*, that is, a system generating practices and representations that can be objectively adapted to their goal without implying conscious strategies (Bourdieu

1980b: 88). Granted that the performative power of ritual is socially determined, and that the ritual has in turn social effects such as differentiation and legitimation or naturalization of artificial dichotomies, it should not be reduced to its social determination. This may be just another example of the "chicken and egg" fallacy, since the structural logic at play here is also at the very basis of society. Bourdieu warns us against the temptation of reducing the two levels of analysis (phenomenological and ideological) to one another, of seeing ritual or practice either as true or as mere false consciousness. This methodological "twofold truth" echoes Tambiah's argument about ritual's duplex existence, "as an entity that symbolically and/or iconically represents the cosmos and at the same time indexically legitimates and realizes social hierarchies" (Tambiah 1981: 153).

RITUAL MEDIATION

Often described as mediation, ritual forces us to question the model of mediation we have been using throughout this book. Are we confronted with another actualization or recontextualization of the same logical fault that generated (and regenerates periodically) the Buddhist field of discourse? The paradigmatic oppositions we encountered are precisely the result of the patterning imposed by the tradition, and this polarization is usually replicated by scholars—who tend to like "fake windows" and to take models, whether theirs or those provided by the tradition, for an accurate description of reality. (See Bourdieu 1977b and 1990b; Bell 1987.)

According to the common interpretation, the Buddhist ritual is an *upāya*, an attempt to bridge the gap between delusion and awakening—that is, the gap described (or created) by the model of the Path (*mārga*). Accordingly, it is described in Chan/Zen as a mediation taking place at the level of practice, despite the theoretical claims for immediacy. Since the gap itself was a theoretical product, however, so must be its bridging. Ritual-as-mediation is not simply a form of action or practice; it is another form of "thought," an implicit ideology (orthodoxy and/or -praxy). We tend to forget that the distinction between theory and practice is itself theoretical: mediation presupposes—and actually produces—the dichotomy. In both cases, theory or "practice," one remains at the level of representations: any theory of practice is bound to fail, inasmuch as it remains theoretical, and is irrevocably removed from the practice it purports to describe. Yet inasmuch as it is irrevocably performative, it is already itself a form of practice, albeit admittedly of a different kind. My analysis presents some analogies to anthropological studies, in which ritual is seen to mediate a dichotomy that was perhaps first created by the observers themselves. The dichotomization process in anthropological literature has been well described—and criticized—by Catherine Bell (1987, 1990). I will return to Bell's argument in the epilogue, since the problems she raises have larger implications. Suffice it to say that, in the case of Chan/Zen, the polarization revealed (or re-produced) by scholarship was first revealed/concealed (and produced) by the tradition itself.

Hidden by intellectual representations or worldviews that conflict or ignore each other, and by claims for mediacy or immediacy, a practice, a *vécu*, is found in all probabilities that remains unaffected by dichotomies such as sudden/gradual. In this sense, the twofold truth is indeed at the same time a twofold falsehood, hiding another dimension of reality behind its theoretical constructions. Ritual raises the same kind of problems as myth. For Lévi-Strauss, myth is above all an attempt to mediate a dichotomy, and primitive thinking is already anthropological, while anthropological discourse itself remains essentially mythological. As any other type of thought, mythical thinking is a passage from continuous reality to discontinuous representation. In a controversial essay, Lévi-Strauss attempts to "naturalize" polarity, to project it from the cultural to the natural sphere, thus undermining the nature/culture dichotomy he had helped to establish (Lévi-Strauss 1985: 101–120). If ritual is precultural, it might after all, as Staal has suggested, be perfectly meaningless and not even aimed at mediating any opposites. At any rate, it does not simply bridge polarities, it also creates them. In Chan at least, ritual is reappropriated, as are various other patterns, in a system of representations that it helps to institute and preserve, becoming simultaneously, like Wumen Huikai's famous kōan, the barrier (Ch. *guan*) that blocks and opens the way, the fault and its closing, the dichotomy and its mediation. Whether or not the polarization is, as Lévi-Strauss (ibid.) claims, ultimately cultural or biological (*etic* or *emic*), the polarity itself is socio-historical, and perhaps cross-cultural. The ritualization of Chan practice— from death rituals to everyday life—has modified significantly the access to the sacred or to ultimate reality. Like death, awakening is no longer an individual experience; it implies a collective participation and a ritual process.[20] Thus ritual is not only taking place in the interstices of Chan practice and doctrine, as commonly believed; it also modifies them significantly, creating an entirely new *problématique*, while pretending simply to function within the old one (Althusser and Balibar 1970: 19–28). By the displacement it operates, ritual creates or reinforces in Chan/Zen two concurrent ideologies: the ideology of transcendence and immediacy, and the ideology of mediation and thaumaturgic immanence. The dissemination of charisma works according to the logic of supplementarity: it

[20] For a similar case in Daoism, see Bell 1988.

paradoxically emphasizes presence by multiplying its supports, but simultaneously defers it endlessly. The presence in the *śarīra*, the flesh-body, or the icon is never perceived as a full presence but as a "suspended animation" that allows for all the oscillations of belief and unbelief, ritualism and antiritualism. On every issue, Chan masters can take two extreme stances and all the intermediary positions. As noted earlier, the iconic or aniconic "trace" can be the sign both of an absence and of a transcendent presence; *śarīra* in particular are simultaneously the self of the Buddha or patriarch—his entire self—and not the self, as it is disseminated in other relics and is also said to be found nowhere. In this way, both the *ātman* and *anātman* theories seem justified. Similarly, words are concealing and/or revealing, efficient and/or inefficient, absolute truth and/or *upāya*. Every aspect of ritual (words, icons, kōans, meditation) seems dual-tracked. Whereas Chan shares the ideology of mediation with the rest of Buddhism, it stands apart from it with its ideology of immediacy. By focusing on the first aspect, we have blurred the demarcation line between Chan and Buddhism, but these lines were constantly reasserted at another, doctrinal or political, level. This justifies us in preserving, as we have done, the denomination of "Chan/Zen," against those who, taking Dōgen and other sectarian figures at face value, claim that there is no Zen sect, only Buddhism. Our discussion has shown precisely that Chan/Zen has at least two faces, and that every face always has several "values."

Epilogue

> Next to the constraint that makes us think that the
> truth of the world gives itself under the sign of undif-
> ferentiation, we must take into account that other
> constraint which *structures* our imaginary.
> —Marcel Gauchet, *Le désenchantement du monde*

The conclusion of a book is usually the place for an attempt to integrate
all the data discussed in previous chapters, to achieve a closure that anticipates the closing of the book by the reader. What could such a conclusion
be when one of the objectives of the book has been to dismantle the "old
theological/imperialistic impulses toward totalization, integration, and
unification" (Jonathan Z. Smith 1987: 18)? This text has been a long hesitation, if not between sound and sense—as in Valéry's definition of the
poem—at least between two irreconcilable models, perhaps two "opposite follies," like those of the Tang calligraphers Chang Xu and Huaisu.[1]
Thus it is perhaps impossible to conclude, to close the text, to bring a
happy ending to this story (for it is no more than a story, as opposed to a
history), to reconcile all the differences, or to close all the parentheses (as
in *Arabian Nights* or Raymond Roussel's *New Impressions of Africa*). I
should at least be able to recapitulate my itinerary, since this is probably
the only totalization possible or permissible. Yet an epilogue is hardly
better; and it is perhaps significant or ominous that, while the primary
meaning of the word is "recapitulation," a secondary meaning (in French)
is "malevolent comments."

Be that as it may, one point of entry into the problematic of this book
was the issue of transference and the impossibility of maintaining two
separate, watertight areas, the "primary" discourse of the tradition and
the secondary discourse of scholarship—in other words, to ensure the objectivity of a historical discourse aiming at an accurate mimesis. I believe
that there is always a contamination, a dissemination from one type of
discourse to the other. Thus, although it refers at times to historical contexts, my own discourse has abandoned its claims to historiographic objectivity. Whereas historical discourse may be defined as "a semiological
apparatus that produces meaning by the systematic substitution of signifieds for the extra-discursive entities that serve as their referents" (White
1987: x), my analysis is primarily concerned with the signifieds (concep-

---

[1] According to Liu Xizai, "Chang Xu assimilates joy and sadness in his teaching, the
monk Huaisu eliminates both." See *Yi kai* (Shanghai: Guji, 1978), 158, quoted in Hsiung
1984: 56.

tual contents), not with their referents. My methodological claim is that Chan can be approached neither simply from the outside like a "social fact" in the Durkheimian sense (i.e., as a "thing"), nor by resorting to some privileged "fusion of horizons" in the Gadamerian sense.

The various chapters of the book display (and play with) the same tension or aporia, only from different angles. The problem of the nature of the data is interwined with that of theory or methodology, insofar as the data themselves derive from the theory or methodology, while the latter are in turn questioned by the data. Proceeding from the Orientalist margins of the scholarly discourse on Chan/Zen, I have attempted to examine some of the issues that the tradition has claimed as central to its practice— such as the "sudden/gradual" debate. These analyses reinforced a rather obvious observation, that of the (perhaps not so) vexing discrepancy between Chan theoretical discourse and its practice. The sudden/gradual case can indeed be perceived as paradigmatic. Chan, I argued, distinguishes itself from other religious trends by its insistence on immediacy and its denial of all traditional mediations. Yet it is clear that these mediations were always present, even (or precisely) when they were most vehemently repudiated. This fault line, which I followed throughout representations of Chan attitudes toward dreams, thaumaturgy, death, relics, ritual, and gods, has been usually silenced or explained away— both by the tradition itself and by its scholarly replication—by means of notions such as the Two Truths. We are usually told that what is perceived "im-mediately" by the advanced adepts as (at the level of) ultimate truth must, because of the immaturity of ordinary believers, be hidden or revealed indirectly through "skillful means," as (at the level of) conventional truth. Like the Dao and its Daoist representatives, the Dharma and the various Buddhas or Chan patriarchs must "soften their light and mingle with the dust." This camouflage would account for the use of ritual and the reintroduction of intermediaries as a subtext or supplement to the teaching of immediacy. This compromise, however, was repeatedly rejected by the most radical (doctrinaire?) adherents, who claimed that Chan might lose its "purity" in its dealing with the world but who were actually using syncretism as a foil to construct their own brand of "pure" Chan/Zen.[2]

The textbook interpretation might still make sense. The very expression "to make sense," however, suggests that sense is not a mere given but rather a product—in other words, that this interpretation itself is essentially *performative*. This raises the issue of ideology and of the twofold truth of the "Twofold Truth," of what appears as the "radical" duplicity

---

[2] See Dōgen's criticism of the Chinese "Three in One" ideology in *Shōbōgenzō Shizen Biku*; trans. Yokoi 1976: 159.

of Chan discourse. The paradoxical nature (or function) of Chan reveals itself precisely in the discrepancy between immediacy and mediation. Since mediation is usually perceived as one of the characteristic features of traditional Buddhism and of the so-called popular religion(s), the rejection of mediations seems at first glance to amount to a rejection of traditional Buddhism(s) and popular religion(s). A closer look at "popular religion," however, has revealed it to be a concept of many hues, covering a wide range of religious trends—some of which are antithetical to Chan, while others seem homologous. Consequently, the earlier distinction between Chan and popular religion, between a "great tradition" and its margins, became a matter of differences within both Chan and popular religion(s). This leaves us with plural, multivocal, differential traditions on both sides of the earlier divide, a divide that retains only a provisional validity. The naive two-tiered model used by most historians of Chan cannot account for these phenomena; it hides rather than explains their intricate relationships. By stressing (if only to deplore it) the influence of one level ("popular religion") on the other (Chan/Zen), it reifies them and gives them undue logical or chronological priority over the relationship itself. Nevertheless, phenomena traditionally considered as resulting from the influence of "popular religion" on Chan actually emerged from within Chan itself and cannot simply be seen as effects of "acculturative syncretism." Of course, one cannot deny that the latter also played a role, inasmuch as the representations of a "pure Chan" and of a monolithic popular religion, in due time, became part of reality. But these representations must not be projected anachronistically as the principles of things in a past in which they had not as yet emerged, and they should not acquire more than a localized explanatory value. At any rate, it seems significant that, having set out to consider the relations between Chan and popular religion, I ended by examining the various reinscriptions of an inner divide *within* Chan itself.

If the classical explanation of Chan "contamination" by popular religion loses most of its explanatory value, what models can we use to understand this inner dialectic of Chan and the (sometimes perverse) effects of the twofold truth model? This model tells us at least one (or two) things—namely, that two models are better than (even a twofold) one. And each of these models can itself be shown to be (at least) double, since it has already been "contaminated" by the other, despite claims that the two truths, perceived as two ontological levels, remain hermetically (hermeneutically?) watertight realms. As Derrida has shown in another text/context, the "pure" level of descriptive or "constative" discourse (Austin 1962: 2) is *always already* contaminated by the "impure" metaphorical level of performative rhetorical discourse, and "context is always, and always has been, at work *within* the place, and not only *around* it" (Derrida

1988: 198). The core is not always limited by the margins but traversed by them. Thus the margins of Chan are found at work in Chan itself, marginalizing various trends while "centering" others. The sudden/gradual controversy and its sectarian outcome—that is, the differentiation between orthodoxy and heterodoxy and the schism between Southern and Northern Chan—can be seen as the paradigmatic example of this dialectical process and its dichotomic radicalization. This is perhaps a case of what Bergson (1935) called the "law of twofold frenzy" (*loi de double frénésie*)—although it seems to be more a tendency than a "law." Likewise, for each case studied (e.g., ritual), we may resort to a variety of models, following, as it were, the process of differentiation of the tradition itself and acknowledging that the truth of the phenomena studied can never be collected in a single (sudden) intuition but has to be experienced through the dialectical oscillation of its alternating positions, at various stages along the process of its dissemination.

The plurality of interpretations also results from the simple fact that the positions considered are always overdetermined and ambiguous. Why does Chan speak the language of immediacy while its very existence means potentially the contrary, that is, the prevailing of mediation? Are we to assess the significance of Chan discourse for its explicit content or rather for the implicit act that permits it? Should we pay more attention to the ritual (ortho- or heteropraxy) than to the doctrine (ortho- or heterodoxy)? This is what we have done here so far, but it is admittedly a preliminary phase, necessary in order to counterbalance the usual emphasis on doctrine. An approach that would simply reverse the hierarchy, however, between doctrine and ritual, or between representation and practice, would remain bound by the same metaphysical constraints. Such is, for example, Staal's position when he advocates the ritualistic approach to Buddhism as a "substitution of paradigms" (Staal 1985). As Merleau-Ponty and Derrida have pointed out, such inversions merely reproduce the ideological effects of the old paradigms. In his analysis of "differential ritual," Turner has warned us against the danger of overlooking "the qualitative difference from either [level] presented by the pattern of their interdependence" (Turner 1969: 50). In other words, the ultimate truth of the two truths—or what Bourdieu calls the phenomenological and ideological levels—is that they are not in any sense ultimate but correlated and *supplementary* (not simply complementary, which would remain too static and non-dialectical). It is not by mere coincidence, nor by deviation (as the advocates of "pure" Chan would have us believe), that rationalism and occultism, philosophy and ritual, a/theology and i/deology, observance of the precepts and transgression (but also sudden and gradual), coexist in practice, if not always in representation. These terms are of course neither overlapping nor symmetrical. Yet they seem intertwined like strands in the warp and woof—and as such require a different (and perhaps warped) approach. One cannot simply isolate the two levels, as D. T. Suzuki and his epigones do, trying to isolate "true" Zen from its Buddhist structure. (See Merton 1970: 1.) Even if Zen can be characterized as what exceeds or subverts the structure, it remains an effect of this structure and cannot exist apart from it, just as ultimate truth cannot exist apart from conventional truth. It is perceived through it and framed by it. When such a metaphysical, antistructural claim is made, it falls back into the structure and turns into ideological discourse. Wittgenstein has argued that such metaphysical discourse is tautological, and that language cannot truly point toward the Other (Wittgenstein 1958). Yet language is also, in some of its uses, *heterological*, and we cannot exclude the possibility that the Other glimmers within the metaphysical closure of language.

One must go one step further. Just as, in society, power affirms itself against the differences that it institutes by denying them through a symbolic inversion or equalization of the levels, the Chan denial of mediations, hierarchy, and difference may be seen as the very source of the latter. In this sense, Chan's freedom from conventions remains an aristocratic *privilege*, a "private law"; it is not the "revolutionary" achievement it claims to be. Perhaps it is precisely because of the constraints of ordinary practice that the theoretical excess was possible. Chan, and Mahāyāna in general, opened a field of discourse that had to be framed by concrete situations. But Chan discourse proved *hybrid* in both senses of the term: its *hybris* led Chan to deny its hybridity in the name of pristine purity and to leave the solid ground of practice for the icy sphere of antinomian metaphysics. This move, however, fulfilled both an *ideological* and a *utopian* function—to use Jameson's distinction—and cannot be reduced to either aspect. The trickster ideal in Chan, for instance, is neither pure subversion nor mere ideological camouflage. Another possible interpretation is that the theoretical discourse opens a space that it cannot keep open, and that it therefore delimits through practices and implicit or explicit provisos.[3]

On the other hand, these structural constraints do not mean that the "twofold truth" of Chan is not also the product of its militant syncretism. Although subitism and "purism" look positive, "like all 'isms,' . . . they are all negatively infused, taking their form antithetically to other 'isms' [some elements of which, paradoxically, they often end by incorporating]."[4] Thus the ritualization of Chan may have something to do with sectarian differentiation, and more precisely with its geographical expan-

---

[3] This theoretical excess, although necessarily bound by practical constraints, might be at times reactivated. See Derrida (1978: 60) on the "dialogue between hyperbole and finite structure."

[4] Kenneth Burke, *The Rhetoric of Religion*, quoted in Boon 1982: 9.

sion and its confrontation with local cults, Daoism and Confucianism. In this sense, the traditional historical explanation remains valid; it simply needs to be relativized.

The coexistence is not necessarily, and indeed was not always, a pacific one, and it can also be interpreted in terms of inner acculturation. The structural tension between the two levels of discourse does not mean that, in specific historical contexts, one level did not come to prevail over the other. We have seen that this was the case in some Chan circles during the Tang with the radical, antinomian interpretation of subitism. In other cases, the ritual seems to have prevailed largely over the doctrine, and one may argue that, in this way, it came actually to "extort the essential on the pretense of demanding the trivial" (Bourdieu 1980b: 117). In other words, behind the official teaching of Chan that filled the adepts' mind and mouth, another teaching was inscribed in their bodies and actualized in their daily practice. This inverted relationship between representation and reality makes practice and ritual (as ritualized practice) privileged vectors of ideology—or sometimes its very source. But it must be stressed that, here again, both ritualized practice and antiritualist doctrine are (at least) twofold; in other words, each can be the ideological mask of the other, or on the contrary manifest a truth distorted by the other.

Much of the Chan tradition—and perhaps of the truth of Chan itself—is essentially dialogical, and consequently it requires a dialogical understanding. As I have argued in the case of Dōgen and the Darumashū, this inner dialogue—or at least its real interlocutor—is usually silenced, erased from the surface of Chan/Zen texts (Faure 1987a: 39). According to Jameson, "every universalizing approach will be found to conceal its own contradictions and repress its own historicity by strategically framing its perspective so as to omit the negative, absence, contradiction, repression, the *non-dit*, the *impensé*" (Jameson 1981: 110). On the other hand, traditions do also, consciously or not, give voice to the other. The univocity, the ideal of the orthodoxy, is always denied by an irrepressible multivocality. Like cultures, according to Boon, sectarian traditions, although "perfectly commonsensical from within, nevertheless flirt with their own 'alterities,' gain critical self-distance, formulate complex (rather than simply reactionary) perspectives on others, confront (even admire) what they themselves are not" (Boon 1982: 19). Consequently, "rituals, myths and religions mutually exaggerate, reciprocally radicalize, their meanings" (ibid.: 10).

It is relatively easy to admit that various voices or levels of discourse may coexist within a single tradition. But how can they coexist within a single individual? Or is there no perfectly *single* individual? Perhaps the discrepancy is attenuated by the psychosomatic (dis)location, that is, the mental inscription of the doctrinal teaching and the bodily inscription of the ritual teaching; but this does not seem sufficient. Neither is the socio-logical explanation that opposes the intellectual elite to the common practitioners. Sōtō scholars have thus tried to oppose Dōgen to the ulte-rior Sōtō tradition. But there is no clear border in the textual tradition to indicate where Dōgen ends and his heirs begin. A psychological expla-nation for the coexistence of rational and magical thinking is provided by Favret-Saada (1980). It is the twofold logic of what she calls *je sais bien, mais quand même*: "I know [that it cannot be true], yet [I somehow believe in it]." According to Favret-Saada, logical and prelogical thinking are not the characteristics of two different categories of people, as van Gennep and Lévy-Bruhl believed, but of linguistic positions that any individual can occupy at various times (Favret-Saada 1980: 291). Paul Veyne has used a similar notion, that of the alternation of "programs of truth."[5] This oscillation is reminiscent of what Jon Elster calls "higher order beliefs" or "beliefs about beliefs," as in Niels Bohr's statement about horseshoes: "I don't believe in them, but I am told that they bring good luck even to those who do not believe in them."[6] Of course, this duplicity is precisely the definition of false consciousness, and one may question the "en-chanted relationship" that Chan entertains with its own practice, preach-ing at the same time an unlocalized teaching, arguing for the return of chaos, and creating fixed points in this chaos (rules, ritual, stages). It is probably impossible to assess the degree of misrecognition—or plain bad faith—in Chan/Zen rituals such as funerals, when not only the beliefs (such as the belief in the actual presence of the dead in an effigy) but the rituals themselves are fluctuating. Furthermore, as Bourdieu himself points out, the actual experience of individuals, while not being the entire truth of what they do, is nevertheless part of the truth of their practices (Bourdieu 1984: 32).

DICHOTOMIES IN QUESTION(S)

As noted earlier, the current anthropological theory of ritual has been criticized as a dichotomizing process by Catherine Bell.[7] Bell shows in

[5] See Veyne 1988: 21–22. On the plurality of these "programs of truth," see ibid.: 27. Similarly, according to Geertz, human beings move, "more or less easily, and very fre-quently, between radically contrasting ways of looking at the world, ways which are not continuous with one another but separated by cultural gaps across which Kierkegaardian leaps must be made in both directions." See his "Religion as Cultural System," in Lessa and Vogt 1979: 88.

[6] Quoted in Elster 1983: 5. See also Umberto Eco's variant—"Superstition brings bad luck"—appropriately placed in exergue of *Foucault's Pendulum* (New York: Harcourt Brace Jovanovitch, 1988).

[7] This chapter was written before I had the chance and privilege to read Bell's recent manuscript, *Ritual Theory, Ritual Practice* (1990). Since some of the questions raised by her

particular how the dichotomy between action and thought, unconsciously projected by the anthropologist, engenders a whole series of secondary dichotomies. Ritual is perceived on a first level as belonging to the sphere of action, and on a second level as an attempt at synthesis or dialectical integration between concepts (thought, worldview) and dispositions (action, ethos). Finally, on a third level, it provides through this synthesis a convenient cultural unit, a unit of meaning for the actor and by the same token for the observer: it therefore integrates actor and observer, that is, also, action and thought, practice and theory, within a dialectical relation. The "resolution" of this dichotomy, however, exists only by maintaining the polarity that it claims to fill, and, according to Bell, such a polarity is fraudulently imported into the object: it is actually a projection of the unconscious categories of thought of the subject.[8]

Does Bell's analysis of ritual and discursive dichotomy apply to my characterization of Chan as dichotomic thinking? Have I created "fake windows" by reading into Chan dichotomies that are the product of my own binary thinking? Is it merely a Californian obsession with earthquakes that led me to imagine that Chan masters were "living on a fault line"? I insisted earlier on the value of the transference between the scholar and the object of scholarship. To be sure, using the same word (here "mediation") to describe two different projects implies some risk of being misled into seeing them "as more alike than they really are" (Staten 1984: 77). Yet such mediation (of "mediation") may also prove useful, if it brings out homologies between two discourses that would otherwise have remained unconscious.

Although Bell never claims that the validity of her analysis goes beyond the anthropological theory of ritual, it is clear that her critique has larger implications. At the risk of reinforcing Zen chauvinism, I would like to argue that Chan/Zen (and, needless to say, my understanding of it) constitutes the exception that confirms the rule. Bell's argument rests on the assumption that the dichotomy is merely a projection of the observer and is not found in the "objective" practice and/or representation of the traditions observed. This may be true in the case of "archaic" societies in which practices and representations are not yet dissociated.[9] It is not so in the case of Chan, where a dichotomy does exist, at least at the

---

earlier article (Bell 1987) were answered in it, and other relevant issues further elaborated, I have felt compelled to include references to this yet unpublished work here.

[8] Bell's analysis, focusing on ritual, would apply in the case of myth as well, considered by Lévi-Strauss as an attempt to solve contradictions between the cultural and the social, the ideal and the factual situation.

[9] To the anthropologist's dismay, such societies have become admittedly very rare. See also Derrida's notion that "arch-writing" (as spacing and *différance*) is present even in "oral" cultures (Derrida 1974: 139–140), or Lévi-Strauss's analysis of the dichotomies of mythical thinking as a form of (mytho-)logic (Lévi-Strauss 1966).

level of representation. One may even argue that, due to centuries of cross-cultural reification, this dichotomy evolved from a mental structure to a reality that now exists "out there." (See Berger and Luckmann 1967.) History seems in that respect endowed with a kind of ontological effect. It is, one hopes, not a mere sleight of hand that allowed us to characterize Chan as a dichotomic thought resulting from a denial of mediation and to reintroduce in a second moment a different, "purified" mediation; or even to describe it as a thought reinvested, subverted by the old mediations of popular religion. As LaCapra points out: "The undoing of binary oppositions does not eliminate the need to investigate their actual role in intellectual, social and political relations where they may be quite constraining intellectually and have strong institutional support" (LaCapra 1989: 7).

There are significant differences between the dichotomies described in the case of Chan and those described (or imagined) by anthropologists in the case of ritual. The main difference is that we find in Chan clear evidence of an autochthonous discourse that is dichotomic—despite, or precisely because of, its vindication of nonduality. Therefore, it is perhaps precisely the possibility of a transference, in other words the existence of affinities or homologies between the discursive logics of the object and the subject, that permits a dialogical progress. The transferential circle cannot be left so easily. It need not, however, be a vicious one, and, as Heidegger said of the hermeneutical circle, perhaps the important point is not so much to exit it as to enter it correctly (Heidegger 1962: 194). It may be after all only appropriate that Chan, like its kōans, questions the questioners, returns to them their own questions and helps them discover (or produce) themselves through them. It is also a typically Chan gesture that does not stop with the unfolding of a mediation, the deployment of a theoretical or praxical scaffolding, but cuts the ground from under one's feet and sweeps away the discursive structure patiently erected. Of course, this gesture itself is soon integrated into another semiotic structure, adding legitimacy to it.

Not unlike sudden Chan itself, Bell's deconstruction of the theory of ritual chooses to bypass the question of mediation by denying the existence of polarities and the need of any dialectic. The dualistic model, however, retains its heuristic value, as long as it is perceived only as a model and not as a description of reality—and it is precisely the confusion of models with reality that Bell criticizes. The value of the model is "performative"; it depends on the fertility of its applications, not on its correspondence with a problematic "original." Referring to Paul de Man's notion of "blindness and insight," Bell shows that she is conscious that any methodological choice implies a cost, and that it always does some violence to the tradition under study. The interest in Bell's approach (her insight) lies in the unmasking of a number of false dichotomies; its cost (her blindness) is that it tends to overlook actual dichotomies. After all, human experience has not been "wrongly divided" only by theorists in comparative religion (Douglas 1970b: 28). Although the various "two-tiered models" of religion inherited from Western and Asian literate traditions can no longer be taken as reflecting the reality experienced by most of the common practitioners, we would fall in the same method-ological scapegoatism that we denounced if we were to deny any validity to the *literati* worldview.

One way to approach this question is to consider that ritual—just as speech, action, or thinking—is both differentiation (i.e., the production of dichotomy) and representation (i.e., a form of thought). According to Lévi-Strauss, the function of ritual is to reestablish the lost continuity (mediation), to bridge the gap produced by mythical representations or intellectual speculations (such as the Two Truths). As ritual meditation, Chan goes against dualism, against the polarity produced by the Twofold Truth, or rather its sudden pole. Thus at the level of representation, grad-ualism can be seen as an attempt to mend the "sudden" tear. On the other hand, traditional Chinese thought, in its hierarchical mode, implied an ontological-epistemological break, whereas "sudden" Chan claims to "fuse the mind" with the Principle, to restore its primordial integrity. This is, however, a rather desperate attempt that leads to the opposite result: a denial of reality, a theoretical gap that can be filled only by ritual. Thus ritualization comes to play the role that thought can no longer play, that it has forbidden itself to play, outside the rare cases when a sudden insight, like a burst of laughter, "spares one a long detour to connect and unify two semantic fields" (Lévi-Strauss 1981: 659).

An important point in Bell's discussion is that neither the polarization nor its resolution is neutral: they always tend to privilege one of the poles and function simultaneously to keep them separated and hierarchized. The attempt to "think together the symbol and the function" (Augé 1982a) is itself generally biased toward the symbol. Although one may resort to the notion of performance (closer to the function/action pole), it is still in order to extract the "true meaning" or significance (albeit not a hermeneutical one in the strict sense). Yet Bell herself seems to set up a polarity between dichotomizing and nondichotomizing approaches—and to privilege the latter. Her emphasis on the function of ritual (Tambiah's "indexical features," referring to social hierarchy) tends to play down the symbolic features (referring to the cosmology enacted by the practi-tioner). As Certeau pointed out, and as Bell herself acknowledges, all such methodological choices imply a violence, an embalming of the ob-ject of study. Should we then be afraid of dichotomizing, when the tra-dition itself does so? We cannot ignore that, however distorted it may be, the representation of reality is also part of that reality. (See Bourdieu 1977b: 5–9.) This does not mean that we have to endorse the claims of the tradition; on the contrary, we also discover (and perhaps imagine) faults where it attempts to appear seamless. At any rate, the polarity or gap between tradition and scholarship is misleading: there is also a continuity between sectors of tradition and sectors of scholarship that are dualist or metaphysical, as there is a continuity between other sectors of tradition and scholarship that are decentered or deconstructive. Perhaps after all there is no going back to the pristine facts, or beyond the "*pensée par couples*" (and copulas): better, then, theoretical copulation than objectivist voyeurism.

The Paradoxes of Mediation

In Chan/Zen at least, ritualization seems at first glance to illustrate the return of repressed mediations, the incongruency between the ideal and the real. If, however, "ritual gains force where incongruency is perceived and thought about" (Jonathan Z. Smith 1982: 63), what happens when the incongruency is the ritualization itself, when ritual disguises itself as nonritual, as in the Chan "encounter dialogues" or in sitting meditation? What goes on when spontaneity itself is ritualized, when immediacy— not a dichotomy—is mediated by ritual, when ultimate truth is framed by conventional truth? One could perhaps argue that immediacy is affirmed at the very historical moment when it is about to disappear, when mediations come to play an increasing role—not only in Chan, but in the larger context of Chinese society: for instance, with the imperial centralization under the Tang and the monetarization of the economy during the Song. Of course, there is probably no direct causal relationship between the ideological realm on the one hand and the socio-political and economical realms on the other, the relative autonomy of the ideological realm being ensured precisely by a complex network of mediations. (See Somers 1986: 984–985.) Nevertheless, it is clear that socio-economic factors have played a role. For example, social factors such as the demand of lay groups may have contributed to the ritualization of Chan,[10] while the concurrence between Chan masters and schools probably contributed to the banalization (and perhaps to a certain extent to the secularization) of Chan. (See Weber 1964: 60–79; Bourdieu 1971a and 1971b.)

Assuming that Chan immediacy is denied, deferred, or supplemented by the return of mediations, can we at least suppose that Chan dichotomic thinking is now unified, that the ontological and epistemological breaks

[10] On the other hand, the lay critique of the monks as "specialists of the occult"—a critique exemplified by Vimalakīrti and Layman Pang—may have contributed to the development of Chan antiritualism. See Gernet 1956: 191–195.

have been mended, and that ritual has succeeded in bridging the gap produced by mythological and logical speculations? This would be to overlook the issue of ideology in the Althusserian sense, that is, the fact that representation does not necessarily correspond to reality and that ritual and mediation in general play an ambiguous role or a double game: they simultaneously mediate and maintain (or even create) the gap. We have here another dialectical reversal: the mediation that attempts to erase the differences is precisely what produces them. For instance, we are confronted with two kinds of denial of duality and "ontological" difference: one that advocates fusion or immediacy (for example, the identity of *saṃsāra* and *nirvāṇa*), and one that works as mediation, as in the case of ritual. The actual effect of these denials, however, is the opposite of their apparent purpose: whereas the claim for immediacy, aiming at an absolutization of the relative, ends up in relativizing the absolute and contributing to secularization, the claim for mediation actually widens the gap; it augments the separation between heaven and earth, between sacred and profane. The paradoxical effect of mediation is to reiterate the differences, both ontological and social, and to consolidate the hierarchy, to "produce the sense of the very thing they defer" (Derrida 1974: 157). As Jameson points out, "Once needs have been sundered from means, in lived experience and in the theory that reflects it, it is impossible to put the two back together again, to restore the 'naive' and primitive, unself-conscious unity of action in the other-oriented cultures." As in the case of contemporary philosophy, the emphasis of Chan "on restoring the concrete, on being in the world, on praxis as a total process, may best be understood against the background of this dissociation" (Jameson 1988: 2:9). This is as true of Chan ideology as it is, according to Bell, of anthropological discourse.

Thus ritual points to the gap at the same time that it attempts to bridge it, it reveals the discrepancy or even produces it. Furthermore, there is no way to show a priority between these two functions, and the two levels of analysis—phenomenological or ideological—can neither be reconciled or bridged, nor bypassed. The thrust of ritual may be the reverse of that of mythical thinking, but in the end (contrary to what Lévi-Strauss thinks) the result is the same. The originary continuity that it yearns for is itself a projection, a derivation, a "trace"; the ultimate is always still *penultimate*. We should keep in mind the elliptical structure of the text or of the ritual, the constant tension of its *double bande*: one, yet two—like Moebius's strip or Escher's drawings. Two antithetic readings are always possible (at least at the conventional level). The question must remain open as to whether practice actually results from a tension between the two poles of discourse, or whether on the contrary the practice itself produces a tension, of which the two poles of discourse, and later the sectarian reifications, are only the terminals. Ritual might simultaneously be a response to a doctrinal split or a theoretical polarity—such as sudden/gradual—and an autonomous polarization, both a consequence and a cause, a denial and a reconciliation of "epistemological couples." The intermediary is at the same time an obstacle, and it may be seen to function as a shifter or a *pivot*: ritual may, for instance, mediate between belief and unbelief by allowing the practitioner to shift from one program of truth to another.[11] Like trance and ritual, meditation is both a deconditioning and a reconditioning process, an instrument of personal freedom and of social control. This may serve as a useful reminder that what we have been calling ritual or practice is an abstraction, an approximation, and that we are actually confronted with specific acts that are rather arbitrarily defined as rites and practices. Even at the microlevel, however, concrete practices seem to reveal a twofold truth, that of their alienating *and* liberating functions. But the grammatical conjunction must not lead us to rest satisfied with a comfortable *conjunctio oppositorum*, a reconciliation of contraries such as that between *saṃsāra* and *nirvāṇa*—supposedly the hallmark of Asian thought. It is an agonistic tension, not a comfortable binary opposition. It is perhaps this tension, this discrepancy, that produces the *play* (*jeu*), the essential undecidability of Chan, its fault and vanishing point.

We may temporarily emphasize differentiation in order to argue that it is the theory that contradicts the practice, not the other way around: in other words, practice cannot simply be seen as reconciliation of a preexisting polarity, not even as maintaining the tension between the poles. In this sense, doctrinal discourse is always ulterior to practice, and necessarily framed by it. Thus the observed practice cannot be reduced to a degeneration (heteropraxy) of another "pure" practice (orthopraxy), the existence of which, at first merely virtual, now acquires reality and is eventually identified with a given ideological or sectarian trend (such as Dōgen's "pure Zen"). Yet the "primacy of practice" vindicated by Althusser (Althusser and Balibar 1970: 70) should not lead us to deny the ideology—on the contrary, since ideology (whether that of Chan or of the scholar) is itself recognized as a form of practice. According to Althusser, the concept of mediation is used only by those who need to fill a gap between "abstract categories" or "theoretical principles" and the "concrete," and as such it functions as a mask and a theoretical imposture.[12] The particularity of Chan, however, is that it simultaneously de-

---

[11] On this to-and-fro motion, see Geertz in Lessa and Vogt 1979: 88. On ritual as a means of shifting between levels of reality—a "pivoting of the sacred"—see van Gennep 1960: 12–13.

[12] Althusser 1990: 77. Whereas Althusser is concerned only with the mediations between

nies and resorts to mediation, and it is rather the denial that appears to function as a theoretical imposture. Even if such is the case, it is precisely on this theoretical level, rather than on that of pre-discursive practices (whatever this may be), that I have chosen to focus. To understand Chan masters as ideologues, the concept of mediation, *pace* Althusser, retains its validity, since it is precisely what they have tried to cover up. Further- more, one cannot deny that practice, while admittedly prior to any po- larization, is *also* ulterior: what started as an *ex post facto* rationalization of the differentiation produced by practice (as a "model of") becomes sub- sequently a kind of cause (a "model for"). Practice thus becomes a con- scious attempt, at least on the part of the most lucid Chan ideologues (such as Zongmi), to provide a mediation. And precisely the ideological masking of mediation, denounced by Althusser, helps us to see more clearly the similar role played by the opposite notion of immediacy. Moreover, it reveals the polemical dimension of Althusser's critique, originally addressed to Sartre. Between Althusser and Sartre (but also Merleau-Ponty, another advocate of mediation), the old gradual/sudden debate seems to replay itself—if on another mode or stave. Admittedly, there is no neutral ground, and every theoretical position is performative. My attempt to negotiate this aporia is to consider that mediation is—also, if not only—differentiation. *Not only* differentiation, because we cannot entirely elude the possibility that, by producing even a "semblance of presence" (Certeau 1982), it may somehow provide, so to say laterally or as a by-product, an access to the other. However remote this possibility may appear, it is sufficient to maintain that the *utopian* aspect of mediation should not be sacrificed to the *ideological*. (See Jameson 1981: 289.)

Thus when confronted with the dominant unifying tendency *and* the doctrinal or sectarian dichotomies of the Chan/Zen tradition, two alter- native responses seem possible: to play down or dismiss dichotomies as ideological constructs (as Bell does for ritual theory), and/or to empha- size them—or even to provoke them if necessary—in order to crack the smooth façade of the orthodoxy. On the one hand, a common thrust is revealed in Chan practices (such as meditation and funerary rituals) that tends to blur doctrinal (sudden/gradual) or sectarian (Chan/non-Chan) distinctions and, almost unnoticed, to alter radically, if not the name, then the very nature of the Chan game; on the other hand, some dichot- omies are heuristically accentuated to show that the fault runs deeper than the doctrinal level, revealing the practical interface or *différend* of irrecon- cilable worldviews.

The simultaneous vision of the two truths means that ultimate truth

---

reality and theoretical knowledge, the question of mediation in Chan (and in Buddhism in general) is both cognitive and soteriological.

must be framed by conventional truth in order to be understood properly. With the most radical trends in Chan, however, one discerns an attempt to pass from an economy of hierarchy to an economy of difference, where the two levels become autonomous and irreconcilable. It is a further departure from the (ideal) archaic substrate, a type of religiosity that does not dissociate the order of representations from that of practices. In this sense, Chan can be said to have paved the way to a process of secularization that flourished in certain trends of neo-Confucianism.

Yet the two truths or two levels of discourse constitute a system. In other words, one cannot have the end without means (as radical Chan claims), or means without end (as sometimes seems the case in "practical" Chan). The two hold only through their essential tension, and conventional truth becomes a necessary *supplement* of ultimate truth (or practice a supplement of innate awakening, as Dōgen argued against what he called the "Senika heresy," referring by this to the mainstream of Song Chan and Japanese Tendai). Subitism has to be mitigated if it is to be more than wishful thinking. But by the same token, there is a displacement or inversion of the means and end: to some extent, the means become the end, the end the means. Likewise, practice already implies a cognitive—theoretical—component, while, at the other end of the spectrum, theory—inasmuch as it is performative—remains a form of practice.[13] Although somewhat blurred, the distinction is never totally canceled, for this would mean the end of the polar structure, that is, of Chan itself. The same is true for Chan scholarship: here again, the two levels (exegesis and ideological critique) hold because of their tension, and the scholar cannot simply reduce the truth claims of the tradition to mere rhetoric, its metaphysics to mere ideology. The ideological truth is itself always *supplementary*; although it constantly threatens the truth claims of the tradition, it can never entirely cancel or supersede them. It can prove the ideological nature of particular metaphysical claims, or the derivative nature of the absolute, but it cannot totally reject the possibility of a heterology—of an irruption of the "Other" into the tautological discourse of metaphysics, the shining through of some kind of transcendence into the most flagrantly ideological discourse—without becoming itself ideological and falling victim to its own criticism. (See Derrida 1972b.)

By fusing (ideally) the two spheres of reality into one, Chan provoked a double dynamic of secularization and of sacralization of the profane. Despite their denial of mediations, or precisely because they had removed other alternatives, Chan masters became or remained the ultimate mediators, straddling the two orders of reality, or transiting from one to the

---

[13] See Althusser 1990: 71. Althusser, however, seems to draw inverse conclusions concerning the "truth" or "inner logic" of theoretical Marxism.

other. Only their statusless status permitted this new kind of mediation. In the same way, their iconoclasm turned out to be, not the radical denial that it claimed to be, but an attempt to purify, to rarefy, the dominant symbols. Likewise, the motto of nondependence on scriptures triggered a process of limitation that aimed in fact at redefining and closing the canon, not at suppressing it altogether (except in the most extreme cases). On the other hand, by interiorizing religious practice, Chan paved the way to the "dialectic of transcendence" (privatization/secularization) that eventually weakened it as a tradition. This perhaps made possible the emergence or persistence of "catholic" aspects such as ritual and the cult of icons, which expressed an ideology of "thaumaturgic immanence." Thus one can discern two tendencies in Chan (at least on the level of representation). The first is an attempt to save the ontological reality, the irreducible *sui generis* nature of Chan insight, at the expense of the second, the anthropological tendency, the variety of elaborations, seen as degenerations or corruption of the primordial "ontic seizure" (Jonathan Z. Smith 1987: 42), thus forgetting that "pure experience" itself has the structure of a "trace."

As Jonathan Smith points out in the case of the canon, scholarship—following the traditional account—has usually limited itself to the theological aspect of the dialectical process (limitation) and overlooked or played down its anthropological aspect (elaboration, differentiation, ingeniousness). One way to explain the coexistence of two different models is thus to see it as the sedimented trace of a dialectical process. Thus liminality becoming structure would explain the emergence of a double discourse, *double bande*, twofold truth (or falsehood). An alternative way to interpret the discrepancy between these two tendencies is to see it, not diachronically, but rather synchronically, as resulting from various vantage points and corresponding "to two different ways of describing one organization too complex to be formalized by a single model" (Lévi-Strauss, quoted in Jonathan Z. Smith 1987: 43). Analyzing conflicting descriptions of the power structure in a village, Lévi-Strauss comments: "Thus, it is from a perspective of power that A sees the village as symmetrical and reciprocal; it is from a position of subordination that B pictures the village as hierarchical. . . . These opposing positions give rise to two discordant ideological maps of geographical and social space."[14] These two ideological maps of the village constitute the two poles between which are arrayed all concrete positions. But these positions are never fixed; they are the object of a constant negotiation, in which the ideological maps themselves play a significant role. Thus the classification

[14] Quoted in Jonathan Z. Smith 1987: 44–45. See also Dumont: "At the superior level there is unity; at the inferior level there is distinction" (Dumont 1970: 239, quoted in Smith ibid.: 55).

is itself performative; it affects the positions that it claims to describe. Likewise, the Chan school existed as an institution, as a concretized *idéel* (see Godelier 1984) that had acquired an objective reality, but also as a fluid, subjective representation of specific individuals who attempted to define and *distinguish* themselves through their sectarian affiliation. It does not really matter whether these two aspects are chronological phases of the tradition or alternative logical (or illogical) positions of an individual. If Chan tradition can be defined, following Smith's terms, as a dialectical process of limitation (theological aspect) and inner differentiation (anthropological aspect), it is time for Chan scholarship, emulating this dialectic, to stress "anthropological" multiplicity, since earlier scholarship has tended to stress the "a/theological" unicity of Chan "classical" orthodoxy. Likewise, if the emphasis on hierarchy and diversity reflects the vision from below, it is perhaps time to look at Chan from the ground and to abandon the detached vision from the "top of the bamboo pole," a vision that remains the privilege of a few Chan acrobats. Or at least it is time to realize that in order to reach the top of this hundred-foot pole— let alone to jump from it—even "walkers of emptiness" such as the Arhat Piṇḍola need to acknowledge its existence. We have come to the point where both the rhetoric of immediacy and its accomplice, the rhetoric of mediation, having been displaced, fail. The leap may take place (or lose place) at the oscillating end of the pole or, as in Daoism (Schipper 1983: 186–191), at the moving core (the "square inch") or the fault of the polarized structure. The goal of this book was to elicit this structure and to (dis)locate its *point(s) de fuite. Hic saltus.*

Glossary

Akiba 秋葉
ako 下炬
ankotsu 安骨
An Lushan 安錄山
Anqing 安靜
An Shigao 安世高
Anzan Kichidō 案山吉道
arabuha kami (kōjin) 荒神
Ayuwang shan 阿育王山

Bai Juyi 白居易
Baizhang Huaihai 百丈懷海
Baogong 寶公
Baojing 寶鏡
baojuan 寶卷
Baolin 寶林
Baoqin 寶欽
Baosheng 寶生
Baotang 保唐
baotong 報通
Baozhi 寶誌
Bassui Tokushō 拔隊得勝
benjue 本覺
Benzaiten 辯才天
Beppō Daiju 別峰大殊
bianwen 變文
biguan 壁觀
Bishamon 毘沙門
bodaiji 菩提寺
bodaimon 菩提門
bonnō soku bodai 煩惱即菩提
bōsō 亡僧
Budai 布袋
Bukkai shōnin 佛海上人
buli wenzi 不立文字
butsuden 佛殿

Caodong 曹洞
Caoshan Benji 曹山本寂
Caoxi (var. Caoqi) 曹溪
Chajang 慈藏

Chan Daokai 單道開
Changbu panguan (Shōbō hangan) 掌簿判官
Changlu Zongze 長蘆宗賾
chanhui 懺悔
channa kuangjie 禪那拄解
chanshi 禪師
Chanyue dashi 禪月大師
Cheng Xuanying 成玄英
Chengguan 澄觀
chenghuang shen 城隍神
Chewu Jixing 徹悟際醒
chigo 稚兒
Chingam Hyeso 神鑑慧昭
chinju 鎮守
chinjusha 鎮守社
chinsō (var. chinzō) 頂相
Chinul 知訥
chishigo kirigami 知死期切紙
Chō Densu 兆殿司
Chōgen 重源
Chogye 曹溪
Chōnen 奝然
chongxuan 重玄
Chōōn Dōkai 潮音道開
chōri 長吏
chuandeng 傳燈
chūin 中陰
Chuji 處寂
Chujin 楚金
chūū 中有

dabi 茶毘
Dadian 大顛
Daer 大耳
Dahui Zonggao 大慧宗杲
Daidō Juen 大同壽圓
Daigenshuri 大權修利
daijinbutsu 代人物
Daijōji 大乘寺
Daikoku 大黑

daimyōjin 大明神
Dainichi Nōnin 大日能忍
daisan 大參
Daitokuji 大德寺
daitōryō 大棟梁
Damei Fachang 大梅法常
Damo 達摩
Damolun 達摩論
Danrin 檀林
Dantian 丹田
Danxia Tianran 丹霞天然
Daoan 道安
daochang 道場
Daoji 道濟
Daosui 道邃
daotong 道通
Daoxin 道信
Daoxuan 道宣
Daoxuan 道璿
Daoyu 道育
Daquan xiuli (*see* Daigenshuri)
Darumashū 達摩宗
dashou 大壽
dazhangfu 大丈夫
Dazhao 大照
Dazhi 大志
Dazhu Huihai 大珠慧海
Deshan Xuanjian 德山宣鑑
dian cao 顛草
dieryi di 第二義諦
Ding jushi 丁居士
diyiyi di 第一義諦
Dizang 地藏
dochidō fugin 土地堂諷經
Dōgen Kigen 道元希元
Dokuan Genkō 独庵玄光
Dōkyō 道鏡
Dong Fangshuo 東方朔
Dongjun 東曔
Dongshan famen 東山法門
Dongshan Liangjie 洞山良介
Dōryō 道了
Dōryō *gongen* 道了權現
Dōsen (*see* Daoxuan 2)
Dōshō 道照
Du Fei 杜朏
dun 頓

dunwu 頓悟
dunwu dunxiu 頓悟頓修
duotai fa 奪胎法
Du Zhenglun 杜正論

Eiheiji 永平寺
Eisai (*see* Yōsai)
ekō 廻向
Enchin 圓珍
engaku 圓覺
engaku 緣覺
Engakuji 圓覺寺
Enni Ben'en 圓爾弁圓
Ennin 圓仁
Enryakuji 延曆寺
ensō 圓相
Enzūin 圓通院

Fachi 法持
Fachong 法沖
fahua sanmei 法華三昧
Famen si 法門寺
Fangbian 方辯
fangbian 方便
Fang Guolong 方國龍
fangshi 方士
Faru 法如
Faxian 法顯
Faxiang 法相
Fayan Wen'yi 法眼文益
Fazang 法藏
Fazhao 法照
Fenggan 豐干
Fengxiang 鳳翔
Fen'yang Shanzhao 汾陽善昭
Fotudeng 佛圖澄
foxinzong 佛心宗
Foyin Liaoyuan 佛印了元
Fozhao 佛照
Fudaraku 補陀洛
Fu dashi 傅大士
Fugen Kōmyō 普賢光明
fugin 諷經
Fuke (*see* Puhua)
Fumon Mukan 普門無關
fusetsu (see *pushuo*)
Fu Xi 傅翕 (*see also* Fu dashi)

Fuyō Dōkai (Furong Daokai)
芙蓉道楷

gandō 龕堂
Ganjin 鑑眞
gantong 感通
ganying 感應
Ganying shizhe 感應使者
Ganzan *daishi* 元三大師
Gaoxian 昌黎
garandō 伽藍堂
garanjin (see *qielanshen*)
Gasan Jōseki 峨山紹(韶)碩
Gedatsu shōnin 解脫上人
Gennō Shinshō 源翁心昭
Genshin 源信
genze riyaku 現世利益
Gidō Shūshin 義堂周信
Gikai (*see* Tettsū Gikai)
Gishin 義眞
gohōjin 護法神
gongan (*kōan*) 公案
gongen 權顯
gorinnotō 五輪塔
Gorohō 五老峰
goroku (see *yulu*)
gozan 五山
Guan Di 關帝
Guangxiao si 光孝寺
guanxin 觀心
guanxin shi 觀心釋
Guanxiu 貫休
Guanyin 觀音
Guifeng Zongmi 圭峰宗密
Guishan Lingyou 潙山靈祐
Guiyangzong 潙仰宗
Gu Kaizhi 顧愷之
Gyōhyō 行表
gyōji 行事
gyōji 行持
Gyōki 行基

Haein-sa 海印寺
Hakuin Ekaku 白隱慧鶴
Hakusan (Shirayama) 白山
Hakusan Myōjin 白山明神

Hakusan myōri daigongen 白山妙理
大權顯
Hanlin 漢林
Hanshan 寒山
Hanshan Deqing 憨山德清
Han Yu 韓愈
hattō 法堂
Hehe 和和
Heze 荷澤
hijiri 聖
hinin 非人
hinko 秉炬
hiya 火屋
Hōnen 法然
hongaku (see *benjue*)
hongaku shisō 本覺思想
Hongbian 弘辯
Hongqian 紅倩
Hongren 弘忍
Hongzhi Zhengjue 宏智正覺
Hongzhou 洪州
honji suijaku 本地垂迹
hōshin 報身
hosshin 發心
hosshin 法身
hosshinmon 發心門
hossu 狒子
Hottō kokushi 法燈國師
huaben 話本
Huaisu 懷素
Huangbo Xiyun 黃檗希運
Huangmei shan 黃梅山
huangu fa 換骨法
Huatai 滑臺
huatou 話頭
Huayan 華嚴
Huian 慧安
Huichang 會昌
Huiguang 惠光
Huihong (*see* Juefan Huihong)
Huike 慧可
Huineng 慧能
Huixiu 慧秀
Huiyuan 慧遠
Huizhong 慧忠
Huode xingjun (Katoku shōkun)
huohe 合和

huo jushi 火居士
Hwaŏm (*see* Huayan)

Idaten 韋駄天 (*see* Weituo)
igan 移龕
igi soku buppō 威儀即佛法
ihai 位牌
ikigami 生神
Ikkei Eishū 一径永就
Ikkyū Sōjun 一休宗純
Inari 稻荷
indō 引導
inka 印可
ishin denshin (see *yixin chuanxin*)

jakugo 垂語
Jakushitsu 寂室
jian 漸
Jianqi shizhe 監齋使者
jianxing (*kenshō*) 見性
jiaochan yizhi 教禪一致
jiaowai biechuan 教外別傳
Jidian *dashi* 濟顛大師
Jigong 濟公
jiji rulü ling 唸々如律令
jinen gedō 自然外道
Jingjue 淨覺
Jingshan Faqin 徑山法欽
jingtu (Jōdo) 淨土
Jingzhong 淨眾
jinushi no kami 地主神
jinzū (see *shentong*)
jiriki 自力
jitengen 事點眼
Jitsuan Yūsan 實菴融參
Jiuhua shan 九華山
Jiuxian Yuxian 酒仙遇賢
Jixiangdan 吉祥旦
Jizō (*see* Dizang)
jōdō (see *shangtang*)
Jōjin 成尋
Jōkei 貞慶
Jōyō 上葉
jōza 上座
Juefan Huihong 覺範慧洪
jueguan 絕觀
Juehua *dashi* 覺化大師

junryō 巡寮
Juzhi (Gutei) 俱胝

kaigen 開眼
kaiguang 開光
kaimyō 戒名
kaisandō 開山堂
kaiyan 開眼
kaji 加持
Kakua 覺阿
Kakuban 覺鑁
Kamo daimyōjin 賀茂大明神
Kangiten 歡喜天
Kang Senghui 康僧會
kanhua chan 看話禪
kanjō 灌頂
kanna zen (see *kanhua chan*)
Kannon (*see* Guanyin)
kannō shisha (see Ganying shizhe)
Kanpō Shidon 乾峰士曇
kansai jisha (see Jianqi shizhe)
kanxin 看心
Kanzan Egen 關山慧玄
karagokoro 唐心
Karaten 迦羅天
kasō 火葬
kasshiki 喝食
Katoku shōkun 火德聖(星)君
kechimyaku (see *xuemo*)
Kegon (*see* Huayan)
Keikai 景戒
Keizan Jōkin 瑩山紹瑾
Kenchōji 建長寺
kenmitsu 顯密
Kenninji 建仁寺
keshin 掛眞
kessei ango 結制安居
kigan 起龕
Kim Dabei 金大悲
Kim *heshang* (*see also* Wuxiang) 金和尙
Kim Yusin 金庾信
kirigami 切紙
Kishimōjin 鬼子母神
kitō 祈禱
kitō jiin 祈禱寺院
kōan (see *gongan*)
Kōbō Daishi 弘法大師

Kōchi Hōin 弘智法印
Kōjin 荒神
Kokan Shiren 虎關師鍊
Kōshōji 興聖寺
Kōun Ejō 孤雲懷奘
Kōyasan 高野山
kuang 拄
kuangchan 拄禪
Kuangye shen 曠野禪
Kuangzhen *dashi* 匡眞大師
kuden 口傳
Kuiji (Cien) 慈恩窺基
Kūkai 空海
kū soku ze shiki 空即是色
kyōge betsuden (see *jiaowai biechuan*)
kyōzen itchi (see *jiaochan yizhi*)

Lan Can 嬾殘
Laozi 老子
Liang Wudi 梁武帝
Li Ao 李翱
Liaoran 了然
Li Daochun 李道純
Liezi 列子
Li Guangzhu 李廣珠
Li Hua 李華
Li Longmin 李龍眠
Li Mi 李泌
ling 靈
Lingmo 靈默
Lingtan 靈坦
ling'yan 靈驗
linian 離念
Linji (Rinzai) 臨濟
Linji Yixuan 臨濟義玄
liru 理入
lishi 理事
Liu Chongjin 劉崇景
Liu Junxi 劉君錫
Liu Mi 劉謐
Liu Qixiang 劉起相
Li Zhi 李贄
Longmen 龍門
Luofu shan 羅浮山
Luohan 羅漢

Malang fu 馬郎婦

Manzan Dōhaku 卍山道白
Mao shan 茅山
mappō 末法
Mawangdui 馬王堆
Mazu 媽祖
Mazu Daoyi 馬祖道一
Meihō Sotetsu 明峰祖哲
Menzan Zuihō 面山瑞方
Miaopu 妙普
Miaoshan 杳山
Miidera 三井寺
mijiao (mikkyō) 密教
Mile (Miroku) 彌勒
Minchō 明兆
Mingwu 明悟
Mingzan 明瓚
mogari 殯
Moheyan 摩訶衍
mokushō zen (see *mozhao chan*)
mondō (see *wenda*)
mozhao chan 默照禪
Mucha 木叉
muchū kenbutsu 夢中見佛
muchū mondō 夢中問答
muchū setsumu 夢中說夢
Mugaku Sogen (*see* Wuxue Zuyuan)
Muhon Kakushin 無本覺心
muhōtō 無縫塔
mui no shinnin 無位眞人
Mujaku Dōchū 無著道忠
Mujaku Myōyu 無著妙融
Mujū Ichien 無住一圓
Mulian 目蓮
Musang (*see* Wuxiang)
Musō Soseki 無窓疎石
mutsugo sasō 沒後作僧
Muyŏm 無染
Myōe 明惠
Myōkaku 妙覺
myōshin 妙心
Myōshinji 妙心寺
Myōshin *shōnin* 妙心上人
Myōzen 明全

Nacha 那吒
nanfeng 南風
Nanhua si 南華寺

Nanquan Puyuan 南泉普願
nanshoku 男色
Nan'yang Huizhong 南陽慧忠
Nan'yue Huairang 南岳懷讓
Nanzenji 南禪寺
nehanmon 涅槃門
neiguan 內觀
nianfo 念佛
Nichira 日羅
nikushinzō 肉身像
Niutou Farong 牛頭法融
Niutou shan 牛頭山
Nyorai-kyō 如來教
nyoshoku 女色
nyūgan 入龕
nyūjō 入定
nyūshitsu 入室

Ōbaku 黃檗
Ōbaku Kōsen 黃檗高泉
onmyōdō 陰陽道
onryō (var. *goryō*) 御靈

Pang Yun 龐蘊
Panshan Paoqi 盤山寶積
Pei Xiu 裴休
po 魄
Pŏpchŏng 法淨
Pozao Duo 破竈墮
Puan Yinsu 普庵印肅
Puhua 普化
Puji 普寂
pushuo 普說
Puxian (Fugen) 普賢
Puzhaowang 普照王

qielanshen 伽藍神
qinggui 清規
Qinghe 清豁
Qingyuan Xingsi 青原行思
Qinniang 琴娘
Qisong 契嵩

Rakan (*see* Luohan)
Rakanji 羅漢寺
Rankei Dōryū (Luanqi Daolong)
    蘭溪道隆

rantō 卵塔
reiken (see *ling'yan*)
reizō 靈像
Renhua 任華
Renjian 仁儉
renyun 任運
rikaigen 理開眼
Rinken 琳賢
Rinzai (*see* Linji)
risshun daikichi 立春大吉
Rizhao 日照
Rokkakudō 六角堂
rokudō 六道
roushen 肉身
Rujing 如淨
rulai chan 如來禪
Ryōan Emyō 了庵慧明
Ryōgen 艮源
Ryōgon-e 楞嚴會
Ryōgon-ju 楞嚴呪
Ryōkan 艮寬

sagan 鎖龕
Saichō 最澄
Saigyō 西行
Saijōji 最乘寺
Sampŏp 三法
sanbō 三寶
Sanbōji 三寶寺
Sanbō Kōjin 三寶荒神
sanjiao yizhi 三教一致
sankyō itchi (see *sanjiao yizhi*)
sanmon 三門
sanpai 三牌
sanzen 參禪
Seimen jisha 青面使者
Seiryōji 清涼寺
Sengcan 僧璨
Sengchou 僧稠
Senglang 僧郎
Sengqie 僧伽
Sengzhao 僧肇
Sennyūji 泉涌寺
sesshin 攝心
sesshō seki 殺生石
shangtang 上堂
Shanmiao (Zenmyō) 善妙
Shanxin 善心

shan'you 善友
Shaolin si 少林寺
Shaozhou 韶州
shari 舍利
shen 神
Shenhui 神會
Shennong 神農
shenseng 神僧
shentong 神通
Shenxiu 神秀
shenyi 神異
shenzuo 神座
shexin 捨身
shi 事
Shide 拾得
Shidō Bunan 至道無難
shihonbata 四本幡
shijie 尸解
shikan taza 祇管打坐
shiki soku ze kū 色即是空
shimon 四門
shin (zhen) 眞
Shinchi Kakushin 心地覺心
shingi (see qinggui)
shinkoku 神國
shinkotsu 眞骨
shinnin kedō 神人化道
Shinra Myōjin 新羅明神
Shinran 親鸞
Shinshū Gyōjun 心宗行順
shisho 嗣書
Shitou Xiqian 石頭希遷
shitsunai 室內
shizi kong (J. shishiku) 獅子吼
Shōbōji 正法寺
Shōgen 昭元
Shōhō shichirō 招寶七郎
shōji soku nehan 生死即涅槃
Shōjō 證定
Shōkokuji 相國寺
Shōten 聖天
Shōtoku taishi 聖德太子
shouxiang 壽像
Shucao 束草
shūdō 衆道
shūdō girei 修道儀礼
Shūgendō 修驗道
shūgyōmon 修行門

Shunjō 俊芿
Shun'oku Myōha 春屋妙葩
shūshō ittō 修證一等
Sizhou 泗州
sōhei 僧兵
Sōjiji 総持寺
sōkō fugin 竈公
sokushinbutsu 即身佛
sokushin jōbutsu 即身成佛
sokushin ze butsu 即心是佛
Song shan 嵩山
Sonin 祖忍
sonshuku 尊宿
Sōtō (see Caodong)
Ssanggye-sa 雙溪寺
Su Dongpo 蘇東坡
Sugawara Michizane 菅原道眞
Suiwei Wuxue 翠微無覺
Sumiyoshi Myōjin 住吉明神
Sun Wukong 孫悟空
Suzuki Bokushi 鈴木牧之
Suzuki Shōsan 鈴木正三

Taigen Sōshin 太源宗眞
tairyō shōsan 對靈小參
Tamonten 多門天
Tang He 唐和
Tanjō Myōjin 丹生明神
Tao Hongjing 陶弘景
tariki 他力
tatchū 塔頭
tencha 奠茶
tengai 天蓋
tengen 點眼
Tengteng 騰騰
Tenkei Denson 天桂傳尊
Tenman daijizai tenjin 天滿大自在
  天神
tenrinnō 轉龍王
Tenryūji 天龍寺
tentō 奠湯
tera koshō 寺小姓
Tetsugen 鉄眼
Tettsū Gikai 徹通義介
ti 體
Tianmu shan 天目山
Tiantai 天台
Tiantong shan 天童山

tiyong 體用
Toba Sōjō 鳥羽僧正
Tōdaiji 東大寺
Tōfukuji 東福寺
Tōjiin 等持院
Tōkoku 洞谷
Tominaga Nakamoto 富永仲基
T'ongdo-sa 通度寺
Tōnomine 多武峰
Tōrei Enji 東嶺圓慈
Tō Tō Tenjin 渡唐天神
Toŭi 道義
Tsūgen Jakurei 通幻寂靈
tsuno daishi 角大師

Ŭich'on 義天
Ŭisang 義湘
ujiko 氏子
Ungai Tōjiku 雲外東竺
unsui 雲水
unyō sansō 右遶三匝

Wang Bi 王弼
Wang Wei 王維
wangxiang 忘想
Wang Yangming 王陽明
Wanhui 邁廻
Wei Gao 韋皋
Weiguan 韋貫
Wei Qu 韋璩
Weituo 韋馱
Wenshu (Monju) 文殊
wenda (see *mondō*)
Wŏnhyo 元曉
Wujie 五戒
Wuliao 無了
Wumen Huikai 無門慧開
Wuming 無名
wunian 無念
wusheng 無生
Wutai shan 五臺山
Wuxiang 無相
wuxiang 無相
wuxiangjie 無相戒
wuxin 無心
Wuxue Zuyuan 無學祖元
wuyi 無意

Wuzhu 無住
Wuzhun Shifan 無準師範

xiang 相
Xiangmo Zang 降魔藏
Xiang'yan Zhixian 香嚴智閑
Xianhua 顯化
xingru 行入
Xingtao (var. Lingtao) 行(令)韜
Xiong'er shan 熊耳山
Xiwangmu 西王母
Xuanzang 玄奘
Xuanze 玄賾
Xuanzong 玄宗
Xuefeng Yicun 雪峰義存
xuemo 血脈
Xuyun (Xu Yun) 虛雲

Yakushi 藥師
yang 佯
Yangshan Huiji 仰山慧寂
Yanguan Qian 塩官濟安
yaotong 妖通
Yifu 義福
yijia 逸家
Yijing 義淨
yijing 易經
Yikong (Gikū) 義空
yingtang 影堂
yinxin 印心
yitong 依通
yixin chuanxin 以心傳心
Yixing 一行
yixing sanmei 一行三昧
yixin sanguan 一心三觀
Yōkōji 永光寺
yong 用
Yongjia Xuanjue 永嘉玄覺
Yongming Yanshou 永明延壽
Yongning si 永寧寺
Yōsai (Eisai) 榮西
youlanpen 盂蘭盆
youxiang 有相
Yuancai 元甹
Yuan *chanshi* 遠禪師
Yuangui 元珪
Yuanwu Keqin 圜悟克勤

Yuanzhao 圓紹
Yueshan Weiyan 藥山惟儼
yuige 遺偈
yulu 語錄
yume no ki 夢記
Yunmen Wen'yan 雲門文偃
Yun'yan Tansheng 雲巖曇晟
Yuquan si 玉泉寺

Zanning 贊寧
zansheng 散聖
Zhang Baiduan 張伯端
Zhang dadi (Chō daitei) 張大帝
Zhang Jingman 張淨滿
Zhang Xu 張旭
Zhanran 湛然
Zhaobao qilang (*see* Shōhō shichirō)
Zhaobao shan 招寶山
Zhaozhou Congshen 趙州從諗
Zhenjing 眞淨
zhenru 眞如

Zhen'yan (Shingon) 眞言
Zhiduan 志端
Zhifeng 志逢
Zhigong 誌公
zhiguan 止觀
Zhikong 志空
Zhishen 智詵
Zhixu 智旭
Zhiyi 智顗
Zhongfeng Mingben 中峰明本
Zhuangzi 莊子
Zhuhong 袾宏
Zhuoan Deguang 拙庵德光
Zhu Tanyou 竺曇猷
Zhu Xi 朱熹
ziran 自然
Zōga 增賀
Zuigon 瑞巖
zuochan (*zazen*) 坐禪
zuojia 作家
Zuoqiao 鑿竅

Bibliography

PRIMARY SOURCES

Abhidharmakośa-śāstra, by Vasubandhu. *T.* 29, 1558. Trans. Louis de la Vallée Poussin, *L'Abhidharmakośa de Vasubandhu.* 6 vols. Brussels: Institut Belge des Hautes Etudes Chinoises, 1971. (*Mélanges chinois et bouddhiques*, vol. 16)

Anityatā-sūtra. See *Wuchang jing.*

Avataṃsaka-sūtra. See *Da fangguang fo huayan jing.*

Ayuwang zhuan 阿育王傳 (*Aśokarājāvadāna*). Trans. An. Faqin 安法欽. *T.* 50, 2042.

Baolin zhuan 寶林傳. In Yanagida Seizan, ed., *Sōzō ichin Hōrinden, Dentō gyokuei shū* 宋藏遺珍寶林傳, 傳燈玉英集. Kyoto: Chūbun shuppansha, 1975.

Baozang lun 寶藏論. Attr. to Sengzhao 僧肇 (384–414). *T.* 45, 1857.

Beishan lu 北山錄, by Shenqing 神清 (fl. 8th c.). *T.* 52, 2113.

Bintui lu 賓退錄, by Zhao Yushi 趙與昔 (1175–1231). *Congshu jicheng* ed. Shanghai: Commercial Press, 1936.

Biyan lu 碧巖錄, by Xuetou Chongxian 雪竇重顯 (980–1052); commentary by Yuanwu Keqin 圓悟克勤 (1063–1135). *T.* 48, 2003.

Butsuga shari ki 佛牙舍利記. *Gunsho ruijū*, 19, 443: 286.

Caoshan lu 曹山錄 [full title: *Fuzhou Caoshan Yuanzheng chanshi yulu* 撫州曹山元證禪師語錄]. *T.* 47, 1987a.

Chang ahan jing 長阿含經 [*Dīrghāgama*]. Trans. Buddhayaśas and Zhu Fonian 竺佛念 (fl. ca. 365). *T.* 1, 1.

Changuan cejin 禪關策進 [1600], by Zhuhong 袾宏 (1535–1615). *T.* 48, 2024.

Chanhai shizhen 禪海十珍 [1685]. *ZZ* 1, 2, 31. (Taibei ed., vol. 112)

Chanjia guijian 禪家龜鑑, by Qingxu Xiujing 清虛休靜 (n.d.). *ZZ* 1, 2, 17. (Taibei ed., vol. 112)

Chanlin baoxun 禪林寶訓, by Jingshan 淨善 (fl. 1174–1189). *T.* 48, 2022.

Chanlin sengbao zhuan 禪林僧寶傳, by Juefan Huihong 覺範慧洪 (1071–1128). *ZZ* 1, 2B, 10, 3. (Taibei ed., vol. 137)

Chanmen baozang lu 禪門寶藏錄 [1293]. *ZZ* 1, 2, 18. (Taibei ed., vol. 113)

Chanmen jing 禪門經. Apocryphon. In Suzuki Daisetsu [D. T.], *Suzuki Daisetsu zenshū* 鈴木大拙全集. Vol. 3. Tokyo: Iwanami shoten, 1980 [1968].

Chanmen juzushi jiesong 禪門諸祖師偈頌. *ZZ* 1, 2, 21. (Taibei ed., vol. 116)

Chanmen shizi chengxi tu 禪門師資承襲圖, by Guifei Zongmi 圭峰宗密 (780–841). *ZZ* 1, 2, 15. (Taibei ed., vol. 110)

Chanxue dacheng 禪學大成. Ed. Xieguan Shengti 謝冠生題. 6 vols. Taibei: Zhonghua fojiao wenhua guan, 1969.

Chanyuan qinggui 禪苑清規, by Changlu Zongze 長蘆宗賾. *ZZ* 1, 2, 16, 5. (Taibei ed., vol. 111) See also Kagamishima Genryū 鏡島元隆, Satō Tatsugen 佐藤達玄, and Kosaka Kiyū 小坂機融, eds., *Yakuchū Zen'en shingi* 訳註禪苑清規. Tokyo: Sōtōshū shūmuchō, 1972.

Chanyuan zhuquanji duxu 禪源諸詮集都序, by Guifei Zongmi. *T.* 48, 2015.

Chanzong zhengmo 禪宗正脉 [1489]. *ZZ* 1, 2B, 19. (Taibei ed., vol. 146)

Chewu chanshi yulu 徹悟禪師語錄. *ZZ* 1, 2, 14, 4. (Taibei ed., vol. 109)

Chixiu Baizhang qinggui 勅修百丈清規, by Dong'yang Dehui 東陽德輝 (d.u.). *T.* 48, 2025.

Chodang chip. See. Zutang ji.

Chuan fabao ji 傳法寶紀, by Du Fei 杜朏 (n.d.). In Yanagida Seizan, ed., *Shoki no zenshi 1*. Tokyo: Chikuma shobō, 1971.

Chuanfa zhengzong ji 傳法正宗記, by Qisong 契嵩 (1007–1072). *T.* 51, 2078.

Chuanxin fayao 傳心法要, by Huangbo Xiyun 黃檗希運 (n.d.). Comp. Pei Xiu 裴休 (797–870). *T.* 47, 2012a and Iriya 1969. See also *Chuanxin fayao* ed. Taibei: Fojiao chubanshe, 1976.

Conglin gonglun 叢林公論 [1189], by Zhean Huibin 者庵惠彬. *ZZ* 1, 2, 18. (Taibei ed., vol. 113)

Conglin liangxu xuzhi 叢林兩序須知 [ca. 1639]. *ZZ* 1, 2, 17. (Taibei ed., vol. 112)

Congrong lu 從容錄, by Wangsong Xingxiu 萬松行秀 (1166–1246). *T.* 48, 2004.

Da banruo boluomiduo jing 大般若波羅密多經. Trans. Xuanzang 玄奘 (596–664). *T.* 7, 220.

Da fangguang fo huayan jing 大方廣佛華嚴經 [*Avataṃsaka-sūtra*]. Trans. Buddhabhadra (359–429): *T.* 9, 278; trans. Śikṣānanda (652–710): *T.* 10, 279.

Da fangguang fo huayan jing suizhou yanyi chao 大方廣佛華嚴經隋疏演義鈔, by Chengguan 澄觀 (736–839). *T.* 36, 1736.

Dahui Pujue chanshi yulu 大慧普覺禪師語錄. *T.* 47, 1998a.

Dahui Pujue chanshi zongmen wuku 大慧普覺禪師宗門武庫. *T.* 47, 1998b.

Dahui shuwen 大慧書問. In Araki Kengo, ed., *Daie sho*. Tokyo: Chikuma shobō, 1969.

Da Ming gaoseng zhuan 大明高僧傳, by Ruxing 如惺 (fl. ca. 1671). *T.* 50, 2062.

Damo dashi wuxing lun 達摩大師悟性論. Attr. to Bodhidharma. *ZZ* 1, 2, 15, 5. (Taibei ed., vol. 110)

Damo dashi xuemo lun 達摩大師血脈論. Attr. to Bodhidharma. *ZZ* 1, 2, 15, 5. (Taibei ed., vol. 110)

Daoxuan lüshi gantong lu 道宣律師感通錄, by Daoxuan 道宣 (596–667). *T.* 52, 2107.

Dapiposha lun 大毘婆沙論 [*Mahāvibhāṣā*]. Trans. Xuanzang. *T.* 27, 1545.

Dasheng beizong lun 大乘北宗論. Anon. *T.* 85, 2836.

Dasheng qixin lun 大乘起信論. Apocryphon. *T.* 32, 1666.

Dasheng wusheng fangbian men 大乘無生方便門. *T.* 85, 2834.

Da Song sengshi lüe 大宋僧史略 [977], by Zanning 贊寧 (919–1001). *T.* 54, 2126.

Da Tang Zhongyue dong Xianjusi gu dade Gui heshang ji dechuang 大唐中嶽東閑居寺故大德珪和尚紀德幢. In *Baqiongshi jinshi buzheng* 八瓊室金石補正 53: 7. *SKSLXB* ed., vol. 7: 4849a–4850b.

Dazhao chanshi taming 大照禪師塔銘, by Li Yong 李邕 (d. 747). *QTW* 262, 6: 3360–3363.

Dazhi chanshi beiming bingxu 大智禪師碑銘并序, by Yan Tingzhi 嚴挺之 (673–742). *QTW* 280, 6: 3596–3598.

Dazhidulun 大智度論. Attr. to Nāgārjuna. Trans. Kumārajīva. *T.* 25, 1509.

Denkōroku 傳光錄, by Keizan Jōkin 瑩山紹瑾 (1268–1325). *T.* 82, 2585. In Tajima Hakudō, ed., *Keizan.* Tokyo: Kōdansha, 1978.

Dīrghāgama. See *Chang ahan jing.*

Dongjing menghua lu 東京夢華錄, by Meng Yuanlao 孟元老 (n.d.). Ed. Iriya Yoshitaka and Umehara Kaoru, *Tōkei mukaroku: Sōdai no tōshi to seikatsu.* Tokyo: Iwanami shoten, 1983.

Dongshan lu 洞山錄 [*Dongshan Liangjie chanshi yulu* 洞山良介禪師語錄]. *T.* 47, 1986a.

Dunwu rudao yaomen lun 頓悟入道要門論, by Dazhu Huihai 大珠慧海 (n.d.). *zz* 1, 2, 15, 5. (Taibei ed., vol. 110). See also Hirano Sōjō, ed., *Tongo yōmon.* Tokyo: Chikuma shobō, 1970.

Eihei shingi 永平清規, by Dōgen. *T.* 82, 2584.

Eihei Shōbōgenzō senbyō 永平正法眼藏借評, by Mujaku Dōchū 無著道忠 (1653–1744). In Kagamishima Genryū, ed., *Dōgen zenji to sono monryū*, 225–289. Tokyo: Seishin shobō, 1961.

Enpō dentōroku 延寶傳燈錄, by Shiban 師蛮 (1627–1710). *DNBZ* 69–70, 534. (1931 ed., vol. 108)

Enzan Bassui oshō goroku 鹽山拔隊和尚語錄, by Bassui Tokushō (1327–1387). *T.* 80, 2558.

Erru sixing lun 二入四行論. Attr. to Bodhidharma. In Yanagida Seizan, ed., *Daruma no goroku: Ninyū shigyō ron.* Zen no goroku 1. Tokyo: Chikuma shobō, 1969(a).

Fayan Wen'yi chanshi yulu 法眼文益禪師語錄. *T.* 47, 1991.

Fayuan zhulin 法苑珠林 [668], by Daoshi 道世. *T.* 53, 2122.

Fen'yang Shanzhao chanshi yulu 汾陽善昭禪師語錄. *T.* 47, 1992.

Foguo Yuanwu chanshi xinyao 佛果圜悟禪師心要. *zz* 1, 2, 25. (Taibei ed., vol. 120)

Fojian chanshi yulu 佛鑑禪師語錄. *zz* 1, 2, 26. (Taibei ed., vol. 121)

Foying ming 佛影銘, by Huiyuan 慧遠 (334–416). In *Guang hongming ji.* *T.* 52, 2103: 197c.

Fozu guangmu 佛祖綱目 [1631], by Zhu Shiyuan 朱時恩. *zz* 1, 2B, 20. (Taibei ed., vol. 146)

Fozu lidai tongzai 佛祖歷代通載 [1344], by Meiwu Nianchang 梅屋念常 (1282–?). *T.* 49, 2036.

Fozu tongji 佛祖統記, by Zhipan 志盤 (fl. 1258–1269). *T.* 49, 2035.

Fu fazang yin'yuan zhuan 付法藏因緣傳. *T.* 50, 2058.

Fujiaobian 輔教編, by Qisong. In Araki Kengo, ed., *Hokyōhen.* Tokyo: Chikuma shobō, 1981.

Fukan zazengi 普勸坐禪儀, by Dōgen. *T.* 82, 2580.

Fusō zenrin sōbōden 扶桑禪林僧寶傳, by Shōton Kōsen (1630–1692). *DNBZ* 70, 535. (1931 ed., vol. 109)

Gakudō yōjinshū 學道用心集, by Dōgen. *T.* 82, 2581.

Gaoseng Faxian zhuan 高僧法顯傳. *T.* 51, 2085.

Gaoseng zheyao 高僧摘要 [ca. 1654], by Xu Changzhi 徐昌治. *zz* 1, 2B, 21. (Taibei ed., vol. 148)

Gaoseng zhuan 高僧傳, by Huijiao 慧皎 (497–554). *T.* 50, 2059.

Genkō shakusho 元享釋書 [1322], by Kokan Shiren 虎關師鍊 (1278–1346). *DNBZ* 62, 470. (1931 ed., vol. 101)

Goke sanshō yōromon 五家參祥要門, by Tōrei Enji 東嶺圓慈 (1723–1794). *T.* 81, 2576.

Guang hongming ji 廣弘明集, by Daoxuan. *T.* 52, 2103.

Guangxiao si yifa taji 光孝寺瘞髮塔記, by Fazai 法才 (n.d.). *QTW* 912, 19: 11996.

Guanxin lun 觀心論 [*Poxiang lun* 破相論], by Shenxiu 神秀 (606–706). *T.* 85, 2833.

Guishan Ling'you chanshi yulu 溈山靈祐禪師語錄. *T.* 47, 1989.

Gunsho ruijū 羣書類從. Comp. Hanawa Hokiichi 川俣馨一 (1779–1819). Shinkō gunsho ruijū. 24 vols. Tokyo: Naigai shoseki, 1937.

Guzunsu yulu 古尊宿語錄 [1403], by Yi Zangzhu 頤藏主. *ZZ* 1, 2, 23. (Taibei ed., vol. 118)

Hanshan dashi meng'yu quanji 憨山大師夢遊全集. *ZZ* 1, 2, 32. (Taibei ed., vol. 127)

Hekizan nichiroku 碧山日錄, by Unsen Taikyoku 雲泉太極 (1421–1472?). Ed. Tsunoda Bun'ei 角田文衛 and Gorai Shigeru 五來重. In Shintei zōho shiseki shūran kankōkai, ed., *Shintei zōho shiseki shūran* 新訂增補史籍集覽. Vol. 26: 235–448. Kyoto: Rinsen shoten, 1927.

Hokuetsu seppū 北越雪譜, by Suzuki Bokushi 鈴木牧之. Ed. Okada Takematsu 岡田武松. Tokyo: Iwanami shoten, 1987 [1936].

Honchō kōsōden 本朝高僧傳, by Shiban 師蛮. *DNBZ* 63, 472. (1931 ed., vols. 102–103)

Honchō sōbōden 本朝僧寶傳. Anon. *DNBZ* 69, 533. (1931 ed., vol. 111)

Hongjie fayi 弘戒法儀 [1613], by Fazang 法藏 (fl. Ming). *ZZ* 1, 2, 11. (Taibei ed., vol. 106)

Hongzhi chanshi guanglu 宏智禪師廣錄. *T.* 48, 2001.

Hōonhen 報恩編, by Tenkei Denson 天桂傳尊 (1648–1735). *T.* 82, 2600.

Hottō Enmyō kokushi yuihō roku 法燈圓明國師遺芳錄. *DNBZ* 47, 298. (1931 ed., vol. 96)

Huanzhu'an qinggui 幻住庵清規 (1317), by Zhongfeng Mingben 中峯明本 (1263–1323). *ZZ* 1, 2, 16, 5. (Taibei ed., vol. 111)

Hyakurenshō 百練抄. In *Shintei zōho kokushi taikei* 新訂增補國史大系. Ed. Kuroita Katsumi. Vol. 11. Tokyo: Yoshikawa Kōbunkan, 1929.

Inryōken nichiroku 蔭涼軒日錄, by Kikei Shinzui 季瓊眞蘂 et al. *DNBZ* 75–78, 596. (1931 ed., vols. 133–137). See also Tamamura Takeji 玉村竹二 and Katsuno Ryūshin 勝野隆信, eds., *Inryōken nichiroku*. Tokyo: Shiseki kankōkai, 1954.

Jianzhong jingguo xudeng lu 建中靖國續燈錄. *ZZ* 1, 2B, 9. (Taibei ed., vol. 136)

Jiatai pudeng lu 嘉泰普燈錄, by Zhengshou 正受. *ZZ* 1, 2B, 10, 1–2. (Taibei ed., vol. 137)

Jingang banruo boluomi jing 金剛般若波羅密經 [*Vajracchedikā*]. Trans. Kumārajīva. *T.* 8, 235.

Jingang sanmei jing 金剛三昧經. Apocryphon. *T.* 9, 273.

Jingde chuandeng lu 景德傳燈錄 [1004], by Daoyuan 道原 (n.d.). *T.* 51, 2076.

Jinshi cuibian 金石萃編 [1805]. Comp. Wang Chang 王昶 (1725–1807). 4 vols. Taibei: Tailian guofeng chubanshe, 1964.

Jishō ki 自證記, by Shidō Bunan 至道無難 (1603–1676). In Kōda Rentarō, ed., *Shidō Bunan zenji shū* 至道無難禅師集. Tokyo: Shunjūsha, 1956.

Jiu Tang shu 舊唐書 [compl. 945]. Attr. to Liu Xu 劉昫 (887–946). 16 vols. Beijing: Zhonghua shuju, 1975.

Jōtō shōgakuron 成等正覺論. In Shinagawa Kenritsu Kanazawa Bunko, ed., *Kanazawa bunko shiryō zensho: Butten I, Zensekihen.* Yokohama: Kanazawa Bunko, 1974.

Jueguan lun 絕觀論. In Suzuki Daisetsu [D. T.], *Suzuki Daisetsu zenshū.* Vol. 2. Tokyo: Iwanami shoten, 1980 [1968].

Jūroku Rakan genzuiki 十六羅漢現瑞記 [1249], by Dōgen. *DZZ* 2: 399.

Kakuzen shō 覺禪鈔, by Kakuzen. *DNBZ* 53–56, 431 (1931 ed., vols. 45–51); *T.* 89–90, 3022.

Keiran shūyō shū 溪嵐拾葉集, by Kōshū 光宗 (1276–1350). *T.* 76, 2410.

Keizan shingi 瑩山清規 [*Tōkoku shingi* 洞谷清規], by Keizan Jōkin (1268–1325). *T.* 82, 2589.

Kenzei ki 建撕記 [ca. 1472], by Kenzei (n.d.). *DNBZ* 73, 587. (1931 ed., vol. 115)

Kinben shigai 金鞭指街, by Mujaku Dōchū. Unpublished ms. Library of the Zen bunka kenkyūsho, Hanazono College, Kyoto.

Koji ruien: Fukyūhan. Shūkyōbu 古事類苑普及版宗教部. 4 vols. Tokyo: Yoshikawa kōbunkan, 1977.

Kōzen gokoku ron 興禪護國論, by Yōsai 榮西 (1141–1215). *T.* 80, 2543.

Kyōun shū 狂雲集, by Ikkyū Sōjun 一休宗純 (1394–1481). In Yanagida Seizan, ed., *Ikkyū. Ryōkan.* Tokyo: Chūōkōron, 1987.

Laozi 老子. Ed. Sibu congkan 四部叢刊. Shanghai: Shangwu yinshuguan, 1937–1938.

Lengqie shizi ji 楞伽師資記, by Jingjue 淨覺 (683–ca. 750). *T.* 85, 2837.

Liandeng huiyao 聯燈會要 [1183], by Wuming 悟明. *ZZ* 1, 2B, 9, 3–5. (Taibei ed., vol. 136)

Liaoyuan ge 了元歌. Attr. to Renjian 仁儉 (n.d.). In *Jingde chuandeng lu* 30. *T.* 51, 2076.

Lidai fabao ji 歷代法寶記 [ca. 774]. Anon. *T.* 51, 2075.

Lidai shenxian tongjian 歷代神仙通鑑. Comp. Xu Dao 徐道. Taibei: Guangwen, 1975.

Liezi 列子. Ed. Sibu beiyao. Taibei: Zhonghua shuju, 1974.

Linjian lu 林間錄, by Juefan Huihong. *ZZ* 1, 2B, 21, 4. (Taibei ed., vol. 148)

Linji lu 臨濟錄 [*Zhenzhou Linji Huizhao chanshi yulu* 鎮州臨齊慧照禪師語錄]. *T.* 47, 1985. See Ruth Fuller Sasaki, trans., *The Recorded Sayings of Ch'an Master Lin-chi Hui-chao of Chen Prefecture.* Kyoto: The Institute for Zen Studies, 1975.

Lishi zhenxian tidao tongjian 歷世眞仙體道通鑑, by Zhao Daoyi 趙道一. *DZ* 139–148.

Liuzu dashi fabao tanjing 六祖大師法寶壇經. Attr. to Huineng 慧能 (d. 713). *T.* 48, 2008.

Lohu yelu 羅湖野錄 [1155], by Xiaoying 曉瑩. *ZZ* 1, 2B, 15, 5. (Taibei ed., vol. 142)

Lun fogu biao 論佛骨表 [819], by Han Yu 韓愈 (768–824). *Jiu Tang shu* 160; *Tang huiyao* 47.

Lun'yu 論語, by Kongzi [Confucius]. In *Harvard-Yenching Institute Sinological Series*. Supplement no. 16: *A Concordance to the Analects of Confucius*. Reprint. Taibei: Chinese Materials and Research Aids Service Center, 1972 [1966].

Madhyamakakārikā. See *Zhonglun*.

Mahāprajñāpāramitā-sūtra. See *Da banruo boluomiduo jing*.

Mahāvibhāṣā. See *Dapiposha lun*.

Mazu Daoyi chanshi guanglu 馬祖道一禪師廣錄. *ZZ* 1, 2, 24, 5. (Taibei ed., vol. 119)

Mengqi bitan 夢溪筆談, by Shen Gua 沈括 (1031–1095). Ed. Umehara Kaoru 梅原郁, *Mukei hitsudan*. 3 vols. Tokyo: Heibonsha, 1978–1981.

Miaofa lianhua jing 妙法蓮華經 [*Saddharmapuṇḍarīka-sūtra*]. Trans. Kumārajīva. *T.* 9, 262.

Mohe banruo boluomi jing 摩訶般若波羅密經 [*Pañcaviṃśatisāhasrikā-pāramitā*]. Trans. Kumārajīva. *T.* 8, 223.

Mohezhiguan 摩訶止觀, by Zhiyi 智顗 (538–597). *T.* 46, 1911.

Muchū mondō 夢中問答, by Musō Soseki 夢窻疎石 (1275–1351). Ed. Satō Taishun. Tokyo: Iwanami shoten, 1974 [1934].

Murōzan onshari sōden engi 室生山御舍利相傳緣起. *Zoku gunsho ruijū*, 27(b) 800.

Nanhai jigui neifa zhuan 南海寄歸內法傳 [691], by Yijing (635–713). *T.* 54, 2125.

Nan'yang Huizhong yulu 南陽慧忠語錄. In Ui Hakuju, ed., *Daini zenshūshi kenkyū*. Tokyo: Iwanami shoten, 1966(b).

Nanzong ding shifei lun 南宗定是非論, by Dugu Pei 獨孤沛. *T.* 85, Annex. Also in Hu Shi, ed., *Shenhui heshang yiji*. Taibei: Hu Shi jinianguan, 1970 [1930].

Nichiiki Sōtō shitsunai tekiteki hitsuden mippō kirigami 日域曹洞室內嫡々秘傳密法切紙. *SZ* 18, *Shūi*.

Nichiiki Tōjō shosoden 日域洞上諸祖傳, by Tangen Jishō 湛元自澄. *DNBZ* 70, 537. (1931 ed., vol. 110)

Nihon Tōjō rentōroku 日本洞上聯燈錄, by Shūnyo 秀恕 (n.d.). *DNBZ* 70–71, 540. (1931 ed., vol. 110)

Nittō guhō junrei kōki 入唐求法巡禮行記, by Ennin 圓仁 (794–864). *DNBZ* 72, 563. (1931 ed., vol. 115). See also Edwin O. Reischauer, trans. *Ennin's Diary: The Record of a Pilgrimage to China in Search of the Law*. New York: Reginald Press, 1955(a); and Shioiri Ryōdō, ed., *Nittō guhō junrei kōki*. 2 vols. Tokyo: Heibonsha, 1970 and 1985.

Nomori kagami 野守鏡. *Gunsho ruijū*, 21, 484.

Nyorai hashari denrai 如來齒舍利傳來. Anon. *DNBZ* 65, 497. (1931 eds., vol 111). See also *Zoku gunsho ruijū*, 25(b), 710.

Ōbaku shingi 黃檗清規, by Ingen Ryūki (Yin'yuan Longqi 隱元隆琦, 1592–1673). *T.* 82, 2607.

Pañcaviṃśatisāhasrikā-pāramitā. See *Mohe banruo boluomi jing*.

Pang jushi yulu 龐居士語錄. *ZZ* 1, 2B, 25, 1. (Taibei ed., vol. 120). See Ruth Fuller Sasaki et al., trans., *A Man of Zen: The Recorded Sayings of Layman P'ang*. New York: Weatherhill, 1971.

Puan Yinsu chanshi yulu 普菴禪師語錄. *ZZ* 1, 2, 25, 3. (Taibei ed., vol. 120)

Pusa chutai jing 菩薩處胎經. Trans. Zhu Fonian. *T.* 12, 384.

Rakan kōshiki 羅漢講式. Anon. *T.* 84, 2731.

Rakan kuyō shikimon 羅漢供養式文, by Dōgen. *DZZ* 2: 402–404.

Rentian baojian 人天寶鑑 [1230], by Chizhao 智昭. *ZZ* 1, 2B, 21. (Taibei ed., vol. 113)

Rōankyō 驢鞍橋, by Suzuki Shōsan 鈴木正三 (1579–1655). Ed. Suzuki Daisetsu. Tokyo: Iwanami shoten, 1977.

Rujing heshang yulu 如淨和尙語錄. *T.* 48, 2002a.

Ru Lengqie jing 入楞伽經 *Laṅkāvatāra-sūtra.* Trans. Bodhiruci. *T.* 16, 671.

Ruzhong riyong 入衆日用, by Wuliang Zongshou 無量宗壽 (n.d.). *ZZ* 1, 2, 16, 5. (Taibei ed., vol. 111)

Saddharmapuṇḍarīka-sūtra. See *Miaofa lianhua jing.*

Samguk yusa 三國遺事, by Ilyŏn 一然. *T.* 49, 2039.

Sanjiao pingxin lun 三教平心論, by Liu Mi 劉謐 (fl. Southern Song). *T.* 52, 2117.

San Tendai Godaisan ki 參天台五臺山記, by Jōjin 成尋 (1011–1081). *DNBZ* 72, 577. (1931 ed., vol. 115)

Sennyūji Fukaki hōshi den 泉涌寺不可棄法師傳, by Shinzui 信瑞 (d. 1279). *DNBZ* 72, 557. (1931 ed., vol. 115)

Shan'an zalu 山庵雜錄 [1375], by Wuwen 無溫. *ZZ* 1, 2B, 21. (Taibei ed., vol. 148)

Shanhui dashi yulu 善慧大師語錄. *ZZ* 1, 2, 25, 1. (Taibei ed., vol. 120)

Shaolin si bei 少林寺碑. *QTW* 279, 6: 3584–3587.

Shasekishū 沙石集, by Mujū Ichien 無住一圓 (1226–1312). Ed. Watanabe Tsunaya. Tokyo: Iwanami shoten, 1975 [1966].

Shenseng zhuan 神僧傳. Anon. *T.* 50, 2064.

Shimen zhengtong 釋門正統 [1237], by Zongjian 宗鑑. *ZZ* 1, 2B, 3, 5. (Taibei ed., vol. 130)

Shiniu tu 十牛圖. *ZZ* 1, 2, 18. (Taibei ed., vol. 113). See also Yanagida Seizan, Kajitani Sōnin 梶谷宗忍, and Tsujimura Kōichi 辻村公一, eds., *Shinjinmei. Shōdoka. Jūgyūzu. Zazengi* 信心銘、正道歌、十牛図、坐禅儀. Tokyo: Chikuma shobō, 1974.

Shinnyokan 眞如觀. Attr. to Genshin 源信 (942–1017). In Tada Kōryū et al., eds., *Tendai hongakuron*, 119–149. Tokyo: Iwanami shoten, 1973.

Shishi yaolan 釋氏要覽 [ca. 1019], by Daocheng 道誠. *T.* 54, 2127.

Shiyue lu 指月錄 [1602], by Qu Ruji 瞿汝稷 (n.d.). *ZZ* 1, 2B, 16. (Taibei ed., vol. 143)

Shōbōgenzō 正眼法藏, by Dōgen. *T.* 82, 2582.

Sho ekō shingi [*shiki*] 諸廻向清規, by Tenrin Fūin 天倫楓隱 (n.d.). *T.* 81, 2578.

Shōichi kokushi goroku 聖一國師語錄, by Enni Ben'en 圓爾辨圓 (1202–1280). *T.* 80, 2544.

Shōsōrin shingi 小叢林清規, by Mujaku Dōchū. *T.* 81, 2579.

Shōtoku taishi denryaku 聖德太子傳曆. *DNBZ* 71, 546. (1931 ed., vol. 112)

Shouleng'yan jing 首楞嚴經. Apocryphon. *T.* 19, 945.

Shūmon mujintō ron 宗門無盡燈論, by Tōrei Enji. *T.* 81, 2575.

Shuo Song 說嵩 [1721], by Jing Rizhen 景日昣. In Chen Yunlong, ed., *Zhongguo mingshan shengji zhi congkan* 21 [n.d.]. 4 vols.

Shutsujō kōgo 出定後語, by Tominaga Nakamoto 富永仲基 (1715–1746). Kyōdo Jikō ed. Tokyo: Ryūbunkan, 1982.

Sifen lü 四分律 (*Dharmaguptaka-vinaya?*). Trans. Buddhayaśas, Zhu Fonian et al. *T.* 22, 1428.

Sifen lü xingshi chao 四分律行事鈔 [630], by Daoxuan. *T.* 40, 1804.

Sijia yulu 四家語錄. *zz* 1, 2, 24, 5. (Taibei ed., vol. 119)

Sita ji 寺塔記, by Duan Chengshi 段成式. *T.* 51, 2093.

Sōkei daishi betsuden 曹溪大師別傳. Anon. *zz* 1, 2B, 19, 5. (Taibei ed., vol. 146)

Sokushin ki 即心記, by Shidō Bunan 至道無難 (1603–1676). In Kōda Rentarō, ed., *Shidō Bunan zenji shū* 至道無難禪師集. Tokyo: Shunjūsha, 1956.

Song gaoseng zhuan 宋高僧傳, by Zanning. *T.* 50, 2061.

Song yue Gui chanshi yingtang ji 嵩嶽珪禪師影室記, by Xu Chou 許籌. *QTW* 790, 17: 10435–10436.

Sonjŏng yukcho Hyenŭng taesa chŏnsang tongnae yŏn'gi 禪宗六祖慧能大師頂相東來緣起. Attr. to Kakhun 覺訓 (fl. ca. 1215). In Chŏn Posam 1989: 327–329.

Ssanggye-sa yŏksa 雙磎寺略史. Unpublished ms. Library of Komazawa University, Tokyo.

Taiping guangji 太平廣記 [978], by Li Fang 李昉 (925–966) et al. Taibei: Guxin shuju, 1980.

Taiping yulan 太平御覽 [983], by Li Fang. Ed. Wang Yunwu 王雲五. 7 vols. Taibei: Shangwu yinshuguan, 1980 [1935].

Tang huiyao 唐會要 [961], by Wang Pu 王溥 (932–982) et al. Ed. Yang Jialo 楊家駱. 3 vols. Taibei: Shijie shuju, 1974.

Tang Yuquan si Datong chanshi beiming bingxu 唐玉泉寺大通禪師碑銘并序, by Zhang Yue 張說 (667–730). *QTW* 231, 5: 2953–2954.

Tetsugen zenji kana hōgo 鐵眼禪師假名法語. Ed. Akamatsu Shinmyō. Tokyo: Iwanami shoten, 1941.

Thūpavaṃsa, by *Vācissatthera*. Ed. N. A. Jayawickrama. London: Luzac and Co., 1971.

Tiansheng guangdeng lu 天聖廣燈錄. *zz* 1, 2B, 8, 4–5. (Taibei ed., vol. 135)

Tiantai shan ji 天台山記. Comp. Xu Lingfu 徐靈府 (ca. 760–841). *T.* 51, 2096.

Tōjō shitsunai danshi kenpi shiki 洞上室內斷紙揀非和記 [1749], by Menzan Zuihō 面山瑞芳 (1683–1769). *sz* 15, *Shitsuchū.*

Tōkoku ki 洞谷記 [*Tōkokki*], by Keizan Jōkin. In Kohō Chisan, ed., *Jōsai daishi zenshū*, 392–463. Yokohama: Daihonzan Sōjiji, 1976 [1937]. See also Sōtōshū Shūmuchō, ed., *Sōtōshū zensho, Shūgen* 2: 503–543. Tokyo: Sōtōshū Shūmuchō, 1970–1973.

Vajracchedikā. See *Jingang banruo boluomi jing.*

Vimalakīrti-nirdeśa. See *Weimojie jing.*

Wanshan tonggui ji 萬善同歸集, by Yongming Yanshou 永明延壽 (904–975). *T.* 48, 2017.

Weimojie jing 維摩詰經 [*Vimalakīrti-nirdeśa*]. Trans. Zhi Qian 支謙 (fl. 3rd. c.). *T.* 14, 474.

Wuchang jing 無常經 [*Anityatā-sūtra*]. Trans. Yijing. *T.* 17, 801.

Wudai huiyao 五代會要 [961], by Wang Pu. Shanghai: Guji chubanshe, 1978.

Wudeng huiyuan 五燈會元 [1252], by Puji 普濟 (1179–1253). *ZZ* 1, 2B, 10–11. (Taibei ed., vol. 138)

Wudeng yantong 五燈嚴統 [1653], by Tongrong 通容 (1593–1661). *ZZ* 1, 2B, 12. (Taibei ed., vol. 139)

Wujia zhengzong zan 五家正宗贊, by Shaotan 紹曇 (n.d.). *ZZ* 1, 2B, 8, 5. (Taibei ed., vol. 135)

Wujia zongzhi zan'yao 五家宗旨纂要 [1657], by Xingtong 性統 (n.d.). *ZZ* 1, 2, 19. (Taibei ed., vol. 114)

Wumen guan 無門關, by Wumen Huikai 無門慧開 (1183–1260). *T.* 48, 2005.

Wuwei sanzang chanyao 無畏三藏禪要, by Śubhakarasiṃha (637–735). *T.* 18, 917.

Wuxin lun 無心論. Attr. to Bodhidharma. *T.* 85, 2831.

Wuzu Fayan chanshi yulu 五祖法演禪師語錄. *T.* 47, 1995.

Xinjin wenji 鐔津文集, by Qisong. *T.* 52, 2115.

Xin Tang shu 新唐書 [1043–1060]. Comp. Ouyang Xiu 歐陽修 (1007–1072), Song Qi 宋祁 (998–1061) et al. 20 vols. Beijing: Zhonghua shuju, 1975.

Xiuchan yaojue 修禪要訣, by Buddhapāli. *ZZ* 1, 2, 15. (Taibei ed., vol. 110)

Xiuxin yaolun 修心要論 [*Zuishangsheng lun* 最上乘論]. Attr. to Hongren (601–674). *T.* 48, 2011.

Xuansha Shibei chanshi yulu 玄沙師備禪師語錄. *ZZ* 1, 2, 31. (Taibei ed., vol. 126)

Xu chuandeng lu 續傳燈錄, by Juding 居頂 (d. ca. 1404). *T.* 51, 2077.

Xuefeng Yicun chanshi yulu 雪峰義存禪師語錄. *ZZ* 1, 2, 24. (Taibei ed., vol. 119)

Xu gaoseng zhuan 續高僧傳, by Daoxuan. *T.* 50, 2060.

Xutang heshang yulu 虛堂和尚語錄. *ZZ* 1, 47, 2000.

Yangqi Fanghui heshang yulu 楊岐方會和尚語錄. *T.* 47, 1994a.

Yangshan yulu 仰山語錄 [*Yuanzhou Yangshan Huiji chanshi yulu* 袁州仰山慧寂禪師語錄]. *T.* 47, 1990.

Yijian zhi 夷堅志, by Hong Mai 洪邁 (1123–1202). 4 vols. Beijing: Zhonghua shuju, 1981.

Youyang zazu 酉陽雜俎, by Duan Chengshi 段成式. Ed. Imamura Yoshio, *Yuyō zasso.* 5 vols. Tokyo: Heibonsha, 1980–1981.

Yuanjue jing 圓覺經. Apocryphon. *T.* 17, 842.

Yuanjue jing dashu chao 圓覺經大疏鈔, by Guifei Zongmi. *ZZ* 1, 14, 3–5; 15, 1. (Taibei ed., vol. 14–15)

Yuanling lu 宛陵錄, by Huangbo Xiyun. See Hirano Sōjō, ed., *Tongo yōmon.* Tokyo: Chikuma shobō, 1970.

Yuanren lun 原人論, by Guifei Zongmi. *T.* 45, 1886.

Yuanwu Foguo chanshi yulu 圓悟佛果禪師語錄. *T.* 47, 1997.

Yunji qiqian 雲笈七籤 [1019], by Zhang Junfang 張君房. *DZ* 677–702.

Yunmen guanglu 雲門廣錄. *T.* 47, 1988.

Yunmen shan zhi 雲門山志. Ed. Chen Xuelu. In Mingwen shuju, ed., *Zhongguo fosi shizhi huikan* 中國佛寺史志彙刊. Vol. 6. Taibei: Mingwen shuju, 1980.

Zenrin shōkisen 禪林象器箋, by Mujaku Dōchū. In Yanagida Seizan, ed., *Zenrin shōkisen; Kattō gosen jikkan; Zenrin kushū benmyō.* Vol. 1. Kyoto: Chūbun shuppansha, 1979.

Zhao lun 肇論, by Sengzhao 僧肇 (384–414?). *T.* 45, 1858.

Zhengfa yanzang 正法眼藏, by Dahui Zonggao 大慧宗杲 (1089–1163). *zz* 1, 2, 23. (Taibei ed., vol. 118)

Zhenzong lun 眞宗論 [*Dasheng kaixin xianxing dunwu zhenzong lun* 大乘開心顯性頓悟眞宗論]. *T.* 85, 2835.

Zhonglun 中論 [*Madhyamakakārikā*], by Nāgārjuna. *T.* 30, 1564.

Zhongxiu Caoxi tongzhi 重修曹溪通志, by Ma Yuan 馬元. In Mingwen shuju, ed., *Zhongguo fosi shizhi huikan*. Vols. 4–5. Taibei: Mingwen shuju, 1980.

Zhuangzi 莊子. Attr. to Zhuang Zhou 莊周; commentary by Guo Xiang 郭象. Ed. Sibu beiyao. Taibei: Zhonghua shuju, 1973. See also *Harvard-Yenching Institute, Sinological Index Series*. Supplement no. 20: *A Concordance to Chuang Tzu*. Cambridge, MA: Harvard University Press. 1956.

Zimen jingxun 緇門警訓, by Rujin 如巹 (fl. ca. 1470–1489). *T.* 48, 2023.

Zizhi tongjian 資治通鑑. Comp. Sima Guang 司馬光. Hong Kong: Zhonghua shuju, 1971.

Zoku gunsho ruijū 續羣書類從 [1822], by Hanawa Hokiichi. 34 vols. Tokyo: Zoku gunsho ruijū kanseikai, 1972.

Zokuzoku gunsho ruijū 續々羣書類從. Ed. Kokusho kankōkai. 16 vols. Tokyo: Kokusho kankōkai, 1906–1909.

Zongjing lu 宗鏡錄, by Yongming Yanshou. *T.* 48, 2016.

Zuiweng tanlu 醉翁談錄 [ca. 1150], by Jin Yingzhi 金盈之. *Xinbian zuiweng tanlu* ed. Shanghai: Gudian wenxue, 1958.

Zutang ji 祖堂集 (K. *Chodang chip*, 952). In Yanagida Seizan, ed., *Sōdōshū*. Kyoto: Chūbun shuppansha, 1974(b).

Zuting shiyuan 祖庭事苑 [1108], by Muan Shanqing 睦庵善卿. *zz* 1, 2, 18, 1. (Taibei ed., vol. 113). See also *Chanxue dacheng*, ed. Xieguan Shengti. Vol. 3. Taibei: Zhonghua fojiao wenhua guan. 1969.

SECONDARY SOURCES

Abe Chōichi 阿部肇一. 1963. *Chūgoku zenshūshi no kenkyū: Nanshūzen seiritsu igo no seiji shakaishi-teki kōsatsu* 中國禪宗史の研究——南宗禪成立以後の政治社會史的考際 [Researches on the History of the Chan School in China]. Tokyo: Seishin shobō.

Ahern, Emily M. 1973. *The Cult of the Dead in a Chinese Village*. Stanford: Stanford University Press.

———. 1979. "The Problem of Efficacy: Strong and Weak Illocutionary Acts." *Man* 14, 1: 1–17.

Almond, Philip C. 1988. *The British Discovery of Buddhism*. Cambridge: Cambridge University Press.

Alper, Harvey, ed. 1989. *Mantra*. Albany: State University of New York Press.

Althusser, Louis. 1990. *Philosophy and the Spontaneous Philosophy of the Scientists and Other Essays*. Ed. Gregory Elliott. Trans. Ben Brewster. London and New York: Verso.

Althusser, Louis, and Etienne Balibar. 1970. *Reading "Capital."* Trans. Ben Brewster. London: NLB.

Amino, Yoshihiko. 1983. "Some Problems Concerning the History of Popular Life in Medieval Japan." *Acta Asiatica* 44: 77–97.

Andō Kōsei 安藤更生. 1960. *Ganjin daiwajō den no kenkyū* 鑒眞大和上傳之研究. [Researches on the Biography of the Great Priest Ganjin]. Tokyo: Heibonsha.

———. 1961. *Nihon no miira* 日本のミイラ [The Mummies of Japan]. Tokyo: Mainichi shinbunsha.

Angenot, Marc. 1984. "Structuralism and Syncretism: Institutional Distortions of Saussure." In John Feteke, ed., *The Structural Allegory: Reconstructive Encounters with the New French Thought*, 150–163. Minneapolis: University of Minnesota Press.

App, Urs. 1987. "Ch'an/Zen's Greatest Encyclopaedist Mujaku Dōchū (1653–1744)." *Cahiers d'Extrême-Asie* 3. 155–174.

———. 1989. "Facets of the Life and Teaching of Chan Master Yunmen Wenyan (864–949)." Ph. D. diss., Temple University.

Araki Kengo 荒木見悟, ed. 1969. *Daie sho* 大慧書 [The Letters of Dahui]. Zen no goroku 17. Tokyo: Chikuma shobō.

———. 1975. "Confucianism and Buddhism in the Late Ming." In W. T. de Bary, ed., *The Unfolding of Neo-Confucianism*, 39–66. New York: Columbia University Press.

———. 1976. *Bukkyō to Jukyō: Chūgoku shisō o keiseisuru mono* 仏教と儒教——中国思想を形成するもの [Buddhism and Confucianism: The Components of Chinese Thought]. Kyoto: Heirakuji shoten.

Ariès, Philippe. 1974. *Western Attitudes Toward Death: From the Middle Ages to the Present*. Trans. Patricia M. Ranum. Baltimore and London: Johns Hopkins University Press.

———. 1981. *The Hour of Our Death*. Trans. Helen Weaver. New York: Alfred A. Knopf.

Ariès, Philippe, and André Béjin, eds. 1982. *Sexualités occidentales*. Paris: Seuil.

Arntzen, Sonja. 1986. *Ikkyū and the Crazy Cloud Anthology: A Zen Poet of Medieval Japan*. Tokyo: University of Tokyo Press.

Augé, Marc. 1975. *Théorie des pouvoirs et idéologie*. Paris: Hermann.

———. 1982a. *The Anthropological Circle: Symbol, Function, History*. Cambridge: Cambridge University Press.

———. 1982b. *Le génie du paganisme*. Paris: Gallimard.

Austin, J. L. 1962. *How to Do Things with Words*. Cambridge, MA: Harvard University Press.

Azuma Ryūshin 東隆眞. 1974. *Keizan zenji no kenkyū* 瑩山禅師の研究 [Researches on the Zen Master Keizan]. Tokyo: Shunjūsha.

———. 1983. "Dōgen zenji to Rakan kōshiki ni tsuite" 道元禅師と羅漢講式について [On Zen Master Dōgen and the Ceremony for the Arhats]. *IBK* 31, 2: 76–83.

Bachelard, Gaston. 1964. *La poétique de l'espace*. Paris: Presses Universitaires de France.

Baity, Philip C. 1975. *Religion in a Chinese Town*. Taibei: Asian Folklore and Social Life Monographs 64.

Bakhtin, Mikhail. 1968. *Rabelais and His World*. Trans. H. Iswolsky. Cambridge, MA: MIT Press.

Bakhtin, Mikhail. 1981. *The Dialogic Imagination: Four Essays*. Ed. M. Holquist. Trans. C. Emerson and M. Holquist. Austin: University of Texas Press.

———. 1986. *Speech Genres & Other Late Essays*. Trans. Vern W. McGee. Austin: University of Texas Press.

Balazs, Etienne. 1968. *La bureaucratie céleste: Recherches sur l'économie et la société de la Chine traditionnelle*. Paris: Gallimard.

Bapat, P. V, and Hirakawa Akira, trans. 1970. *Shan-Chien-P'i-P'o-Sha: A Chinese Version by Saṅghabhadra of Samantapāsādikā*. Bhandarkar Oriental Series 10. Poona: Bhandarkar Oriental Research Institute.

Bareau, André. 1962. "La construction et le culte des stūpa d'après le Vinayapiṭaka." *BEFEO* 50: 229–274.

———. 1963. *Recherches sur la biographie du Buddha dans les sūtrapiṭaka et les vinayapiṭaka anciens*. Publications de l'Ecole Française d'Extrême-Orient 53. Paris: Ecole Française d'Extrême-Orient.

———. 1971. *Recherches sur la biographie du Buddha dans les sūtrapiṭaka et les vinayapiṭaka anciens: II. Les derniers mois, le parinirvāṇa et les funérailles*. 2 vols. Paris: Ecole Française d'Extrême-Orient.

———. 1975. "Les récits canoniques des funérailles du Buddha et leurs anomalies: Nouvel essai d'interprétation." *BEFEO* 62: 151–190.

Barthes, Roland. 1970. *L'empire des signes*. Paris: Flammarion.

———. [1971] 1989. *Sade, Fourier, Loyola*. Trans. Richard Miller. Berkeley: University of California Press.

Bastian, Adolf. 1871. *Die Voelker des Oestlichen Asien: Studien und Reisen*. Jena: Hermann Costenoble.

Bastide, Roger. 1972. *Le rêve, la transe, la folie*. Paris: Flammarion.

Bataille, Georges. 1954. *L'expérience intérieure*. Paris: Gallimard.

———. 1970–. *Oeuvres complètes*. Vol. 6. Paris: Gallimard.

Bauer, Wolfgang. 1976. *China and the Search for Happiness: Recurring Themes in Four Thousand Years of Chinese Cultural History*. New York: Seabury Press.

Bell, Catherine. 1983. "Medieval Taoist Ritual Mastery: A Study in Practice, Text and Rite." Ph.D. diss., University of Chicago.

———. 1986. "Charisma and Classification: Chinese Morality Books." Unpublished paper.

———. 1987. "Discourse and Dichotomies: The Structure of Ritual Theory." *Religion* 17: 95–118.

———. 1988. "Ritualization of Texts and Textualization of Ritual in the Codification of Taoist Liturgy." *History of Religions* 27, 4: 366–392.

———. 1989a. "Religion and Chinese Culture: Toward an Assessment of 'Popular Religion.'" *History of Religions* 29, 1: 35–57.

———. 1989b. "Ritual, Change, and Changing Ritual." *Worship* 63, 1: 31–41.

———. 1990. *Ritual Theory, Ritual Practice*. Cambridge: Cambridge University Press (forthcoming).

Benjamin, Walter. 1968. *Illuminations*. Trans. Harry Zohn. New York: Schocken Books.

Benl, Oscar. 1960. "Die Anfänge der Sōtō-Mönschsgemeinschaften." *Oriens Extremus* 7, 1: 31–50.

Benveniste, Emile. 1966, 1974. *Problèmes de linguistique générale*. 2 vols. Paris: Gallimard.

Berger, Peter L. 1969. *The Sacred Canopy: Elements of a Sociological Theory of Religion*. New York: Anchor Books.

Berger, Peter L., and Thomas Luckmann. 1967. *The Social Construction of Reality*. New York: Anchor Books.

Bergson, Henri. 1935. *The Two Sources of Morality and Religion*. New York: Henry Holt.

Berling, Judith A. 1980. *The Syncretic Religion of Lin Chao-en*. New York: Columbia University Press.

———. 1985. "Self and Whole in Chuang Tzu." In David. J. Munro, ed., *Individualism and Holism: Studies in Confucian and Taoist Values*. Ann Arbor: Center for Chinese Studies, University of Michigan.

———. 1987. "Bringing the Buddha down to Earth: Notes on the Emergence of *Yü-lu* as a Buddhist Genre." *History of Religions* 21, 1: 56–88.

Berque, Augustin. 1986. *Le sauvage et l'artifice: Les Japonais devant la nature*. Paris: Gallimard.

Beyer, Stephan. 1977. "Notes on the Vision Quest in Early Mahāyāna." In Lewis R. Lancaster, ed., *Prajñāpāramitā and Related Systems: Studies in Honor of Edward Conze*, 329–340. Berkeley: Buddhist Studies Series, University of California.

Biardeau, Madeleine, and Charles Malamoud. 1976. *Le sacrifice dans l'Inde ancienne*. Paris: Presses Universitaires de France.

Bielefeldt, Carl. 1979. "Dōgen's *Shōbōgenzō Sansuikyō*." In Michael Charles Tobias and Harold Drasdo, eds., *The Mountain-Spirit*, 37–49. Woodstock, NY: Overlook Press.

———. 1985. "Recarving the Dragon: History and Dogma in the Study of Dōgen." In William R. LaFleur, ed., *Dōgen Studies*, 21–53. Honolulu: University of Hawaii Press.

———. 1986. "Chang-lu Tsung-tse's *Tso-ch'an i* and the 'Secret' of Zen Meditation." In Peter N. Gregory, ed., *Traditions of Meditation in Chinese Buddhism*, 129–161. Honolulu: University of Hawaii Press.

———. 1988. *Dōgen's Manuals of Zen Meditation*. Berkeley: University of California Press.

———. 1989a. "Ennin's Treatise on Seated Zen." *Ten Directions* 10, 1: 7–11.

———. 1989b. "No-Mind and Sudden Awakening: Thoughts on the Soteriology of a Kamakura Zen Text." In Robert E. Buswell, Jr., and Robert M. Gimello, eds., *Paths to Liberation: The Mārga and Its Transformations in Buddhist Thought*. Studies in East Asian Buddhism, 7. Honolulu: University of Hawaii Press (forthcoming in 1991).

———. 1989c. "Putting the Cart Before the Horse: Reflections on Ennin's *Treatise on Seated Zen*." *Ten Directions* 10, 1: 7–21.

Birnbaum, Raoul. 1984. "Thoughts on T'ang Buddhist Mountain Traditions and their Context." *T'ang Studies* 2: 5–23.

———. 1986. "Seeking Longevity in Chinese Buddhism: Long Life Deities and their Symbolism." *Journal of Chinese Religions* 13–14: 143–176.

———. 1989. "Deity Cults, Sacred Geography, and Buddhist Practice in Medieval China." Unpublished paper.

Blake, William. 1966. *Complete Writings*. Ed. Geoffrey Keynes. Oxford: Oxford University Press.

Bloch, Marc. 1983. *Les rois thaumaturges: Etude sur le caractère surnaturel attribué à la puissance royale, particulièrement en France et en Angleterre.* Paris: Gallimard.

Bloch, Maurice, and Jonathan Parry, eds. 1982. *Death and the Regeneration of Life.* Cambridge: Cambridge University Press.

Blondeau, Anne-Marie, and Kristofer Schipper, eds. 1988. *Essais sur le rituel.* Louvain: Peeters.

Blonski, Marshall, ed. 1985. *On Signs.* Baltimore: Johns Hopkins University Press.

Bloom, Harold. 1973. *The Anxiety of Influence: A Theory of Poetry.* Oxford: Oxford University Press.

Bloss, Lowell W. 1973. "The Buddha and the Nāga: A Study in Buddhist Folk Religiosity." *History of Religions* 13, 1: 36–53.

Bodiford, William M. 1989. "The Growth of the Sōtō Zen Tradition in Medieval Japan." Ph.D. diss., Yale University.

Boltz, Judith M. 1987. *A Survey of Taoist Literature.* Berkeley: Institute of East Asian Studies, University of California.

Bond, George O. 1980. "Theravāda Buddhism's Meditation on Death and the Symbolism of Initiatory Death." *History of Religions* 19, 3: 237–258.

Boon, James A. 1972. *From Symbolism to Structuralism: Lévi-Strauss in a Literary Tradition.* New York: Harper and Row.

―――. 1982. *Other Tribes, Other Scribes: Symbolic Anthropology in the Comparative Study of Cultures, Histories, Religions and Texts.* Cambridge: Cambridge University Press.

―――. 1986. "Symbols, Sylphs, and Siwa: Allegorical Machineries in the Text of Balinese Culture." In Victor W. Turner, ed., *The Anthropology of Experience*, 239–260. Urbana and Chicago: University of Illinois Press.

―――. 1990. *Affinities and Extremes: Crisscrossing the Bittersweet Ethnology of East Indies History, Hindu-Balinese Culture, and Indo-European Allure.* Chicago: University of Chicago Press.

Borgen, Robert. 1986. *Sugawara Michizane and the Early Heian Court.* Cambridge, MA: Harvard University Press.

Borges, Jorge Luis. 1981. *Borges: A Reader.* Ed. Emir Rodriguez Monegal and Alastair Reid. New York: E. P. Dutton.

Boswell, John. 1980. *Christianity, Social Tolerance and Homosexuality.* Chicago: University of Chicago Press.

Bourdieu, Pierre. 1971a. "Genèse et structure du champ religieux." *Revue française de Sociologie* 12: 295–334.

―――. 1971b. "Une interprétation de la théorie de la religion selon Max Weber." *Archives européennes de Sociologie* 12: 3–21.

―――. 1977a. "The Economics of Linguistic Exchanges." *Social Science Information* 16, 6: 645–668.

―――. 1977b. *Outine of a Theory of Practice.* Cambridge: Cambridge University Press.

―――. 1979. "Symbolic Power." *Critique of Anthropology* 13: 77–85.

―――. 1980a. "The Production of Belief: Contribution to an Economy of Symbolic Goods." *Media, Culture and Society* 2, 3: 261–293.

―――. 1980b. *Le sens pratique.* Paris: Minuit.

———. 1982. *Ce que parler veut dire: L'économie des échanges linguistiques.* Paris: Fayard.

———. 1984. *Distinction: A Social Critique of the Judgement of Taste.* Trans. Richard Nice. Cambridge, MA: Harvard University Press.

———. 1985a. "The Genesis of the Concepts of *Habitus* and of *Field*." *Sociocriticism* 2: 11–24.

———. 1985b. "The Social Space and the Genesis of Groups." *Social Science Information* 24, 2: 195–220.

———. 1989. *Questions of Culture.* Stanford: Stanford University Press.

———. 1990a. *In Other Words: Essays Towards a Reflexive Sociology.* Trans. Matthew Adamson. Stanford: Stanford University Press.

———. 1990b. *The Logic of Practice.* Trans. Richard Nice. Stanford: Stanford University Press.

Braudel, Fernand. 1980. *On History.* Trans. Sarah Matthews. Chicago: University of Chicago Press.

Braverman, Arthur, trans. 1989. *Mud and Water: A Collection of Talks by the Zen Master Bassui.* San Francisco: North Point Press.

Brill, A. A., trans. [1938] 1966. *The Basic Writings of Sigmund Freud.* New York: Modern Library.

Broughton, Jeffrey Lyle. 1975. "Kuei-feng Tsung-mi: The Convergence of Ch'an and the Teachings." Ph.D. diss., Columbia University.

———. 1983. "Early Ch'an Schools in Tibet." In Robert Gimello and Peter N. Gregory, eds., *Studies in Ch'an and Hua-yen,* 1–68. Honolulu: University of Hawaii Press.

———. 1988. "Proto-Ch'an Texts." Unpublished ms.

Brown, Carolyn T., ed. 1988. *Psycho-Sinology: The Universe of Dreams in Chinese Culture.* Lanham: University Press of America.

Brown, Peter. 1978. *The Making of Late Antiquity.* Cambridge, MA: Harvard University Press.

———. 1981. *The Cult of the Saints: Its Rise and Function in Latin Christianity.* Chicago: University of Chicago Press.

———. 1982. *Society and the Holy in Late Antiquity.* Berkeley: University of California Press.

———. 1988. *The Body and Society: Men, Women, and Sexual Renunciation in Early Christianity.* New York: Columbia University Press.

Bugault, Guy. 1967. *La notion de "Prajñā" ou de sapience selon les perspectives du Mahāyāna: Part de la connaissance et de l'inconnaissance dans l'anagogie bouddhique.* Paris: Editions de Boccard.

Bukkyō minzoku gakkai 仏教民俗学会, ed. 1977. *Katō Shōichi sensei koki kinen ronbunshū: Bukkyō to girei* 加藤章一先生古稀記念論文集 — 仏教と儀礼 [Buddhism and Ritual: Essays Offered to Prof. Katō Shōichi on the Occasion of his Retirement]. Tokyo: Kokusho kankōkai.

Bush, Susan H., and Victor H. Mair. 1977–1978. "Some Buddhist Portraits and Images of the Lü and Ch'an Sects in Twelfth- and Thirteenth-century China." *Archives of Asian Art* 31: 32–51.

Buswell, Robert E., Jr. 1983. *The Korean Approach to Zen: The Collected Works of Chinul.* Honolulu: University of Hawaii Press.

Buswell, Robert E., Jr. 1987. "The 'Short-cut' Approach of *K'an-hua* Meditation: The Evolution of a Practical Subitism in Chinese Ch'an Buddhism." In Peter N. Gregory, ed., *Sudden and Gradual: Approaches to Enlightenment in Chinese Thought*, 321–377. Honolulu: University of Hawaii Press.

———. 1988. "Ch'an Hermeneutics: A Korean View." In Donald S. Lopez, Jr., ed., *Buddhist Hermeneutics*, 231–256. Honolulu: University of Hawaii Press.

———, ed. 1989a. *Chinese Buddhist Apocrypha*. Honolulu: University of Hawaii Press.

———. 1989b. *The Formation of Ch'an Ideology in China and Korea: The Vajrasamādhi-Sūtra, A Buddhist Apocryphon*. Princeton: Princeton University Press.

Bynum, Caroline Walker. 1987. *Holy Feast and Holy Fast: The Religious Significance of Food to Medieval Women*. Berkeley: University of California Press.

Bynum, Caroline W., Steven Harrel, and Paula Richman, eds. 1986. *Gender and Religion: On the Complexity of Symbols*. Boston: Beacon Press.

Cahill, James. 1987. "Tung Ch'i-ch'ang's 'Southern and Northern Schools' in the History and Theory of Painting: A Reconsideration." In Peter N. Gregory, ed., *Sudden and Gradual: Approaches to Enlightenment in Chinese Thought*, 429–446. Honolulu: University of Hawaii Press.

Carré, Patrick. 1985. *Les entretiens de Houang-po, maître Tch'an du IXe siècle*. Paris: Les Deux Océans.

Carrithers, Michael, Steven Collins, and Steven Lukes, eds. 1985. *The Category of the Person: Anthropology, Philosophy, History*. Cambridge: Cambridge University Press.

Carroll, Lewis. 1963. *Alice's Adventures in Wonderland and Through the Looking Glass*. Harmondsworth: Penguin Books.

Casalis, Mathieu. 1983. "The Semiotics of the Visible in Japanese Rock Gardens." *Semiotica* 44, 3–4: 349–362.

Cedzich, Ursula-Angelica. 1985. "Wu-t'ung: Zur bewegten Geschichte eines Kultes." In G. Naundorf et al., eds., *Religion und Philosophie in Ostasien: Festschrift für Hans Steininger*, 33–61. Würzburg: Königshausen and Neumann.

———. 1990. "Unravelling the Cult Behind the Scripture: The Case of the *Nan-yu chi*." Unpublished paper.

Certeau, Michel de. 1970. *La possession de Loudun*. Paris: Julliard.

———. 1975. *L'écriture de l'histoire*. Paris: Gallimard.

———. 1980. *La culture au pluriel*. Paris: Christian Bourgeois.

———. 1982. *La fable mystique: XVIe-XVIIe siècle*. Paris: Gallimard.

———. 1984. *The Practice of Everyday Life*. Trans. Steven Rendall. Berkeley: University of California Press.

———. 1986. *Heterologies: Discourse on the Other*. Trans. Brian Massumi. Minneapolis: University of Minnesota Press.

———. 1988. *The Writing of History*. Trans. Tom Conley. New York: Columbia University Press.

Chan, Hok-lam, and Wm. Theodore de Bary, eds. 1982. *Yüan Thought: Chinese Thought and Religion Under the Mongols*. New York: Columbia University Press.

Chan, Wing-tsit. 1953. *Religious Trends in Modern China*. New York: Columbia University Press.

———, trans. 1963. *Instructions for Practical Living and Other Neo-Confucian Writings by Wang Yang-ming*. New York: Columbia University Press.

Chapin, Helen B. 1933. "The Ch'an Master Pu-tai." *JAOS* 53: 47–52.

Chappell, David W. 1980. "Early Forebodings of the Death of Buddhism." *Numen* 27, 1: 122–154.

———. 1983. "The Teachings of the Fourth Ch'an Patriarch Tao-hsin (580–651)." In Whalen Lai and Lewis R. Lancaster, eds., *Early Ch'an in China and Tibet*, 89–129. Berkeley: Asian Humanities Press.

———. 1986. "From Dispute to Dual Cultivation: Pure Land Responses to Ch'an Critics." In Peter N. Gregory, ed., *Traditions of Meditation in Chinese Buddhism*, 163–197. Honolulu: University of Hawaii Press.

———, ed. 1987. *Buddhist and Taoist Practice in Medieval Chinese Society: Buddhist and Taoist Studies II*. Honolulu: University of Hawaii Press.

Charles, Michel. 1985. *L'arbre et la source*. Paris: Seuil.

Chartier, Roger. 1988. *Cultural History: Between Practices and Representations*. Trans. Lydia G. Cochrane. Ithaca: Cornell University Press.

Chavannes, Edouard. 1910. *Le T'ai Chan: Essai de monographie d'un culte chinois*. Paris: Ernest Leroux. Reprint. Taibei: Chengwen, 1970.

———. 1919. "Le jet des dragons." *Mémoires concernant l'Asie orientale* 3: 53–220. Paris: Ernest Leroux.

Chen Yuan 陳垣. 1977. *Zhongguo fojiao zhi lishi yanjiu* 中國佛教之歷史研究 [Studies in the History of Chinese Buddhism]. Taibei: Jiuxiang chuban.

Ch'en, Kenneth S. 1973. *The Chinese Transformation of Buddhism*. Princeton: Princeton University Press.

———. 1976. "The Role of Buddhist Monasteries in T'ang Society." *History of Religions* 15, 3: 209–230.

Cheng, François. 1977. *L'écriture poétique chinoise: Suivi d'une anthologie des poèmes des T'ang*. Paris: Seuil.

Chidester, David. 1990. *Patterns of Transcendence: Religion, Death, and Dying*. Belmont, CA: Wadsworth.

Childs, Margaret H. 1980. "*Chigo Monogatari*: Love Stories or Buddhist Sermons?" *Monumenta Nipponica* 35, 2: 127–151.

———. 1985. "Kyōgen-kigo: Love Stories as Buddhist Sermons." *Japanese Journal of Religious Studies* 12, 1: 91–104.

Chŏn Posam 全寶三. 1989. "Yukcho chŏnsang ŭi tongnaesŏl kwa kŭ sinangsa-chŏk ŭiŭi—Yukcho Hyenŭng taesa chŏnsang tongnae yŏn'gi rŭl chungsim ŭro" 六祖頂相의 東來說과 그信仰史的意義 [The Theory of the Coming to the East of the Head of the Sixth Patriarch and its Meaning from the Standpoint of the History of the Faith]. In Kim Chigyŏn, ed., *Yukcho tan'gyŏng ŭi segye* 六祖壇經의世界 [The World of the *Platform Sūtra*], 317–342. Seoul: Minjoksa.

Chou Yi-liang. 1944–1945. "Tantrism in China." *HJAS* 8: 241–332.

Chung Muo-hwan 鄭茂煥. 1987. "*Zenshū rokuso Enō daishi chinsō tōrai engi kō*" 「禅宗六祖慧能大師頂相東来縁」考 [A Study of the Story of the Sixth Patriarch's Head Brought to the East]. *IBK* 36, 1: 81–83.

Cleary, Christopher [J. C.]. 1977. *Swampland Flowers: The Letters and Lectures of Zen Master Ta Hui*. New York: Grove Press.

———. 1986. *Zen Dawn: Early Texts from Tun Huang*. Boston and London: Shambhala.

Cleary, Thomas, trans. 1990. *Transmission of Light [Denkōroku]: Zen in the Art of Enlightenment by Zen Master Keizan*. San Francisco: North Point Press.

Cleary, Thomas, and J. C. Cleary. 1977. *The Blue Cliff Record*. 3 vols. Boulder and London: Shambhala.

Clifford, James, and George E. Marcus, eds. 1986. *Writing Culture: The Poetics and Politics of Ethnography*. Berkeley: University of California Press.

Cockburn, Aidan and Eve, eds. 1983. *Mummies, Disease, and Ancient Cultures*. Abridged ed. Cambridge: Cambridge University Press.

Collcutt, Martin. 1981. *Five Mountains: The Rinzai Zen Monastic Institution in Medieval Japan*. Cambridge, MA: Harvard University Press.

———. 1982. "The Zen Monastery in Kamakura Society." In Jeffrey P. Mass, ed., *Court and Bakufu in Japan: Essays in Kamakura History*, 191–220. New Haven: Yale University Press.

———. 1983. "The Early Ch'an Monastic Rule: *Ch'ing-kuei* and the Shaping of Ch'an Community Life." In Whalen Lai and Lewis R. Lancaster, eds., *Early Ch'an in China and Tibet*, 165–184. Berkeley: Asian Humanities Press.

Collins, Steven. 1982. *Selfless Persons: Imagery and Thought in Theravāda Buddhism*. Cambridge: Cambridge University Press.

Conze, Edward. 1957. *Vajracchedikā Prajñāpāramitā*. Rome: Istituto Italiano per il Medio ed Estremo Oriente.

———. 1974. "The Intermediary World in Buddhism." *The Eastern Buddhist* (n.s.) 7, 2: 22–31.

———, trans. 1973. *The Perfection of Wisdom in Eight Thousand Lines and its Verse Summary*. Bolinas, CA: Four Seasons Foundation.

Corbin, Henri. 1958. *L'imagination créatrice dans le soufisme d'Ibn' Arabî*. Paris: Flammarion.

———. 1967. "Le songe visionnaire en spiritualité islamique." In Roger Caillois and G. E. von Grunebaum, eds., *Le rêve et les sociétés humaines*, 380–406. Paris: Gallimard.

———. 1983. *Face de Dieu, face de l'Homme: Herméneutique et soufisme*. Paris: Flammarion.

Covell, Jon Caster. 1980. *Unraveling Zen's Red Thread: Ikkyū's Controversial Way*. Seoul: Hollym International Corporation.

Croissant, Doris. 1986. "Das Unsterbliche Leib: Ahneffigie und Reliquienporträt in der Porträtplastik Ostasiens." Unpublished paper.

Culler, Jonathan. 1981. *The Pursuit of Signs: Semiotics, Literature, Deconstruction*. Ithaca: Cornell University Press.

———. 1982. *On Deconstruction: Theory and Criticism after Structuralism*. Ithaca: Cornell University Press.

Dars, Jacques, trans. 1987. *Contes de la montagne sereine*. Paris: Gallimard.

Dayal, Har. [1932] 1975. *The Bodhisattva Doctrine in Buddhist Sanskrit Literature*. Delhi: Motilal Banarsidass.

de Bary, Wm. Theodore, ed. 1970. *Self and Society in Ming Thought.* New York: Columbia University Press.

———, ed. 1975. *The Unfolding of Neo-Confucianism.* New York: Columbia University Press.

DeBernardi, Jean. 1987. "The God of War and the Vagabond Buddha." *Modern China* 13, 3: 310–332.

Delahaye, Hubert. 1983. "Les antécédents magiques des statues chinoises." *Revue d'esthétique* (n.s.) 5: 45–53.

Delehaye, Hippolyte. [1905] 1962. *The Legends of the Saints.* Trans. Donald Attwater. New York: Fordham University Press.

Deleuze, Gilles, and Félix Guattari. 1983. *On the Line.* Trans. John Johnston. New York: Semiotext(e).

de Man, Paul. 1979. *Allegories of Reading: Figural Language in Rousseau, Nietzsche, Rilke and Proust.* New Haven: Yale University Press.

———. 1983. *Blindness and Insight: Essays in the Rhetoric of Contemporary Criticism.* Minneapolis: University of Minnesota Press.

———. 1986. *The Resistance to Theory.* Minneapolis: University of Minnesota Press.

Demiéville, Paul. 1927. "Sur la mémoire des existences antérieures." *BEFEO* 27: 283–298.

———. 1949. "Le *touen* et le *ts'ien* (le 'subit' et le 'graduel')." In *Annuaire du Collège de France,* 177–182. Paris: Collège de France. Repr. in Demiéville, *Choix d'études sinologiques (1929–1970),* 94–99. Leiden: E. J. Brill, 1973(b).

———. 1952. *Le concile de Lhasa: Une controverse sur le quiétisme entre les bouddhistes de l'Inde et de la Chine au VIIIe siècle de l'ère chrétienne.* Paris: Presses Universitaires de France.

———. 1954. "La *Yogācārabhūmi* de Saṅgharakṣa." *BEFEO* 44: 339–436.

———. 1956. "La pénétration du bouddhisme dans la tradition philosophique chinoise." *Cahiers d'histoire mondiale* 3, 1: 19–38. Repr. In Demiéville, *Choix d'études sinologiques (1929–1970),* 241–260. Leiden: E. J. Brill, 1973(b).

———. 1957. "Le bouddhisme et la guerre: Post-scriptum à l' *Histoire des moines-guerriers du Japon* de G. Renondeau." In *Mélanges publiés par l'Institut des Hautes Etudes Chinoises,* 347–385. Paris: Presses Universitaires de France.

———. 1961. "Deux documents de Touen-houang sur le Dhyāna chinois." In *Essays on the History of Buddhism presented to Professor Zenryū Tsukamoto,* 1–27. Kyoto: Nagai Shuppansha. Repr. in Demiéville, *Choix d'études bouddhiques (1929–1970),* 320–346. Leiden: E. J. Brill, 1973(a).

———. 1965. "Momies d'Extrême-Orient." *Journal des savants* (Special issue): 144–170. Repr. in Demiéville, *Choix d'études sinologiques (1929–1970),* 407–432. Leiden: E. J. Brill, 1973(b).

———. 1970a. "Le bouddhisme chinois." In *Encyclopédie de la Pléiade, Histoire des religions,* Vol. 1: 1249–1319. Paris: Gallimard.

———. 1970b. "Recueil de la Salle des Patriarches (*Tsou-t'ang tsi*)." *T'oung Pao* 56: 262–286.

———, trans. 1972. *Entretiens de Lin-tsi.* Paris: Fayard.

———. 1973a. *Choix d'études bouddhiques (1929–1970).* Leiden: E. J. Brill.

Demiéville, Paul. 1973b. *Choix d'études sinologiques (1929–1970)*. Leiden: E. J. Brill.

———. 1974. "L'iconoclasme anti-bouddhique en Chine." In *Mélanges d'Histoire des Religions offerts à H. C. Puech*, 17–25. Paris: Presses Universitaires de France.

———. 1976. "Une descente aux enfers sous les T'ang: la biographie de Houang Che-k'iang." In *Etudes d'histoire et de littérature chinoises offertes au professeur Jaroslav Prušek*, 71–84. Paris: Presses Universitaires de France.

———. 1978. "Appendice sur 'Damoduolo' (Dharmatrā[ta])." In Jao Tsong-yi et Paul Demiéville, eds., *Peintures monochromes de Tun-huang (Dunhuang baihua)*, 43–49. Paris: Ecole Française d'Extrême-Orient.

———. 1980. "Notes on Buddhist Hymnology in the Far East." In Somaratna Balasooriya et al., eds., *Buddhist Studies in Honour of Walpola Rahula*, 44–61. London: Gordon Fraser.

———. 1984. *Poèmes chinois d'avant la mort*. Ed. Jean-Pierre Diény. Paris: L'Asiathèque.

———. 1985. *Buddhism and Healing: Demiéville's Article "Byō" from Hōbōgirin*. Trans. Mark Tatz. Lanham: University Press of America.

———. [1947] 1987. "The Mirror of the Mind." In Peter N. Gregory, ed., *Sudden and Gradual: Approaches to Enlightenment in Chinese Thought*, 13–40. Honolulu: University of Hawaii Press.

Derrida, Jacques. 1967. *De la grammatologie*. Paris: Minuit.

———. 1972a. *Marges*. Paris: Minuit.

———. 1972b. *Positions*. Paris: Minuit.

———. [1967] 1974. *Of Grammatology*. Trans. Gayatri C. Spivak. Baltimore: Johns Hopkins University Press.

———. 1977. "Ja, ou le faux bond." *Digraphe* 11: 84–121.

———. 1978. *Writing and Difference*. Trans. Alan Bass. Chicago: University of Chicago Press.

———. 1979. "Living on: Borderlines." In Harold Bloom et al., eds., *Deconstruction and Criticism*, 75–175. New York: Seabury.

———. 1981a. *Dissemination*. Trans. Barbara Johnson. Chicago: University of Chicago Press.

———. 1981b. "D'un ton apocalyptique adopté naguère en philosophie." In Philippe Lacoue-Labarthe and Jean-Luc Nancy, eds., *Les fins de l'Homme: A partir du travail de Jacques Derrida*, 445–479. Paris: Galilée.

———. 1987. *Psyché: Inventions de l'autre*. Paris: Galilée.

———. 1988. *Limited Inc*. Trans. Samuel Weber. Evanston: Northwestern University Press.

Detienne, Marcel. 1979a. *Dionysos Slain*. Trans. Mireille and Leonard Muellner. Baltimore: Johns Hopkins University Press.

———. 1979b. *Les maîtres de vérité dans la Grèce ancienne*. Paris: Maspero.

———. 1986. *The Creation of Mythology*. Trans. Margaret Cook. Chicago: University of Chicago Press.

Detienne, Marcel, and Jean-Pierre Vernant. 1978. *Cunning Intelligence in Greek Culture and Society*. Trans. Janet Lloyd. Atlantic Highlands: Humanities Press.

Dobbins, James C. 1990. "The Biography of Shinran: Apotheosis of a Japanese Buddhist Visionary." *History of Religions* 30, 2: 179–196.

Donner, Neil. 1987. "Sudden and Gradual Intimately Conjoined: Chih-i's T'ien-t'ai view." In Peter N. Gregory, ed., *Sudden and Gradual: Approaches to Enlightenment in Chinese Thought*, 201–226. Honolulu: University of Hawaii Press.

Doré, Henri. 1914–1938. *Researches into Chinese Superstitions*. Trans. M. Kennely. 11 vols. Shanghai: T'usewei Press.

Douglas, Mary, 1970a. *Natural Symbols: Explorations in Cosmology*. Harmondsworth: Penguin Books.

———. 1970b. *Purity and Danger*. Harmondsworth: Penguin Books.

Drège, Jean-Pierre. 1981a. "Clefs des Songes de Touen-houang." In Michel Soymié, ed., *Nouvelles contributions aux études de Touen-houang*, Vol. 3: 205–249. Geneva: Droz.

———. 1981b. "Notes d'onirologie chinoise." *BEFEO* 70: 271–289.

Dreyfus, Hubert L. 1984. "Interpretation in Late Heidegger and Recent Foucault." In G. Shapiro and A. Sica, eds., *Hermeneutics: Questions and Prospects*. Amherst: University of Massachusetts Press.

Dreyfus, Hubert L., and Paul Rabinow. 1983. *Michel Foucault: Beyond Structuralism and Hermeneutics*. Chicago: University of Chicago Press.

———. 1986. "What is Maturity? Habermas and Foucault on 'What is Enlightenment?'" In David C. Hoy, ed., *Foucault: A Critical Reader*, 109–121. New York: Basil Blackwell.

Duara, Prasenjit. 1988. "Superscribing Symbols: The Myth of Guandi, Chinese God of War." *Journal of Asian Studies* 47, 4: 778–795.

Dudbridge, Glen. 1978. *The Legend of Miao-shan*. Oxford Oriental Monographs 1. London: Ithaca Press.

Dumont, Louis. 1960. "World Renunciation in Indian Religions." *Contributions to Indian Sociology* 4: 33–62.

———. 1970. *Homo Hierarchicus: The Caste System and its Implications*. Trans. Mark Sainsbury. Chicago: University of Chicago Press.

Dumoulin, Heinrich, S. J. 1953. *The Development of Chinese Zen after the Sixth Patriarch in the Light of the Mumonkan*. Trans. Ruth Fuller Sasaki. New York: The First Zen Institute of America.

———. 1984. "The Person in Buddhism: Religious and Artistic Aspects." *Japanese Journal of Religious Studies* 11, 2–3: 143–167.

———. 1988–1990. *Zen Buddhism: A History*. 2 vols. New York: Macmillan.

Dunne, George H., S. J. 1962. *Generation of Giants: The Story of the Jesuits in China in the last Decades of the Ming Dynasty*. London: Burns and Oates.

Dupont, Florence. 1989. "The Emperor-God's Other Body." In Michel Feher, ed., *Fragments for a History of the Human Body*, Pt. 3: 397–420. New York: Urzone.

Dupront, Alphonse. 1987. *Du sacré: Croisades et pélerinages, Images et langages*. Paris: Gallimard.

Durkheim, Emile. 1960. *Les formes élémentaires de la vie religieuse*. Paris: Presses Universitaires de France.

Durkheim, Emile, and Marcel Mauss. 1963. *Primitive Classification*. Trans. Rodney Needham. Chicago: University of Chicago Press.

Durt, Hubert. 1983. "Daigenshuri." In *Hōbōgirin*, 6: 599–609. Paris: Adrien Maisonneuve.

Durt, Hubert. 1987. "The Meaning of Archeology in Ancient Buddhism: Notes on the Stūpas of Aśoka and the Worship of the 'Buddhas of the Past' according to Three Stories in the *Samguk Yusa*." In *Buddhism and Science: Commemorative Volume for the 80th Anniversary of the Founding of Tongguk University*, 1223–1241. Seoul: Tongguk University.

Duyvendak, J. J. L. 1947. "The Dreams of the Emperor Hsüan-tsung." In *India Antiqua*, 102–108. J.-Ph. Vogel Festschrift. Leiden: E. J. Brill.

Eberhard, Wolfram. 1967. *Guilt and Sin in Traditional China*. Berkeley: University of California Press.

———. 1971. *Moral and Social Values of the Chinese: Collected Essays*. Taibei: Chinese Materials and Research Aids Service Center.

Ebersole, Gary L. 1989. *Ritual Poetry and the Politics of Death in Early Japan*. Princeton: Princeton University Press.

Ebrey, Patricia. 1989a. "Cremation in Sung China." Unpublished paper.

———. 1989b. "State Response to Popular Funeral Practices in Sung China." Unpublished paper.

Eck, Diana. 1985. *Darśan: Seeing the Divine Image in India*. Chambersburg, PA: Anima Books.

Ecke, Gustav, and Paul Demiéville. 1935. *The Twin Pagodas of Zayton: A Study of Later Buddhist Sculpture in China*. Cambridge, MA: Harvard University Press.

Eisenstadt, S. N. 1968. *Max Weber on Charisma and Institution Building*. Chicago: University of Chicago Press.

Eliade, Mircea. 1959. *The Sacred and the Profane: The Nature of Religion*. Trans. Willard R. Trask. New York: Harcourt, Brace.

———. 1969a. *The Quest*. Chicago: University of Chicago Press.

———. 1969b. *Yoga: Immortality and Freedom*. Trans. Willard R. Trask. Princeton: Princeton University Press.

———. 1974. *Shamanism: Archaic Techniques of Ecstasy*. Trans. Willard R. Trask. Princeton: Princeton University Press.

Elias, Norbert. 1982. *Power and Civility: The Civilizing Process: Volume II*. Trans. Edmund Jephcott. New York: Pantheon Books.

———. 1983. *The Court Society*. Trans. Edmund Jephcott. New York: Pantheon Books.

Elison, George. 1973. *Deus Destroyed: The Image of Christianity in Early Modern Japan*. Cambridge, MA: Harvard University Press.

Elster, Jon. 1979. *Ulysses and the Sirens*. Cambridge: Cambridge University Press.

———. 1983. *Sour Grapes: Studies in the Subversion of Rationality*. Cambridge: Cambridge University Press.

Eoyang, Eugene. 1971. "The Historical Context of Tun-huang Pien-wen." *Literature East and West* 15, 3: 339–357.

Evans-Wentz, W. Y., ed. 1954. *The Tibetan Book of the Great Liberation*. London: Oxford University Press.

Falk, Nancy. 1977. "To Gaze on the Sacred Traces." *History of Religions* 16, 4: 281–293.

Faure, Bernard. 1983. "Shen-hsiu et *l'Avataṃsaka*." *Zinbun: Memoirs of the Research Institute for Humanistic Studies* 19: 1–15.

————. 1986a. "Bodhidharma as Textual and Religious Paradigm." *History of Religions* 25, 3: 187–198.

————. 1986b. "Le maître de dhyāna Chih-ta et le 'subitisme' de l'école du Nord." *Cahiers d'Extrême-Asie* 2: 123–131.

————. 1986c. "The Theory of One-Practice Samādhi (*i-hsing san-mei*) in Ch'an Buddhism." In Peter N. Gregory, ed., *Traditions of Meditation in Chinese Buddhism*, 99–128. Honolulu: University of Hawaii Press.

————. 1986d. *Le Traité de Bodhidharma: Première anthologie du bouddhisme Chan.* Paris: Le Mail.

————. 1987a. "The Daruma-shū, Dōgen and Sōtō Zen." *Monumenta Nipponica* 42, 1: 25–55.

————. 1987b. "Space and Place in Chinese Religious Traditions." *History of Religions* 26, 4: 337–356.

————. 1987c. *La vision immédiate: Nature, éveil et tradition selon le Shōbōgenzō.* Paris: Le Mail.

————. 1988. *La volonté d'orthodoxie dans le bouddhisme chinois.* Paris: Editions du C.N.R.S.

————. 1989. *Le bouddhisme Ch'an en mal d'histoire: Genèse d'une tradition religieuse dans la Chine des T'ang.* Paris: Ecole Française d'Extrême-Orient.

————. 1990. "Alternative Images of Pilgrimage: Sung-shan and Ts'ao-hsi." In Susan Naquin and Chün-fang Yü, eds., *Pilgrimage and Sacred Sites in China.* Berkeley: University of California Press (forthcoming).

Favret-Saada, Jeanne. 1980. *Deadly Words: Witchcraft in the Bocage.* Cambridge: Cambridge University Press.

Feher, Michel, ed. 1989. *Fragments for a History of the Human Body.* 3 vols. New York: Urzone.

Feng, Youlang. 1989. "On the Chan Sect." *Chinese Studies in Philosophy* 20, 2: 3–38.

Feteke, John, ed. 1984. *The Structural Allegory: Reconstructive Encounters with the New French Thought.* Minneapolis: University of Minnesota Press.

Filliozat, Jean. 1963. "La mort volontaire par le feu et la tradition bouddhique indienne." *Journal Asiatique* 251: 21–51.

Fingarette, Herbert. 1972. *The Secular as Sacred.* New York: Harper and Row.

Fischer, Michael. 1986. "Ethnicity and the Post-Modern Arts of Memory." In James Clifford and George E. Marcus, eds., *Writing Culture: The Poetics and Politics of Ethnography*, 194–233. Berkeley: University of California Press.

Foard, James. 1977. "Ippen Shōnin and Popular Buddhism in Kamakura Japan." Ph.D. diss., Stanford University.

————. 1980. "In Search of a Lost Reformation: A Reconsideration of Kamakura Buddhism." *Japanese Journal of Religious Studies* 7, 4: 261–291.

Forte, Antonino. 1976. *Political Propaganda and Ideology in China at the End of the Seventh Century: Inquiry into the Nature, Authors and Function of the Tun-huang Document S. 6502 Followed by an Annotated Translation.* Naples: Istituto Universario Orientale.

Foucault, Michel. 1972. *The Archeology of Knowledge: & The Discourse on Language.* Trans. Sheridan Smith. New York: Pantheon Books.

————. 1973a. *Madness and Civilization: A History of Insanity in the Age of Reason.* New York: Vintage/Random House.

Foucault, Michel. 1973b. *The Order of Things: An Archeology of the Human Sciences.* New York: Vintage/Random House.

———. 1977. *Language, Counter-memory, Practice: Selected Essays and Interviews.* Ed. Donald F. Bouchard. Ithaca: Cornell University Press.

———. 1979. *Discipline and Punish: The Birth of the Prison.* Trans. Alan Sheridan. New York: Vintage/Random House.

———. 1980. *Power/Knowledge: Selected Interviews and Other Writings, 1972–1977.* New York: Pantheon Books.

———. 1984. "Space, Knowledge and Power." In Paul Rabinow, ed., *The Foucault Reader,* 239–256. New York: Pantheon Books.

———. 1986a. *The Care of the Self: History of Sexuality 3.* Trans. Robert Hurley. New York: Vintage Books.

———. 1986b. "Of Other Spaces." *Diacritics* 16, 1: 22–27.

Foucault, Michel, and Ludwig Binswanger. 1984–1985. *Dream and Existence.* Trans. Forrest Williams and Jacob Needleman. *Review of Existential Psychology and Psychiatry* 19, 1. (Special issue)

Foulk, Theodore Griffith. 1987a. "The 'Ch'an School' and its Place in the Buddhist Monastic Tradition." Ph.D. diss., University of Michigan.

———. 1987b. "Zen Buddhist Ceremony and Ritual." Unpublished ms.

———. 1988. "The Zen Institution in Modern Japan." In Kenneth Kraft, ed., *Zen: Tradition and Transition: A Sourcebook by Contemporary Zen Masters and Scholars,* 157–177. New York: Grove Press.

———. 1989. "Ch'an Monastic Practice, 700–1300." Unpublished paper.

Foulk, Griffith, Elisabeth Horton, and Robert Sharf. 1990. "The Meanings and Functions of Ch'an and Zen Portraiture." *Cahiers d'Extrême-Asie* (forthcoming).

Frame, Donald M., ed. 1963. *Montaigne's Essays and Selected Writings.* New York: St. Martin's Press.

Frank, Bernard. 1986. "Vacuité et corps actualisé." In *Le temps de la réflexion VII: Corps des dieux,* 141–170. Paris: Gallimard.

Freedman, Maurice. 1974. "On the Sociological Study of Chinese Religion." In Arthur Wolf, ed., *Religion and Ritual in Chinese Society,* 19–41. Stanford: Stanford University Press.

Freund, Julien. 1986. "Le polythéisme chez Max Weber." *Archives de sciences sociales des religions* 61, 1: 51–61.

Fu, Charles Wei Hsun. 1973. "Morality or Beyond: The Neo-Confucian Confrontation with Mahāyāna Buddhism." *Philosophy East and West* 23, 3: 375–396.

Fujii Masao 藤井正雄, ed. 1977. *Bukkyō girei jiten* 仏教儀礼辞典 [A Dictionary of Buddhist Ritual]. Tokyo. Tōkyōdō.

Funaoka Makoto 般岡誠. 1984. "Nihon Zenshūshi ni okeru Darumashū no ichi" 日本禅宗史における達摩宗の位置 [The Position of the Daruma School in the History of the Japanese Zen Sect]. *Shūgaku kenkyū* 26: 103–108.

———. 1987. *Nihon zenshū no seiritsu* 日本禅宗の成立 [The Constitution of the Japanese Zen Sect]. Tokyo: Yoshikawa Kōbunkan.

Furuta Shōkin 古田紹欽. 1979. *Bassui* 抜隊. Nihon no goroku 11. Tokyo: Kōdansha.

Gadamer, Hans-Georg. 1982. *Truth and Method*. New York: Crossroad.

Gallagher, Louis J., trans. 1953. *China in the 16th Century: The Journals of Matthew Ricci: 1583–1610*. New York: Random House.

Gauchet, Marcel. 1981–1982. "Des deux corps du roi au pouvoir sans corps: Christianisme et politique." *Le Débat* 14: 135–157; 15: 147–168.

———. 1985. *Le désenchantement du monde*. Paris: Gallimard.

Geary, Patrick. 1978. *Furta Sacra: Thefts of Relics in the Central Middle Ages*. Princeton: Princeton University Press.

———. 1986. "Sacred Commodities: The Circulation of Medieval Relics." In Arjun Appadurai, ed., *The Social Life of Things: Commodities in Cultural Perspective*, 169–191. Cambridge: Cambridge University Press.

Geertz, Clifford. 1973. *The Interpretation of Cultures*. New York: Basic Books.

———. 1983. *Local Knowledge: Further Essays in Interpretive Anthropology*. New York: Basic Books.

Gernet, Jacques. 1949. *Les entretiens du maître de dhyāna Chen-houei du Ho-tsö*. Paris: Adrien Maisonneuve.

———. 1956. *Les aspects économiques du bouddhisme dans la société chinoise du Ve au Xe siècle*. Paris: Ecole Française d'Extrême-Orient.

———. 1959. "Les suicides par le feu chez les bouddhistes chinois du Ve au Xe siècle." In *Mélanges publiés par l'Institut des Hautes Etudes Chinoises*, Vol. 2: 528–558. Paris: Presses Universitaires de France.

———. 1981. "Techniques de recueillement, religion et philosophie: A propos du *jingzuo* néo-confucéen." BEFEO 69: 289–305.

———. 1982. *Chine et Christianisme: Action et réaction*. Paris: Gallimard.

———. 1985. *China and the Christian Impact: A Conflict of Cultures*. Trans. Janet Lloyd. Cambridge: Cambridge University Press.

———. 1987. "Sur le corps et l'esprit chez les Chinois." In *Poikilia: Etudes offertes à Jean-Pierre Vernant*, 369–377. Paris: Ecole des Hautes Etudes en Sciences Sociales.

Giddens, Anthony. 1976. *New Rules of Sociological Method*. New York: Basic Books.

Giesey, Ralph E. 1960. *The Royal Funeral Ceremony in Renaissance France*. Geneva.

———. 1987. *Cérémonial et puissance souveraine: France, XVe-XVIIe siècles*. Paris: Armand Colin.

Gimello, Robert M. 1976. "Apophatic and Kataphatic Discourse in Mahāyāna: A Chinese View." *Philosophy East and West* 26, 2: 116–136.

———. 1982. "The Sudden/Gradual Polarity: A Recurrent Theme in Chinese Thought." *Journal of Chinese Philosophy* 9: 471–486.

———. 1989a. "Ch'an Buddhism, Learning, and Letters During the Northern Sung: The Case of Chüeh-fan Hui-hung (1071–1128)." Unpublished paper.

———. 1989b. "Chang Shang-yin on Wu-t'ai Shan." Unpublished paper.

Gimello, Robert M., and Peter N. Gregory, eds. 1983. *Studies in Ch'an and Hua-yen*. Honolulu: University of Hawaii Press.

Ginzburg, Carlo. 1982. *The Cheese and the Worms: The Cosmos of a Sixteenth-Century Miller*. New York: Penguin Books.

Girard, René. 1965. *Desire, Deceit, and the Novel: The Self and Other in Literary Structure*. Baltimore: Johns Hopkins University Press.

Girard, René. 1977. *Violence and the Sacred*. Trans. P. Gregory. Baltimore: Johns Hopkins University Press.

Girardot, Norman J. 1983. *Myth and Meaning in Early Taoism: The Theme of Chaos (Hun-tun)*. Berkeley: University of California Press.

Godelier, Maurice. 1973. *Horizon, trajets marxistes en anthropologie*. 2 vols. Paris: Maspero.

———. 1984. *L'idéel et le matériel: Pensée, économies, sociétés*. Paris: Fayard.

Gombrich, Richard. 1966. " The Consecration of a Buddhist Image." *Journal of Asian Studies* 26, 1: 23–36.

Gómez, Luis O. 1977. "The Bodhisattva as Wonder-Worker." In Lewis R. Lancaster, ed., *Prajñāpāramitā and Related Systems: Studies in Honor of Edward Conze*, 221–261. Berkeley: Buddhist Studies Series, University of California.

———. 1985. "Contributions to the Methodological Clarification of Interfaith Dialogue among Buddhists and Christians." In G. W. Houston, ed., *The Cross and the Lotus: Christianity and Buddhism in Dialogue*, 127–208. Delhi: Motilal Banarsidass.

———. 1987. "Purifying Gold: The Metaphor of Effort and Intuition in Buddhist Thought and Practice." In Peter N. Gregory, ed., *Sudden and Gradual: Approaches to Enlightenment in Chinese Thought*, 67–165. Honolulu: University of Hawaii Press.

Gonda, J. 1970. *Eye and Gaze in the Veda*. Amsterdam: Verhandelingen der Koninklijke Nederlandse Akademie van Wetenschappen.

Goody, Jack. 1977. *The Domestication of the Savage Mind*. Cambridge: Cambridge University Press.

———. 1986. *The logic of Writing and the Organization of Society*. Cambridge: Cambridge University Press.

Gorai Shigeru 五来重. 1976. *Bukkyō to minzoku: Bukkyō minzokugaku nyūmon* 仏教と民俗—仏教民俗学入門 [Buddhism and Popular Customs: An Introduction to Buddhist Folklore]. Tokyo: Kadogawa shoten.

———. 1979. *Zoku bukkyō to minzoku* 続仏教と民俗. Tokyo: Kadogawa shoten.

———. 1983. "Sō to kuyō" 葬と供養 [Funerals and Services]. *Tōhōkai* 112: 34–42.

Gourevitch, Aaron J. [1972] 1985. *Categories of Medieval Culture*. Trans. G. L. Campbell. London: Routledge and Kegan Paul.

Grabar, André. 1984. *L'iconoclasme byzantin*. Paris: Flammarion.

Granet, Marcel. 1968. *La pensée chinoise*. Paris: Albin Michel.

Granoff, Phyllis, and Koichi Shinohara, eds. 1988. *Monks and Magicians: Religious Biographies in Asia*. Oakville, New York and London: Mosaic Press.

Grapard, Allan. 1982. "Flying Mountains and Walkers of Emptiness: Toward a Definition of Sacred Space in Japanese Religion." *History of Religions* 20, 3: 195–221.

———. 1986. "Lotus in the Mountain, Mountain in the Lotus." *Monumenta Nipponica* 41: 21–50.

———. 1987. "Linguistic Cubism: A Singularity of Pluralism in the Sannō Cult." *Japanese Journal of Religious Studies* 14, 2–3: 211–233.

Gregory, Peter Nielsen. 1983. "Tsung-mi's 'Inquiry into the Origin of Man': A Study of Chinese Buddhist Hermeneutics." Ph.D. diss., Harvard University.

———, ed. 1986. *Traditions of Meditation in Chinese Buddhism*. Honolulu: University of Hawaii Press.

———, ed. 1987: *Sudden and Gradual: Approaches to Enlightenment in Chinese Thought*. Honolulu: University of Hawaii Press.

Greimas, A. J. 1985. "The Love-Life of the Hippopotamus: A Seminar with A. J. Greimas." In Marshall Blonski, ed., *On Signs*, 341–362. Baltimore: Johns Hopkins University Press.

Grimes, Ronald. 1982. *Beginnings in Ritual Studies*. Lanham: University Press of America.

Groethuysen, Bernard. [1927] 1968. *The Bourgeois: Catholicism versus Capitalism in Eighteenth-Century France*. New York: Holt, Rinehardt and Winston.

Groner, Paul. 1984. *Saichō: The Establishment of the Japanese Tendai School*. Berkeley: Buddhist Studies Series, University of California.

Groot, J. J. M. de. 1893. *Le Code du Mahāyāna en Chine, son influence sur la vie monacale et sur le monde laïque*. Amsterdam: J. Müller.

———. [1910] 1982. *The Religious System of China: Its Ancient Forms, Evolution, History and Present Aspects; Manners, Customs and Social Institutions Connected Therewith*. 6 vols. Taibei: Southern Materials Center.

Grunebaum, G. E. von, and Roger Caillois, eds. 1966. *The Dream and Human Societies*. Berkeley and Los Angeles: University of California Press.

Guth, Christine M. E. 1987. "The Divine Boy in Japanese Art." *Monumenta Nipponica* 42, 1: 1–24.

Gyatso, Janet. 1988. "The Relic Text as Prophecy: The Semantic Drift of *Byang-bu* and Its Appropriation in the Treasure Tradition." Unpublished paper.

Ha, Tae-hung, and Grafton K. Mintz, trans. 1972. *Samguk Yusa: Legends and History of the Three Kingdoms of Ancient Korea*. Seoul: Yonsei University Press.

Habermas, Jürgen. 1981. "Modernity Versus Post-Modernity." *New German Critique* 22: 3–14.

———. 1986. "Taking Aim at the Heart of the Present." In David C. Hoy, ed., *Foucault: A Critical Reader*, 103–108. New York: Basil Blackwell.

Hackmann, Heinrich. 1908. "*Pai-chang ch'ing-kuei:* The Rules of Buddhist Monastic Life in China." *T'oung Pao* 9: 651–662.

Haguenauer, Charles. 1937. "Du caractère de la représentation de la mort dans le Japon antique." *T'oung Pao* 33: 158–183.

Hall, John W., and Toyoda Takeshi, eds. 1977. *Japan in the Muromachi Age*. Berkeley: University of California Press.

Hamerton-Kelly, Robert G., ed. 1987. *Violent Origins: Walter Burkert, René Girard and Jonathan Z. Smith on Ritual Killing and Cultural Formation*. Stanford: Stanford University Press.

Han Kidu 韓基斗. 1984. "Keitoku Dentōroku ni miru Shiragi Zen" 景徳伝灯録 に見る新羅禅 [Silla Buddhism as Reflected in the *Jingde chuandeng lu*]. *Zen bunka kenkyūsho kiyō* 13: 129–144.

Han Yuan 憨園. 1978. "Zhongguo fota zhi guizhi" 中國佛塔之規制 [Historical Monographs on the Temple Stūpa of Chinese Buddhism]. In Zhang Mantao, ed., *Zhongguo fojiao sita shizi*, 311–323. Taibei: Dasheng wenhua.

Hansen, Valerie. 1989. "The Popular Pantheon During the T'ang-Sung Transition." Unpublished paper.

———. 1990. *Changing Gods in Medieval China*. Princeton: Princeton University Press.

Hanuki Masai 葉貫磨哉. 1962. "Tōmon zensō to shinnin kedō no setsuwa" 洞門禅僧と神人化度の説話 [Legends concerning Zen Monks of the Sōtō Sect and their Predication to the Gods]. *Komazawa shigaku* 10:44–51.

Harada Kōdō 原田弘道. 1988. "Chūsei Sōtōshū to Rakan shinkō" 中世曹洞宗と羅漢信仰 [The Medieval Sōtō Sect and the Arhat Cult]. *IBK* 37, 1: 232–238.

Harada Masatoshi 原田正俊. 1987. "Tō Tō tenjin gazō ni miru zenshū to Muromachi bunka" 渡唐天神画像にみる禅宗と室町文化 [The Zen Sect as Seen in the Images of Michizane in China and Muromachi Culture]. In *Yokoda Ken'ichi sensei koki: bunkashi ronsō* 横田健一先生古稀記念―文化史論叢, Vol. 2: 376–395. Tokyo: Sōgensha.

Harari, Josué, ed. 1979. *Textual Strategies: Perspectives in Post-Structuralist Criticism*. Ithaca: Cornell University Press.

Harootunian, H. D. 1988. *Things Seen and Unseen: Discourse and Ideology in Tokugawa Nativism*. Chicago: University of Chicago Press.

Harrison, Paul. 1988. "Buddhism: A Religion of Revelation After All?" *Numen* 34, 2: 256–264.

Hasebe Kōichi 長谷部好一. 1972. "Zenmon no girei (1)" 禅門の儀礼 [The Ritual of the Zen School]. *Aichi Gakuin Zen kenkyūsho kiyō* 2: 40–52.

Hastings, James, ed. 1924. *Encyclopaedia of Religion and Ethics*. London: Scribners.

Heesterman, J. C. 1985. *The Inner Conflict of Tradition: Essays in Indian Ritual, Kingship, and Society*. Chicago: University of Chicago Press.

Heidegger, Martin. 1962. *Being and Time*. Trans. John Macquarrie and Edward Robinson. New York: Harper and Row.

———. 1971. *On the Way to Language*. Trans. Peter D. Hertz. New York: Harper and Row.

Henderson, John B. 1984. *The Development and Decline of Chinese Cosmology*. New York: Columbia University Press.

Henmi Baiei 逸見梅栄. 1974. "Sōjiji no butsuzō" 総持寺の仏像 [The Buddhist Icons at Sōjiji]. In Keizan zenji hōsan kankōkai, ed., *Keizan zenji kenkyū*, 1103–1107. Tokyo: Keizan zenji hōsan kankōkai.

Hertz, Robert. [1907] 1960. "A Contribution to the Study of Collective Representations of Death." Trans. Rodney and Claudia Needham. In Rodney Needham, ed., *Death and the Right Hand*, 27–86. Glencoe, IL: The Free Press.

———. 1970. *Sociologie religieuse et folklore*. Paris: Presses Universitaires de France.

———. [1909] 1973. "The Preeminence of the Right Hand: A Study in Religious Polarity." In Rodney Needham, ed., *Right and Left: Essays on Dual Symbolic Classification*, 3–31. Chicago: University of Chicago Press.

Hinsch, Bret. 1990. *Passions of the Cut Sleeve: The Male Homosexual Tradition in China*. Berkeley: University of California Press.

Hirakawa, Akira. 1963. "The Rise of Mahāyāna Buddhism and its Relationship to the Worship of Stūpas." *Memoirs of the Research Department of the Tōyō Bunko* 22: 57–106.

Hirano Sōjō 平野宗浄, ed. 1970. *Tongo yōmon* 頓悟要門 [*The Essential Gate to Sudden Awakening (Dunwu yaomen)*]. Zen no goroku 6. Tokyo: Chikuma shobō.

Hirazuka Ryōsen 平塚良宣. 1987. *Nihon ni okeru danshoku no kenkyū* 日本における男色の研究 [A Study of Male Homosexuality in Japan]. Tokyo: Ningen no Kagakusha.

Hirose Ryōkō 広瀬良弘. 1983. "Sōtō zensō ni okeru shinjin kedō akurei chin'atsu" 曹洞禅僧における神人化度, 悪霊鎮圧 [The Pacification of Evil Spirits and the Conversion of Gods by Sōtō Monks]. *IBK* 21, 2: 233–236.

———. 1985a. "Chūkinsei ni okeru Sōtō zensō no katsudō to sōsai ni tsuite" 中近世における曹洞禅僧の活動と葬祭について [On the Activity of Sōtō Zen Monks and Funerals in the Pre-Modern Period]. *Shūgaku kenkyū* 27: 143–150.

———. 1985b. "Chūsei koki ni okeru zensō, zenji to chiiki shakai: Tōkai Kantō chihō no Sōtōshū o chūshin to shite" 中世後期における禅僧, 禅寺と地域社会—東海関東地方の曹洞宗を中心として [Zen Monks and Zen Monasteries in the Late Medieval Period and Regional Society]. In Kawamura Kōdō and Ishikawa Rikisan, eds., *Dōgen zenji to Sōtōshū*, 214–249. Tokyo: Yoshikawa kōbunkan.

Hōbōgirin: Dictionnaire encyclopédique du bouddhisme d'après les sources chinoises et japonaises. Vols. 1–6. Paris: Adrien Maisonneuve, 1927–1983.

Hori, Ichirō. 1962. "Self-mummified Buddhas in Japan: An Aspect of the Shūgendō ('Mountain Asceticism') Sect." *History of Religions* 1, 2: 222–242.

Horkheimer, Max, and Theodor M. Adorno. 1972. *Dialectic of Enlightenment*. Trans. John Cumming. New York: Seabury Press.

Horner, I. B., trans. 1938–1966. *The Book of Discipline (Vinaya Piṭaka)*. 6 vols. London: Luzac and Company.

Hoy, David C., ed. 1986. *Foucault: A Critical Reader*. New York: Basil Blackwell.

Hsiung, Ping-ming. 1984. *Zhang Xu et la calligraphie cursive folle*. Paris: Collège de France.

Hsu, Sung-peng. 1979. *A Buddhist Leader in Ming China: The Life and Thought of Han-shan Te-ch'ing, 1546–1623*. University Park: Pennsylvania State University Press.

Hu Shih. 1932. "The Development of Zen Buddhism in China." *The Chinese and Political Science Review* 15, 4: 475–505. Repr. in Hu Shi, *Ko Teki Zengakuan*, 691–722. Ed. Yanagida Seizan. Kyoto: Chūbun shuppansha, 1975.

———. 1953. "Ch'an (Zen) Buddhism in China: Its History and Method." *Philosophy East and West* 3, 1: 3–24.

Hu Shi 胡適 [Hu Shih], ed. [1930] 1970. *Shenhui heshang yiji* 神會和尚遺集 [Collected Works of Master Shenhui]. Taibei: Hu Shi jinianguan.

Hu Shi. 1975. *Ko Teki Zengakuan* 胡適禅学案 [The Writings of Hu Shi on Chan]. Ed. Yanagida Seizan. Kyoto: Chūbun shuppansha.

Huang, Chi-chiang. 1986. "Experiment in Syncretism: Ch'i-sung (1007–1072) and Eleventh-Century Chinese Buddhism." Ph.D. diss., University of Arizona.

Huang Tsung-hsi. 1987. *The Record of Ming Scholars*. Ed. Julia Ching. Honolulu: University of Hawaii Press.

Hubert, Henri, and Marcel Mauss. 1964. *Sacrifice: Its Nature and Function*. London: Cohen and West.

Huizinga, Jan. 1952. *Homo Ludens*. London: Routledge and Kegan Paul.

Huntington, Richard, and Peter Metcalf. 1979. *Celebration of Death: The Anthropology of Mortuary Ritual*. New York: Cambridge University Press.

Hyers, Conrad. 1973. *Zen and the Comic Spirit*. Philadelphia: Westminster.

Ichikawa Hakugen 市川白弦, Iriya Yoshitaka 入矢義高, and Yanagida Seizan 柳田聖山, eds. 1972. *Chūsei zenke no shisō* 中世禅家の思想 [The Thought of Medieval Zen Masters]. Tokyo: Iwanami shoten.

Imaeda Aishin 今枝愛心. 1966. "Chūsei zensō no seikatsu" 中世禅僧の生活 [The Life of Medieval Zen Monks]. *Kokubungaku: kaishaku to kanshō* 31, 12: 215–223.

———. 1970. *Chūsei zenshūshi no kenkyū* 中世禅宗史の研究 [Studies in the History of the Medieval Zen School]. Tokyo: Tōkyō Daigaku shuppankai.

———. 1974. "Keizan zenji no rekishi-teki ichi: Hakusan Tendai to no kanren o chūshin to shite" 瑩山禅師の歴史的位置 [The Historical Situation of Keizan]. In Keizan zenji hōsan kankōkai, ed., *Keizan zenji kenkyū*, 81–99. Tokyo: Keizan zenji hōsan kankōkai.

———, ed. 1979. *Zenshū no shomondai* 禅宗の諸問題 [Questions concerning the Zen School]. Tokyo: Yuzankaku.

Imamura Yoshio 今村与志雄, ed. 1980–1981. *Yuyō zasso* 酉陽雑俎 [*Youyang zazu*]. 5 vols. Tokyo: Heibonsha.

Inoue Hisashi 井上ひさし. 1971. *Dōgen no bōken* 道元の昌険 [The Adventure of Dōgen]. Shinchō bunko. Tokyo: Shinchōsha.

Inoue Ichii 井上以智為. 1941. "Kan'u shibyō no yūrai narabini hensen" 關羽祠廟の由来並に變遷 [The Origin and Development of Temples Dedicated to Guan Yu]. *Shirin* 26: 41–51, 242–283.

Iriya Yoshitaka 入矢義高, ed. 1958. *Chūgoku koten bungaku zenshū* 中国古典文学全集 [Complete Works of Classical Chinese Literature]. Vol. 7. Tokyo: Heibonsha.

———, ed. 1969. *Denshin hōyō. Enryōroku* 伝心法要, 宛陵録 [The *Chuanxin fayao* and the *Yuanling lu*]. Zen no goroku 8. Tokyo: Chikuma shobō.

———. 1973a. "Chinese Poetry and Zen." *The Eastern Buddhist* (n.s.) 6, 1: 54–67.

———, ed. 1973b. *Hō Koji goroku* 龐居士語録 [The Recorded Sayings of Layman Pang]. Zen no goroku 7. Tokyo: Chikuma shobō.

Irokawa Daikichi. 1985. *The Culture of the Meiji Period*. Trans. ed. Marius B. Jansen. Princeton: Princeton University Press.

Isambert, François-André. 1979. *Rite et efficacité symbolique: Essai d'anthropologie sociologique*. Paris: Cerf.

————. 1982. *Le sens du sacré: Fête et religion populaire*. Paris: Editions de Minuit.

————. 1986. "Le 'désenchantement' du monde: Non-sens et renouveau du sens." *Archives de sciences sociales des religions* 61, 1: 83–103.

Ishida Jūshi 石田充之, ed. 1972. *Kamakura bukkyō seiritsu no kenkyū: Shunjō risshi* 鎌倉仏教成立の研究—俊芿律師 [The Vinaya Master Shunjō: Researches on the Constitution of Kamakura Buddhism]. Kyoto: Hōzōkan.

Ishii Shūdō 石井修道. 1974. "Busshō Tokkō to Nihon Darumashū: Kanazawa bunko hokan *Jōtō shōgakuron* o tegakari toshite" 仏照徳光と日本達摩宗—金沢文庫保管「成等正覚論」をてがかりとして [Fozhao Deguang and the Japanese Bodhidharma School]. *Kanazawa bunko kenkyū* 20, 11: 1–16, 20, 12: 1–20.

————. 1987. *Sōdai zenshūshi no kenkyū* 宋代禅宗史の研究 [Researches on the History of the Chan School during the Song]. Tokyo: Daitō shuppansha.

Ishikawa Rikisan 石川力山. 1982. "Chūsei Sōtōshū no chihō tenkai to Gennō Shinshō" 中世曹洞宗の地方展開と原翁心昭 [The Regional Development of the Medieval Sōtō Sect and Gennō Shinshō]. *IBK* 31, 1: 227–231.

————. 1983. "Chūsei Sōtōshū kirigami no bunrui shiron (1)" 中世曹洞宗切紙の分類試論 [Essay on the Classification of the *kirigami* of Medieval Sōto, 1]. *KDBGKK* 41: 338–350.

————. 1984a. "Chūsei Sōtōshū kirigami no bunrui shiron (4)." *KDBGR* 15: 152–169.

————. 1984b. "Chūsei zenshū to shinbutsu shūgo: Tokuni Sōtōshū no chihōteki tenkai to kirigami shiryō o chūshin ni shite" 中世禅宗と神仏習合—特に曹洞宗の地方的展開と切紙資料を中心にして [The Medieval Sōtō Sect and the Shintō–Buddhist Syncretism]. *Nihon bukkyō* 60–61: 41–56.

————. 1984c. "Darumashū no sōjōbutsu ni tsuite" 達摩宗の相承物について [On the *Tradita* of the Daruma School]. *Shūgaku kenkyū* 26: 109–115.

————. 1985a. "Chūsei Sōtōshū kirigami no bunrui shiron (6)." *KDBGR* 16: 102–152.

————. 1985b. "Chūsei Sōtōshū to reizan shinkō" 中世曹洞宗と霊山信仰 [The Medieval Sōtō Sect and Mountain Cults]. *IBK* 33, 2: 26–31.

————. 1986a. "Chūsei Sōtōshū kirigami no bunrui shiron (7)." *KDBGKK* 44: 250–267.

————. 1986b. "Chūsei Sōtōshū kirigami no bunrui shiron (8)." *KDBGR* 17: 179–213.

————. 1987a. "Chūsei Sōtōshū kirigami no bunrui shiron (9)." *KDBGKK* 45: 167–198.

————. 1987b. "Chūsei Sōtōshū kirigami no bunrui shiron (10)." *KDBGR* 18: 163–192.

————. 1987c. "Chūsei zenshū to sōsō girei" 中世禅宗と葬送儀礼 [The Medieval Zen Sect and Funerary Rituals]. *IBK* 35, 2: 299–304.

————. 1987d. "Zen no sōsō" 禅の葬送 [Zen Funerals]. *Nihongaku* 10: 139–149.

————. 1989. "Shinshū to zenshū no aida: *Jōdo shinshū hyakutsū kirigami* o meguru shomondai" 真宗と禅宗の間—「浄土真宗百通切紙」をめぐる諸問題 [Relationships between the Shin Sect and the Zen Sect]. *Zengaku kenkyū* 67: 79–109.

Itō Kokan 伊藤古鑑. 1940. "Zenshū no butsuzō ni oite" 禅宗の仏像において [On the Icons of the Zen Sect]. *Zengaku kenkyū* 34: 97–110.

Iyanaga Nobumi. 1983. "Daijizaiten." In *Hōbōgirin*, Vol. 6: 713–765. Paris: Adrien Maisonneuve.

———. 1985. "Récits de la soumission de Maheśvara par Trailokyavijaya— d'après les sources chinoises et japonaises." In Michel Strickmann, ed., *Tantric and Taoist Studies in Honour of R. A. Stein*, Vol. 3: 633–745. Brussels: Institut Belge des Hautes Etudes Chinoises.

Izard, Michel, and Pierre Smith, eds. 1982. *Between Belief and Transgression: Structuralist Essays in Religion, History, and Myth*. Trans. John Leavitt. Chicago: University of Chicago Press.

Jakobson, Roman. 1963. *Essais de linguistique générale: Les fondations du langage*. Paris: Minuit.

Jameson, Fredric. 1972. *The Prison-House of Language: A Critical Account of Structuralism and Russian Formalism*. Princeton: Princeton University Press.

———. 1981. *The Political Unconscious: Narrative as a Socially Symbolic Act*. Ithaca: Cornell University Press.

———. 1985. "The Realist Floor-Plan." In Marshall Blonski, ed., *On Signs*, 373–383. Baltimore: Johns Hopkins University Press.

———. 1988. *The Ideologies of Theory: Essays 1971–1986*. 2 vols. Minneapolis: University of Minnesota Press.

Jan Yün-hua. 1964. "Buddhist Historiography in Sung China." *Zeitschrift der deutschen morgenländischen Gesellschaft* 114, 2: 360–381.

———. 1965. "Buddhist Self-Immolation in Medieval China." *History of Religions* 4, 2: 243–268.

———. 1966a. "Buddhist Relations between India and Sung China." *History of Religions* 6, 1: 24–42; 6, 2: 135–168.

———. 1966b. *A Chronicle of Buddhism in China (580–960 A.D.): Translations of the Monk Chih-p'an's 'Fo-tsu t'ung-chi.'* Santiniketan: Visva-Bharati.

———. 1972. "Tsung-mi: His Analysis of Ch'an Buddhism." *T'oung Pao* 8: 1–54.

———. 冉雲華. 1979. "Donghai dashi Wuxiang zhuan yanjiu" 東海大師無相傳研究 [A Study of the Biography of the Korean Master Wuxiang]. *Dunhuang xue* 4: 47–60.

———. 1982. "Chinese Buddhism in Ta-tu: The New Situation and New Problems." In Hok-lam Chan and Wm. Theodore de Bary, eds., *Yüan Thought: Chinese Thought and Religion under the Mongols*, 375–417. New York: Columbia University Press.

———. 1983. "Seng-ch'ou's Method of Dhyāna." In Whalen Lai and Lewis R. Lancaster, eds., *Early Ch'an in China and Tibet*, 51–63. Berkeley: Asian Humanities Press.

Jankélévitch, Vladimir. 1960. *Le pur et l'impur*. Paris: Flammarion.

Jayawickrama, N. A. 1971. *The Chronicle of the Thūpa and the Thūpavaṃsa*. London: Luzac and Company.

Jochim, Christian. 1988. "'Great' and 'Little,' 'Grid' and 'Group': Defining the Poles of the Elite–Popular Continuum in Chinese Religion." *Journal of Chinese Religions* 16: 18–42.

Johnson, David. 1985. "The City God Cults in T'ang and Sung China." *HJAS* 45: 365–457.

————, ed. 1989. *Ritual Opera, Operatic Ritual: "Mu-lien Rescues his Mother" in Chinese Popular Culture*. Berkeley: Chinese Popular Culture Project, University of California.

Johnson, David, Andrew J. Nathan, and Evelyn S. Rawski, eds. 1985. *Popular Culture in Late Imperial China*. Berkeley: University of California Press.

Jorgensen, John. 1987. "The 'Imperial' Lineage of Ch'an Buddhism: The Role of Confucian Ritual and Ancestor Worship in Ch'an's Search for Legitimation in the mid-T'ang Dynasty." *Papers on Far Eastern History* 35: 89–133.

Jullien, François. 1982a. "L'absence d'inspiration: Représentations chinoises de l'incitation poétique." *Extrême-Orient, Extrême-Occident* 1: 31–71.

————. 1982b. "Le plaisir du texte: L'expérience chinoise de la saveur littéraire." *Extrême-Orient, Extrême-Occident* 1: 73–119.

————. 1984. "L'oeuvre et l'univers: Imitation ou déploiement (Limites à une conception mimétique de la création littéraire dans la tradition chinoise)." *Extrême-Orient, Extrême-Occident* 3: 37–88.

————. 1985. *La valeur allusive: Des catégories originales de l'interprétation poétique dans la tradition chinoise (Contribution à une réflexion sur l'altérité culturelle)*. Paris: Ecole Française d'Extrême-Orient.

————. 1986. "Naissance de l'"imagination': Essai de problématique au travers de la réflexion littéraire de la Chine et de l'Occident." *Extrême-Orient, Extrême-Occident* 7: 23–81.

————. 1989. *Procès ou création: Une introduction à la pensée des lettrés chinois*. Paris: Seuil.

Jung-kwang. 1979. *The Mad Monk: Paintings of Unlimited Action*. Ed. Lewis R. Lancaster. Berkeley: Lancaster-Miller.

Kagamishima Genryū 鏡島元隆, ed. 1961. *Dōgen zenji to sono monryū* 道元禅師とその門流 [Dōgen and his Disciples]. Tokyo: Seishin shobō.

————. 1978. *Manzan. Menzan* 卍山. 面山. Nihon no Zen goroku 18. Tokyo: Kōdansha.

Kagamishima Genryū, Satō Tatsugen 佐藤達玄, and Kosaka Kiyū 小坂機融, eds. 1972. *Yakuchū Zen'en shingi* 訳註禅苑清規 [An annotated translation of the *Chanyuan qinggui*]. Tokyo: Sōtōshū shūmuchō.

Kaltenmark, Max. 1960. *"Ling-pao:* Note sur un terme du taoïsme religieux." In *Mélanges publiés par l'Institut des Hautes Etudes Chinoises*, Vol. 1: 559–588. Paris: Presses Universitaires de France.

Kamata Shigeo 鎌田茂雄. 1964. "Hoku Shū no haibutsu to Zen" 北周の廃仏と禅 [Chan and the Anti-Buddhist Repression of Northern Zhou]. *Shūgaku kenkyū* 6: 556–561.

————, ed. 1971. *Zengen shosenshū tojo* 禅源諸詮集都序 [The *Chanyuan zhuquanji duxu*]. Zen no goroku 9. Tokyo: Chikuma shobō.

————. 1986. *Chūgoku no bukkyō girei* 中国の仏教儀礼 [Chinese Buddhist Rituals]. Tokyo: Daizō shuppansha.

Kamata Shigeo, and Tanaka Hisao 田中久夫, eds. 1971. *Kamakura kyū-bukkyō* 鎌倉旧仏教 [Ancient Buddhism during Kamakura]. Tokyo: Iwanami shoten.

Kantorowicz, Ernst H. 1957. *The King's Two Bodies: A Study in Medieval Political Theology*. Princeton: Princeton University Press.

Kaplan, Steven. 1986. "The Ethiopian Cult of the Saints." *Paideuma* 32: 1–13.

Kapstein, Matthew. 1989. "The Illusion of Spiritual Progress: Remarks on Indo-Tibetan Buddhist Soteriology." Unpublished paper.

Karatani, Kōjin. 1988. "One Spirit, Two Nineteenth Centuries." *The South Atlantic Quarterly* 87, 3: 615–634.

Katō, Shuichi. 1967. "Tominaga Nakamoto, 1715–46: A Tokugawa Iconoclast." *Monumenta Nipponica* 22, 1–2: 177–210.

Katz, Steven T., ed. 1978. *Mysticism and Philosophical Analysis*. New York: Oxford University Press.

Kawaguchi Kōfu 川口高風. 1984. "Ryōjūin ni anchisareru Sōtōshū ryōso no goreikotsu" 霊鷲院に安置される曹洞宗両祖の御霊骨 [The Relics of the Two Patriarchs of the Sōtō School Enshrined at Ryōjūin]. *Aichi gakuin daigaku kenkyūsho kiyō* 13: 9–30.

Kawai, Hayao. 1990. *The Buddhist Priest Myōe: A Life of Dreams*. Trans. Marc Unno. Venice, CA: Lapis Press (forthcoming).

Kawakami Susumu 河上貢, Yoshikawa Motome 吉川需, and Furuoka Hiroshi 吉岡滉, eds. 1979. *Zenshū no bijutsu: Zen-in to teien* 禅宗の美術 — 禅院と庭園 [The Art of the Zen School: Zen Temples and Gardens]. Nihon bijutsu zenshū 13. Tokyo: Gakken.

Kawamura Kōdō 河村孝道 and Ishikawa Rikisan, eds. 1985. *Dōgen zenji to Sōtōshū* 道元禅師と曹洞宗 [Zen Master Dōgen and the Sōtō Sect]. Tokyo: Yoshikawa kōbunkan.

Keizan zenji hōsan kankōkai 瑩山禅師奉讃刊行会, ed. 1974. *Keizan zenji kenkyū* 瑩山禅師研究 [Studies in the Zen Master Keizan]. Tokyo: Keizan zenji hōsan kankōkai.

Kelsey, W. Michael. 1981. "Salvation of the Snake, the Snake of Salvation: Buddhist–Shintō Conflict and Resolution." *Japanese Journal of Religious Studies* 8, 1–2: 83–113.

Kidder, Edward J. 1972. *Early Buddhist Japan*. New York: Praeger.

Kobori, Sohaku, trans. 1970–1971. "*Sokushin-ki*, by Shidō Munan Zenji." *The Eastern Buddhist* (n.s.) 3, 2: 89–118; 4, 1: 116–123; 4, 2: 119–127.

Kobori, Sohaku, and Norman Waddell, trans. 1970. "*Sokushin-ki*, by Shidō Munan zenji." *The Eastern Buddhist* (n.s.) 3, 2: 89–118.

Kodera, Takashi James. 1980. *Dōgen's Formative Years in China: An Historical Study and Annotated Translation of the Hōkyō-ki*. London: Routledge and Kegan Paul.

Koepping, Klaus-Peter. 1985. "Absurdity and Hidden Truth: Cunning Intelligence and Grotesque Body Images as Manifestations of the Trickster." *History of Religions* 24, 3: 191–214.

Kōhō Chisan 孤峰智璨, ed. [1937] 1976. *Jōsai daishi zenshū* 常濟大師全集 [Collected Works of the Great Master Jōsai (a.k.a. Keizan)]. Yokohama: Daihonzan Sōjiji.

Komatsu Kazuhiko 小松和彦. 1985. *Kamigami no seishinshi* 神々の精神史 [A Spiritual History of the Gods]. Tokyo: Hokutō shuppan.

Komazawa Daigaku Zenshūshi Kenkyūkai 駒沢大学禅宗史研究会, ed. 1978.

Enō kenkyū 慧能研究 [Researches on Huineng]. Tokyo: Taishūkan shoten.

Kosugi Kazuo 小杉一雄. 1937. "Nikushinzō oyobi yuikaizō no kenkyū" 肉身像及遺灰像の研究 [Studies in "Flesh-body Icons" and "Ash Icons"]. *Tōyō gakuhō* 24, 3: 93–124.

Kraft, Kenneth. 1981. "Musō Kokushi's *Dialogues in a Dream* (Selections)." *The Eastern Buddhist* (n.s.) 14, 1: 75–93.

Kristeva, Julia. 1969. *Semeiotike: Recherches pour une sémanalyse*. Paris: Seuil.

Kunishita Hirosato 圀下大慧. 1921–1922. "Gensho ni okeru teishitsu to zensō to no kankei ni oite" 元初に於ける帝室と禅僧との関係に就いて [The Relations between the Imperial House and Zen Monks at the Beginning of the Yuan]. *Tōyō gakuhō* 11: 547–577; 12: 89–124, 245–249.

Kuroda Toshio 黒田俊雄. 1980. *Jisha seiryoku: Mō hitotsu no chūsei shakai* 寺社勢力——もう一つの中世社会 [The Power of Temples and Shrines]. Iwanami shinsho 117. Tokyo: Iwanami shoten.

———. 1981. "Shintō in the History of Japanese Religion." Trans. James C. Dobbins and Suzanne Gay. *Journal of Japanese Studies* 7, 1: 1–21.

———. 1983. *Ōbō to buppō: Chūseishi no kōzu* 王法と仏法——中世史の構図 [The Imperial Law and the Buddha Dharma]. Kyoto: Hōzōkan.

———. 1989. "Historical Consciousness and *Hon-jaku* Philosophy in the Medieval Period on Mount Hiei." In George J. Tanabe, Jr., and Willa Jane Tanabe, eds., *The Lotus Sūtra in Japanese Culture*, 143–158. Honolulu: University of Hawaii Press.

Kushida Ryōkō 櫛田良洪. 1977. "Shittan denju ni tsuite: Hōbōdaiin shiryō o megutte" 悉曇伝授について [On the Transmission of Siddham]. In Bukkyō minzoku gakkai, ed., *Bukkyō to girei* 仏教と儀礼, 65–105. Tokyo: Kokusho kankōkai.

Kushida Ryōkō hakushi shōju kinenkai, ed. 1973. *Kushida hakushi shōju kinen: Kōsōden no kenkyū* 櫛田博士頌寿記念——高僧傳の研究 [Researches on the Biographies of Eminent Monks]. Tokyo: Sankibō busshorin.

LaCapra, Dominick. 1983. *Rethinking Intellectual History: Texts, Contexts, Language*. Ithaca: Cornell University Press.

———. 1985. *History and Criticism*. Ithaca: Cornell University Press.

———. 1987. *History, Politics, and the Novel*. Ithaca: Cornell University Press.

———. 1988. "A Review of a Review." *Journal of the History of Ideas* 49, 4: 677–687.

———. 1989. *Soundings in Critical Theory*. Ithaca: Cornell University Press.

LaCapra, Dominick, and Steven L. Kaplan, eds. 1982. *Modern European History: Reappraisals and New Perspectives*. Ithaca: Cornell University Press.

LaFleur, William R. 1983. *The Karma of Words: Buddhism and the Literary Arts in Medieval Japan*. Berkeley: University of California Press.

———, ed. 1985. *Dōgen Studies*. Honolulu: University of Hawaii Press.

Lagerway, John. 1987. *Taoist Ritual in Chinese Society and History*. New York: Macmillan.

Lai, Whalen. 1980. "Further Developments of the Two Truths Theory in China." *Philosophy East and West* 30, 2: 139–162.

———. 1983. "The Transmission Verses of the Ch'an Patriarchs." *Han Hsüeh yen-chiu* 1, 2: 593–624.

Lai, Whalen. 1985. "Ma-tsu Tao-i and the Unfolding of Southern Zen." *Journal of Japanese Religions* 12: 173–192.

Lai, Whalen, and Lewis R. Lancaster, eds. 1983. *Early Ch'an in China and Tibet.* Berkeley: Asian Humanities Press.

Lakoff, George, and Mark Johnson. 1980. *Metaphors We Live By.* Chicago: University of Chicago Press.

Lamotte, Etienne. 1944–1980. *Traité de la Grande Vertu de Sagesse.* 5 vols. Louvain: Institut Orientaliste. (1: 1944, 2: 1949, 3: 1970, 4: 1976, 5: 1980)

———. 1958. *Histoire du bouddhisme indien: Des origines à l'ère Śaka.* Louvain: Institut Orientaliste.

———. 1960. "Mañjuśrī." *T'oung Pao* 48, 1–3: 1–96.

———. 1962. *L'enseignement de Vimalakīrti.* Louvain: Institut Orientaliste.

———. 1966. "Vajrapāṇi en Inde." In *Mélanges de Sinologie offerts à Monsieur Paul Demiéville,* 113–159. Paris: Presses Universitaires de France.

———. 1987. "Religious Suicide in Early Buddhism." *Buddhist Studies Review* 4, 2: 105–118.

Lancaster, Lewis R. 1974. "An Early Mahāyāna Sermon About the Body of the Buddha and the Making of Images." *Artibus Asiae* 36, 4: 287–291.

———, ed. 1977. *Prajñāpāramitā and Related Systems: Studies in Honor of Edward Conze.* Berkeley: Buddhist Studies Series, University of California.

———. 1984. "Elite and Folk: Comments on the Two-Tiered Theory." In George A. DeVos and Takao Sofue, eds., *Religion and the Family in East Asia. Senri Ethnological Studies* 11: 87–95 (Special issue).

Lanselle, Rainier, trans. 1987. *Le poisson de jade et l'épingle au phénix: Douze contes chinois du XVIIe siècle.* Paris: Gallimard.

Lanternari, Vittorio. 1982. "La religion populaire: Prospective historique et anthropologique." *Archives de sciences sociales des religions* 53, 1: 121–143.

Laufer, Berthold. 1931. "Inspirational Dreams in Eastern Asia." *Journal of American Folk-Lore* 44, 172: 208–216.

La Vallée Poussin, Louis de, trans. 1923–1931. *L'Abhidharmakośa de Vasubandhu.* 6 vols. Paris: Paul Geuthner. English trans. by Leo Pruden, *Abhidharmakośabhāsyam.* 3 vols. published. Berkeley: Asian Humanities Press, 1988–1989.

Leach, Edmund. 1972. "Pulleyar and the Lord Buddha." In William A. Lessa and Evon Z. Vogt, eds., *Reader in Comparative Religion: An Anthropological Approach,* 302–313. 3d ed. New York: Harper and Row.

———. 1983. "The Gate Keepers of Heaven: Anthropological Aspects of Grandiose Architecture." *Journal of Anthropological Research* 39: 243–268.

Le Bras, Gabriel. 1966. "Quelques problèmes sociologiques de l'histoire du bouddhisme." *Archives de sociologie des religions* 11, 21: 119–124.

Lee, Peter H., trans. 1969. *Lives of Eminent Korean Monks: The Haedong Kosŭng Chŏn.* Harvard-Yenching Institute Studies 25. Cambridge, MA: Harvard University Press.

Le Goff, Jacques. 1980. *Time, Work and Culture in the Middle Ages.* Trans. Arthur Goldhammer. Chicago: University of Chicago Press.

———. 1984. *The Birth of Purgatory.* Trans. Arthur Goldhammer. Chicago: University of Chicago Press.

————. 1988. *The Medieval Imagination*. Trans. Arthur Goldhammer. Chicago: University of Chicago Press.

Lessa, William A., and Evon Z. Vogt, eds. 1979. *Reader in Comparative Religion: An Anthropological Approach*. 4th ed. New York: Harper and Row.

Lessing, Ferdinand D. 1954. "The Eighteen Worthies Crossing the Sea." In *Contributions to Ethnography, Linguistics, and History of Religions*, 111–128. Stockholm: Statens Etnografiska Museum.

Leung, Angela K. 1983. "L'amour en Chine: Relations et pratiques sociales au XIIIe et XIVe siècles (1)." *Archives de sciences sociales des religions* 56, 1: 59–76.

————. 1984. "Sexualité et sociabilité dans le *Jin Ping Mei*, roman érotique chinois de la fin du XVIème siècle." *Social Science Information* 23, 4–5: 652–676.

Levering, Miriam. 1982. "The Dragon Girl and the Abbess of Mo-shan: Gender and Status in the Ch'an Buddhist Tradition." *Journal of the International Association of Buddhist Studies* 5, 1: 19–35.

————. 1987a. "Buddhism in Sung Culture: The Ch'an Master Ta-hui Tsung-kao." Ph.D. diss., University of Tennessee.

————. 1987b. "Ta-hui and Lay Buddhists: Ch'an Sermons on Death." In David W. Chappell, ed., *Buddhist and Taoist Practice in Medieval Chinese Society*, 181–214. Honolulu: University of Hawaii Press.

Lévi, Jean. 1986. "Les fonctionnaires et le divin: Luttes de pouvoirs entre divinités et administrateurs dans les contes des Six Dynasties et des Tang." *Cahiers d'Extrême-Asie* 2: 81–110.

————. 1987. "Les fonctions religieuses de la bureaucratie céleste." *L'homme* 101: 35–57.

————. 1989. *Les fonctionnaires divins: Politique, despotisme et mystique en Chine ancienne*. Paris: Seuil.

Lévi, Sylvain, and Edouard Chavannes. 1916. "Les seize Arhat protecteurs de la Loi." *Journal Asiatique* 8: 5–48, 189–304.

Lévi-Strauss, Claude. 1963. *Structural Anthropology*. Trans. Claire Jacobson and Brooke Grundfest Schoepf. New York: Doubleday.

————. 1966. *The Savage Mind*. Chicago: University of Chicago Press.

————. 1974a. *Structural Anthropology, Volume Two*. Chicago: University of Chicago Press.

————. [1955] 1974b. *Tristes tropiques*. Trans. John Russell. New York: Atheneum.

————. [1971] 1981. *The Naked Man: Introduction to a Science of Mythology: 4*. Trans. John and Doreen Weightman. New York: Harper and Row.

————. 1985. *The View from Afar*. Trans. Joachim Neugroschel and Phoebe Hoss. New York: Basic Books.

————. 1987. *Introduction to the Work of Marcel Mauss*. Trans. Felicity Baker. London: Routledge and Kegan Paul.

————. 1988. *The Jealous Potter*. Trans. Bénédicte Chorier. Chicago: University of Chicago Press.

Levin, M. 1930. "Mummification and Cremation in India." *Man* 30: 29–34, 44–48, 64–66.

Lévy, André. 1978. *Inventaire analytique et critique du conte chinois en langue vulgaire*. 2 vols. Paris: Collège de France.

———, trans. 1985. *Fleur en Fiole d'Or (Jin Ping Mei cihua)*. 2 vols. Bibliothèque de la Pléiade. Paris: Gallimard.

Levy, Howard S., trans. 1975. *Two Chinese Sex Classics: The Dwelling of Playful Goddesses; Monks and Nuns in a Sea of Sins*. Ed. Lou Tsu-k'uang. Asian Folklore and Social Life Monographs 75. Taibei: Orient Cultural Service.

Lévy, Paul. 1968. *Buddhism: A "Mystery Religion"?* New York: Schocken Books.

Lévy-Bruhl, Lucien. [1949] 1975. *The Notebooks on Primitive Mentality*. Trans. Peter Rivière. Oxford: Oxford University Press.

Lewis, Gilbert. 1980. *Day of Shining Red: An Essay on Understanding Ritual*. Cambridge: Cambridge University Press.

Lewis, I. M. [1971] 1989. *Ecstatic Religion: A Study of Shamanism and Spirit Possession*. London and New York: Routledge and Kegan Paul.

Li Lincan 李霖燦. 1982. *Nanzhao Daliguo xinde shiliao zonghe yanjiu* 南詔大理國新的資料綜合研究 [Synthetic Researches on New Documents on the Dali Kingdom in Nanzhao]. Taibei: Guoli gugong bowuyuan.

Liebenthal, Walter. 1952. "The Sermon of Shen-hui." *Asia Major* (n.s.) 3, 2: 132–155.

———. 1955. "Chinese Buddhism during the 4th and 5th Centuries." *Monumenta Nipponica* 11, 1: 44–83.

Liu, James J. Y. 1975. *Chinese Theories of Literature*. Chicago: University of Chicago Press.

———. 1982. *The Interlingual Critic: Interpreting Chinese Poetry*. Bloomington: Indiana University Press.

Liu Ts'un-yan. 1962. *Buddhist and Taoist Influences in Chinese Novels*. Vol. 1: *The Authorship of the Feng Shen Yen I*. Wiesbaden: Otto Harrassowitz.

Lopez, Donald S., Jr., ed. 1988. *Buddhist Hermeneutics*. Honolulu: University of Hawaii Press.

———. 1990. "Inscribing the Bodhisattva's Speech: On the *Heart Sūtra's* Mantra." *History of Religions* 29, 4: 351–372.

Luk, Charles (Lu K'uan-yü). 1964. *The Secrets of Chinese Meditation: Self-cultivation by Mind Control as Taught in the Ch'an, Mahāyāna and Taoist Schools in China*. London: Rider and Company.

———. 1966. *The Śūraṅgama Sūtra (Leng Yen Ching)*. London: Rider and Company.

———. 1971. *Practical Buddhism*. Wheaton, IL: Theosophical Publishing House.

Lynn, Richard John. 1987. "The Sudden and the Gradual in Chinese Poetry Criticism: An Examination of the Ch'an-Poetry Analogy." In Peter N. Gregory, ed., *Sudden and Gradual: Approaches to Enlightenment in Chinese Thought*, 381–427. Honolulu: University of Hawaii Press.

Lyotard, Jean-François. 1984a. *Driftworks*. Ed. Roger McKeon. New York: Semiotext(e).

———. 1984b. *The Postmodern Condition: A Report on Knowledge*. Trans. Geoff

Bennington and Brian Massumi. Minneapolis: University of Minnesota Press.

———. 1985. "Histoire universelle et différences culturelles." *Critique* 456: 558–568.

———. 1988. *The Differend: Phrases in Dispute.* Trans. Georges van Abbeele. Minneapolis: University of Minnesota Press.

Lyotard, Jean-François, and Jean-Loup Thébaud. 1985. *Just Gaming.* Trans. Wlad Godzich. Minneapolis: University of Minnesota Press.

Macé, François. 1976. "Origine de la mort et voyage dans l'au-delà selon trois séquences mythiques du *Kojiki* et du *Nihonshoki*." *Cahiers d'études et de documents sur les religions du Japon* 1: 75–113.

———. 1986. *La mort et les funérailles dans le Japon ancien.* Paris: Presses Orientalistes de France.

———. 1988. "Les funérailles des souverains japonais." *Cahiers d'Extrême-Asie* 4: 157–165.

Magliola, Robert. 1984. *Derrida on the Mend.* West Lafayette, IN: Purdue University Press.

Mair, Victor. 1986a. "The Origins of an Iconographical Form of the Pilgrim Hsüan-tsang." *T'ang Studies* 4: 29–41.

———. 1986b. "Records of Transformation Tableaux (*pien-hsiang*)." *T'oung Pao* 72: 3–43.

Makita Tairyō 牧田諦亮. 1956. "Hōshi oshō den kō: Chūgoku ni okeru bukkyō reiken juyō no ichi keitai" 宝誌和尚伝考 ── 中国における仏教霊験受容の一形熊 [Reflections on the Biography of the Priest Baozhi]. *Tōhō gakuhō* 26: 64–89.

———. 1957. *Chūgoku kinsei bukkyōshi kenkyū* 中国近世仏教史研究 [Studies in the History of Modern Chinese Buddhism]. Kyoto: Heirakuji shoten.

———. 1958. "Tonkōbon *Sandaishi den* ni tsuite" 敦煌本「三大師伝」について [On the Dunhuang Recension of the *Biographies of the Three Great Masters*]. *IBK* 7, 1: 250–253.

———. 1981. *Chūgoku bukkyōshi kenkyū: Daiichi* 中国仏教史研究第一 [Studies in the History of Chinese Buddhism, Vol. 1]. Tokyo: Daitō shuppansha.

———. 1984. *Chūgoku bukkyōshi kenkyū: Daini* [Studies in the History of Chinese Buddhism, Vol. 2]. Tokyo: Daitō shuppansha.

Makita Tairyō, and Fukui Fumimasa 福井文雅, eds. 1984. *Tonkō to Chūgoku bukkyō* 敦煌と中国仏教 [Dunhuang and Chinese Buddhism]. Tokyo: Daitō shuppansha.

Malamoud, Charles. 1989. *Cuire le monde: Rite et pensée dans l'Inde ancienne.* Paris: Editions La Découverte.

Malamoud, Charles, and Jean-Pierre Vernant, eds. 1986. *Le Temps de la réflexion VII: Corps des dieux.* Paris: Gallimard.

Marcus, George E., and Michael M. J. Fischer. 1986. *Anthropology as Cultural Critique: An Experimental Moment in the Human Sciences.* Chicago: University of Chicago Press.

Marshall, Roderick. 1989. *Falstaff: The Archetypal Myth.* Longmead, Shaftesbury, Dorset: Element Books.

Masefield, Peter. 1986. *Divine Revelation in Pāli Buddhism*. London: George Allen and Unwin.

Maspero, Henri. 1950. *Les religions chinoises: Mélanges posthumes sur les religions et l'histoire de la Chine*. 2 vols. Paris: Presses Universitaires de France.

———. 1981. *Taoism and Chinese Religion*. Amherst: University of Massachusetts Press.

Mather, Richard. 1976. *Shih-shuo hsin-yü: A New Account of Tales of the World*. Minneapolis: University of Minnesota Press.

Matignon, J.-J. 1902. *Superstition, crime et misère en Chine*. Lyon: Stock.

Matsumoto Akira 松本昭. 1985. *Nihon no miirabutsu* 日本のミイラ仏 [Japanese Mummified Buddhas]. Tokyo: Rokkō Shuppan.

Matsumoto Shōten 松本昭典. 1969. "Sōtō zen no denpan katei ni okeru kitōkan no hensen ni tsuite: Shoki kyōdan to shingi to no kōshō o chū-shin to shite" 曹洞宗の伝播過程における祈禱観の変遷について [On the Changes concerning the Conception of Prayer during the Process of Expansion of Sōtō Zen]. *IBK* 17, 2: 345–348.

Matsunaga, Alicia. 1969. *The Buddhist Philosophy of Assimilation: The Historical Development of the Honji-Suijaku Theory*. Tokyo and Rutland, VT: Charles E. Tuttle.

Matsuura Shūkō 松浦秀光. 1971. *Zenshū kojitsu gemon no kenkyū* 禅宗古実偈文の研究 [Researches on the Versified Literature of the Chan School]. Tokyo: Sankibō busshorin.

———. 1972. *Zenke no sōhō to tsuizen kuyō no kenkyū* 禅家の葬法と追善供養の研究 [Researches on Funerals and Commemorative Ceremonies of the Chan School]. Tokyo: Sankibō busshorin.

———. 1976. *Zenshū kojitsu sonzō no kenkyū* 禅宗古実尊像の研究 [Researches on the Icons of the Chan School]. Tokyo: Sankibō busshorin.

———. 1985. *Sonshuku sōhō no kenkyū* 尊宿葬法の研究 [Researches on the Funerary Rituals for Eminent Priests]. Tokyo: Sankibō busshorin.

Mauss, Marcel. 1950. *Sociologie et anthropologie*. Paris: Presses Universitaires de France.

———. 1967. *The Gift: Forms and Functions of Exchange in Archaic Societies*. Trans. Ian Cunnison. New York: W. W. Norton.

———. 1968–1969. *Oeuvres*. Ed. Victor Karady. 3 vols. Paris: Minuit.

———. 1979. *Sociology and Psychology*. Trans. B. Brewster. London: Routledge and Kegan Paul.

Mauss, Marcel, and Henri Hubert. 1972. *A General Theory of Magic*. Ed. D. Pocock. London: Routledge and Kegan Paul.

McCallum, Donald F. 1990. "Zenkōji and its Icon: A Study in Medieval Japanese Religious Art." Unpublished ms.

McFarland, H. Neill. 1987. *Daruma: The Founder of Zen in Japanese Art and Popular Culture*. Tokyo and New York: Kōdansha International.

McRae, John R. 1983. "The Ox-head School of Chinese Buddhism: From Early Ch'an to the Golden Age." In Robert M. Gimello and Peter N. Gregory, eds., *Studies in Ch'an and Hua-yen*, 169–253. Honolulu: University of Hawaii Press.

———. 1986. *The Northern School and the Formation of Early Ch'an Buddhism.* Honolulu: University of Hawaii Press.

———. 1987. "Shen-hui and the Teaching of Sudden Enlightenment in Early Ch'an Buddhism." In Peter N. Gregory, ed., *Sudden and Gradual: Approaches to Enlightenment in Chinese Thought*, 227–278. Honolulu: University of Hawaii Press.

———. 1988a. "Religion as Revolution in Chinese Historiography: Hu Shih (1891–1962) on Shen-hui (684–758)." Unpublished paper.

———. 1988b. "The Story of Early Ch'an." In Kenneth Kraft, ed., *Zen: Tradition and Transformation: A Sourcebook by Contemporary Zen Masters and Scholars*, 105–124. New York: Grove Press.

———. 1989. "Bracketing the Emergence of Encounter Dialogue: The Transformation of the Spiritual Path in Ch'an Buddhism." In Robert E. Buswell, Jr., and Robert M. Gimello, eds., *Paths to Liberation: The Mārga and its Transformations in Buddhist Thought.* Studies in East Asian Buddhism, 7. Honolulu: University of Hawaii Press (forthcoming in 1991).

Merleau-Ponty, Maurice. 1960. *Eloge de la philosophie et autres essais.* Paris: Gallimard. English trans. by John Wild, James Edie, and John O'Neill, *In Praise of Philosophy and Other Essays.* Evanston: Northwestern University Press, 1970.

———. 1964a. *The Primacy of Perception and Other Essays on Phenomenological Psychology, The Philosophy of Art, History and Politics.* Ed. James M. Edie. Evanston: Northwestern University Press.

———. 1964b. *Signs.* Trans. Richard McCleary. Evanston: Northwestern University Press.

———. 1968. *The Visible and the Invisible.* Ed. Claude Lefort. Trans. Alphonso Lingis. Evanston: Northwestern University Press.

Merton, Thomas. [1968] 1970. *Zen and the Birds of Appetite.* New York: New Directions.

Michihata Ryōshū 道端良秀. 1957. *Tōdai bukkyōshi no kenkyū* 唐代仏教史の研究 [Researches on the History of Tang Buddhism]. Kyoto: Hōzōkan.

———. 1979. *Chūgoku bukkyō shisōshi no kenkyū* 中国仏教思想史の研究 [Researches on the History of Chinese Buddhist Thought]. Kyoto: Heirakuji shoten.

———. 1980. *Chūgoku bukkyō to shakai to no kōshō* 中国仏教と社会との交渉 [The Interaction between Chinese Buddhism and Society]. Kyoto: Heirakuji shoten.

———. 1983. *Rakan shinkōshi* 羅漢信仰史 [A History of the Arhat Cult]. Tokyo: Daitō shuppansha.

———. 1984. "Tonkō bunken ni mieru shigo no sekai" 敦煌文献にみえる死後の世界 [The Afterlife as Seen in the Dunhuang Documents]. In Makita Tairyō and Fukui Fumimasa, eds., *Tonkō to Chūgoku bukkyō*, 501–536. Tokyo: Daitō shuppansha.

Mills, D. E., trans. 1970. *A Collection of Tales from Uji: A Study and Translation of Uji Shūi Monogatari.* Cambridge: Cambridge University Press.

Miyakawa Hisayuki. 1979. "Local Cults around Mount Lu at the Time of Sun

En's Rebellion." In Holmes Welch and Anna Seidel, eds., *Facets of Taoism: Essays in Chinese Religion*, 83–102. New Haven: Yale University Press.

Miyasaka Yūshō 宮坂宥勝, ed. 1964. *Kana hōgo shū* 段名法語集 [A Collection of Sermons in *Kana*]. Nihon koten bungaku taikei 83. Tokyo: Iwanami shoten.

Miyata Noboru 宮田登. 1970. *Miroku shinkō no kenkyū: Nihon no okeru dentōteki meshiakan* ミロク信仰の研究—日本における伝統的メシア観 [Researches on the Cult of Maitreya]. Tokyo: Miraisha.

———. 1979. *Kami no minzokushi* 神の民俗史 [A Folkloric History of the Gods]. Iwanami shinsho 97. Tokyo: Iwanami shoten.

Mochizuki Shinkō 望月信亨, ed. 1958–1963. *Bukkyō daijiten* 仏教大辭典 [Great Dictionary of Buddhism]. 10 vols. Tokyo: Sekai seiten kankō kyōkai. Reprint. Taibei: Horizon Publishing Company, 1977.

Mōri Hisashi. 1977. *Japanese Portrait Sculpture*. Tokyo and New York: Kōdansha International.

Morrell, Robert E. 1985. *Sand and Pebbles (Shasekishū): The Tales of Mujū Ichien, A Voice for Pluralism in Kamakura Buddhism*. Albany: State University of New York Press.

———. 1987. *Early Kamakura Buddhism: A Minority Report*. Berkeley: Asian Humanities Press.

Morris, Ivan, trans. 1963. *The Life of an Amorous Woman (Kōshoku ichidai onna), by Ihara Saikaku*. New York: New Directions.

———, ed. 1970. *Madly Singing in the Mountains: An Appreciation and Anthology of Arthur Waley*. New York: Walker and Company.

Motobe Enjō 本部圓靜. 1979. "Muchū kenbutsu ni tsuite" 夢中見仏について [On Seeing the Buddha in a Dream]. *IBK* 28, 1: 373–376.

Murayama Shūichi 村山修一. 1976. *Kodai bukkyō no chūseiteki tenkai* 古代仏教の中世的展開 [The Medieval Development of Ancient Buddhism]. Kyoto: Hōzōkan.

Mus, Paul. 1935. *Barabuḍur: Esquisse d'une histoire du bouddhisme fondée sur la critique archéologique des textes*. 2 vols. Hanoi: Imprimerie d'Extrême-Orient. Reprint. New York: Arno Press, 1978. Paris: Arma Artis, 1990.

Musil, Robert. 1988. *The Man Without Qualities*. 2 vols. London: Pan Books.

Myerhoff, Barbara. 1982. "Rites of Passage: Process and Paradox." In Victor Turner, ed., *Celebration: Studies in Festivity and Ritual*, 109–135. Washington, D.C.: Smithsonian Institution Press.

Nagai Masashi 永井政之. 1985a. "Chūgoku minshū no bosatsukan: Fukuan Inshuku no baai" 中国民衆の菩薩観—普庵印粛の場合 [The Chinese Popular Conception of the Bodhisattva: The Case of Puan Yinsu]. *Nihon bukkyō gakkai nenpo* 51: 225–250.

———. 1985b. "Chūgoku zen no minshū kyōka ni tsuite: Chōrō Sōsaku no baai" 中国禅の民衆教化について—長蘆宗賾の場合 [On Popular Predications in Chinese Zen]. *IBK* 34, 1: 291–298.

Nagao, Gadjin. 1989. *The Foundational Standpoint of Mādhyamika Philosophy*. Trans. John P. Keenan. Albany: State University of New York Press.

Naitō Masatoshi 内藤正敏. 1974. *Miira shinkō no kenkyū* ミイラ信仰の研究 [Researches on the Cult of Mummies]. Tokyo: Yamato Shobō.

Najita, Tetsuo, and Irwin Scheiner, eds. 1987. *Japanese Thought in the Tokugawa Period 1600–1868: Methods and Metaphors*. Chicago: University of Chicago Press.

Nakamura, Kyoko, trans. 1973. *Miraculous Stories from the Japanese Buddhist Tradition: The Nihon Ryōiki of the Monk Kyōkai*. Cambridge, MA: Harvard University Press.

Nakao Ryōshin 中尾良心. 1984. "Dainichibō Nōnin no zen" 大日房能忍の禅 [The Zen of Dainichibō Nōnin]. *Shūgaku kenkyū* 26: 221–235.

Naquin, Susan. 1988. "Funerals in North China: Uniformity and Variations." In James L. Watson and Evelyn Rawski, eds., *Death Ritual in Late Imperial and Modern China*, 37–70. Berkeley: University of California Press.

Naundorf Gert, Karl-Heinz Pohl, and Hans Hermann Schmidt, eds. 1985. *Religion und Philosophie in Ostasien: Festschrift für Hans Steininger zum 65. Geburtstag*. Würzburg: Königshausen and Neumann.

Needham, Joseph, ed. 1974–1983. *Science and Civilization in China*. Vol. 5. Cambridge: Cambridge University Press.

Nei Kiyoshi 根井浄. 1986. "Chūsei no Fudaraku tōkai" 中世の補陀落渡海 [The Crossing Over to Potalaka in the Medieval Period]. *IBK* 34, 2: 209–214.

Ng, Vivien. W. 1987. "Ideology and Sexuality: Rape Laws in Qing China." *Journal of Asian Studies* 46, 1: 57–70.

Ngo, Van Xuyet. 1976. *Divination, magie et politique dans la Chine ancienne*. Paris: Presses Universitaires de France.

Nisard, Charles. [1864]. 1965. *Histoire des livres populaires ou de littérature de colportage*. 2 ed. New York: Burt Franklin.

Nishimura, Sey. 1985. "The Prince and the Pauper: Dynamics of a Shōtoku Legend." *Monumenta Nipponica* 40, 3: 299–310.

Nishiwaki Tsuneki 西脇常記. 1990. "Shari shinkō to sōden ni okeru : sono jojutsu: Ekō *Zenrin sōbōden* jojutsu no rikai no tame ni" 舎利信仰と僧伝における―その序述 [The Cult of Relics and its Description in the Biographies of Monks]. *ZBKK* 16: 195–222.

Norman, H. C., ed. 1912. *The Commentary on the Dhammapada*. 3 vols. London: Pāli Text Society.

Nosco, Peter, ed. 1984. *Confucianism and Tokugawa Culture*. Princeton: Princeton University Press.

Nōtomi Jōten 納富常天. 1985. "Kamakura jidai no shari shinkō: Kamakura o chūshin to shite" 鎌倉時代の舎利信仰―鎌倉を中心として [The Cult of Relics during the Kamakura Period]. *IBK* 33, 2: 447–451.

Nukariya Kaiten 忽滑谷快天. 1930. *Chōsen zenkyōshi* 朝鮮禪教史 [A History of Korean Zen]. Tokyo: Shunjūsha.

Ōbata Hironobu 小畠宏允. 1976. "*Rekidai hōbōki* to kodai Chibetto no bukkyō" 「歴代法宝記」と古代チベットの仏教 [The *Lidai fabao ji* and Ancient Tibetan Buddhism]. In Yanagida Seizan. *Shoki no zenshi 2: Rekidai hōbōki*, 325–337. Tokyo: Chikuma shobō.

O'Flaherty, Wendy Doniger. 1973. *Ascetism and Eroticism in the Mythology of Śiva*. New York: Oxford University Press.

O'Flaherty, Wendy Doniger. 1976. *The Origins of Evil in Hindu Mythology*. Berkeley: University of California Press.

———. 1984. *Dreams, Illusions and Other Realities*. Chicago: University of Chicago Press.

Ōkubo Dōshū 大久保道舟, ed. 1966. *Dōgen zenji den no kenkyū* 道元禅師傳の研究 [Studies in the Biography of the Zen Master Dōgen]. Tokyo: Chikuma shobō.

———, ed. 1971. *Kohon kōtei Shobōgenzō* 古本校訂正眼法藏. Tokyo: Chikuma shobō.

Okuda Isao 奥田勲. 1978. *Myōe: Henreki to yume* 明惠：遍歴と夢 [Myōe: Pilgrimages and Dreams]. Tokyo: Tōkyō Daigaku Shuppankai.

Ong, Roberto K. 1985. *The Interpretation of Dreams in Ancient China*. Bochum: Studienverlag Brockmeyer.

———. 1988. "Image and Meaning: The Hermeneutics of Traditional Chinese Dream Interpretation." In Carolyn T. Brown, ed., *Psycho-Sinology: The Universe of Dreams in Chinese Culture*, 47–54. Lanham: University Press of America.

Ong, Walter. 1982. *Orality and Literacy: The Technologizing of the Word*. London and New York: Methuen.

Ooms, Herman. 1984. "Neo-Confucianism and the Formation of Early Tokugawa Ideology: Contours of a Problem." In Peter Nosco, ed., *Confucianism and Tokugawa Culture*, 27–61. Princeton: Princeton University Press.

———. 1985. *Tokugawa Ideology: Early Constructs, 1570–1680*. Princeton: Princeton University Press.

———. 1987. "From Tokugawa Religion to Tokugawa Ideology." Unpublished paper.

Orzech, Charles D. 1989. "Seeing Chen-yen Buddhism: Traditional Scholarship and the Vajrayāna in China." *History of Religions* 29, 2: 87–114.

Ōtani Kōshō 大谷光照. 1937. *Tōdai no bukkyō girei* 唐代の佛教儀禮 [Buddhist Ritual of the Tang]. 2 vols. Tokyo: Yūkōsha.

Ouwehand, Cornelius. 1964. *Namazu-e and their Themes: An Interpretive Approach to Some Aspects of Japanese Folk Religion*. Leiden: E. J. Brill.

Overmyer, Daniel. 1976. *Folk Buddhist Religion: Dissenting Sects in Late Traditional China*. Cambridge, MA: Harvard University Press.

———. 1980. "Dualism and Conflict in Chinese Popular Religion." In Frank Reynolds and Theodore M. Ludwig, eds., *Transitions and Transformations in the History of Religions: Essays in Honor of Joseph M. Kitagawa*, 153–184. Leiden: E. J. Brill.

———. 1988. "Buddhism in the Trenches: Attitudes Toward Popular Religion in Indigenous Scriptures from Tun-huang." Unpublished paper.

Pachow, W. 1986. "A Hermeneutical Approach to Supernatural Phenomena in Buddhist History (Contd.)." *Chinese Culture* 27, 2: 73–100.

Padoux, André. 1988. *L'énergie de la parole: Cosmogonies de la Parole Tantrique*. Paris: Soleil Noir.

Parry, Jonathan. 1982. "Sacrificial Death and the Necrophagous Ascetic." In

Maurice Bloch and Jonathan Parry, eds., *Death and the Regeneration of Life*, 74–110. Cambridge: Cambridge University Press.

Paul-Lévy, Françoise, and Marion Segaud. 1983. *Anthropologie de l'espace*. Paris: Centre Georges Pompidou.

Pedersen, Kusumita Priscilla, trans. 1975. *"Jishōki." The Eastern Buddhist* (n.s.) 8, 1: 96–132.

Pelliot, Paul. 1923. "Notes sur quelques artistes des Six Dynasties et des T'ang." *T'oung Pao* 22: 215–291.

Péri, Noël. 1916. "Le dieu Wei-t'o." *BEFEO* 16: 41–56.

———. 1917. "Hārītī, la Mère-de-démons." *BEFEO* 17: 1–102.

Peterson, Willard J. 1988. "Squares and Circles: Mapping the History of Chinese Thought." *Journal of the History of Ideas* 49, 1: 47–60.

Pfister, Louis, S.J. 1932–1934. *Notices biographiques et bibliographiques sur les Jésuites de l'ancienne mission de Chine, 1552–1773*. 2 vols. Shanghai: Mission Catholique.

Pflugfelder, Gregory M. 1990a. "The Forbidden Chrysanthemum: Male–Male Sexual Behavior in Meiji Law." Unpublished paper.

———. 1990b. "Male–Male Sexual Behavior in Tokugawa Legal Discourse." Unpublished paper.

Pokora, Timoteus. 1985. "'Living Corpses' in Early Medieval China: Sources and Opinions." In G. Naundorf et al., eds., *Religion und Philosophie in Ostasien: Festschrift für Hans Steininger*, 344–357. Würzburg: Königshausen and Neumann.

Pollack, David. 1985. *Zen Poems of the Five Mountains*. New York: Crossroad.

———. 1986. *The Fracture of Meaning: Japan's Synthesis of China from the Eighth through the Eighteenth Centuries*. Princeton: Princeton University Press.

Powell, William. 1986. *The Record of Tung-shan*. Honolulu: University of Hawaii Press.

———. 1988. "The Dicang Festival at Jiuhua shan and its Theoretical Implications." Unpublished paper.

———. 1989. "A Pilgrim's Landscape Text of Chiu Hua Shan." In Susan Naquin and Chün-fang Yü, eds., *Pilgrimage and Sacred Sites in China*. Berkeley: University of California Press (forthcoming).

Prebish, Charles S. 1975. *Buddhist Monastic Discipline: The Sanskrit Prātimokṣa Sūtras of the Mahāsāṃghikas and Mūlasarvāstivādins*. University Park and London: Pennsylvania State University Press.

Preston, David. 1988. *The Social Organization of Zen Practice: Constructing Transcultural Reality*. Cambridge: Cambridge University Press.

Prip-Møller, J. [1937] 1982. *Chinese Buddhist Monasteries: Their Plan and its Function as a Setting for Buddhist Monastic Life*. Hong Kong: Hong Kong University Press.

Przyluski, J. 1935–1936. "Le partage des reliques du Bouddha." *Mélanges chinois et bouddhiques* 4: 341–467.

Rabinow, Paul, ed. 1984. *The Foucault Reader*. New York: Pantheon Books.

———. 1986. "Representations are Social Facts: Modernity and Post-Modernity in Anthropology." In James Clifford and George E. Marcus, eds., *Writing Culture: The Poetics and Politics of Ethnography*, 234–261. Berkeley: University of California Press.

Rabinow, Paul, and William M. Sullivan, eds. 1979. *Interpretive Social Science: A Reader*. Berkeley: University of California Press.

Radin, Paul. 1972. *The Trickster*. New York: Schocken Books.

Rawlinson, Andrew. 1986. "Nāgas and the Magical Cosmology of Buddhism." *History of Religions* 16, 2: 135–153.

Reader, Ian. 1986. "Zazenless Zen? The Position of Zazen in Institutional Zen Buddhism." *Japanese Religions* 14, 3: 7–27.

Reischauer, Edwin O. 1955a. *Ennin's Diary: The Record of a Pilgrimage to China in Search of the Law*. New York: Reginald Press.

———. 1955b. *Ennin's Travels in T'ang China*. New York: Reginald Press.

Ren, Jiyu. 1984b. "A Brief Discussion of the Philosophical Thought of Chan Buddhism." *Chinese Studies in Philosophy* 15, 4: 3–69.

———. 1984b. "On Hu Shih's Mistakes in his Study of the History of the Chan Sect." *Chinese Studies in Philosophy* 15, 4: 70–98.

Renou, Louis, and Jean Filliozat. [1953] 1985. *L'Inde classique: Manuel des études indiennes*. 2 vols. Paris: Ecole Française d'Extrême-Orient.

Reynolds, Frank E. 1977. "The Several Bodies of the Buddha: Reflections on a Neglected Aspect of the Theravāda Tradition." *History of Religions* 16, 4: 374–389.

Rhie, Marylin M. 1977. *The Fo-kuang ssu: Literary Evidence and Buddhist Images*. New York: Garland Publications.

Rhys Davids, T. W., and Hermann Oldenberg, eds. 1881. *Vinaya Texts*. Oxford: Clarendon Press.

Ricci, Matthew. [1942] 1953. *China in the Sixteenth Century: The Journals of Matthew Ricci, 1583–1610*. Trans. Louis J. Gallagher, S.J. Ed. Nicolas Trigault. New York: Random House.

Ricoeur, Paul. 1977. *The Rule of Metaphor: Multi-disciplinary Studies of the Creation of Meaning in Language*. Trans. Robert Czerny. Toronto: University of Toronto Press.

———. 1981. *Hermeneutics and the Human Sciences: Essays on Language, Action and Interpretation*. Trans. John. B. Thompson. Cambridge: Cambridge University Press.

———. 1983. *Temps et Récit*. Vol. 1. Paris: Seuil. Trans. Kathleen McLaughlin and David Pellaw, *Time and Narrative*. Vol. 1. Chicago: University of Chicago Press.

Riffaterre, Michael. 1983. *Text Production*. Trans. Térèse Lyons. New York: Columbia University Press.

———. 1984. *Semiotics of Poetry*. Bloomington: Indiana University Press.

———. 1990. *Fictional Truth*. Baltimore: Johns Hopkins University Press.

Robinet, Isabelle. 1977. *Les commentaires du Tao tö king jusqu'au VIIe siècle*. Paris: Institut des Hautes Etudes Chinoises, Collège de France.

———. 1979a. *Méditation taoïste*. Paris: Dervy-Livres.

———. 1979b. "Metamorphosis and Deliverance from the Corpse in Taoism." *History of Religions* 19, 1: 37–70.

Rorty, Richard. 1985. "Le cosmopolitisme sans émancipation: En réponse à

Jean-François Lyotard." *Critique* 456: 569–580. [Followed by a discussion between Jean-François Lyotard and Richard Rorty, 581–584.]

Rosaldo, Renato. 1989. *Culture and Truth: The Remaking of Social Analysis.* Boston: Beacon Press.

Rouget, Gilbert. 1980. *La musique et la transe: Esquisse d'une théorie générale des relations de la musique et de la possession.* Trans. Derek Coltman, *Music and Trance: A Theory of the Relations between Music and Possession.* Chicago: University of Chicago Press, 1985.

Rousseau, Jean-Jacques. 1956. *Oeuvres complètes.* Vol. 1. Bibliothèque de la Pléiade. Paris. Gallimard.

Roussel, Raymond. 1963. *Nouvelles impressions d'Afrique.* Paris: Jean-Jacques Pauvert.

Ruegg, David Seyfort. 1969. *La théorie du Tathāgatagarbha et du Gotra: Etude sur la sotériologie et la gnoséologie du bouddhisme.* Publications de l'Ecole Française d'Extrême-Orient 70. Paris: Ecole Française d'Extrême-Orient.

———. 1971. "On the Knowability and Expressibility of Absolute Reality in Buddhism. *IBK* 20, 1: 495–489 [*sic*].

Said, Edward. 1979. *Orientalism.* New York: Vintage Books.

———. 1985. "Orientalism Reconsidered." *Cultural Critique* 1: 89–108.

Saigō Nobutsuna 西郷信綱. 1972. *Kodaijin to yume* 古代人と夢 [The Ancients and Dreams]. Tokyo: Heibonsha.

Saikaku, Ihara. 1956. *Five Women Who Loved Love.* Trans. Wm. Theodore de Bary. Rutland, VT: Charles E. Tuttle.

———. 1990. *The Great Mirror of Male Love.* Trans. Paul Gordon Schalow. Stanford: Stanford University Press.

Saintyves, Pierre. 1987. *Les contes de Perrault. En marge de la Légende Dorée. Les reliques et les images légendaires.* Paris: Robert Laffont.

Saitō Kōjun 斎藤光純. 1973. *"Shakuen shirin"*「釈苑詞林」[The *Shiyuan Cilin*]. In Kushida Ryōkō hakushi shōju kinenkai, ed., *Kushida hakushi shōju kinen: Kōsōden no kenkyū* 櫛田良洪博士頌壽記念 — 高僧伝の研究 [Researches on the Biographies of Eminent Monks], 823–849. Tokyo: Sankibō busshorin.

Sakauchi Ryūyu 坂内竜雄. 1974. "Sōtōshū ni okeru mikkyō no juyō" 曹洞宗における密教の受容 [The Reception of Esoteric Buddhism in the Sōtō Sect]. *Shūgaku kenkyū* 16: 35–40.

Sakurai, Kiyohiko, and Tamotsu Ogata. 1983. "Japanese Mummies." In Aidan and Eve Cockburn. eds., *Mummies, Diseases and Ancient Cultures*, 211–223. Cambridge: Cambridge University Press.

Sakurai Shūyū 桜井秀雄. 1979. "Sōtō monge ni okeru 'kirigami' sōjō no ichi kōsatsu" 曹洞門下における「切紙」相承の一考察 [A Study on the Transmission of *Kirigami* in the Sōtō Sect]. *Shūkyōgaku ronshū* 9: 169–184.

Sanford, James H. 1977. "*Shakuhachi* Zen: The Fukeshū and Komusō." *Monumenta Nipponica* 32, 4: 411–440.

———. 1980. "Mandalas of the Heart: Two Prose Works by Ikkyū Sōjun." *Monumenta Nipponica* 35, 3: 273–298.

———. 1981. *Zen-Man Ikkyū.* Harvard Studies in World Religions 2. Chico, CA: Scholars Press.

Sanford, James H. 1988. "The Nine Faces of Death: 'Su Tung-p'o's *Kuzō-shi*." *The Eastern Buddhist* 21, 2: 54–77.

Sangren, P. Steven. 1983. "Female Gender in Chinese Religious Symbols: Kuan Yin, Ma Tzu, and the 'Eternal Mother.' " *Signs* 9: 4–25.

———. 1984. "Great Tradition and Little Traditions Reconsidered: The Question of Cultural Integration in China." *Journal of Chinese Studies* 1: 1–24.

———. 1987. *History and Magical Power in a Chinese Community*. Stanford: Stanford University Press.

———. 1988. "Rhetoric and the Authority of Ethnography: 'Postmodernism' and the Social Reproduction of Texts." *Current Anthropology* 29, 3: 405–435.

Sargent, Galen Eugene. 1957. "Tchou Hi contre le bouddhisme." In *Mélanges publiés par l'Institut des Hautes Etudes Chinoises*, Vol. 1: 1–157. Paris: Presses Universitaires de France.

Sasaki, Ruth Fuller, trans. 1975. *The Recorded Sayings of Ch'an Master Lin-chi Hui-chao of Chen Prefecture*. Kyoto: The Institute for Zen Studies.

Sasaki, Ruth Fuller, Yoshitaka Iriya, and Dana R. Fraser, trans. 1971. *A Man of Zen: The Recorded Sayings of Layman P'ang*. New York: Weatherhill.

Satō Shunkō 佐藤俊晃. 1985. "Sekidōzan shinkō to Nōto Keizan kyōdan" 石動山信仰と能登瑩山教団 [The Cult of Mt. Sekidō and the Community of Keizan in Noto]. *Shūkyōgaku ronshū* 12: 73–102.

———. 1986–1987. "Sōtōshū kyōdan ni okeru 'Hakusan shinkō juyōshi no mondai" 曹洞宗教団における「白山信仰」受容史の問題 [The Problem of the Reception of the "Hakusan Cult" in the Sōtō Community]. *Shūgaku kenkyū* 28: 148–151; 29: 157–160.

———. 1987. " 'Chinju Hakusan' kō" (1) 「鎮守白山」考 [Reflections on the "Tutelary God of Hakusan"] *Sōtōshū kenkyū kiyō* 19: 114–124.

Satō Taishun 佐藤泰舜, ed. [1934] 1974. *Muchū mondō* 夢中問答 [*Dialogues in a Dream*]. Tokyo: Iwanami shoten.

Sawada Mizuho 澤田瑞穂. 1975. *Bukkyō to Chūgoku bungaku* 仏教と中国文学 [Buddhism and Chinese Literature]. Tokyo: Kokusho kankōkai.

Saward, John. 1980. *Perfect Fools: Folly for Christ's Sake in Catholic and Orthodox Spirituality*. Oxford: Oxford University Press.

Schafer, Edward H. 1951. "Ritual Exposure in Ancient China." *HJAS* 14, 1: 130–184.

———. 1965. "Incubi and Succubi." In "Notes on T'ang Culture II." *Monumenta Serica* 24: 135–139.

Schalow, Paul Gordon. 1987. "Bald Headed Sects: The Priestly Tradition of Homosexual Love in Japanese Buddhism." Unpublished paper.

———. 1989. "Kūkai on the Tradition of Male Love in Japanese Buddhism." In José Cabezón, ed., *Buddhism, Sexuality and Gender*. Albany: State University of New York Press (forthcoming).

Schipper, Kristofer M. 1966. "The Divine Jester: Some Remarks on the Gods of the Chinese Marionette Theater." *Academia Sinica, Bulletin of the Institute of Ethnology* 21: 81–94.

———. 1974. "The Written Memorial in Taoist Ceremonies." In Arthur

P. Wolf, ed., *Religion and Ritual in Chinese Society*, 309–324. Stanford: Stanford University Press.

———. 1978. "The Taoist Body." *History of Religions* 17, 3–4: 355–386.

———. 1983. *Le corps taoïste: Corps physique, corps social.* Paris: Fayard.

———. 1985. "Vernacular and Classical Ritual in Taoism." *Journal of Asian Studies* 45: 21–57.

Schmidt, J. D. 1974. "Ch'an, Illusion, and Sudden Enlightenment in the Poetry of Yang Wang-li." *T'oung Pao* 60, 4–5: 230–281.

Schmidt-Glintzer, Helwig. 1985. "Eine Ehrenrettung für den Süden: Pao-chih (418–514) und Fu Hsi (497–569): Zwei Heilige aus den Unteren Yangtse Tal." In G. Naundorf et al., ed., *Religion and Philosophie in Ostasien: Festschrift für Hans Steininger*, 247–265. Würzburg: Königshausen and Neumann.

Schmitt, Jean-Claude. 1976. "'Religion populaire' et culture folklorique." *Annales: Economies, sociétés, civilisations* 31, 5: 941–953.

———. 1990. *La raison des gestes dans l'Occident médiéval.* Paris: Gallimard.

Schneider, Richard. 1987. "Un moine indien au Wou-t'ai chan: Relation d'un pélerinage." *Cahiers d'Extrême-Asie* 3: 27–39.

Schopen, Gregory. 1975. "The Phrase '*sa pṛthivīpradeśaś caiyabhūto bhavet*' in the *Vachracchedikā*: Notes on the Cult of the Book in Mahāyāna." *Indo-Iranian Journal* 17, 3–4: 147–181.

———. 1987. "Burial 'Ad Sanctos' and the Physical Presence of the Buddha in Early Indian Buddhism: A Study in the Archeology of Religions." *Religion* 17: 193–225.

———. 1988. "On the Buddha and his Bones: The Conception of a Relic in the Inscription of Nagarjunikonda." *JAOS* 108: 527–537.

———. 1990. "Monks and the Relic Cult in the *Mahāparinibbānasutta*: An Old Misunderstanding in Regard to Monastic Buddhism." In Gregory Schopen and Koichi Shinohara, eds., *From Banaras to Beijing: Essays on Buddhism and Chinese Religion in Honor of Jan Yün-hua*. Oakville: Mosaic Press (forthcoming).

Schurhammer, Georg, S. J. 1982. *Francis Xavier: His Life, His Times.* Vol 4: *Japan and China, 1549–1552.* Rome: Jesuit Historical Institute.

Seidel, Anna. 1969. *La divinisation de Lao tseu dans le taoïsme des Han.* Paris: Ecole Française d'Extrême-Orient.

———. 1978. "Buying one's Way to Heaven: The celestial Treasury in Chinese Religions." *History of Religions* 17, 3–4: 419–431.

———. 1981. "Note à propos du terme 'Trésor national' en Chine et au Japon." *BEFEO* 69: 229–261.

———. 1983a. "Dabi." In *Hōbōgirin*, Vol. 6: 573–585. Paris: Adrien Maisonneuve.

———. 1983b. "Imperial Treasures and Taoist Sacraments: Taoist Roots in the Apocrypha." In Michel Strickmann, ed., *Tantric and Taoist Studies in Honor of R. A. Stein*, Vol. 2: 291–371. Brussels: Institut Belge des Hautes Etudes Chinoises.

———. 1987. "Traces of Han Religion in Funeral Texts found in Tombs." In Akitsuki Kan'ei 秋月観暎, ed., *Dōkyō to shūkyō bunka* 道教と宗教文化 [Taoism and Religious Culture], 21–57. Tokyo: Hirakawa shuppansha.

Seidel, Anna. 1988. "Corruptible Body, Incorruptible Body, Substitute Body: Modes of Immortality in China and Japan." Unpublished paper.

Sekiguchi Shindai 関口真大. 1967. *Daruma no kenkyū* 達摩の研究 [Researches on Bodhidharma]. Tokyo: Iwanami shoten.

————. [1957] 1969. *Daruma daishi no kenkyū* 達摩大師の研究 [Researches on the Great Master Bodhidharma]. Tokyo: Shunjūsha.

Serres, Michel. 1982. *Hermes: Literature, Science, Philosophy*. Trans. Josué V. Harari and David F. Bell. Baltimore: Johns Hopkins University Press.

Sharf, Robert H. 1989. "Being Buddha: A Performative Approach to Ch'an Enlightenment." Unpublished paper.

Shih, Robert. 1968. *Biographies des moines éminents (Kao Seng Tchouan) de Houei-kiao: Première partie: biographies des premiers traducteurs*. Louvain: Institut Orientaliste.

Shiina Kōyū 椎名宏雄. 1968. "Sūzan ni okeru Hokushū zen no tenkai" 嵩山における北宗禅の展開 [The Development of Northern Chan on Song shan]. *Shūgaku kenkyū* 10: 173–185.

————. 1972. "Tōdai zenshū no reizan ni tsuite" 唐代禅宗の礼懺についつ [The Repentance Ritual in the Chan School during the Tang]. *IBK* 20, 2: 764–769.

Shils, Edward, 1981. *Tradition*. Chicago: University of Chicago Press.

Shimode Sekiyo 下出積與. 1986. *Hakusan shinkō* 白山信仰 [The Hakusan Cult]. Tokyo: Yūzankaku shuppan.

Shinagawa Kenritsu Kanazawa Bunko 神奈川県立金沢文庫, ed. 1974. *Kanazawa bunko shiryō zensho: Butten, zensekihen I* 金沢文庫資料全書—仏典第一禅籍篇 [Documents of the Kanazawa Library: Buddhist Scriptures, Section on Zen Texts, Vol. 1]. Yokohama: Shinagawa Kenritsu Kanazawa Bunko.

Shinohara Hisao 篠原久雄, ed. 1980. *Eihei daishingi: Dōgen no shudō kihan* 永平大清規—道元の修道規範 [The Great Rule of Eihei: Dōgen's Norms for Practice]. Tokyo: Daitō shuppansha.

Shinohara Hisao 篠原久雄, and Tanaka Ryōshō 田中良昭, eds. 1980. *Tonkō butten to zen* 敦煌仏典と禅 [Buddhist Scriptures of Dunhuang and Chan. Tokyo: Daitō shuppansha.

Shinohara, Koichi. 1988. "Two Sources of Chinese Buddhist Biographies: Stūpa Inscription and Miracle Stories." In Phyllis Granoff and Koichi Shinohara, eds., *Monks and Magicians: Religious Biographies in Asia*, 119–228. Oakville, New York and London: Mosaic Press.

Shioiri Ryōdō 塩入良道, ed. 1970. *Nittō guhō junrei kōki* 入唐求法巡礼行記. Vol. 1. Tōyō bunko 157. Tokyo: Heibonsha.

————, ed. 1985. *Nittō guhō junrei kōki*. Vol. 2. Tōyō bunko 442. Tokyo: Heibonsha.

Sivin, Nathan. 1978. "On the Word Taoist as a Source of Perplexity: With Special Reference to the Relations of Science and Religion in Traditional China." *History of Religions* 17, 3–4: 303–330.

Sloterdijk, Peter. 1987. *Critique of Cynical Reason*. Trans. Michael Eldred. Minneapolis: University of Minnesota Press.

Smart, Ninian. 1981. "Problems of the Application of Western Terminology to Theravāda Buddhism with Special Reference to the Relationships between the Buddha and the Gods." In Nathan Katz, ed., *Buddhist and Western Philosophy*, 444–449. New Delhi: Sterling Publishers.

Smith, Bryan. 1989. *Reflections on Resemblance, Ritual, and Religion*. New York: Oxford University Press.

Smith, Jonathan Z. 1978. *Map is Not Territory: Studies in the History of Religions*. Leiden: E. J. Brill.

———. 1982. *Imagining Religion: From Babylon to Jonestown*. Chicago: University of Chicago Press.

———. 1987. *To Take Place: Toward Theory in Ritual*. Chicago: University of Chicago Press.

Snodgrass, Adrian. 1985. *The Symbolism of the Stūpa*. Ithaca: Southeast Asian Program, Cornell Univeristy.

Somers, Robert M. 1986. "Time, Space, and Structure in the Consolidation of the T'ang Dynasty (A.D. 617–700)." *Journal of Asian Studies* 45, 5: 971–994.

Soper, Alexander C. 1948. "Hsiang-kuo ssu: An Imperial Temple of Northern Sung." *JAOS* 68, 1: 19–45.

———. 1959. *Literary Evidence for Early Buddhist Art in China*. Ascona: Artibus Asiae.

Soymié, Michel 1956. "Le Lo-feou chan: Etude de géographie religieuse." *BEFEO* 48: 1–132.

———. 1961. "Sources et sourciers en Chine." *Bulletin de la Maison Franco-Japonaise* (n.s.) 7, 1: 1–56.

———. 1984. "Quelques représentations de statues miraculeuses dans les grottes de Touen-houang." In Soymié, ed., *Contributions aux Etudes de Touen-houang*, Vol. 3: 77–102. Publications de l'Ecole Française d'Extrême-Orient 135. Paris: Ecole Française d'Extrême-Orient.

———. 1987. "Notes d'iconographie bouddhique: Des Vidyārāja et Vajradhara de Touen-houang." *Cahiers d'Extrême-Asie* 3: 9–26.

Spence, Jonathan D. 1984. *The Memory Palace of Matteo Ricci*. New York: Penguin Books.

Spiro, Audrey. 1988. "New Light on Gu Kaizhi: Windows of the Soul." *Journal of Chinese Religions* 16: 1–17.

Spiro, Melford E. 1970. *Buddhism and Society: A Great Tradition and its Burmese Vicissitudes*. Berkeley: University of California Press.

Sponberg, Alan. 1989. "Attitudes Toward Women and the Feminine in Early Buddhism." In José Cabezón, ed., *Buddhism, Sexuality, and Gender*. Albany: State University of New York Press (forthcoming).

Sponberg, Alan, and Helen Hardacre, eds. 1988. *Maitreya, The Future Buddha*. Cambridge: Cambridge University Press.

Staal, Frits. 1979. "The Meaninglessness of Ritual." *Numen* 26, 1: 2–22.

———. 1985. "Substitutes de paradigmes et religions d'Asie." *Cahiers d'Extrême-Asie* 1: 21–57.

———. 1986a. "The Sound of Religion," (I) *Numen* 33, 1: 33–64.

———. 1986b. "The Sound of Religion." (II) *Numen* 33, 2: 185–224.

Stalleybrass, P., and A. White. 1986. *The Politics and Poetics of Transgression*. Ithaca: Cornell University Press.

Starobinski, Jean. 1971. *Les mots sous les mots: Les anagrammes de Ferdinand de Saussure*. Paris: Gallimard.

Staten, Henry. 1984. *Wittgenstein and Derrida*. Lincoln and London: University of Nebraska Press.

Stein, Rolf A. 1970. "La légende du foyer dans le monde chinois." In Jean Pouillon and Pierre Maranda, eds., *Echanges et communications: Mélanges offerts à Claude Lévi-Strauss à l'occasion de son 60ème anniversaire*, 1280–1305. The Hague: Mouton.

———. 1974. "Etude du monde chinois: Institutions et concepts." *Annuaire du Collège de France*, 499–517. Paris: Collège de France.

———. 1975. "Etude du monde chinois: Institutions et concepts." *Annuaire du Collège de France*, 481–495. Paris: Collège de France.

———. 1978. "Etude du monde chinois: Institutions et concepts." *Annuaire du Collège de France*, 639–654. Paris: Collège de France.

———. 1979. "Religious Taoism and Popular Religion from the Second to the Seventh Centuries." In Holmes H. Welch and Anna Seidel, eds., *Facets of Taoism: Essays in Chinese Religion*, 53–81. New Haven: Yale University Press.

———. 1981. "Porte (Gardien de la): Un exemple de mythologie bouddhique, de l'Inde au Japon." In Yves Bonnefoy, ed., *Dictionnaire des mythologies et des religions*, Vol. 2: 280–284. Paris: Flammarion.

———. 1986. "Avalokiteśvara/Kouan-yin, un example de transformation d'un dieu en déesse." *Cahiers d'Extrême-Asie* 2: 17–77.

———. [1977] 1987. "Sudden Illumination or Simultaneous Comprehension: Remarks on Chinese and Tibetan Terminology." In Peter N. Gregory, ed., *Sudden and Gradual: Approaches to Enlightenment in Chinese Thought*, 41–65. Honolulu: University of Hawaii Press.

———. 1988. "Grottes-matrices et lieux saints de la déesse en Asie orientale." Publications de l'Ecole Française d'Extrême-Orient 151. Paris: Ecole Française d'Extrême-Orient.

———. 1990. *The World in Miniature: Container Gardens and Dwellings in Far Eastern Religious Thought*. Trans. Phyllis Brook. Stanford: Stanford University Press.

Steiner, George. 1975. *After Babel: Aspects of a Theory of Translation*. New York: Oxford University Press.

Stevens, Keith. 1976–1977. "Chinese Preserved Monks." *Journal of the Hong Kong Branch of the Royal Asiatic Society* 16–17: 292–297.

Stock, Bryan. 1983. *The Implications of Literacy: Written Language and Models of Interpretation in the Eleventh and Twelfth Centuries*. Princeton: Princeton University Press.

Strickmann, Michel. 1977. "The Mao Shan Revelations: Taoism and the Aristocracy." *T'oung Pao* 63, 1: 1–64.

———. 1979. "On the Alchemy of T'ao Hung-ching." In Holmes H. Welch and Anna Seidel, eds., *Facets of Taoism: Essays in Chinese Religion*, 123–192. New Haven: Yale University Press.

———. 1980. "History, Anthropology, and Chinese Religions." *HJAS* 40: 201–248.

———. 1981. *Le taoïsme du Mao chan: Chronique d'une révélation*. Paris: Presses Universitaires de France.

———, ed. 1981–1985. *Tantric and Taoist Studies in Honour of R. A. Stein*. 3 vols. Brussels: Institut Belge des Hautes Etudes Chinoises.

———. 1988. "Dreamwork of Psycho-Sinologists: Doctors, Taoists, Monks." In Carolyn T. Brown, ed., *Psycho-Sinology: The Universe of Dreams in Chinese Culture*, 25–46. Lanham: University Press of America.

———. 1989. "The Animate Icon." Unpublished paper.

Strong, John S. 1979. "The Legend of the Lion-Roarer: A Study of the Buddhist Arhat Piṇḍola Bhāradvāja." *Numen* 26, 1: 50–88.

———. 1983. *The Legend of King Aśoka: A study and Translation of the Aśokāvadāna*. Princeton: Princeton University Press.

Sugimoto Shunryū 杉木俊竜. [1938] 1982. *Zōtei Tōjō shitsunai kirigami narabi ni sanwa no kenkyū* 増訂洞上室内切紙并参話の研究 [Researches on the Esoteric *Kirigami* and *Sanwa* of the Sōtō Sect]. Tokyo: Sōtōshū Shūmucho.

Sullivan, Lawrence E. 1986. "Sound and Senses: Toward a Hermeneutics of Performance." *History of Religions* 26, 1: 1–33.

Suzuki Bokushi 鈴木牧之. 1986. *Snow Country Tales: Life in the Other Japan*. Trans. Jeffrey Hunter. New York: Weatherhill.

———. [1936] 1987. *Hokuetsu seppu* 北越雪譜 [Snow Country Tales]. Ed. Okada Takematsu 岡田武松. Tokyo: Iwanami shoten.

Suzuki, D[aisetsu] T[eitarō]. 1949–1953. *Essays in Zen Buddhism*. 3 vols. London: Rider and Company. Reprint. New York: Grove Press, 1961.

———. 1953. "Zen: A Reply to Hu Shih." *Philosophy East and West* 3, 1: 25–46.

———. 1965. *The Training of the Zen Buddhist Monk*. New York: University Books.

———. 1968–1971. *Suzuki Daisetsu Zenshū* 鈴木大拙全集 [The Complete Works of D. T. Suzuki]. Ed. Hisamatsu Shin'ichi, Yamaguchi Susumu, and Furuta Shōkin. 30 vols. Tokyo: Iwanami shoten.

———. 1968. *Zen shisōshi kenkyū, Daini: Daruma kara Enō ni itaru* 禅思想史研究第二 [Studies on the History of Chan Thought, Part 2]. *Suzuki Daisetsu Zenshū*, Vol. 2, Tokyo: Iwanami shoten.

———. 1976. "Dōgen, Hakuin, Bankei: Three Types of Thought in Japanese Buddhism." *The Eastern Buddhist* (n.s.) 9, 1: 1–17; 9, 2: 1–20.

———. [1930] 1977. *Studies in the Lankavatara Sutra*. Taibei: Southern Materials Center.

Suzuki Shōkun 鈴木省訓. 1987. "Rinzai zen no shingi shisō" 臨済禅の神祇思想 [The Rinzai Zen Conception of the Gods]. *Nihon bukkyō gakkai nenpō* 52: 219–230.

Suzuki Taizan 鈴木泰山. [1942] 1983. *Zenshū no chihō hatten* 禅宗の地方発展 [The Regional Development of the Zen School]. Tokyo: Yoshikawa Kōbunkan.

Suzuki Tetsuo 鈴木哲雄. 1984. *Tō Godai no zenshū: Kōnan Kōsai hen* 唐五代の禅宗—湖南, 江西篇 [The Chan School during the Tang and The Five Dynasties: Hunan and Jiangxi]. Tokyo: Daitō shuppansha.

———. 1985. *Tō Godai Zenshūshi* 唐五代禅宗史 [A History of the Chan School during the Tang and the Five Dynasties]. Tokyo: Sankibō busshorin.

Tachibana Kyōdō 橘恭堂. 1964. "Nihon zenshū kyōdan to shomin no sōsō-girei" 日本禅宗教団と庶民の葬送儀礼 [The Zen Community in Japan and the Funerary Rituals of the People]. *Zengaku kenkyū* 54: 220–227.

———. 1980. "Zenshū to minzoku" 禅宗と民俗 [The Zen Sect and Popular Customs]. In Gorai Shigeru et al., eds., *Bukkyō minzokugaku,* 328–342. Tokyo: Kōbundo.

Tada Kōryū 多田厚隆 et al., eds. 1973. *Tendai hongakuron* 天台本覚論 [The Tendai Debate on Innate Awakening]. Nihon shisō taikei 9. Tokyo: Iwanami shoten.

Tada, Michitarō. 1981. "Sacred and Profane: The Division of a Japanese Space." *Zinbun: Memoirs of the Research Institute for Humanistic Studies* 17: 17–38.

Tajima Hakudō 田鳥柏堂, ed. 1978. *Keizan* 瑩山. Nihon no Zen goroku 5. Tokyo: Kōdansha.

Takahashi Shūhei 高橋秀栄. 1984. "Sanbōji no Darumashū monto to rokuso Fugen shari" 三宝寺の達摩宗門徒と六祖普賢舎利 [The Darumashū Believers of Sanbōji and the Relics of the Six Patriarchs and of Samantabhadra]. *Shūgaku kenkyū* 26: 116–121.

Takahashi Tetsu. 1965. *Secret Heirloom Picture Scrolls.* Tokyo: Kantō shobō.

Takakusu, Junjirō. 1928–1929. "Le voyage de Kanshin au Japan (742–754), par Aomi-no Mabito Genkai (779)." BEFEO 28: 1–41, 441–472; 29: 47–62.

———, trans. [1896] 1970. *A Record of the Buddhist Religion as Practiced in India and the Malay Archipelago (A.D. 671–695), by I-tsing.* Taibei: Cheng Wen.

Takao Giken 高雄義堅. 1975. *Sōdai bukkyōshi no kenkyū* 宋代仏教史の研究 [Researches on the History of Song Buddhism]. Tokyo: Hyakkaen.

Takase Shigeo 高瀬重雄, ed. 1977. *Hakusan. Tateyama to Hokuriku shūgendō* 白山, 立山と北陸修験道 [Hakusan, Tateyama, and the Shūgendō of North-eastern Japan]. Tokyo: Meicho shuppan.

Takeuchi Kōdō 竹内弘道. 1985. "Shinshutsu no Kataku Jinne tōmei ni tsuite" 新出の荷沢神会塔銘について [On the Recently Found Stele Inscription of Heze Shenhui]. *Shūgaku kenkyū* 27: 313–325.

Tamamura Takeji 玉村竹二. 1976–1981. *Nihon zenshūshi ronshū* 日本禅宗史論集 [Essays on the history of the Zen school in Japan]. 4 vols. Tokyo: Shibunkaku shuppansha.

Tamamuro Taijō 圭室諦成. 1963. *Sōshiki bukkyō* 葬式仏教 [Funerary Buddhism]. Tokyo: Daihōrinkaku.

Tambiah, Stanley J. 1968. "The Magical Power of Words." *Man* 3: 175–208.

———. 1970. *Buddhism and the Spirit Cults of Northeast Thailand.* Cambridge: Cambridge University Press.

———. 1976. *World Conqueror and World Renouncer: A Study of Buddhism and Polity in Thailand against a Historical Background.* Cambridge: Cambridge University Press.

———. 1981. "A Performative Approach to Ritual." In *Proceedings of the British Academy,* Vol. 65: 113–169. New York: Oxford University Press.

———. 1985. *The Buddhist Saints of the Forest and the Cult of Amulets: A Study in Charisma, Hagiography, Sectarianism, and Millennial Buddhism.* Cambridge: Cambridge University Press.

———. 1990. *Magic, Science, Religion, and the Scope of Rationality.* Cambridge: Cambridge University Press.

Tanabe, George Joji, Jr. 1983. "Myōe shōnin (1173–1232): Tradition and Reform in Early Kamakura Buddhism." Ph.D. diss., Columbia University.

Tanabe, George Joji, and Willa Tanabe, eds. 1989. *The Lotus Sūtra in Japanese Culture*, Honolulu: University of Hawaii Press.

Tanaka Ryōshō. 1981. "Relations between the Buddhist Sects in the T'ang Dynasty through the ms. P. 3913." *Journal Asiatique* 269: 163–169.

———. 田中良昭. 1983. *Tonkō zenshū bunken no kenkyū* 敦煌禅宗文献の研究 [Researches on Documents of the Chan School from Dunhuang]. Tokyo: Daitō shuppansha.

Taussig, Michael T. 1980. *The Devil and Commodity Fetishism in South America*. Chapel Hill: University of North Carolina Press.

Taylor, Mark C. 1984. *Erring: A Postmodern A/theology*. Chicago: University of Chicago Press.

Teiser, Stephen F. 1988. *The Ghost Festival in Medieval China*. Princeton: Princeton University Press.

———. 1989. "The Growth of Purgatory." Unpublished paper.

Terada Tōru 寺田透, and Mizuno Yaeko 水野弥穂子, eds. 1975. *Dōgen*. 2 vols. Tokyo: Iwanami shoten.

Thomas, Keith. 1971. *Religion and the Decline of Magic*. London: Charles Scribner's and Sons.

Todorov, Tzvetan. 1978. *Symbolisme et interprétation*. Paris: Seuil.

———. 1984. *Mikhail Bakhtin: The Dialogical Principle*. Trans. Wlad Godzich. Minneapolis: University of Minnesota Press.

———. 1987. *Literature and its Theorists: A Personal View of Twentieth-Century Criticism*. Trans. Catherine Porter. Ithaca: Cornell University Press.

Togawa Anshō 戸川安章. 1974. *Dewa sanzan no miirabutsu* 出羽三山のミイラ仏 [The Mummified Buddhas of the Three Mountains of Dewa]. Tokyo: Chūō shoin.

Tokiwa Daijō 常盤大定. 1923. *Shina bukkyō shiseki* 支那佛教史蹟 [Historical Vestiges of Chinese Buddhism]. Tokyo: Bukkyō shiseki kenkyūkai.

———. 1943. *Shina bukkyō no kenkyū* 支那佛教の研究 [Studies in Chinese Buddhism]. Tokyo: Shunjūsha.

———. [1938] 1972. *Shina bukkyō shiseki tōsaki* 支那佛教史蹟踏査記 [Record of Exploration of the Historical Vestiges of Chinese Buddhism]. Tokyo: Kokusho kankōkai.

Tokiwa Gishin, trans. 1973. *A Dialogue on the Contemplation-Extinguished: Translated from the Chüeh-kuan lun, an Early Chinese Zen Text from Tun-huang*. Kyoto: Institute for Zen Studies.

Tominaga Nakamoto 富永沖基. 1982. *Shutsujō kōgo* 出定後語 [Emerging from Samādhi]. Tokyo: Ryōbunkan.

———. 1990. *Emerging from Meditation*. Trans. Michael Pye. Honolulu: University of Hawaii Press.

Tracy, David. 1981. *The Analogical Imagination: Christian Theology and the Culture of Pluralism*. New York: Crossroad.

———. 1987. *Plurality and Ambiguity: Hermeneutics, Religion, Hope*. San Francisco: Harper and Row.

Tsuji Zennosuke 辻善之助. 1944–1955. *Nihon bukkyōshi* 日本佛教史 [A History of Japanese Buddhism]. 10 vols. Tokyo: Iwanami shoten.

Tsukamoto Zenryū 塚本善隆. 1975. *Tsukamoto Zenryū chosakushū* 塚本善隆著作集 [Collected Works of Tsukamoto Zenryū]. Vol. 3: *Chūgoku chūsei bukkyō shiron kō* 中国中世仏教史論攷 [A Historical Study of Medieval Chinese Buddhism]. Tokyo: Daitō shuppansha.

————. 1976. *Chūgoku Jōdo kyōshi kenkyū* 中国浄土教史の研究 [Researches on the Chinese Pure Land Doctrine]. Tokyo: Daitō shuppansha.

Turner, Victor W. 1969. *The Ritual Process: Structure and Anti-structure*. Chicago: University of Chicago Press.

————. 1974. *Dramas, Fields, and Metaphors: Symbolic Action in Human Society*. Ithaca: Cornell University Press.

————. 1975. *Revelation and Divination in Ndembu Ritual*. Ithaca: Cornell University Press.

————. 1987. *The Anthropology of Performance*. New York: PAJ Publications.

Turner, Victor W., and Edith Turner. 1978. *Image and Pilgrimage in Christian Culture: Anthropological Perspectives*. New York: Columbia University Press.

Tyler, Royall. 1984. "The Tokugawa Peace and Popular Religion: Suzuki Shōsan, Kakugyō Tōbutsu, and Jikigyō Miroku." In Peter Nosco, ed., *Confucianism and Tokugawa Culture*, 92–119. Princeton: Princeton University Press.

Ueda Shizuteru 上田閑照, and Yanagida Seizan 柳田聖山. 1982. *Jūgyūzu: Jikō no genshōgaku* 十牛図—自己の現象学 [The Ten Oxherding Pictures: A Phenomenology of the Self]. Tokyo: Chikuma shobō.

Ui Hakuju 宇井伯壽 [1941] 1966a. *Daini zenshūshi kenkyū*. Tokyo: Iwanami shoten.

————. [1943] 1966b. *Daisan zenshūshi kenkyū*. Tokyo: Iwanami shoten.

————. [1935] 1966c. *Zenshūshi kenkyū* 禅宗史研究 [Researches on the History of the Chan School]. Tokyo: Iwanami shoten.

Valéry, Paul. 1927. *Monsieur Teste*. Paris: Gallimard.

————. 1946. *Mon Faust*. Paris: Gallimard.

————. 1970. *Analects*. Trans. Stuart Gilbert. Bollingen Series XLV: 14. Princeton: Princeton University Press.

van Gennep, Arnold. [1909] 1960. *The Rites of Passage*. Trans. M. B. Wizedom and G. L. Caffee. Chicago: University of Chicago Press.

van Gulik, Robert. [1961] 1974. *Sexual Life in Ancient China: A Preliminary Survey of Chinese Sex and Society from ca. 1500 B.C. till 1644 A.D.* Leiden: E. J. Brill.

Varley, H. Paul, trans. 1980. *A Chronicle of Gods and Sovereigns: Jinnō Shōtoki of Kitabatake Chikafusa*. New York: Columbia University Press.

Vernant, Jean-Pierre. 1965. *Mythe et pensée chez les Grecs: Etudes de psychologie historique*. 2 vols. Paris: Maspero.

————. 1974. *Mythe et société en Grèce ancienne*. Paris: Maspero.

————. 1979. *Religions, histoires, raisons*. Paris: Maspero.

————. 1981. "Death with Two Faces." Trans. J. Lloyd. In S. C. Humphreys and H. King, eds., *Mortality and Immortality*, 285–291. London: Academic Press.

Vernant, Jean-Pierre et al., eds. 1974. *Divination et rationalité*. Paris: Seuil.

Veyne, Paul. 1984. *Writing History*. Trans. Mina Moore-Rinvolucri. Middletown: Wesleyan University Press.

————. 1988. *Did the Greeks Believe in their Myths? An Essay on the Constitutive Imagination.* Trans. Paula Wissig. Chicago: University of Chicago Press.

————. 1990. "Propagande expression roi, image idole oracle." *L'homme* 114: 7–26.

Visser, Marinus Willem de. 1923. *The Arhats in China and Japan.* Berlin: Oesterheld.

Vita, Silvio. 1988. "Li Hua and Buddhism." In Antonino Forte, ed., *Tang China and Beyond: Studies on East Asia from the Seventh to the Tenth Century*, 97–124. Kyoto: Istituto Italiano di Cultura.

Vos, Frits. 1979. "Tung-fang Shuo, Buffoon and Immortal in Japan and Korea." *Oriens Extremus* 26, 1–2: 189–203.

Wachtel, Nathan. 1971. *La vision des vaincus: Les Indiens du Pérou devant la Conquête espagnole.* Paris: Gallimard.

Waddell, Norman, trans. 1977–1978. "Dōgen's *Hōkyō-ki.*" *The Eastern Buddhist* (n.s.) 10, 2: 102–139; 11, 1: 66–84.

————, trans. 1979. "Being Time: Dōgen's *Shōbōgenzō Uji.*" *The Eastern Buddhist* (n.s.) 12, 1: 114–129.

Waddell, Norman, and Masao Abe, trans. 1971. "Dōgen's *Bendōwa.*" *The Eastern Buddhist* (n.s.) 4, 1: 88–115.

————, trans. 1972. "Dōgen's *Shōbōgenzō Zenki* and *Shōji.*" *The Eastern Buddhist* (n.s.) 5, 1: 70–80.

Waghorne, Joanne Puzzo, and Norman Cutler, eds. 1985. *Gods of Flesh, Gods of Stone: The Embodiment of Divinity in India.* Chambersburg, PA: Anima Books.

Wagner, Rudolf. 1988. "Imperial Dreams in China." In Carolyn T. Brown, ed., *Psycho-Sinology: The Universe of Dreams in Chinese Culture*, 11–24. Lanham: University Press of America.

Wakeman, Frederic, Jr. 1988. "Mao's Remains." In James L. Watson and Evelyn Rawski, eds., *Death Rituals in Late Imperial and Modern China*, 254–288. Berkeley: University of California Press.

Waley, Arthur, trans. 1923. *The Temple and Other Poems.* London: George Allen and Unwin.

————. 1931–1932. "New Light on Buddhism in Medieval India." *Mélanges chinois et bouddhiques* 1: 355–376.

————. 1949. *The Life and Times of Po Chü-i, 772–846 A.D.* New York: Macmillan.

————. 1952. *The Real Tripiṭaka and Other Pieces.* New York: Macmillan.

————. 1969. "Two Posthumous Articles." *Asia Major* 14, 2: 242–246.

————. [1955] 1970. "Some Far Eastern Dreams." In Ivan Morris, ed., *Madly Singing in the Mountains: An Appreciation and Anthology of Arthur Waley*, 364–371. New York: Walker and Company.

Wang Hongjin, ed. 1988. *Tales of the Shaolin Monastery.* Trans. C. J. Lonsdale. Hong Kong: Joint Publishing.

Wata Kenju 和田謙壽. 1960. "Minzokugakuteki tachiba kara mita Sōtōshū no hatten ni tsuite" 民俗学的立場からみた曹洞宗の発展について [The Development of the Sōtō Sect from an Ethnographical Perspective]. *Shūgaku kenkyū* 2: 124–131.

Watanabe Shōhei 渡部正英. 1975. "Zenshū to minshū to no ni tsuite" 禅宗と

民衆とのについて [On the Chan School and the People]. *Sōtōshū kenkyūin kenkyūsei kenkyū kiyō* 12: 148–161.

———. 1986. "Shomin shinkō to Zenshū jiin no gyōji" 庶民信仰と禅宗寺院の行事 [Popular Beliefs and the Ceremonies of Zen Temples]. *IBK* 34, 2: 175–182.

Watanabe Tsunaya 渡邊綱也, ed. 1966. *Shasekishū* 沙石集 [Collection of Sand and Pebbles]. Tokyo: Iwanami shoten.

Watson, Burton, trans. 1963. *Hsün Tzu: Basic Writings.* New York: Columbia University Press.

———, trans. 1968. *The Complete Works of Chuang Tzu.* New York: Columbia University Press.

———. 1988. "Zen Poetry." In Kenneth Kraft, ed., *Zen: Tradition and Transition: A Sourcebook by Contemporary Zen Masters and Scholars,* 105–124. New York: Grove Press.

Watson, James L. 1976. "Anthropological Analyses of Chinese Religion." *China Quarterly* 66: 355–364.

———. 1982. "Of Flesh and Bones: The Management of Death in Cantonese Society." In Maurice Bloch and Jonathan Parry, eds., *Death and the Regeneration of Life,* 155–186. Cambridge: Cambridge University Press.

———. 1985. "Standardizing the Gods: The Promotion of T'ien Hou (Empress of Heaven) along the South China Coast." In David Johnson, Andrew J. Nathan, and Evelyn S. Rawski, eds., *Popular Culture in Late Imperial China,* 292–324. Berkeley: University of California Press.

———. 1988. "The Structure of Chinese Funerary Rites: Elementary Forms, Ritual Sequence, and the Primacy of Performance." In James L. Watson and Evelyn Rawski, eds., *Death Rituals in Late Imperial and Modern China,* 3–19. Berkeley: University of California Press.

Watson James L., and Evelyn Rawski, eds. 1988. *Death Rituals in Late Imperial and Modern China.* Berkeley: University of California Press.

Watt, Paul B. 1984. "Jiun Sonja (1718–1804): A Response to Confucianism within the Context of Buddhist Reform." In Peter Nosco, ed., *Confucianism and Tokugawa Culture,* 188–214. Princeton: Princeton University Press.

Weber, Max. 1951. *The Religion of China: Confucianism and Taoism.* Trans. H. H. Gerth. Glencoe, IL: Free Press.

———. 1958a. *From Max Weber.* Trans. H. H. Gerth and C. Wright Mills. New York: Oxford University Press.

———. 1985b. *The Religion of India: The Sociology of Hinduism and Buddhism.* Trans. H. H. Gerth and D. Martindale. Glencoe, IL: Free Press.

———. 1964. *The Sociology of Religion.* Trans. Ephraim Fischoff. Boston: Beacon Press.

———. 1978. *Economy and Society: An Outline of Interpretive Sociology.* Ed. Guenther Roth and Claus Wittich. Berkeley and Los Angeles: University of California Press.

———. 1986. "Parenthèse théorique: Le refus religieux du monde, ses orientations et ses degrés." *Archives de sciences sociales des religions* 61, 1: 7–34.

Wechsler, Howard J. 1985. *Offerings of Jade and Silk: Ritual and Symbol in the Legitimation of the T'ang Dynasty.* New Haven: Yale University Press.

Weinstein, Stanley. 1973. "Imperial Patronage in the Formation of T'ang Buddhism." In Arthur Wright and Denis Twitchett, eds., *Perspectives on the T'ang*, 265–306. New Haven: Yale University Press.

——. 1974. "The Beginnings of Esoteric Buddhism in Japan: The Neglected Tendai Tradition." *Journal of Asian Studies* 34, 1: 177–191.

——. 1987. *Buddhism under the T'ang*. New York: Cambridge University Press.

Welch, Holmes H. 1963. "Dharma Scrolls and the Succession of Abbots in Chinese Monasteries." *T'oung Pao* 50, 1–3: 93–149.

——. 1967. *The Practice of Chinese Buddhism, 1900–1950*. Cambridge, MA: Harvard University Press.

——. 1968. *The Buddhist Revival in China*. Cambridge, MA: Harvard University Press.

Welch, Holmes H., and Anna Seidel, eds. 1979. *Facets of Taoism: Essays in Chinese Religion*. New Haven: Yale University Press.

Weller, Robert P. 1987. *Unities and Diversities in Chinese Religions*, Seattle: University of Washington Press.

Wen Fong. 1958. *The Lohans and a Bridge to Heaven*. Washington, D.C.: Freer Gallery, Occasional Papers.

White, Hayden. 1973. *Metahistory: The Historical Imagination in Nineteenth-Century Europe*. Baltimore: Johns Hopkins University Press.

——. 1978. *Tropics of Discourse: Essays in Cultural Criticism*. Baltimore: Johns Hopkins University Press.

——. 1987. *The Content of the Form: Narrative Discourse and Historical Representation*. Baltimore: Johns Hopkins University Press.

Wieger, Léon. 1951. *Bouddhisme chinois: Extraits du Tripiṭaka, des commentaires, etc.* Paris: Catharsia.

Wittgenstein, Ludwig. 1958. *Philosophical Investigations: The English Text of the Third Edition*. New York: Macmillan.

——. 1971. "Remarks on Frazer's *Golden Bough*." *The Human World* 3: 18–41.

Wolf, Arthur P., ed. 1978. *Studies in Chinese Society*. Stanford: Stanford University Press.

Wright, Arthur F. 1990. *Studies in Chinese Buddhism*. Ed. Robert M. Somers. New Haven: Yale University Press.

Wu, Pei-yi. 1975. "The Spiritual Autobiography of Te-ch'ing." In Wm. Theodore de Bary, ed., *The Unfolding of Neo-Confucianism*, 67–92. New York: Columbia University Press.

——. 1978. "Self-examination and Confession of Sins in Traditional China." *HJAS* 39, 1: 5–38.

Xu Guolin 許國林. 1937. *Dunhuang shishi xiejing tiji yu Dunhuang zalu* 敦煌石室寫經題記與敦煌雜錄 [List of Titles of Dunhuang Manuscripts and Varia from Dunhuang]. 2 vols. Shanghai: Shangwu yinshuguan.

Xu Yun. 1988. *Empty Cloud: The Autobiography of the Chinese Zen Master Xu Yun*. Trans. Charles Luk. Longmead: Element Books.

Yamaguchi Zuihō 山口瑞鳳. 1973. "Chibetto bukkyō to Shiragi no Kin oshō" チバット仏教と新羅の金和尚 [The Silla Priest Kim and Tibetan Buddhism]. In Kim Chigyŏn 金知見 and Ch'ae Inyak 蔡印約, eds., *Shiragi bukkyō kenkyū* 新羅仏教研究 [Researches on the Buddhism of Silla], 3–36. Tokyo: Sankibō busshorin.

Yamazaki Hiroshi 山崎宏. 1967. *Zui Tō bukkyōshi no kenkyū* 隋唐仏教史の研究 [Researches on the History of Buddhism during the Sui and the Tang]. Kyoto: Hōzōkan.

———. 1971. *Shina chūsei bukkyō no tenkai* 支那中世仏教の展開 [The Development of Medieval Chinese Buddhism]. Kyoto: Hōzōkan.

Yampolsky, Philip B. 1967. *The Platform Sūtra of the Sixth Patriarch*. New York. Columbia University Press.

———. 1988. "The Development of Japanese Zen." In Kenneth Kraft, ed., *Zen: Tradition and Transformation: A Sourcebook by Contemporary Zen Masters and Scholars*, 140–156. New York: Grove Press.

Yanagida Seizan 柳田聖山. 1961. "*Zenmonkyō ni tsuite*" 「禅門経」について [On the *Chanmen jing*]. In *Tsukamoto hakushi shōju kinen: Bukkyō shigaku ronshū* 塚本博士記念—仏教史学論集 [Essays on Buddhist Historiography], 869–882. Tokyo: Tsukamoto hakushi shōju kinenkai.

———. 1963. "*Den hōbōki to sono sakusha*" 「伝法宝紀」とその作者 [The *Chuan fabao ji* and its Author]. *Zengaku kenkyū* 53: 45–71.

———. 1967. *Shoki zenshū shisho no kenkyū* 初期禅宗史書の研究 [Researches on the Historiographical Works of the Early Chan School]. Kyoto: Hōzōkan.

———, ed. 1969a. *Daruma no goroku: Ninyū shigyō ron* 達摩の語録—二入四行論 [The Recorded Sayings of Bodhidharma: The *Erru sixing lun*]. Zen no goroku 1. Tokyo: Chikuma shobō.

———. 1969b. "Fuke no fūkyū" 普化の風狂 [The Eccentric Style of Puhua]. In *Tōyō bunka ronshū* 東洋文化論集 [Essays on Eastern Culture], 1083–1097. Tokyo: Waseda daigaku shuppansha.

———. 1970. "Daruma zen to sono haikei" 達摩禅とその背景 [The Chan of Bodhidharma and its Background]. In Ōchō Enichi 横超慧日, ed., *Oku Gi bukkyō no kenkyū* 北魏仏教の研究 [Researches on the Buddhism of the Northern Wei], 115–177. Kyoto: Hōzōkan.

———, ed. 1971. *Shoki no zenshi 1: Ryōga shiji ki; Den hōbō ki* 初期の禅史—楞伽師資記, 伝法宝記 [The History of Early Chan I: *Lengqie shizi ji; Chuan fabao ji*]. Zen no goroku 2. Tokyo: Chikuma shobō.

———. 1972a. "The Life of Lin-chi I-hsüan." *The Eastern Buddhist* (n.s.) 5, 2: 70–94.

———, ed. 1972b. *Rinzai roku* 臨済録 (The Recorded Sayings of Linji). Tokyo: Daitō shuppansha.

———. 1973. *Zen no yuige* 禅の遺偈 [The Departing Verses of Chan/Zen]. Tokyo: Chōbunsha.

———. 1974a. "Hokushū zen no shisō" 北宗禅の思想 [The Thought of Northern Chan]. ZBKK 6: 67–104.

———, ed. 1974b. *Sōdōshū* [*Chodang chip*] 祖堂集. Kyoto: Chūbun shuppansha.

———. 1974c. *Zen goroku* 禅語録 [The Recorded Sayings in Chan]. Tokyo: Chūōkōronsha.

———, ed. 1975. *Sōzō ichin Hōrinden, Dentō gyokuei shū* 宋藏遺珍寶林傳, 傳燈玉英集. Kyoto: Chūbun shuppansha.

————, ed. 1976. *Shoki no zenshi 2: Rekidai hōbōki* 初期の禅史―歴代法宝記 [The History of Early Chan II: *Lidai fabao ji*]. Zen no goroku 3. Tokyo: Chikuma shobō.

————, ed. 1977. *Chokushū Hyakujō shingi sakei* 敕修百丈清規左艦. 2 vols. Kyoto: Chūbun shuppansha.

————. 1978. "Shinzoku tōshi no keifu: Jo (1) 新続灯史の系譜 [The Lineage of the "Histories of the Lamp"]. *Zengaku kenkyū* 59: 1–39.

————, ed. 1979. *Zenrin shōkisen; Kattō gosen jikkan; Zenrin kushū benmyō* 禅林象器箋、葛藤語箋十巻、禅林句集辨苗. 2 vols. Kyoto: Chūbun shuppansha.

————. 1980. "*Zekkanron* to sono jidai" 絶観論とその時代 [The *Jueguan lun* and its Times]. *Tōhō gakuhō* 512: 367–401.

————. 1981a. *Chūsei hyōhaku* 中世漂泊 [Wanderings through the Middle Ages]. Kyoto: Hōzōkan.

————. 1982b. "Shinzoku tōshi no keifu: Jo (2)" *Zengaku kenkyū* 60: 1–70.

————. 1982a. "Kūbyō no mondai" 空病の問題 [The Problem of *Śūnyata* Sickness]. In Bukkyō Shisō Kenkyūkai, ed., *Bukkyō shisō* 仏教思想, Vol. 7: 755–798. Kyoto: Heirakuji shoten.

————. 1982b. "The Search for the Real Dōgen: Challenging Taboos concerning Dōgen." *Young East* 8, 1: 3–19.

————. 1983a. "The Development of the 'Recorded Sayings' Texts of Chinese Ch'an Buddhism." Trans. John. R. McRae. In Whalen Lai and Lewis R. Lancaster, eds., *Early Ch'an in China and Tibet*, 185–205. Berkeley: Asian Humanities Press.

————. 1983b. "The *Li-tai fa-pao chi* and the Ch'an Doctrine of Sudden Awakening." Trans. Carl Bielefeldt. In Whalen Lai and Lewis R. Lancaster, eds., *Early Ch'an in China and Tibet*, 13–49. Berkeley: Asian Humanities Press.

————. 1984. "Dōgen to Chūgoku bukkyō" 道元と中国仏教 [Dōgen and Chinese Buddhism]. *ZBKK* 13: 3–128.

————. 1985. "Goroku no rekishi: Zen bunken no seiritsu shiteki kenkyū" 語録の歴史―禪文献の成立史的研究 [A History of the "Recorded Sayings" Genre]. *Tōhō gakuhō* 57: 211–663.

————, ed. 1987. *Ikkyū. Ryōkan* 一休, 良寛. Daijō butten: Chūgoku. Nihon hen, Vol. 26. Tokyo: Chūōkōron.

————. 1988a. "Jinne no shōzō" 神会の肖像 [The Portrait of Shenhui]. *Zen bunka kenkyūsho kiyō* 15: 215–243.

————. 1988b. *Zen no bunka: Shiryōhen: Zenrin sōbōden yakuchū (1)* 禅の文化―資料篇―禅林僧宝伝訳注 [Zen Culture: Documents: Annotated Translation of the *Chanlin sengbaozhuan*]. Kyoto: Kyōto daigaku jinbun kagaku kenkyūsho.

————. 1989. "Shoki zenshū to *Hokekyō*" 初期禅宗と法華経 [The Early Chan School and the *Lotus Sūtra*]. *Bukkyō shigaku kenkyū* 32: 81–103.

Yang, C. K. 1961. *Religion in Chinese Society: A Study of Contemporary Social Functions of Religions and Some of their Historical Factors*. Berkeley: University of California Press.

Yang Hsüan-chih. 1984. *A Record of Buddhist Monasteries in Lo-yang*. Trans. Wang Yi-t'ung. Princeton: Princeton University Press.

Yang Lien-sheng. 1963. *Studies in Chinese Institutional History*. Cambridge, MA: Harvard University Press.

Yates, Frances. 1966. *The Art of Memory*. Chicago: University of Chicago Press.

Yetts, W. Perceval. 1911. "Notes on the Disposal of Buddhist Dead in China." *Journal of the Royal Asiatic Society* 43: 699–725.

Yi Nǔnghwa 李能和. [1918] 1955. *Chosǒn pulgyo t'ongsa* 朝鮮佛教通史 [A General History of Korean Buddhism]. 3 vols. Tokyo: Kokusho kankōkai.

Yin Shun 印順. 1971. *Zhongguo chanzong shi* 中國禪宗史 [A History of the Chan School in China]. Taibei: Huiri jiangtang.

Yokoi, Yuho. 1976. *Zen Master Dōgen: An Introduction with Selected Writings*. New York and Tokyo: Weatherhill.

Yoshikawa Tadao 吉川忠夫. 1985. *Chūgoku kodaijin no yume to shi* 中国古代人の夢と死 [The Dreams and Death of the Ancient Chinese]. Tokyo: Heibonsha.

Yoshizu Yoshihide 吉津宜英. 1985. *Kegon Zen no shisōteki kenkyū* 華厳禅の思想的研究 [Researches on the Philosophy of Huayan Chan]. Tokyo: Daitō shuppansha.

Yu, Anthony, trans. 1977–1983. *The Journey to the West*. 4 vols. Chicago: University of Chicago Press.

Yü Chün-fang. 1981. *The Renewal of Buddhism in China: Chu-hung and the Late Ming Synthesis*. New York: Columbia University Press.

———. 1982. "Chung-feng Ming-pen and Ch'an Buddhism in the Yüan." In Hok-lam Chan and Wm. Theodore de Bary, eds., *Yüan Thought: Chinese Thought and Religion under the Mongols*, 419–477. New York: Columbia University Press.

Yuasa, Nobuyuki, trans. 1981. *The Zen Poems of Ryōkan*. Princeton: Princeton University Press.

Zeuschner, Robert B. 1983. "The Concept of *li-nien* ("being free from thinking") in the Northern Line of Ch'an Buddhism." In Whalen Lai and Lewis R. Lancaster, eds., *Early Ch'an in China and Tibet*, 131–148. Berkeley: Asian Humanities Press.

Zhang Mantao 張曼濤, ed. 1978. *Zhongguo fojiao sita shizhi* 中國佛教寺塔史志 [Historical Monographs on the Temple *Stūpa* of Chinese Buddhism]. Taibei: Dasheng wenhua.

Zhang Shengyan 張聖嚴. 1975. *Min matsu chūgoku bukkyō no kenkyū: Tokuni Chikyoku o chūshin to shite* 明末中国仏教の研究――特に智旭を中心として [Researches on Chinese Buddhism at the End of the Ming]. Tokyo: Sankibō busshorin.

Zürcher, Erik. 1959. *The Buddhist Conquest of China: The Spread and Adaptation of Buddhism in Early Medieval China*. 2 vols. Leiden: E. J. Brill.

———. 1980. "Buddhist Influence on Early Taoism." *T'oung Pao* 66, 1–3: 84–147.

Index

Errata

PAGE	FOR	READ
140, n. 30, line 4	Li Guangzhou	Li Guangzhu
152, n. 6, line 1	*Shoushen ji*	*Soushen ji*
154, par. 3, line 5	*Datong kusi*	*Datong gusi*
166, par. 2, line 3	*gan*	*kan*
262, n. 12, lines 3–4	Kōkuzō	Kokūzō
321, left col., line 5	Anqing	Anjing
323, right col., line 47	*huohe*	*hehe*
324, left col., line 23	*jiji rulü ling*	*jiji ru lüling*
325, left col., line 37	Liu Chongjin	Liu Chongjing
328, right col., line 20	Yanguan Qian	Yanguan Ji'an
329, left col., line 10	*zansheng*	*sansheng*
331, line 12	Zhao Yushi	Zhao Yuxi
331, lines 32 and 40	Guifei	Guifeng
332, line 20	*suizhou*	*suishu*
333, line 32	*guangmu*	*gangmu*
337, line 4	Chizhao	Zhizhao
337, line 35	*Shiyue*	*Zhiyue lu*
338, line 12	*yingtang*	*yingshi*
339, line 14	*Xinjin*	*Tanjin*
353, line 33	*The Secular as Sacred*	*Confucius: The Secular as Sacred*
355, line 34	*sourveraine*	*souveraine*
365, line 42	Lagerway	Lagerwey
367, line 18	University of Tennessee	Harvard University
376, line 13	Ren, Jiyu. 1984b	Ren Jiyu. 1984a
379, line 26	Nagarjunikonda Inscription	Nāgārjunikoṇḍa Inscriptions
382, line 32	Brook	Brooks
397, right col., line 28	of Kukai	of Kūkai
397, right col., line 30	of Shito Xiqian	of Shitou Xiqian
400, left col., line 51	Zongmi (Guifei)	Zongmi